The Exile of James Joyce

Hélène Cixous

Translated from the French by Sally A. J. Purcell

John Calder

LONDON

First published in Great Britian 1976
by John Calder (Publishers) Ltd.
18 Brewer Street London W1R 4AS
Copyright © 1972 Hélène Cixous
Translation copyright © 1976 John Calder (Publishers) Ltd.
Published in French, 1972, by Bernard Grasset, 61 Rue des St. Peres, Paris 6ᵐᵉ

This edition originally published in the United States by
David Lewis, Inc., 216 West 89th St., New York, N.Y. 10024

Table of Contents

Introduction

Realism or Symbolism

As a native of Ireland, Joyce has often been accused of being a middle-class author whose work is a denial of history and attempts to make itself a mediaeval *summa* rather than a realistic portrayal of his times. It is true that Joyce wrote no historical novel, and it is true that *Finnegans Wake* is an encyclopedia of mythology; but Joyce is profoundly an Irishman and his work is truly the product of his own inner Ireland. Joyce's Ireland is not that of Yeats and perhaps even less that of Eamonn de Valera.

What he retains from it is less its legendary past or its political future, than its present, that of the beginning of the twentieth century; from a reading of *Dubliners* and *Ulysses* one can discover all urban Ireland and Dublin society. As a social document it still retains its value today. But that is only the framework for the story of a developing consciousness, that of the artist, and, in *Ulysses,* that of an ordinary Dubliner—and by extension that of Dublin itself. There will always be a realistic basis to this spiritual or intellectual history, but neither is it presented objectively, nor does it distort the real; in the center of the work Joyce places individuals, and around the individuals, the three circles of family, homeland and Church are interpreted by those whom they surround and who at the same time serve to define them.

The family, the economic and social problems, are thus both concrete elements of surrounding reality—an end in itself, but limited—and the means by which the artist's mind is sharpened. In this, any realism is at once overtaken and assimilated, to become the surface of a symbolism which is made less and less publicly significant as it is more and more charged with personal meaning, until, with *Finnegans Wake*, it becomes a Joycean form of occultism, initiation to which is achieved by a progress *through* Joyce enabling one to reach reality.

How far and to what degree can one speak of "realism" in Joyce's art?

When Joyce writes *A Portrait*, he already possesses that "double consciousness of one watching himself live" (J. J. Mayoux, *Joyce*, p. 44), which enables him to reconstitute by memory a time which is experienced and now past. This retrospective glance at his own history reveals both the *image* he has of himself (not himself), and the exterior forces which have caused him to develop in opposition to them; what he sees is the social alienation of his family and of Ireland to which he has responded by withdrawing, by declaring his *difference*, while still, in the tones of the romantic and idealistic *fin-de-siècle* artist, claiming the role of moral reformer within this very society that he rejects.

Stephen's lucidity develops throughout the five chapters of *Portrait*, that history of a consciousness in evolution: its growth is measured by the extending of his comprehension of the outside world and of the relationships between the self and society. Since these things can only be defined by relation to each other, we must admit that objective reality can only be discovered by a sort of deductive reading; if Dublin is seen by Stephen, we must know how Stephen sees in order to place reality and the subjective starting-point correctly. Now Stephen does not claim to be "objective", and Joyce does not grant him infallibility; on the contrary, Joyce does not fail to point out the occasional deformations and errors of his character's thought, not by intervening but by giving Stephen a sense of self-criticism almost equal to his critical sense, expressing itself almost by implication, as it were in the margins of his judgements. In *A Portrait*, Stephen oscillates between bitter irony and an insipid or idealistic romanticism; these destroy each other to the advantage of the author's "impartial" view which registers the young man's efforts to escape the traps and pitfalls of society. While *Stephen Hero* was written solely in a tone of aggressive violence and its hero indulged in numerous monologues in indirect style, encumbered with an overdone sensitivity, the *Portrait* is coloured less by the critical intention than by time, space and retrospect; the attention is decentralised, although Stephen is still in the foreground, towards the many and revealing scenes, whose ambiguity we can see: thus we can understand the range and meaning of the first chapter of *Portrait* better than the principal character involved can. He loosely bundles together objective facts and his own interpretation of them, which is still hesitant and limited because he has only a small child's experience and does not know whether he is at the centre of the world or on its outermost edge. To obtain a true picture of the reality of this Ireland, therefore, one must take into account the part played by aesthetic transformation and refer also to the available biographical documents. This can be done thanks to the books of Stanislaus Joyce, *My Brother's Keeper* and especially the *Dublin Diary* of 1903–4, which is about the years when James passed from being aware of his genius to giving it free play, and thanks to the Ellmann biography. Finally, the analysis of Shakespeare's life, starting from an interpretation of his work made by Stephen in *Ulysses*, gives the keys of the critical method the author suggests to whoever is interested in the secrets of creation.

Life and the Work

The relationships between the artist's life and his work form the subject of a long and complicated chapter in *Ulysses:* in "Scylla nd Charybdis" Joyce, by the intermediary of a Stephen who is partially himself, sets out certain patterns of these relationships in the form of psychological laws, taking the Shakespeare type as his example. But why Shakespeare?

There is no lack of reasons for such a choice. On the one hand, it is a matter of expounding in this chapter a theory the elements of which existed already, though less objectively, in the *Portrait of the Artist as a Young Man,* and are to be found scattered throughout *Ulysses.* On the other hand, Shakespeare constitutes one of the mythical figures in *Ulysses*, being used by Joyce ironically as the double of his protagonists, unexpectedly as the mask of an ordinary Dubliner, as a subject of aesthetic discussion among the students of Stephen's circle, as a symbol of "the artist of genius" (the certainties and details of whose life are unknown to us), as the type of a man who has pursued the hazardous path of life and is capable of summing up his experience in a work of art, as the author of some works which provide an occasional leitmotif (*Hamlet, Macbeth, Othello,* and *Lear* form part of the common store of references from which Joyce and his characters indifferently draw), and finally as a human type both individual and representative.

Stephen elaborates his critical biography before a fairly competent audience, at the National Library in Dublin, wishing to convince others yet at the same time not claiming absolute conviction himself: one feels that Shakespeare is less the subject than the pretext for this brilliant analysis. It is a pretext for Stephen to provoke and fascinate those whom he considers his opponents, a pretext for Joyce to set out via Stephen in almost systematic form a number of themes which he has often used but not formulated before. A part of Joyce's critical plan was to analyse the mechanics of his own creation. In his three major works, *Portrait*, *Ulysses*, and *Finnegans Wake*, there is a central character who is the artist, who serves as his mouthpiece. The need to be totally comprehensive necessitates the inclusion within the work of the very instruments of its genesis—thus one must always look for both the finished form and that which precedes it, the form in progress. Similarly, one will find the finished man as well as the man in the process of forming himself, at every stage of development.

Stephen, for example, is the artist as a young man; he is far from having ended the cycle of his experiences at the beginning of *Ulysses*, while Bloom is nearly at the end of his, yet will not reach the true end of his evolution until the penultimate chapter, "Ithaca". Until the end, Stephen and Bloom will keep (to some degree) the malleability of those who are still in search of their permanent identity and seeking to define it in their relationships with other people and with themselves.

In life, existence and its incidentals precede creation. The work is a product not only of the artist's imagination but also of his personal problems. This is why, in order to tell the story of Shakespeare, Stephen interprets the work as the consequence of particular experience, transformed by art: one can thus find the man via the work.

In the same way, to Joyce life and art are consubstantial. But only after a *particular moment*, a turning point, does Joyce grasp the implications of this and find himself able to comprehend the lived experience, no longer as a series of events succeeding each other in time, but in the suspension of memory; what had been a life becomes a kind of "history" defined by its own laws, with a structural system, and this crystallisation takes place at a certain moment of Joyce's life which is recorded in the play *Exiles*, which we shall examine in the second part. All these things are given to us, but given in the haphazard disorder of reality; a number of actual theorems are to be found in the fifty pages of this play, and if they are collected together, it will be seen that in their totality they portray in a lively fashion Joyce's idea of the nature of man and artist. It must be pointed out first of all that for Joyce there is no question of making a moral portrait, but a portrait of the artist as he is defined by his personal and social situation and by the practice of his art: the work is a function of the biographical happenings; but very soon for Joyce the opposite of this relationship becomes necessary, and life comes to depend on the exercise of the art.

Who is Shakespeare? Joyce presents him as young man, husband, father, writer, courtier. He is determined by circumstances first, and then by his actions, before beginning to be determined by his art.

The important thing to point out here is that Joyce confers significant form on his life *a posteriori,* and that it is his interpretation of his own life that constitutes the work of art; it is the modulations of episodes from lived experience into themes of literature that give the work its tone of originality. In "Circe" and "Charybdis and Scylla" can be seen a fairly complete picture of Joyce's favourite themes; the fact that these are excerpted from a biography of Shakespeare and from a parody of that biography contributes two indirect meanings. One is the universal validity of this system of critical deduction, since what is valid for Shakespeare is surreptitiously taken over by Stephen, behind whom Joyce is but half hidden; and on the other hand this very universality of experience shows that Joyce in fact tends to reject the overly individual characteristics and to make a "portrait" rather than a realistic study of a man. Neither Joyce nor Stephen believes himself to be Shakespeare, or believes in the Shakespeare he evokes; on the contrary, they believe in the artist as a person who is formed as much by a vocation as by a series of encounters with the outside world—chance encounters at first, which soon appear necessary and are then methodically repeated. The artist is indeed, as Stephen says in *Portrait,* "a product of this race and this country and this life," but the phrase must be understood as meaning, it is not this race, this country, this life, that "produce" Stephen or Joyce, but the artist who produces himself *against* or *outside of* these determining factors.

Race, country and life are called by other names as well: race, in particular, only takes on its full meaning if it is seen to contain the more precise concept of "Church"; by "race" in the ethnic sense Joyce means the Celtic race. This is no empty word, for there is in Joyce a current of anti-Celtic racialism opposed to the Celtophilia so in favour with his contemporaries, that of Yeats and A.E., of Griffith and the Sinn Fein. What does "race" mean for Joyce? "A race of clodhoppers," he says in *Portrait* and in *Ulysses,* not by insisting on the poverty or the coarseness of the peasants, but by emphasising the fact that their primitive cast of mind provides a breeding-ground for every superstition, the most thriving being the Catholic Church.

"This country" is Ireland, battered, colonised, and in Joyce's eyes incapable of regaining her true freedom.

"This life," at the time Stephen is speaking, still means his "first" life, his childhood and adolescence in Dublin, with his family.

Reality and its interpretation, object and subject, destiny and choice are connected, sometimes to the point of confusion, in this work whose originality can be summed up thus: Joyce not only feeds the work of art on his life (a property common to all work), but also fashions his life so that its reality may already be the image of what is to be written in its image. Stanislaus Joyce says in *My Brother's Keeper* (p. 223) that James had decided to make his life "an experiment," to be "the artificer" of "his own style of life." Ellmann's biography shows to what extent Joyce's life was already a work of art in itself.

The Determining Moment

The general, exterior form of the artist's life as seen by Joyce has, as we have said, a rhythm of out-going and return. The motive of this movement out in the first phase, and then of the conscious withdrawal back, is a particular form of unhappiness: the artist as a young man leaves his native town because he feels himself shut out and threatened, and because he is, by his own fault, trapped in a situation so dangerous to his personal integrity that he has to take to flight in order to save himself. The vocation begins under sinister conditions. The details of Shakespeare's story as told by Stephen are typical: scarcely transposed, they are the same as those which drive Richard Rowan, Stephen Dedalus, and James Joyce from Dublin. Stephen calls the youthful errors which necessitate flight "the portals of discovery," using, as one can guess, a variation on the myth of the fall, the *felix culpa* which drives man from paradise while promising a redemption to come. This morality of sin as necessary is scarcely original, for it can be found in Milton or Blake as well as Saint Augustine. But Joyce makes use of it for profane purposes: Stephen declares "the mistakes of genius are voluntary," justifying after the event with Satanic pride certain errors of his own inspired less by his will than by defiance, or the shame of being the victim rather than the criminal. This is also the situation of Shakespeare, victim rather than guilty perpetrator of an unfortunate marriage, and victim of a family of unscrupulous brothers. Joyce selects a series of "moments of contact" around which crystallise whole networks of emotions (in the realm of life) or of symbols (in art). These moments can be easily identified by their recurrence in the work: that which is accidental when it first appears becomes coincidental the second time and determines a whole mechanism of repetition so that any gesture, act or word connected with the first event will, if evoked or repeated, set off the complete mechanism. We shall see, for example, the theme of unjust punishment appear and develop throughout Joyce's work from the beginning of *Portrait* onwards. It is certain that if Joyce imagined the succession of these experiences as a movement in space and time, as the "slow and dark birth of the soul" (*Portrait,* p. 203), or as the "changing forms" of the soul, "entelechy, form of forms" (*Ulysses,* p. 178), he did so because he imagined the work of art simultaneously as a spatio-temporal journey towards the point where the artist would know himself as such, and as the recording of this journey in the memory. Present, past and future collaborate in constituting the person of the man of genius, a process both active and passive in which, as Stephen says of Shakespeare, he acts and is acted upon, he meets others and meets himself.

And here Joyce's intention of using life for the purposes of art comes in: he wishes to find in the reality of the outside world that which was in his inner world *in potentia.* In other words, the latter is to give to the former its desired shape and pattern. Joyce finds everywhere his chosen, personal targets—the family, the Church, his country—and represents these institutions in his work by means of type characters, or by way of a system of correspondances, abstract themes or symbolic objects. From his encounters with these three adversaries springs a series of themes which will be the object of our study in the first part. These comparatively personal themes are raised by art to a universality such that what was only a private grievance of Joyce's may become relevant for everyman.

Part One: The Family Cell

I. The Family and its Portrayal

A Dublin Family

The history of the Joyce family assumed distressing forms which marked James Joyce for life: from 1882 they declined in the social scale in a rather spectacular fashion, from a comfortable middle-class level to genuine poverty, and this decline could not be excused by reason of any noble political misfortune, but was due to the irresponsibility of John Joyce.

Because of his bad record (says Stanislaus Joyce)[1], it was at first doubtful whether my father would be granted any pension, but on the personal intercession of my mother, the people at the top, whoever they were, assigned to him a pension equal to about one third of his salary, and amounting to eleven pounds a month. At about the same time his house property in Cork, or what was left of it, was sold, apparently to make good defalcations, but it was so heavily mortgaged that little or nothing came to him from the sale. We left Blackrock abruptly and moved up to Dublin. My father was still in his early forties, a man who had received a university education and had never known a day's illness. But though he had a large family of young children, he was quite unburdened by any sense of responsibility towards them. His pension, which could have taken in part the place of the property he had lost and been a substantial addition to an earned income, became his and our only means of subsistence.

[1] Stanislaus Joyce, *My Brother's Keeper* (New York, 1958).

Nor could it be considered a nobly borne or pitiful poverty. John Joyce aggravated his inefficiency by a chronic alcoholism which enabled him to turn the catastrophic aspect of the situation into farce; but his family could not hide their misery. James reacted by making a kind of ironic trophy out of his wretchedness; Stanislaus, his younger brother, finding publicity intolerable, developed the sense of honour which his father lacked. In real life, James became accustomed to insecurity, and probably profited from it in the form of experience to be used artistically; the difficulty of everyday life led him to the building of imaginary replacements. The gap between original social status and present sordid reality left him suspended in a sort of no-man's-class, not actually belonging to any social stratum, and thus provided the distance necessary for a critical observation of material situations. This feeling of having no place in society[2] is ironically parallelled by the physical displacement caused by moving house so often.[3]

So much moving should prevent any attachment to a particular place, where one lives for long enough to take it over in the memory. The decline and displacement are the germs of that theme of exile which is, in Joyce's work, at the origin of every movement. Thus, it is not possible for one's points of stability to be concrete objects: if there is any sense of possession or property, it can only be imaginary or of the inner world. What is to be inalienable in the future is precisely these family memories and the possession of the inner world, whose importance and integrity James is determined to defend. He becomes attached to himself, and gives himself a world from which no father can disinherit him. He sets up a permanent place in a universe over which history has no power, the universe of art and culture. Indeed, it would not be wrong to suppose that even Joyce's metaphors are responses to the unpleasant nature of real images. Necessity makes him walk, and he is to create a character who dreams of flying. The complete lack of actual space belonging to him is doubtless at the origin of the need for infinite space manifested in the character of the artist. The gradual disappearance of

[2]"Our neighbours in Millbourne Lane except in the other half of the villa, were farmhands and navvies who lived in dilapidated cottages. Though there were certainly no signs of wealth about the children of our family, the infant proletarians from the cottages were unfriendly, and displayed their hostility by name-calling in chorus and stone-throwing. It was quite unprovoked, due solely to that innate animosity, observable everywhere in the lower classe, to anybody who is not yet quite so lousy as they are". (*My Brother's Keeper*, p. 72.)

[3]Stanislaus counts nine changes of address in eleven years: "In the beginning, two furniture vans and a float were needed for the moving; in the end it was just a float." (*Ibid.*, p. 69.)

family possessions to the sales or the pawnshop creates in him an intentional indifference to personal property, logically accompanied by the tendency to attribute almost magic qualities to the few material objects he does possess. An object finds its home only in Joyce's closely-guarded subjective world; only those objects marked with the seal of the work will be precious. Later Joyce collected objects as signs, as he felt himself to be their owner by right of "interpretation" of their meaning—talisman rings, a waistcoat, Nora's bracelet, or again those photographs of the Mestrovic sculptures, pinned up not from any love of sculpture but out of love for malicious allusion, showing three hideous women and labelled thus by Joyce: a bald peasant woman giving birth, labelled "dura mater"; a woman suckling a skeletal child, called "pia mater"; and an ugly old woman naked, labelled "Helen of Troy", at the age Dante saw her in Canto V of the *Inferno*.

What normally assures the coherence of a family simply does not exist for the Joyces: the ritual of meals or of worship together is very soon given up, because they cannot afford proper family meals. What, then, can the meaning of the family be for Joyce? By its numerical abundance, it has a tribal aspect, and family events are of two kinds: the two eldest sons see many siblings born and die. Life is on the rather primitive level of its natural cycles, which Joyce is to use in *Finnegans Wake*. Then there are the quarrels between John Joyce and his wife, from which the sons soon learn a disgust for violence and for resignation and a feeling for the degradation incurred by a person who yields to his baser passions such as anger; this becomes the subject of "Counterparts," one of the stories in *Dubliners*. A complete devaluation of morality ensues; family solidarity becomes a defence against the neighbours' eyes and the gossip Joyce was to parody so well in *Ulysses* and *Finnegans Wake*. The social pose is almost a necessity for these children.

As for the sanction of the Church, it is made a mockery of by the mediocrity of this union it has consecrated; by it the sacrament is deconsecrated. If one has to put on a show for others as a means of self-defence, the solitude of the individual within the family, on the contrary, separates them all. Out of the (approximately) eighteen members of the Joyce family, only James and Stanislaus had any feeling of relative sympathy. In 1904 Joyce wrote to Nora, "We were seventeen in family. My brothers and sisters are nothing to me. One brother alone is capable of understanding me."[4] This was not exactly true, for his brothers and

---

[4]*Letters*, vol. II, p. 48, 29 Aug. 1904.

sisters formed the chorus to sing of the family sufferings around him and to inspire in him the wish, hence the reason, for flight. Later he summoned two of his sisters to Italy, motivated partly by the desire to reconstitute, as ever, his own Dublin.

He is both alone and safe and yet threatened by the family cell. Joyce will never be able to do without the protecting circle. They flatter him and stifle him; he escapes but has to reconstruct this family, because it is still part of himself and is, further, a kind of Dublin. There he establishes his personality, he rules, he loves and is loved, he rests from his greatness, he sings, is nicknamed "Sunny Jim," temporarily discards his social pose, sympathises—but never hesitates to exploit others or to demand a double ration when others are hungry. He is well off there. And the tribe is astonishingly faithful to this man who acts as if all doors were open and all gestures easy to make, who dances and mimics his troubles, who makes them into metaphors and displays them in public, even down to his tastes in dress—while his brothers and sisters live in strictest constraint, keep silent, practise resignation, enter orders, accept hunger as their lot, and live in simple ignorance. Humility seems natural to this Catholic family.

But it must be borne in mind that this family, beginning with Joyce himself in 1882, are unfortunate rather than tragic, for they still have an over-strong vitality and instinct for self-preservation. They share intimately but not excessively the political and economic misfortunes of Ireland. They are defined as Catholics as opposed to the Protestants, with whom nevertheless the elder Joyce can maintain good relations, but who remain always "the others"—people such as the Vance family of Martello Terrace, whose daughter Eileen was Joyce's first (and doubtless only) innocent love. The real enemies are the English, and there can be no confusion possible on this point; for Joyce they are shopkeepers and merchants, people obsessed with hygiene, imperialists who tend to consider Ireland as a kind of picturesque Australia near at hand, where the explorer may observe the vestiges of druidic civilisation— hence James' deep dislike for the Oxford undergraduate brought back by his friend Gogarty, Mr. Trench, more Gaelic than the Irish.[5] Joyce reacted so strongly to his feeling of cultural alienation that he came to prefer the teaching of the Jesuits to that of lay teachers in so far as the latter implied mental Anglicisation. Thus in a curious way he agrees with his father's view, for the attitude of John Joyce towards the Jesuits

[5]V. Chevenix Trench, an original of Haines in *Ulysses*, who used to encourage his Irish friends to revive their language.

was that of the business-minded bourgeois who judges according to class criteria.

Music, sport, beer and debts form the typically Dublinesque leitmotif of family conversations. The underhand pressures exerted by the Church via the mother, and their chronic poverty sometimes cause explosions; and later the Joyce brothers discover that this is not characteristic of their own home only, that the same happens elsewhere.

Thus Joyce's childhood unfolds in a family setting marked by falls and crises. For him, the family is experienced in pity and fear. As the eldest, it must be he who bears the crushing burden of family responsibility for his father. The house and its misery repel him, and he knows that in claiming himself as a unique being, he is rejecting and denying his family. One must choose; it is a question of life and death. And Joyce will always choose his own life rather than that of others—with lucidity, but not without paying the price. He cannot fail to feel guilty; and yet he is sure that he was right in saving himself first, feeling sacrifice to be useless because these days it is impossible for one man to try to save the others. Salvation is either collective and economic, or the work of the individual soul for itself, Joyce knows. When in his reflection on the subject he identifies himself with Jesus, he sees himself not as Saviour but as a villainous little dark-skinned Jew, in torment; the Passion finds its justification in itself and in the folly of mankind, not in a sacrifice for others. It is masochistic and an "act of passion" much more than it is generous.

Before becoming able to eliminate all hesitation, he had had to experience instability, or the absence of all security. What could established stability offer to a young Joyce? Neither father, homeland, art nor culture, for these were all in the hands of the enemy. There is God. But God is the supreme absence: in Ireland his Church has allied itself with the English, with reactionaries. Ireland, he used to say, is caught between two masters, the Pope and the English imperialism. The Joyce family had chosen to pay its homage to Rome. Confessors are there like hated ghosts, guiding the mother to such an extent that Joyce never knows whether he is addressing her or her spiritual counsellor.

The disagreement in the house over questions of morality ceases to exist in the political sphere. The tone is set by John Joyce the father, a boastful, voluble Cork man, who sees history as a comedy rather than a nightmare. Picturesque detail and commentary appeal to him most. Events are to be lived through personally, and to have mock-heroic effects drawn from them, for the subsequent amusement of one's drinking companions. For this father Parnell had been less a political personality of the first importance than a favourite hero, whose adventures could border on the romantic or the disreputable, at the whim of the narrator.[6] After the death of the Hero, John Joyce loses interest in history, just as though in a serial the noble hero had been killed off too early in the story. The pretext for the plot then becomes boring. Parnell was the "Irish Dream": one could identify with him, he was too handsome to be true, and yet he did what every Irishman of John Joyce's age surely dreams of doing—committed adultery. And with the wife of an English captain!

But when the dream has crumbled away, reality loses its charms. After Parnell, John Joyce seems to have given up the game—an end to tears and noble theatrical emotions! The Irish revolution, with its crowd-impulses, was not a show at which one could applaud the good and hoot at the bad without danger to oneself. John had a theatrical sense of politics rather than a realistic or ideological concept; he was inspired by personal enmities; the anticlericalism inherited from his father and the sarcastic pleasure he took in disliking his in-laws would inspire him more than did the fate of his country. John Joyce called a halt to his active life towards 1889, and enlivened the rest of his time with boasting and revised versions of his mémoirs.

None of the members of the family who remained in Ireland took any part in the liberation of the country. The two eldest, James and Stannie, claimed to have a European "vocation", but neither of them was a nationalist. "Politics" was one of those "big words" which the two brothers soon learned to distrust:

> In early youth, my brother had been in love, like all romantic poets, with vast conceptions, and had believed in the supreme importance of the world of ideas. His gods were Blake and Dante. But then the minute life of the earth claimed him, and he seems to regard with a kind of compassion his youth deluded by ideals that exacted all his service, "the big words that make us so unhappy," as he called them. *(My Brother's Keeper, p. 53)*

[6]"When the property in Cork was sold, he had gone with my father on what I think was his last visit to his native town. In *A Portrait of the Artist,* the visit takes place later and awakens in Stephen a raw sense of unrest and spiritual discomfort, but my brother's letters home at the time were written in a tone of amusement, even when he described going from one bar to another. While we were living in Millbourne Lane, there was a further visit of a few days in summer to Glasgow, at the invitation of a captain of one of the Duke liners, who was a friend of my father's. The great joke of the visit, which was spoiled by rain, was that my father, soused to the gills, on the return trip, had a heated and noisy argument about politics with the captain, an anti-Parnellite. Fortunately the captain was a teetotaller on board though not on shore. 'By God, man,' my father would conclude in telling this wonderfully good story, 'if he had been drinking he would have thrown me overboard.' " *(My Brother's Keeper)*

It was each one's business to *survive*. Joyce was the eldest of sixteen or seventeen children,[7] and his experiences in the family would be enough to destroy a merely luke-warm optimist; they were hungry every day, while belonging to a class that eats when hungry. But somehow there existed a strange harmony, due perhaps to the father's undeniable charm and the mother's resignation. Even in their darkest years they had the consolation of the piano, father and son would sing, and the mother listen, with joy.

All this was to go towards the creation of the Joycean atmosphere, composed of an invincible sense of humour and of emotion, and of a redeeming sentimentalism, transfiguring the sordidness. The Joyce family established, on a smaller scale, a system of individual relationships very like that of Irish society, politically unimportant, economically and mentally under-developed, as it was about 1900. But it still had the Irish qualities of lyricism and vivacity that can be found in an O'Casey *(Juno and the Paycock)* or a Brendan Behan.

The Role of the Family in the Works of Joyce

The family as a unity does not exist in Joyce's works until *Finnegans Wake;* in *Portrait* and in *Ulysses,* it appears as a rather chaotic arrangement centred around the father and constantly threatened with collapse. Paradoxically, it is within the family circle that the feeling of separation is most direct and clear; in *Stephen Hero* there was still some vague complicity between Stephen and the younger brother Maurice, but Maurice has disappeared from the *Portrait.* This feeling of separation constitutes a direct criticism of marriage and conjugal existence.

The family as a living group and as a network of personal relationships plays an exceptionally large role in Joyce's work: his characters, who have rightly been called solitary, are surrounded by a crowd of living people or ghosts, with relation to whom their own position becomes established and identified, in more depth than it would be by their relations to their contemporaries. For Joyce, the person hidden behind his professional and social image is the product of his racial and family

[7]The figure varies with James or Stannie, either because they really did not know the number of still-born children, or because inexactitude here strengthens the attitude of deliberate indifference.

past. Once it has been said that Stephen is Irish and Bloom a Dublin Jew, everything that may explain their behaviour, thoughts or problems (except the factor of profession or vocation), comes from their blood relationships. Yet there are numerous different points of view possible for an observer of family structures. A sociologist or ethnologist might take for his central study the mature couple, with ancestors and descendants extant. For Joyce, the family long remains the first obstacle in the way of freedom for the young artist, and this is the situation of the son who is at the centre of the structure until *Ulysses*.

The family in *Portrait* makes Stephen into a rebellious son who clashes with his mother and despises his father. Again, the conditions of family life are associated in Stephen's mind with the conditions of life in Dublin, to such an extent that images from the kitchen and images from the street are superimposed in the imagination of the young man who is experiencing the town and the family in similar fashions: the disastrous economic situation is trying for Stephen, not only physically, as it is for the other children, but also spiritually, as it is for both James and Stanislaus. Stephen is infuriated by the ugliness of their poverty, which produces "a sordid, lying vision." "He was. . . . angry with the change of fortune which was reshaping the world about him into a vision of squalor and insincerity. Yet his anger lent nothing to the vision. He chronicled with patience what he saw, detaching himself from it and tasting its mortifying flavour in secret" (*Portrait*, p. 67).

He reacts as always by opposition: in his reveries he sees nothing but a white, Mediterranean house, its walls covered with trellises, where there lives, not a large poverty-stricken family, but a young girl alone, waiting for him. Next he tries to save his family, following his first vocation, that of redeemer, at an age when he is still a romantic and an idealist; he tries

> to build a breakwater of order and elegance against the sordid tide of life without him and to dam up, by rules of conduct and active interests and new filial relations, the powerful recurrence of the tides within him. Useless. From without as from within the waters had flowed over his barriers: their tides began once more to jostle fiercely above the crumbled mole. (*Portrait*, p. 98)

This attempt as Joyce describes it shows how the youthful artist's imagination works: life in its ugliness is as concrete and as irresistibly oncoming and as dangerous as the tide. The grey sea, the dirty yellow waters of the harbour, or the snot-green of Dublin Bay, rising. Stephen sets up aesthetic concepts in opposition to the threatening dirty water

—as though he wished to cure the family of its misery by harmonious phrases rather than by financial aid; in his naïveté, he still believes in a spiritual compensation, which is his form of religion. In fact, it would probably be more logical to say that the squalor of life around him brought out this taste for order and elegance in Stephen's mind; in a second phase, after the temptation of order and the religious life (be it that of Art or that of the Church), Stephen adopts the opposite attitude, because he no longer feels it possible to resist the sordidness.

He behaves now as James Joyce behaved: the foulness and the failure are put down to experience, for the sake of art; on the one hand, the things that he loathes become a means of distancing oneself, a justification for the most extravagant sensual or voluptuous imaginings, since one need not fear actually coming to believe in them. Stephen's poetic ecstasies, moving like Dante towards the Rose in the centre of seraphic choirs,[8] are attenuated by reality; instead of the infinite ardent spaces, the poet finds himself looking at the wall, at "the great overblown scarlet flowers of the tattered wallpaper," and hearing "common noises, hoarse voices, sleepy prayers." On the other hand, he quickly comes to differentiate the possible from the impossible and beauty from reality. And he decides not to flee from "the snares of the world" (*Portrait,* p. 162), but to yield to them and thus to know purity, beauty and integrity only relatively, in relation to their contraries. He rejects order because it is a lie or an escape; he instinctively rejects the "grave, and ordered and passionless life, . . . a life without material cares" that the Jesuits offer him, because "the chill and order of the life repelled him" (*Portrait,* pp. 160–1); he associates order with cold, a deathly sensation, and disorder becomes characteristic of life: "He smiled to think that it was this disorder, the misrule and confusion of his father's house and the stagnation of vegetable life, which was to win the day in his soul" (*Portrait,* p. 162).

At this level, then, the "misrule and confusion of his father's house" represents the necessary obstacle upon which to start building that moral resistence which forms the artist's soul. Joyce was in reality much more patient, or indifferent, than Stanislaus; then what had been indifference became the rule as soon as he discovered the principle of the *felix culpa,* the necessity of sin, the doctrine of progress by opposition to evil, which he extended to all real or imaginary spheres. From this point of view, misery and all the unpleasantness of life, humiliation,

[8]"The rose-like glow sent forth its rays of rhyme; ways, days, blaze, praise, raise. Its rays burned up the world, consumed the hearts of men and angels." (*Portrait,* p. 217.)

hunger, loneliness, all foster art. Apart from his fear of thunder, nothing made Joyce retreat; and we can see here that that form of heroism Stanislaus admired in him had its origin in an acute sensitivity to the future that was to be composed with the present. For the artist as centre of the world, the family setting, first perceived as the "amniotic liquid that surrounds the child,"[9] soon becomes the first place of dispossession and banishment; the united substance of which the small Stephen made a part is rent and torn, and different characters come forward, invested with an authority drawn from sources outside the family. Each adult is simultaneously a relative and a representative of some mysterious and often constraining power. Father, mother, and the aunt Dante[10] speak in the name of Dublin, of the Church, of politics; Ireland's past and present are thus transposed into realistic scenes of family meals, which take on an allegorical value: the well-known Christmas dinner in the first chapter of *Portrait* can be considered as a sociological allegory in miniature of the year 1891.

In the *Portrait*, every event of national or family import is related back to the family setting by Stephen as interpreter of reality; he still has Ireland in mind in the plans he makes. At the end of the book, he is preparing to "forge the uncreated conscience of (his) race"—he feels that his future and that of Ireland are somehow connected, and the link between the artist and his nation is essential.

By the beginning of *Ulysses* we can see an evolution taking place, not an evolution of progress towards the future and in the interests of Ireland, but rather one of retrogression and narrowing of the world. Stephen has turned towards the past and enclosed himself in the "Parnell pose" more than ever and the family has now become so scattered that father and son can go all day without meeting, that each wishes to repudiate the other, that Stephen can meet one of his sisters by accident and that they no longer share the same house. What remains of the family is a misty past, the ghost of the mother, and a father who behaves as though his children were ghosts themselves. Joyce is no longer interested in offspring, or in history, or in Ireland.

The family as pattern develops as the author's life evolves: at this time Joyce's main preoccupation was his life with Nora. Simon Dedalus, although still a faithful and attractive representation of John Joyce, retires into the background and only counts henceforth as titular father.

---

[9] J.-J. Mayoux, *Joyce* (Paris, 1965), p. 46.

[10]"Dante" was just the Joyce children's version of the word "Auntie," meaning Mrs. Conway, the original of Mrs. Riordan.

The place of this father who could well do without his son is taken by Bloom, the father without a son, who longs for children. In *Portrait*, Stephen was a projection of Joyce. On June 16, 1904, the day that constitutes *Ulysses*, Joyce was in actual fact twenty-two, the same age as Stephen. But *Ulysses* was written between 1914 and 1920, when Joyce was Bloom's age and passionately interested in Bloom, while he was losing interest in Stephen; Bloom's problems are more vital than Stephen's.

Instead of a large family, Joyce now presents the married couple, Mr. and Mrs. Bloom, and their relationship which in many ways is similar to that of Jim and Nora, which is to become the material of art: again the life fosters and feeds the work of art, and the author plays two roles. He uses himself as model for the son and for the father. This decentralisation of the family and this move towards the creation of archetypes (Adam and Eve) constitute the first step towards *Finnegans Wake*. This also determines important changes in tone: the artist was a rebellious son, but his youth serves as excuse for him; Joyce could permit himself some measure of self-criticism. The mature man, married and father of a daughter already nubile, is a vulnerable figure with no excuses—he is what he has made himself. Neither hero nor artist, his greatness is that of his humility in relation to himself.

It is in this doubtless that Bloom's originality lies, in his lack of any outstanding quality. Borgès used to say that Shakespeare was like all men except in that he was like *all* men; and in this sense Bloom is a Dublin Jewish Shakespeare: he is like all ordinary men, innocently imperfect, by virtue of his sympathy, tolerance and indulgence for others. Bloom has the modesty of those who care for others, and this lessens his personal existence. On the surface he exists as little as do those who are ghosts through absence or forgetfulness whom Stephen discusses in "Charybdis and Scylla." Mediocre, banal, and ridiculous—like everyone else: this is the conclusion Joyce wants the reader to reach, this the antiromantic stage of his work. The suppression of all possibility of difference, either by virtue or by vice, by any accidental good luck or misfortune, characterises Joyce's progress towards the universal mean—Bloom and Molly, husband and wife, are no longer specifically Dubliners or lower-middle-class in particular.

The family was used first in Joyce's work as a microcosm of Dublin, reproducing on a smaller scale the relationships of the individual in a limited society. The family, a social group or unit in *Portrait* and *Ulysses*, gradually becomes the organic group it is in *Finnegans Wake*, in which the individual has less importance the more the family represents the process of human development. The individual becomes blurred as the *type* emerges, and the family is no longer defined by its place in society but by its function as a self-renewing moment in human time.

Joyce proceeds to a detemporalisation of the couple in such a way that the Blooms might already belong to the archetypal world of *Finnegans Wake*, where Dublin is no longer one specific city of people, but a geographical site in the shape of a man, above which float shadows miming the history of many centuries, while the sins, desires, rivalries and basic curiosities of the eternal human family remain and renew themselves again.

The ephemeral and trivial life of one citizen observed under the microscope is but a particle of Life as a natural phenomenon observed with the telescope; history is replaced by "this nonday diary" in which the sounds of the street and the noise of pubs are swallowed up in the rustling of trees and the lapping of the river, where the family is no more than an interplay of primitive sexual attitudes or "herotisms" (*Finnegans Wake*, p. 614), ruled by A.L.P., a type of original woman (her initials forming the first letter of the Hebrew alphabet, *aleph*) and by H.C.E. the male figure who plays the parts of father, lover, builder, sinner, "Allmen" (*Finnegans Wake*, p. 419), with their three children, the twins and the fair Iseut. The family is no longer a small circle inside a large one, but is the symbol of humanity; history and society lose their primacy before the importance of "der Fall Adams."[11] Since, as Harry Levin says, H.C.E. is the archetypal father upon whom falls the responsibility for the misfortunes of humanity seen as one family,[12] history and society exist only as modifications of family relationships, which are dominated by the father. It can be seen that Joyce, having reached his fifties, H.C.E.'s age, was detaching himself from reality in order to understand life from the standpoint of those ageless human problems whose shadow, projected through Time, may be mistaken for History.

The fate of the father in the archetypal family is similar to that of John Joyce: he falls. And in his fall are contained all other falls from Adam's to that of the drunken mason Finnegan, who falls from his scaffolding and is killed, and that of John Joyce who falls down to the bottom of the social order. But the father in the thirties is no longer John, it is James Joyce, and his contribution to the portrait of the father is his unhappy

[11] *Finnegans Wake*, p. 70. This can mean the "case" or "trial" of Adam if one takes the German meaning of the pun, or the biblical Fall if it is English.

[12] See Harry Levin, *James Joyce, A Critical Introduction*, (Faber, London, 1960, 2nd. ed.), pp. 136–7.

discovery of the part played by the daughter as woman in the life of her father as lover. Love and guilt come together in the theme of incest, as they had been united thirty-five years earlier in the theme of sexual sin.

The family has never been so closely and narrowly centred on itself, it seems; for Joyce only the father and his creation still have some reality, while the woman still continues to wander about in the background. H.C.E.'s family consists of five people, in theory, but in fact everything is attached around one of two groups, one consisting of the father and the daughter as rejuvenation of the mother, and the other comprising the two brothers. In searching for the figurative sense of this family we realise that Joyce is still treating himself and his art under the organic appearance of human development; and surely the complex relationships between Joyce and his daughter Lucia must have provided inspiration for this ardent, guilty father who refused, against the general opinion, to admit his daughter's madness, insofar as he could not but feel himself responsible. On the other hand, the conflict of the sons, opposing yet complementary, can be considered as the allegorical setting out, in personal forms, of conflicts which weigh upon the father's conscience. Their perpetual struggle is evocative of all the mental dramas and wars of history, that end only when one side suppresses the other, for a while. Shem and Shaun turn into Jacob and Esau, Brutus and Cassius, Wellington and Napoleon, Wyndham Lewis and James Joyce, Jim and Stanislaus, de Valera and Joyce, all couples whose progress is made by mutual opposition and mistakes until they are at last absorbed in one body lying by the Liffey, on the site of Dublin; although the family evolves in time, it perpetuates itself in space, for geography remains while history changes. If *Finnegans Wake* is nothing but the father's dream, we return to John Joyce and the artist as god at the end of the family's tale.

Joyce's life was to have two rhythms, two places of action, two plots, which will not surprise anyone who is aware of the ambiguity of the human personality.

In a first, fairly brief period, Joyce learns all his lessons from history and from his experiences as a human being, in one particular world located in Dublin and centered on his family. Then comes the time to "steady himself" and "earn a living." He could be a priest or teacher if he adopted their creed. But he has seen too much for that. The Church, drink, brutalisation, fear of the unknown, masochism, have seeped into the nature of the Irish and of the Joyces over a long period, and they are deadly perils. Ireland signifies death and James Joyce does not want to die. But death comes to seek him out in Paris: "Mother dying, come home, Father." So Joyce comes home to see his mother die. She took several months "to die like an animal," as Gogarty says.

And Joyce is back again in the isle of death; some months pass before he can make good his escape. His mother's death frees him and makes it possible for him to be born as artist. He has virtually abandoned the political renaissance. He is to be, not an Irishman, but Joyce. Henceforth, history can happen without him, and sometimes against him, often spoiling his time or his plans. He lives until 1941, passing through two world wars and the Irish revolution, but does not speak about politics again. In 1914, during the first war, he clears his account with Ireland, with mother, wife, and treacherous friends in a play, so hermetically personal as to be almost unplayable, called *Exiles*. His vision of the world concerns an un-historicised human race, and his ethical views correspond curiously with the morality of a man trained and influenced by theologians. The city disgusts him, but there are still the people; if he dislikes the people, there is still Man.

And it is Man, Everyman, that mediaeval character eternally one and the same, who moves him to pity—so much so that at last he remains Man, and is Joyce. And Joyce becomes his own first subject and first object.

Thus in 1918, when the western world emerges again, Joyce publishes in a journal of limited circulation, the *Little Review*, the first episode of *Ulysses*, dealing with Stephen Dedalus, the discontented man, coming to terms with his selfish history. Stephen is attacked by ghosts that are forms of his own death, at a time when death is not an individual matter but a wholesale slaughter in which the creatures are more like beasts than men. The generation of the twenties and thirties is trying to assimilate the phenomenon of war and its sequel. But nothing is allowed to hinder Joyce, who takes great care not to let himself return into the reality of national powers, having once escaped; he spends the troubled times in unreal or neutral towns such as Trieste and Zurich, where one can pretend not to know of other people's death.

In 1920, all is going well; Joyce is in Paris, France has won and is recovering, and will soon be able to take notice of *Ulysses*—in fact, will take great pleasure in it, in order to forget the nightmare. Stephen wants to escape from the nightmare of History. He does not mean contemporary history but History in general as manifestation of the absurdity of violent action. His examples are not Irish, nor even Euro-

pean. By now Joyce hears only the voices of his own work. His "micro-
history" is the time marked out by his petty wars and great victories.
His calendar no longer coincides with that of the outside world; fron-
tiers are removed and space "disoriented." Joyce wanders incessantly
according to his whims or the changing seasons, replacing by an almost
pathological nomadic urge the "paralysis" of Ireland that he had so
despised.[13] It is unusual for a writer to have moved about so much
without disturbing the creative mechanism. It is as though he had been
constantly moving, driven by some half-conscious wish always to be
rootless, as though he had wanted to live out his flight from Egypt, his
exile, like the wandering Jew—but where was the promised land?
There was no land for Joyce. He rejected the appeal, the attachment
to any material object outside himself. The only thing to exist is that
which he is *going to create;* the only place both dear and necessary to
him is the "space" of the book and the only time that of the work in
progress. The important thing is not to bring to an end but to persevere. . . .

Joyce finds his place in movement, in a perpetual "progress" which
seeks no end because the only end is death and every halt an image of
death. The "progress," in the sense of projection towards the future, is
active, is work. One must create and not let oneself be moulded. Joyce's
"time" passes in the mind of the artist; there are breaks, caused by
illness or lawsuits for example, but essentially it is a continuity. No-one
can stop Joyce from living and creating, except himself. His body takes
its revenge: his eyes weaken, his children remind him that they are
individuals differing from him, his daughter goes mad. But everything
continues, the Joycean machine carries on, no longer set in motion by
circumstances but by its inventor alone. One might almost say that
Joyce's response to History is a book in which he mocks its power. For
in 1939, as he finishes *Finnegans Wake,* Joyce feels cheated and threatened. Hitler has dared to start war and distracts the attention of the
public with his sadistic grimacings, while Joyce is publishing the most
modern work ever written. Europe is being fobbed off with endless
speeches while Joyce is transforming language. And he fears lest *Finnegans Wake* disappear in the ruins of yet another war, lest there be
no-one left to read *Finnegans Wake.* This would be the harm. Joyce has
long since given up being interested in the decline of values; *Ulysses*

[13]Ellmann has made an impressive collection of Joyce's addresses in *Letters,* vol. II.

had already settled accounts with humanism. After Bloom, the deluge, but Joyce had already prepared *Finnegan* as an ark to contain all human myths and types; the world, in its blind lust to seek its own destruction, could wipe itself out, for *Finnegans Wake* had saved its symbols, its notations, and its cultural patterns.

II. John Joyce:
The Father's Side

The Network of Interdependence

Financially comfortable, only son of an only son who was rich and a gentleman of leisure, John Joyce passed on to his son James one virtue which was apparently a family characteristic, a good sense of humor and an eye for the ridiculous. For three generations one can trace the taste for striking an attitude in public, the Rabelaisian defiance[1] capable of transformation into dramatic talent; both John and James were good actors. The heads of the Joyce family also shared a curious lack of practical sense which brought them in two generations or less from a state of relative well-being to total poverty. Grandfather Joyce managed to go bankrupt twice, and John Joyce continued the tradition by investing the rest of the family fortunes in the Dublin and Chapelizod Distillery Company, nominating himself secretary. Three years

[1] "My grandfather's portraits and photographs show him to have been a handsome man —the handsomest man in Cork, according to my father. He was the only child of an only child, as my father was. The source of my brother's peculiar form of self-exploitation for an artistic purpose, that sublimation of egoism, may well be here in these three generations of only sons. A brilliant young man of promise, my grandfather lived beyond his means. He was fond of hunting, and at one period in his brief career, seems to have owned a race-horse; I fancy from certain vague hints of my father's that he must have been a gambler. One was that, marrying at the same time as a friend of his, they had a bet of ten guineas on which of the two would have a son first. My father won the bet for him, but shortly after birth lost this useful talent for making easy money." (*My Brother's Keeper*, p. 42.)

later he discovered that the shareholders had been swindled by an unscrupulous director; which discovery brought him the congratulations of his fellow-victims. John Joyce was to be very often applauded and congratulated during his life. He later successfully entered the service of the National Liberal Club, and was even offered a chance of election, but preferred to live on the income from his property in Cork, which would allow him to go sailing, to drink his fill, and to sing, sometimes in concerts and at other times in the pub opposite the concert-hall. John always held some sort of sinecure, thanks to family connections, in various employments which controlled Dublin's economy—the tax-office, brewery, or politics—and this was how he gained experience of the hidden side of public affairs, of the side that is ridiculous and like a parody when compared with the glittering surface of finance, policy and power. This knowledge of the underside of things, which provides so much of *Dubliners* and *Ulysses,* has its origin in this parasitic activity of the father. To John, also, James owes his sense of the heroi-comical anecdote, and especially the living presence of Dublin, for John, although a Cork man, knew all about its citizens, their ancestry, and the mythical history of their misdemeanours, as though he were Asmodeus himself. Dublin was like a vast theatre for both John and James, where they could be simultaneously author, actor, and prompter. John Joyce was a personality in Dublin society well known for his gift of commentary. In the privacy of his family, he was cruel, sombre, irritable, his pleasant humour turned to sarcasm,[2] drunk four or five days in the week, and cruel to his wife from the beginning of their marriage, when she had been a pretty girl of nineteen, up to her death as a prematurely aged woman of forty-four.

James has two images of his father, and the one of John the born charmer redeems that of the guilty father; the two images are inseparable—hence the ambiguity of Joyce's attitudes towards the father. Love and indulgence are both strongly present, but the eldest son's love for the father was genuine, and was moreover returned. In reality it was John who betrayed James when the latter eloped with Nora Barnacle without paternal or ecclesiastical consent. John had seduced May, but he had married her. The old sinner still keeps his respect for established institutions; and there was to be no reconciliation until James in his turn produced a son. Thus the Joyce line was assured of continuing; Giorgio

---

[2]"What a loving son!" he would say when Stanislaus tried to avoid him (*My Brother's Keeper,* p. 78), and James echoes this in *Stephen Hero* (p. 207), "By God, you're a loving pair of sons, you and you brother!"

was to inherit the vices and virtues of his forbears, a good voice, a tendency to drink, failed career as a singer, etc. John and James felt the responsibility of perpetuating the succession.

For some time Dublin is still too near to them for the sons to be able to overcome the feeling of shame their father's behaviour causes them. But it must be emphasised that James never repudiated his father in real life, and hardly even in his work. It has often been said that the dominant father- or uncle-figure in *Dubliners* was inspired by John Joyce, but this is not entirely true; the fathers and uncles of the boys in *Dubliners* have, it is true, many of John Joyce's characteristics, and Tom Kernan, representative of a tea firm, is indeed modelled on him,[3] but he is much more agreeable and amusing in his decline than are the hypocrites around him, and if he does wrong, he harms himself most. On the contrary, it is seldom pointed out that Gabriel Conroy, in "The Dead", makes an after-dinner speech very similar to those which John Joyce knew so well how to make; he is a great talker, like John, and a worried husband like James.

There is a tendency to take Farrington, the ferocious drunkard in "Counterparts", for John, and it is true that this scene might have taken place in the Joyces' home, except that neither James nor Stanislaus would have crawled or cried, "I'll say an Ave for you"; but the story of Farrington[4] originates in a real incident, and the model for the unworthy father was Uncle Murray, May Joyce's brother.

The parents of Richard Rowan, the artist who personates Joyce in *Exiles,* do not copy John and May, but are exact reproductions of John's parents, the father a "smiler" and the mother—older, richer and harder than her husband—who never acknowledged her son's marriage.[5] It is, however, certain that the selfish fathers in *Dubliners, Portrait* and *Ulysses* are images of John Joyce; but one must again point out that when these images are harsh or cruel, they are borrowed from Stanislaus. Simon Dedalus, as we shall see later on, is John as seen by Stannie. James borrows from the younger brother's hatred in this way because the characters he first brings on stage are romantic child or adolescent figures, oppressed by the world and the family; Stephen as son is not James but a mixture of James and Stannie, the artist and the rebellious son.

[3] See "Grace," in *Dubliners.*
[4] See later examination of "Counterparts."
[5] "His own mother had been opposed to the match—'They are troublesome people, John'—and when his son, her only child, married, she went back to Cork. He never saw her again. She died alone." (*My Brother's Keeper*, p. 52.)

James loved his father for two reasons: because he had, as J.-J. Mayoux rightly remarks (*op. cit.*, p. 49), "a taste for dissociating himself from commonly-held opinions, for turning them upside down," to such an extent that no pressure would have forced him to change (and it was doubtless enough for someone to criticise his father, for Joyce to adopt an indulgent attitude and make allowances for him); and because James (and, privately, Stannie too) considered his father as a victim of his position as an Irish Catholic and of his country's history. If the mother represented the Church with its gentle insistence that the victim should agree to his own death, the father wanted to live but lacked the means of support. The father was apparently the agent of destruction, but in reality it was the mother as accomplice of insidious ecclesiastical forces that preach renunciation.

It would be easy to make a quick diagnosis of Joyce's case from a psycho-analytical standpoint; one could define the situation of Joyce as son in his attitudes to father and mother in the classic terms of the Oedipus complex and the impossibility of resolving it; but, on the contrary to what Ellmann says in his biography, Joyce does not identify with the father in order to pay court to the mother. If there is any identification, it happens rather at the level of infantile regression to which his alcoholism had brought John Joyce; John felt himself to be guilty and condemned as such by his wife, and if James identifies himself with John, it is by sharing this guilt, which for him has different causes —father and son were accused of having killed May Joyce, the former by his ill-treatment, the latter by his refusal of the Catholic faith.

Because she seems to have only a small role in his work, it is sometimes forgotten how much Jim did love his mother. His mother-fixation is clear: on the one hand he cannot do without her, he needs her to participate in his most private life, to obtain her approval; and on the other, he is always tenderly careful and solicitous, without going as far as self-sacrifice, in her interests. Filial and paternal in his attitudes towards her, he cannot but associate her image in his mind with those of mourning, death, and Ireland in the guise of the "poor old woman" carrying milk who appears in "telemachus."

The mother-fixation reveals an ambiguity of feelings, of simultaneous guilt and mistrust. In order to be himself he has to injure the person who clumsily wishes for his good. The mother's death cannot be lived out like a normal event: the theme of matricide is transposed into the work, as we shall see, and becomes a pathological motif. In reality, it is his mother's death that frees Jim from any bondage to the Church. Inversely and correlatively, the Church has to be, as it were, exorcised in his work—it must have no further hold over his soul, so that he may rid himself of his mother's presence.

From these complexual relationships Joyce draws a general attitude which sets the tone of his work and inspires him in his researches on the participation of the artist in his art. The Dedalus family might have suggested to a Zola a dark realistic study, but the Joyce family, on the contrary, is turned into a miniature universe whose difficulties are treated with a humour unblunted by bitterness. Anger arouses the spirit of satire, and the gap between dream and reality fosters the spirit of parody.

Stephen's melancholy is real, but he makes use of it to parody himself as Hamlet. Truth or reality cannot be fully revealed unless pathos is tempered with irony—hence the creation of the hero-type who is only the mask covering the vulnerable sensitive person, who may be called "impostor," as Shaun calls Shem in *Finnegans Wake*. This very false invulnerability is the source of self-mockery, since the person is not deceived by his own heroic persona; the Stephen of *Ulysses* makes asides denouncing his own sufferings and duplicity. The multifarious game of pretences begins with the need for dissimulation which Stephen in *Portrait* calls "silence and cunning," and ends in *Finnegans Wake* with the pleasure of denunciation. The youthful Joyce suffered from victimisation and humiliation, and his idol was Ibsen, the great, solitary moralist and reformer. By the end of his life he had far outdistanced Ibsen: defensive dissimulation had been replaced by a gallery of self-portraits, of comic "confessions" by a man who loathed the idea of confession (one must, however, point out that Joyce confesses in a language so difficult that few readers are able to understand all the joyous or shameful secrets he pours out in *Finnegans Wake*).

When James Joyce was born in 1882, John was nothing more than a clerk in a tax-office, with no possible social dignity. It was therefore necessary to invent one's own, which John proceeded to do by giving up work and by arrogating to himself the status of Gentleman. Unfortunately, a gentleman is one who is independant and of private means, while John's only income was now his pension. But he was, as it seems, gifted. "He is generous, however, and when he claims to have 'some ideas of a gentleman' he does not seem to be ridiculous," notes Stanislaus, in the diary he kept in Dublin.[6] An unscrupulous debtor, he passes on to James the art of shameless borrowing; James, on the contrary,

---

[6] *Dublin Diary*, September 1903.

would not admit charity—to require tribute in the name of some imaginary right allows one to remain calm and uninvolved. Ellmann recounts how Joyce took great care to protect his self-respect against any patronising attempts to take him over. For instance, there is the well-known incident of the pair of old shoes which Ezra Pound, in a spirit of friendship and quite without malice, sent to Joyce by the intermediary of T.S. Eliot, who did not know what was in the box. Joyce, on opening it, was so mortified by the grotesque contents that he at once felt obliged to invite Eliot and Wyndham Lewis out to dinner, where he spent enough to have bought several pairs of new shoes. This gentlemanly self-respect impelled him to give excessive tips when he did go out, in spite of Nora's advice to the contrary. One can see here how much Joyce had been influenced by his father, whose likeness in *Stephen Hero* has a disturbing resemblance to the sort of person the son had become:

> On account of a certain income and of certain sociable gifts Mr. Dedalus had been accustomed to regard himself as the centre of a little world, the darling of a little society. This position he still strove to maintain but at the cost of a reckless liberality from which his household had to suffer both in deed and in spirit. (*Stephen Hero*, III)

John set up against the unfortunate reality of his material downfall a personal code of honour, composed of bravado, disguised idleness, a certain amount of courage, as must be admitted, and much cowardice disguised as authority. By avoiding real action, he also avoided having to realise his failure, being in this more fortunate than the miserable men in *Dubliners* who have failed and must know it. But he could not deceive himself; he could only change the form of the failure. Consciousness of his social inconsequence, he feels an increased need for self-assertion when he comes home to his waiting victims, and at once the mechanism of aggression is set in motion: the bad master fears his slaves. John Joyce fears his sons, and in order to crush any potential rebellion or diminution of his prestige, he shouts and bangs the table. He is caught—the house is both his kingdom and his prison now. His marriage, under conditions which he made worse by his hostility to his wife's family, had been rather like marriage into a class below him, and, as in every situation of this nature (underdeveloped, colonised country, alien, unsympathetic culture), the only riches are the poor man's wealth, children—and the Joyces had many children. John probably still longed for the only son, and so James as the eldest profited by this, being the only one to be treated with any pride or generosity. Stannie's situa-

tion as second son often enabled him to share or copy the fortunes of
the eldest; he was sent to school in the wake of James, and soon became
his faithful follower. The others formed an unhappy squad, whose presence rather embarrassed their father—he did not really know what to
do with them, as is cruelly illustrated by the story of Isabel in *Stephen
Hero;* the little girl had been packed off to a convent, where she made
the mistake of falling seriously ill:

> Stephen's father did not like the prospect of another inhabitant in his
> house, particularly a daughter for whom he had little affection. He was
> annoyed that his daughter would not avail herself of the opportunity
> afforded her in the convent but his sense of public duty was real if spas-
> modic and he would by no means permit his wife to bring the girl home
> without his aid. The reflection that his daughter, instead of being a help
> to him, would be a hindrance, and the suspicion that the burden of respon-
> sibility which he had piously imposed on his eldest son's shoulders was
> beginning to irk that young man troubled his vision of the future. (*Ste-
> phen Hero*, III)

Individual portions became smaller with each new addition to the
family. There must be a choice between sensibly limiting the numbers
of the family and wilfully increasing the difficulties of existence. But at
the same time John Joyce needed this large family: the concept became
quantitative, that the more children there were, the more he was truly
father. But the more children there were, the more enemies he had
about him. John's power rested upon this subject people who suffered
his tyranny, and whenever one of them escaped into independence,
"Pappie" was weakened. The house was, as we can see, the theatre
more of an antagonism between father and children than of any married harmony.

This does not mean that the latter relationship was unimportant, but
it is less violently presented, because the woman can always find some
pattern of existence within the home, however repressed and constrained it be. The home becomes a battlefield of clashing encounters,
with changing alliances between the apparent powers and real power,
with genuine victims and those who pretend to be oppressed. The head
of the family only has the right to use violence in order to conserve his
authority from attacks on all sides. He seems, and claims, to be master
of the situation, but has in fact always been its prisoner. This is why, in
the evening, the family hearth was made to witness vengeances, plotted
and muttered over, expressed in grunting and swearing. He had in the
beginning spared his wife from these, but that mercy was long since

forgotten. His wife annoyed him by "her dutiful symbolism" (*Stephen Hero*, III). He is only the centre of the family group because he is indicated as responsible to its real head, who is perpetually absent yet rules and judges them—God. This goes so far that John Joyce has some difficulty in forgiving his wife for having let herself be married, and comes to feel himself the unfortunate victim of a complete misalliance, hating as much as he does the Murrays, his wife's family. As for God, not daring to attack him directly, he attacks instead his representatives, showing thus the anticlericalism inherited from his own father.

The worst of the conjugal state is that the burden grows heavier all the time: each child increases May's sufferings, as she moves on to consecrated multiple motherhood, while John at her expense allows free rein to his uncontrollable selfishness. May is, indeed, more patient than other women would have been: Nora Barnacle's mother had not had so much consideration for her good-for-nothing husband, and she bears some resemblance to Mrs. Mooney in *Dubliners*, who also separated herself, with the Church's blessing, from a worthless, drunken husband. But May Joyce did not leave John. It would have been useless, anyway, since the increasing number of children already constituted such a barrier between them. She became simply "the mother of children," John being only their legal maker; and this role was sufficient for him. The role of protector he was quite happy to pass on to his eldest son.

> He imagined that while he strove to retain this infatuating position his home affairs would, through the agency of a son whom he made no effort to understand, in some divine manner right themselves. This hope when indulged in would sometimes embitter his affection for a son whom he therefore acknowledged as superior. (*Stephen Hero*, III)

Stanislaus' Dublin diary is here revealing—it shows us John Joyce in flight or in fury before his silent and unyielding wife. But if we read beyond Stanislaus' hate for his father, we can see that the more piteous, unhappy and lonely of the two is John. He is responsible for his own misfortune, but in the context of the deteriorated values and broken social and family structures of Ireland in 1900. May herself probably realised that the father of her children was only the unfortunate "double" of the charming young gallant she had married.

When his mother died, Stanislaus felt as though he were standing at the bedside of someone murdered:

Now for the first time waking in the quietness and subdued light of the room . . . she had the importance that should always have been hers. An ever-watchful anxiety for her children, a readiness to sacrifice herself to them utterly, and a tenacious energy to endure for their sakes replaced love in a family not given to shows of affection. She was very gentle towards her children . . . Pappie, who had no relatives and was free and selfish, demanded of Mother, who had many, alienation from them . . . she was never altogether alienated from them. . . . Perhaps if she had done so she would have been just as unloved by one so eminently selfish as Pappie, or if not as unloved certainly as cruelly treated. It is in her favour that in the middle of worries in which it is hard to remain gentle or beautiful or noble Mother's character was refined as much as Pappie's was debased. . . . Yet I cannot regard Mother and Pappie as ill-matched for with Pappie Mother had more than mere Christian patience, seeing in him what only lately and with great difficulty I have seen in him. It is strange, too, that the true friendships Pappie made (with Mr. Kelly for instance) were confirmed at home and, I think, under Mother's influence, his friends being scarcely less friendly towards Mother than towards himself. Up to the last Mother had a lively sense of humour and was an excellent mimic of certain people. Though worn and grave, Mother was capable at unusual times of unusual enegy. She was a selfish drunkard's unselfish wife.[7]

She is defined by her weakness, and therein lies her strength: there is a formidable alliance between the apparently suffering, victimised woman and the Church that stands behind her as last refuge and fortress—an alliance of good conscience and of rights. If the woman's strength is composed of her weakness and the silent blackmail she practises, the husband's "strength" (or brutality) is his weakness, his silent admission of defeat, and the fertility of the one both confirms and threatens the virility of the other. The relationships between Jim's parents are marked throughout by the insidious victory of this passive resistance, the woman's characteristic.

John Joyce's wife died at the age of forty-four, probably of cancer. James, who had returned from Paris, at his father's call, helped to lessen her long agony. He sang for her, looked after the children, and brought a more pleasant family atmosphere back to the house, while John went out drinking.

John disliked whatever interfered with his life, including trouble and sickness. His wife symbolised for him everything that brought him back to the horror of reality and of his own guilt. We have a strange impression of the parent-couples in James's earlier works: the husband exists,

---

[7] *Dublin Diary*, pp. 23–4.

with great intensity, and a whole series of fragments of his personality
are "projected", as though John's immense vitality had been divided up
amongst a number of different characters whose scandalous, noisy and
lively behaviour are an echo of his life. But the wife, repressed, betrayed, or beaten, still takes her silent revenge. There is a reversal of
sadism in which the victim takes revenge on the torturer by adopting
most completely the role of victim; by keeping silent one can accuse,
by letting oneself be crushed one can also punish, and by dying the
woman can suddenly assume the place that in life was denied her—the
martyred wife disappears indeed, but not without trace. Dead, she is
shame, overwhelming memory, a most living reproach. If she rests in
peace, she leaves no peace in the conscience of others. She has thwarted
the youthful ambitions and dreams of the man. Her passivity and silence are the weapons of her power. In fact, she is not herself so much
as a vast authority, hostile to John and disguised under an appearance
of fragility—she speaks not for herself but in the name of God. She asks
nothing for herself, she accepts her own destruction, accepts her lack
of comfort and care, but she greedily watches over the family's "souls,"
Stanislaus, Jim, and John, despite their very different relations with
May, band together when it becomes necessary to preserve and defend
themselves against the infiltration of the Church into their home. Since
John offered the least resistance, it was also he who behaved in the most
violent fashion—every victory in this field was for him a kind of infidelity. May is a faithful wife, true, but none the less she adores a God
other than her master on earth, and if the priest demands it she is
capable of deception and treachery.

> Mother saw that the reading of life in our home was unchristian and,
> consequently, deceived herself to make her life submissive to that Priest-
> worship in which she was reared. She even asserted her Catholicism that
> by speaking much she might convince herself, and this is called insincerity.
> Mother's religion was acquiescence and she had the eye of unbelievers
> constantly upon her.[8]

The household lives in a permanent state of spiritual siege and in the
end it is the mother who wins, by undergoing her passion. It must be
pointed out that May Joyce was isolated by the very faith she professed,
for the only members of the family who could have communicated with
her were, as the Superintendant of the seminary said of Charlie, the

[8] *Dublin Diary*, p. 25.

religiously minded son, "particular-ly stupid"; her confessor, now her confident and adviser, counselled her to remove the two eldest from the house, "before they corrupt the other children."[9] Jim was furious; gradually he grew away from his mother, who listened with such docility to the accusations of her spiritual counsellors. His love for a mother who was constantly telling him that in the eyes of the Church he was "extremely cowardly" became a menace to the artist's spiritual vocation. The last pages of *Portrait* are the sad echo of this situation. Jim's mother grew into a ghostly figure of gentle reproach; even her goodness to him, when associated with the memory of her sufferings, gave rise to the only doubt he was to feel, and hence to violent reactions: the more his mother loves him the more he must harden himself and take to flight, until he even appears to detest her. His mother comes to him in one of the dreams in Paris which he makes into an epiphany:

> She comes at night when the city is still; invisible, inaudible, all unsummoned. She comes from her ancient seat to visit the least of her children, mother most venerable, as if he had never been alien to her. She knows the inmost heart; therefore she is gentle, nothing exacting; saying I am susceptible of change, an imaginative influence in the hearts of my children. Who has pity for you when you are sad among the strangers? Years and years I loved you when you lay in my womb.[10]

Twenty years later, Joyce uses this dream in "circe," where the ghost of Stephen's mother appears in Bella Cohen's house in the form of a decaying body, and says, "Years and years I loved you, O my son, my firstborn, when you lay in my womb." And she says "with the subtle smile of death's madness," "I was once the beautiful May Goulding. I am dead. . . . Who saved you the night you jumped into the train at Dalkey with Paddy Lee? Who had pity for you when you were sad among the strangers? . . . Repent, Stephen." (*Ulysses*, p. 520). The furious reaction of the son who cries out "The ghoul! Hyena!" shows how disturbing the mother's image was for Joyce; in *Portrait*, Stephen clashes with a living mother and refuses to yield. But it seems that Joyce had always considered his mother's solicitous care as an involuntary attempted murder: in *Stephen Hero* the young man, annoyed because

---

[9] *My Brother's Keeper*, p. 203.

[10] Epiphany 34, quoted in Scholes and Kain, *The Workshop of Daedalus*, (Northwestern U.P., 1965) p. 44. Stanislaus tells us that this was a dream Joyce wrote down during his stay in Paris, 1902–3. In the dream, the appearance of the mother is confused with that of Our Lady.

his mother is weeping over the perdition of his soul, reprimands her and tells her that she ought to be pleased that he is alive.

> —I never thought I would see the day when a child of mine would lose the faith. God knows I didn't. I did my best for you to keep you in the right way.
>
> Mrs. Dedalus began to cry. Stephen, having eaten and drunk all within his province, rose and went towards the door:
>
> —It's all the fault of those books and the company you keep. Out at all hours of the night instead of in your home, the proper place for you. I'll burn every one of them. I won't have them in the house to corrupt anyone else.·
>
> Stephen had now halted at the door and turned towards his mother who had now broken out into tears:
>
> —If you were a genuine Roman Catholic, mother, you would burn me as well as the books.
>
> —I knew no good would come of your going to that place. You are ruining yourself body and soul. Now your faith is gone.
>
> —Mother, said Stephen from the threshold, I don't see what you're crying for. I'm young, healthy, happy. What is the crying for? It's too silly. (*Stephen Hero*, p. 138)

And in *Ulysses* (p. 520), the time present of the epiphany (which dates from 1903) is transformed by death into time past, and thus puts the whole episode on the level of an ambiguous symbolism: it is a dead woman who tells Stephen that she bore him in her womb; death and the mother are confused and Stephen feels that his mother's love is like the embrace of death. The tension between mother and son is far greater than that between father and son. This is because Joyce never expected anything from his father, while the mother's love was both necessary and stifling. His brothers and sisters agree that he depended on their mother, as only James Joyce knew how. "He was her favourite. Jim was completely dependent on her not only for a mother's care, but especially for moral support. He wanted her to believe that he would make a success of his life as a writer."[11] In fact, since he was a child he had tried to involve her in his own passion for culture. When Stannie was not yet old enough to go to school, Joyce at the age of eight or nine would take his school books along on family walks during the holidays, so that his mother could hear his lessons for him. Later, he read her his essay on *Art and Life*, as Stephen Hero does; he brings her in between art and life.

[11]Interview with Mrs. Schaurek, Joyce's sister, in the Dublin *Evening Herald*, Monday, July 15, 1963.

His mother had not asked to see the manuscript: she had continued to iron the clothes on the kitchen table without the least suspicion of the agitation in the mind of her son. . . . At last unable to control his agitation, he had asked her pointblank would she like him to read out his essay.

—O, yes, Stephen—if you don't mind my ironing a few things.

—No, I don't mind.

Stephen read out the essay to her slowly and emphatically and when he had finished reading she said it was very beautifully written but there were some things in it which she couldn't follow. . . . (*Stephen Hero*, p. 83)

Why should he try to convince his mother if not because basically he is grieved that the nobility of his enterprise is not admired and imitated, and because he is also seeking the approval of a woman whom "he by no means considered a fool"? Unfortunately the *rapprochement* is on both sides more diplomatic than disinterested, each one seeking to convert the other to his religion, art or Catholicism as the case may be. The mother begins to find out that "beauty"[12] can have connotations other than the purely sexual. She sighs, and imagines art to be a way of forgetting real life, and Stephen must protest:

Art is not an escape from life. It's just the very opposite. Art, on the contrary, is the very central expression of life. An artist is not a fellow who dangles a mechanical heaven before the public. The priest does that. The artist affirms out of the fulness of his own life. He creates . . . (*Stephen Hero*, p. 85)

Whereupon Mrs. Dedalus reads several scenes from Ibsen, is moved by *The Wild Duck* and eventually says that the author has "an extraordinary knowledge of human nature" (*Stephen Hero*, p. 86). The father, seeing a book in his house for the first time in years, is disappointed; he had hoped for a slight excursion into pornography, but Ibsen is a moralist (it will be noticed that his son had not offered it to him to read). His wife seeks to make him share her feelings (and her worries); but the intellectual exchange takes place between mother and son, for the purposes of mutual persuasion. His artistic vocation clashes with her obedience, and eventually Joyce sees his mother as both victim and the symbolic type of the woman who is afraid to think freely and has made herself the accomplice of a puritanical, superstitious religion. Nothing

[12]"His mother who had never suspected probably that 'beauty' could be anything more than a convention of the drawingroom or a natural antecedent to marriage and married life was surprised to see the extraordinary honour which her son conferred upon it. Beauty, to the mind of such a woman, was often a synonym for licentious ways" (*Stephen Hero*, p. 83).

illustrates more clearly how Jim's attitude to his mother had changed,
than the scene[13] which took place a week after May Joyce's death: Jim
spent a whole day reading a bundle of letters which John had written
to her before their marriage, in order to gain useful information for his
future work. "Well?" asked Stannie, who was familiar with the impersonal, experimental side of Jim's nature. "Nothing," replied Jim dryly.
Nothing of interest for the artist, that is. Beyond all human sympathy
or need, Joyce *observed*. His mother, once dead, becomes a symbolic
character only.

Reading the letters Joyce wrote from Paris in 1903, at the age of
twenty-one, we see that unlike Stephen, who leaves his father's house
"to seek misfortune" (as he says to Bloom, *Ulysses* p.545), Joyce left his
mother's house, and had no rest before he was brought back, almost at
once, for Christmas. His letters are a mixture of imperious begging,
self-pity with no consideration for the worry his mother naturally feels
for him, and eloquent descriptions of his own hunger, careless of that
of others. The letter of March 20, 1903, is a good example: he makes
sarcastic remarks about poverty, talks of his work in dispassionate tones,
and suddenly changes his tone and stops play-acting, with the words:
"You will oblige me very much if you will write to me and tell me what
you think of me. I shall read your letter with great anxiety." All this ends
with a postscript in the margin, telling her to get new spectacles, and
to go out walking for her health; one can deduce that the mother as
beloved object only exists, for Joyce, in the margins of his life and *after*
his own concerns. But no matter—even if she is only a reminder of his
conscience, the tone is tender and sincere. Apart from his deep love for
Nora and his children, Joyce was never to express sympathy for anyone
but his mother, or for his "substitute" mother-figures. Joyce had no
need of the adulation of the crowd, and was, to Stannie's great admiration, independent of all criticism, but he was to remain always dependent upon one person's judgement that was always the same. There was
indeed nothing secret about this, and his relatives would remark on his
behaviour in this respect. His sister Eileen, who lived with the Joyces
in Trieste for six years, Eileen "the catholicissima," as Joyce called her,
made these perspicacious remarks in an interview shortly before her
death:

> When my mother was dead, Aunt Josephine looked after us from a
> distance, and Jim turned all his affection to her. He was like that. We used
> to make fun of him, about Aunt Josephine. He needed somebody. Not

[13]Described in *My Brother's Keeper*, p. 248.

long after my mother died it was he met Nora Barnacle and married her a few months later. After that, of course, Nora was the only woman in his life.[14]

It will be seen, on considering Joyce's life as a whole, that when his mother is dead, he carries out a series of substitutions; after 1903 he chose Aunt Josephine as replacement-figure. Stanislaus' Diary of 1903-4 shows with what rapidity and intensity Jim turned to her; and now it is she who must answer the question "What do you think of me?"

When Nora appears, Joyce has no more need of Aunt Josephine, and asks the same question of Nora. Aunt Josephine naturally fades into the background, but she still remains necessary to some extent, because Nora and Jim form a unity, and he needs to ask Aunt Josephine some-times "What do you think of *us*?" Often, over a period of ten years, he confides to her his moral confusion and at times even the temptation to leave Nora.

Time passes; Jim and Nora settle into an equivocal relationship, in which many quarrels and clashes break out and are ritually brought to an end by threats from Nora and eventual forgiveness. Jim knows more or less clearly that Nora will always forgive him in the end, and so he can remain peaceful despite frequent reproaches.[15]

And he takes his question to a higher level, to another mother-figure, Miss Weaver, whose generosity enables him to be free from financial worries while writing *Finnegans Wake*. It would be wrong to believe that the importance and form of this question were for Joyce simply the

[14]Interview, 15 July 1963. Aunt Josephine was one of the people Jim made into receiv-ers of his confidence and affection. It is typical, because the *Evening Herald* is a Dublin paper, to publish such a blatant lie in 1963. It has to be that Joyce married Nora in 1904, as though only the sacrament could justify their genuine fidelity. They are thus made respectable by the Church. But in fact, their marriage did not take place until 1931. Eileen tells us further: "We called him back from Paris when we thought she was dying. But she lived on for months and he stayed with us. We were very pleased to have him because he was the only one who could be a bit of comfort to her. He sang and played the piano for her, and left the door open so that she could hear. She liked that. It made her more calm. When she died it was terrible for Baby, that is Mabel, the youngest, who was only little at the time. She was distracted. Jim said that the only thing that could spoil her mother's happiness up in heaven would be to see her crying, so she stopped then.

"And was his own distress genuine?"

"He still wept for her in Trieste, years later. You see, Mother was wonderfully under-standing with him. She always wanted him to go on with his studies and his writing. We had no money at all and the whole family said that Jim was the eldest and ought to go out to work to help his family. But Mother would never stand for that idea, she always did what she could to help him follow his own way."

[15] They quarrelled for two main reasons: Nora loathed drunkenness, and reproached James for not wanting to settle down in middle-class comfort, while he despaired at her indifference to his work.

results of childish frustration, indefinitely prolonged.

A general study of behaviour in this context reveals the sense of that act of questioning which elicited a different response from each adoptive mother. May Joyce herself had been a substitute, and Joyce acted towards her as he did towards the Church; one can guess what complexity of anguish underlies the repetition of the question: Joyce chooses to be the prisoner at the bar of one person's opinion alone. Only the chosen mother is to have this right over him, a right which he accords her, though knowing that it renders him vulnerable. It may, in fact, go so far as to threaten to destroy his art; and this is why, during their stay in Trieste, reprimanded by Nora and accused of scribbling instead of earning a living, he threw *Stephen Hero* into the fire with an heroic, theatrical gesture, and it was only saved, already partially burned, by his young sister who rescued it from the stove. Similarly, much later, when Miss Weaver timidly questioned the legibility of some pages in *Finnegans Wake*, Joyce justified himself with such painful vehemence that he became nearly speechless.

Nevertheless, although Joyce left himself open to attack, he never let himself be martyred; although he desired to be given absolution, he would still have chosen, had he not received it, to pursue his own way, for art was his life and life the breath of art. But it was necessary to go very close to destruction, to adopt endlessly an attitude of guilt and isolation, which had been chosen but which were also attributed to other, outside causes. His mind worked here with a devilish subtlety; thus, too, when Stephen persuades his mother to read Ibsen, his admitted intention is pure, but his secret intention is, typically, to set a trap for his mother, hoping to be betrayed:

> He did not consider his mother a dullard but the result of his second disappointment in the search for appreciation was that he was enabled to place the blame on the shoulders of others—not his own: he had enough responsibilities thereon already, inherited and acquired. (*Stephen Hero*, p. 83)

Thus Joyce exploits a social, family situation as the basis for the orientation and colouring he gives to his work, making use of the dramatic resources of the human context, exaggerating on the blacker side if necessary. If one compares the childhood of Joyce as related by Stanislaus or as reconstituted by Ellmann with the childhood of Stephen Dedalus, it will be seen that Joyce has of set purpose exaggerated the loneliness of the central figure and the hostility of his surroundings, in order to bring out more strongly the romantic prestige of the artist. He has, on the other hand, appreciably diminished the disgusting aspect of his father's behaviour, underlining instead his liveliness, his almost naïve egoism, and the varied talents of the successful man. If he appears to be victimised, in the person of Stephen, he is much rather a victim of his mother in her capacity as an ally of the Church; it is as though Stephen preferred the Byronic act to the melancholy of Hamlet. Joyce instinctively hates death and the privilege of the dead or dying to exercise their blackmail on the living. John Joyce is on the side of the living; and moreover offers very little resistance to the growing authority of his son. He is more a comrade or even an accomplice than a father. His egoism confirms and strengthens that of his son, and it is in the same spirit, with the same appetite for life, that they undertake their famous journey to London to spend the money James had received for his first published article. All the details of the anecdote have their significance. The article was a criticism of Ibsen's play *When We Dead Awake*, and it appeared in the *Fortnightly Review* of April 1, 1900, the play having been put on in December 1899. Joyce was then eighteen. The article follows the lecture he gave at University College in January 1900, on *Drama and Life*, which will be dealt with later; the two analyses concern the same subject, one which was to be Joyce's central preoccupation until the end of *Portrait*, namely, the relationships between art, life and death, and the distance which can or should be established between art and these two poles of humanity. The fascination and the impassioned precision with which Joyce analyses the play, and the passages which he selects for quotation, foreshadow with an astonishing prescience the psychological pattern of Dedalus' evolution from 1904 to 1914. In reading these twenty closely packed pages we find that it was this play of Ibsen's which provided the model for the scenes dealing with artistic vocation in *Portrait*, as well as strengthening the young man's hostility to marriage: Rubek the sculptor is divided between two women, his wife Maia and Irene, who modelled for the central figure in his masterpiece and then disappeared without trace. Five years have passed since Irene's disappearance and his marriage to Maia, since which time Rubek has made nothing but portrait busts, on commission.

Irene had posed for *The Day of Resurrection*. It is she again who poses to Joyce's imagination for the girl on the beach, the day of resurrection for the artist as a young man; she offered herself to the artist in her tranquil nakedness, as the bird-girl appears to Stephen, and by the contemplation of that body the "young living soul" is given. Irene says she has given her soul to Rubek. The union of model and artist in art gives birth to the "child" of the soul, that is the statue. We recognize here all the themes which will return in *Exiles*, especially the idea of the two marriages: the one, between the artist and the source of his inspiration, creates the work of art within the imagination that projects it into material form, and in this marriage the artist is both masculine and feminine; the other is between a man and a woman who wants to live her own life, who mocks his art as Nora was to mock Joyce's; in this marriage the wife is sterile, and destructive.

Joyce takes his stand clearly on the side of art, against married life with its deceptions and its misunderstandings—rather naïvely, though, for it is clear that he, like Ibsen, finds it natural for art to be accomplished only on the heights or in the abyss, and not in the comfort of tourist hotels. Naturally enough, he shares his gains with John Joyce, the artist who missed his vocation, who stands outside the family circle. Out of his twelve guineas, he gives his mother a pound (which must have meant a good meal for the whole family). The rest is spent by two mesmerised provincials in the big city—they go to see Duse playing in Ibsen and d'Annunzio, both of whom inspire the unquiet adolescent; Jim returns in triumph and declares to Stannie, who notes it down in his diary, that "it is not poetry but the music-hall that is the real critic of life."

But why are "poetry" and "the music-hall" considered as opposites? There is, firstly, a certain scorn for the "poet" as merely passive dreamer (which Ibsen himself expresses in the play). Opposed to the poet is literature's wrestler, the playwright: he acts and speaks, for or against, he influences others. The music-hall is comedy in song, just like John Joyce's life. And by leaving for London, James chose comedy and left behind him the pathos of his mother's house. Stanislaus notes down his declaration, and then two lines further on, without commentary, this remark, the less funny side of the comedy—"Both Jim and Pappie seem to be a little proud of having spendthrift blood in them." One cannot help noticing that the choice of the theatre contrasts with the sense of duty, which evolves later. In this first act of independence can already be seen patterns of associations and equivalents which govern Joyce's life throughout, and soon come to govern his whole work too: his selfishness, which is partly inspired by the desire for self-preservation, attaches him to his father. Father, desire for pleasure, guilty conscience, game and theatre, all these themes form the chain of his life throughout the work.

Life is a musical comedy when John Joyce is the commentator.

For May Joyce life is a requiem. The characteristics of Mother, incomplete satisfaction, tragic remorse, and difficulty of reality, are hostile to creation. Jim had received twelve guineas; if we are to measure the place he allotted to responsibility in his life by the gift of a pound to his mother, it would take up less than one-twelfth of the space. This is all the more striking in view of the relative misery of his life after Dublin, but already at the age of eighteen he had the sense of parody. This is why he gives no more than a tiny and almost secret place in his work to poetry, considered as acceptance of suffering. On the contrary, he determinedly takes his stand on the side of the comical—which predetermines the place and role of mother and father in his work. Three connections between real life and the work are to be emphasized: the father as seen by Jim sets the tone of comedy in every one of Joyce's books and is moreover the only real model present throughout. There is also present from time to time another father figure, harsh and cruel, who is not to be confused with the mocking reincarnation of John in Simon Dedalus—the sinister father is John as seen by Stannie.

And finally, although in real life Joyce was much closer to his mother than to his father, and although she was a refuge more central than any other for Jim, May Joyce scarcely exists in the work, where her complicity with the Church brings down upon her the scorn of a son who is not identical with Jim. Absent from *Dubliners*, scarcely present in *Portrait*, she has become a ghost in *Ulysses*, as though Joyce were carrying out some kind of conscious relegation. The reduction of the mother and her role shows that she constitutes a threat to James as artist, by the paralysing forces that she represents.

The Music-Hall is the Real Critic of Life

John Joyce is the comic Virgil guiding his son through his hell, his inspiration and guide through Dublin. "The humour of Ulysses is his," said Joyce, "the characters are his friends. The book is his spitting image." Joyce here pays his homage to the tale-teller and singer of Dublin; but John Joyce is not only a kind of Irish bard, author of a number of comic songs. He is a protean figure, ungraspable yet always the same throughout his middle-class picaresque adventures. His journey about himself makes him the pattern for Bloom; the variety of his activities is such that it is possible to make a comic inventory of them, as though of titles and honours:

—What was he? Cranly asked after a pause.

Stephen began to enumerate glibly his father's attributes:

—A medical student, an oarsman, a tenor, an amateur actor, a shouting politician, a small landlord, a small investor, a drinker, a good fellow, a story-teller, somebody's secretary, something in a distillery, a tax-gatherer, a bankrupt and at present a praiser of his own past. (*Portrait*, p. 241)

John Joyce as seen by his son becomes a Rabelaisian character with his truculence and insolence, a Panurge always ready to mock others, turning under his son's amused gaze into a hero of parody. Three main characteristics animate this comic hero's life: rebellion against the Church and the family, rejection of old age, a passion and talent for singing.

A swearer, young at heart, a good tenor voice, John Joyce stands thus immortalized in the character of Simon Dedalus and his doubles. These three characteristics are complementary: the rebelliousness expresses in a fashion which remains always good-humoured a regret for past liberty, now gilded over by the memory. John's defence against reality is to turn his back on it, to live in memory in the times of his youth, before he had a wife, children, responsibilities. And when melancholy threatens to bring him back to the present, he takes refuge in his singing. His voice does not age, his tenor remains unrivalled. Like Ulysses, like Stephen, he defends himself with his own weapons against the surrounding world.

Like Ulysses? It is indeed partly by way of John that the artist perfects his technique of transposing the epic on to the level of average contemporary humanity: in "grace" (in *Dubliners*), John is the Bloom-like hero of a parody of an epic, constructed with the same minute attention to detail that characterises the whole of *Ulysses*. It is not the *Odyssey*, but rather Dante's *Inferno*, whose theme is appropriate for what Gogarty maliciously called the elder Joyce's "zigzag career," and for James's state of mind at the time of this novella's composition in 1905. For between 1903 and 1906 Joyce was going through his Dante phase. He had learned Italian from Father Ghezzi at the University and quoted Dante at every opportunity, to the extent that Gogarty nicknamed him Dante. It is of significance that he was able to compose around one grotesque episode in his father's life, a miniature epic in which the father plays the part of Dante; this is the final stage of that ironic withdrawal with respect to the self, to be able to put the great epic poem of Christianity to the service of his art and of its "scrupulous pettiness," exercised upon the inspired drunkenness of John: Tom Kernan in the pub lavatory suffers a fall which is the first of a series that ends with Earwicker, in *Finnegans Wake*, and does so as naturally as any hardened drinker who has no idea that he is setting in motion again the progress of the *Divine Comedy*.

Tom, like John, is a gentleman; his ascension, from the *Inferno* where he lies, face downwards, his eyes closed and his clothes smeared with filth, to his bed which serves as Purgatory to the Jesuit church in Gardiner Street, all happens in an atmosphere of polite cordiality, because the characters are all gentlemen together. Squalor is rejected as being too facile, and the beginning takes place ceremoniously despite the unworthiness of the surroundings: "Two gentlemen who were in the lavatory at the time tried to lift him up." From then on a whole set of people undertakes to lift him up, beginning with a young cyclist, quite anonymous, who kneels down beside the injured man and calls for water. A purification, perhaps? The constable trying to make out his report also kneels down. Tom, like Tim Finnegan in the ballad, is revived with alcohol. Then the right-thinking gentlemen reaffirm their solidarity and tolerance towards their own world in which Mr. Kernan is still respected, like John Joyce: "He had never been seen in the city without a silk hat of some decency and a pair of gaiters. By grace of these two articles of clothing, he said, a man could always pass muster" (*Dubliners*, p. 218). John Joyce had the same concern for various details of his clothing. Mr. Power, much younger and more debonair than Tom, is still concerned for him as a personality, but Mr. Kernan's decline is already started on its Joycean curve downwards. Mr. Power, a converted Protestant without real convictions, wants to make him "turn over a new leaf," though we never find out exactly why. So he appeals to the specialists in conversion of drunkards, Mr. Cunningham, the double here of Shakespeare, and Mr. McCoy, a friend of Bloom's in *Ulysses*, who are competent people. For Mrs. Kernan, "religion was a habit, and she suspected that a man of her husband's age would not change greatly before death" (*Dubliners*, p. 223).

Mr. Kernan is in bed with an injured tongue (his wife considers it to be divine punishment), and around him his friends plot to destroy the old drunkard and "make a new man of him." The innocent drink stout, but the guilty one is not able to; Mr. Power "officiates," but Mr. Kernan, being in a state of sin, cannot communicate. Mr. Kernan is thirsty; he is only human, after all, and wants to live: "And have you nothing for me, duckie?" he asks. "O, you! The back of my hand to you!" replies Mrs. Kernan pitilessly; the Church and the home are places of correction for recalcitrant husbands.

Kneel! says the wife to her husband; and one day she eventually triumphs and takes a vicarious revenge. The finest day of Mrs. Kernan's life apart from her wedding day is when Mr. Kernan undergoes his penance, thanks to the machinations of the worthy and mysterious Mr. Power,[16] who repeats "we'll make a new man of him" and "all's well that ends well."

And the happy ending brings the recalcitrant one to heel; he "beats his retreat," and goes to listen to a preacher, "a powerful-looking figure, the upper part of which was draped with a white surplice, . . . struggling up into the pulpit." Father Purdon resembles the vast policeman of the opening scene. He speaks "in a business-like way" that echoes through the transept full of men with carefully brushed hats and shared guilty consciences. If the victim of the plot suffers nothing more than sermonising, and, as Mrs. Kernan says, it could do no harm, this is because the Kernans have already passed through all the Dante-like circles of marriage, following a downward, Dublin path as opposed to the ascent of the Florentine, going by degrees from innocence to complete alienation (the gentlemen's lavatory); a man like Mr. Kernan can no longer hope for any restoration. Salvation existed prior to marriage, and the wedding is seen as the first step in the process of self-loss. This could have been material for tragedy, but for Joyce tragedy is a literary complaisance that falsifies reality. It is the ridiculous alienation of the Dubliner that leads John Joyce and his like through *Dubliners* and *Portrait* from the simple, trustful marriage to the deadly surrender, from the Dublin "marriage à la mode" that is concluded in "the Boarding House" to the catastrophe of "the Dead." Tom's hat has been rehabilitated, his soul can be refurbished by the Jesuits.

On the pretext of relating the banal history of a drunkard's conversion, Joyce denounces both the devaluation of belief and the impure motives of the Dublin Catholics, giving the main role to the man whose salvation is their great concern; Tom Kernan, John Joyce's double, reveals with drunken unawareness the comedy they make of salvation. Marriage, a good conscience, the "right way," and penitence become laughable in contrast with the profound reality of the impenitent. Compromise is necessary for the recapture of Tom; and again like John, he plays hard to get. "Pappie's religion is the funniest thing about him"[17] noted Stannie in his diary. Yet Stannie rarely felt like laughing at Pappie's behaviour; it must be admitted, though, that John at least had the

---

[16] Some critics see in the choice of this name an allusion to an insidious wish for power.
[17] *Dublin Diary*, 29 Sept. 1904.

courage of his inconsequentiality and blasphemy, and very little worry about the Last Judgement, as can be seen from the anecdote which was the original source for "grace,"[18] which made Stannie laugh out loud two years afterwards. If Tom Kernan is less openly blasphemous than John, it is because Joyce wants to prove that by an imitation redemption the drunkard is doomed in this present life if not for eternity, because he is subject to a woman without the gentle resignation of May, one who will not stop short of intrigue in order to reach her pious ends. Kernan

[18] We quote large extracts from Stannie's Diary in order to show what work Joyce did on this reported reality: "The last time Pappie went to Confession and Communion was highly amusing. I bawled laughing at the time. It was about two years ago. Mr. Kane and Mr. Boyd and Mr. Chance were to attend a retreat in Gardiner Street, and Pappie, who would never do anything so vulgar for himself, was persuaded by Mr. Kane to attend it too. He did so, and came home very drunk for two nights after each sermon. On the second night Chance brought him home. He was to go to confession next evening. I heard the conversation downstairs.

Chance: Holy Communion on Sunday morning and then at half five go to renew baptismal vows. They'll give you candles—and then all together we'll—

Pappie (very drunk): Oh, I bar the candles, I bar the candles! I'll do the other job all right, but I bar the candles.

Chance: Oh, that'll do all right—only a formality—but what hour'll we call for you tomorrow night to go to Confession? Matt Kane and myself are going at half seven.

Pappie: Oh, I don't know, I don't know—I'll—well, call at half seven then. Will that suit you?

Chance: Splendidly. And you'll come then?

Pappie: Oh yes! Oh yes! Old fellow, I'll go, never you fear, I'll go—can you go to whoever you like?

Chance: Oh yes! They've all equal power, all the same.

Pappie: I don't mind, you know. I don't care. I'll go to the first felleh that's open. I haven't got much to tell him, you know. D'you think I have much to tell him?

Mother: I do. God forbid I had as much.

Chance: Oh, that's not the point.

Mother: Oh no! That's not the point, of course.

Chance: It doesn't matter how much you have to tell him it'll all be wiped off; you'll have a clean sheet.

Pappie: I don't mind, you know. I'd go in to the first bloody felleh that's open and have a little chat with him.

Chance: Right! That's right! Now don't forget I'll be here at 5:30.

Pappie went as he had promised to Confession on Saturday night and went out early to Holy Communion on Sunday morning . . . I can imagine how much he disliked acting so thoroughly vulgarly. But his vanity would not let this idea remain with him, and he told me at the breakfast table (there was a special breakfast on the occasion) how Father Vernon (the Jesuit who had conducted the triduum) told him, 'You're not such a bad fellow after all. Ha! ha! ha! ha!' That day after dinner Pappie went to the winding-up lecture at about 4:30 and came home not quite sober with Chance a little before seven. He wanted to borrow money from Mother and was becoming impatient when Mother made a difficulty about giving it, ridiculed her family, and when Mother shook her head at him, went out blaspheming and banging the door behind him. I laughed and said something bitter and satirical. It was certainly the shortest conversion on record. Mother said nothing, but looked patient. (Michaelmas Day, 1904)."

will be saved willy-nilly by the pious athletes, keepers of his soul's peace (and history does not even tell us that he got drunk the next morning, as John Joyce did). John's antipathy to the clergy was a well-established fact at home; they were, in fact, one of his favourite targets, for he knew that he upset his wife by attacking them. In his Trieste notebook, James notes down twice in the list of his father's characteristic expressions, "He calls a prince of the church a tub of guts." And again, "He calls Canon Keon frosty face and Cardinal Logue a tub of guts. Had they been laymen he would condone their rancid fat."[19]

Tom Kernan would not be able to use such language; he is too much surrounded by right-thinking friends. John's conversion has a certain bravado about it, even if he and his sons do consider it as a brief defeat, but Kernan's is piteous and would sadden us were it not for the spirit of John that inspires in the victim a last glimmer of resistance: Kernan gives way on every point but one, which concerns his dignity: "I bar the candle." Everyone laughs, and Tom (or John) is saved within the little circle of his friends, at least, by the laughter he knows how to cause.

In his Trieste notebook Joyce puts down as a first definition of Pappie, "He is an Irish suicide,"[20] or as Gallaher would say, he has his head in the bag. The piquant list of Pappie's characteristic remarks includes this note: "The verses he quotes most are:

> Conservio is captured! He lies in the lowest dungeons
> With manacles and chains around his limbs
> Weighing upwards of three tons."

This grotesque rhyme, repeated in *Ulysses* by His Eminence Simon Stephen Cardinal Dedalus, is basically a caricature of John Joyce. John Conservio Joyce is a man of regrets, bitterly bemoaning his captivity. The interview published in *A James Joyce Yearbook*[21] consists of the elder Joyce's recollections of his youth, with much retrospective ornamentation. Yet it is Stephen rather than Joyce who, in answer to Cranly's question says that his father, after having tried his hand at a score of pseudo-employments, is now (since the days when he wielded the authority have gone) a "praiser of his own past." This praise is less a matter of boasting than of keeping alive his own past into which he has projected his own youthful image.

[19] Quoted in *Workshop*, p. 104. Simon Dedalus causes great offence by using the expression, in *Portrait*, p. 33.
[20] *Workshop*, pp. 103–4.
[21] Ed. Maria Jolas (Paris, 1949).

The good old days were characterized by a life of pleasure, sport, and song, but as yet no woman. John boasts of the additional decorations memory brings, like a true Cork man who has been drinking whiskey all his life. It seems to act as a preserving liquid. "I had a devil of a good tenor in those days—and they were great days, My God! they were." The great events are all of the same stamp, for example the celebrations following an unexpected success of John's at the polls: "And by God Almighty such drinking of champagne I never saw in my life. We could not wait to draw the corks, we slapped them against the marble-topped counter." "Oh dear, dear, God, those were great times." This was John Joyce, inexhaustible mixture of God, devil and story-telling. "There is not a field in County Cork that I don't know"; and "my God when I think of the times I used to have!" John was king of Cork in those days. "Youth" for John Joyce, Simon Dedalus and their like is a retrospective memory and projection of their imagination for such frustrated men, because present and future are the battlegrounds of their defeat; in the past they are still lively and free, without responsibilities, without children.

The birth of a son is a very traumatic experience; difficult days begin, the son *watches* the father and forces him to be nothing more than what he actually is—the son lives in time present, in the reality of hunger, and obliges the father to think of the future, keeps bringing him back to the enclosure of guilt and of death. If the son steals the father's imaginary youth, the father in revenge confiscates the real youth of the son—this, at any rate, is the way Joyce expresses it in *Portrait*. In reality it was Stannie who began to feel old at the age of nineteen, while Jim offered no vulnerable places to Pappie's attack. Stephen, accompanying his father to the latter's native town, is treated by the youthfully irresponsible Simon not as a baby, but as a grown man; the father declares that he is the same age as his son, because:

—We're as old as we feel, Johnny, said Mr. Dedalus. And just finish what you have there and we'll have another. Here, Tim or Tom or whatever your name is, give us the same again here. By God, I don't feel more than eighteen myself. There's that son of mine there not half my age and I'm a better man than he is any day of the week.

—Draw it mild now, Dedalus. I think it's time for you to take a back seat, said the gentleman who spoken before.

—No, by God! asserted Mr. Dedalus. I'll sing a tenor song against him or I'll vault a five-barred gate against him or I'll run with him after the hounds across the country as I did thirty years ago along with the Kerry Boy and the best man for it.

—But he'll beat you here, said the little old man, tapping his forehead and raising his glass to drain it.

—Well, I hope he'll be as good a man as his father. That's all I can say, said Mr. Dedalus." (*Portrait*, p. 95)

If the father by such comparisons tries to usurp the son's youth, it is because he needs to be reassured that he is still alive. The father further denies the son his painfully developing manhood.

Another, a brisk old man, whom Mr. Dedalus called Johnny Cashman, had covered him with confusion by asking him to say which were prettier, the Dublin girls or the Cork girls.

—He's not that way built, said Mr. Dedalus. Leave him alone. He's a level-headed thinking boy who doesn't bother his head about that kind of nonsense.

—Then he's not his father's son, said the little old man.

—I don't know, I'm sure, said Mr. Dedalus, smiling complacently.

—Your father, said the little old man to Stephen, was the boldest flirt in the city of Cork in his day. Did you know that? (*Portrait*, p. 94)

By his dallying in and conserving the imaginary pre-marital past, the father suppresses his son's existence, and of his own accord admits this:

—That was before you were born.

—Ay, or thought of, said Mr. Dedalus. (*Portrait*, p. 95)

In *Ulysses*, Simon completely effaces Stephen from his memory especially at the time of his imaginary rejuvenation in the Sirens' bar; he no longer sees the hindering son, and is obviously displeased when someone recalls him to mind:- "Lenehan: Greetings from the famous son of a famous father. —Who may he be? asked Mr. Dedalus" (*Ulysses*, p. 256).

Thus to kill the son, to forget time, to associate life with memory, is to refuse one's successor the right to live as himself in the present, to force him to agree to an underhand exchange which drives the real young man out of his own age and causes him to renounce the still-fresh memories of his childhood, to wander through life like Shelley's moon, companionless, without even the right to have an individual image of himself.

Stephen watched the three glasses being raised from the counter as his father and his two cronies drank to the memory of their past. An abyss of fortune or temperament sundered him from them. His mind seemed older than theirs: it shone coldly on their strifes and happiness and regrets like a moon upon a younger earth. (*Portrait*, p. 96)

The son has no right to turn back or linger in childhood, for the father pushes him out of the nest of his memories. The chapter following the return to Cork in *Portrait* gives the son the symbolic role of the father —Stephen feeds his mother, brother, and the father himself, with the money of a prize he has won. In real life, John Joyce did indeed long to abdicate from his fatherly duties and return to his world of song; Jim had inherited the burden, which he later shared with Stannie, Jim playing the part of the father, Stannie supplying the elements of surliness and common-sense. The father sells the right to rule in exchange for the right to dream, and from then on lives on two time-scales: that of evoked memory and mythic action, and that of abdication and of anger to disguise his shame.

There is in *Portrait* an intimate scene between Stephen and Simon in Cork, its details both "sad and happy"; we see Stephen watching his father, in a scene of narcissism, lingering over his toilet and humming a ballad whose words are a commentary on his unspoken dreams of flight and escape. His movements are bird-like and Stephen's gaze conjures up the shape of a peacock in the mirror:

> His father was standing before the dressing-table, examining his hair and face and moustache with great care, craning his neck across the water-jug and drawing it back sideways to see the better. While he did so he sang softly to himself with quaint accent and phrasing:
>
> > "Tis youth and folly
> > Makes young men marry,
> > So here, my love, I'll
> > No longer stay;
> > What can't be cured, sure,
> > Must be injured, sure,
> > So I'll go to
> > Amerikay.
> >
> > "My love she's handsome,
> > My love she's bonny:
> > She's like good whiskey
> > When it is new;
> > But when 'tis old
> > And growing cold
> > It fades and dies like
> > The mountain dew". (*Portrait*, p. 88)

This vain bird is a ridiculous double of the hawk-god that is the artist's emblem, and he too longs to escape from the nets of Ireland. He escapes on a more humble level into an imaginary world that he shares with other disillusioned Dubliners—that of the pub. Here he can satisfy two vital needs, that of being admired and preserved in the eyes of others at the height of his glory, that of singing to an audience capable of appreciating his talent. The song is his literature, his substitute for all that he has lost or been refused.

John flees from the Church, which summons him in his wife's dutiful voice; he feels himself to be the victim of an emotional swindle, for although she is subject to him, her religious, believing side escapes him completely. At home he is judged, but at the pub he is safe. The pub becomes the rallying-place of rebels, of men who long for their spiritual freedom. There is communication, mutual reassurance, boasting among men, showing off like peacocks, mutual encouragement, admiration, healing of wife-wounded vanity; hence the numerous scenes, in *Portrait* and in *Ulysses*, in which the man after a domestic quarrel goes out to his fellow-creatures, to the only place that will welcome his mortified masculine self-respect, the pub, that temple reversed whose service is always an act of fraud and sacrilege. The libations are dedicated to the dream of liberty, and there is always present a temptress whose role is defined by its opposition to that of the legitimate spouse: she is there solely to embody the possibility of transgression. While symbolising the man's defiance of his wife, she does not constitute any real danger because she also belongs to the same world of confession. But she plays her reassuring part as "symbolically sinful"; in real life the man is unwilling to pass from the possibility of transgression to its execution, but it is sufficient for him to have accomplices in the comedy of soothing his vanity. There is pretence on both sides, and in their false but emotionally charged confrontation there is to be found (in exchange for as little as the price of a pint) reassurance for self-esteem that has been sorely tried by moral and religious prohibitions—yet there is never any risk of incurring retribution.

Protected by the expanse of the bar, she flirts, flattering the customer according to the classical tactics of eroticism, pretending that the bar really is a barrier, that marriage really is a chain, and committing gentle violence by dressing up a succulently sinful possibility as a virtuous woman. The roused imagination feeds on symbolic gestures such as "counting the buttons" on a blouse or rubbing the glasses, for the whole of this pleasure is limited by prudence.

She was a genteel young person of a very tempting figure. While she was polishing glasses she indulged in flirty, gossipy conversation with the young men: . . . She reproved Mr. Garvey once or twice for levity and asked Stephen wasn't it a shame for a married man. Stephen said it was and began to count the buttons on her blouse. The barmaid said Stephen was a nice sensible young man not a gadabout fellow and smiled very sweetly. (*Stephen Hero*, p. 251)

It all boils down to a comedy of looks, for there is no touching; they need the illusion of prestige without having to fear the punishment. If the Irishman has to choose between self-denial and hell, he prefers to deny himself in this life. He therefore has recourse to expedients in order to create a fictitious character for himself. This simulation has a double aspect: it can only be effective if the pretender remains at a distance, for proximity would at once spoil the deception, but paradoxically this entails the impossibility of attaining satisfaction. Furthermore, the necessity of communicating only by looks and words makes the comedy into a romance; by making use of the "speaking look," one introduces the element of mystery, of inaccessibility and disguise. Joyce produces effects ranging from the very subtle to the most broadly comical. The barmaid's glance reflects the man that the husbands would love to be, but dare not; in the eyes of the sirens each man sees himself as a Don Juan or Blazes Boylan. The mistress here is as crafty as Calypso, but without frightening the customer; it is she who authorises what under the mask of convention and propriety is simply unhappy lust. The pub is the setting for a petty voyeurism, and only those who have, like Stephen, won their way to freedom or are outcasts from society's bed, like Bloom, will venture their human reality into a real bordello.

Everything is allowed, provided that it remain superficial. The barmaids and the gentlemen watch their dreams reflected in the mirrors and glasses. It is agreed and understood that the world of the pub is unreal. One pretends that one is young, frisky and frivolous, that one has never seen a woman before; one acts as though one did not own a house and a real wife, as though one were really a great free-thinking devil of a fellow, as though God did not exist, as though one were as innocent as a new-born baby. It is possible to act in a bold, daring fashion while remaining innocent, for nobody believes anybody else among the giant-killers of the Ormonde. The women lead the men on to confess, without their being aware of it.

—Oh welcome back, Miss Douce.
He held her hand. Enjoyed her holidays?

—Tiptop.

He hoped she had nice weather in Rostrevor.

—Gorgeous, she said. Look at the holy show I am. Lying out on the strand all day.

Bronze whiteness.

—That was exceedingly naughty of you, Mr. Dedalus told her and pressed her hand indulgently. Tempting poor simple males.

Miss Douce of satin douced her arm away.

—Oh go away, she said. You're very simple, I don't think.

He was.

—Well now, I am, he mused. I looked so simple in the cradle they christened me simple Simon. (*Ulysses*, pp. 254-5)

To the end of the bar to him she bore lightly the spiked and winding seahorn, that he, George Lidwell, solicitor, might hear. (*Ulysses*, p. 275)

As in real life, woman signifies carnal desire, but here in the Sirens' bar, it is for the pleasure of the whole company

Wonderful really. So distinct. Again. George Lidwell held its murmur, hearing: then laid it by, gently.

—What are the wild waves saying? he asked her, smiled.

Charming, seasmiling and unanswering Lydia on Lidwell smiled.

(Here, the men are "gentlemen," and the women are both "ladies" to whom one can pay gallant attentions without being ridiculous or imprudent, and admirers of the gentlemen's talents. They pay court and are courted; they have all the virtues of the convinced virgin and of the knowledgeable woman; they are discreetly behaved and quickly alarmed.)

Miss Douce withdrew her satiny arm, reproachful, pleased.

—Don't make half so free, said she, till we are better acquainted.

George Lidwell told her really and truly: but she did not believe.

First gentleman told Mina that was so. She asked him was that so. And second tankard told her so. That that was so. (*Ulysses*, p. 271)

But they have another aspect, the maternal. They know that the men pretend to be cruel and immoral seducers, and so they in their turn pretend to be frightened. They know that men are just big babies, and show the appropriate solicitude. These sirens are very devoted women, who sacrifice their dreams for others, for with Boylan or the viceroy they would no longer play at trying to escape, but would have recourse to real weapons. The pub is the scene of metamorphoses as much as Bella Cohen's house is . But with the latter the possibility of metamorphosis is terrifying; with the former, man is free and the liquid is neither amniotic fluid nor holy water. In the house of Circe men are beasts, or else their own masochism turns them into what they would (not) be, into martyrs, cardinals, prophets, saints, women. In the house of Circe there is mimic castration in all forms; at the Ormonde, mimic masturbation.

> On the smooth jutting beerpull laid Lydia hand lightly, plumply, leave it to my hands. All lost in pity for croppy. Fro, to: to, fro: over the polished knob (she knows his eyes, my eyes, her eyes) her thumb and finger passed in pity: passed, repassed and, gently touching, then slid so smoothly, slowly down, a cool firm white enamel baton protruding through their sliding ring. (*Ulysses*, p. 280)

Words, the monstrous floods of words that are the charms of Circe's temple, are replaced by mimicry, and by objects, in a symbolism of touch and manipulation. The sirens' code is based on the principle that the pub as phenomenon is the home of innocence and satisfaction. Everything, people as well as objects, in the pub is perfectly clean and neat, glasses polished, tables wiped, sandwiches under cover. Things are only what they are and the men are simply gentlemen. If you order a beer, you will get a drink and not a magic potion. But the other world is there, accessible to the initiated; to reach beyond apparent objectivity, one has to decipher the signs, to use one's eyes in order to surprise the double face of things and the double meaning of the signs. Thus all developments entail equivocation: the innocent exterior is the mask of a delicious perversity. The spiked and winding seahorn can mean the sea, but begins to stand for other things too; the language of the waves has no words, but its rhythm is that of the blood. And while Boylan is knocking on Molly Bloom's door with his stick, and bulky Ben Dollard singing the ballad of the *Croppy Boy*, the young Irish rebel, Bloom watches the movement of Lydia's skilful hand. The song ends and the young rebel meets his heroic death.

Boylan the flamboyant bachelor comes in abruptly, disturbing the dreams of the wave-rocked bar. A Don Juan who is all too real, he saddens Simon Dedalus, Leopold Bloom, the two barmaids and the solicitor by his sudden arrival, and the "slow cool dim seagreen sliding depth of shadow *eau de Nil*" engulfs the married gentlemen of Dublin. Disenchantment grips all hearts, and suddenly all together they pick up the fragments left by the sparkling bachelor and take comfort in a comically vicarious participation in Boylan's legendary conquests; they act out an adultery, then Simon sings and by the beauty of his voice recovers the esteem that Boylan had momentarily dulled. They give themselves up to an orgy of exciting memories in compensation, and end by choosing a scapegoat to act as a symbolic cuckold for all, feeling the necessity to identify with the "cock" Boylan. Bloom buys drinks for everyone. And while Boylan meets Molly, Dedalus and company act out an imaginary adultery, Dedalus waving his pipe to stand for the conquering hero's "haw haw horn."

> Mr. Dedalus struck, whizzed, lit, puffed savoury puff after.
> —Irish? I don't know, faith. Is she, Simon?
> Puff after stiff, a puff, strong, savoury, crackling.
> —Buccinator muscle is.. . . What? . . . Bit rusty . . . O, she is . . . My Irish Molly , O.
> He puffed a pungent plumy blast.
> —From the rock of Gibraltar. . . . all the way. (*Ulysses*, p. 263)

After which everyone feels better, and a singing contest is started, a concert of peacocks, seducers and seduced. Dedalus expresses sympathy for the "tympanum of her ear" (i.e., of any lady listening) and Father Cowley, not to be outdone, alludes to "another membrane." While Bloom eats animals' intestines, Dedalus sings "Down among the Dead Men" and "All is Lost Now." All is indeed lost, except for the ephemeral illusion of youth, lasting till the song ends. But Joyce maliciously sends Dedalus back into his trap, by giving him a priest as accompanist.

> Go on, Simon.
> —Ah, sure my dancing days are done, Ben . . . Well . . .
> Mr. Dedalus laid his pipe to rest beside the tuningfork and, sitting, touched the obedient keys.
> —No, Simon, Father Cowley turned. Play it in the original. One flat.
> The keys, obedient, rose higher, told, faltered, confessed, confused.
> Upstage strode Father Cowley.
> —Here, Simon. I'll accompany you, he said. Get up. (*Ulysses*, p. 265)

III. The Fear of Marriage
and the Dream of Freedom

Joyce's Marriage

By a strange coincidence, it was in 1931 that Joyce married, in London, Nora Barnacle, with whom he had been living for twenty-seven years; and the same year saw the death of John Joyce, who had been for his sons the frightening figure of the murderously tyrannical husband.[1] Joyce's "regularisation" of their situation was carried out for material rather than social reasons: there was no longer any risk of being suspected of conformism, but it was necessary to envisage the eventuality of his death and to think about protecting his children. His Dublin friend Byrne was a witness to the marriage; and thus, even so late and performed in a foreign country, Joyce's marriage constitutes a backward glance towards Ireland, as though Dublin, his childhood, family and native land were making, in spite of Jim, a gesture of recognition; it is as though Joyce, having denied the legal bond any legality, was showing by his choice of Byrne as witness, his wish to re-integrate a certain cultural pattern.

In fact, by 1931, Joyce no longer risks being transformed by marriage into a successor of his father; he is no longer afraid of Nora, society, the Church, or public opinion, and his gesture has only the strictly limited value he gives it: that of a "legal fiction." He has been a well-known,

---

[1]See his letter of 29 Aug. 1904 to Nora: "My mother was slowly killed. . . . by my father's ill-treatment, by years of trouble, and by my cynical frankness of conduct."

accepted writer for fifteen years, and all the traps have been sprung. The word "marriage" no longer hides any dangerous secret meaning.

To the young Joyce marriage had signified the threat of responsibilities to be borne, or of modifications to be made in the self, in a sense that was anything but pleasing to such an autocrat. It is normal that the problem should have taken its place in his mind at an early stage, for the home and the tribe are the holy places of marriage. But the whole of Ireland is caught in a tormenting, exhausting involvement: the alliance with the Church is unforgiving; marriage and the flesh can only be opposed, but the problems created by puritanism, which we shall deal with later, would only constitute, so to speak, the "classical" obstacles, stemming in the last analysis from the psychology of the Catholic married couple, if they did not also form part of a complicated local situation that alienates the man. The Irish husband of 1900 is a man with very few chances for self-accomplishment outside his own home. Constrained and oppressed since childhood by the system of confession, he has no right to enjoy a private life. He cannot achieve freedom or success by merely taking possession of material or financial riches—the woman's presence is always necessary. What possessions could a Joyce own in 1904? Caught between the family with its moral and vital imperatives, and a social and economic dependence in a colonial political system, he becomes the slave of his home, family and nation—there is always a master above him. Every job John Joyce took compromised his nationalist honour; sinecures are the height of self-betrayal, and this was John Joyce's speciality, employee in a tax office, for instance, bringing in a quarter of the amount the family needed! For James, submission to the Church would solve his financial problems, but as he explains to Nora, who wanted to push him into a career at the Catholic university, there can be no question of compromising his "moral nature." Honour and fear are linked together at the origin of Joyce's refusal to marry.

At the time Joyce considered himself as a "socialist artist"; he explains this several times, and again later in May 1905 when he was in Trieste, because he felt insulted by his old friends' criticisms. He entrusts his defence to Stannie for the moment:

> I cannot tell you how strange I feel sometimes in my attempt to live a more civilised life than my contemporaries. But why should I have brought Nora to a priest or lawyer to make her swear away her life to me? And why should I superimpose on my child the very troublesome burden of belief which my father and mother superimposed on me?[2]

[2] To Stanislaus, 2 or 3 May 1905. *Letters*, vol. II, p. 88.

In conclusion, Jim would be acting here for Nora's own good; in fact, he only believes this for a moment. What he says is not untrue, but it is only a small part of a great complex system of justification he builds up. Nora's good is a weak point in this system, and so he makes great efforts to strengthen it with long arguments. His own manifestly selfish worries are hardly touched upon, mentioned as though by accident, as in the hasty remark on the occasion of one of his speeches on the genius of Ibsen, on a postcard sent to Stanislaus from Trieste: "I am studying Danish again with constancy. Do you know that Ibsen's married life ended by his leaving his wife?"[3]

In 1904 Joyce and Nora left for Europe. From their meeting in June 1904 until their departure, he had seen her quite regularly and written her many letters. Some are simply love-notes, but the majority of the longer ones show that Joyce was primarily seeking to define himself, to make a self-portrait and autobiography so that she might know him. The tone can be firm, when he expounds on the break he had made with the powers of society, or sad and distressed when he feels that she has not understood him. It appears that he wanted to make Nora the companion of his life, and with his usual frank and systematic turn of mind he at once set to work to form and inform her. It is equally clear that in his plans for their life together, he conceives the partnership in completely egocentric terms of HIS life, HIS future, HIS past, HIS work. Nora is for him the object of a very real tenderness, and her place is determined by its relation to him.

> No human being has ever stood so close to my soul as you stand, it seems, and yet you can treat my words with painful rudeness. ("I know what is talking now" you said). When I was younger I had a friend to whom I gave myself freely—in a way more than I give to you and in a way less. He was Irish, that is to say, he was false to me. . . . Believe me, my dear Nora, I honour you very much but I want more than your caresses. You have left me again in an anguish of doubt. J.A.J.[4]

The end of this letter describes adequately the type of relationship Joyce had imposed from the beginning. The letter begins with a paragraph describing his unhappiness; as always, when he feels that he has been hurt by someone he loves, he seeks to hurt them by displaying his misery and suffering: "My dear Nora, I have just finished my midnight dinner for which I had no appetite . . . I felt sick just as I did last night.

[3]MS. Cornell, June 1905.
[4]MS. Cornell, 29 Aug. 1904, 60 Shelbourne Road. *Letters*, vol. II, pp. 49-50.

I am much distressed," and then, having prepared the ground, he attacks:

> I may have pained you tonight by what I said but surely it is well that you should know my mind on most things? My mind rejects the whole present social order and Christianity—home, the recognised virtues, classes of life, and religious doctrines. How could I like the idea of home? My home was simply a middle-class affair ruined by spendthrift habits which I have inherited. . . . (*Ibid.*)

One can see what has happened, and what status Joyce gives Nora: she has talked to him of settling down, and he replies that the home has no meaning for him, that there are seventeen in his family and that brothers and sisters mean nothing to him. He does not for a moment dream of turning back to what he calls "the system," so it is up to Nora, if she can, to change her wishes. He, Joyce, is struggling against "incredible difficulties" but heroically "despises them": "I make open war upon the Catholic Church by what I write and say and do. I cannot enter the social order except as a vagabond." The balance-sheet of his relations with society gives a rather negative result: understood by only one brother, and one friend (in fact J.F.Byrne), who deceived him. He honours Nora with exceptional confidence, in a form which may well surprise her: she stands close to his soul. Nearer, and yet less near, than the lost friend; in this love the woman is to be the confidante of his secret thoughts. It is neither middle-class nor courtly, this love: Joyce has invented a form of love that suits his soul and mind (he was forever talking of "soul" and "mind"), his private lands where he would admit none but her. But very soon, from 1905 onwards, he has to give up the idea of sharing his mind with her, because "with one entire side of my nature she has no sympathy". More and more she becomes close to his soul. One cannot fail to recognise in all these idealistic formulations a desire for a holy union. Joyce to some extent plays the part of God, and wishes to raise Nora to his level. On the other hand he rejects Christianity because it has compromised itself by becoming part of the social order. The enemy is the Church in society. Joyce retains a deep longing for the sacred: thus, in this same letter, he refers to a holy night, which is in his language a kind of marriage. It is not a question of a night of pleasure, and sexuality is here reduced to tenderness; but it is a night that Joyce has transformed into an exalting imitation of ritual, while Nora sees in it nothing but a degradation close to parody:

> I consider it as a kind of sacrament and the recollection of it fills me with amazed joy. You will perhaps not understand at once why it is that I honour

you so much on account of it as you do not know much of my mind. But it. . . . left in me a final sense of sorrow and degradation—sorrow because I saw in you an extraordinary, melancholy tenderness which had chosen that sacrament as a compromise, and degradation because I understood that in your eyes I was inferior to a convention of our present society.[5]

Ceremony indeed there had been, but Nora had believed that she was only yielding to Joyce's selfish fancies. Again, because she does not understand him, she always guesses that he is inspired by desire much more than by love; when Jim says "I want more than your caresses," he wants her soul and is prepared to give his own in exchange. But in the context of Dublin, Jim's periphrases and private language are not easy to grasp. All their misunderstandings stem from his refusal to use symbolic words and his wish for Nora to understand him by implication, that she should leave unspoken the words (marriage, love, only, fidelity) which he cannot say without derogating from his own moral code. This is the implication of this passage from a letter written at the Martello tower in Sandycove:

My dear, dear Nora. . . . In a way I have no right to expect that you should regard me as anything more than the rest of men—in fact in view of my own life I have no right at all to expect it. But yet I seemed to have expected it if only because I myself had never regarded anyone as I regarded you.[6]

This was not to hinder Jim from considering Nora as his wife and living with her through all the problems of a lower-middle-class couple such that it could have served as a model for the similar couple in *Ulysses*. Nevertheless, if Nora accepts the compromise quickly, it is Jim who takes more time to assimilate it, probably less from hatred of social convention than from fear of being limited or diminished by the constant presence of a woman. When they were back in Europe in 1905, Jim wrote to Stannie, who had become the confidant of his mind now that Nora was unable to be. He shares his thoughts with him, and throughout numerous letters to his brother is portrayed the conflict in which he was struggling. For the first time in his life, Jim found himself in a situation where the choice did not impose itself as evident: he admired and respected Nora, but they were making each other miserable. In 1905, after some difficult months, he was thinking of separation, because "her effect on me has so far been to destroy (or rather to

[5] *Letters*, vol. II, p. 49.
[6] MS. Cornell, 10 Sept. 1904. *Letters*, vol. II, p. 51.

weaken) a great part of my natural cheerfulness." But he was still quite ready to believe that this was merely a passing uneasiness. He was coming to feel less and less romantic and had no intention of driving Nora to take "a douche in the Serpentine" like Harriet Shelley. In a very long letter to Stanislaus[7] he tries to draw up the balance-sheet of their nine months of life together; he oscillates from page to page, sets out that he has been working, written three novellas, five hundred pages of *Stephen Hero*, and engendered a child; but on the other hand Nora is ill, complains, suffers from the coldness and hostility of the Triestine women and from her own idleness, is often in tears, sulks, and spends days sometimes without speaking. But Jim does not reproach her at all. He says, following his own rule, "I feel it is better that people should be happy." He is emotionally touched by Nora's plight to the same degree that he feels himself lessened by her; and basically, under the mask of reasonable consideration, he fears the misfortune that Ibsen denounces in the case of Rubeck and Maia:—"I want to avoid as far as is humanly possible any such apparition in our lives as that abominable spectre which Aunt Josephine calls 'mutual tolerance'." Having said this, he at once feels hope returning. Much as he may deny it, the agitation in his soul is caused by a form of idealism: love must remain exceptional and ecstatic, otherwise it degenerates into "tolerance," which is obligatory for those couples blessed and sanctioned by the Church. The freedom of his union with Nora must therefore be the guarantee of the purity of their love. Jim is, however, still not fooled into believing this freedom real, since habit cannot fail to make it "conjugal."

This ill-begun experiment in unmarried love was thus to end in a legal marriage in 1931. But here appearances are deceptive: even though Joyce only married Nora in 1931, because marriage is a bourgeois institution, or (as Ellmann thinks) because he was able to exert pressure on Nora because of the falsity of their situation, or because he was afraid of marriage, or because non-religious marriage was meaningless, it is a fact that Jim and Nora lived as a married couple with the same type of relationship as any legally married pair. Furthermore, it was Nora and not Joyce who after 1909 was to make blackmailing threats of separation. Perhaps this rather contradictory state of mind explains the negative forms taken by the theme of marriage in Joyce's work: in *Dubliners* he establishes typical patterns on the level of the epiphany to portray little bourgeois comedies after the style of his father's anecdotes.

[7]MS. Cornell, 12 July 1905, Via S. Nicolo, Trieste. *Letters*, vol. II, pp. 92-8.

In *Portrait*, the image of marriage the infant and later pubescent Stephen projects is much more disturbing: marriage is seen as the source of misfortune to individual and family alike, and Joyce treats it as an obsession, accompanying it with images of terror or abject submission. By contrast Stephen imagines a marriage in the world of art, and a marriage of redemption and purification in which he sees himself as the Spouse of Ireland, saving his race by half-ritual, half-sexual magic —this becomes comical in its opposition to the reality. Joyce's irony shows clear at the expense of the rebel artist. Finally, it is in a mood of frank comedy or parody that Joyce creates in *Ulysses*, out of his own experiences turned to ridicule, the archetypal couple, "one of Joyce's great inventions,"[8] with their train of small misfortunes and humiliations, adultery, bedroom secrets, their double solitude, all accepted because this is life. All the picture lacks is the wedding day. In *Ulysses*, which represents in one day a whole example of man's life, Joyce takes us to a birth, a death, to all the meals that space out the time, and conducts us to all the places where man lives, alone or in society: he follows Everyman Everywhere and in Every temptation. And all is so complete, the living man is so closely enchained that some time passes before we realise this curious absence, absence not of the married state but of the ceremony. The conjugal state is, in the prime sense of the word, almost the natural state: one *is* in it. But if one turns back to *Portrait* or *Dubliners*, one still does not find the wedding day. There are, indeed, formal scenes of asking for a lady's hand, worthy of a Tchekhov, and especially those "reversed" scenes which show the manoeuvres of the woman to seduce the chosen man; sometimes society participates in the offer, grotesquely as in *The Boarding House*, sometimes the woman, by herself but eternally woman, conducts the campaign, with the magical charm of Molly.

Marriage as Epiphany: Analysis of "The Boarding House"

When Joyce wrote his long letter to Stannie on 12 July 1905, worrying about the future of his life with Nora, he announced to him at the same time the appearance of a fifth novella, *The Boarding House;* later he was to classify it in the seventh place in his collection, between *Two Gal-*

[8] J.-J. Mayoux, in *Critique*, Aug.-Sept. 1960, p. 683.

lants, a sordid tale of procuring, and *A Little Cloud,* the story of a middle-class marriage, of an artist *manqué* victim of a heartless wife. *The Boarding House* is neither darkly sordid nor cruelly pathetic, but both sordid and pathetic in the grotesque mood; the characters' ambitions and dreams are medicocre, in proportion to the good or bad fortune that befalls them.

The Marriage of Bob Doran is conducted in terms of a hunt and a kill. This could be tragic, but the story is in fact discreetly comic. The execution is that of an animal fit to eat. The whole affair is placed under the sign of the butcher's cleaver, wielded by Mrs. Mooney, an energetic woman with a marriageable daughter. Joyce sets the tone and the leitmotif with the opening words, "Mrs. Mooney was a butcher's daughter," and from then on the tale proceeds, apparently like a realistic short story, but in fact with a perpetual exchange between the narrator's objectivity and the landlady's secret thoughts, forming a kind of indirect interior monologue, like this reflection of Mrs. Mooney's about her husband: "It was no use making him take the pledge: he was sure to break out again a few days after." So, there was once an ogress who was an expert on meat, fresh or otherwise, and kept young men in her house, fattening them up in order to choose, when the day came, the best one for sacrifice. As it happens, the lady has a daughter with grey-green eyes, called Polly, who looks like "a little perverse madonna" when she sings for Madam's young men provocative songs, whose boldness she is not supposed to understand, such as:

> I'm a . . . naughty girl
> You needn't sham:
> You know I am.

But song is not real life—or is it? And Polly is not naughty. And Bob Doran is not a villain either. He saw first of all in Polly her madonna aspect, not her perversity. Is it Polly's fault if she has feminine hands and smells pleasant, and if on her bath night a gust blew out her candle and she had to come down timidly in her night-clothes to get it relighted? Of course, this process could be interpreted symbolically, but, after all, Polly is only nineteen and a candle is only a candle. True, but Bob Doran is a man, believing in the good Lord and therefore in the Devil, and Polly is tempting. Again, he is an old bachelor, and the young girl is already as crafty as a woman: when he comes in late, she warms up his dinner, and with great care makes punch for him, if it is a cold night. Perhaps marriage might not be so bad . . . but Mr. Doran feels uneasy; his world is reduced to two buildings which swallow up the freedom he had so far guarded jealously, the boarding house and the church. The third place of alienation for him is Mr. Leonard's great Catholic wine-merchant's office, where he has been employed for thirteen years. The future that was opening before him grows narrow; the priest and the landlady have concluded their traditional alliance.

One fine Sunday in summer when the bells are calling the Dublin crowds to mass, Mrs. Mooney is preparing to "intervene." Mr. Doran is already half-choked by the inquisition he had to undergo the previous evening; the victim is about to pass from the confessional to the tribunal, and will not come out alive. The priest has dragged all of poor Bob's secret life out of him: "The recollection of his confession of the night before was a cause of acute pain to him; the priest had drawn out every ridiculous detail of the affair, and in the end had so magnified his sin that he was almost thankful at being afforded a loophole of reparation. The harm was done." The priest has prepared the victim to be polite and grateful to the executioner. Mrs. Mooney too acts energetically: "she dealt with moral problems as a cleaver deals with meat." She exercises a characteristic economy, of money and of time, leaving herself forty-three minutes to "have the matter out," from seventeen minutes past eleven until twelve, and at twelve she will go to report to God on having accomplished her task: "She would have lots of time to have the matter out with Mr. Doran and then catch short twelve (Mass) at Marlborough Street"; while she awaits her prey, Mrs. Mooney keeps her sense of proportion, though: from 11.17 to 11.20 the servant collects the scraps of bread for making Tuesday's bread-pudding. In this house everything is put under lock and key, butter, breadcrumbs, happiness, time . . .

A tacit pact rules both the Mooney house and the Church. There is complicity in manufacturing feelings of guilt in those to be sacrificed. The Saturday night is supposed to bring them counsel. Yet there is a difference between Polly and Bob, based on sex rather than age: according to conventional morality, Bob as a man is automatically guilty; Polly is a woman and therefore innocent victim. "It is all very well for the man . . . but the girl has to bear the brunt." Even if Bob protests feebly to himself that "it was not altogether his fault," he cannot defend himself against public accusation; "the weight of social opinion" is on the woman's side. And why not marry Polly? Because the man still feels distrust, in the same unimaginative way that Mrs. Mooney does. Doran is not fooled, and he is not sure that he really loves her. "He could not make up his mind whether to like her or despise her for what she had done." "Once you are married, you are done for," whispers his bachelor

instinct, and his Dubliner conscience replies "But the sin is there"—his
fate is already settled. And as he prepares to go slowly downstairs, his
fragmented spirit undergoes the correct transformation. A fatal logic
beats time to his inner meditation as he goes down from his third floor
to the last floor where there waits "the implacable face . . . of his
discomfiture," and Joyce weaves Mrs. Mooney's web by marking the
end of each paragraph like another step by a beaten man. How is one
to make honourable reparation, wonders Doran at the third landing—
he is still free. "For her only one reparation could make up for the loss
of her daughter's honour: marriage." Doran feels like a man walking
towards death, while Mrs. Mooney is already savouring the hour of
victory: "Nearly the half-hour! . . . The decisive expression of her great
florid face satisfied her, and she thought of some mothers she knew who
could not get their daughters off their hands." Then old Mr. Leonard
rises, like a jack-in-the-box, into Doran's imagination: "Send Mr. Doran
here, please!" Doran panics. "What could he do now but marry her or
run away?"

If he were Stephen Dedalus, he would not hesitate, but he is only
an ordinary Irishman, and even if he had boasted of his free-thinking when he was young, "that was all passed and done with." Bob
thinks like a good Irish Catholic already: "His sense of honour told
him that reparation must be made for such a sin." His timid soul
momentarily thinks of flight as he begins to go downstairs: "He
longed to ascend through the roof and fly away to another country
where he would never hear again of his trouble," yet "a force
pushed him downstairs step by step." Indeed, Bob is no daring
Icarus; his glasses mist over, he gives in. This is scarcely surprising,
for after all he is already weakened by thirteen years of servitude.
His efficient, clerkly soul does not resist: he is passively married to
Polly. Mrs. Mooney takes over the speaking role: "Come down, dear.
Mr. Doran wants to speak to you."

"But delirium passes," he used to say to himself. The moment of
happiness had lasted for those few secret nights when they used to go
upstairs on tiptoe, when silence and cunning protected their happiness
in an *equally shared* guilt. But the married couple no longer have this
exalting complicity in sin together—the man is alone, accused, condemned, tied down, while Polly, now a sanctified, non-perverse
madonna, patient, almost cheerful, has already forgotten the pre-nup-
tial comedy in favour of her "hopes and visions of the future." She is
happy, and Doran is Irish, as Joyce would say.

When Joyce sent the story to Stannie, he simply said, "There is a neat phrase of five words in *The Boarding House:* find it."[9] This little phrase was probably, as Robert M. Adams suggests,[10] the description of Polly, "like a little perverse madonna." Whispered thus to the person who was at the time his only friend and confidant, the phrase becomes both the key and leitmotif of the novella, and constitutes a permanent symbol, that of woman as deceptive virginal figure. Polly Mooney's perversity is rewarded; but we shall find Bob later in the place where all such marriages lead. The man caught in the trap has lost in advance any privileges of conjugal life. Joyce was very sensitive to the degradation brought about by "natural forces," manipulated by woman in league with the Church, just as Stephen in "Charybdis and Scylla" condemns Shakespeare's "sin" in letting himself be "tumbled in a cornfield" by a woman stronger than himself. This is why, in dedicating *The Boarding House* to Stanislaus, whose opinion in the matter is the same as his own, he knows that it will be doubly understood by his brother, as a typical Dublin scene and as a parable in which he defends his decision to reject marriage.

It was July 1905; just over a year before, Jim had met Nora, and he imagined that he had not been caught by the Polly trick. The date, 12 July 1905, is not without meaning, for the son of Jim and Nora was born on 27 July 1905, fifteen days after the capture of Bob Doran. Joyce is not Doran, but the temporal coincidence is not inconsequential, given that Joyce never hides very far away from his work. Joyce was at the time well and healthy, not married, not red-haired, not thirty-five years old like Doran. But . . .

> Polly was a slim girl of nineteen; she had light soft hair and a small full mouth. Her eyes, which were grey with a shade of green through them, had a habit of glancing upwards when she spoke with anyone, which made her look like a little perverse madonna.

And Nora was a slim girl of nineteen . . . Polly and Nora have too many elements in common, and those precisely the most secret, which no-one would know while Jim and Nora were alive. When Joyce wanted his secrets to be sought for and unearthed, he never failed to leave a trail for those who would with patience and energy discover them, by digging through objective reality. One whole part of the work is so alive that one sometimes forgets that it is not Joyce, but a fictitious character,

[9]12 July 1905. *Letters,* vol. II, p. 92.
[10]Robert M. Adams, *Surface and Symbol, The Consistency of James Joyce's Ulysses* (O.U.P., New York, 1962), p. 200.

speaking. The genesis of these "slices of life" is not easy to establish, the text clings so closely to the living person; one can no longer distinguish object from subject or divide art and life. It may be that Jim's life is putting up a defence against being afraid of Nora by writing against her.

Jim's letters to Nora have only been preserved by chance. Joyce did not intend to make posthumous confidences; and these letters, accessible in the Cornell collections, are innocent of art and artifice alike. Ellmann published them in two large volumes that appeared in December 1966, and critical suspicions were confirmed; Nora is the model for Polly and for Gretta Conroy. Not only is Polly Mooney the physical portrait of Nora, but Polly's life and past are also inspired by Nora's, as can be verified from the long letter Joyce wrote to Stanislaus from Pola,[11] sketching out Nora's earlier history. It can be seen at once that Nora and Polly have the same family background: the mother had got rid of the alcoholic father with the same Christian fortitude. Polly has those same eyes that troubled James Joyce so much. The identification becomes less sure when we come to the question of guilt insinuating itself into innocence: Joyce constantly compared Nora to Our Lady, not because Nora was a pure, venerable Marian figure, but because Joyce was still passionately attached to the Church whose interdicts he rejected and yet desired—so much so that he could not have loved a woman without taking for his starting-point the first image of woman impressed on his mind from childhood upwards, that of Our Lady. How this emotional replacement began is a problem with which we shall deal later, but its existence must be mentioned here, because it dictates all relationships with women in Joyce's life and work; he often tells Nora that she has "marked his life as strongly as the Virgin previously had oriented it." She exalts, strengthens, tempts and attracts him; he longs to be open and honest before her, shameless and as much, as entirely, himself as possible. But he longs also to be the spouse and ravisher of the Virgin, to feel the terrifying joy of sacrilege and the glorious joy of replacing the Holy Spirit.

Joyce uses Nora to provoke God; she is instrumental if not an accomplice; she loses the possibility of innocence as she becomes gradually initiated into his defiance. In 1904, she had to be a madonna with a gift for perversity; in 1905 she may well have acquired from Jim a certain practical ability. But Polly's perversity has an immediate quality which Nora's never had. In the manuscript of the first version[12] Joyce had

[11]MS. Cornell, 3 Dec. 1904. *Letters,* vol. II, pp. 71–3.
[12]Now in Yale University Library.

written "a little hypocritical madonna," but Nora was no hypocrite, and neither is Polly, although she is preparing to be. Nora hardly trespasses on Jim's integrity, whatever he says to the contrary, but Polly, or rather marriage, drove Bob to drink; in spite of thirteen years of abstinence working for a wine firm, thirteen years of resisting temptation, Bob is completely destroyed by captivity: we find him again in *Ulysses*, at Barney Kernan's, in the chapter "Cyclops" (p. 294), in which he is dead drunk. Paddy Leonard says that Doran is often in this condition, and seen in dubious company too. He has been seen in the most low places, impossibly drunk: "And calling himself a Frenchy for the shawls, Joseph Manuo."

In his interesting book of research, Robert Adams turns Doran's borrowed name inside out in order to find its hidden meaning.[13] He claims that Bob is Joseph the "cuckold-carpenter," because Polly is the madonna. He therefore concludes from the choice of name that Polly is unfaithful; but this would be too easy and nothing obliges us to accept it. Doran simply has the overwhelming feeling of being caught in a trap, and so he is in the process of betraying Polly, while Polly is probably getting her consolation at church. If adultery there is, it is adultery of a psychological kind dating from before the marriage and the guilty party is God. Polly has no need to be Molly to turn Doran into a drunkard. As for his name, Adams has sought in vain in Paris and Trieste, and sieved through all European languages, including Hungarian, without finding a trace of Manuo. The trail leads into mystery. If Manuo does not exist, this may well be a joke—Doran exists and is unhappy; he wishes not to be Doran, so in his drunkenness, he invents himself a name, the name of a man who does not exist. Being dead drunk, he no longer exists in his own eyes; he adopts a virile nationality and calls himself *Frenchy*.[14] He invents himself a French-style name of virility, and the name *Man* is the first to suggest itself. (Cf.Little Chandler's famous trip to the Isle of Man, in the following novella, *A Little Cloud*). In the end, Bob Doran becomes a blasphemer, like John Joyce, and on very bad terms with God:

> And so says Bob Doran, with the hat on the back of his poll, lowest blackguard in Dublin when he's under the influence:
> —Who said Christ is good?
> —I beg you parsnips, says Alf.

[13]Adams, *op. cit.*, p. 200.
[14]Joyce makes him into Belluomo in the "Proteus" episode of *Ulysses*, remembering his own observation-visit in 1903.

—Is that a good Christ, says Bob Doran, to take away poor little Willy
Dignam?

. . . Bob Doran shouts out of him.

—He's a bloody ruffian I say, to take away poor little Willy Dignam.
(*Ulysses*, p. 296)

We can feel Joyce being deeply and strangely threatened, not by
Nora as a person so much as by the images of aggression she suggested
to his mind and by the fact that she was expecting a child destined to
make great changes in their relationship;[15] the next novella concerns
a young husband whom his wife detests and who struggles against
wishing that his son were dead.

It will be seen that from this point of view the woman becomes an
instrument of death. She who was modest and self-effacing in love now
becomes demanding for her child's sake. Jim hastened to solve this
problem, but crises occurred from time to time which threatened to put
an end to their union; each time that Nora had a child, she and Jim
would come into conflict and every time his instinctive reaction was to
seek escape in flight. They came so near to catastrophe in Trieste in
1905 because *Dubliners*, which Joyce was trying to publish with Grant
Richards, seemed unlikely ever to appear. And on 27 July 1905 Nora
had brought forth another Dubliner in exile. The child and *Dubliners*
at once became opposed, not because Joyce was not pleased to become
a father, but because Nora was taking much more interest in the child
than in the written new work. As always, he signified the existence of
the conflict by symbolic gestures of refusal: two months after the child's
birth, it still had no name, as though Joyce were in a way refusing to
acknowledge his creation publicly (though he had said from December
onward that he would recognise it), or as though he could not prevent
himself from feeling jealous of a human gestation and birth for taking
only nine months. Hence the rather worrying biographical details of the
3 and 4 December 1905: on the third Joyce sent *Dubliners* to Grant
Richards, and on the fourth he wrote to Aunt Josephine that he was
thinking of leaving Nora:

> I have hesitated before telling you that I imagine the present relations
> between Nora and myself are about to suffer some alteration . . . I daresay
> I am a difficult person for any woman to put up with but on the other hand
> I have no intention of changing. Nora does not seem to make much differ-

---

[15]In his Trieste notebook, Joyce noted down under "Giorgino," "Before he was born
I had no fear of fortune."

ence between me and the rest of the men she has known and I can hardly believe that she is justified in this. I am not a very domestic animal—after all, I suppose I am an artist—and sometimes when I think of the free and happy life which I have (or had) every talent to live I am in a fit of despair. At the same time I do not wish to rival the atrocities of the average husband and I shall wait till I see my way more clearly.[16]

Joyce had a five-month-old son when he wrote that letter. It seemed that the roles of father and artist were irreconcilable. Very soon he began to defend against all comers his paternity in art; he was not John Joyce's son for nothing. But he was watchful. Children of flesh and blood were never to be a major concern of his, except when the work would permit of it. Only after *Finnegans Wake* was Lucia to become the object of a genuine obsession, not of normal fatherly care.

Jim both provokes and fears the inevitable rivalry between Nora and his writing, as we can trace in the shaming admissions of *Exiles*, the play in which he puts himself on trial, intending to acquit himself in the end, but meaning first to admit and accept all the wrongs he has done. Bertha, alias Nora, the companion of the writer Richard Rowan, has two rivals whom she assimilates together: the one is Beatrice who has inspired Richard from afar and is the pale, cold embodiment of the artist's relationship to his inspiration; and the other is Richard's work itself, which deprives Bertha of the real presence of the man she calls *my* lover, when he sits up all night in the study, giving himself to the work rather than to the woman who longs for him.

Basically the union of Jim and Nora is not radically different from the type of marriage that horrified the eighteen-year-old Jim; both forms of human relationship are scarcely discreet disguises for masculine selfishness of the John Joyce type. He needs always to feel free, within a certain constancy; and it is necessary for Nora to be always a woman met casually, to remain like the little blue flower one picks after the rainstorm. Joyce must eliminate "duties" and "rights," so that she may never be able to call upon the occult powers of the Church or of motherhood. Nora has to be as submissive, within the framework of this imitation freedom whose yoke she alone bears, as May Joyce was to John.

Eventually Jim was to succeed so well in destroying the characteristics of marriage that little or nothing remained of the couple's subjection to the function of procreation; he was only tempted to leave Nora when she took on the appearance of the mother, signifying constraint.

[16]MS. Cornell, to Mrs. William Murray, from Trieste. *Letters*, vol. II, pp. 128–9.

The children had to be sacrificed to Jim's happiness with Nora, and this was what happened in Joyce's lifetime: Lucia and Giorgio had to pay for their parents' decision to be first and foremost Nora and Jim, in order that Jim might freely be James Joyce.[17] This is why Nora's maternal feelings gradually atrophied as she became more and more Jim's companion. Later Joyce would see the double consequences of this wilful deformation of marriage: on the one hand, the children of a couple who live like Adam and Eve in a world unlike Eden are indirectly afflicted by an overwhelming freedom (when they needed Nora's protection she could only answer that she had but one "child" —her husband); and on the other, Lucia as she grew up found Nora to be "father's companion" rather than "mother." This was a cause of that tragically violent jealousy whose movements can be perceived in *Finnegans Wake*. The couple Jim and Nora is succeeded by that of Jim and Lucia; *Finnegans Wake* is a work of fatherhood and incest, whose language echoes that of the daughter.

Marriage Obsessively Viewed, by Stephen

The theme of marriage changes in tone completely when it becomes a problem for Stephen Hero and Stephen artist: what was merely a comic parody of a typical middle-class marriage, target of Jim's and Stannie's allied sarcasm, becomes for Stephen such an obsessive problem that any approach, real or imaginary, to the sacrament or any idea of a future married life will set off aggressive behaviour-patterns in the "hero," and later, in the "artist," genuine hallucinations. Stephen's complexity as a character has two origins: firstly, his personal problems are often strangely divided, and Joyce takes advantage of the confusion reigning in the mind of his double, as it still was in his own. And secondly, Joyce himself had not yet succeeded, even by the time of *Portrait*, in establishing an equilibrium which would allow him fully to sustain the note of irony. The vocation and everyday life make opposing demands, because of the sacerdotal nature Joyce attributes to the former, and the sublimation of everyday material into the matter of art.

[17]"Our children (much as I love them) *must not* come between us. If they are good and noble-natured it is because of *us*, dear. We met and joined our bodies and souls freely and nobly and our children are the fruit of our bodies." (31 Aug. 1909). *Letters*, vol. II, p. 242.

Marriage as eventual vocation is the centre of that psychological crisis during which Stephen's choices are made.

The problem hidden behind the ambiguous speeches of Stephen Hero and the unexplained visions of Stephen Dedalus is as follows: what is the relationship between sex, marriage and love? (This limiting the social aspect.) What are the connections between sex and the individual freedom that the artist in particular needs? To what extent can woman and the artist's vocation be conciliated?

In *Stephen Hero* Joyce begins by eliminating the hypothesis of a social and sexual equality which would answer all the problems; Lynch was resigning himself to a return into "the company of the unsatisfied" when he was saved by meeting Stephen. Henceforth he becomes the amused if unenterprising confidant of the artist's attempted or successful satisfactions, which Joyce treats in the comic vein. Stephen, being a hero, decides to attempt the impossible, to induce a middle-class Dublin girl, Emma Clery, to share his views on sexual emancipation. Joyce was not that young Stephen; he took, as he told Stannie, an amused pleasure in following his hero's amorous adventures. The grotesque side of the adventure served simply as a pretext for expounding a theory which he considered more as a challenge than anything else; he was in fact less preoccupied with sexual freedom in an adventure than with moral freedom within a permanent relationship. The hero's acts of daring are the naïve expression of what the author calls his "moral nature."

To be an artist is, by vocation, to be destined for a fate different from that of other men. For Joyce the "vocation" is the discovery of one's "moral nature," which is what, when mature, will produce the works of art. Joyce's letters and Stanislaus' diary show how methodically Jim organised his life around this conviction. Some words appear and recur so frequently that they eventually form a mental image of "the artist" by himself. Their association brings to light a triple relationship whose contradictory complexity is to determine various important aspects of the work. These key words are "artist," associated sometimes with "puberty," and other times with "nature," which is often qualified as "moral." Joyce as a young man would repeat to Stannie, as he later would to Nora, that his conduct was governed by one law only, the necessity of acting in accordance with this "moral nature," whatever the obstacles in its way might be. Joyce had an idea of what constituted the safety of his artistic integrity, and bent all his will to protecting it, for it was more precious to him than anything else in the world. Evi-

dently, his artistic nature *quā nature* must be determined by the subject; yet it seems that the principle of fidelity to oneself entails a need
for liberty, which in its turn is to be defined as opposition to all social
institutions. Which is as much as to say that only supreme egocentricity
is acceptable, because the artist cannot enter into any structure or be
a part of any whole.

Theoretically, all this is perfectly logical; but in practice, as soon as he
had discovered his nature, Joyce found himself beset by problems,
which he calls "struggles," and which do not always find peaceful solution. The most thorny of these problems is that of sex. As Ellmann
emphasises, "he formulated this vocation soon after he passed from
childhood to adolescence."[18] The words "artist" and "puberty" are
connected as the natural elements and terms of organic development:
but what Joyce calls "the impulses of my nature," that is, sexual desires,
clash with the moral pattern and ideal of purity of his childhood. To
deny eroticism would be a lie and denial of oneself; and so he realises
that in order to be honest he must sacrifice that imaginary part of
himself, his virginity.

At fourteen, marked by the teachings of the Church, and already
beginning to haunt the bawdy-houses of Dublin, he has two revelations
that date from the same period, that he is an "artist" and that he is a
"debauchee." Since the two revelations are simultaneous, he concludes
that they both constitute part of his being, and that they must be
reconciled and justified by each other, in order that their co-existence
may be fruitful. Joyce does not question either of these aspects of his
moral nature: the artist should be a complete being, uniting the aspirations of the spirit and of the flesh. Once the reconciliation has been
effected (the episode of the girl on the beach), it is necessary to integrate
also the third natural aspect of the soul, the intimate connection of art
with the theological form. The artist should be both a debauchee and
a high-priest of art; he would then be integrating human experience on
a higher level than the priest does because of the totality of his experience.

There is a tendency to see in *Portrait* the progress of the artist in
search of himself and the gradual, immediately applied formulation of
an aesthetic. In fact, Stephen is just as preoccupied by sexual problems
as he is by problems of artistic creation, and he frequently confuses the
two. Sexuality and creation are further accompanied by the opposing
notions of purity and impurity. On the imaginary level the artist has

[18]Introduction to *Letters*, vol. II, pp. 37–8.

soon found his way and formulated his own aesthetic. But art is not separate from life, and the first part of the programme calls for concretisation in reality. And here the obstacles begin to pile up for Joyce, as for his representative in *Portrait*; for to be "natural" in debauch one needs a partner. The matter would be trivial, and the bawdy-house quite sufficient, were it not that the introduction of debauchery into aesthetics causes Joyce (and especially Stephen) to wish instinctively for the debauch to be beautiful. The whole structure is thus threatened with collapse, and Joyce could not fail to see the comic side of the matter, as in this dialogue between the hero and his confidant:

> You know, Lynch, said Stephen, we may as well acknowledge openly and freely. We must have women.
> —Yes I agree. We must have women.
> —Jesus said, "Whoso looketh upon a woman to lust after her hath already committed adultery with her in his heart": but he did not condemn "adultery." Besides it is impossible not to commit "adultery."
> . . . —I must go to where I am sure of my ground.
> —But that costs money; and besides it is dangerous. You may get a dose that will last you your life. I wonder you have not got it before this.
> —Ah, yes, isn't it a nuisance. And yet I must go somewhere. . . . She is a human being, you know. I can't say I consider harlots as human beings. *Scortum* and *moechus* are both neuter nouns" (*Stephen Hero*, p. 195).

The creative artist sees himself as pure from every contact with this world, which gives us the portrait of Stephen obsessed with the filthy miasmas of Dublin; sex also is obviously an impure contact with others. Yet Stephen is unable to renounce either. This clash of the real and the imaginary produces, without his realising it, a series of visions revelatory of his agitation; some are almost comical in expression, others are terrifying. The whole is dominated by a feeling so old that it is to be found, expressed in exactly the same fashion, in the first sketch for *Portrait*, dated 1904: a real hatred, which Joyce then entirely shared, for "grotesque virginities." He mocks his contemporaries as "young fools" who are so subject to the Church that they keep their "absurd virginity" until they marry; he expresses himself very clearly on this point in *Stephen Hero*:

> Stephen's aestheticism united with a sane and conscienceless acceptance of the needs of young men . . . being a shrewd animal himself, he (Lynch) had begun to suspect from Stephen's zeal and loftiness of discourse at least an assertion of that incorrigible virginity which the Irish race demands alike from any John who would baptise it or from any Joan who

would set it free as the first heavenly proof of fitness for such high offices. (*Stephen Hero*, p. 154)

When Joyce was editing *Stephen Hero* in 1905, he expressed the same anger; he was not a person to forget annoyances, and once a formula had pleased him or an annoyance inspired him, it acquired a kind of freedom to appear throughout his work, right up to *Finnegans Wake*. The sentences of the nameless artist of 1904 are taken up word for word by Stephen Hero, so important are they to Joyce. We find the same hatred for the "young men" who are subject to their teachers, amongst whom it is impossible for him "to find his soul's sufficient good.

> ... Impossible that a temperament ever trembling towards ecstasy should submit to acquiesce, that a soul should decree servitude for its portion over which the image of beauty had fallen as a mantle" (*Stephen Hero*, p. 197).

It is important to recall the degree to which ecstasy in art depends on the spiritual liberty of the person, and to what degree this liberty is a function of moral independence, verified in sexual experience: the latter is only one means of reaching beauty, and the image (though not the reality) of free love is "a part of the soul."

Similarly, in the "portrait of the artist" in *Stephen Hero* and especially in *Portrait* we find a series of sketches, almost Goya-like in their ugliness, of his contemporaries as nightmare figures, their "bovidities." These allegorical sketches are a translation of what Stephen (and Joyce) thinks of them: the moral seems always to be immediately visible in the concrete gesture. The following analysis attempts to elucidate these equations between physical and moral attitudes in *Portrait*.

From *Stephen Hero* to *Portrait* a change takes place, not in the feelings but in their literary form: instead of diatribes and scholastic quibbles, there is a series of pictures, instead of speeches there are projected images as seen by Stephen, who is generally detached and often in retreat, hiding behind the object he sees, or there are symbolic dreams whose meaning Stephen seeks but whose explicit interpretation Joyce refuses to give us. The young man suffers, surrounded as he is by contemporaries who are ready and willing to become "domestic animals."

The word "animal" brings us back into the troubled world, where Bob Doran was led to the slaughter. The 1904 Stephen had already attacked bovidity. It is natural for a man so marked by Catholicism to draw, whether consciously or not, his metaphors and comparisons from the animal world. The visionary universe of Stephen in *Portrait* looks out on the world of animality insofar as the animal traditionally represents the lower aspect of man, the species; on the other hand the animal is the living being without reason, and this is why Stephen, when attacked by the demon of the flesh, sees himself as an animal. This is also why, observing the unconscious placidness of those around him, he confuses them with animals. Thus the animal symbolises the lucidity of the artist and the torpor of the ordinary adolescent; this would make the use of the symbol contradictory if Joyce did not add to the strength and precision of the fundamental comparison by a whole play of original obsessions, of beheading, of the bowed head, of the death's head.

These three visions, symbolising fear of death and refusal to submit, come almost simultaneously to Stephen at the beginning of chapter V of *Portrait*. The chapter proceeds on two levels, one a superficial realism, maintained by the presence of other people (hence the almost rhetorical clarity of the dialogues) and the other an uncontrollable dream-state where Stephen wanders lost in the mists of "the dull phenomenon that is Dublin." The latter is expressed through an indirect inner monologue, interrupted at times by images which at first have no meaning for him, but in which superstition reveals his as yet unidentified thoughts, fears, and longings. The universe of Dublin as he believes he sees it is in fact the world as he wishes to see it subjectively; his contemporaries act out before him, even in their most simple actions, a destiny which he refuses. And because Stephen wants to escape, everything seems to be closing in on him. Because he refuses to bow down, others appear to him in this servile posture. This hallucinatory aspect is in fact a "metaphorisation" of violent occurrences in the intellectual world which can only be imagined. Joyce makes much use of this process in *Portrait* and in *Ulysses*, where the awakened conscience is in a state of osmosis with the dream-world, finding its apogee in "Circe." Joyce himself possessed this consciousness on the edge of dream, which is related both to the poetic vision and to an almost pathological hypersensitivity. When Joyce was preparing to leave Dublin with Nora, he was haunted by a dream that recurred with traumatic insistency;[19] it was a death's head, symbolising for him God and Dublin. Stephen, like Joyce, is in that state of mental vulnerability which precedes the making of a gesture that will change the whole course of his life; at such a time everything becomes charged with meaning—the universe and

[19]Cf. letter to Nora, 1 Sept. 1904, from St. Peter's Terrace, Cabra, Dublin. *Letters*, vol. II, p. 50.

other people take on positive or negative values, and one sees life or death at every turn.

Stephen lives through his last dizzy days in Dublin, imagining it to himself as though he had already left it, or, on the contrary, as though Dublin were not going to let him go. The feverish strength of his imagination is such that places shift about *within* his consciousness.

Thus, when one reads:

> He saw the heads of his classmates meekly bent as they wrote in their notebooks the points they were bidden to note, nominal definitions, essential definitions and examples or dates of birth or death, chief works, a favourable and an unfavourable criticism side by side. His own head was unbent for his thoughts wandered abroad and whether he looked around the little class of students or out of the window across the desolate gardens of the green an odour assailed him of cheerless cellar-damp and decay. (*Portrait*, p. 177)

One feels actually present at the English lecture at University College; but in fact Stephen has stopped in the street in front of a placard listing the lectures, and sees what is going on far away, and watches himself watching. As though by chance, everyone's head but his is bowed. He feels that these are "humble worshippers" before the tabernacle, and thus makes the transition in his mind from University to Church, escaping in thought from a place where in reality he is not. Submission, rebellion, escape, are all shown in images here within the framework of the University: the bowed heads represent intellectual abdication.

These bowed heads are succeeded by a severed head, in a second vision called up by the first. It is the head of his friend Cranly, seen not as the rough young man from Wicklow that he is in reality but as the head of a dead priest:

> Why was it that when he thought of Cranly he could never raise before his mind the entire image of his body but only the image of the head and face? Even now against the grey curtain of the morning he saw it before him like the phantom of a dream, the face of a severed head or death-mask, crowned on the brows by its stiff black upright hair as by an iron crown. It was a priest-like face, priest-like in its pallor, in the wide winged nose, in the shadowings below the eyes and along the jaws, priest-like in the lips that were long and bloodless and faintly smiling. (*Portrait*, pp. 177–8)

It becomes the focus for a whole web of significances. Cranly, the recipient of his meditations, is the silent only son of an old mother. Stephen associates this severed head with the Church and with death without knowing why. By stirring up his feelings and memory, he reaches an even stranger image through which he associates these two things with a vague female figure also:

> Stephen . . . would have told himself that it was the face of a guilty priest who heard the confessions of those whom he had not power to absolve but that he felt again in memory the gaze of its dark womanish eyes.
>
> Through this image he had a glimpse of a strange dark cavern of speculation but at once turned away from it, feeling that it was not yet the hour to enter it.

One can perceive the suggestive art and the knowledge of the mechanism of association which Joyce uses in setting out the first elements of the network of obsessions. Then it all stops, as though by accident (and the keys to the enigma are not given until later), after the "long talk with Cranly on the subject of my revolt." As Stephen notes it down in his diary for March 20, "He had his grand manner on. I supple and suave. Attacked me on the score of love for one's mother."

Justifying his refusal to marry Nora when she was pregnant, Joyce wrote to Stannie that "the struggle against conventions in which I am at present involved was not entered into by me so much as a protest against the conventions as with the intention of living in conformity with my moral nature."[20]

Such was the declaration in real life which was to become Stephen's fine Satanic formula, "I will not serve that in which I no longer believe, whether it call itself my home, my fatherland, or my church" (*Portrait*, p. 247). This declaration comes at the end of a painful conversation with Cranly, mainly on the subject of love. Cranly has been asking, "Do you love your mother?" and "Have you never loved anyone?" And Stephen replies, "I tried to love God. It seems now that I failed. It is very difficult." Stephen, like Satan, has tried to love God and failed. It may be that Joyce could not succeed in loving Nora as much as himself, either. The refusal of love is both subjective and objective: there is refusal to love and refusal to be loved. In Joyce's case, the refusal was by no means complete; he needed a permanent accomplice. For Stephen, it is essential not to love and not to be loved; this is why the images of marriage and woman are represented in a way that suggests death rather than happiness. The enterprise is not easy for the young artist, who is still very young and has a mother so devoted that one might be deluded into believing in mother-love; and loneliness is painful when one is always being tempted to love in the romantic vein. So,

[20]MS. Cornell. *Letters*, vol. II, p. 99, 19 July 1905.

it is necessary to persuade oneself once and for all that no love is possible in Ireland, and if one is the only person to believe this, then one makes the loneliness into the inflexible cover for a decisive mind.

The first stage consists of denying reality and replacing it with a ghostly world in which people are reduced to virtual non-existence except insofar as they are seen, deformed, disincarnated or even suppressed by the young man; the process is described thus in *Stephen Hero*:

> He was egoistically determined that nothing material, no favour or reverse of fortune, no bond of association or impulse or tradition should hinder him from working out the enigma of his position in his own way. He avoided his father sedulously because he now regarded his father's presumptions as the most deadly part of a tyranny, internal and external, which he determined to combat with might and main. He argued no further with his mother, persuaded that he could have no satisfactory commerce with her so long as she chose to set the shadow of a clergyman between her nature and his. (*Stephen Hero*, pp. 213–4)

To give up speaking is the first formulation of the rule he later promulgates in *Portrait*: "Using for my defence the only arms I allow myself to use—silence, exile, and cunning" (p. 247). These are defensive arms, but the defensive is in fact the cunningly organised and hidden offensive. In *Portrait*, the silence is conveyed by absence: we see Stephen with his family for the last time, at the beginning of chapter V, in a short and picturesque scene which becomes overwhelmingly charged with irony when one realises that in the book it is a farewell scene: the unseen father insults his son, in the manner of John Joyce, and Stephen departs, with a "Good morning, everybody, . . . smiling and kissing the tips of his fingers in adieu" (p. 175). This is his rehearsal for leaving home properly. Nothing more is heard of his father and mother; he resolutely buries himself in the world of his thoughts, which, he had said in *Stephen Hero*, "disturbed his brain." The process of effacing other people continues throughout the chapter until he declares to Cranly that he will not serve "home, fatherland or church." The formulaic expression removes all living content from the heroic attitude; people are replaced by the "big words," and ingratitude or lack of love are made easier. Throughout chapter V, Stephen lives "in a dusk of doubt and self-mistrust, lit up at moments by the lightnings of intuition, but lightnings of so clear a splendour that in those moments the world perished about his feet as if it had been fire-consumed" (*Portrait*, p. 176).

By the end of the chapter, Stephen has associated figures, visions and characters in such a way that the origin of his sickness is revealed: it is soon obvious that the real individuals represent more abstract figures or institutions, and that Stephen more or less consciously interprets, always in the same way, a multitude of tiny incidents, thoughts or scenes. Cranly, the nameless Temptress, the Church, the priest, the mother, all become conspirator-figures, whom Stephen treats with the same angry mistrust. What relates them together? The first practical problem to solve, for Stephen as for Cranly, is that of marriage. They both hear a clear-voiced servant singing a popular song:

"Cranly stopped to listen, saying:
—*Mulier cantat.*
The soft beauty of the Latin word touched with an enchanting touch the dark of the evening, with a touch fainter and more persuading than the touch of music or of a woman's hand." (*Portrait*, p. 244)

The voice and the Latin words evoke in Stephen's mind "the figure of a woman as she appears in the liturgy of the church." The artist is ravished in contemplation of an image of pure beauty. The actual woman is invisible. For Cranly the verses have a concrete meaning and he takes them literally:

"Cranly repeated in strongly stressed rhythm the end of the refrain:

And when we are married,
O, how happy we'll be
For I love sweet Rosie O'Grady
And Rosie O'Grady loves me.

—There's real poetry for you, he said, there's real love.
. . . .—Do you consider that poetry? Or do you know what the words mean?
—I want to see Rosie first, said Stephen.
—She's easy to find, Cranly said."

Stephen's reply is intentionally cynical but it has also a hidden meaning: for Stephen there will always be two women, the imaginary inaccessible and the provocative real—he must keep away from her because she asks for too much without wishing to give anything; she asks, in particular, a Platonic love, in the twentieth century! This is one of the themes, both serious and mocking, that never lost their fascination for Joyce; he peoples it with a ridiculous Dante and a perverse Beatrice. In *Stephen Hero* he sets up as opposed to Dante the figure of the modern lover who is obliged to have recourse to a feudal terminology to express his love:

> As he could not use it with the same faith and purpose as animated the feudal poets he was compelled to express his love a little ironically. This suggestion of relativity, he said, mingling itself with so immune a passion is a modern note: we cannot swear or expect eternal fealty because we recognise too accurately the limits of every human energy. (*Stephen Hero*, p. 177)

Joyce is in fact hidden behind that Stephen; he used feudal terminology himself in his love poems without reluctance; and yet he reminded Nora of "the limits of every human energy." But Nora did not act the part of Beatrice. But in *Portrait* as in *Stephen Hero* the beautiful inspiration would much rather have Dante than the modern lover.

From lack of Dante, however, and while she waits for marriage, she "flirts," as Stephen puts it with bitter jealousy, with priests; at this stage one can no longer tell what really infuriates Stephen and what is only pretext to cover his real resentments. But it is incontestable that Stephen conflates Cranly and the priest who in all innocence has the favour of E.C. Throughout short wordless scenes he interprets her looks and signs to Cranly and constructs in his imagination a whole clandestine idyll between them with himself as the mocked, deceived victim.

Joyce is already using here procedures similar to the montage of the cinema, which he was to utilise to such remarkable effect in *Ulysses*: thus the scenes which Stephen's glance creates in space are acted out in the same places which permit the observer to be both watchful and acting too. The first scene and the introduction of the protagonists is the model of all the others: "She" stands silently among her companions, under the arcade of the library, waiting for the rain to stop. A group of men students are standing round Cranly, leaning against a pillar out of the rain. Stephen intentionally goes and stands out in the rain, below the group, and from the step watches the girls. "She has no priest to flirt with, he thought with conscious bitterness" (*Portrait*, p. 215). The rain stops and the girls depart. Stephen, apparently pleased by her reserved behavior, changes his mind and forgives her: "And if he had judged her harshly?"

He goes home with in his mind an image of her in her purity, "her life simple and strange as a bird's." The bird is a good sign of his turn of mind, since he claims the protection of the bird-god Thoth. He spends a miraculous night with the image of the beauty he has seen; the chapter begins with a seraphic ecstasy and follows the wanderings of his reverie. He writes a poem after the visitation of his spirit by the angel Gabriel, and a rosy light grows intense in his spirit, a light that is "her heart, strange that no man had known or would know." The rose breathes out rhymes to him. In the virgin womb of his imagination the word was made flesh, and from this mingling of glow, virginity, word, soul, spirit and heart a poem is born. The poet longs to win his Beatrice; he imagines himself as a heretic Franciscan, whispering in her ear. But "no, it was not his image, it was like the image of the young priest in whose company he had seen her last, looking at him out of dove's eyes" (*Portrait*, p. 219). The gentle vision is broken up by anger and its fragments scattered all around. These fragments become deformed reflections of her image on all sides, kitchen girl, flower girl, passer-by, prostitute, all shouting with laughter. He seems to attract mockery rather than sympathy from women. Yet he at once transforms the humiliation into aggressiveness: if women are not to be for him, then it is he who does not want anything to do with *them*, because they are so vulgar, so unlike the ideal bird, more like the common bat:

> She was a figure of the womanhood of her country, a bat-like soul waking to the consciousness of itself in darkness and secrecy and loneliness, tarrying awhile, loveless and sinless, with her mild lover and leaving him to whisper of innocent transgression in the latticed ear of a priest. (*Portrait*, p. 220)

And the priest is but a "priested peasant."

He organises the defences for his own self-esteem, and his imagination, impelled by anger, makes up associations which debase both love and its object. As priest of the imagination he could change an ordinary girl into "the radiant body of everliving life" (p. 221). The priest of religion cannot receive in confession "her soul's shy nakedness." Stephen renounces the idea of possessing her heart or soul, and keeps nothing but the images and words. Henceforth he tries to strengthen his decision by accumulating proofs of her "guilt." Cranly also is involved in this complex secret operation insofar as he is always the advocate of Christian values, mother-love, marriage, etc., and his pale severed head represents the mask of the enemy. Stephen reflects that Cranly's mask has the face of a priest and behind it is death; in its eyes, since Cranly is conscious and intelligent, lurks a presence, not that of Cranly himself since he has chosen death, but that of the person to whom he has sacrificed his ideas, the woman.

In the following scene everything has already been arranged, it is only a matter of rehearsal: Cranly, leaning against a pillar of the library colonnade, salutes someone. "She passed out from the porch of the library and bowed across Stephen in reply to Cranly's greeting. He also?" (*Portrait*, p. 232). The priest of the eternal imagination walks away to the far end of the colonnade to dream, since reality is denied him. He first summons up a whole harem of memory, "languid grace, the softness of chambering", and tastes "in the language of memory ambered wines, dying fallings of sweet airs, the proud pavan, and saw with the eyes of memory." He wants to forget her, but her image is not to be lost in these entanglements. Then the true miracle of the imagination takes place:

> It was not thought nor vision though he knew vaguely that her figure was passing homeward through the city. Vaguely first and then more sharply he smelt her body. A conscious unrest seethed in his blood. Yes, it was her body he smelt, a wild and languid smell, the tepid limbs over which his music had flowed desirously and the secret soft linen upon which her flesh distilled odour and a dew. (*Portrait*, p. 233)

If we have here not imagery but distinct physical sensations, then it must have resembled a phenomenon of hysteria. For how could one perceive the scent of a person who was not there except by magic or by some kind of hypnosis that has no connection with poetry? Stephen is sketching out an attempt at replacing everything else from within his own head, and succeeds for one feverish moment. Then he is brought back to reality by a louse crawling over his neck. Everything falls back into place now: the louse is a kind of grotesque messenger of reality. "His mind bred vermin. All the images it had awakened were false." In reality he is not attractive, nor does he desire to be: "Well then, let her go and be damned to her! She could love some clean athlete who washed himself every morning to the waist and had black hair on his chest. Let her" (*Portrait*, p. 234). And he knows, as his thoughts turn back to Cranly, that Cranly with his priestly head and his athlete's body would be able to love Rosie O'Grady.

> Stephen saw his pale face, framed by the dark, and his large dark eyes. Yes. His face was handsome and his body was strong and hard. He had spoken of a mother's love. He felt then the sufferings of women, the weaknesses of their bodies and souls; and would shield them with a strong and resolute arm and bow his mind to them. (*Portrait*, p. 245)

This is not an admission of defeat; Stephen compensates for his feeling of inferiority by sowing a subtle scorn in his words—"bow his mind

to them"—for there could never be any question of the artist's bowing his head or his mind.

> Away then: it is time to go. A voice spoke softly to Stephen's lonely heart, bidding him go and telling him that his friendship was coming to an end. Yes; he would go. He could not strive against another. He knew his part.
>
> Probably I shall go away, he said.

This inaudible inner speech, surprised by Joyce inside Stephen's head, sounds slightly false. One is not quite sure who is speaking, the Stephen who has just begun his superb mythological flight, or the little Stephen who hid under the table lest the eagles pull out his eyes (yet refused to apologise); is it the hero or the coward? For the motivation behind the decision is not really clear. There is first the necessity of self-preservation; for only when a spectacular farewell scene becomes imperative does Stephen begin to introduce as his main reason for leaving the need he feels to save the conscience of his race—wondrously naïve hypocrisy! Joyce leaves no shadows of doubt about Stephen's most secret inner self, that is not yet expressed and not yet distorted; thus the reader witnesses the precise moment at which Stephen's fate is determined, and the voice of Stephen at that moment is not the voice of Dedalus. It is the voice of John Joyce's son, the pupil of the Jesuits, the adolescent student with his erotic dreams. Ireland's last words have made up his mind for him, for to stay one would have to believe in Cranly's "real poetry," and to make this poetry real one would have to succeed in loving Rosie O'Grady. To love Rosie requires a strong body and a back that bends easily—one needs to be sufficiently sure of one's masculinity not to consider marriage as a test, to be able to yield one's authority to "another," that is, to God, for love of the woman who is God's faithful slave and who wants to turn man into God's minion too. For physical love, insinuates Stephen, the head is not needed; all one wants is a strong body and manly limbs. Ideas do not make children:

> Whatever else is unsure in this stinking dunghill of a world a mother's love is not. Your mother brings you into the world, carries you first in her body. What do we know about what she feels? But whatever she feels, it, at least, must be real. It must be. What are our ideas or ambitions? Play. Ideas! Why, that bloody bleating goat Temple has ideas. MacCann has ideas too. Every jackass going the roads thinks he has ideas.

Stephen, hearing Cranly speak thus, senses not only the latter's hostility, but also the Irish fear of life, its abdication from the chance of making history, of changing or owning the world. Cranly is his mother's son; and Stephen has just confided to him that he has broken with his mother by his refusal to do his Easter duty—his mind refuses to bow down and worship. This break with the mother is the equivalent of the break with Ireland and with religion.

Cranly would "bow his mind" if he could make up for the loss of his spiritual prestige by physical conquest. But Stephen's body is weak and soft, while his back is as unbending and straight as his ashplant; Stephen moreover has "ideas" which he does not consider as merely "play." They are indeed much more "real" than Rosie. Stephen holds fast to that which forms the reality of his poetry, which is to say that he thinks freely—with absolute freedom. To marry Rosie would mean for him not only the loss of his masculinity and authority but also, and above all, the loss of his right to think and to love images.

The vision of the meek students foretold the rigidity of Stephen's own refusal: he was not to bow the head before authority. The vision of Cranly's severed head suggests two ironic interpretations: on the one hand the Cranly who imitates the priests devotes himself to a type of chastity which is symbolised by the suppression of the body; and on the other hand Stephen sees Cranly as a John the Baptist, precursor of himself, using grotesque analogies such as these: Cranly lives on figs, "read wild honey," says Stephen. Cranly's mother is old, "read Elizabeth." But if Cranly is St. John the precursor, then Stephen is Jesus. He had been Satan. And it is true that in *Stephen Hero* Stephen declares that Satan is "Christ as a romantic youth." Thus Joyce introduces into the grandiose image of the son of Dedalus who is preparing to forge the conscience of his race the image of the son of God who cried in agony upon the cross. Satan, Jesus, Stephen, Icarus, are all destined to fall. The supreme Artist is not present, but Joyce the Creator tells this story of his young son with a delicate taste for iconoclasm.

Stephen at last appoints himself the mission of saviour, with strangely formulated ambitions that are more grotesque than serious: while Cranly plays at being the chivalrous knight, Stephen wants to act as the defender of his race, on the spiritual plane. He transposes his frustrated youthful desires into a wish to be the potential and spiritual genitor; in this way he can rival his contemporaries whose success he envies, "but him no woman's eyes had wooed" (*Portrait*, p. 238). His dream is "to cast his shadow over the imaginations of their daughters, before their squires begat upon them, that they might breed a race less ignoble than their own" *(ibid)*. One can see in this plan for premarital influence a curious deviation from the artist's role, due to Stephen's naïve pride and to Joyce's ironical attitude towards his missionary. Stephen becomes a subversive actor in the comedy. But the idea of the precursor remained peculiar to Joyce, whose vocation as creator was parallelled by a vocation as pioneer.

Marriage as Archetype: The Comic Captivation of Bloom

The story of *The Boarding House* is basically *petit-bourgeois* by the fact of the marriage arranged for two people by others whose main interest is "to get rid of them"; the mother-in-law is traditionally a figure of comedy and hostility. The story of Molly Tweedy and Poldy Bloom, which also ends in a *petit-bourgeois* marriage, has a completely different purpose and design; Molly and Bloom have been really in love, their adventure is archetypal, and beyond the apparent vulgarity and banality there is a poetry that dares not speak its name, though it often approaches romantic love and what Stephen Hero called "the feudal terminology." There is, indeed, another aspect which is the antithesis of romanticism, which is the mythical side, the tale of Venus and Adonis. The marriage of Bloom and Molly evokes two opposite myths, that of Adam and Eve and that of Shakespeare and Ann Hathaway. The relationships of the two couples are mirror-images of each other, Joyce ingeniously suggesting both simultaneously. In the same way Joyce and Nora were both Adam and Eve and Shakespeare and Ann. This is partly because Joyce claimed not to know which of them had originally taken the initiative, and at some moments was not far from seeing Nora as a Venus, even a Venus in expensive furs, when at other times she represented the Virgin Mary. This doubt, both agreeable and intolerable to him, eventually suggested the fusion of the two couples in *Ulysses*, where Eve marries Adam, although Adam believes that he is marrying *her:* Molly wants to marry Bloom, and Bloom loves and wants Molly.

All that remains is to induce the young man to ask. This would be a rather sordid manoeuvre if Molly had not in fact been seduced by Bloom. She uses Eve's own methods of persuasion to get what she wants, because she feels that Bloom understands women; in his own way he is a poet. Molly's weakness for poets is however by no means an indirect homage to the art as such but rather a sign of practicality: poets

are liable to make better husbands than insensitive men—Boylan makes
no distinction between poetry and cabbages. It is only normal that
Molly should prefer to such a vulgar man the man who treats her as
though she were a flower. She knows by experience that it is better to
be adored than dominated. Joyce insists with malicious pleasure on this
secret power of Molly's, which turns her into a man-tamer in the
"Circe" episode. In reality it was he who enjoyed to be treated like a
beaten dog. When Molly is sure that she can make Bloom do what she
wants, she has only to "lead him on to say yes"; the woman's manoeuvre
consists of trapping the man's energy and binding him like a captured
animal under the pretext of giving oneself as a gift. Molly Bloom is the
comic example of the predatory woman; the women seduce and marry
the men, yet manage to leave them the illusion that the conquest is all
their doing.

Molly's final "yes" in *Ulysses* is not the reply to a romantic proposal
of marriage but the expression of a dissimulated will for power. Joyce,
Nietzsche and Mr. Duffy have all the same mistrust of women. The book
ends on a naïve glorification of the alliance between God and woman,
expressed by Molly in metaphysical murmurings which lead her into a
comfortable acquiescence. God, woman and the sun are inevitable,
unchangeable manifestations of Nature, and nothing alters their
rhythm or their being; Molly's sleepy mind formulates this as a proclamation of faith: "I suppose that's what a woman is supposed to be there
for" (i.e., physical love), and "they might as well try to stop the sun from
rising tomorrow." This is Molly's reply to atheism:

> as for them saying theres no God I wouldnt give a snap of my two fingers
> for all their learning why dont they go and create something I often asked
> him atheists or whatever they call themselves go and wash the cobbles off
> themselves first then they go howling for the priest and they dying and
> why why because theyre afraid of hell on account of their bad conscience

The transitions in Molly's thought are made by purely verbal rather
than logical bridges; thus she passes from the proof of God's existence
from nature through the theme of the sun to the fatal capture of man
by woman:

> the sun shines for you he said the day we were lying among the rhodo-
> dendrons on Howth head in the grey tweed suit and his straw hat the day
> I got him to propose to me yes first I gave him the bit of seedcake out of
> my mouth and it was leapyear like now yes 16 years ago my God after that
> long kiss I near lost my breath yes he said I was a flower of the mountain
> yes so we are flowers all a womans body yes that was one true thing he said

in his life and the sun shines for you today yes that was why I liked him
because I saw he understood or felt what a woman is and I knew I could
always get round him and I gave him all the pleasure I could leading him
on till he asked me to say yes"

Thus Molly, with the aid of the Creator, tempted Bloom towards his
fall on the Edenic rock of Howth. The pattern of the temptation is
eternally the same: the woman entices the man, feeds him with an
apple or seedcake or hot punch, herself using only the language of
glances and flowers; woman and nature are by a dangerous stratagem
associated in the idea of marriage. The woman hides the cage in the
flowers and the man is taken in by the apparently natural innocence,
without seeing that God and his cage are hidden under the rhododendrons. Molly makes Bloom realise that he wants her, as Polly seduces
the man who believes himself to be her seducer. She chooses to be
chosen. Food and pleasure are seen as the promises of the first kiss, and
the man who only wanted to quieten his hunger has to walk voluntarily
into marriage. Even the youthful Stephen in *Portrait* associates all his
desires and needs with the same circle of images, empty belly, hunger,
joy and fear, desire as cyclic progress and return, titillation, greedy
looks, open glances, the tiny star that explodes like a firework, as in
"Nausicaa".

What Joyce emphasises is first the simplicity of the masculine mind
confronted with woman's wiles, and then the practical nature of the
girls who want to be married and not merely courted, the calculated
or instinctive use of their physical charms as bait; what he does not
emphasise is something which seems to him too evident to need saying,
but which is nevertheless revealing for a study of his thought: that man
is attracted by women because, as Stephen Hero crudely puts it, "we
must have women." The youthful Stephen also, borrowing a phrase of
Jim's which Stannie records, calls them "marsupials."

The young women of the beginning of this century were quite experienced, and one can understand that Jim should sometimes have
been worried about Nora's aptitude for sensuality, since he did not wish
her to be solely "the companion of his pleasures." He was never convinced that it had been he who first seduced Nora.[21] His previous
experiences had all been of the venal kind. To be a conqueror, it would

[21]Letter to Stannie from Zurich. *Letters*, vol. II, p. 66, 11 Oct. 1904. Joyce in his first
letter from exile confides to his brother a detail that must have been on his mind, in a
postscript written in bad French: "Finalement elle n'est pas encore vierge; elle est
touchée."

be necessary to be a Don Juan, but Joyce was only a comedy Don Juan, like the Shakespeare whom Stephen describes; he was to express all these half-amused, half-bitter reflections into Molly's speech.

He portrays the Molly of the "Penelope" episode in these terms:

> The chapter begins and ends with the female word *yes.* It turns like the huge earthball slowly surely and evenly round and round spinning. Its four cardinal points being the female breasts, arse, womb and—expressed by the words *because, bottom, woman, yes.* . . . It seems to me to be perfectly sane full amoral fertilisable untrustworthy engaging shrewd limited prudent indifferent *Weib. Ich bin des Fleisch das stets bejaht.*[22]

"The flesh that always says yes" is like a caricature of the Faustian spirit that always says no. It is also a shell, a parody emptied of all spiritual content. In reality Molly doubtless is the earthball with its natural movement, ruled over by predictable astral influences. But Molly is a flower to Bloom, as Nora was for Jim, and in a world of flowers the marriage of Bloom and Molly commemorates the difficult but lasting union of Jim and Nora:

> and how he kissed me under the Moorish wall and I thought well as well him as another and then I asked him with my eyes to ask again yes and then he asked me would I yes to say yes my mountain flower and first I put my arms around him yes and drew him down to me so he could feel my breasts all perfume yes and his heart was going like mad and yes I said yes I will Yes. (*Ulysses*, p. 710)

Bloom may have been thinking then, as Joyce put it, that "Her soul! Her name! Her eyes! They seem to me like strange beautiful blue wildflowers growing in some tangled, rain-soaked hedge. And I have felt her soul tremble beside mine, and have spoken her name softly to the night . . ."[23]

And Bloom echoes:

> Her eyes upon me did not turn away. Ravished over her I lay, full lips full open, kissed her mouth. Yum. Softly she gave me in her mouth the seedcake warm and chewed. Mawkish pulp her mouth had mumbled sweet and sour with spittle. Joy: I ate it: joy. Young life, her lips that gave me pouting. Soft, warm, sticky gumjelly lips. Flowers her eyes were, take me, willing eyes.

Bloom is not a second Joyce: he has never adored Molly as though she were the Virgin, and has never adored her soul; in his prosaic existence

---

[22] *Letters*, vol. I, p. 170.
[23] *Letters*, vol. II, p. 267, 19 Nov. 1909. (To Nora from Dublin.)

interrupted by poetic outbursts, he is both Joyce being passionate and Joyce mocking his own passion. When Molly says "yes I will Yes," a nanny-goat traverses the landscape "sowing currants," as though Joyce were taking great care to remove all romanticism from the embraces of Molly and Bloom, by punctuating all such episodes with appearances of animals, to bring this pagan union down to its merely fleshy, animal level. Goats, flies and dogs share, as it were, in the passionate relationships of this moving but comical couple; a transposition of Joyce's personal and secret myths lies at the foundation of this odd marriage which was begun with kisses and now exists only on memories and on a basic fidelity which is superior to all infidelities—as that of Jim and Nora resisted Joyce's own infidelities and their domestic quarrels. What saves the Blooms is the total absence of God (and particularly of a vengeful god)—Bloom is half-Jewish and a convert and Molly only nominally a Catholic, with no real religion. They have no accounts to settle with the deity, for Bloom is really an atheist and Molly an amoral pantheist. There is no "third person" except some ephemeral suitors who do not in fact ever separate Molly and Bloom.

Woman is deified soul and body, and man has for her feelings of adoration and humiliation. "The figure of woman as she appears in the liturgy of the church," the statue of Venus (*Ulysses*, p. 73) which Bloom examines in comic imitation of Sacher-Masoch's Severin in ecstasy before a statue, the "image of the world's beauty" for Joyce, she precedes man and follows him, like Ann Hathaway whose sixty-seven years of life enclose those of Shakespeare. Finally the dominant figure in these evoked figures is that of the Mother: as wife, mistress, goddess or schoolgirl, she remains the inspirer, the giver of life. To judge by Joyce's letters to Nora (and, indeed, nothing allows us to doubt their truth and sincerity), the poet needs to receive into his soul the beauty he finds in her eyes and soul, in order that he may create.[24] But his especial need is to be forever taken up and purified and finally brought back into the world, so much does he feel that every passing day and thought bring impurity and the fall. The processes of redemption and of creation are linked in parallel patterns. To write, and to live in order to write, is to fall, and this entails the necessary association of corruption with the possibility of writing. Joyce translates this into terms of purification corresponding to the exaltation of the imagination, to the height from which he has fallen. In life the roles are shared out thus: man rises, falls,

---

[24]See Nora's letters written to Jim in 1909 when he was visiting Galway, the home town of his "little runaway." *Letters*, vol. II, p. 241.

is raised again, by woman. Stephen's creative process is an exact reproduction of Joyce's own secret superstitions.

The interest of these feelings would have a purely biographical significance, were it not that they provide an insight into the very origin
of Molly, a character which inspired Jung to say that Joyce understood
the feminine soul as though he were the devil's grandmother. Here we
touch on one of the secrets of Joyce's creation: when he was young, he
admitted that he knew nothing about woman and that only a woman
could understand the mystery of another woman. This was why he
submitted his problems about Nora to Aunt Josephine, feeling her to be
more qualified in the subject than himself.[25] Joyce also admired Ibsen
for the latter's "extraordinary knowledge of woman's nature"—a rather
naïve admiration if we remember that it was expressed in his article on
"Ibsen's New Drama," written when he was only eighteen years old
and his knowledge of "woman's nature" somewhat limited. Nevertheless, the praise was not wrong or mendacious to Joyce: the lines Ibsen
gives one of his women characters, and which Joyce quotes with enthusiasm, show that Joyce recognised in Irene the woman of his own
dreams, a dramatic mixture of mystical spirituality and visual eroticism,[26] organised about a favourite theme of Joyce's, nakedness.

Later Joyce creates Molly. She is as realistic as Bloom, and she has the
same origin, being a daughter of Jim and Nora. She could be defined as
Bloom is, but she is more than everywoman, she is all women, and in
this lies her uniqueness.

Nora was probably the original and model for Molly without knowing
it, through her meek submission to Jim's boundless curiosity. But Jim
too is the model for Molly: he gives Molly the thoughts that his behaviour might be expected to arouse in a young woman's mind. There is
nothing original about the phenomenon of suggestion; on the other
hand, the idea of using as scientific documents the reactions one has
intentionally provoked, foreseen and wished for in another person is
purely Joycean. When Severin insists to his Wanda that he should become her slave in order to adore her more completely, Wanda, who

[25] *Letters*, vol. II, p. 95, 12 July 1905.

[26] "In Irene's allusion to her position as model . . . Ibsen gives further proof of his
extraordinary knowledge of women. No other man could have so subtly expressed the
relations between the sculptor and his model. . . .

Irene—I exposed myself wholly and unreservedly to your gaze . . . and never once did
you touch me.

Rubek—(looks impressively at her) I was an artist, Irene.

Irene—(darkly) That is just it. That is just it." (*The Critical Writings of James Joyce*, ed.
Mason and Ellmann, p. 54).

loves him, finds the idea repugnant. But gradually she comes to like the idea until she takes it over herself and satisfies Severin's desire, herself deriving pleasure from this abandoned behaviour. Severin's abjection has created, or at least brought out, Wanda's cruelty. Joyce made Nora read Sacher-Masoch for inspiration; and similarly Bloom has made Molly read Rabelais, although she must have been as indignant and offended as Nora was. Thus Nora turns into Joyce's Wanda, and from her Molly draws her superb and terrible pride:—

"sure they wouldnt be in the world at all only for us they dont know what it is to be a woman and a mother how could they where would they be all of them be if they hadnt all a mother to look after them . . ."

Without her, he would not exist; this is the ineluctable way of procreation, for a father can be a legal fiction or a ghost. The mother establishes an incontestable power curiously like that of God: "who was the first person in the universe before there was anybody". . . (*Ulysses*, p. 708).

Without her and without Him, man would not exist.

IV. Dreaming of Freedom

The Illusion of Freedom

When Joyce and his father visited Mullingar in July 1900 and spoke to a friend who had gladly accepted matrimony, Joyce drew from the conversation the following epiphany:

> Mullingar: a Sunday in July: noon.
> Tobin (walking noisily with thick boots and tapping the road with his stick) . . . "O there's nothing like marriage for making a fellow steady. Before I came here to the *Examiner* I used to knock about with fellows and boose . . . Now I've a good house and . . . I go home in the evening and if I want a drink . . . well, I can have it . . . My advice to every young fellow that can afford it is: marry young."

This epiphany in its realism is clearly one of those whose nature had been first defined in *Stephen Hero* (pp. 216–7): their form is that of fragments of a monologue or dialogue which only take on a deep meaning insofar as they are detached from any context; they are, as one might say, epiphanies of the inane, or, as Stephen put it, the translation in "vulgarity of speech or of gesture" of the reality of Ireland. Tobin appears as an individual contented with the bourgeois way of life, deprived of any trace of romanticism; marriage is for him simply the means of regulating a pointless existence and of keeping a tranquil conscience. I used to be . . . I am now . . . is there any real progress? Tobin's little speech shows that for him marriage differs from celibacy simply by an improvement in his drinking conditions.

The damaged manuscript of *Stephen Hero* (p. 251) ends on a recasting of this scene into the mould of caricature. Tobin has become the self-assured Mr. Garvey. He probably intends less to advise than to boast. Stephen and his friend Nash meet him in the bar, flirting with the barmaid with all the ease of a married man, for to be married enables one to pay gallant compliments and behave saucily. Mr. Garvey is a free man: his ritual integration into ecclesiastically-controlled society confers upon him all the privileges of bourgeois hypocrisy. The existence of the spouse guarantees the solidity of his world. Mr. Garvey walks with confidence (a characteristic which pleased Joyce), and he hammers the road with his stick as though he were sure of being on the right road, as though to emphasise the advice he gives to Stephen and Nash: "There's nothing like marriage . . ." Mr. Garvey has a practical mind, he has his feet firmly on the ground, like his stick, the symbol of his boastful virility. Mr. Garvey can drink in his own house if he wants to, he is happy. But all the same he tells his young friends to meet him in the bar, when he boasts to them of the benefits of marriage.

And in a bar, too, Little Chandler, who chose to follow this advice, meets the man who chose not to—who comes back from London covered in glory, a free man, to dazzle others less fortunate.

Joyce wrote 'A Little Cloud', the story of Little Chandler and Big Gallaher, in February 1906 in Trieste.[1] This novella, by its use of the antithetical motif of freedom and imprisonment corresponds to the novellas of exotic dreaming and frustration such as "Araby" and "The Sisters"; the heros of the latter two are small boys whose imaginations have been excited by the desire for romantic adventures and mystery. Little Chandler is one of that class of dreamers whose hopes have been disappointed by the reality which is Dublin; though he is not a small boy victimised by a heartless uncle or perverse priest. He is a failed poet, a casualty of marriage. He suffers, as do all Joyce's Dubliners, from a sickness which acts as the unifying theme of the fifteen stories, paralysis. The title has both symbolic and ironic meaning: "the little cloud" is an allusion to the rainstorm called up by the prophet Elijah to put an end to the literal and metaphorical dryness of the land.[2]

---

[1]Joyce was well acquainted with the Gallaher family, members of which make episodic appearances in *Ulysses*; Ellmann points out that Fred Gallaher, a Dublin journalist, was obliged to leave for London after some unidentified scandal. "He belonged to that gallery of stocky and insensitive men to whom Joyce was to add Buck Mulligan and Boylan," says Ellmann.

[2]Tindall, *A Reader's Guide to James Joyce* (London, 1959), pp. 26–7.

The response takes on first of all the form of a little cloud the size of a man's hand, and ends by filling the whole sky; there is no cloud in the Dublin sky on the extraordinary day when the man who has fulfilled his dreams and become "a brilliant figure on the London Press" meets his old friend who is still ardently dreaming of success. A kindly light glows on the dirty or huddled shapes on the park benches. Little Chandler, full of the present joy, hastens towards his appointment at Corless's, like the small boy hurrying to the bazaar Araby. "A light began to tremble on the horizon of his mind," the light of hope. Everything is light and dreams of freedom in the beginning of the evening, everything is exotic colour, from Gallaher's vivid orange tie to the red and green shining of the wine-glasses; but troubled feelings begin to arise in the little man's mind. They first express themselves in the notion of exile: "There was no doubt about it: if you wanted to succeed you had to go away," and end in the renunciation of "Could he not escape from his little house? Could he not go to London? There was the furniture still to be paid for." It all begins with a little cloud of melancholy, and ends with the great storms of hatred and rage seen in the cold eyes of his wife Annie. "Little Chandler . . . stood back out of the lamplight." "A Little Cloud" symbolises the fallen dream, the idea of powerlessness. "It was useless! He was a prisoner for life." By its symbolism this novella fits into the general design, which Joyce considered, as he told his editor, as "a chapter in the moral history" of Ireland, and a denunciation of "the soul of that . . . paralysis which many consider a city."[3]

As well as the motifs which make it an integral part of a coherent whole, the novella has its own particular tone and key-themes, and its own final revelation, illumination or epiphany, which orients its meaning; the epiphany takes shape, signifying that it is too late for Little Chandler to leave, because he is married. His wife's real face appears in the last scene, having been absent and forgotten during the few hours of his free, intoxicated dreaming. She closes in the future, and her eyes full of hatred are the prisoner-poet's only horizon. All the subsidiary motifs lead up to this terrifying vision: that of melancholy (the word occurs seven times), whose repetition by its very excess suggests Joyce's surreptitious irony at the would-be poet's expense, that of virility and immorality. Thus Joyce builds up a set of ironic allusions whose general effect is to reduce words to the level of anecdotes and horrors to that of the laughable, increasing the imaginary distance between the idealistic grandeur and the actual pettiness. The happy evening ends in a

[3] 1904 letter to Curran; *Letters*, vol. I, p. 55.

domestic quarrel, poetry has no place in marriage, and the tension is built up right from the beginning, from the title, "A Little Cloud."

Parody of a Failed Byron

"A Little Cloud" is a prospectus of Joyce's intentions: the story he is going to tell plays on the opposition of large and small as physical symbols of a real or imaginary moral stature. And the little man is dominant, because everything is small, narrow, petty and diminished in this world which Little Chandler has already lost, he who would have liked to be a great poet.

Chandler is one of those men who lived curled up in a foetal position, not daring to move lest they be flung out into the outside world. He secretes his own protective cocoon, with childlike, womanlike care. He is still gently nestling within his illusions, preparing his secret self to be born to the glorious destiny of a poet. He has metaphysical inclinations, he "thinks of life" and the thought fills him with sadness. Real life is "vermin," an image of disgust for him, and one which also haunts Stephen. Hordes of children run or crawl or squat like mice in the same ghostly streets where the heroic Stephen also walks. Chandler gives no thought to this life; reality is sordid and he has propped up his life in his lonely little room where "poetry consoles him." The little man is too shy to read poetry out to his wife, but furtively, in secret, he leafs through the book of himself. He is shamefully timid because his love for poetry is naturally a treason against reality (that is, against his wife) committed by the dream.

The evening is romantic and golden because the little man is on his way to meet "the great man" who "has seen the world." The big world holds a door ajar for Little Chandler to peep inside. In the distance he sees London, the town, the women, success, the accepted vices, elegant masculinity. By a psychological substitution he assimilates himself to Gallaher. From the height of his fame and prestige he suddenly sees in its true littleness the place where he lives "his own sober inartistic life," and something happens: he begins to have not only a thought but also ideas. He has opened his babyish eyes and has just discovered how far he can see. He is no longer just a Dubliner in Dublin, he is a Dubliner in revolt. Is this the promise of a new birth? Is another person going to escape like Stephen Dedalus? Little Chandler considers himself: thirty-two years old, young, sensitive, fastidious, able to fly away, in fact. Little Chandler "tries to weigh his soul," finds melancholy, tenderness, a conventional imagination, "recurrences of faith and resignation"; mature enough to pass for a poet, bearing "an infant hope," the little man has just discovered that his mind has an horizon—which in itself is surely an invitation to travel. Already he reads the favourable criticisms of the poems he will one day write, and Joyce plays on the lyric notes of irony at his own expense. *Chamber Music* sounds slightly like *Chandler Music*, "the gift of easy and graceful verse," as the English critics were going to say. Chandler knows himself and would not aim at the glory of a Byron; he would be quite contented to be James Joyce, the sentimental poet.

Joyce himself declares to Stanislaus, his Dublin representative to the editor Elkin Matthews, after three of his love poems had been accepted by Richards, who had not bee impressed by *Dubliners*, that "A page of *A Little Cloud* gives me more pleasure than all my verses."[4] Although Ellmann questions Joyce's good faith here and claims that he is exaggerating his indifference,[5] it is probable that Joyce was telling the truth. Again, biographical information sheds light on the novella: Joyce was determined to deprecate his poetry, and when Stanislaus wanted to keep the originally suggested title, *Chamber Music*, Jim considered it "too self-satisfied," and wanted rather "a title which to some extent would repudiate the book, but without completely depreciating it." But Joyce maintained always an ambiguous attitude to poetry: it seems perfect for secret loves and for song, but it has nothing to do with that Reality which is Joyce's main preoccupation. Poetry is the writer's own personal pleasure and delight, but Chandler the frustrated poet is far from having what Joyce called "an artistic temperament,'. He has only the gentle melancholies of the little poetic scribbler who is married; energy, anger, and cunning are not for him. He is even ridiculous in his way of delicately distilling his occasional thoughts. He is much too virtuous to win Joyce's approval, he hardly drinks, and as Gallaher says, he is "the very same serious person that used to lecture me on Sunday mornings when I had a sore head and a fur on my tongue."

We can see here Joyce's pleasure in creating characters with characteristics borrowed from people who in real life were very different. All the sensitivity of Little Chandler is similar to that of Stephen and echoes Joyce's own; but where Joyce would feel violent hatred, Little Chandler

---

[4] *Letters*, vol. II, p. 182, 18 Oct. 1906.
[5] Ellmann, *James Joyce*, p. 240.

feels only dreary exasperation—his timid and puritanical nature is quite alien to Joyce. Finally, the little man's capture by the correct middle-class conventions, his employment at the King's Inns, and his Catholic marriage with a masterful woman, all set him down definitively among the failures. All Joyce's own resentment against Ireland is concentrated in this novella, which is contemporaneous with Chapter XXV of *Stephen Hero*.[6] Joyce had reached a temporary halt at this chapter because of his discouragement at the publication difficulties of *Dubliners*; and in this chapter Stephen formulates his theory of the epiphany as "sudden spiritual manifestation, whether in the vulgarity of speech or of gesture or in a memorable phase of the mind itself" (*Stephen Hero*, p. 216). This theory had come to Stephen like an epiphany after a long and bitter meditation upon women, when walking through the dusk, he overheard fragments of a banal conversation which seemed to him to symbolise the indirect blackmail the Irish woman practises on the man. Similarly, in the world created by the artist, "A Little Cloud" corresponds to the treatment as epiphany of a young, ambitious, but weak-willed young man's marriage; the details and the banality bring forth the sudden spiritual manifestation: thus, we see Little Chandler reading Byron, for which Stephen in *Portrait* had been punished. But while Stephen's spiritual solidarity is explained by his "byronic satanism," Chandler's sedentary, middle-class conformism only shows up the vanity of his dreams: he is only a little Dubliner with no characteristics of the rebel or of the Don Juan, and his call to exile can easily be satisfied by the meagre compensations his self-esteem receives.

At Corless's he takes his first steps towards the imitation of Gallaher and his forbidden knowledge of "life." He finds it difficult to think himself into the journalist's rough way of life, it is true: Gallaher is "vulgar," and Little Chandler feels dissatisfied because his hero is not entirely to his taste. But the little man wants to grow larger, and he makes some laudable efforts. The subjects of conversation quickly converge upon the same terms of contrast; wherever he begins, Little Chandler ends up small and alone, faced with the image of his own reduced manliness. They talk of travel: Gallaher tells him to go abroad and see the world, and Chandler says that he has once been on a trip to the Isle of Man. They talk of Paris, and Gallaher tells him about the Moulin Rouge, but these places are "Hot stuff! Not for a pious chap like you, Tommy." But Gallaher is wrong, for the pious and serious little clerk has an unspoken desire to hear all about these forbidden places.

[6]Ellmann, *op. cit.*, p. 231.

Chandler is a timid man. He dares not read out poetry to his wife, he dares not answer when prostitutes call out to him, he dares not speak, drink, or move, but he is dying to. At night he walks through the ill-famed streets of Dublin to smell the presence of sin, just like Stephen Dedalus—with the difference that Stephen is scarcely an adolescent and Chandler a man of thirty-two when he wanders "the darkest and narrowest streets," where "a sound of low fugitive laughter made him tremble like a leaf."

Is life or literature the first temptation? Who exactly *is* Gallaher for Chandler? Is he the journalist who can get him published or the experienced man who "in a calm historian's tone. . . . proceeded to sketch for his friend some pictures of the corruption which was rife abroad"? Gallaher enumerates the mysteries, as the priest did to the child in "The Sisters". Human Nature is just as immoral in Paris as in London or Berlin; there is only Dublin that is virtuous, and Dublin's dirt is purely superficial, nothing to do with immorality. Chandler is ashamed of Dublin: "How dull you must find it," he says, but in fact it is Chandler himself who finds it dull and dreams, though without admitting it, that he is Gallaher and Dublin is Paris. But this is only a dream. Gallaher will not let his expansive personality be taken over: he brutally recalls to Chandler the latter's married state: "Hogan told me you had . . . tasted the joys of connubial bliss."

Chandler is grieved that Gallaher makes this separation between them; his friend's congratulations fling him back into his own monotonous existence, and his whole self rebels. If he cannot emulate Gallaher, he will refuse to admit that he would like to do so; Joyce manoeuvres this about-turn in silence. Nothing is said, but Little Chandler is thinking like the fox in the fable, "I cannot be Gallaher, so I tell myself that I do not wish to be Gallaher, and I persuade myself of this." Besides, "Gallaher was his inferior in birth and education." He pretends that all that prevents him from revealing his greatness is his timidity. He raises himself up to his full height, and takes the decisive step from insincerity to resentment. He expresses his hostility not in wishing that Gallaher were dead but by wishing for him to become Chandler: the hero can be punished "like everyone else," he will "put his head in the sack." The secret intentions of the two friends are curiously parallel: Gallaher has wished Chandler a long life, which under the circumstances is a very ill wish, for the longer Chandler lives, the longer he will be the slave of his living death, and Chandler has predicted that Gallaher will also be caught.

They are not playing now; Gallaher fails to appreciate the perverse prophecy because "he knows the game too well." This time they are not a mutual admiration society; Gallaher feels threatened, as though Chandler's words could put a spell on him, and he declares that he intends to live, that marriage would be for him simply the acquaintance of "a good fat account at the bank," and finally despatches the little man with a grimace of disgust at the idea of monogamy: "Must get a bit stale, I should think," he says, and on this vulgar comment brings the brilliant evening to a close. Chandler is tied to one woman, and will never have the inconstancy of a fully living man: his wife, is, moreover, that Annie with pinched lips who looks sourly at him from her photograph and who has given him a new setting for his life. How can he be the husband of the cold-eyed Annie, with her treacherously conjugal behaviour and her refusal to be treated as a wife? She is the acid test of Chandler's manly heroism, for after a year of marriage she has become his enemy and rejected him in order to be the mother of her son, opposed to him. Alone in their room with its "pretty furniture," bought on the hire system, Chandler progresses from gentle melancholy to evaluation of the scrupulous pettiness which impregnates everything around him, as was Joyce's intention. Again he seeks to escape. Alone, he again begins to admire Gallaher's courage. Supposing that it were not too late? Even if he cannot be Gallaher, he at least has his writing. What about Annie, and all the furniture of the prison, objects of hers? All except the book lying on the table, a volume of Byron.

He reads "Whilst I return to view my Margaret's tomb . . ." Byron's words, but supposing the names changed, suppose Chandler mourning Annie? And perhaps he could write a poem about it, which would be the beginning of his fame. . . .

But Annie's son keeps crying, and cries louder than the poetry or the dream. "He couldn't do anything"; if he is in prison it must be because he is guilty, and the guilt is still fresh in his memory; he had wanted to live, and in order to live had imagined Annie dead. His arms tremble with anger, and like Farrington, the brutal hero of "Counterparts," he takes his revenge on the baby, by shouting "Stop!" But he cannot avoid his punishment; his conscience has already brought him into perishable time present, and he fears that the baby may die. Annie-Mother-Church opens the cell door and shouts "What have you done to him?", and her voice is full of hatred. Her words bind Chandler again in overwhelming remorse: "My little man! My little mannie! . . . . There now, love! . . . Mamma's little lamb of the world!" Annie, like a furious

Virgin Mary, rocks her only man, her son the lamb.[7] Ashamed and in tears, Little Chandler withdraws from the circle of lamplight where mother and son are consoling each other. All this would be scrupulously and intolerably petty were it not for the ironic relief provided by Joyce and Byron. Joyce when he wrote this had a son the age of Chandler's son, and it would hardly be surprising for him to have caricatured some scene from his life as father hindered by his offspring. The author is included in the mockery; Joyce is remembering his own Byronic phase, but he has now reached the stage of the moralist, not that of the romantic.

Although he now knows by experience what "wedded bliss" signifies, he does not present celibacy as an ideal state opposed to marriage, but the bachelors are much more an object of mockery to him than are the married people.

Joyce's Satire against Bachelors

Robert Hand, the journalist who betrays his friend Richard Rowan in the play *Exiles*, Hugh Boylan called Blazes Boylan, son of a horse-dealer and impresario for concert tours, and Malachi Mulligan, called Buck Mulligan, are members of a small group of men for whom Joyce feels the profoundest antipathy; he takes pleasure in plotting their downfall, opposing them to adversaries with whom he sympathises, the artist Bloom, and Stephen. These men, who share between them all the faults Joyce detests, are bachelors. Yet it is not their unmarried state that determines their behaviour, nor is this state in itself considered as a vice. But the typical portrait which emerges from a comparison and study of these men shows that Joyce associates the defensive egoism of the man who wants to enjoy life without paying the price with a complete lack of humanity, which is manifest in all their behaviour: they are brutal, their intelligence is without warmth or scruples, they are ath-

---

[7]Letter to Stannie, from Rome: "A woman's love is always maternal and egoistic. A man, on the contrary, side by side with extraordinary cerebral sexualism and bodily fervour (from which women are normally free) possesses a fund of genuine affection for the "beloved" or "once beloved" object. I am no friend of tyranny, as you know, but if many husbands are brutal the atmosphere in which they live (vide Counterparts) is brutal and few wives and homes can satisfy the desire for happiness." (*Letters*, vol. II, p. 192, 13 Nov. 1906.)

letic and proud of their physical and fleshly accomplishments.[8] Stephen reproaches Mulligan for his cruelty and brutishness, just as Molly considers her lover Boylan as a brute who treats her as though she were a mare, and whose sensuality is completely lacking in any sensibility. Incapable of love or friendship, they all have the coarse gaiety of Doherty, their forebear who figured in the first sketches for *Portrait*, of whom Stephen thought that "his coarseness of expression was no spiritual blasphemy but the mask of a coward."[9]

Their common model is Oliver Gogarty, who was for Joyce the embodiment of the mediocre mind, triumphant by the power of money. Gogarty is the enemy Joyce chose to act as a scapegoat throughout his work—in *Finnegans Wake* he is represented by Shaun. Hypocrite, faithless friend and traitor, he wears the mask of cordiality and radiates petty worldly and social success. He is the anti-Joyce and the anti-Bloom. He is inevitable, being as complementary as Shaun is for Shem; in the beginning came the expulsion of Joyce by Gogarty from the Martello tower at Sandycove where they were both living in 1904. Their former friendship had been broken off, and Joyce had decided to turn their antagonism into an obsessive theme for the purposes of his creation. Gogarty is Joyce's favourite enemy because he claimed to be non-conformist, in imitation of the artist, but in fact had only the banal ambitions of a rich man's self-confident son. Nothing angered Joyce more than Gogarty's marriage. His letter of 12 August 1906[10] shows how necessary to him Gogarty was: the latter played the role of bourgeois that Joyce might be reassured of his own firm socialism—"I am curious to know how he looked in a tall silk." With "A Little Cloud" still fresh in his mind, Joyce wished Gogarty all the worst fortune, as Chandler had wished Gallaher: "However to be charitable I suppose we had better wish Mr. and Mrs. Ignatius Gallaher health and long life." Joyce will not admit of submission to the Irish conventions, and Gogarty's marriage shows that he is right—only such people marry in a world like this. The true socialist refuses tyranny:

> Can you not see plainly from facts like these that a deferment of the emancipation of the proletariat, a reaction to clericalism or aristocracy or bourgeoisism would mean a revulsion to tyrannies of all kinds. Gogarty

[8]Cf. the name of Robert Hand, as indirect indication of a way of life which considers other people simply as objects to be manipulated.

[9]Cf. the portrait of Doherty quoted in Ellmann, *op. cit.*, p. 390; and W. Litz, *The Art of James Joyce*, pp. 132-5.

[10]*Letters*, vol. II, p. 148.

would jump into the Liffey to save a man's life but he seems to have little hesitation in condemning generations to servitude . . .

Joyce's motives are always very complex, since he mixes up his need to justify his own life (it was Nora who told him of Gogarty's marriage) with his need to be able to use everything as the matter of fiction. In the end the Gogarty affair took on such proportions that Joyce was able to draw from it all his grievances against the treacherous friend who had to some extent encouraged him in his resolutions on the subject of exile. To Gogarty he owes the theme of betrayal, which, extended as the myth of the rival brothers, is almost as important as the theme of the mother devouring her young. Joyce manufactured his "false friends," and Gogarty was sufficiently unlike him to be made into the perfect anti-self. This exchange of feelings was a conscious process, and had been going on since his Dublin days, as can be seen from his confidences to Stannie: "If you look back on my relations with friends and relatives you will see that it was a youthfully exaggerated feeling of this maldisposition of affairs which urged me to pounce upon the falsehood in their attitude towards me as an excuse for escape."[11]

What "maldisposition of affairs" does he mean? In the previous paragraph Jim had explained to Stannie that he was a "socialist artist," but that since the State did not need his artistic services, he was obliged to earn his living as best he could; some people had accused him of contradicting himself on this point, because his socialism should impel him to become a Civil Servant—his exile would then have a real, material reason behind it, the necessity of earning a living without becoming part of the "system" in Ireland. There is no question here, it will be observed, of leaving "to forge in the smithy of his soul the uncreated conscience of his race."

Thus the bachelor is caught in Joyce's cunningly woven net; and if Mulligan is a projection of Gogarty's blasphemous vitality, Blazes Boylan inherits his strong man's self-confidence—and is destined to perish from the poisoned arrows of Joyce's satire.

In all Joyce's work there is only one survivor from the shipwreck of matrimony, the only one who can look and be looked at, who can furthermore touch and take possession without fear of punishment. The league of prisoner-husbands gapes at him enviously, for amongst the tamed birds he is the cock, the only one to exercise his masculine rights, protected by his bachelor independence—Blazes Boylan, Molly's lover,

[11] *Letters*, vol. II, pp. 88-9, 2-3 May 1905.

"the worst individual" strutting the streets of Dublin, Don Juan with a straw hat and walking stick, who on this 16th of June has a rendezvous with Mrs. Bloom, whose impresario and lover he is. "One rapped on a door, one tapped with a knock, did he knock Paul de Kock, with a loud proud knocker, with a cock carracarracarra cock. Cockcock" (*Ulysses*, p. 276). Among the men who envy his liberty and the women who gaze at him, the free man walks in Bachelor's Walk:

> By Bachelor's walk jogjaunty jingled Blazes Boylan, bachelor, in sun, in heat, mare's glossy rump atrot, with flick of whip, on bounding tyres: sprawled, warmseated, Boylan impatience, ardentbold. Horn. Have you the? Horn. Have you the? Haw haw horn. (*Ulysses*, p. 263)

Boylan pays only a brief visit to the bar of dreamers and seers. The sirens forget their alluring role to watch the seducer, he who looks like a stallion, not like a bird, fish, or toad, animals the sirens hate:

> Those things only bring out a rash, replied, reseated (Miss Douce). I asked that old fogey in Boyd's for something for my skin.
> . . . . Don't let me think of him or I'll expire. The hideous old wretch! That night in the Antient Concert Rooms.
> . . . . O! shrieking, Miss Kennedy cried. Will you ever forget his goggle eye?
> . . . . O greasy eyes! Imagine being married to a man like that, she cried. With his bit of beard!
> Douce gave full vent to a splendid yell, a full yell of full woman, delight, joy, indignation. (*Ulysses*, pp. 252-3)

Boylan is not an invalid, or paralysed, or mummified like most of the victims of marriage in *Ulysses*. He, Bloom, and Stephen are constantly moving, but of the three Boylan is the only one whose movement is determined by his "impatience." Stephen is on a quest but also in flight, a voluntary exile but also banished. Bloom, only half-alive, moves the living part of himself through the streets of Dublin; his route and his schedule are not determined by the organisation of his own business, but are connected with Boylan's activities, since his appearance is the signal for Bloom's discomfiture. This is why the rhythm of Boylan's time-scale is unique in *Ulysses*; the bachelor lives in time present or in the immediate future, while the married men flocked together and leaning on the bar are wandering in the formless time of idle memory. The gallant Blazes Boylan has an appointment, someone is waiting for him, he is hurrying to meet a woman, and he is not afraid; he does not put off the time of the meeting, he fears no decoy or scarecrow, for he is real and will lose no feathers in the combat. The siren-barmaids are a mere introductory morsel, but his appetite is not to be whetted by the sound of a garter rebounding against flesh:—

> Smack. She let free sudden in rebound her nipped elastic garter smack-warm against her smackable woman's warmhosed thigh.
> —*La cloche*! cried gleeful Lenehan. Trained by owner. No sawdust there.
> She smilesmirked supercilious (wept! aren't men?) but, lightward gliding, mild she smiled on Boylan. (*Ulysses*, p. 260)

But at the end of the day Boylan is relegated to the inferior place that he occupies in humanity as seen by Joyce; as Ellmann says,[12] in the "Penelope" episode Molly, faithful in spite of herself, ends the day by yielding to her husband and sending Boylan back to his proper insignificance. In the works of Joyce, the soul always has the superiority over the body, and masculinity is something to be mocked. The bachelor in the straw hat makes a lot of noise but exists very little, in effect. No bachelor could compete with the complete man, even Jesus could not, since he lacked the experience of conjugal life, according to Joyce.

[12]Ellmann, *op. cit.*, p. 390.

V. Variations on the Theme of Transubstantiation

Begging for one's Food

We have had very little food—no meal at all in fact—and having taken some tea and dry bread, I washed and went out. Pappie came in sober, without money, and in ill-humour . . . I was inclined to be irritated, as we are this way through his having spent £2 10s. on himself in the last ten days." (*Dublin Diary*, p. 58)

This year we have lived . . . on practically starvation rations. There has been a very small breakfast, perhaps, no dinner, and no tea, and at about seven o'clock I find the house intolerable and go down town. (*Dublin Diary*, p. 97)

By the end of 1903, John Joyce had no further financial resources (see Ellmann, pp. 148-9), James was working out his aesthetic theories, the pious brother Charlie had taken to drink and used to spend nights at the police station, and the five daughters had to beg occasional pennies from a sarcastic, insulting father. Stannie alone was working, though with distaste, at the School of Pharmacy, and kept this job until 20th January 1904, when he decided to cultivate his own misery in the bosom of the general idleness of the rest of the family. He was awaiting the revelation of his destiny, as Stephen awaits the image of his fate in *Portrait*. The depths of misery were reached when John Joyce pawned the piano. There was now nothing left in what Stannie called "the house of the bare table." This was henceforth to be the sign of the Joyces' house; often days passed with no proper meals for the family. There was nothing left but tea, often brewed up several times until it resembled nothing so much as urine—as the Joyce children, who were not without a sense of humour, would point out. Joyce used to joke that only hunger had ever been able to arouse murderous instincts in his pacifist soul; and his visit to Paris in 1903 is immortalised as an epiphany in the scene of *Ulysses* where he recasts as a cinematographic inner monologue a real incident which at the time had caused him to feel bitter resentment towards his mother:

> With mother's money order, eight shillings, the banging door of the post office slammed in your face by the usher. Hunger toothache. *Encore deux minutes.* Look clock, Must get. *Fermé.* Hired dog! Shoot him to bloody bits with a bang shotgun, bits man spattered wall all brass buttons. Bits all khrrrrklak in place clack back. Not hurt? O, that's all right. Shake hands. See what I meant, see? O, that's all right. Shake a shake. (*Ulysses*, p. 44)[1]

Anger, hunger, emptiness, absence and irony are necessarily linked. It is not merely a question of a physiological sickness, but of a lack felt deeply at all levels of being. Hunger becomes for Jim the object of pride, and something to be joked about; when Gogarty maliciously asked him what illness had kept him in bed for two days, he replied "I was suffering from inanition." Joyce lived through his hunger in his own fashion, and in a sense finally nourished a certain part of his art on his own hunger. It was necessary first to sample physical distress, the kind Stanislaus mentions so often in his diary (and so seldom in his book).

> Food is good and warmth is good. This is a good house to learn to appreciate both in. We do weeks on one chance insufficient meal, and a collation in the days I have been stripped of my garments, even of my heavy boots, willingly stripped, to pawn them and feed on them. What kind of adults will we be? I am becoming quite morbid on the point and regard food as an energy-stuff. (*Dublin Diary*, p. 64)

Joyce too was capable of violence; but after the death of the mother whom he incessantly tormented with his complaining, he began inventing gargantuan fantasies, proceeding from his hunger, and describing

[1]Cf. letter to May Joyce, 21 Feb. 1903, from Paris:-"Dear Mother Your order for 3s/4d of Tuesday last was very welcome as I had been without food for 42 hours (forty-two). Today I am twenty hours without food . . . With the utmost stretching your order will keep me Monday midday . . . then, I suppose, I must do another fast. I regret this as Monday and Tuesday are carnival days and I shall probably be the only one starving in Paris.—Jim." And, 8 March 1903, "Sunday. I cannot cash your order today. I do not understand in the least what you write about Gaze's. When you spend only three minutes at a letter it cannot be very intelligible. In any case Gaze's was shut. My next meal therefore will be tomorrow."(*Letters*, vol. II, pp. 29 and 34.)

them comically to Stannie. In the worst and most discouraging moments of his exile in 1905 his hunger was so great that it dislocated all other values, even the sacred values of art; and this is why in his later life every occasion for rejoicing, that is, every victory over death, became automatically associated with a need to eat, as a revenge on the world that had tried to devour him alive. The multiplication of anniversaries to be commemorated by picnics or banquets stems both from Joyce's, pleasure in ritualising life and from his need to symbolise thus the end of the lean years.[2]

During the lean years in Italy, the happiest times Jim and Nora spent were when a money order from Stanislaus permitted them to have a vast meal, sending him a detailed account of the menu afterwards: one must eat to live, a rule of prime importance which Jim very touchingly applied to Nora, leaving her with a store of cocoa, for example, when he went back to Dublin for a short visit in 1909, because cocoa is a complete and health-giving food. Later cocoa was to become the starting-point of a whole chain of symbolism and comedy in *Ulysses*, but it began as the tonic that the couple and their children lived on. As Stanislaus said, one learns to appreciate the value of food; and the cocoa is indeed doubly nourishing, because for Joyce literally everything can become material for his work. The books of Joyce relate meals of every kind, go into great detail about hungers that are satisfied, appetites that are transcended, or not: there is breakfast at the Martello tower at the expense of the artist, there are kidneys for Bloom, cream and butter for Molly, lemon platt for baby Tuckoo on the first page of *Portrait*, cocoa at the cabmen's shelter for Stephen and Bloom in the "Eumeus" episode, the mouthful of damp seedcake Molly puts into Leopold's mouth while kissing him. It is not unlikely that real hunger and mythical meals coincide to suggest a number of symbolic scenes throughout the work of Joyce. Starting from actual lived experience, he works out two types of symbols, illustrating the themes of material or spiritual hunger, and of communion: the hunger for possession is represented by the many versions of Eve's temptation of Adam, and the longing for communion by the scenes of communal sharing. Soul and body find their imaginary or material food—but the table is not yet laid for the young man in

[2] Cf. letter to Stannie from Rome:—"Yesterday being the anniversary of my espousal and of the day of the gladness of my heart, we went out into the country and ate and drank . . . Here is the full and exact list of what we ate yesterday: 10.30 a.m. Ham, bread and butter, coffee, 1.30 p.m. Soup, roast lamb and potatoes, bread and wine; 4-p.m. Beef-stew, bread and wine; 6-p.m. Roast veal, gorgonzola cheese and wine; 8.30 p.m. Roast veal, bread and grapes and vermouth; 9.30 p.m. Veal cutlets, bread, salad, grapes and wine." (*Letters*, vol. II, p. 172, 9 Oct. 1906.)

Portrait, who has to begin by surviving at the expense of the rich and well-fed.

The rational solution would be to work in order to earn one's living, as did the contemporaries of Jim and Stannie who were not possessed of a fortune like that of Gogarty.

The pleasant solution would be to live by one's writing, an ambition which Joyce toyed with in moments of discouragement in Dublin or Trieste, when he would make up for the refusals or silence of prospective editors by dreaming of a cottage he would share with Stannie, paying the rent with the money coming in from the sale of his poems and of *Dubliners*. But in reality he was never able to live on the proceeds of his art; when he was eighteen and used to affect pride as a counterweight to his misery, this fact grieved him a good deal—and all the more so because the rival cult to his own (that is, the Catholic Church) was able to feed its priests very well, and furthermore invited him to its table; for Jim, the important matter was to survive while remaining what he was, an artist. There were two possible routes open, the father's and the mother's. John Joyce had long been trying to make his son take up some useful, well-paid employment, but at last resigned himself to seeing them all working as petty menials, clerks, etc. The mother offered the bait with which the Church tried to trap James (and Stephen)—she would be only too happy to see him as a priest. But the unfortunate parents know "what a nice bloody atheist this fellow has turned out" (*Stephen Hero*, p. 237). Stephen's father is no atheist, but a realist; there is nothing mystic about his admiration for the Jesuits, but he feels a bourgeois appreciation of their social skill. The Jesuits, as opposed to the Christian Brothers, know about life. They are God's businessmen:

> —Christian brothers be damned! said Mr. Dedalus. Is it with Paddy Stink and Micky Mud? No, let him stick to the Jesuits in God's name since he began with them. They'll be of service to him in after years. Those are the fellows that can get you a position.
> —And they're a very rich order, aren't they, Simon?
> —Rather. They live well, I tell you. You saw their table at Clongowes. Fed up, by God, like gamecocks. (*Portrait*, pp. 71-2)

Simon echoes all the praises of the Jesuits in "Grace":

> —There's no mistake about it, said Mr. McCoy, if you want a thing well done and no flies about, you go to a Jesuit. They're the boyos have influence. . . .
> —The Jesuits are a fine body of men, said Mr. Power.

One can trust the Jesuits because they are "men of the world like ourselves."[3] Thus Mr. Kernan's friends know that the preacher at the retreat will be understanding. Father Purdon, tall and rather red-faced, will speak to them as man to man, in language they can follow, not in God's language, because he is "a man of the world," and because "the vast majority are forced to live in the world."[4] The gentlemen who want to verify their accounts with God are gathered together in the Gardiner Street church, a microcosm of the outside world. "The gentlemen sat in the benches, having hitched their trousers slightly above their knees and laid their hats in security. They sat well back and gazed formally at the distant speck of red light which was suspended above the high altar."

There is a whole world, the world of business, between this pleasant, decent retreat which does not ill-treat those who are voluntarily taking part in it, and that other retreat which made the boy Stephen a prey to all the images of hell. But this is just what is displeasing to him, for nothing easy can satisfy Stephen, he must be always either victorious or vanquished. How can he believe in this imitation Redemption? How can he feel for the distant red speck of light the ecstasy that he felt before the celestial rose? It is not sufficiently large or terrible or beautiful for the artist's soul. This is why Joyce maliciously names the preacher Purdon, partly because Purdon sounds like pardon, and partly because Purdon Street was a place of ill-fame in Dublin,[5] near the house of Bella Cohen; that was a religion lacking in devilish charms.

In 1902 Joyce, B. A. of University College, was offered by Father Darlington the chance to give evening classes at the university, teaching French to "little clerks." This would doubtless have brought in enough money to feed him, and have been fairly easy work, but Joyce refused. The Jesuit was astonished that anyone should choose to be "a man of letters"—surely there was a risk of dying of hunger before one became famous and successful?

> After much rubbing of his chin and many blinkings of the eyes, Father
> Butt asked what were Stephen's intentions . . .

[3]Cf. "Look at their church, too," said Mr. Power. "Look at the congregation they have." "The Jesuits cater for the upper classes," said Mr. Power.

[4]"O, it's just a retreat, you know," said Mr. Cunningham. "Father Purdon is giving it. It's for business men, you know."

"He won't be too hard on us, Tom," said Mr. Power persuasively.

. . . "O, you must know him, Tom," said Mr. Cunningham stoutly. "Fine, jolly fellow! He's a man of the world like ourselves."

[5]Robert Adams, *Surface and Symbol in Ulysses*, pp. 13-15.

—Literature, said Stephen.

—Yes, yes . . . of course . . . but meanwhile, I mean . . . of course you will continue your course until you have got a degree—that is the important point.

—I may not be able to, said Stephen. I suppose you know that my father is unable to . . .

—Now, said Father Butt joyfully, I'm so glad you've come to the point . . . That is just it. . . . There might be . . . it has just occurred to me . . . an appointment here in the college . . . One or two hours a day . . . that would be nothing . . . I think, yes . . . we shall be . . . let me see now. It would be no trouble for you . . . no teaching or drudgery, just an hour or so here in the office in the morning.

Stephen said nothing. Father Butt rubbed his hands together and said:

—Otherwise there would be a danger of your perishing . . . by inanition . . . (*Stephen Hero*, pp. 231–2)

In fact, Jim and the Jesuits have not the same concept of hunger, or of life, as Stannie points out.[6] The Reverend Fathers concern themselves more with the hunger of the stomach, Jim with that of his soul. This seems like a Jesuit paradox. Joyce explains to his brother that every compromise destroys: it is better to borrow from false friends and be a parasite, declaring loudly that one must eat, than to enter into a system of lies. Money is always powerful; it is a language of exchange and of alienation, it uses polyvalent money-signs, its power is both material and spiritual. He who is paid has been bought by him who pays. And thus Stephen Dedalus, because in part he does what Jim was not willing to do, finds himself in the hands of Mr. Deasy, who is not a Jesuit and cannot buy Stephen's soul, but who tries to have some proprietary rights over his mind—he pays Stephen to advise him. Stephen is employed as a teacher and then treated as a disciple by a decrepit sage for whom he feels only pity. So he moves away.

In *Stephen Hero*, Father Butt only offers Stephen the post of auxiliary teacher after having advised his mother to "put him on the books of a brewery." Maurice concludes from this that "they can do nothing for a case like yours which presents certain difficulties of temperament."[7] Stephen feels that "they want to buy him." In order to emphasise this

[6]*My Brother's Keeper*, pp. 200–1.

[7]"Stephen gave details of his interview to Maurice:

—Don't you think they are trying to buy me? he asked.

—Yes, that's evident, But I'm surprised at one thing . . .

—What is that?

—That the priest lost his temper when speaking to Mother. You must have annoyed the good man a great deal.

—How do you know he lost his temper?

aspect of the event, Joyce changes the conditions of the "purchase" in *Portrait*—it is not a teaching post this time but the Jesuit robe itself that is offered to the brilliant pupil. But Stephen has already discovered by experience how useless it is to submit oneself to any systems that relate to the family or religion; he knows that the satisfaction of his hunger will not satisfy his artistic nature, that is made for the enjoyment of a proud solitude.

Stephen had, in fact, made the attempt in *Portrait* of reconciling family life with his own autonomy and the responsibilities of the former with his needs as an artist, by using the first money he earned by his scholarly talents in an attempt to re-establish contact with "the others." The first act that he performs as artist and master of himself shows that he is now autonomous with regard to food: with the money from his literary prize, he inaugurates "a brilliant career"[8] by a symbolic expenditure; he thinks for a moment of buying a coat for his mother, and eventually chooses to take his parents to dine at Underdone's.[9] His gesture signifies that henceforth no-one may touch him; he is his own protector. The father has difficulty in keeping up with his son and jokes, "Take it easy like a good young fellow. We're not out for the half-mile, are we?" Indeed we are not; but precedence and authority have been reversed, and Simon has lost his seniority; he had come to Cork, in the previous chapter, to sell the last of the family inheritance, and at the bar has recovered some superficial prestige, claiming eternal youth and youthful vigour still. But an abyss had opened between father and son. Stephen's thirty-three pounds represent an important sum, which was supposed to suffice for his needs at college, but he spends it extravagantly, needing to feel the money "run through his fingers," and to make abundance and rejoicing reign in the family circle, however briefly. He buys presents for everyone and draws up "a form of commonwealth for the household by which every member of it held some office, opens a loan bank for his family" (*Portrait*, p. 98); in short, for a brief period he creates a perishable but well-organised world of plea-

---

—O, he must have when he suggested to her to put you on the books of a brewery. That gave the show away. Anyhow we can see what right these men have to call themselves spiritual counsellors of their flocks." (*Stephen Hero*, p. 233.)

[8] "The friendly teller . . . wished him a brilliant career in after life." (*Portrait*, p. 96.)

[9] "Stephen looked at his thinly clad mother and remembered that a few days before he had seen a mantle priced at twenty guineas in the windows of Barnado's.

—We had better go to dinner, said Stephen. Where?

—Dinner? said Mr. Dedalus. Well, I suppose we had better, what?

—Some place that's not too dear, said Mrs. Dedalus." (*Portrait*, p. 97.)

sure, in which one can sense his need to direct, to arrange, to replace chaos with a happy republic, as it were. Behind this attempted reorganisation can be felt the embryonic socialism which appeared in Joyce's life at this age, too. The result is naturally negative, the bank makes a loss and closes. And Stephen is scarred more by the spiritual failure than by the material bankruptcy, for "He had not gone one step nearer the lives he had sought to approach nor bridged the restless shame and rancour that had divided him from mother and brother and sister" (*Portrait*, p. 98).

Once again he has to admit that he is alone and different; he feels himself to be a "fosterchild and fosterbrother." No spiritual or material communion is possible with a family whose misery and ugliness offend him and whose poverty weighs heavy upon him. In reality the shared communion is intolerable, and Stephen stops believing in the family.

An Alternative: The Economy of Grace, The Church

White pudding and eggs and sausages and cups of tea accompany Stephen's redemption at the end of chapter III of *Portrait*; it may be that a simple, beautiful life is beginning for him, under the favourable constellation of this simple, wholesome food. He has not been able to love his family, but perhaps he will be able to love God; he receives Communion, and "It was true. . . . The past was past. *Corpus Domini nostri*. The ciborium had come to him." And in chapter IV Stephen begins a new life, marked out by the times and forms of devotion. This time the order of life is personal and spiritual; it is no longer dictated by the family and the mother. Stephen's problems are formulated in terms of mathematics, but this time the calculations are of a spiritual order: he wonders how to translate into intelligible terms the relationships between human time and eternity.[10] And because of this accountancy Stephen, like Joyce, quite soon repeals the contract he has made with God. In order to gain eternal life by daily exercises of piety, he divides

---

[10]"Every thought, word, and deed, every instance of consciousness could be made to revibrate radiantly in heaven; and at times his sense of such immediate repercussion was so lively that he seemed to feel his soul in devotion pressing like fingers the keyboard of a great cash register and to see the amount of his purchase start forth immediately in heaven, not as a number but as a frail column of incense or as a slender flower." (*Portrait*, p. 148.)

up the day into minutely scrupulous portions, invents an arithmetic of devotion, and multiplies his prayers into hundreds. But on the other hand, he wonders how there can be any connection between the love that God has had for him from all eternity, before the creation of the world in fact, and the brevity of human emotions. He is troubled by the disproportion between divine universality and his own relatively infinitesimal existence.

> Life became a divine gift for every moment and sensation of which, were it even the sight of a single leaf hanging on the twig of a tree, his soul should praise and thank the Giver. The world for all its solid substance and complexity no longer existed for his soul save as a theorem of divine power and love and universality. So entire and unquestionable was this sense of the divine meaning in all nature granted to his soul that he could scarcely understand why it was in any way necessary that he should continue to live. (*Portrait*, p. 150)

Faced with the idea of God, the world becomes an epiphany, a mathematical abstraction. Relativity dissolves reality: the world, nature and mankind no longer have any "reason" to exist in reality, being as they are merely the shadows of God's designs. Mystic contemplation leads Stephen into an ecstasy in which he loses himself completely. Already his keen sense of being different and separated from others had made him feel at times that he was "invisible."[11] He disappears completely, becomes simply an anonymous quantity that could be replaced by any other quantity—a feeling which would be intolerable for the artist who considers himself to be irreplaceably different from all other beings; this loss of the self is again a bankruptcy and a failure. Joyce humorously shows us the images that distract Stephen from his Creator:

> But he could no longer disbelieve in the reality of love, since God Himself had loved his individual soul with divine love from all eternity. Gradually, as his soul was enriched with spiritual knowledge, he saw the whole world forming one vast symmetrical expression of God's power and love. (*Portrait*, p. 149)

Unable to love, he yet discovers that he is loved by God; he was loved even before he existed, and this love is a great embarrassment to Stephen—he cannot reject it as he rejected his mother's love, for it is eternal. Basically, he feels dangerously in a state of grace. He begins to

[11]"At times as he walked through the streets of Dublin he felt that he was really invisible." (Trieste Notebook, quoted in *Workshop*, p. 95).

think in Satanic terms, no longer in terms of punishment, in order to catch God in the wrong.

> It is not sufficient to be loved as from all eternity, he wants to be fully and eternally pardoned also. Even if his devotion is changed into spiritual energy, the quantity of energy expended "did not wholly reward his zeal of prayer, since he could never know how much temporal punishment he had remitted" (*Portrait*, p. 147).
>
> He could only feel degradation, as though the fervent relationship were all one-sided, as it is. He was humiliated by the feeling of his own useless-ness and vanity compared with the infinite gift he had received; and since everything had been given to him from all eternity, it was necessary for him to confiscate or limit these gifts for himself, in order to be able to give thanks for them. He came at last to a mortification of all the senses, cloak-ing an ill-concealed innate masochism.
>
> It surprised him however to find that at the end of his course of intricate piety and self-restraint he was so easily at the mercy of childish and un-worthy imperfections. His prayers and fasts availed him little for the sup-pression of anger at hearing his mother sneeze. (*Portrait*, p. 151)

In fact, the consumption of energy naturally increases, and so in due proportion do the feelings of anguish and the conviction that he has been deceived. Stephen is discovering that sanctity is harder to reach than damnation, and he is filled with Satanic pride.

> "It gave him an intense sense of power to know that he could, by a single act of consent, in a moment of thought, undo all that he had done" (*Portrait*, p. 152).

Next Stephen invents the titillating game of temptation, replacing the exhausting efforts towards purification by a flirtation with the fall that is possible; he tests the power of his resistance and attributes it to the easiness of obtaining grace, subject as it is to the costly caprices of God. Often after confession he is asked to name some sin of his past life before being absolved. He quickly sees the circle of confession, repent-ance, and absolution as a vicious circle; God's grace causes man to revolve like a chained beast. Stephen prefers to fall, insofar as a fall is always followed by a recovery and a striving upward. Humiliation profits him nothing. Then he is offered the opposite situation, that of being the priest who confesses, absolves, and wields more power than kings or emperors:

> The power of the keys, the power to bind and loose from sin, the power of exorcism, the power to cast out from the creatures of God the evil spirits that have power over them; the power, the authority, to make the great

God of Heaven come down upon the altar and take the form of bread and wine. (*Portrait*, p. 158)

This would settle all the problems of accommodation, communication, and pride in self. But there would be a price to pay: one would have to renounce oneself in order to become God's elect. Stephen does not want such an exalted position any more than he wants the penitent's humiliation. Like Joyce, Stephen is not an atheist, but like Satan, he refuses to love God although he recognises his presence, judging insufficient any proofs of his reality or goodness. In any case, if God does exist, his manifestations hinder Stephen from living fully. It would be absurd to be fed and kept at the expense of a faith he did not share and which would endanger his soul, threatening it with impurity, with paralysis. This is why he refuses to take Communion. His respect for worship, either of God or of art, is reinforced by a fear which is the very height of pride: if by chance the eucharist were real and effective, he would run the risk of being saved in spite of himself or damned for taking it insincerely, so he chooses the risk of absolute error:

> —And is that why you will not communicate, Cranly asked, because you are not sure of that too, because you feel that the host, too, may be the body and blood of the son of God and not a wafer of bread? And because you fear that it may be?
> —Yes, said Stephen quietly, I feel that and I also fear it.
> . . .—But why do you fear a bit of bread?
> —I imagine, Stephen said, that there is a malevolent reality behind the things I say I fear."
> . . . . Freedom! Cranly repeated But you are not free enough yet to commit a sacrilege. Tell me would you rob?
> —I would beg first, Stephen said. (*Portrait*, pp. 243ff)

The Artist's Defence and Right to Ingratitude, The Proud Beggar

Thus Joyce reacts by refusing to enter religion, in two ways: first he eliminates all links of gratitude to others, refusing to say thank-you. He borrows with no intention of returning; he invites himself to meals, an inconvenient guest but one indifferent to politeness. But this is only a provisional expedient. When young, he made use of it only insofar as those from whom he took things deserved (at least in his opinion) to be tricked. Thus the position of the borrower is curiously changed: Joyce took an obvious delight in extracting money from people he hated. Thus he often turned to Gogarty, the enemy, taking ironic pleasure in using his poverty as a weapon of mockery. As in this epiphany:

> Dublin: in O'Connell Street: in Hamilton Long's, the chemist's.
> Gogarty: Is that for Gogarty?
> The Assistant: Yes, sir . . . Will you pay for it now?
> Gogarty: No—put it on the account; send it on. You know the address.
> The Assistant: Ye-es.
> Gogarty: 5 Rutland Square.
> The Assistant: (half to himself as he writes) 5., . . . *Rutland* . . . Square.
> (quoted in *Workshop*, p. 50)

When one lives at 5, Rutland Square, one does not need to pay cash. Respectability, stability, credit, a permanent address, everything the Joyces lack—and Jim takes pleasure in caricaturing all this by acting the part of the unreliable, unstable character of "no fixed abode," who lives on those he mocks; the most subtle and crafty game is played with those who think they can catch him. In his Trieste notebook, Joyce dissects Gogarty, and notes down, among a score of other characteristics, all displaying his hatred, "His money smells bad."[12]

His money smells bad, but Jim borrows it shamelessly, and Gogarty is delighted, because any excuse to have some hold over Joyce is welcome. His generosity is a crafty attempt to gain possession. But who can boast that he owns Joyce? Doctor O.St.John Gogarty realises that he has miscalculated—he has not bought Joyce's silence by his generosity in buying him drinks, he has acquired nothing but the role of the most unsympathetic, most unattractive and least likeable citizen of Dublin with the name and attributes of Buck Mulligan, a Satanic Hilarion to Stephen as St. Antony, a hellenising Walt Whitman opposed to the fierce mediaevalist brandishing Aquinas. ("Do I contradict myself? Very well then, I contradict myself.") (*Ulysses*, p. 20.)

Joyce had worked out his system of begging with remarkably good business sense: the problem was, how could one borrow without getting into debt? However difficult this seems, there is in fact nothing easier to solve. It is sufficient to consider borrowed money as really money due to him, to replace I.O.U. by I.A.J. (I am Joyce)—thus it is the business

[12]Cf. other remarks on Gogarty (*Workshop*, p. 98): "He discovered the vanity of the world and exclaimed 'The mockery of it!" (cf. *Ulysses*, p. 5); and "Heaven and earth shall pass away but his false spirit shall not pass away."

of his creditors to thank him, for he immortalises them in his work. Joyce's unshakeable sense of irony turns his mendicant condition into the material of his art, and ingratitude into his prerogative; his borrowings were conducted with a certain sense of justice, too, for it was true that Gogarty's money smelt bad. We can perceive the resentment Jim must have felt if we consider their agreement about the occupation of the Martello tower: Gogarty came from a very rich family yet played at being a romantically poverty-stricken student. He had furnished the tower with left-over furniture from 5, Rutland Square; while Joyce, whose family did not even possess a kettle,[13] had to pay the rent with the money he had won from a university prize, and was expected to do the housework too. Gogarty's opinions show us his character; and here we can see both in the first episode of *Ulysses*, as told in his autobiography:—

> One morning . . . I was shaving on the roof of the Tower . . . when up comes Joyce.
>
> "Fine morning, Dante. Feeling transcendental this morning?" I asked.
>
> "Would you be so merry and bright if you had to go out at this hour to teach a lot of scrawny-necked brats?"
>
> Touché. He had me there: not a doubt about it. Why don't I think about other people's problems? I must develop a little sympathy: suffer with them; realize their difficulties. I am glad that he has a job, though it is only that of a teacher . . .
>
> "Yes", I said, "that is enough to obscure the Divine Idea that underlies all life. But why be atrabilious about it?" He gave me a sour look . . .
>
> "I suppose you will bear that in mind and attach it to me when you come to write your *Inferno?*" I said . . .
>
> Joyce was the most damned soul I ever met. He went to hell and he could not get out. He could not help it . . . he was stubborn and contemptuous. He could not follow in his father's footsteps, for they were too zigzag. His father was . . . an old alcoholic wag. His mother was a naked nerve; and Joyce himself was torn between a miserable background and a sumptuous education.[14]

Which meant, as Joyce realised, that Gogarty considered him to be "educated above his station." Later, "unappreciated and laughed at in

[13]"He told her to tell her father that Mr. Kettle called. 'You won't forget now—Mr. Kettle—what you boil water in.' Baby was telling this as a joke, and Eva [who] was sitting on the fender at the fire boiling water, said, 'Unfortunately he didn't know it's Mr. Teapot we boil the water in.'" (*Dublin Diary*, pp. 28–9.)

[14]Gogarty, *It Isn't this Time of the Year at all,* quoted in *Workshop*, p. 213.

Dublin, he eloped with Nora Barnacle, a maid from Finn's Hotel." It is
obvious how much Joyce would enjoy entrapping and befooling this sort
of person.

His other borrowings tended in the same direction. He would take
from the rich and from those he considered to be hypocrites. Thus, he
would borrow without too many scruples from George Roberts in the
following clownish fashion:— "Dear Roberts—Be in the 'Ship' tomorrow at 3.30 with £1. My piano is threatened. It is absurd that my superb
voice should suffer. You recognise a plain duty—Well then—James
Overman."[15] George Roberts, who died in 1935, was one of the found-
ers of the Irish national theatre, and a director of Maunsel and Co. (later
Maunsel and Roberts), who published Synge, Yeats, and Lady Gregory,
and who were about to publish *Dubliners*.

Joyce established much the same relations with Yeats[16] and George
Russell (A.E.).

> How now, sirrah, that pound he lent you when you were hungry?
> Marry, I wanted it.
> Take thou this noble.
> Go to! You spent most of it in Georgina Johnson's bed, clergyman's
> daughter. Agenbite of inwit.
> Do you intend to pay it back?
> O, yes.
> When? Now?
> Well . . . no.
> When, then? (*Ulysses*, p. 186)

With A.E. Joyce can invent pleasing variations on the theme of debt:
A.E., I.O.U. is the refrain of the penniless poet. His borrowings from
A.E. bring out the other aspect of Joyce's revenging irony: A.E. called
him a "devilish proud beggar" and did not consider him as a genius, and
Joyce attacked his pretentions to virginity and virtue. Stephen uses the
borrowed pound to visit Georgina Johnson, his first conquest. The best
example of the refined irony that constitutes Stephen's charm is his
brilliant way of using his actual pedantry both to strengthen his aggressive attitude to others and to mock sensibly his own irritability: see, for
instance, his famous telegram to Mulligan, in which are summed up the
ambiguities of their nameless mutual hatred: "Telegram! Malachi Mulli-

[15]Undated letter-card in pencil, postmark 13 July 1904. *Letters*, vol. I, p. 56.
[16]Cf. Yeats' letter to Joyce, 2 Oct. 1904:—"I am very sorry I cannot help you with
money. I did my best to get you work as you know, but that is all I can do for you." (*Letters*,
vol. I, p. 58.)

gan, the Ship, lower Abbey street. The sentimentalist is he who would enjoy without incurring the immense debtorship for a thing done. Signed: Dedalus."

The Ship is the pub where Mulligan said he would meet Stephen (in the "Telemachus" episode), on learning that it was the latter's pay-day; he intended to extract Stephen's last farthing from him, having taken already the key of the Martello tower, the money to pay the milk-woman, and his handkerchief. Stephen refused to be treated in so domineering a fashion, but sent this Delphic message instead, a quotation from that supreme egoist, Sir Austin Feverel.[17] Joyce gives his definition of irony as applied to life, without formulating it in so many words, but by leaving the words to speak their double meanings, as in real life, in the "Charybdis and Scylla" episode: "Do you think it is only a paradox, the quaker librarian was asking. The mocker is never taken seriously when he is most serious. They talked seriously of mocker's seriousness" (*Ulysses*, p. 195). The paradox of mockery is that it is the reverse of innocence and its very frankness is the height of hypocrisy; if the mocker says, "I am not serious," no one believes him; such is the conclusion of the quaker, who is the embodiment of seriousness.

"They talked *seriously* of mocker's seriousness," notes Stephen; this is the height of the ridiculous. For if the mocker denounces himself, it is in order that people will not believe him, so that he may then mock and play upon their incredulity; thus behind the truth (declared as a lie), the serious people will imagine that they see the real lie, which is in fact nothing but the truth hidden under the evidence of its own existence. Stephen is never taken seriously because he mocks seriously. Joyce was taken seriously by Gogarty, Cosgrave, Yeats, A.E., and the others, because no-one thought of seeing behind the mask the extraordinary irony. Sometimes it was understood, when the incredibly grave attitude of those who judged him made Joyce burst into his "homeric" laughter, especially in the company of Stannie. The telegram is a reply to the complaints of Gogarty-Mulligan about his ingratitude. But what a reply! In the first place it is taken from Meredith, that specialist in Victorian cant; it is signed "Dedalus," but remains impersonally phrased. Who is "the sentimentalist"? Mulligan does not consider it aimed at him, for he is not sentimental. So, is it Dedalus himself who would enjoy? Who is it? Their friends are in agreement that it is Jim, or Stephen. But for

---

[17]Cf. *My Brother's Keeper*, p. 98, where Stanislaus relates how he drew Jim's attention to this aphorism, which was for him "a sudden illumination" on the nature of sentimentality. The remark would also suit Joyce himself very well.

Stephen the man who has robbed him is Mulligan. And he refuses to say thank-you. "Have you drunk the four quid?" asks Mulligan when Stephen arrives. Neither Stephen nor Joyce has succeeded in making those around them realise that the artist is not responsible for his debts. Ireland herself is Stephen's debtor, because he gives her new life by his art.

Two Profane Interpretations of Communion

The eucharist, which Joyce (and Stephen) adopted as a metaphor of the first operation necessary for his art, and which he considered as the gesture which makes reality reveal its essence, was for Stannie a ritual survival of cannibalism. The brutality of the younger brother's profane declarations was probably encouraged by the religious seriousness with which the elder made his sacrilegious borrowing. In any case, the discussions Jim and Stannie had about communion caused Joyce to found his aesthetic system on the notion of transubstantiation, and to take up the theory of cannibalism to make comic use of it in *Ulysses*.

"Don't you think," Jim would ask," there is a certain resemblence between the mystery of the Mass and what I am trying to do? I mean that I am trying in my poems to give people some kind of intellectual pleasure or spiritual enjoyment by converting the bread of everyday life into something that has a permanent artistic life of its own." (*My Brother's Keeper*, p. 121)

This was simply another way of defining the epiphany, but it also integrated the brief instant of spiritual manifestation into the total framework of an ordered piece of work, just as the Mass follows a specific order in celebrating the divine mysteries. In *Portrait* the same formulation of the creative principle is taken up again, almost word for word; but the context changes what was simply a comparison inspired by some fidelity to the forms if not to the content of worship into a childlike pretension to the power of the magus: Stephen sees himself as "a priest of the eternal imagination, transmuting the daily bread of experience into the radiant body of everliving life." and he thinks this in a moment of anger and jealousy caused by seeing his beloved flirting with "a priested peasant, with a brother a policeman in Dublin and a brother a potboy in Moycullen." The variations of the vocabulary in real life and in the *Portrait* show the author's intention of mockery; the words confided to Stannie confine themselves prudently to analogy, while Stephen makes no difference between the two acts, except that he reverses the powers of priest and artist, attributing the power of giving immortality to the priest of art. Passing from "the permanence of art" to "the life eternal," Stephen questions the very definition of art, until he makes art disappear and turn into a religion of the imagination, when one would have expected just the opposite. The artist of the *Portrait*, wishing to rival the Church, takes literally that form of symbolism which Joyce (and Stephen himself, in *Ulysses*) mocked, and the "daily bread" is devalued in favour of the "radiant body," reality loses and mystical transcendence gains. As Stephen says of hermetic writers in *Ulysses* (p. 184), "they creepy-crawl after Blake's buttocks into eternity of which this vegetable world is but a shadow." And it is true that in *Portrait*, where the world is the world Stephen sees, it is at the most a shadow and nothing more.

Bloom's frankly materialist view of the world he inherits from Stannie: the eucharist is truly a mystery for him, for despite his three baptisms he does not understand what the rituals of the Mass mean. He innocently follows the ceremony that takes place at All Saints' Church; and while Stephen is sharply aware of himself in his capacity as priest of art, Bloom does not realise that Joyce is playfully changing him, in the "Lotos-eaters" chapter, into a Buddha. His secret correspondent Martha has sent him a flattened yellow flower in the envelope of the letter addressed to his pseudonymous self, Henry Flower. Standing in front of a poster about Chinese missions, Bloom thinks of "Buddha their god . . . taking it easy with hand under his cheek" (*Ulysses*, p. 78). The smell of the cold stones draws him in, just in time to see the communion itself: "Shut your eyes and open your mouth. What? *Corpus.*" Some scraps of Latin float into his mind and he discovers the etymology of the word *corpse*. "They don't seem to chew it; only swallow it down. Rum idea: eating bits of a corpse why the cannibals cotton on to it." "He stood aside watching their blind masks pass down the aisle, one by one, and seek their places" (*Ulysses*, p. 79). And Bloom approves of the communion, not because he is a convert, but because the host is obviously a powerfully sedative drug: "Now I bet it makes them feel happy." Stephen scorns the bowed heads and closed eyes, but Bloom thinks "There's a big idea behind it, kind of kingdom of God is within you feel. . . . They do. I'm sure of that. Not so lonely." Stephen on the other hand fears *not* being alone. Chemistry and botany are the dominant arts in this episode: drugs and remedies for body and soul are rivals of the host.

Any remedy for the misery of the lonely man seems good to Bloom, even if its efficacity is based on the patient's credulity. The holy wine in the chalice makes him think "Pious fraud but quite right." And so nothing hinders the fraud if it is beneficent; and now nothing hinders Joyce from transforming Bloom's body into an innocent eucharist, as he bathes in the red-brick mosque: Bloom sees himself as an Eastern god, his body floating in the bath as in a ciborium, and reflects, "This is my body," hence I am Christ. He sees "the limp father of thousands, a languid floating flower" (*Ulysses*, p. 85). Bloom is Buddha too. This is a living body[18], and Bloom washes it with lemon-scented soap that he has just bought at the chemist's; the chemist's shop with all its medicinal plants recalls the reality of transubstantiation, and the herbalist's chemistry is analagous to that of the priest or poet. One can say that the eucharist is a chemical mutation or see in chemical precipitation a form of eucharist, and this confusion of the ordinary and the divine is the goal that Joyce has set his art.

[18]The body of Dignam which is buried in the following chapter, "hades," is in Bloom's imagination nothing more than "meat gone bad."

VI. The Artist as Cannibal

Prolegomena

In *Finnegans Wake*, Mercius, one of the types of Shem, the artist and penman, boasts to his brother Justius of being a "pariah, cannibal Cain" (p. 193). This was what Joyce had been, fully and selfishly, his whole life long, making use of others to feed his work; few men can have exploited the artist's "right to selfishness" with so much indifference to the needs of others, or scrupled so little to use not only their exterior appearances but also their most secret thoughts and most cherished moments of privacy; few men can have shown so little gratitude to those who lent themselves to him and to his work, from motives of admiration if not from love.

His father and mother, his brother Stannie and his wife Nora were the most skilfully used as models and sources for different characters in his work, but Joyce treated them in different ways: it is important that he publicly acknowledged his debt of imagination to his father, and went so far as to admit that *Ulysses* is, in a sense, that father's portrait. On the contrary, his mother is reduced to a hated ghost haunting her son with emblems of death. We know that May Joyce was devoted to James until her death, and that he loved her; but he wiped out from his artistic memory the mother's love and transformed her into a figure standing for the Church and death. Gossip accused him of having hastened her death by his cynical behaviour, and he commits a matricide throughout the work which tortures him with remorse.

Nora was the model for all his women, from the impertinent little
girls to Molly Bloom. We shall return to Nora's contribution later, but
it is important to remark here that if Joyce does absorb her wholly in
the work, even to her smallest looks and words, he takes good care not
to point this out, because of his respect for her.[1]

The victim who suffered most from the cannibal was certainly Stanislaus, from whom Jim took or borrowed everything, from his clothes[2] to
his smallest ideas, for nearly twenty years, without thinking of showing
any gratitude. Stanislaus, his life, personality and desires, were all taken
over by Joyce, until about 1915, with the full consent of the victim. Such
was the moral, material and intellectual aid contributed by the younger
brother that James found it necessary to make him disappear without
trace as soon as he felt that his willing servant was beginning to escape
from his grasp. Ellmann has pointed out that Joyce did not like to
acknowledge important intellectual debts, yet would not hesitate to pay
exuberant homage to minor writers whose worth did not constitute any
threat to his own: thus he allowed Edouard Dujardin a small ration of
glory for having suggested to him the idea of the interior monologue
—the great Joyce could make this generous gesture to a little-known
writer, who would be flattered and not at all dangerous. He would
indeed have needed to be courageous to admit that in 1905 Stanislaus
had given him a first specimen of the style and the idea (see below). In
fact, he made use of Stanislaus by annexing him to his own life, until
Stannie by his involuntary absence (being interned from 1915 to 1919)
became useless and therefore temporarily non-existent; when he was
released by the Austrian authorities in 1918, there was no place left for
him in his brother's life or works.[3] They met again, briefly and coldly,
in 1919, then James left for Paris and the publication of *Ulysses*. The
brothers only saw each other three times after that. Stannie felt himself
exiled from the world that James brought into being; but Joyce would
not easily let go the people he considered his own property (either
because they offended or because they reassured him by their exis-

---

[1]This respect was in fact limited, and he knew this, because after his death his letters
would permit criticism to find Nora throughout the work.

[2]Cf. *Dublin Diary*, 16 Aug. 1904, "It is really unfair when I need so little and keep my
things so long, that that little should not be left with me. Pappie has my coat, gloves and
laces, Jim my rain cloak and this morning wanted my hat, and these are clothes that are
much older than their own."

[3]When Jim wrote *Stephen Hero*, Stannie played the not inconsiderable part of Maurice
Dedalus, but after 1913 it is as though Jim were expelling Stannie from their world.
Stanislaus, once Jim's only audience and critical adviser, was largely replaced by a real
public, and Jim was less financially dependent.

tence). Stannie, guardian, servant and accomplice as long as they were together, became the accuser, traitor and false brother in Joyce's secret and personal mythology; he was the necessary prey that never escapes.

The Ambiguity of the Brothers' Relationship

Stannie, born on 17 December 1884, was three years younger than James, as soon as he was old enough to follow him, became the latter's disciple and confidant, then his best and most faithful ally within the family and in Dublin during their adolescence, then his guardian, food-supply, literary agent and adviser for ten years, all these roles being carried out with extraordinary devotion. Jim and Stannie were a pair of brothers whom Joyce liked to imagine as "unlike twins," "a pair of accomplasses,"[4] the elder, nicknamed "Sunny Jim," always merry, roaring with laughter, tall and thin, and Stannie short and stocky, athletic, "saturnine," gloomily sharing Dean Swift's *saeva indignatio*, rigid in his ideas, and rough and obstinate through fear of not being faithful to what he really thought. In Trieste Italo Svevo compared their shapes to Don Quixote and Sancho Panza, but by that time Stannie had begun to weary of his hero, and the ambiguous feelings they had for each other had reached the stage of antagonism. To be the brother of a genius was a hard task for a gifted younger brother, but to be Jim's brother was still more difficult: Stannie was torn by conflicting emotions, while Jim sheltered behind his usual duplicity. Hate and love, frankness and hypocrisy are the cardinal points of the self-examination Stannie carries out in the diary he kept between 1903 and 1905, largely in order to find out who he was himself, what sort of person he could be or wanted to be without Jim and relying only on himself.

In 1903 Stanislaus hoped that his brother, then twenty-one, might become "the Rousseau of Ireland," with Stanislaus as his first disciple and commentator. In 1903 he observed what he does not hesitate to call the budding of his brother's genius. He kept a diary, and the main character in it was always Jim, not Stanislaus. The first line, the first

[4]Like the twins Dolph and Kev in *Finnegans Wake*, p. 295: "And makes us a daintical pair of accomplasses; you, allus for the Kunst and me for something with a handel to it."

word of *Dublin Diary*, gives away his secret: everything concerns Jim, begins with him, and on the second page continues:

> Jim's character . . . is developing . . . Jim is a genius of character. When I say "genius," I say just the least little bit in the world more than I believe . . . he is perhaps a genius though his mind is minutely analytic. He has, above all, a proud, wilful, vicious selfishness, out of which now by times he writes a poem or an epiphany, now commits the meannesses of whim or appetite . . . He has extraordinary moral courage—courage so great that I have hopes that he will become one day the Rousseau of Ireland . . . His great passion is a fierce scorn of what he calls the "rabblement"—a tiger-like, insatiable hatred. He has a distinguished appearance and bearing and many graces: a musical singing and especially speaking voice (a tenor), a good undeveloped talent in music, and witty conversation. He has a distressing habit of saying quietly to those with whom he is familiar the most shocking things about himself and others, and, moreover, of selecting the most shocking times, saying them, not because they are shocking merely, but because they are true.

This scrupulous moral portrait, painted by Stannie at the age of nineteen, shows vividly the strange relationship between the brothers, making Stanislaus "his brother's jackal," as their father maliciously said.

On the third page, Jim says this, Jim sings well, Jim is exceptionally intelligent . . . and a little further on, "I think that I shall never sing well." Intelligent without being brilliant, honest with the troubled diligence of one who fears his own weaknesses and has to struggle to be honest, Stannie was also a rebellious son, with none of the prodigal son's glory, and was in his way nearer to Rousseau in his wish to strip his character bare for the sake of humility than was his Byronic brother Jim. Again,

> Jim is often silly-mannered and impolite. I have no doubt that he is a poet, a lyric poet, that he has a still greater mastery of prose. He may be a genius—it seems to me very possible—but that he has not yet found himself is obvious. (*Dublin Diary*, February 1904)

Stannie is obviously fascinated by Jim, whose development is more important to him than his own. "Jim says that his ambition in life is to burn with a hard and gem-like ecstasy. Mine is then—it would be said —to burn with a hard and Jim-like ecstasy."

Stannie was to exist only as a function of Jim, not as his double or echo, for he often disagrees with him. He does not lack judgement, has his own opinions, tastes and choices, but everything he thinks, says or does, is given meaning by perpetual reference to Jim, as we can see:

My life has been modelled on Jim's example, yet when I am accused
. . . of imitating Jim, I can truthfully deny the charge. It was not mere aping
as they imply, I trust I am too clever and my mind too old for that. It was
more an appreciation in Jim of what I myself really admire and wish for
most. . . . I follow Jim in nearly all matters of opinion, but not all . . . Jim,
I think, has even taken a few opinions from me. (*Dublin Diary*, 13 August
1904)

In his introduction to Stanislaus' book *My Brother's Keeper*,[5] Ellmann
rightly refers to the "sense of bondage" felt by Stanislaus and expressed
by the choice of title. If the day of Stannie's death, the 16th June, seems
almost tragical in its ironical coincidence with Bloomsday, anniversary
of his brother's immortal creation, this is because the real brother suffered throughout his life from being refused the right to be himself. At
the age of seventy, fourteen years after Jim's death, Professor Joyce, as
he was respectfully called, was still his brother's Cain. At least he would
declare this, in order, as Ellmann says, "to disarm criticism." Stannie
always saw himself first and foremost as he was seen by others. When
he looked at himself, his glance would rebound on to the mirror, because in seeking himself there, he would always see Jim first. And he
knew that for other people he was "Jim's brother." From Stannie Stephen inherits a feeling of annoyance at not being himself, but often only
the son of a famous father, in the eyes of Dublin. Stannie was expected
to imitate his brother, had no right to differ in fact, and was then
accused of aping him. The fatal irony was that he was so well suited to
be Jim's double that he became sometimes the initiator rather than the
imitator, and found himself accused of servility. Everything was attributed to Jim, and taken away from Stannie. Eventually he can no
longer tell whether he should imitate the brother he admires or separate himself from him; he is sincere in his respect for Jim, but feels
unavoidably bitter at having to be merely Jim's reflection; in order not
to become petty and mean he adopts an excessive humility, and under-
estimates himself because others underestimate him, despising those
who do appreciate his worth:

Aunt Josephine tells me that I underrate myself and that I am not an
egoist. The fact that I think so constantly about myself should prove to her
that I am. Yet I take myself at Jim's valuation of me, because it is my own,
perhaps. (*Dublin Diary*, p. 53)

[5]This account of the brothers' life until 1903 was broken off by the author's death in
1955, and published in 1958.

To adopt Jim's opinion as his own is the height of humility, but it leads to revolt against those who, like Aunt Josephine, do appreciate him. Stannie even says, "I am not sure but I think a little less highly of him because he has a high opinion of me" (p. 54).

Stanislaus is often motivated by the need to go a little further than Jim, in order to be a little himself; this can be seen in the episodes of open warfare with the Jesuit masters, related in *My Brother's Keeper,* (pp. 101ff. and 117ff.) and in his elimination of "the idea of God" along with "the idea of sin"—"I support Home Rule for the Universe," he would say. And Jim claimed to be God the one and only. It was often enough for Stannie to discover some mode of thought or behaviour not yet used by Jim, for the latter to take it over. It was not Jim's genius, but his insatiable faculty for despoiling other people's personalities, that prevented Stannie from living fully. Jim despoiled him without a word of thanks:

> What he calls the domestic virtues are words of contempt in his mouth. He does not recognise such a thing as gratitude. He says it reminds him of a fellow lending you an overcoat on a wet night and asking for a receipt. (Gratitude is, after all, such an uncomfortable sentiment—thanks with a grudge at the back of it). As he lives on borrowing and favours, and as people never fail to treat him . . . as a genius while he treats them as fools, he has availed himself of plenty of opportunity for showing ingratitude. (*Dublin Diary*, pp. 49–50)

Why keep a diary except for revealing one's self? In principle it replaces the confident or confessor, but Stannie's diary alone had a reader, and the confidences inevitably sounded false since that reader was Jim: "He has always read these notes, for there was always much in them about him, and if I was calling them anything I would call them 'My journal in imitation of Jim' (August 1904)."

Stanislaus had come to submit his hesitations, sufferings, troubles and ridicule to the one person from whom he should have kept away this little individual cache. He felt this, indeed, and his discomfort expressed itself in his conviction that he was a hypocrite, falling far short of Jim's pure honesty. He was tempted to destroy his incomplete confessions, and did so once; but the fact that he followed out this alienation of himself shows how much he was dependent on Jim's judgement. He attempts some self-justification, as in, "My diary is not very startlingly frank, for I am not over-communicative even to myself. . . . One of my chief reasons for keeping these notes is to prevent myself becoming stupid" (*Dublin Diary*, p. 51).

It is true that Stannie writes in order to prove to himself that he too can wield a pen, but especially because the diary is one long letter to Jim; for Stanislaus it is a way of reminding his brother that he has no intention of becoming the priest of any deity, and that pen and paper can be used by anyone; it is also a way of pointing out that they are keeping a watch on each other, and that if there is fraternisation, it is not for the love of Jim, but for intellectual esteem for genius and their shared hatred of Ireland. One of the excuses he makes for his servility is that it would be worth while to imitate Jim without loving him, because Jim holds the secret of life; thus Stannie claims that he is making use of Jim, as Jim makes use of him. He makes Jim into a master of thought, a spiritual guide, although he keeps the right to pass judgement to himself:

> He has said that what women admire most in men is moral courage, and that people are unhappy because they cannot express themselves, and these things I recollect and at times consider, and though they seem small, they affect me greatly. (*Dublin Diary*, p. 50)

On the other hand, it is important that he began his new diary after his mother's death in August 1902. A previous diary has disappeared. The chronicle of Joyce the genius was written under very curious circumstances, typical of the Joyces' world and of the connection between the two brothers: Stanislaus wrote on the back of his brother's old essays, because in the Joyce household it was necessary to save even scraps of waste paper, but also as though obscurely wanting to write his works symbolically behind those of James.

Stanislaus' researches involve repressed but recurrent attempts at flight and escape:—"Know thyself—but if, when I know myself, I should discover I know a self not worth knowing, what then O Oracle?" He is in search of himself but afraid of what he might find; he is afraid of seeing a hateful self rise up, yet he is also "tempted seven times a day to play a part," and this temptation is only strong because Jim does not play a part, or claims not to. But the choice of role to play is beyond him.

But Stanislaus had a perversely intuitive notion of how important he was to Jim, and he writes also in order to please Jim and to make himself indispensable.

> Anything I owe to Jim I owe to his example, for he is not an encouraging person in criticism. He told me when I began keeping a diary that I would never write prose and that my diary was most uninteresting except in the parts that were about him. (Indeed it was a journal of his life with detailed

conversations . . . between him and Irish men of letters . . . I burnt it to make a holocaust. Perhaps Jim owes something of his appearance to this mirror held constantly up to him). (*Dublin Diary*, p. 25)

Joyce took a sarcastic pleasure in knowing that he was being watched, as his reactions show: "Jim's criticisms of these notes of mine are characteristic. One of them is this: 'An' do ye be sittin' up here, scratchin' your arse, an' writin' thim things'. He pronounces 'arse' something like 'aerse'."

Joyce thought a great deal of the diary, and must have found it not only a portrait of himself by one like him, but also a document of human value on the psychology of the Double, and besides this an excellent source of all kinds of information to be used in his own work:

> I am tempted seven times a day to burn these notes. I yielded to the temptation in summer, 1903, and burnt a long and full diary which I had kept for two years. Jim said he was very sorry I burnt it, as it would have been of great use to him in writing his novel, and if it would have been of use, I am sorry too.[6]

In fact the brothers' feelings for each other were normally ambivalent. Stannie would pretend not to like Jim, an attitude which made his devotion appear greater;

> There was never any friendship for Jim in my relations with him for there was never any real trust. . . . I think I may safely say I do not like Jim. I perceive that he regards me as quite commonplace and uninteresting—he makes no attempt at disguise—and though I follow him fully in this matter of opinion, I cannot be expected to like it. (*Dublin Diary*, pp. 36 and 47)

But we feel that he protests too much, and that his lack of brotherly love is far from being an established fact. And indeed, Jim has scarcely left Dublin before Stannie shows the real affection that he keeps hidden, along with his opposition to Dublin society:

> People like Jim easily . . . perhaps because he is so much alive. He seemed to me the person in Ireland who was most alive. . . . Jim turned a number of the Irish literary clique against him by announcing his dislike for work and his intention to do it only when he must. . . . People forget that . . . Jim is never idle except when studying for an exam, but always spiritually very much alive. (*Dublin Diary*, pp. 103 and 99)

[6]Cf. letter to Stannie, 13 Jan. 1905: "Send me all documents dealing with University College period from your diary etc." (quoted in *Diary* also.)

He could hardly live without Jim; and being left alone in Dublin, he re-examined his attitudes, concluding that he did love Jim, but disliked Jim's way of oppressing him:

> I wrote once that I disliked Jim, but I see now how I was led to believe a lie. With reference to anyone whom we know, we may like or dislike more than one thing; we may like that person's character, for instance, and yet dislike what he does or the way he does it. Jim had done many things which I disliked and had slighted me a few times before I wrote. Now that I think of it, I suggest I may have been irritated by the demands which, quite unknown to me, Jim's presence made on my character; but more than all this, the idea of affection between characters so distrustful and mutually so little affectionate repelled me as it does now. I think I understand Jim, however, and like him in the way of admiration. As for my interest in Jim, it has become chronic, for it has always been my habit to try to live Jim's intellectual life as well as my own. (*Dublin Diary*, p. 101)

The only person whose esteem would be really pleasing for him is the pitiless brother who laughs at all his efforts. So Stannie writes against himself, for that one and only reader, hiding his distress under a mask of assumed objectivity. He considered Jim noble, brave, and even heroic, but modified his hero-worship when his hero was actually in Dublin.

> I am wrong in saying I dislike Jim. I have no liking for him but I see that his life is interesting. My opinion of myself is what I write, and is so low probably because I have a very high standard . . . Perhaps this high standard implies a high temper of mind. I am more inclined to believe that it is the reflection of Jim's nature. (*Dublin Diary*, p. 63)

Stannie was prevented from expressing freely the genuine liking that he felt for Jim by the latter's refusal to treat him with anything other than cool amusement: Jim would not recognise his own need for Stannie, yet his dependence on his brother was equalled only by his dependence on Nora. He had hardly arrived in Trieste before he started summoning Stannie to his side, first by "invitation," and later in such urgent terms that the invitation became more like an order. At length Stannie made up his mind, and arrived in Trieste in 1905. From that moment he became literally (morally and materially) his brother's keeper; in particular he campaigned against Jim's drinking habits, fearing that he would destroy himself. He would seek him out in bars, and sometimes found it necessary to use violence to get him home;[7] over-

---

[7]Cf. Ellmann, *op. cit.*, p. 223.

coming his disgust, he would thrash Jim in order to save him. Cain loved
Abel more than he loathed him. One can imagine his distress on seeing
"that lively genius" menanced by the destructive forces of drink. Jim
would mock Stannie's anger, and yet derive pleasure from it, for Stanislaus in beating him was taking his place in Jim's archetypal pattern and
trap, for Jim needed to be the suffering victim, even if guilty. And
Stannie sees, in spite of himself, that the role of saviour and chastiser
is allotted to him. Relations between the brothers were altered in a
fashion which was intolerable to him, and he had to play the roles he
detested: father of his brother, protector of the family, servant, source
of food, guardian of the disintegrating home (for Joyce and Nora nearly
separated in 1906, and it was Stannie who brought about their reconciliation)—they lived through him. Jim was killing Stanislaus and pretending to be the suffering martyr himself; he would borrow Stannie's
trousers to go out drinking in, when his own were worn out, just as he
used to in Dublin; and while Jim lived out his life in borrowed clothes,
Stanislaus, despoiled of his own, was then accused of being a killjoy. At
Trieste he was still the cashier, postman, and feeder of the household.

Alcohol, the father's drink, Circe's philtre, turned Pappie into a criminal and Jim into a swine. Stannie's diary reveals a violent hostility to
Dublin's foremost vice; alcohol had degraded his father and threatened
to destroy his brother. And there is something very touching about
Stannie's attempts to keep his brother away from the drink. He is
constantly warning him, that treacherous friends will make him drink
in order to drag him down to their level. As Ellmann tells us (in his
introduction to *My Brother's Keeper*) it was during these summers in
Trieste that there evolved one of the fables of *Finnegans Wake*, the tale
of the ant and the grasshopper, or the Mookse and the Gripes, the Ondt
and the Grace-hoper; Stannie was the ant and Jim the grasshopper,
singing and writing all summer at the expense of the ant's carefully
saved money. Not only did Stannie look after the feeding of the family,
but he also helped Jim in his disputes with editors, persuaded him to
bring out *Chamber Music* in 1907, reread, commented and advised.

But Jim did feel some affection for his faithful brother, although he
took care to hide it with jovial insults; they exchanged innumerable
postcards whenever Stannie was away, those from James asking for
money orders or carrying on a conversation in their own private language. Joyce would share his troubles and his boastful pride with Stanislaus, confiding to him the most intimate details about his relationship
with Nora, and even his extravagant but typical plans for them all to live
together in "a little cottage near Dublin" with Nora and the child,

sharing their money and means of livelihood.[8] This suggestion was first made in July 1905 just before Giorgio was born, and could thus have been put into practice by Easter 1906. Joyce insisted on the idea and repeated it in subsequent letters: two months later, Stannie had still not replied, and James reminded him thus: "You did not seem to take my statement—viz, that my present absurd life is no longer possible for me —very seriously. Therefore I repeat the remark: and may I also remind you that I have a habit . . . of following up a conviction by an act."[9] At last Stannie came to join Jim, because a teaching post at the Berlitz school had just fallen vacant. The idea of the cottage had been entirely a selfish dream, as he had quite rightly realised; but there was also Jim's need to recreate the family, starting from himself and Stannie. The tone of the invitation has become threatening, as usual. Only Stannie could have tolerated the cruelty of which James was capable when he felt himself to be endangered.

James grew more cool towards his brother in about 1909, and there had probably been some clash with Nora. Joyce had twice gone by himself to Dublin in 1909, leaving the family in the care of his brother; he had never been reluctant to practice emotional blackmail whenever the need for money became urgent, and to beg in tones of comical supplication for the uncle to take pity on the weeping wife and the poor little nephew who is so hungry. It may be that Stannie was tempted to take Jim's place more completely while the latter was away; for Cain's diary does not tell us to what extent he came to confuse himself with his brother. But on the contrary, Jim's works begin to give more scope to the brother-figure, and the younger brother appears as "false" (in both senses of the word), and treacherous. James, having deprived Stanislaus of his own freedom to live, is replaced in the role of depriver by the dispossessed himself. This may be seen as the height of masochism, but we cannot tell how much is theft and how much gift in the incessant ambiguity of the brothers' life together. We cannot tell whether Stanislaus' self-sacrifice was motivated by love or by loathing. The only certainty is that neither of them was ever simply Cain or simply Abel. What have you done with your brother? God asked Cain.

Stannie was really a false Cain; he began as Jim's Abel, and only after ten years of being the real keeper and undergoing great troubles did he become Cain. It is obvious that his extraordinary self-abnegation was

[8]This plan or dream was dear to Joyce's heart, for Bloom inherits it in the "Ithaca" episode, and we find it again in *Finnegans Wake*, p. 179.
[9]*Letters*, vol. II, p. 107, 18 Sept. 1905.

ambiguous, that by denying himself he was assimilating himself to the master; by self-sacrifice he made himself indispensable. Jim's unscrupulous behaviour and the irresistible fascination he had for Stanislaus only came to an end when Providence intervened in 1915 to bring about the vital separation, when Stanislaus was interned and Jim enjoying creative freedom. Which is Cain to Abel? Stannie as a character was somewhat embarrassing, since Jim needed him as a disciple and yet denied his fidelity; he was the brother whose brother James did not wish to be, his likeness whom he feared to resemble; yet he wished there to be some resemblance so that Stannie could be used as another self, the self which one denies and scorns. Stannie's function in the life as in the work is ambiguous: he is neither entirely himself nor entirely Jim, nor entirely anyone else. Joyce reduces all virtual relationships from the starting-point of the real relationship of brotherhood.

In reality, Jim was the eldest; but in the work there is repeated shifting between the roles of elder and younger. Cain is older than Abel, as Esau is older than Jacob. Beside these two biblical myths Joyce sets up a third, in which the inversions of rights and duties allow for a number of ambivalent combinations. In real life the brothers stood together against the world of Dublin, but were very clearly opposed within the family structure. The biblical distribution of blessings, which benefited Jacob the younger brother at the expense of Esau, is cunningly transposed in the life of the Joyces. Esau is as crafty as Jacob here and pretends to sell his birthright as eldest son in order to gain a double ration of life, his own and his brother's, in exchange for the blessings of a "bland old Isaac" (*Finnegans Wake* I), who in reality never had anything but curses to give his two sons.

The egg Humpty-Dumpty that falls with a noise of thunder on the first page of *Finnegans Wake* commemorates the fall of the father who breaks in two parts, "humptyhillhead" and "tumptytumtoes," and also the last type of the family war which has broken many an eggshell throughout Joyce's works, setting free the divine bird who breaks more than a code to bring out its message. And it is Jhem or Shem who comes forth from the ruins. Almost before they can stand, the brothers recommence their war, which started in the quarrel between James and Stanislaus, and which animates the whole of *Finnegans Wake*. When Joyce called his brother "my whetstone," he was founding his work on a pun or word-play, as Christ, he liked to recall, had founded His Church on a play on words. When after Jim's death, Stanislaus spoke of himself and defined himself as a man twice exiled, by being faithful to his brother, and by being unfaithful to him, in these words, "You know . . . Cain," he was expressing the highest and most disturbed kind of alienation: loyal to the role James had assigned to him and to the invented character so that Jim could be Joyce, Stanislaus *becomes doubled* and speaks for Jim (hence against himself) in the book which relates the brother's development.

Stannie's Contribution to Joyce's Works

It was obvious for Joyce's Dublin friends that his friendship or affection were never disinterested: he would try out his theories or sharpen his ideas and emotions on them. In "Circe," Stephen calls Lynch "my whetstone," upon whom since the days of *Portrait* he has been sharpening the dagger definitions of his aesthetics.[10] In real life Lynch (that is, Cosgrave) was the last of a series of whetstones which Joyce in the person of Stephen enumerates when expounding to an incredulous audience his version of Shakespeare's life; Stephen passes without transition from Shakespeare's life to his own with the introduction of the two bad brothers Richard and Edmund, whom he thinks the critics are wrong in ignoring. "A brother is as easily forgotten as an umbrella. ... Where is your brother? Apothecaries' hall. My whetstone. Him, then Cranly, Mulligan: now these."[11]

Stanislaus lent himself willingly to this task, although having the disagreeable feeling that he was simply being used as an instrument: "He used me, I fancy, as a butcher uses a steel to sharpen his knife." Gogarty had nicknamed Jim Kinch (imitation of the scraping of a knife blade) and Stannie Thug (the strangler, tough and unsubtle). Both brothers were sharp-witted, but Stannie would lend himself to sharpening his brother's wit, as though he felt some obscure satisfaction at being an instrument of an instrument, and contributing indirectly to the wounding of the enemy (that is, of Irish hypocrisy wherever it was found). Kinch as knife is an object, accomplice in the satirical enterprise. Thug lends his strength and some sharp words to aid Kinch; and Stanislaus provides Jim with many of his characters' names, participating thus in his own way in his brother's creative life. His real contribution to Joyce's work and vision of the world is not merely limited to having suggested

[10]In 'Charybdis and Scylla', *Ulysses*, p. 183, Stephen mocks his own sharpness with "Unsheathe your dagger definitions. Horseness is the whatness of allhorse."

[11]*Ulysses*, p. 207. At the time of *Ulysses*, in 1904, Stanislaus was working at Apothecaries' Hall and trying, though in vain, to acquire some learning, while Jim, like Stephen, was making speeches in the high places of Dublin wit.

the titles *Chamber Music* and *Stephen Hero*. By his diary, his personality and his opinions, he participates directly, providing names and titles as though he felt a strange compulsion to give names to Jim's creatures; his wit was of the epigrammatic type natural to Irish satire, which is related closely to pastiche: "I suggested many names to him: Pappie is *Sighing Simon*, Jim, *Stuck-up Stephen*, myself, *Morose Maurice*, the sister, *Imbecile Isabel*, Aunt Josephine, *Blundering Brigid*, Uncle Willie, *Jealous Jim.*" These details are of importance for Stannie most of all, but he also contributed more than anyone else did to the formative stages of *Portrait* and *Dubliners*.

To begin with, Stannie's vision of Dublin people was painted in very much more sombre colours than Jim's was; and his hatred for Ireland and the Irish were articles of faith which Joyce adopted for the use of his Stephen.

> The Irish are morally a cowardly, chaos-loving people, quarrelsome and easily deceived, dissipated in will and intellect, and accustomed to masters, with a profitless knowledge of their own worthlessness which causes them constantly to try to persuade themselves and others that they are what they are not. The lying, untrustworthy, characterless inhabitants of an unimportant island. (*Dublin Diary*, p. 57)

He declared that the Irish have three national vices: drunkenness, masturbation and lying. His hatred for the Church in general and the Jesuits in particular went much further than Jim's did, and provided Joyce with the majority of the anticlerical episodes in *Portrait* and all the fine speeches in *Stephen Hero*. One can recognise here Stephen's doubts expressed in terms of violent defiance:

> I remember the trite moral the vulgarian priests who were my masters, the Jesuits, would draw from my case. My mind must be very lax and my thoughts very desultory, for I permit myself to think lazily and quite without sincerity, would I change with them? . . . I could easily cultivate the domestic virtues, throw up the sponge, and become a non-commonplace citizen. What in the end am I trying to do with this head-piece of mine? But if my mind has been lax, it suddenly rises up and is glad, for I would not change with them. I have no certitude in me. If they are right, then I lose all. If I am right, they certainly suffer nothing. . . . I can answer them no questions, but I do not believe their blessed fable of Jesus Christ nor in the Church they have built out of it, and though I am quite without principles myself and accuse myself of inconsistency, a personal honour will not let me try to believe for policy's sake. This enlivening of my faith in unbelief seems to me not unworthy. (Dec. 1904, *Dublin Diary*, pp. 97–8)

His departure from the Church was much more radical than Jim's, as can be seen from these two passages, one from the diary:

Is thought the motion of grey matter in the head, or is it dependent on but distinct from that motion, just as life is dependent on the action of the heart but is yet not a heart-beat nor a succession of them? . . . The catechism remarks that St. Paul says of apostates, that "it is impossible for them to be renewed again to penitence", that is, their conversion is extremely difficult. It asks, "Why is the conversion of apostates so very difficult?" Answer: "The conversion of apostates is very difficult because by this apostasy they sin against the Holy Ghost, crucify again the Son of God, and make a mockery of him". This wholesale begging of the question and neat shutting to of a false door, so that others may be deceived as to how the free ones escaped, are an admirable mixture of simplicity and roguery and very typical of the Catholic Church.

And the other from *My Brother's Keeper:*

I don't know, I said . . . I know that the host is supposed to be the real body and blood of Christ, that people have been burnt for not believing that it is . . . Well I don't believe it. . . . To make a long story short, I am not going to Communion any more because I don't believe that the host is the real body and blood of Christ . . . And if it is, because I have no appetite.

Jim stood stock-still, raised his chin in the air like a dog about to bay, and gave one of his loud shouts of laughter. . . . Then: "Well, do as you please. I certainly don't want to influence you".

I added more calmly that I was satisfied in my mind that Communion was a ritual survival of cannibalism.

Joyce takes this up again to use in Bloom's non-violent humanitarianism, as has been seen above.

But it was especially his affection for his cousin Katsy Murray and his relationship with Pappie that made Stannie into the model for Stephen Dedalus.

Kathleen Murray, their cousin, then thirteen years old, had "a very rich nature," so rich that she had momentarily attracted Jim's attention —but he had doubtless been discouraged by the fact that it was not possible for him to express himself as his "moral nature" dictated to the daughter of Aunt Josephine. Stanislaus experienced the same forbidden emotions: "I admired Katsy. I thought her nature luxurious and proud —the pride of the flesh."

Stanislaus' early years provide the material for those of Stephen Dedalus. It can be seen from his diary that the capricious young temptress who made Stannie's heart dance like a floating cork was partially the model for E.C. in *Portrait*. And one cannot help finding all the more touching the young man's sufferings because his idyll takes place in July 1904, at the same time that Jim was easily making the conquest of Nora; although, of course, Nora was nineteen years old and willing to be seduced, while Katsy was still only a child.[12]

Stephen is an artist; and this is why, using his brother's timid emotions as a starting-point, Joyce reconstitutes the inner world of desire to find its ironical expression in the Villanelle of the Temptress. This is how Joyce's own proud shyness manages to project itself into a character made up from Stannie's awkwardness and timidity. There is indeed a sentimentalism shared by both brothers, although they both find it embarrassing and seek to deny it; their life in the family had been too painful to permit of any lyric notes, or would have made them sound ridiculous. Thus Jim would go away and hide in order to write his poems to Nora, and Stanislaus, keeping his own youthful passions hidden, suggested he call them *Chamber Music;* this was a mocking reference to James's susceptibility to Nellie, the sympathetic prostitute who admired his work and who had offered "to accompany him on the 'po' on one occasion when he was about to sing."[13] This was an example of brotherly complicity on Stannie's part, since he knew that the poems were written for very correct, respectable ladies, and that Jim was far from being a Casanova. Katsy was a living person, sweet and cruel, who treated Stanislaus casually and unkindly, just as Stephen in the first part of *Portrait* is ill-treated by little Eileen.[14] Stanislaus worshipped her and bowed to her wishes in a way curiously reminiscent of Jim's devotion to Nora. Stannie also thought, however, that Jim had never conducted an affair so clumsily as this one with Miss Barnacle; he was ashamed of

[12]Stanislaus' diary for 23 July 1904: "There's Katsy! I saw her tonight from the Annesley Bridge. She ran quickly across the road in the dark and back again. I started at the sight of her. I had been sullen all night. . . . Where did she go? Into Elmore's, run out on her last message before going to bed? No, into my heart and scuttled round it and out again, the little mouse".
    Cf. "She passed out from the porch of the library. . . . She had passed through the dusk. And therefore the air was silent save for one soft hiss that fell . . ." (*Portrait*, p. 232.)
    [13]It was Stanislaus, too, who arranged the poems in order for publication.
    [14]Stanislaus' diary, 31 July 1904:—"Katsy went all night with Eileen. They ran past quickly on the path and Katsy turned her face to me laughing. I felt as if she was trampling over my liking for her like a charge of cavalry." Cf. *Portrait*, p. 76: "He remembered how. . . . all of a sudden, she had broken out into a peal of laughter and had run down the sloping curve of the path."

the weakness which Jim was showing, yet which he would never have condoned normally, when he was priding himself on his lordly detachment: "Many things he has expressed I remember, for they seemed to me to be just while they seemed to suit me. His contempt, for example, for enthusing, for strenuousness, for flirting and sentimentality, which he says he leaves to clerks."

The younger brother must have been greatly surprised to see his Don Juan brother behaving so clumsily with Nora. "He walks out at night with Miss Barnacle, and kisses her, while she calls him 'my love,' though he is not a clerk." Don Jim is no longer recognisable. And the brothers begin quietly to drift apart: they enthuse. Stannie exclaims "My sly saint!", and Katsy replies scornfully:

> "Your sly saint! I like that! What dog died, may I ask, and left you anything?" The phrase is not coarse in her mouth, it is a phrase in their house. Aunt Josephine, who was there, laughed; I laughed and went on talking again. I was checked and hurt but I did not let it be seen. It would be ridiculous to inflict my sensitiveness on others. I did not call her 'my sly saint' again, because I did not want to have the incident repeated."

To which Stanislaus reacts like Stephen when mocked: he wonders whether he is really in love. "My mind is discontented because I do not know whether I love Katsy."

As far as feelings are concerned, Shem and Shaun, or Jim and Stannie, are identical; their difference lies in their ways of dissimulating the feelings. Jim chooses the heroic pose and acts like Don Juan, while Stannie takes unhappy refuge in a destructive "Feverelism," seeing himself as the hero's servant.

> Jim has the first character of the hero—strange to say, he is noble; and the first character of the lyric poet—he is most susceptible. His affairs have the proper air of reality. His second last was his cousin Katsy Murray—a child. His present Mary Sheehy. Mary . . . is romantic. . . . She wants Hero.

Mary wants Hero, but what does Katsy want? Might she accept his servant? Poor Stannie has not yet dared to say in his diary that the servant must love where the hero has loved. Jim was attracted by Katsy and so Stannie gave up to his brother all his cousinly rights in her: Katsy was not for one whose very existence was so feeble that he was hardly real. He turned to consider the play of Love and Genius next:

> The wise virgins delight in the society of the necessitous young genius. They are happy when he comes in. They laugh at him, or with him, or for

him, making the heart of the dullard envious. And he is suspected of wild ways. They flatter him . . . the servant sees.

He does not realise that for Jim heroism does not go beyond fine talk and acting, and that pride is the best excuse for anyone who fears failure.

Reading his protestations of innocence and recitals of complaisant guilt, we see that Stanislaus prefers being someone else's double to liking himself at all; he hates himself for reasons more serious than that of intellectual inferiority. He feels that he resembles his father, that is, that he is an Irishman and an Irishman's son, than which he can imagine nothing worse. "I loathe my father," he says. "I loathe him because he is himself, and I loathe him because he is Irish—*Irish*, that word that epitomises all that is loathsome to me" (12 April 1904).[15] It is all the fault of Ireland, for it would be better not to have been born than to be born son of John Joyce. There is suicide, of course, but Stanislaus refuses the romantic conventions and facilities. He chooses another form of de- struction, that of suicide by assimilation of himself to Jim and violent rejection of his father. Stephen Dedalus' dislike for his father in *Portrait* is that of Stannie, not of Jim, for the father in real life. For Stannie, to live means to kill the father. He tells himself as much, he reminds himself constantly: "Remember, I dislike Pappie very much. . . . I am resolved not to deceive myself on this point, and this resolution may, perhaps, be the beginning of a spiritual life for me." This is not without interest, that for Stannie life begins in opposition to the father; his diary closes with a page of characteristic bitterness, arising partly from his violent hatred for his father, partly from annoyance with himself for having lived peacefully with Pappie for several days, and partly from a "stomach anger." Stannie had spent all day looking for his father in Dublin, like a furious prototype of the Dedalus children looking for their father, in *Ulysses*. The hours pass into an increasing emptiness and violence; the house turns into a court of law where a John Joyce who seems very like H.C.E. is supposed to be defending himself, but the accused makes no reply, because he is drinking his own health in some pub which his son has not yet discovered. The family grows angry and restive, insults fly about, for an empty belly knows no manners. Stannie laments:

[15]Cf. also, "I dislike Pappie for the same reason that I dislike my country—he has made me live in hostility and unhappiness."

What to do in such a house? Answer advertisements? . . . After ten Pappie came in with a few pence left. We . . . had fasted 14 hours. I heard his drunken intonations in the dark downstairs, and then the saddening flow. This is a true portrait of my progenitor: the leading one a dance and then the disappointing, baffling, baulking, and turning up drunk—the business of breaking hearts. (*Dublin Diary*, p. 114)

We see him in the "Wandering Rocks" episode of *Ulysses*, spied on by his daughter Dilly; Simon tells her to stand up straight. He, after all (as he comes out of the Scotch House, probably), can at least keep his back straight. The child is hungry—has rickets? Father gives her alms.

—Here, Mr. Dedalus said, handing her two pennies. Get a glass of milk for yourself and a bun or something.
. . .—Did you get any money? Dilly asked.
—Where would I get money? Mr. Dedalus said. There is no-one in Dublin would lend me fourpence.
—You got some, Dilly said, looking in his eyes.
—How do you know that? Mr. Dedalus asked, his tongue in his cheek.
(*Ulysses*, p. 232)

There are plenty of portraits of Pappie in Stannie's diary; he returns to the idea as often as he does to that of Jim, trying very hard to justify himself and to be impartial, but honestly hating him, yet ready to admit some good qualities in him. This example is one of many, trying to be objective:

He is domineering and quarrelsome and has in an unusual degree that low, voluble abusiveness characteristic of the Cork people when drunk. . . . He is ease-loving and his ambition in life has been to be respected and to keep up appearances. However unworthy this may sound, it has been so difficult of attainment and he has struggled for it with such tenacious energy against the effects of his constant drunkenness that it is hard to despise it utterly. He is lying and hypocritical. He regards himself as the victim of circumstances and pays himself with words. His will is dissipated, and his intellect besotted, and he has become a crazy drunkard. He is spiteful like all drunkards who are thwarted, and invents the most cowardly insults that a scandalous mind and a naturally derisive tongue can suggest. He undoubtedly hastened Mother's death. . . . For his children he has no love or care but a peculiar sense of duty arising out of his worship of respectability. . . . He boasts of being a bit of a snob. His idea of the home is a well-furnished house in which he can entertain and his children grow up under their mother's care, and to which, having spent the evening in drinking, . . . he can return to lord it and be obeyed.

But often Stannie bursts out in furious accusations:

> I fail to see the magnificent generosity in standing a drink . . . Moreover
> I understand that the greater number stand drink at somebody else's
> expense, Jim for instance at the expense of anyone he can "touch," Pappie
> all his life at the expense of his wife and children. (3 Apr. 1904)

It is unfortunately true that the father's drinking and absenteeism
were responsible for a great deal of suffering: Charlie died of tuberculosis in hospital, for instance, and out of eight children surviving, four died
young, undernourished, ill cared for, not looked after at all. In 1905,
Stanislaus finished his diary of accusation against Pappie. Jim had left,
in order to survive; but in the violence of Stanislaus' tone can be felt the
horror and misery of one who must henceforth stand alone in the
labyrinth of emotions, facing a monster who kills his children in order
to satisfy his own needs, calm his fears, and save his own skin.

> I attribute the following to Pappie:
> (1) the undermining of his children's health, and their rotting teeth, to
> absolutely irregular feeding and living. . . .
> (2) the handicap of his children's chances in life . . .
> (3) Mother's unhealth, unhappiness, weakening mind, and death, to his
> moral brutality . . . and to his execrable treatment of her even up to her
> last day; and (4) indirectly, Georgie's death, for if Georgie had been prop-
> erly doctored or in hospital, he would have lived. (*Dublin Diary*, p. 113)

This delightful list is still an underestimate, too.

> "Moral brutality" does not convey to the stranger mind the eternity of
> abuse. . . . It was a constant threat of his to Mother, "I'll break your heart!
> I'll break your bloody heart!" It must be admitted that this was exactly
> what he did. . . . He uses the threat to us now, but adds, "I'll break your
> stomach first though, ye buggers. You'll get the effects of it later on. Wait
> until you're thirty and you'll see where you'll be." *(Ibid)*

Endearments of Pappie when sober, to his children, might be: "Ye
dirty pissabed . . . ye black-looking mulatto . . . ye bloody, gummy
toothless bitch, I'll get ye a set of teeth, won't I . . .[16] . . . Ye ugly bloody
corner-boy, you've a mouth like a bloody nigger."
If the tone of this speech makes the family tragedy seem more like
farce or cheap horror, one must remember that John Joyce carried out
his threats, for with the help of nature and heredity, his children did die.

---

[16]The Joyce children never had any dental care, and years later, for Jim in exile, the
dentist was a longed-for redeemer-figure; for how can one write when one has had
toothache since childhood?

This might be coincidence, but such a father threatening his sons had already a frightening intuitive resemblance to the furious primitive figure whose voice is heard in *Ulysses* and *Finnegans Wake*. The worst part of it was that if the father did attack the sons it was because he felt some real esteem for them, and because he knew that they were watching him and passing judgement. So he behaved like an angry Biblical patriarch, cursing them in his own fashion and prophesying that his own sufferings would fall upon them. Stanislaus reacted with a methodical campaign against his father, while James left home. John Joyce was criminally irresponsible; he was The Enemy to his family, and his sons mounted guard against him.

> We—Jim, Charlie, and I—relieve one another in the house like policemen as the girls are not safe in it with Pappie. A few nights ago, not knowing I was in—I do most of the duty—he attempted to strike some of them. He catches at the thing nearest to hand—a poker, plate, cup or pan —to fling. (29 March 1904)

And so the children would go elsewhere to look for advice or for their one fresh cup of tea for the week—a replacement which constitutes an indirect insult to the father. Uncle Willie Murray and his family lived at Bray; he was the very image of the wicked uncle, a strange character, cruel and frightening, who turned his own children into cowardly slaves and hypocrites. He was John Joyce's favourite target for insult and hostility,[17] and John would interminably state his wish to pulverise Uncle Willie (possibly because the latter was a living portrait of his own moral degeneracy). In their house there took place a typical incident illustrative of the two brothers' attitudes to Pappie:

> Why should I respect my father, and why, when Jim tells me how he stood up and left when Uncle Willie confessed to him that he hated Pappie, should his pride seem to me the working of an old-fashioned nobility in Jim's perverse and modern character—and a sign of its aristocracy? I envied him that impulse because I am envious. And yet Jim called Pappie "that little whore up in Cabra" before Ellwood for selling the piano on him. Pappie's mind too works towards Jim's with the same backward motion. I know Jim acted purely on impulse. Is it sometimes noble to act on prejudice? Or are they stupid? (*Dublin Diary*, p. 33)

[17]"Where are ye going, Cha-a-arlie? Down to the Murrays, I hope? . . . Going down to sponge on them for porter, eh? Sucking porter . . . You seem to be very fond of them . . . Ye can go and stay with the Murrays, then. Ye can go and sponge on them as your brother did." (*Dublin Diary*, p. 99.)

In fact Jim instinctively took up his father's defence, and he had to admit that his attitude was not "rational," hence it was insincere. Stannie himself recognised that even if he "did not feel the slightest real affection for him," yet there was still "a spark of admiration for his vitality."

This ambivalence of Stannie's feelings suggested to Jim the portrait of Simon Dedalus as seen by Stephen. The drunken brutality finds its place in one of the novellas, in which Joyce amalgamated Pappie and Uncle Willie, taking over Stannie's feelings of hatred in order to portray more effectively the brutal father.

"Grace" showed the comic side of John Joyce's drunken ways; "Counterparts" shows the obverse of that provisional redemption. We follow Farrington's degradation, beginning with a series of humiliations at the office where he works as a rather unsatisfactory lawyer's clerk; he is threatened with dismissal, and reacts by plunging deeper into guilt. He has not completed his work, and goes out for consolation in the form of a glass of beer. The damp dark night draws on, and his thoughts stray to "the glare and rattle of the public-house." He too is a dreamer, but his imagination goes no further than the nearest bar. Then he commits a supreme offence, quite worthy of John; the boss shouts at him, "Do you take me for a fool?" and he replies, "I don't think, sir, that that's a fair question to put to me." The reply would have made John into a hero, but Farrington has to apologise, and he knows now that "Mr. Alleyne would never give him an hour's rest; his life would be a hell to him." He finds consolation in relating his heroic reply to an audience of friends at Davy Byrne's, and then goes on to other pubs, unable to satisfy his vital thirst for freedom and personal integrity. He can but compensate for his feelings of inferiority by taking revenge on others who are hungrier than himself, or by imitating the power that he detests by acting like a tyrant in his own home. He takes revenge on Ireland and the Church, on Mr. Alleyne and on his own thirst, by beating his son. His wife is a little woman who bullies her husband when he is sober and is bullied by him when he is drunk. They have five children; and while Farrington is being humiliated and made to feel small in the street outside and at the office, Ada goes to church and the children stay in alone beside the dying fire; mother prays and father shouts. The end of Farrington's day is a grotesque caricature of the couple's misfortune and unhappy situation. It is difficult to match the destructive tones of the violent epiphany which is James's version of the savagery Stanislaus tells him:

—Where's your mother?
—She's out at the chapel.
—That's right. . . . Did she think of leaving any dinner for me?
—Yes, pa. I . . .
—Light the lamp. What do you mean by having the place in darkness? Are the other children in bed?

Then there follows a caricature of Pappie and of his trick of imitating other people's voices:

> The man sat down heavily on one of the chairs while the little boy lit a lamp. He began to mimic his son's flat accent, saying half to himself: "At the chapel. At the chapel, if you please!" When the lamp was lit he banged his fist on the table and shouted:
> —What's for my dinner?
> —I'm going . . . to cook it, pa, said the little boy.
> The man jumped up furiously and pointed to the fire.
> —On that fire! You let the fire go out! By God, I'll teach you to do that again!
> He took a step to the door and seized the walkingstick which was standing behind it.
> —I'll teach you to let the fire out! he said, rolling up his sleeve in order to give his arm free play.
> The little boy cried "O, pa!" and ran whimpering round the table, but the man followed him and caught him by the coat. The little boy looked about him wildly but, seeing no way of escape, fell upon his knees. . . .
> O, pa! he cried. Don't beat me, pa! And I'll . . . I'll say a *Hail Mary* for you . . . I'll say a *Hail Mary* for you, pa, if you don't beat me . . . I'll say a *Hail Mary* . . .

The confusion of values takes place at the lowest possible level, and we do not know which vice calls most for our indignation. The sadistic father is of course the first target, but Jim intervenes by introducing a whole network of attenuating circumstances. Because the world that day had administered a severe correction to Farrington and gradually made him unsure of his manliness; because he was beaten twice at the pub in a test of strength by "a stripling" (an Englishman, too, an acrobat and knockabout *artiste* at the Tivoli); because the two young women whom he ogled in the pub were also at the Tivoli and spoke with London accents; because he had been threatened with dismissal at work; because he seems to be losing everything, wife, job, strength, and even the compensations of vanity; because commerical Ireland, with its

Northern accent, had already betrayed him ten times that day; Farrington is not simply the unnatural father that he has become, but he is a
victim, alone in his anger and pain. Who from now on will treat him as
brave or strong? He seizes the walking-stick, to supplement his declining manliness, and strikes the only person who is weaker than he is, as
though unconsciously wanting to reach the depths of his degeneracy.
As he beats the little boy with his stick he loses the last refuge of his
shattered self-esteem, the possibility of self-respect. And Jim brings
everything back to his obsessive theme: it is all the woman's fault.
Farrington would be the most degraded model of Irishman, were it not
for Ada his wife; they form an archetypal pair. It is not a crime for Ada
to go to church, but it is a crime for her to go to church leaving her five
children at the mercy of a drunkard. We can imagine the scene that
Joyce did not need to write: the return of Mrs. Farrington, her religious
duty smugly accomplished, reassuring her conscience and her faith by
accusing the guilty husband of being a bad father. Mother had gone to
look after her soul's salvation, and Tom is left to make his father's
dinner; the two enemies look for some redemption in separation. Tom
prevents them from forgetting that they are supposed to be one; he is
a living proof of life's treachery. But even so, his integrity and innocence were broken long ago, he is already perverted by the morality
of guilt and conditioned by beatings; he is not one of those who grit their
teeth in order not to cry out in fear and pain, like Stephen Dedalus at
Clongowes, but Tom is destined to become another Little Chandler.
When he falls to his knees before Farrington, ready to ransom himself
with a prayer, one can no longer see where there can be any place for
charity or truth, between the panic and the punishment.

"Counterparts" could be seen as a naturalist or an anticlerical work,
a pretext for attacking the Church indirectly by showing it to be the
original guilty party; but in fact, Joyce invented none of it. The story was
told to him by Stanislaus, who records it in his diary. The scene in which
charity and pity are so severely wounded is perfectly true: "Alice told
me that on one occasion Bertie, then an infant of six or seven, begged
Uncle William not to beat him and promised to say a "hail Mary" for
him if he didn't."

Stanislaus reacts like a true Joyce child: "Such appalling cowardice on
both sides nearly made me ill. I laughed as if I had been hurt." Jim
would have said the same. Stannie contributes the epiphany-like incident and the violence, while Jim superimposes the cultural pattern and
adopts the story into his personal mythology. It remains true, though,

that the most unpleasant side of Farrington comes more directly from Uncle Willie than from Pappie; and this may be one of the reasons why parents are replaced by uncle and aunt in the novellas of childhood in *Dubliners.*

Jim always had a contempt for secrecy, and these notes were in the beginning ironical observations of slips, and little errors and gestures . . . by which people betrayed the very things they were most careful to conceal. "Epiphanies" were always brief sketches, hardly ever more than some dozen lines in length, but always very accurately observed and noted. . . . This collection served him as a sketchbook. . . . But it was in no sense a diary . . . Jim never kept a diary at any time of his life. That dreary habit was mine, and I have kept it up because I began it, as other people do cigarette smoking. (I consider my mania less harmful.) (*My Brother's Keeper*, p. 142)

When Stannie was beginning this "mania" as a reaction against a reality that did not include him and as a way of establishing some communication with his "Morose Maurice" character, Jim was spying out reality, hunting far beyond acts and affectations, revealing motives and cowardice behind the pretences. Stanislaus too was very busy in his inner world, seeking to glimpse the truth of being through the cracks of lies. Jim transcribed into his working notebooks some of Stannie's expressions, to be used in his works. His selection was guided by his appreciation of the accurately observed characteristic which neatly sums up the person; and he takes over ridiculous, furious or unhappy bits of Stannie's own thoughts and feelings as well. The portraits of Byrne, Cosgrave and Gogarty, of whom Stannie was always saying that they were treacherous and unreliable friends, are seen through the eyes of the vigilant and hostile Stannie rather than by Jim, who used them as models for Cranly, Mulligan, and Lynch. Stannie's warnings become the arguments Stephen uses to support his feeling that he is betrayed. Stannie's hatred for Gogarty was certainly more clearsighted than Jim's, but then Jim would cheerfully play the hypocrite.

Gogarty is treacherous in his friendship towards Jim. While never losing an opportunity of "keeping in touch" with celebrities to whom he is introduced, he affects to care nothing for them, or for his own reputation, or anyone else's. He affects to be careless of all things, and carries this out by acting generously towards Jim in regard to money. (*Dublin Diary*, p. 29)

Bryne, too, is seen by Stannie as he is, and furnishes the first sketch of Cranly:

J.F. Byrne . . . never thinks until someone begins to speak to him. Then he deliberates behind an impenetrable mask like a Cistercian bishop's face, and one is given to understand great mental activity. . . . The more subtle the conversation becomes, the more brutally he speaks. He is fond of the words "bloody" and "flamin." My latest name for him is "Thomas Square-Toes." *(Ibid.)*

These portraits are not the most considerable of the direct contributions. The most important is surely this page of inner monologue, improvised *con brio* by Stannie when alone and unhappy, and sounding like the first stammerings of a Bloom as he falls asleep:

It feels like as if I was smashing my foot off at the ankle. That's only imagination I know, but if I force the boot off I may injure my foot still more by straining it, and I won't be able to put a foot under me at all at all tomorrow. . . . Oh, if only I hadn't jumped at that ditch I'd have been all right by now and could have gone as I intended tomorrow. . . . Probably injuring my foot by walking on it, too. I don't care a curse. I want to go and I'll go. . . . I can't even press my foot on the floor; it strains my whole leg. I'm sick into the bargain, this thing has made me sick . . . See, I'm all trembling. I wish I had a light; this room of mine is so dark. I'll call Charlie? No . . . Poppie, then, or Eileen? Oh, I forgot; they're down at Fairview, out with the Murrays and Katsy, while I'm here. In any case I hate to have anyone attending on me. It seems to me peevish and weak. There! It's off, that wasn't so hard. My foot seems to be singing a song, a stinking, painful song, but I'll be into bed in a minute now—The pain isn't so intense, but the darkness here! the uncomfortableness of the bed! my unluckiness—I hate to be invalided up. *(Dublin Diary,* p. 109)

This page, where we hear a familiar voice, was written in 1905, when Joyce was away, but Stannie continuing to send him his notes.

We shall have a still higher opinion of this unwinding of Stannie's "stream of consciousness" when we see that it ends with a fragmentary meditation on the theme of genius, and finally loses itself in sleep; twenty-five years before the *Wake*, Finnegan could already be found, sleeping in Stanislaus' bed:

I'll think about something. What'll I think about? . . . Genius. Well, Genius! What's this everybody said about Genius? . . . How long? How long will this keep on? How stupid of me to forget that about genius, because it was good—clever— . . . this bed is very warm now—The skin seems tightening around my head—slowly! slow-ly! Oh! that was clever—wish I had said that—Aa-a-multitude—M—said that—What was his name? . . . I can't—I can't think—remember

—Dawn!—A—ah!—sink!—. . . . multitude—ude—And so, sleep. (*Dublin Diary*, p. 110)

Perhaps this passage was one of the reasons why Joyce gradually effaced Stannie from his works, never having been one to acknowledge his debts. In any case, the evolution of Stannie's role in Jim's work, from *Stephen Hero* to *Finnegans Wake* tells a tale of cannibalism; Joyce digests his brother, and although Stanislaus inspires many of the main characters, he is less and less visibly there.

Joyce Making Use of Stannie

In the first work, *Stephen Hero*, Stannie has a full existence, with the name he had invented for himself, and playing his accustomed part as the brother with his usual gruff but loyal humour. A bond of mutual comfort and of shared intellectual interests seems to develop between Morose Maurice and Stephen; within the Dedalus family "the free-thinker" and "the surly one" join their separate solitudes together:

> Maurice ate dry bread, muttered maledictions against his father and his father's creditors, practised pushing a heavy flat stone in the garden, and raising and lowering a broken dumb-bell, and trudged to the Bull every day that the tide served. In the evening, he wrote his diary or went out for a walk by himself. Stephen wandered about morning, noon and night. The two brothers were not often together. One dusky summer evening they walked into each other very gravely at a corner and both burst out laughing: and after that they sometimes went for walks together in the evening and discussed the art of literature. (*Stephen Hero*, p. 156)

With Maurice Stephen works out his theory of aesthetics, and Maurice is a lively and receptive disciple, although he is already succeeded in the last chapters, and replaced in *Portrait*, by Lynch, who has no real sympathy nor sincerity of reactions. The collaboration was as extensive as it was in real life; the two brothers made experiments and had fervent discussions on life, art and religion. Joyce quite obviously felt genuine gratitude and respect for Stanislaus at the time of *Stephen Hero*. This portrait of Maurice is a good and direct, yet tactful, likeness: Maurice is the younger brother, but full of wit and enthusiasm:

> Neither of the two youths had the least suspicion of themselves; they both looked upon life with frank curious eyes (Maurice naturally serving himself

with Stephen's vision when his own was deficient) and they both felt that
it was possible to arrive at a sane understanding of so-called mysteries if
one only had patience enough. On their way in every evening the heights
of argument were traversed and the younger boy aided the elder bravely
in the building of an entire science of esthetic. *(Ibid.)*

The relationship between the brothers was broken up by their parents, disturbed to see the elder boy corrupting his brother, although in
reality Maurice, like Stannie, was much more seditious than Stephen-
Jim. He was able to separate himself without terror and without crisis,
by himself, from the religion which Stephen found it so difficult to deny;
he was even able to exercise his dry, savage humour on it, and to show
a tranquil lack of respect which worried Stephen; Maurice's liberation
seems almost too easy—as Joyce thought about Stannie's. "He could not
admit that freedom from strict religious influences was desirable. It
seemed to him that anyone who could contemplate the condition of his
soul in such a prosaic manner was not worthy of freedom . . ." (*Stephen
Hero*, p. 56).

We note here again Joyce's characteristic need for a *bonum arduum;*
for him, freedom begins as a movement towards liberation, and is never
an acquired possession, but always precarious.

Chapters XXI and XXII of *Stephen Hero* show the gradual separation
of the brothers; Maurice is more or less downgraded, for having shown
selfish and petty inclinations and preoccupations and for having favoured dull and mediocre friends; he denounces their lack of good faith
and their need to dictate, but Stephen is sceptical. Although he is
neglected, Maurice remains faithful: he advises Stephen to publish his
poems. And then the brothers spend a calm and harmonious summer
talking and wandering over the North Bull rocks, away from the false
friends, on the very spot where Stephen was to have his vision of the
girl in *Portrait*. The role of Maurice was deliberately equivalent to that
of Stannie.

In *Portrait*, Maurice disappears completely and is absorbed into Stephen's personality, in order to emphasise Stephen's loneliness, but all
Stannie's thoughts are taken over and attributed to the artist; in particular Maurice's opposition to his father, and his militant anticlericalism,
are inherited by Stephen.

It is true that Stanislaus was fanatically opposed to fanaticism, and
that Joyce was a great lover of contradictions; it is true that the heretical
and angry rebellious son is not Joyce but the younger boy, but in the
portrait of the rebellious artist there is nothing at all representative

which does not derive something from Stannie's life in Dublin. His connection with the Jesuits, his refusal to obey the Church, and his bitter revolt against the family as the source of all oppression, are all shown as they were experienced by Stannie. It was he, and not Jim, who refused to do his Easter duty:

> On one of these strolls I announced out of the blue that I would refuse to do my Easter duty. Jim made a half-hearted attempt to dissuade me; he asked me,
> "Why?"
> "Because I don't believe it and I'm not going to pretend that I do," said I, excited in spite of myself. (*My Brother's Keeper*, p. 121)

Stannie is the model of the young rebel of daring opinions; in life he really carried out those great scandalous acts of independence and self-affirmation which Joyce only accomplished through stylistic or oral parodies. Joyce did not think in terms of absolutes, for the good reason that any morality of the absolute smacked too much of the church for his liking. Stannie had been accused of heresy by his master at school: "A master in Belvedere college said I was talking heresy once when I declared that I did not think any act was ever inspired by a simple motive. He said I should believe that Christ died for the pure love of us. I remained silent" (*Dublin Diary*, p. 46).

Stephen wanders alone and dreaming through the skies and streets of Dublin, just as Stannie used to wander for hours, gathering the same grey harvest of half-dead images and sounds.

> I took pleasure in observing the contrasts in colour—a study in grey. The dark grey of the church, the grey of the side-walk, the terra-cotta colour of the houses, the freshened green of the clipped grass in the gardens and of the leaves on the trees at the end of them, each holding a drop in its centre, the grey—dark and light—of the dresses of the women passing under them. The road was quiet and busy with trams and many people walking quickly. I took pleasure in the sameness of colour in the streets I went through, marking the slight change. The stone roadway and path now almost dry, the dark brown houses with one startling colour—the bright yellow front of a dairy—the druggists . . . in front, with dark ivy climbing over the house above the shop. . . . (*Dublin Diary*, p. 59)

Certain types of incident reported by Stannie are the originals of important scenes in *Portrait:*

> I remember . . . a young boy mitched and was found out. A Jesuit named Father Ryan . . . flogged him in the morning. Afterwards at lunch time

Ryan came over to him in the class-room, smiling and playful. Ryan seldom smiled and was never playful. "So you stayed away because you were afraid of me" he said, and began tickling the boy till he wiggled out of him and ran away. Ryan's complexion was pale . . . he became red. (*Dublin Diary*, 90–1)

Stephen's hatred for old age that boasts of its experience of life is also Stannie's: he used to repeat "I detest old age." The little old Cork man (the youthful grandfather) who makes a long speech on the greatness of Simon Dedalus (*Portrait*, p. 100) is the same as Pat Casey who figures in an epiphany-like page of Stannie's diary, overcome with drink and emotion, stammering out an epic drunken eulogy.

Yet again, Stannie is the originator of Stephen's last flamboyant break with his family: Stannie-Stephen denies his father completely. The scene which Mulligan recalls at the beginning of *Ulysses*, where Stephen is rebuked for not having knelt down at the bedside of his dying mother, did in fact take place, but under different circumstances: when May Joyce was in a coma, Uncle John Murray ordered the two brothers to kneel down and pray. They paid no attention, but the scene remained in Jim's mind, while for Stannie religion had long ceased to be a matter of consolation or of remorse; he was able to separate his real grief from any meaning which might be given to that refusal. Yet the brothers used to think bitterly that their mother should have rebelled.

Apart from this, there are scarcely any traces of Stannie left in *Ulysses;* any serious heroism has been eliminated by Stephen's sarcasm, and there only remain the melancholy observations Stannie used to make when preoccupied by his physical ailments. The use made of him has degenerated from the spiritual plane to the corporeal. His idiosyncrasies were to flower in Mr. Bloom, and caricature was already on the way.

Stannie was the first living version of Bloom at his most paralysed, inhibited and unfortunate: he dreams of happiness as Bloom dreams of Palestine, and in his diary speaks like a romantic Bloom. "I love listening to barrel-organs, not piano-organs. . . . They remind me of the south of France, of oranges, of Spain, that I want to live in."

His absurd habit of watching himself in mirrors or of attributing his minor ailments to physiological causes, and his irritating way of explaining everything, all produced a pseudo-scientific sort of observation which could easily be Bloom's, like this passage taken from the diary Joyce used in the composition of *Stephen Hero*, and quoted in his Pola notebook: "I have been unhappy all day: I find that the cause is I have been walking on my heels instead of from the ball of my foot."

There is a whole page where Stannie examines in detail his stomach troubles, and it is difficult to tell whether this is meant to be comical or sad. Again, his thoughts of gallant adventure which never go any futher than an exchange of looks seem early versions of Bloom's daydreams in "Calypso" and "Nausicaa":

> On the Whitworth Road beyond the deep channel where the railroad runs to my right, a nurse is playing with a black dog in the grounds of the Drumcondra Hospital. I can see that she is pretty and young. I would like to be near her, to—But the wish is impossible. Therefore let it pass. . . .
>
> I have noticed many brides and women with child at this time. Is it possible that human beings couple and parturate at seasons, like birds and animals?. . . .
>
> Sunday is the worst day of the week—Dull Sunday. And my Sunday, wherein all the dullness of the week is outdone! That nurse! I would like to lie with her in a bed, now, at mid-day, to see her almost stripped in the daylight. Mid-day lechery! But where's the use of this? Though to be sure mid-day lechery is not unusual. (*Dublin Diary*, pp. 79–80)

Another time he invents a new way of spending a honeymoon. "The happy couple spends a week in bed." His metaphysical reflections are worthy of Bloom's digressions in "the Underworld":

> Death is a very complete ending, an irrelevant, unanswerable, brutal argument, a decision at last in an unready life. There will be the memory of me when I am gone, for a little while. What good is remembrance to me? I shall not remember. The additions to my life and knowledge were daily getting longer, but death has drawn two neat red lines under them and written down nought as the total. (*Dublin Diary*, p. 56)

In fact, Stannie was capable of humour at his own expense; but Joyce preferred to take him seriously, in order to extract full enjoyment from the grotesque aspect of his private thoughts.

Joyce immortalised Stannie as Mr. Duffy, a rather unsympathetic character in *Dubliners,* though having the politeness to christen him James. Not only is Mr. Duffy's personality created from a number of Stannie's little idiosyncrasies, but also the moment of revelation when he discovers that he is nothing more than a dead man is adapted from a moving incident in Stannie's life, taken over, disfigured and desecrated by the unscrupulous Joyce.

In 1901, Stannie had made the brief acquaintance of a lady, one evening at the concert at the Rotunda—an encounter which had no real consequences for him, but which seemed important enough to be written up in his diary. A brown-eyed handsome woman of about forty had been persistently watching him, for no particular reason. She had spoken to him, freely and without ulterior motive. At the end she had shaken hands with him and smiled. Why should he recall this pleasant, unequivocal incident? Stannie was too clearheaded to imagine that he was irresistibly attractive, but that evening a lovely woman had looked at him and spoken to him as though he really were somebody. The lady had not known that he was the brother of Another, but had spoken really and truly to him. Stanislaus notes this down as an epiphany of his own, as something that gives him reality.[18]

He makes a note of it and Jim takes it from him. He steals Stannie's moment of reality from him, and turns it into "A Painful Case". Everything is changed: Jim is present, spying on Stannie and the lady, but instead of a serious young man confronted by a benevolent and beautiful unknown, he sees a stylised type, a man who is lifeless and destructive of life. As in the romances, he is the person whom Jim consigns to the very bottom of the scale of noble values; and, as in the fables, Stannie is the person who pulls the chestnuts out of the fire—as it happens, the fire of hell. But they are a reversed image of Don Quixote and Sancho, for it is Sancho-Stannie who attacks the windmills and who acts out the fate of Mr. Duffy, while the knight has a strong sense of the ridiculous and knows the futility of attacking windmills.

It all happens as though Don Quixote and Sancho had exchanged masks, and the parody is not a matter of literature but of reality. Jim and Stannie carry out their picaresque journeys in the traditional fashion, as companions, but the Doleful Countenance is that of Sancho-Stannie, whom his brother would sometimes ask, in his usual rough way, "to please turn my face away as it bored him." He would sometimes add, even more cruelly, "I wouldn't like to be a woman and wake up to find your 'goo' (face) on the pillow beside me in the morning."

It will be understood that such remarks did nothing to smooth the young brother's path: "Women admire most in a man moral courage,

[18]"The concert hall was crowded and among the audience I was one of the most enthusiastic. After a while I became aware that a lady who was sitting beside me looked at me several times. She was a handsome, dark-haired woman, between thirty and forty years old. I noticed her fair skin and the large pupils and the very pure whites of her brown eyes. . . . At the end she shook hands with me, smiling placidly. Afterwards I met her by chance at least once that I remember. She stopped me in the street; I was not yet eighteen and should not have had the audacity to accost her." (*My Brother's Keeper*, pp. 173–4.)

and I wish most of all to be worthy to be admired, yet reject the wish itself as unworthy when I have framed it." Stanislaus would like to be a hero, and worthy of admiration, but unfortunately, this means wishing to be Jim, and being ashamed of oneself; thus, by an act of inverted courage and a desperate sort of pride, Stanislaus declares himself a coward, and decides that for him the point of honour will consist in daring to be himself: "I do not permit myself to force my nature to exaggerated ways and to imitation of the brave."

Thus, in order to be his own master, Stanislaus perseveres, cultivates himself as he is, unlike Jim, mediocre, unhappy and completely lost; he does not know himself, he is blind and cannot tell who he is. He often repeats this theme; and Joyce takes pleasure in creating as his double Mr. Duffy, who is even more lonely, blind, and self-centred.

> Mr. Duffy is the type of the male celibate. . . . but he is also intended to be a portrait of what my brother imagined I should become in middle age. The portraiture has "the grim Dutch touch" he spoke of. He has used many characteristics of mine in composing Mr. Duffy, such as intolerance of drunkenness, hostility to socialism, and the habit of noting short sentences on a sheaf of loose pages pinned together. The title Jim suggested for these distillations of tabloid wisdom was *Bile Beans*. (*My Brother's Keeper*, p. 174)

> A white mist is falling in slow flakes. The path leads me down to an obscure pool. Something is moving in the pool; it is an arctic beast with a rough yellow coat. I thrust in my stick and as he rises out of the water I see that his back slopes towards the croup and that he is very sluggish. I am not afraid but thrusting at him often with my stick drive him before me. He moves his paws heavily and mutters words of some language which I do not understand.

Commenting on this epiphany,[19] Stanislaus explains that he is himself the beast which Joyce tries to push away with his stick in the dream. Jim was not afraid, but wanted to be free of the beast; he always interpreted his own dreams, and since his adolescence had been in the process of transforming his brother into Shaun. In "A Painful Case," James Duffy "lived at a little distance from his body, regarding his own acts with doubtful side-glances." Stannie-Duffy was not yet the enemy; Jim had not yet turned him completely into Shaun in order to be all the more fully Shem. But between this epiphany and the novella can be traced one of the most ambiguous and complex stages of the relation-

[19] *Workshop*, p. 26, from Buffalo MS. Dated 1901 by Stanislaus.

ship between Jim and his Likeness. Stannie admired Jim for knowing how to conduct his life, but Jim rather scorned Stannie, and let him know this indirectly, because Stannie was afraid of life and shunned the signs of living. The key words of "A Painful Case" are "touch" and "together," with their opposite, "alone."

Joyce has turned the bank-clerk into a hermit figure who lives at Chapelized without imagining that the name means "the chapel of Iseut." Mr. Duffy is writing the life of Mr. Duffy. Physically he resembles Stannie. He lives "in an old sombre house," and from his windows can see "the disused distillery" or the "shallow river" that bounds the dead world that is Dublin. He lives "as far as possible from the city of which he was a citizen," and as far as possible from real life. He only has contact with members of his family when one of them dies; escorting them to the cemetery is a social duty which is quite safe, for there is no risk of being contaminated by life.

His room is arranged like an austere chapel, with everything in it black or white, and strictly functional. Mr. Duffy is alone with his books and his notes, the desk acting as his confessional, and from time to time he writes down another sentence: the confession is not a long one, since he has virtually no sins to conceal. From the desk escapes the smell of an over-ripe apple. Mr. Duffy lives in the society of people like himself: a poet preoccupied with himself (the complete Wordsworth) and a destructive man, *Michael Kramer*.[20] Mr. Duffy died long ago without noticing the fact; yet some part of himself, the writer, has a vague idea that this is the case, for in an ironical moment he had, like Stannie, pasted "the headline of an advertisement for *Bile Beans . . .* on to the first sheet" of his diary.

> He had an odd autobiographical habit which led him to compose in his mind from time to time a short sentence about himself containing a subject in the third person and a predicate in the past tense. He never gave alms to beggars, and walked firmly, carrying a stout hazel. (This is Stannie's own step, "I walk with long, confident steps, but my soul within is bent with weariness.")[21]

Mr. Duffy only exists in the third person and in the past tense: "There

[20]Joyce had also given Mr. Duffy some of his own characteristics, such as his interest in Nietzsche and his translation of *Michael Kramer*, in order to raise his intellectual level.

[21]"I reject . . . adventures—such adventures as one meets with by drinking and going the round of the town, and prefer rather to remain discontented and barren than to satisfy a false appetite." (*Dublin Diary*, p. 33.)

was once Mr. Duffy," and that suffices. He is free from doubts and from "physical or mental disorder." He walks firmly, practises a sensible economy—when one is so little extant, one cannot waste *anything* without risking annihilation. He is a cashier and a man of orderly life, and in his world there are no unnecessary gestures to make. Yet Mr. Duffy has an enemy, his own body. He distrusts it, and keeps careful watch on it, for it is the body that obliges one to stay in contact with other people, for the flesh has its needs, and must be fed. To eat one must sit down at table, and there one risks making acquaintances or at least contacts. In order to avoid any encounter of this kind, Mr. Duffy has arranged his life discreetly around solitude.[22] Or rather, he has organised his absence from life by giving it the form of order. His life rolls out evenly and ritually: his lunch is always beer and arrowroot biscuits, his only dissipation the music of Mozart.

Like Stanislaus, he wanders the streets alone. He is a frugal man, accepting the conventions because they make for orderliness; yet between the first person and the third person, between his confessing personality and his bank-clerk self, he leads a second, mysterious existence, called his "spiritual life." Nobody has access to it. In the secret life of James Duffy, everything is possible: it might even be possible for him to be a hero. In any case he would rob his bank, "in certain circumstances. . . ."

In this world of possibilities one day Stanislaus had met a lady, and James Duffy meets Mrs. Sinico. She has an exotic name (Triestine, in fact), dark blue eyes, and a firm gaze. She sits beside the virtuous Duffy at a concert. The concert hall is the only place where the hero can feel truly in communion with himself, for Mr. Duffy's great concern in life is "to live his spiritual life without any communion with others." The encounter with the lady brings Duffy into the realm of "adventure," and without knowing it he has found his *Araby*. The voyage begins, by proxy, for while Captain Sinico is tossing on the high seas between Dublin and Holland, Mr. Duffy is oscillating between communion and confession. Speech constitutes the first step towards alienation, because in such expansiveness one may give (and thus lose) oneself. Mr. Duffy ventures forth, encouraged by the lady's "full bosom" and "almost maternal solicitude." One does not mistrust a mother figure, after all. And thus our hero falls into the trap:

"Little by little he entangled his thoughts with hers. He lent her

[22]"I prefer idling alone, therefore I hate 'knocking about town'." (*Ibid.*, p. 38).

books, provided her with ideas, shared his intellectual life with her. She listened to all . . . With almost maternal solicitude she urged him to let his nature open to the full: she became his confessor." Mr. Duffy has come back into Dublin by the back door, as it were, without realising the fact.[23] With the adulation and approval of a woman who hangs on his every word, he opens his soul to the air, like an exotic plant. Mrs. Sinico is warmth personified, and creates an atmosphere of fullness. This seems like happiness, even like love; but Mrs. Sinico is not the beloved object. She is simply the go-between for James Duffy's "I" and his "self," and through her the two parts of his personality become joined. Thanks to her ardent and motherly kindness, Mr. Duffy can "listen to the sound of his own voice" in her discreet little room at night.

His soul becomes transfigured, grows wings; his voice is both his own and that of some mysterious impersonal self:

> "He thought that in her eyes he would ascend to an angelical stature; and, as he attached the fervent nature of his companion more and more closely to him, he heard the strange impersonal voice which he recognised as his own, insisting on the soul's incurable loneliness. We cannot give ourselves, it said: we are our own."

Our own, indeed, for Mr. Duffy and himself belong to no-one but Mr. Duffy.

But Mrs. Sinico is only an ordinary woman; the blue-eyes mother turned out to be nothing more. She even dares to touch the angelic Duffy, and this contact is for him a sacrilege; someone has dared to treat him as though he were a man of flesh and blood, and the charm is broken. She is punished for having renewed the sin of Eve in desiring the forbidden fruit, and driven from Paradise. Duffy returns to his orderly, neat room, and Mrs. Sinico leaves the park where they had had their first rendez-vous. "Every bond is a bond to sorrow," he said, borrowing this aphorism from Stannie's diary.

His life resumes its normal, deadly course. Mr. Duffy writes in his confessional notebook: "Love between man and man is impossible because there must not be sexual intercourse, and friendship between man and woman is impossible because there must be sexual intercourse."

Time passes and Duffy perseveres. He has definitively renounced the warmth of human contacts; as Stephen Dedalus pointed out, did not

---

[23]Cf. Stephen, "Cannot repent. This means to leave church by back door of sin and re-enter through the skylight of repentance." (*Portrait*, p. 249.)

Christ himself repudiate his mother? The communion without religion is a communion with himself beside the water-carafe in the restaurant. Communication between Duffy and the world is re-established by the evening paper that he reads with his dinner. Time passes, laid out between silence, absence, and the written word, and the inner landscape is reduced to a few pages of writing.

Is Mr. Duffy happy when he is again "disincarnated"? He seemed to be at peace with himself, when Mrs. Sinico reappeared, like a vampire tempting him in the desert of himself. This is a second terrible encounter, which shakes the order of his universe, and is shocking a second time, coming as it does unexpectedly. The first time she had taken his hand, and this time she strikes his eyes: she is there in the *Mail*, quite unmistakably. Again she bursts upon his world—she is the flesh, and this time is manifested as her mutilated body. Mr. Duffy loses his appetite —the ignoble sensations of life sicken him. He reads "Death of a Lady at Sidney Parade." Mrs. Sinico has been knocked down by a train, and it seems to be an accident. No-one is to blame but Mrs. Sinico herself: She "had been in the habit of crossing the lines late at night"; she "had been in the habit of going out at night to buy spirits." She had not actually been killed by the train: "Death . . . due to shock and sudden failure of the heart." "No blame attached to anyone."

So, his "soul-mate" had only been human after all! Worse, even, she had been subject to human weaknesses. Mr. Duffy feels befouled:

> The whole narrative of her death revolted him and it revolted him to think that he had ever spoken to her of what he held sacred. . . . Just God, what an end! Evidently she had been unfit to live, without any strength of purpose, an easy prey to habits, one of the wrecks on which civilization has been reared. But that she could have sunk so low!

We know that Stanislaus' horror of alcoholism verged on real terror. Mr. Duffy is "pure," and alone in his pure chapel he congratulates himself on such a virginity: he is safe. But now he really meets Mrs. Sinico for the first time, and everything moves very quickly, because time has become disjointed. The dead woman's hand stops the regular progress of time present and impels Duffy's soul towards memory: "As the light failed and his memory began to wander he thought her hand touched his." Death takes Duffy by the hand and abolishes the distance between the man and himself. He flees, and the cold air creeps into the sleeves of his coat. The presence of the dead woman freezes his flesh; Mrs. Sinico is taking her revenge. Poe could not do better in making our flesh creep. And at last Mr. Duffy realises that there was a man, long ago, whom the Superman eliminated; and the man is cold, and afraid, his stomach hurts and his whole body is painfully beginning to cry out and to exist. His habits give way; it is now a question of life or death. He drinks a hot punch, and then another, proposing a funeral toast to the dead woman. Too late he makes his communion, tasting the drink which had led his soul's companion down to the railway line. Now he goes completely off the rails. Is there time for him to change his way of life? Joyce uses all his reserves of imagery for the theme of the "path laid out for one," which will appear as a leitmotif in *Portrait* and *Ulysses.*

But Mr. Duffy is dead: he never lived, only talked and scribbled words. To live is to exist for and with someone, and Mrs. Sinico was ready to give her life up to him, if only he had said the word. Instead, he had simply talked to himself in her presence, using her as a sounding-board. He was very much afraid of being real, and had abolished every concrete trace of existence, but only finds this out when he reads the narrative of his own death: refusal, routine, ritual, in the end nothing. Nothing is over now, because nothing ever began. And by dramatic irony, now she is dead Mrs. Sinico initiates Duffy into the meaning of life. Duffy learns that he is dead, and as he makes this discovery, in the lonely park where he had left her, feeling that she would prove a deadly enemy, he meets again in memory the womanly ghost.

> He entered the Park by the first gate and walked along under the gaunt trees. He walked through the bleak alleys where they had walked four years before. She seemed to be near him in the darkness. At moments he seemed to feel her voice touch his ear, her hand touch his. He stood still to listen.

For the first and the last time, he is listening to a voice other than his own. For one time only he is letting himself be touched by someone else. "He felt his moral nature falling to pieces," and opened his eyes. Death and night are all about him, but Mrs. Sinico, because she has been alive, is present, and has left some traces of herself in the memory. No-one will remember him, though. It was necessary for a woman to die for Mr. Duffy to understand that his neat room had always been his tomb and that his refusals were only a way of signing his death-warrant. And no-one will read his epitaph. He has nothing left but his useless body, no-one wants him, and he is "outcast from life's feast." He has banished himself. In a last epiphany, everything is shown to him and taken away again, in the brief moment when his weak voice enters upon silence and the last echo of the name Sinico dies away: love, life and happiness pass him by in the dark. In the shadow of the park wall he sees "human figures," who remind him of how life begins. The "exotic plant" of his angelic nature fades at once, and although Dublin glows invitingly in the cold night, Duffy is far away from Dublin. He has passed from the white of non-existence to the black of absolute self-loss. The river is grey, life is hateful to him, and he watches the furtive loves down by the wall. Joyce gives him an ephemeral hallucination, heavy with sexual symbolism:

> Beyond the river he saw a goods train winding out of Kingsbridge Station, like a worm with a fiery head winding through the darkness, obstinately and laboriously. It passed slowly out of sight; but still he heard in his ears the laborious drone of the engine reiterating the syllables of her name.
>
> He turned back the way he had come, the rhythm of the engine pounding in his ears. He began to doubt the reality of what memory told him. He halted under a tree and allowed the rhythm to die away. He could not feel her near him in the darkness nor her voice touch his ear.

The train steams past, but Mr. Duffy has refused the journey and the merchandise of life. In a last spasm, he has a hallucination, changing the gourd for the tree, death for life, the killing train for the departing train, and the pen for the fiery-headed worm that signifies escape and freedom, both death and life. Then he hears nothing more; he feels that he is alone; and he takes up his way of death again.

What distinguishes Stannie from his caricature is the lucidity which Mr. Duffy only reaches with great difficulty and which he regrets when it is too late. After all, even if Duffy does speak like Stanislaus, the latter is only eighteen and hates himself, while Duffy is old enough to be his father and adores himself. There is still time for Stannie to escape, to Spain or Italy. One cannot really see how some critics have considered Duffy as an imaginary James caught in the deadly net of Dublin: Harry Levin makes the "timid socialist clerk" a *persona* of Jim, for the reason that he is translating Hauptmann's play *Michael Kramer,* as Joyce himself had once done;[24] Magalaner argues in the same way, in a long and interesting study comparing Duffy with Michael Kramer, and emphasising the irony of the translator who cannot see the character in the play signalling to him that he is in danger. In reality Hauptmann and Nietzsche are, as Stannie himself says, introduced into the little cave in Chapelized where Duffy imagines he lives (when in fact he is dead and

---

[24]M. Magalaner, *Time of Apprenticeship, The Fiction of Young James Joyce* (New York, 1959), pp. 35–7; Harry Levin, *James Joyce, a Critical Introduction* (London, 1960), p. 42.

rotting), in order to serve as prophets who are unheeded. If Jim is present in person here, it must be as an evil omen and no more.

Duffy springs from Stanislaus' moral unhappiness, augmented by the pettiness of the Dublin mind and emphasised by the subtle irony of Joyce. When Magalaner says that Duffy's attitude to women is the same as that of Stephen Dedalus, and hence is Joyce's own, it must be emphasised that the equation is not simply between Stephen and James Joyce, but between Stephen and both of the brothers; the withdrawals and frustrations are Stannie's, and the daring deeds and satisfactions are Jim's. Jim wants to live, and Stanislaus, at the age of eighteen, is afraid of dying; in the end both brothers escape, the one by wanting to live, the other by willing himself to survive, the eldest exaltedly and the younger apprehensively. Stanislaus has not progressed beyond the elementary fears of not being sure of his existence, of not liking himself, of suppression. Life is so far away from him that he is still trying to say "I am," and this is why any giving or any creation of links with others is impossible to him. He feels that he is so poor that any diminution of the self is a perilous threat. Stannie and Duffy are types of the centripetal man, of the person who has so much trouble in keeping himself sufficiently extant that he is constantly in search of himself. Others are only to be encountered if they make no demands on such a person.

The echo of Stannie's voice has no warmth in it, one must admit; the real voice is infinitely more vibrant and nostalgic. The younger brother's powerless will has become Duffy's selfish desire for power. Again, Joyce completed his definition of the only life desirable by including the notion of the necessity of sin, but found something immaculate about his brother which in the world of artistic creation would act as a sterilising agent. Jim always claimed that by falling one learns to fly, and discerned true cleanliness only beyond befoulment. He reproached Stannie for following so obstinately a virtue in which he did not believe; yet Stannie was not wrong when he saw the experimental side of Jim's zeal for "living," and when he perceived in Jim's rejection of the moral sense an attempt to manifest his personal freedom by exercising it in wrongdoing. For Stannie, the will was the same, but it took the opposite alternative: where Jim "did wrong," Stannie introduced virtue in spite of everything, a procedure which never failed to annoy Jim who considered it as hypocrisy. It may be, indeed, that this virtue became a mask from the time when Stannie ceased to be wholly devoted to his Cain, the time when Joyce was trying to reverse their roles:

In his love of life I find something experimental, something aesthetical
... If he was not an artist first, his talent would trouble him constantly like
semen. For the things that go to make up life, glory, politics, women (I
exclude whores), family wealth, he has no care ... His nature is naturally
antagonistic to morality. Morality bores and irritates him. He tries to live
on a principle of impulse. The justification of his conduct is the genuine-
ness of the impulse. The Principle is itself an impulse, not a conviction.
... He demands an absolute freedom to do as he pleases. He wants the
freedom to do wrong whether he uses it or no, and for fear he should be
deceiving himself by any back thought he is vindicating his right to ruin
himself. He accepts no constraint, not even self-constraint, and regards a
forced growth, however admirable in itself, as an impossible satisfaction.
(*Dublin Diary*, pp. 68–9)

Hence the litany to Stannie as Shaun pronounced by a chorus of
twenty-eight charming girls in *Finnegans Wake* (p. 237) as a perverse
prayer to the pretender to virtue. Here Stanislaus is in chains, a confessor, pure, puerile, stainless, useless, rustless, everything Joyce detested:
"Enchainted, dear sweet Stainusless, dearer dearest, we herehear,
aboutobloss, Ocoelicola, thee salutamt, unclean you art not. Out-
caste thou are not ... You are pure. You are pure. You are in your
purity ..."

Part Two: Private and
Public Heroism

VII. Opposing Ideologies

The Formative Years as History

Joyce's formative years are defined not by attachment to a culture or a tradition but by the troubled intellectual climate of pre-revolutionary Ireland, and more particularly by the social and historical conditions, in which he was deeply involved. His first works are polemic, and stake out a lucid and sometimes violent personal opposition to the accepted intellectual solutions. From the age of eighteen, Joyce made a clean break with his contemporaries and chose his own way; but this was not a choice suggested by some sudden romantic inspiration, nor the choice made by the typical adolescent who only feels master of himself when engaged in furious opposition to the world. Joyce's attitude was the product of a number of experiments and encounters with his surroundings, the logical conclusion of a dialogue which he had argued out passionately because everything was at stake, art, society, history, the role of the artist, the future of Ireland, as well as the fate of style and aesthetic philosophy; and one can follow him step by step through this process of self-formation.

On February 2, 1882, James Augustine Joyce was born, at Rathgar, into a basically middle-class family.

In 1882 the Red Irish, the "Invincibles," assassinated two Englishmen, representatives of Her Britannic Majesty, Lord Cavendish, the Secretary for Ireland, and his under-secretary Burke, in Phoenix Park. In that same Phoenix Park fifty years later was to take place the slaugh-

ter of "literature," like a ritual memory of the murder of 1882. It is the
scene of Earwicker's crime, the transgression of the father, in *Finnegans Wake;* and the passage from political murder to sexual aggression
here typified is a perfect symbol of Joyce's relationship with history.

Joyce's birth in 1882 sets him in a world which is still seeking its own
identity, a world defined by violence and despair. Later in life, he could
not be unaware that he was born in the year of the Phoenix Park
murders, that his birth was already marked by disorder and parricide
as Ireland tried to shake off the fatherly oppressor, even at the cost of
blood and terror. Alienation must be the fate of a man born in such a
country; his compatriots' presence weighs heavy on him, and a common
destiny is unavoidable: one begins as an *angry* Irishman. The youthful
Joyce had to begin his own life under the same yoke that all the young
men bore; it was impossible to say "I am Joyce" without first saying "I
am an Irishman," and the first person was treated as a kind of plural,
"we," against a "them"—the English. And for a Joyce from Cork, the
English are the imperialists, the "Romans," the usurpers who ruin and
hinder Ireland from developing a modern economical structure, who
starve it body and soul. They are foreigners. And they speak English as
though it belonged to them by right. At the University the young man
learns suddenly that to be Irish is only to be one among all the others:
English is the language of his people and his father, a lively and picturesque language, and yet his English masters query the authenticity
of his vocabulary. This was the worst of all; it was to make Joyce into
the greatest writer in modern English, at the expense of the language
itself; knowing its resources thoroughly, he was to fling sixteen thousand
different words into his *Ulysses,* as though issuing a challenge to all his
contemporaries for whom it was "the mother tongue," for as an Irishman he felt ill-treated, exploited, and despoiled. This language, that of
the masters, built up throughout centuries of English history and culture, gave access to a culture and a history in which the Irishman played
no part, except that of despised and down-trodden victim. Ireland had
been speaking English for centuries, and its past was a closed book to
the Irish themselves, because they were no longer speaking their own
language; they had only the language of the present, of their loss and
humiliation. The child who learned to speak English knew that it involved a loss of dignity for him. The *Portrait* opens with this double
birth, that of the child's consciousness awakening to the adult world,
and simultaneously that of the son, disinherited like his father, coming
to face the aggressive power that is England.

The child who begins to speak is guilty straightaway, from the very fact of speaking; and whether he likes it or not he has to make use of a foreign language, betraying his own origins. The young Joyce's relations with the language were already charged with sinister overtones, and this may explain the importance he attributes at the beginning of his autobiographical meditation to a capture of the world by means of words; this is why the epiphany was at first a wish to perceive reality and at the same time a desire to do without words, although as the language crystallised into epiphany it exerted an irresistible attraction on the young artist. Phrases petrify into objects, so that he who perceives them can possess and make use of them.

Lacking a national life of his own and a living language, the Irishman has only the Gaelic as means of self-assertion. But it is unfortunately the language of a dead civilisation, mortal and deadly, giving off the dulling, paralysing charms of a legendary, unreal past, haunted by fairies and primitive heroes of superstition. It has no more currency in a modern state. The young Irishmen of the turn of the century championed it with all the fanatic ardour of their nationalism, without realising that if by chance they succeeded in their intentions and managed to rehabilitate the Gaelic they would be more cut off than before from the English-speaking world; and this was what Joyce pointed out, in contradiction of Yeats and the Gaelic League. The young intellectuals who dreamed of re-establishing a literary tradition interrupted for centuries, by means of the language of the bards, were creating an art of "revival," but it only revived a culture which was not viable, because confined to prose, nourished on romanticism and idealism, and tending towards occult symbolism, which could never be the concern of more than a chosen few. W. B. Yeats was writing at this time against the spirit of the Irish republic and turning towards the old dream of "the isle of saints," without realising it; and his revolutionary poems of 1916 would be written in English.[1]

The young Joyce repudiated his inheritance with a sure sense of political reality and national psychology; his wish was to make Ireland participate again in history, because he could see that the balance of power was such that his country must make contact with Europe or perish. The first part of his work is still to some degree an appeal to the Irish and a demonstration that they are not necessarily the forgotten islanders they have chosen to be. But his words apparently fell on stony ground, and Europe made itself without Eire; the Irish returned to their

---

[1] See Ellmann, *Eminent Domain* (New York, O.U.P., 1967); and Kain, *Dublin in the Age of William Butler Yeats and James Joyce* (Oklahoma U.P., 1962), for these themes.

saints and superstitions. Joyce, who had tried to bring his art forward into the modern world, became the heretic whose books were banned; by contradiction and opposition, he can be seen as giving sense and direction to the obstinate retrograde motion of his country.

Inversely, it must be emphasised, in condemning him so strongly, his country gave him the chance to set himself up in all his individuality and originality as opposed to the society whose system of values he rejected.

If he claimed to have no wish to be the bard or ideologist of his race (a task for which he was by no means suited), he still used irreconciliable Ireland as a background to the action in his work. He grasped the world in its objectivity. And the more marked the contrast was, the more the meaning of contemporary attitudes was emphasised.

When George Russell (A.E.) rejected his work from the slim volume *New Songs*[2], which contained a selection of poems by the white hopes of the new Irish literature, Joyce was obscurely offended, and delegated his resentment to the Stephen of *Ulysses*. But at the same time he made much of his own superiority over "all these tearful Irish writers." Against them he set his heroic solitude; for in Ireland heroism was seen in devotion to a group. In exile he could be unique in his strongmindedness.

He was not invited into the poets' circle—because they knew he would refuse, he implies.

The First Poem

No honourable and sincere man, said Stephen, has given up to you his life and his youth and his affections from the days of Tone to those of Parnell, but you sold him to the enemy or failed him in need or reviled him and left him for another. And you invite me to be one of you. I'd see you damned first. (*Portrait*, p. 202)

In 1889, Joyce was seven years old, when Parnell the hero, the only strong Irish figure, was accused in a newspaper campaign of having approved of the Phoenix Park murders. Everyone turned against him and hunted him down; Ireland, "the old sow that eats her farrow,"

[2]Dublin and London, 1904, poems by Russell and his circle.

(*Portrait*, p. 203) finished him off in one mouthful, and the Church planned and stagemanaged his fall. For ten years Parnell had been carrying on an affair with the wife of Captain O'Shea; the army, the middle-class and the guardians of morality discovered this and brought the hero down to a sordid end. His second-in-command, the faithful Healy, turned his back on Parnell because his fear of public scorn and scandal was stronger than his loyalty to a cause which had suddenly become human. Parnell died in 1891, insulted, rejected, alone, a year after his marriage to Kitty, and that death made him into a tragic hero.[3]

James Joyce was nine years old when Parnell died, Ireland's spokesman and hope, "the king," as he was called, dying the death of an outcast; and then came the real "dispersion," as though the people had lost their prophet. This made Joyce decide on the sort of person he must be. In a conflict or in a war, he would choose moral solitude, even at the cost of—a prudent exile. Joyce chose Parnell and rejected Healy, and wrote his first poem. Already he felt disgust for public opinion, and issued his challenge. At nine years old he learnt what he would declare at fifty, that life offers the temptation of cowardice, that fear destroys, and that the best may be betrayed by their own brothers. The title of this lost poem was, significantly, *Et tu, Healy!* The first exclamation, the first cry the child gives is Caesar's *Tu quoque, mi fili:* the bitterness is already there, and the rhetoric. Joyce makes use of the historical allusion, as he was later to set culture between reality and the work.

Joyce's first written work was thus a poem on history, "involved," high minded, idealistic, and perhaps even sincere (for John Joyce was a convinced supporter of Parnell). And the child grew up in an Ireland infected by the memory of Parnell. The experience of death was already intimately connected with the ideas of falling, loss of hope, and the tragic ironies of history.

People tend too often to forget Joyce's personal integrity, which never gave way to easy compromise, whatever the cost. Joyce had a serious view of the publicly spoken word, so much so that he was first an orator, an advocate, before becoming a writer. Far from enmeshing himself in the obscure retreats of sentimentality and being satisfied with the contemplation of a safely protected inner world, he was always in touch, open to the outside world, taking sides and supporting causes.

[3]For Parnell's history, see Kain, *op. cit.*, pp. 114–7. Parnell's affair with Kitty O'Shea had long been public knowledge, but Kitty's divorce in 1890 sparked off the scandal, in which morality was used as a political instrument. Cf. J. Abels, *The Parnell Tragedy* (Bodley Head, 1966); E. S. L. Lyons, *The Fall of Parnell* (London, 1960); Tony Gray, *The Irish Answer* (London, 1966).

His first works are directed at the world, at his contemporaries, and in his youth he was still in the fight, although not optimistic about the result. He spoke up as confidently as though he still felt that he might change the world, and as though he had experienced the Irish situation to the full—but also as though he had wished to make sure before leaving that the situation was hopeless, as though he had measured himself, lonely and powerless, against it before declaring that he wanted no part in it. All action was useless, the heroes died for nothing. This attitude was far from the "Red Easter" of 1916, and Parnell's ghost was to haunt the uneasy Irish conscience for a long time to come.

The First Incident: "The Countess Cathleen"

A new battle and a new setback occurred in 1899: Yeats's play, *The Countess Cathleen,* was jeered at by Joyce's friends, because it "insulted" religion; in fact, the theme was simply the myth of Parnell restated, but the heroic role is played by a woman, which makes matters worse. Joyce, then a student, was yet again the only one to refuse to accept hypocrisy and to defend the right of the individual against the pressure of the mob, in matters of morality. He wrote a series of essays giving free rein to his anger and to his refusal to submit to the judgement of the majority, defining himself both as artist and as victim designate, both as pariah and as human being with freedom of opinion. He sought his spiritual masters outside Ireland, reading Giordano Bruno, Dante, d'Annunzio, Flaubert, Arthur Symons on the symbolist movement, George Moore, and Yeats. When in Paris in 1903 he added Aristotle to his knowledge of Aquinas. He knew personally, but disliked, George Russell and his theosophist group. But no Irish writer could give him what he found in a Flaubert or Ibsen. One can see him in these essays organising his future order, starting from a series of negative attitudes which become more and more clearly personal, centering around words which he defines in his own way. Between 1900 and 1904 we see taking shape his ideas on "life," "drama," "truth," "freedom" and "isolation," expressed with originality and, it must be admitted, a certain romanticism.

In 1900 he enthusiastically launched into polemic; at the age of eighteen, he belonged to two worlds that existed side by side, that of University College, Dublin, and that of his family. Both imposed intolerable constraint on him, as undergraduate and as son; both resembled a court of law, and put him on trial, although at University College he was the advocate of his own cause, and prosecuting counsel against mediocrity and stupidity. He played his double role noisily and enthusiastically: Joyce was not going to pass unnoticed. The university world should be the home of free thought, of open, European culture[4], and it is a closed circle—aggressively so, because the masters wish to defend outworn, reactionary ideas and values; and it impregnates all thought with its tyrannical scholastic ethic, ready to see heresy everywhere.[5]

We see that 1900 was to be a year in which Joyce manifested himself "theatrically," conducting dialogues and altercations with his fellow-students. He expressed all his thought in the form of an attack or a reply, feeling the need to define and defend his own free will and intellectual life, endangered by the pressure of the academic system. The tone and subject chosen for his declarations are both very clear: his first public proclamation was a paper on "The Drama and Life," which was, quite legally, subjected to slight critical censure before it appeared, and then rejected as morally "dubious" by the president of the Literary and Historical Society.[6] The subject chosen was directly related to Joyce's state of mind at the time, as we shall shortly demonstrate; but it must first be recalled how coherent his methods of procedure were. In the same year his article on Ibsen, a criticism of the play *When We Dead Awake* was published by the *Fortnightly Review*. It would be impossible to overemphasise the young man's moral victory, publishing as he was at the age of eighteen a study of a writer unknown in Dublin, a writer whom he had chosen as his master, perhaps hoping one day to succeed him. Literature was to constitute his revenge on the University; and as a final gratification, Ibsen had requested his translator Archer to thank the young man for the article.[7]

It is hardly surprising that in the next two years he completed the affirmation of his opposition to Ireland, and coupled it henceforth with the affirmation of his own detachment, his wish to belong to that select group of spirits superior to the common herd, superior, that is, to the

[4]Cf. *Exiles*, where Robert Hand says to the writer Richard Rowan, "If Ireland is to become a new Ireland she must first become European. And that is what you are here for."

[5]On Joyce's years at University College, see Ellmann, *James Joyce*, pp. 58–77; Kevin Sullivan, *Joyce among the Jesuits* (Columbia U.P., 1958); J.T. Noon, *Joyce and Aquinas* (Yale U.P., 1957).

[6]Ellmann, *op. cit.*, pp. 72ff.

[7]"Before Ibsen's letter Joyce was an Irishman; after it he was a European." (Ellmann, *op.cit.*, p. 78.)

majority of the Irish and indeed to the majority of the world. In 1901 an outspoken article of his against conformity, *The Day of the Rabblement,* his open challenge and declaration of scorn, was refused publication, so he had it privately printed; and in 1902 he "discovered" James Clarence Mangan, a *poète maudit* who formed the subject of an important paper.

The two essays are of especial importance because at the end of the year Joyce put into execution his first decision as a free adult, and left for Paris.

Day of the Rabblement

It was his cry of anger and defiance. In 1899 he had applauded Yeats when the latter was considered a heretic; but in 1901 he was violently proclaiming his dissociation from a literature which was sinking deeper and deeper into unreality, outworn heroism and reactionary "Irishness," and turning its back on progress. It was Joyce the young European who had just translated Gerhart Hauptmann's *Vor Sonnenaufgang,* and who was protesting against the sleepy twilight of the Irish Literary Theatre, protesting in the name of art:

If an artist courts the favour of the multitude he cannot escape the contagion of its fetichism and deliberate self-deception. . . . The Irish Literary Theatre by its surrender to the trolls has cut itself adrift from the line of advancement. Until he has freed himself from the mean influences about him—sodden enthusiasm . . . vanity and low ambition —no man is an artist at all. But his true servitude is that he inherits a will broken by doubt and a soul that yields up all its hate to a caress . . .[8]

One can recognise here the model of that Satanic Stephen who chose to live in doubt, even if it were to cost him the eternity of hell, rather than to take refuge in a security which demanded the renunciation of his aspirations. Joyce protested vigorously against the three types of "rabblement" who kept the Irish theatre in a state of servitude, the uncultured rabble, the cultured rabble, and the placid, intensely moral

[8] *The Day of the Rabblement,* 15 Oct. 1901, in *Critical Writings,* pp. 96ff. Yeats had refused the translation as being inadequate, and said that the Abbey Theatre had not the means to put on German plays at that time. See *Letters,* vol. II, p. 58, 2 Oct. 1904.

theatre-going public, whom he calls *Bestia Trionfante*, a term of scorn borrowed from Giordano Bruno's book *Spaccio della Bestia Trionfante*. He accuses Yeats, Moore, and Russell of being afraid of the public. The true artist is a man who can do without the approval of the multitude, declares the nineteen-year-old artist, with an admirable strength of mind which he never belied in later life. Opening fire, he invokes the patronage of the heretic Giordano Bruno, who was burned in 1600 ("terribly burned," as Stephen Dedalus later said), and this is no vain affectation. "No man, said the Nolan, can be a lover of the true or the good unless he abhors the multitude; and the artist, though he may employ the crowd, is very careful to isolate himself."

Joyce's words here are remarkable for their assurance and for the will they express, the will towards personal integrity as a means of protecting the *power* of one's destiny, the strength and purity of one's intentions. The isolation which he was to adopt as a rule of life was not based on masochism, but was simply an hygienic necessity, because contact with mediocrity is always unhealthy, and the temptation of cowardice is dangerously near. The young man is prudent in a way which has nothing to do with the haughty loneliness of the romantic on his pedestal, or rather his sublimated narcissism.

When S. L. Goldberg in his little book on Joyce[9] claims that to begin with Joyce's ideas came from the romantics, and in particular from Shelley, one must point out that he is not doing the young Joyce justice in crediting him with "the same confusion" that we find in the *Defense of Poetry;* his critical essays prior to 1904 are superbly constructed and already pregnant with the aesthetic theories of the mature Joyce.

From the very beginning Joyce's idea of the personality of the artist was the very opposite of the "Shelley image." It would be difficult to find two more opposing temperaments, as Joyce himself said in his essay "Force," written at University College in 1898 (*Critical Writings,* pp. 17ff.). The imagination that is too powerful *escapes* from the author and bears him away to lands of *ineffable* beauty which his faculties can scarcely comprehend; without more ado Joyce rejects Shelley. For Joyce used to say of himself, quite justly, that he had no imagination, but simply a good memory and the gift of observation, and for him the "ineffable" was the enemy, because Joyce wished to be a writer who *said everything*. Shelley as exile is indeed dear to Stephen, but he is only a phantom, like any other exile; he is a convenient mask for Stephen Hero to use for a time, but he is too distant from Joyce to become

---

[9]Goldberg, *James Joyce* (Oliver & Boyd, London), pp. 5–6.

one of the permanent heroes who recur throughout the work from 1904 to 1941. And after the 1914 *Portrait*, Shelley the serious romantic gives way to Byron the ironical romantic. Joyce prefers the role of Don Juan to that of Prometheus, however unbound. Very little of the Shelley myth actually leaves any trace in Joyce's work, nothing more than a phrase, which pleased Joyce and therefore became part of his own property, "the mind in creation becomes a fading coal," and some allusions made by Stephen in *Portrait* (p. 101) to the wandering lonely moon.

This feeling of loss, the image of the self-consuming fire, is natural to the true creative artist, for creation is experienced as life and as loss of substance; this is why the same words occur in the essay on Mangan in the *Portrait*, and in *Ulysses* (p. 192).

Shelley is still too much the Old Etonian for Joyce to feel much affinity with him, as the Trieste Notebook amusingly indicates: "Shelley (Percy Bysshe)" it carefully notes, as though Joyce were emphasising the aristocratic name: "He spoke his ecstatic verses with an English accent."[10] One could scarcely ask for more laconic clarity from the critic!

The youthful Dubliner feels no idealism: truth counts more than beauty, simplicity more than grandeur, irony more than hope. James Joyce wills himself to be a realist. He knows that he is threatened by lies that stifle, and he does not take a selfish pleasure in his isolation; not for him the egocentric monologue. On the contrary, he needs to talk, and to convince. But he refuses to be bought over or to be rendered innocuous. He has amazingly little ambition, and no care to win over allies who may be useful, but he has chosen never to betray himself. This firmness is seen in its true light when one realises how much Joyce needed other people at this time, simply in order to keep himself from cold and starvation.

First Portrait of a Poet

The essay on *James Clarence Mangan* (1902) is really just a pretext for Joyce to talk about himself and to clarify ideas on aesthetics which are later taken up in *Stephen Hero;* he defines his concepts of romanticism

[10]Trieste Notebook, quoted in *Workshop*, p. 105.

and classicism, literature and actuality, all within the wider framework of a criticism of the concept of history, inspired by much reading of Blake.

Joyce begins with homage to Mangan, the poet who walked in the streets like one who was a stranger in his native land, "alone, like one expiating an ancient sin." Mangan walks alone, but the attention of the public is attracted by his eccentric garments, his high conical hat and his loose trousers many sizes too large (like Jim's tennis shoes and Rousseau's robe, acting as lightning-conductors for gossip and slander, for those who criticise the garments will leave the person alone). He is a strange person who speaks all languages perfectly (except "Timbuctoo-ese," which he does not know very well), in whom "East and West meet," for whom "the song of Ireland or of Istambol" have the same refrain, a prayer for peace to return to the "moonwhite pearl" of his soul. This is like the opalescence of Jim's soul which Nora brought to its full brilliance; and the song of Istanbul reminds the reader of the Oriental dreaming in *Dubliners* and *Ulysses;* here is revealed the sentimental side of Joyce, the softening of emotion which he always associated with the Song of Songs, not only because it was beautiful but because it was *distant.* When the emotion has passed, the theoretical man takes up the dreams, and once and for all places poetry, the superior form of lyric art, outside, and away from, actuality:

Poetry, even when apparently most fantastic, is always a revolt against artifice, a revolt, in a sense, against actuality. It speaks of what seems fantastic and unreal to those who have lost the simple intuitions which are the tests of reality; and, as it is often found at war with its age, so it makes no account of history. . . . History or the denial of reality, for they are two names for one thing, may be said to be that which deceives the whole world. (*Critical Writings,* p. 81)

History is the straitjacket of art, that is, of reality, he says in effect. "History is fabled by the daughters of memory," said Blake, in *A Vision of the Last Judgement,* and Joyce repeats the idea here and in *Ulysses* (p. 25). "They are only men of letters who insist on the succession of the ages, and history or the denial of reality, . . . two names for one thing."

The real can thus only be grasped *outside* actuality, outside the tradition. Everything which is form imposed from without by time (history) or place (nationality) is artificial, and condemned to perish in the sterile order of memory and of literature, while the "splendour of truth," called Beauty, gives and participates in life. Referring to Flaubert's letter of 18 March 1857 to Mlle. Leroyer de Chantepie, Joyce also knows that because he is an artist and not merely a "man of letters," "the principal difficulty for me is still nonetheless *style;* the form, the indefinable beauty that results from the concept itself, which is, as Plato said, the splendour of truth." What Flaubert expresses here, Joyce made his business too: "he entered upon the great study of style." For Joyce, the idea was to find out the style of reality. The whole of this long essay serves to sketch out the first steps towards that conception of classicism and romanticism which Joyce establishes much more clearly in *Stephen Hero;*[11] what he expresses here, rather hindered by confusion in the form, is a kind of defence of the romantic attitude, the "impatience" which he feels is at the origin of the work of art. Art (that is, "every method which concerns itself with present things to transform and fashion them in such a way that a quick intelligence may overtake them and reach the profound meaning that is not yet expressed") must not do any violence to this impatience, but must seek its source in the artist himself and in the themes he uses; in other words, Joyce calls romanticism the secret emotion that provokes to the act of creation, and "art" or classicism the ability to order the real material in such a way as to bring out its significance; he is close to the formulation of the "epiphany," which is, as we can see here, at the very heart of "classicism."

Drama and Life: Life is the Air Art Breathes

Father William Delany, having failed to make Joyce agree to change the relevant passages in his essay, finally allowed him to say what he needed to say, although it was iconoclastic and quite indifferent to the tradition of the humanities. On 20 January 1900, Joyce read to the Literary and Historical Society of University College the paper printed in his collected *Critical Writings* entitled "Drama and Life" (pp. 39ff). It is sharply and firmly written, in a neat effective style, and should be read in its entirety; its arguments towards a *petitio principii* are analysed below.

[11]"The classical temper, . . . ever mindful of limitations, chooses rather to bend upon these present things and so to work upon them and fashion them that the quick intelligence may go beyond them to their meaning which is still unuttered. In this method the sane and joyful spirit issues forth and achieves imperishable perfection, nature assisting with her goodwill and thanks." (*Stephen Hero*, p. 83.)

Joyce distingushes Drama from Literature, but on the other hand associates to the point of assimilation Drama and the Art of writing. This is the first point in his essay, and it must be borne in mind, for it is here that Joyce for the first time puts his theories of the aesthetics of writing into clear and definitive relation with realism. Goldberg glances indulgently at the essay, in which he sees a Shelleyesque confusion[12] and contradictions of thought, because Joyce had not yet clearly sorted out his ideas; but this apparent confusion of subtlety outgrowing itself is due to the originality of the thesis and to the necessity of using a terminology which is here being defined for the first time. In any case, Joyce's first point is that drama is not literature; and he goes on to explain this in a vision of humanity which is both historical and metaphysical:

> Human society is the embodiment of changeless laws which the whimsicalities and circumstances of men and women involve and overwrap. The realm of literature is the realm of these accidental manners and humours —a spacious realm; and the true literary artist concerns himself mainly with them.

For Joyce, the "literary artist" or man of letters is a writer of an inferior category whose province is that of the contingent and accidental. "Drama has to do with the underlying laws first, in all their nakedness and divine severity, and only secondarily with the motley agents who bear them out" (*Critical Writings*, p. 40).

In other words, "literature" interests itself only in the phenomena and artifices of history. In *Stephen Hero* (p. 82), he is more explicit:

The term "literature" now seemed to him a term of contempt and he used it to designate the vast middle region that lies between apex and base, between poetry and the chaos of unremembered writing. Its merit lay in its portrayal of externals; the realm of its princes was the realm of the manners and customs of societies—a spacious realm.

On the contrary, Art or Drama seeks to join itself to the permanence of human nature:

> The artist who could disentangle the subtle soul of the image from its mesh of defining circumstances most exactly and re-embody it in artistic circumstances chosen as the most exact for it in its new office, he was the supreme artist. (*Stephen Hero*, p. 82)

[12] *Op.cit.*, pp. 6–7.

The adjectives Joyce uses to qualify the radical purity (i.e., not morally, but *really*, pure) of the human material are only there because there no others suitable enough. Further on he comments that:

> by drama I understand the interplay of the passions to portray truth.
> . . . However subdued the tone of passions may be, however ordered the
> action or commonplace the diction, if a play or a work of music or a picture
> presents the everlasting hopes, desires, and hates of us, or deals with a
> symbolic presentment of our widely related nature, albeit a phase of that
> nature, then it is drama . . . Whatever form it takes must not be superimposed or conventional.

Which is as much as to say, in summing up, for the appreciation of the methodical development of his theory, that art *moves* and sets in motion the passions (that is, every kind of emotion), in order to describe the truth of man; art does not encumber itself with forms, formalities or limits, but exists everywhere that man *recognises the truth*, even when the words are common or vulgar as they are in a number of epiphanies. Any representation of the Real is "Drama" for Joyce, and symbolism is only one of art's many possible ways of expressing life.

On the other hand, that literature which is simply decadent art "is kept alive by tonics" and conventions; it is analogous to hypocrisy in human relationships, and to compromise with circumstances. Whereupon Joyce joins battle with Ireland, inviting his audience to become the audience of the Drama, of Ibsen, but especially of the interplay of truth and freedom. "Let us clear our minds of cant. . . . Let us criticize in the manner of free people, as a free race, recking little of ferula and formula. The Folk is, I believe, able to do so much." (At this stage, Joyce was still willing to believe in the potentialities of the people.)

He establishes certain fundamental propositions:

1) On the relationship between the artist and Art: in the Drama there is no room for the individual whims of the author, or for his obvious presence; the artist disappears, "foregoes his very self and stands a mediator in awful truth before the veiled face of God." (We are approaching the theory of the "invisible artist," absent from the work).

2) The Drama is answering a need: man needs to create, and drama is the most immediate form of creation because there is no material other than reality itself, neither wood, stone, nor canvas being necessary. Drama and life co-exist simultaneously, because "every race has made its own myths and it is in these that early drama often finds an outlet."

3) The Drama has no utilitarian function, moral or religious.

4) "Beauty" is only "an arbitrary quality (that) often lies no deeper than form," and art cannot be pinned down to this. It is the *truth* that is the object of Art.[13]

Taking up point (3) and developing it further, Joyce proclaims, "It is this doctrine of idealism in art which has in notable instances disfigured manful endeavour, and has also fostered a babyish instinct to dive under blankets at the mention of the bogey of realism."

The time of heroism, of the epic, of romanticism, is past; but there is still real life. "Still, I think out of the dreary sameness of existence, a measure of dramatic life may be drawn. . . . Life we must accept as we see it before our eyes, men and women as we meet them."

Joyce has caused us to forget that the subject of the essay was originally Ibsen—though this is not quite true, because it is Joyce himself who intends to be the inspirer of the spirit of the Drama. "What will you do in our Society, Miss Hessel?" asked Rörlund—"I will let in fresh air, Pastor," answered Lona. Joyce ends his declaration by quoting these last lines of Act I from Ibsen's *Pillars of Society;* and says no more. His success was ambiguous; he was both applauded and considered to be mad. Soon the end of his university career would come. Apprehensively applauded, treated as madman or heretic, he could be reasonably proud of himself, at the beginning of a brilliant career. He wrote a play entitled *A Brilliant Career,* dedicated "to my soul," which has unfortunately disappeared—doubtless because he had no wish to speak out about himself to the extent of stifling in his own self-preoccupation.[14]

Critical freedom is the exercise of reason in connection with reality; it is that objectivity which in *Stephen Hero* Joyce calls the "classical spirit." His use of the word "classical," like that of the word "drama," is ambiguous; he defines it with great care, taking it away from its usual, conventional meaning. "Classical" qualifies the expression of the epiphany; the transition from manifested reality to writing takes place through a *classical* formulation of the concretely perceived significance, that is, through the artist's effort to be faithful to the reality, eliminating all intrusions, even going so far as self-abnegation: "A classical style, he said, is the syllogism of art, the only legitimate process from one world to another" (*Stephen Hero,* p. 83).

[13] *Critical Writings,* pp. 40–1.

[14] "a realistic drama, in four acts . . . a rehash of ingredients borrowed, unconsciously I am sure, from *When We Dead Awaken, A Doll's House,* and *The League of Youth.*" (*My Brother's Keeper,* p. 115.)

Heroism and Satire: The Artist's Holy Office

During the summer of 1904 Joyce, as he announced to Nora, was declaring open war on those impostors of the soul, the merchants of "pure Beauty." He rejected the Revival in favour of real life and its secrets that he knew. *The Holy Office* is a strong blow from a belligerent Dublin fist, directed at the right-thinking gentlemen. In it, Joyce calls himself *Katharsis-Purgative*, and denounces the lies of those who "dream their dreamy dreams," to their faces. They crawl, kneel or crouch in communion, and he stands fearlessly unbowed, sovereign, "self-doomed," keeping the integrity of his soul. This defiant message was so important to him that he later had it printed and distributed individually to the subjects of his satire. Poverty caused the attack to be delayed for a while, and it was not until a year later, in Pola, that he could afford to have his satire printed. He probably regretted not having taken his revenge before leaving Ireland, but it was of course better to attack once one was out of reach. He sent the printed sheets to Stannie in Dublin, and the imperturbable Stannie, obeying the master's orders, took it round from door to door, delivering to the individuals concerned the purge Joyce had concocted for them. It must be emphasised that those he scorns most as "sick men" are the "bards," the very men who should be defending the intellectual health of the country. He is ashamed of Irish art.

In his Trieste Notebook, he notes down under the heading "Ireland" intellectual decadence as its first characteristic: "Its learning is in the hands of the monks and their clerks and its art in the hands of blacklegs who still serve those ideas which their fellow artists in Europe have rebelled against." Art is in league with the Church and the reactionary elements.

Also, "One effect of the resurgence of the Irish nation would be the entry into the field of Europe of the Irish artist and thinker, a being without sexual education" (and hence incomplete).

The Holy Office is a satire of the Irish intellectual and his sexual inhibition, cornered between bed and pulpit. The Holy Office suggests confession, submission, loss; it is the Holy Office of Rome, the Inquisition; in short it is Censure, responsible for entangling the Irishman in notions of sin, of what is "right and proper," it is the censorious power which even today bans Joyce's books in Ireland, and which already considered James and Stanislaus as heretics; it is mental or intellectual censure, synonymous with the "paralysis" of the *Dubliners*. This malady, for Joyce, is the true gnawing syphilis that eventually blinds.

In the satire, Joyce groups together Yeats, Russell, Synge, Gogarty, Colum, George Roberts, accusing them all of hypocrisy and of lying to themselves; he wonders why from reading their works one gets the impression that they have no bodies. A.E., alias Russell, studied the spirit world through the good graces of Mme. Blavatsky, the occultist, author of *Isis Unveiled,* and took refuge in the beyond, as Yeats took refuge in the past.

> That they may dream their dreamy dreams
> I carry off their filthy streams
> For I can do those things for them
> Through which I lost my diadem,
> Those things for which Grandmother Church
> Left me severely in the lurch.
> Thus I relieve their timid arses,
> Perform my office of Katharsis.
> My scarlet leaves them white as wool
> Through me they purge a bellyful.

He explains that he is also the vicar general of man-hating or hysterical virgins, for whom he performs a similar service:

> Whenever publicly we meet
> She never seems to think of it;
> At night when close in bed she lies
> And feels my hand between her thighs
> My little love in light attire
> Knows the soft flame that is desire.

Awakener of souls and bodies, Katharsis-Purgative contemplates from a distance "those souls that hate the strength that mine has/ Steeled in the school of old Aquinas." And the satire passes up to the range of noble apostrophe, leaving far behind the servants of any cult; Joyce stands alone and pure, "firm as the mountain-ridges where/ I flash my antlers on the air."

This masculine image pleased Jim so much that it was later taken up seriously and adopted by Stephen in *Stephen Hero* (p. 39): "There was his ground and he flung them disdain from flashing antlers." Joyce added gesture to insult by his elopement with Nora, for whom he was writing secret, tender poems of love in which he used seriously the same expressions which in *The Holy Office* had served to mock hypocritical virginities. "My tender captive. . . . my love is in a light attire," he sang, in *Chamber Music;* alone with Nora, he no longer adopted the pose of Devirginiser General. With such phrases, he can be heard, simply modifying the tone of voice in order to move from the grave to the grotesque.

His horror of the hypocrisy of the flesh, which formed part of his intense need for honesty to himself, was certainly excessive, because it constituted a *reply* to the excessive denaturing of the human which took place in Ireland; and as long as he stayed in Dublin Joyce was aggressive and exhibitionist, by the necessity imposed upon him by the constant warfare he was waging. He flaunted his immoralities, and probably went beyond his own desires, from an increasing need to break down, to befoul and to beat the sensibilities of friends and acquaintances. Stannie did not follow him in his gallant adventures, his use of women as the instrument of his revenge on society (for it was always Dublin, and its attitudes, which he tried to reach and to maltreat, by way of women Dublin whose lying prudery and hypocrisy he wanted to break through); and this was why James would confide in Gogarty the traitor, knowing that Gogarty could be relied upon to publicise his behaviour.

> Jim says he has an instinct for women. He scarcely ever talks decently of them, even of those he likes. He talks of them as of warm, soft-skinned animals. "That one'd give you a great push." "She's very warm between the thighs, I fancy," "She has great action, I'm sure." (*Dublin Diary*, 29 Feb. 1904)

In reality he must have been a boaster much more than a doer. And in this respect his relationship with the prostitute Nellie, as seen by the prurient Gogarty, becomes very interesting, a spicy and almost epiphany-like account of Joyce's real sexual behaviour. Stannie's report is as objective as always:

> Gogarty tells Jim's affairs to everyone he knows. He told a whore called Nellie that Jim was going in for the Feis (a singing competition), and that he had to feed himself on what he got from books he sold, there was so little at home. At this Nellie was astonished, and having taken a liking for Jim, said that if he came in to her she'd give him whatever she had, but "you couldn't suggest that to him, he's too—in' proud." She has a great admiration for Jim's voice. . . ." I could sit listening to you all night, Kiddie." Having, I suppose, a taste for chamber-music, she offered to accompany Jim on the "po" on one occasion when he was about to sing. Jim who has never lain with this whore by the bye, likes her. In moments of excitement she exclaims, "God's truth I hate you. Christ, God's truth I do hate you."

Jim took up the argument again later, from a distance, having chosen and safely removed Nora for himself. In his letters to Stanislaus he would comment on the ludicrous happenings in Dublin; reading of an enquiry carried out by the Sinn Fein and published in Griffith's newspaper, on the question of venereal disease, he expressed his anger at the inability of any Irish movement, however politically "engaged," to avoid the national psychological sickness: even this one had felt the need to affirm its loyalty to the Church, and Joyce asks:

WHAT is "venereal excess"? If I put down a bucket into my own soul's well, sexual department, I draw up Griffith's and Ibsen's and Skeffington's and Bernard Vaughan's and Saint Aloysius's and Shelley's and Renan's water along with my own. And I am going to do that in my novel *(inter alia)* and plank the bucket down before the shades and substances above mentioned to see how they like it: and if they don't like it I can't help them. I am nauseated by their lying drivel about pure men and pure women and spiritual love and love for ever . . .[15]

Even Oscar Wilde is included, not for his homosexuality, but because Joyce has been disappointed by the *Portrait of Dorian Grey,* finding it too weak and timid; the *Portrait* of Stephen was to be much more frank and honest.[16] Joyce claimed that he would never "confess" even if he had to suffer in Reading Gaol (though it must be admitted that he never took any risks, even in his later clashes with the British authorities).

Having left Dublin and run away with Nora, working in a bank or at the Berlitz school, circumstances put an end to the Don Juan phase; the comedy of scandal and of shocking people was only meaningful as provocation. But as his exile became more and more a real and established fact, Joyce moved on from this stage of retarded puberty and found more noble aims for his heroism. His hostility towards the hypocritically pure strengthens for him the theme of Parnell's fall, which had been his introduction to public life; and in Italy, he was to become more preoccupied with political actualities—here we can place the beginning of his great socialist period.

[15] *Letters,* vol. II, p. 191, 13 Nov. 1906.
[16] Compare what he says about Rousseau in *Stephen Hero*—there is "confession and profession." Wilde's profession was distasteful to Joyce, who always remained very orthodox on this subject—see the "Circe" episode.

VIII. Politics as Temptation

Introduction

There are two principal myths; the one, the older and more personal, is the myth of Parnell which Joyce adapted into his life and work, and the other is his socialist creed, which he vociferously proclaimed between 1903 and 1906 and which formed the subject of a great part of his discussion with Stannie.

Socialism, being a part of the here-and-now, could not be used as material for his works in a pure state, and a political ideology demands a minimum of activity from its converts; but we shall examine Joyce's notion of socialist behaviour. This did not last; but on the contrary, Parnell as part of history can be made use of in as many different ways as the combination of imagination and past events suggests to the artist.

This is why Parnell occupies a more important place in Joyce's work than socialism does; and the interpretation Joyce gave to the Parnell myth allowed him also to escape from the possible consequences of undue involvement in the present.

Vanity of Public Heroism: Parnell's Fall and After

Between 1889 and 1891 the family would have talked much about Parnell. Joyce was at school at Clongowes with the two sons of Richard Piggott,[1] the forger who had written the letter attributed to Parnell, expressing approval of the Phoenix Park assassinations. In 1889, Piggott was unmasked[2] and committed suicide; at school, the Jesuit fathers forbade the other pupils to mention the matter to his sons. In the Christmas holidays of 1889 it became known that Captain O'Shea was seeking a divorce; John Joyce and his friend John Kelly discussed it at meals. Tim Healy, in a last moment of loyalty, declared that the Leader would not be deserted "in sight of the Promised Land"; but Davitt, Gladstone, and the bishops joined forces, then Tim Healy and some others of the party defected, and, as Yeats said in *Parnell's Funeral,* "we devoured his heart." The affair took on the proportions of a legend, and the vocabulary of the people was altered: Healy and Piggott were cast as traitors and villains, and Parnell's misfortune was a result of "treachery." The victim, having been the saviour and the Moses of his people, became the prey of the hunters; and Joyce took up this dramatic terminology, adding other examples until the Parnell affair became for him an archetypal theme. And Parnell died on the 6 October, 1891.[3]

The life and death of Parnell are not simply political events; their meaning goes beyond that of the historical moment and concerns the relationships between man, society, and God. The Joyce brothers deduced from it all that God favours the party standing for injustice and hypocrisy—to such an extent that the man who aspires to freedom and justice must be God's enemy. If God killed Parnell, then God should die. In the eyes of Christian morality, Parnell had insulted God by his adultery, but, as Mr. Casey said, "can we not love our country then? Are we not to follow the man that was born to lead us?" (*Portrait,* p. 38).

Joyce reached "the age of reason" just in time to register in his mind what the powers were that governed the world around him. He understood the relationships and contradictions of these powers by the disturbances they caused in the family, and very soon he discovered a situation that could not be resolved, the situation illustrated by the two brushes Dante has in the first chapter of the *Portrait.* The energy which

[1] Cf. Ellmann, *op. cit.,* pp. 31–4.
[2] He had made a mistake in the spelling of "hesitancy," a fortunate mistake which Joyce plays upon in *Finnegan.*
[3] Ellmann (p. 33) gives Oct. 7, but wrongly. Parnell died on Oct. 6, in Brighton.

could free Ireland from the English imperialism manifests itself in a traditionalist society which cannot shake off its own fetters, and there is not yet an open industrial society to act as a conscious counterweight. Everything seemed to conspire at the same time to trouble the child's growing consciousness, for in 1891 James had to leave Clongowes Wood College because his father could no longer afford to pay the fees. Already he experienced the humiliation of expulsion. On October 6, Parnell died, and the child felt that he had been twice betrayed by a trusted father-figure. He experienced his expulsion both as innocent victim and as guilty criminal, as we can see from the feelings of naïve shame expressed in *Portrait* (chapter I); in the child's world the father is judge and protector. To the ritual question "What is your father?" Stephen replies "A gentleman," instead of saying "A magistrate," as he should. The psychological difficulties involved in overcoming the conflict of emotions here were so great that their trace remains in Joyce's work twenty years later.[4]

The fall of Parnell coincided with the definitive collapse of John Joyce's finances; he had been a loyal supporter of Parnell, although often reproached for his political activity (purely oratorical). An *a posteriori* view of this coincidence between the fall of Parnell and that of John Joyce shows up the heroic-comic aspect of it, but in 1891 the predominant emotions, for both father and son, were those of anger and bitterness. Joyce was not able to laugh about it until *Finnegans Wake.* Parnell was seen as Caesar in the poem *Et Tu Healy,* and Joyce continued to see him as the noble, cold, aloof one whose fascination lay in his absolute indifference to popular fanaticism, whether of adoration or of hatred.

Later the martyrdom was transposed into the killing of Jesus, with Healy as Judas, and the image of crucifixion all the more attractive because it belonged to the Pharisee Church of Ireland. Joyce savoured his resentment in the *Portrait,* reintegrating the tragedy into the course of Irish history and giving free rein to his own anticlericalism. At the same time he satisfies his dreams of heroism by identifying himself with the hero. Politics and the dramatic are mingled in the first chapter of *Portrait,* at the end of the first phase of the artist's growth; the loss of peace, confidence and security, the beginning to question the adult world, and the encounter with the first of the harmful "big words" all determine the first decision to retreat, the first definition of the artistic

[4]"Houses of decay, mine, his and all. You told the Clongowes gentry you had an uncle a judge . . ." (*Ulysses,* p. 41).

condition. The experience was violent and tragic, and complex, for in the opposition of values Joyce learned that politics or history must be incompatible with personal integrity. The first phase of consciousness was marked by the discovery of what "politics" means.

Stephen's childhood, described in the first chapter of *Portrait*, is an age of mystery and of revelations; the child meets or receives "things," sensations, words, touches, which seem to contain the secret of the universe. He passively obeys his masters and parents who make him dance, sing, work, and struggle. Innocent and inquisitive, he amasses a small hoard of words and scenes which he does not understand, of childish images and dreams, and insistently examines and questions them in the hopes that they will open the gates of reality to him. He is not yet able to gather all these fragments together into a significant whole: and Joyce juxtaposes a series of episodes which have been selected by Stephen's memory and lively imagination, but which have as yet no meaning for him. The first question is raised by a children's song which Stephen has distorted in reciting it:

> "O, the wild rose blossoms
> On the little green place.

He sang that song. That was his song.

> O, the green wothe botheth." (*Portrait*, first page)[5]

By chance the rose is frequently brought to mind in these years when there imprint themselves into his mind the images which he is to use as symbols all his life; and the child is attracted both by the words, which give him pleasure in sentences by their sound and rhythm, and by the colours, which he divides into bright and dull. After the roses which are green in his song come the red and white roses which he discovers at school; these distinguish the rival teams in the mathematics class, in a mimic representation of the Wars of the Roses. Stephen is a Yorkist and the white rose loses because he is set too difficult a problem. But for him the real problem is one of vocabulary, of colours and of reality, of finding what is the real relationship between the two roses (and all other roses too). "He could not get out the answer for the sum but it did not matter. White roses and red roses: those were beautiful colours to think of" (*Portrait*, p. 12).

Things are arranged as his sensibility dictates; to begin with these

[5]The distortion may be meant as a sign of literary appropriation: in its new form the song becomes really *his*.

colours are beautiful, and he feels that the beauty is more important than the victory of the Yorkists; but he blushes to think of all the bets laid on him and on victory against Lancaster, for:

> The cards for first place and second place and third place were beautiful colours too. . . . he remembered the song about the wild rose blossoms on the little green place. But you could not have a green rose. But perhaps somewhere in the world you could. *(Ibid.)*

His dreams and meditations on beauty become stronger and he reaches the obstacle of impossibility: he can imagine roses of every colour but green. At once the impossibility inspires in him the desire to *find*, no matter where. There is no green rose in Ireland. From this imaginary wandering develop themes that gradually form a network: the war, the English colours, the green of Ireland which has no flower to represent it, are all hidden behind the poetry of flowers, and a meeting place which will not be that of the world of school is being prepared. Stephen is to discover that national and social peace is as impossible to find as a green rose; it only exists in nursery rhymes. In real life, green is the colour of Parnell whose symbol is the ivy leaf, and the transference from one thing to another happens naturally through the association of the colours: "That was like the two brushes in Dante's press, the brush with the green velvet back for Parnell and the brush with the maroon velvet back for Michael Davitt" (*Portrait*, p. 15).

Dante is Mrs. Conway, an impressive and superstitious lady who taught the Joyce children reading, writing and geography, as well as their prayers, a fear of thunder and a fanatical Catholicism. In 1889 she provoked a split in the Joyce household by declaring herself violently against Parnell; and Stephen observed the instability of human passions:

> He wondered which was right, to be for the green or for the maroon, because Dante had ripped the green velvet back off the brush that was for Parnell one day with her scissors and had told him that Parnell was a bad man. He wondered if they were arguing at home about that. That was called politics. (*Portrait*, pp. 16–7)

The question is not without its troubling aspect because Dante had also called Stephen bad and threatened him that the eagles would come and pull out his eyes, as punishment for a very small sin, long before.

At this stage "politics" is simply a cover for certain disagreeable facts —and a source of argument and dispute. It divides the family into three parties, his father and Mr. Casey forming one, Dante another, and the third being the indifferent or hesitant mother and Uncle Charles.

The word only takes on more precise meaning when Stephen comes home for the Christmas holidays. As he is now nine years old, and is home again after a long absence and an illness, he is allowed a place at the grownups' table for the Christmas dinner. The atmosphere is tense and everyone keeps to his own corner; Dante is obviously angry with Stephen's father; and Stephen listens, observing everything. He is on his father's side because his father is amusing and pleasant. Then they sit down to eat, and the meal table becomes a battlefield where Stephen discovers that the word "politics" has nothing to do with beauty and poetry, but is synonymous with treachery. The worst is that "politics" seems to have no meaning except when it is connected with religion, and according to Dante God is against Parnell, yet Stephen's father is for Parnell.

Parnell is dead, but it is Christmas and the Christ Child is about to be born. Christmas is the Saviour's day, but the Saviour for Ireland was Parnell. The house is decorated with holly, but also with ivy, the symbolic plant of the Parnellite party. Some of the signs are ambiguous and full of warning; the dinner makes Stephen's mouth water, but brings trouble and confusion into his mind, and in the feverish atmosphere about him float words and associations of words and ideas which trouble and obsess the child, bringing back unpleasant memories:

> Why did Mr. Barrett in Clongowes call his pandybat a turkey? But Clongowes was far away: and the warm heavy smell of the turkey and ham and celery rose from the plates and dishes and the great fire was banked high and red in the grate and the green ivy and red holly made you feel so happy and when dinner was ended the big plum pudding would be carried in, studded with peeled almonds and sprigs of holly, with bluish fire running around it and a little green flag flying from the top.
> It was his first Christmas dinner. (*Portrait*, p. 30)[6]

This is also his first experience as an adult: history and religion become confused. At the end of the meal there should appear a pudding decorated with the Irish flag, but in reality the fortunate symbols are replaced by tragic scenes. The King of the Jews and the uncrowned King of Ireland are to be slain after a meal at which they are dismem-

[6]In his article on "The Perceptions of James Joyce" (*Atlantic Monthly*, CCI), John V. Kelleher studies the symbolism of colours in the *Portrait*, and points out that the dominant red and green, standing for vitality, are associated with home. The red becomes the red of rage and madness after the meal, and the green does not reappear until the vision of the girl on the beach in Ch. IV.

bered; birth and death mingle, joy turns to bitterness. At the end the
door slams, the father is left weeping and the patriotic Mr. Casey is in
tears. The pudding will never be served; the green flag will never fly
over the world. The adults' conversation involves the dishes of a ritual
meal that seems related to the cannibalism of hatred rather than to that
of the eucharist. It is a special dinner, but there are ghostly guests
present too; the table is laid for the last supper of the family, and for
that of History. The menu is only apparently innocent, and the communion made here is perfidious and treacherous. Simon Dedalus is in
a blaspheming mood, and is not merely teasing but serious, about politics: the turkey is an excuse for him to indulge in some anticlerical
sarcasm, for he is, like his son, a great player on words.

> Mr. Dedalus rooted with the carvers at the end of the dish and said: —
> There's a tasty bit here we call the pope's nose. If any lady or gentle-
> man. . . .
> He held a piece of fowl up on the prong of the carving-fork. Nobody
> spoke. He put it on his own plate, saying:
> —Well, you can't say but you were asked. I think I had better eat it
> myself. (*Portrait*, p. 33)

Once the pope's nose has been eaten, Simon Dedalus and his friend
Mr. Casey know no bounds to their disrespect; Stephen is silently a
witness to a disconsecration of all the myths and people he has been
taught at school to respect. His father has a gift for mimicry, and Stephen cannot help but laugh, because it is so comical; but Dante does not
laugh. We can recognise here some of John Joyce's favourite expressions, with the satirical tone of the *Holy Office*.

> —Respect! he said. Is it for Billy with the lip or for the tub of guts up in
> Armagh? Respect!
> —Princes of the Church, said Mr. Casey with slow scorn.
> —They are the Lord's anointed, Dante said. They are an honour to their
> country.
> —Tub of guts, said Mr. Dedalus coarsely. He has a handsome face, mind
> you, in repose. You should see that fellow lapping up his bacon and cab-
> bage of a cold winter's day. O Johnny! (*Ibid.*)

The lesson of the vocabulary is a brutal one: the word "politics" and
the word "religion" are in conflict.

In *Portrait*, the death of Parnell which breaks the adult world apart
before the child's eyes is presented as a political and national tragedy,
not as subjective representation of the loss of confidence in one's father.

The well-known scene of the Christmas dinner is cunningly arranged and its symbolism set on a level other than that of time past; it is not said that Mr. Dedalus' finances are in a poor condition. Stephen is present as a witness, and as a schoolboy; he is still at the college and wears its uniform, although the boy Jim had already left; he sits down amongst men who are his peers, to take his share in a ritual meal. On this evening of peace and of a new birth, the boy discovers the existence of violence and death; Christ recrucified is projected into his imagination by the men's words, "Poor Parnell! My dead king!" Stephen's first contact with history in the *Portrait* is a nightmare. For how can one keep one's senses when Dante condemns as a traitor the man whom Simon Dedalus and John Casey worship? When faithful, loving people do not hesitate to have recourse to violence and cruelty, and when Mr. Casey the hero of the resistance boasts of having spat in the eye of an old woman who was saying the same things as Dante says, when he is obviously about to blind Dante in the same efficient way, and she is just as obviously preparing to use the same weapons? "God and religion before everything! Dante cried. God and religion before the world." "Mr. Casey raised his clenched fist and brought it down on the table with a crash. —Very well then, he shouted hoarsely, if it comes to that, no God for Ireland!" This forceful formulation remained impressed upon the boy's mind, and all the more strongly so because he had long admired Mr. Casey as a true nationalist. When one knows Joyce's extreme hatred for violence, one can see that the association of the Church with intolerance was the breaking point of his relationship with the Church.

The Church meddled in politics.[7] From its world of indulgence and charity there came many deadly sins, hatred and anger burst out, and insults poured forth; how was one to respect the Church or believe in politics after such an experience? The most serious piece of intelligence for the son of a man who always commended loyalty was that the priests had betrayed Parnell. And as for Parnell's sin, Stephen could not but palliate it, since he had committed a similar sin himself, or had at least been unjustly accused, by Dante and by Father Dolan at Clongowes. So where is justice to be found?

And if religion can be the same as politics, what about morality? Father Dolan, accusing Stephen of having broken his glasses on pur-

---

[7]"—I'll pay your dues, father, when you cease turning the house of God into a polling-booth.
—A nice answer, said Dante, for any man calling himself a catholic to give to his priest.
—They have only themselves to blame, said Mr. Dedalus suavely. If they took a fool's advice they would confine their attention to religion." (*Portrait*, p. 31.)

pose, called him a "lazy little schemer." So Stephen is a villain, Parnell is a bad man; who are the good people, he wonders? And "the apple of God's eye," as Dante calls the priests, how can they also be "sons of bitches"? "—Sons of bitches! cried Mr. Dedalus. When he was down they turned on him to betray him and rend him like rats in a sewer. Low-lived dogs! And they look it! By Christ! They look it!" (*Portrait*, p. 34).

The image of the victim at bay before the pack is impressed upon Stephen's mind. He feels an instinctive sympathy with Parnell. There is yet another point in common between himself and Parnell, a mystery from which Joyce was to derive much subtle effect, that they were both guilty of something to do with a woman. When Stephen was small Dante forbade him to play with Eileen because Eileen was a Protestant and the Protestants used to make fun of the litany of the Virgin: "Tower of Ivory, they used to say, House of Gold! How could a woman be a tower of ivory?" This question could not fail to strike one who was always seeking to penetrate the mysteries of words. He thought about it and found an answer, discovering without knowing it a classic literary procedure. "Eileen had long white hands. One evening when playing tig she had put her hands over his eyes: long and white and thin and cold and soft. That was ivory: a cold white thing. That was the meaning of *Tower of Ivory.*" Kitty O'Shea also had a mysterious name, but it was not polite, and Mr. Casey would not "sully this Christmas board" by repeating it. Stephen began to imagine all kinds of profane mysteries, and to wonder what could be the litany of Kitty O'Shea. The question becomes absorbed into an infinitely more vast and complicated scheme within the *Portrait*, but here we only consider the aspects of it that were upsetting for the boy Stephen, the mingling of accusation and suffering undergone, and the mysterious female figure who plays some as yet ill-defined role in the tragedy.

The Hero's Fate: Betrayal by his Own

The one sure thing is that Parnell is a victim; he is dead now, or as Simon says, "he was killed." But Dante's reproaches have obscured the true development of events; Joyce deduced from them several laws of relevance to his art, one of which is that treachery is a form of punishment, whether just or not, associating the martyr with the idea of guilt.

The second law is that the hero is betrayed by his own people; objectively, Parnell is handed over to the English as Jesus was to the Romans, both by the people who had been willing to recognise them as Divine King. What Stanislaus called "Judasry" was a source of disgust and resentment to Joyce. The themes become centred round the character of Parnell, in such a way that the order of cause and effect is reversed and the boy no longer knows whether martyrdom is a consequence of sin or not, since values have become so confused. The confusion must have been involuntary to begin with, before it took its final shape as a literary theme in Joyce's work, and it can be summed up thus:—the victim of treachery and injustice is put to death, and those who condemn him are the official representatives of divine justice. Thus one can be both hero and guilty party at the same time, depending on whether one's allegiance is to Church or country.

This theme is represented in Joyce's mind by a series of images, as familiar to him as any trick of style or habit. He had a terrifying vision of Parnell at bay, facing a mob of howling dogs and surrounded; the memory of the Christmas dinner of 1891 remained with him throughout his life and work, the shouting and weeping became associated with the obsessive theme of moral solitude, of treachery and of inevitable guilt. "Parnell, insulted, stoned and hunted down by the people to whom he gave and devoted himself, accompanies the figure of Christ and of Joyce in his loneliness, surrounded by hatred. The image of the hunted beast at bay is often associated with those which have gone before, and the antlers of the stag, shining vaguely in the half-light, are the symbol of his defiance, his challenge," says J.-J. Mayoux (*op. cit.*, p. 48). Joyce was so attached to this image that he used it every time he felt himself to be in a dangerous position; his "Parnell complex" would come into play as an instinctive mixture of pride and fear. He was already using it in the first sketch for the *Portrait*, in 1904, and we have seen how he stands forth, flinging disdain from his flashing antlers on the pack around him, in the *Holy Office*, written at the beginning of his exile. He soon comes to state more precisely the quality and meaning of this handsome challenge.

The image of the stag had originally a noble meaning, but it also had a decidedly less noble function: Joyce's stag bounds over the heights where Ibsen had taken refuge from the attacks of the hound-pack; and Joyce combines, not without humour, proud courage and a measure of prudence. Treachery enrages him, and the pose of martyr pleases him, but he detests the idea of crucifixion.

Parnell and Ibsen, the two heroes of Joyce's youth, are figures in the struggle for independence. One acts and the other writes; one comes down among the "rabblement" and risks his life while the other builds towers and makes his pronouncements and appeals from a height which puts him safely out of reach of the multitude. The one is hunted down and dragged through the mud, while the other ends his life peacefully, on the way to oblivion. If he had to choose, Joyce, who was always physically a coward, opted for the word as weapon rather than the fist; and because he realised the ambiguity of his own motives, he gradually established an ironic amount of distance between himself and his heroic image. He even admitted to Stannie that his moral courage was perhaps only the reverse of his physical cowardice. What he used to call his "politeness," the coldness which really used to alarm athletes like Gogarty, was in fact the cunning of weakness disguised:

> Have you heard of the earthquake in Calabria? I enriched the fund for the sufferers by a crown. Some phenomena of nature terrify me. It is strange that a person can be morally intrepid, as I certainly am, and abjectly cowardly in the physical sense. Some nights I look at my girl's arms with pity and think that perhaps my politeness is also a form of physical cowardice.[8]

In reality, Joyce had no wish to be a *poète maudit*. His only distress during these early years was caused by the difficulties attendant on publication. His letters to Stannie throughout 1905 are revealing: he has no doubt of his genius, but fears the obstacles put in his way by editors, printers and false friends. Heroism as useless sacrifice he detests.[9] The image of the stag is a skilful metaphor to be used in the literary offensive; for it must be remembered that until at least 1914 Joyce was openly writing with the intention of taking revenge on various traitors, whom he had clearly warned, named, and pointed out, following the ancient tradition of Irish satire, which was always designed literally to harm the enemy. The conception of the *Portrait*, and to begin with also that of *Ulysses*, was consciously aggressive, but with words only.[10]

Thus the stag image evolves from noble to grotesque. As a literary

[8]*Letters*, vol. II, p. 108, 1 Sept. 1905.

[9]"Your satirical surprise at my proposed 'dedication' of 'Dubliners' to you arises, I imagine, from an exaggerated notion you have of my indifference to the encouragement I receive. . . . I am not prepared to be crucified to attest the perfection of my art. I dislike to hear of any stray heroics on the prowl for me." (*Letters*, vol. II, p. 83, 28 Feb. 1905.)

[10]Sarcasm and resentment dictated the choice of pseudonyms in the work: thus, Joyce never forgave Cosgrave for not having helped him in a brawl on Stephen's Green, in which Joyce was hurt, and so Cosgrave is given the name of Lynch, after the mayor of Cork who executed his own son.

symbol, it can lend itself to opposite meanings as circumstances dictate. When Joyce left Dublin in 1904 he felt strong in his moral courage; and when he returned in 1909 to found the first cinema, his purpose was also to visit his friends and to test their loyalty, hoping to catch them unawares. But he succeeded only too well, and in spite of himself managed to rouse up treachery against himself. The failure of his commercial enterprise may well be attributed to the barbarity of the "backward Irish," but he finds himself at the centre of a more serious situation (which provided him in fact with powerful opportunities for pathos for several days), for the envious Cosgrave had managed to persuade him that Nora had earlier been unfaithful to him.

Joyce, who had been showing off his visiting card as "journalist on the *Piccolo della Sera,*" impressing his fellow-citizens and generally behaving like the *parvenu* Gallaher in "A Little Cloud," was completely dumbfounded by this news. The cinema went bankrupt and closed; but he did nothing about it. With dreadful irony, he who had posed as the noble animal facing the ravening hounds with derision and pride had returned to the place of his triumph, only to be gored, and to find himself decorated with cuckold's horns. This was the image as he saw and transcribed it. The meaning of adultery changes radically; with the great Parnell, it had been the symbol of defiance and challenge, but now it becomes charged with humiliation; from this experience in 1909 springs, complete, the figure of Bloom. Parnell is banished now for his romantic adultery, and with him goes Ibsen, whose "amoralism" is no longer as attractive to Joyce as it was. In their place Joyce chooses Shakespeare, a man sufficiently great by his genius, yet sufficiently human to play the part of Jim and of Bloom in Dublin streets.

Parnell is no longer useful to Joyce as an image of himself; and at this time Joyce begins to work out the biography of his other double, the Shakespeare betrayed by his brothers, as he appears in "Charybdis and Scylla," and as he is seen in Circe's mirror, wearing horns. The pack has ceased chasing the stag.

From childhood, Parnell is one of the artist's personal myths; he appears twice in the first chapter of *Portrait,* firstly as a ghost in the fever-dreams of a small, very ill child, and later as unconscious model to the more mature schoolboy.

In the first chapter of *Portrait,* Stephen identifies and confuses himself with Parnell, in three symbolic scenes. History has deprived Parnell of his role as political leader and made him into an archetypal hero-victim, whose personal life rather than his ideology is attacked and abused. Thus in his fever-dreams Stephen substitutes himself for Parnell as victim of injustice from others, in this case from his masters, teachers and fellow-pupils.

Stephen is ill, or "he has been made ill," just as for Simon Dedalus the death of Parnell is seen in terms of assassination. In his fever he has three nightmares in which he satisfies a whole crowd of unhappy and angry feelings: the first dream deals with consolation and compensation within the family. Since the world of school is conspiring against him because he is not as he should be, he dreams that he is going home for the holidays. There is holly and ivy, it is Christmas, and everyone is there to welcome him. "His mother kissed him; was that right? His father was a marshal now: higher than a magistrate. Welcome home, Stephen!" This scene, apparently clear, has a subtly sinister network of associations, as is demonstrated below.

The second scene is a naïve account of Stephen's death and burial, where revenge takes the form of remorse inflicted: "All the fellows would be at the mass, dressed in black, all with sad faces. Wells too would be there but no fellow would look at him. . . . And Wells would be sorry then for what he had done" (*Portrait*, p. 24).

The third dream happens in the evening. Stephen hears the noise of waves, and a ship comes in to harbour. He sees a multitude of people, and they cry out in lamentation "Parnell! Parnell! He is dead!" "They fell upon their knees, moaning in sorrow."[11]

The next section takes us into the political reality of the family Christmas dinner.

Stephen's three dreams occur on the same day, and Joyce indirectly indicates the date. He opens his desk and changes the number pasted inside from 77 to 76, because he is living for the future, fleeing from the present and thinking only of the approach of Christmas with its peace and warmth. Thus the day when he dreams his own death is the 76th before Christmas, which is approximately October 6th. Joyce's allusion becomes plain, for in the adults' calendar on that day Parnell died. In the book there is no question of Parnell's death, for a number of complex reasons, which Joyce only indicates by his conspiratorial and meaningful silence, thus: to begin with, at Clongowes, Parnell was Satan, and his death must have been pleasing to the good Fathers. Secondly, the boys were cut off from the outside world, and the most important thing for them was their work, the Humanities rather than humanity. Thirdly, echoes of the Parnell affair must have penetrated to

[11]Parnell's remains were brought back by sea, to Kingstown (Dun Laoghaire).

Clongowes, and the Fathers would try to suppress all dangerous ru-
mours or gossip. At Christmas, when dissension is sown among the
family, already they are only insulting and arguing over a corpse, a man
who has been dead a mere 76 days. And the reader does not even notice
that the Christmas dinner mimes the horror of the hunt and the kill, he
simply receives all the intensity of feeling from it. What was the meaning for Stephen of the 76th day before Christmas?

On that day the boy had experienced the treachery of the world, the
absence of his father, fear and yet need for his mother, self pity, and the
cowardice of others, so bitterly that he felt that he wanted to die. All
his secret problems and worries suddenly overwhelmed him at once,
and life had almost managed to drown him. Wells had pushed him into
the filthy water where the rats were because he had not been willing
to let himself be dispossessed, but also because Stephen was guilty,
guilty of having kissed his mother. "O, I say, here's a fellow says he kisses
his mother every night before he goes to bed," cried Wells (*Portrait*, p.
14), and all the others laughed. Is it right or wrong to kiss one's mother?
wondered Stephen, and the processes of physical disgust took him over.
He began to doubt everything: "What did that mean, to kiss? . . . Why
did people do that with their two faces?" The mother-image becomes
mysteriously veiled over with shame, as though love were wrong. The
father does not defend his son as he should, by the prestige of his social
function. He is not a magistrate. And Stephen feels deserted. He thinks
vaguely of the ghost the other pupils talk about, a marshal who had been
killed at Prague and who in the fashion of ghosts had appeared to his
servants at the very moment when he received his death wound many
miles away. From this Stephen progresses to the substitution of dreaming that his father is a marshal. But in his dream he suppresses the real
marshal's death, because he must not kill the imaginary one. But death
still hovers about the father-figure, and it seems better to have a dead
father who was a marshal than a live one who is only "a gentleman."

It is not the father but the son who dies, and his death falls upon the
shoulders of a fellow-pupil, Wells. Similarly in the following dream, the
crowds mourn the death of Parnell.

Joyce does not say even that Parnell dies like the marshal, while his
spiritual servant and worshipper the young Stephen has premonitory
dreams. No more is said, but Joyce attains here the perfection of the art
of allusion; all the reality is given to us, but as objectively as in real life,
and so we perceive and comprehend it in more or less depth, as in real
life. Everything depends on our desire and on our ability to approach

the real. And if we examine this closely, we can but admire the play upon identities here and their confusion.

Yet this very examination makes it clear that it is a matter of literature here, that Parnell is used to define Stephen and to increase his stature, and that we are far from any objective political idealism.

Parnell's influence can also be traced in the behaviour of the more mature schoolboy as he learns about intellectual rebellion; like Parnell, he is accused, spied upon, punished by unjust masters, accused of heresy and persecuted by his fellows, who are only too glad to have some pretext for expressing openly their jealousy and resentment. In the first chapter of *Portrait* Joyce shows Stephen struggling with the cruelties of the little society of the boarders at Clongowes, unable to understand their customs and their language. His dialogues with fellow-pupils are more like interrogations than conversations. He is asked whether he kisses his mother before he goes to bed, and answers "I do." Then, when everyone laughs, he says, "I do not." But somehow both answers are wrong, and this causes him to feel intolerably overwhelmed and crushed; the general laughter and mockery show that he must be in the wrong, but he does not know why. He embarks upon the vicious circle of accusations; everything that he does seems to violate in some way the secret laws of the society he is in, and he is treated as idle, and then as a liar.

> —Why is he not writing, Father Arnall? (shouts the prefect of studies).
> —He broke his glasses, said Father Arnall, and I exempted him from work.
> —Broke? What is this I hear? What is this your name is! said the prefect of studies.
> —Dedalus, sir. (*Portrait*, p. 50)

Then he is called a "lazy little schemer," and this last accusation is the most serious; he may contravene laws by ignorance, but now it seems that his wickedness is plain to see on his face: "Out here, Dedalus. Lazy little schemer. I see schemer in your face." *(Ibid.)* This is too much: it is possible, though frightening, to be guilty without knowing it, but one cannot be a schemer without knowing it; so Stephen concludes that Father Dolan, who is threatening him, either is mistaken or must be determined to punish him. He would think that the prefect of studies were mistaken, but Dolan seems too keen, too anxious, and after all the Church had stopped at nothing to bring down Parnell in disgrace.

The tone rises quickly, then comes the priest's paroxysm of sadistic rage and the execution. Stephen learns all shame and fear at once, and all the power of wrong, the ferocious pain of the blow that makes his whole hand curl up, fear stronger than pride, indignation, and fury. He cries, and the scene ends with a pantomime in which any respect he might still have for the priest curls up like his wounded hand. "Kneel down, cried the prefect of studies." Henceforth, Stephen, like Parnell, is to belong to "a priestridden Godforsaken race" (*Portrait*, p. 38). He feels pursued by unjust hatreds which are all the more cruel because there is no possibility of foreseeing or avoiding them; at any moment the horrid scene could be repeated, and he would be powerless, because the punishment is always unjustified. He knows only that it is always the same: mental and physical torture, putting him into the position of confession. "Kneel down! . . . Get at your work, all of you, cried the prefect of studies from the door. Father Dolan will be in every day to see if any boy, any idle lazy little loafer wants flogging. Every day. Every day" (*Portrait*, p. 51). This is like history: Every day! Schemer! Kneel down! Get to work! The threat makes the rebel. In his undergraduate essay, "Force," Joyce said "all subjugation by force, if carried out and prosecuted by force is only so far successful in breaking men's spirits and aspirations. . . . it is, in the extreme, productive of ill-will and rebellion" (*Critical Writings*, p. 17). Again in *Ulysses*, it is Joyce who says to the Cyclopean Citizen in the words of Leopold Bloom, "It's no use. Force, hatred, history, all that." And Bloom is simply giving History the other two names Joyce always gave it, Force and Hatred. Or it is the absence of Reason; Bloom's "It's no use" is the same as the boy Stephen's question "What is politics?"

Wells, the inquisitor who asked such difficult questions, has pushed him into a ditch of foul water, and injustice is connected with feelings of disgust, because there were rats in the water, and of slimy cold. Stephen falls ill as a result of this treatment. "He was not foxing. No, no: he was sick really. He was not foxing. And he felt the prefect's hand on his forehead. . . . That was the way a rat felt, slimy and damp and cold" (*Portrait*, p. 22).

Just as the figure of Parnell is surrounded by specific metaphors and attributes, so is Stephen Victim pursued by the rats. Everything aimed against him is thought of as cold and slimy. Fear and disgust at injustice automatically set off his defence mechanism. He is called upon to confess, but what shall he confess? If innocence appears as the highest form of lie, and if he has a schemer's face, this may be because he does not look humble. If he seems to be a schemer it is because he is not guilty, because he is not resigned to a servile existence. He is one of those for whom justice is above God, if God shows himself to be unjust. Stanislaus was not wrong to see something of Rousseau in Jim's determination never to suffer any diminution of his rights or of his integrity. And Stephen despite his fear, risks everything in going to demand justice, because he knows that if he accepts the undeserved punishment he will be really guilty, his silence will crush him, and he will despise himself. So he appeals to the supreme authority, Conmee the Rector. And here we see the limit of Joyce's "revolutionary" impulse as expressed in the step Stephen takes: the boy explains the fact, and the rector gives him credit for it. But justice has not truly been done; the rector belongs to that *cold* world of betrayal. "The rector held his hand across the side of the desk where the skull was and Stephen, placing his hand in it for a moment, felt a cool moist palm" (*Portrait*, p. 58).

All that matters for Stephen (and for Joyce) is that the truth of his words should be recognised; he never sought to speak in the name of all, as Parnell did. What he did borrow from Parnell was the drama of his fall; Ibsen had nothing of the tragic victim about him. At the beginning of his artistic life, Joyce was in need of romanticism; history arranged things well.

The Socialist Pose

Jim calls himself a socialist in politics; "Jim boasts—for he often boasts now—of being modern. He calls himself a socialist but attaches himself to no school of socialism" (*Dublin Diary*, p. 49). But what was Joyce's political "socialism"? Yet another form of individualism, it seems, a conception of himself which took an original form and did not last long; its contents were scarcely political at all, containing for example no trace of Marxism. If he had any political opinion, it was rather a sceptical realism, which throughout his life caused "healthy" reactions to international problems and situations; he generally resolved them by absence and abstention. If Marx did fascinate him, it was because Marx was Jewish and because through Marx he already perceived something of Bloom.

I thought of beginning my story *Ulysses*. . . . (am reading Ferrero) . . . He has a fine chapter on Antisemitism. By the way, Brandes is a Jew.

He says that Karl Marx has the apocalyptic imagination and makes Armageddon a war between capital and labour. The most arrogant statement made by Israel so far, he says, not excluding the gospel of Jesus is Marx's proclamation that socialism is the fulfilment of a natural law.[12]

His socialism was not burdened by a great need for activity either. He had taken care to evolve his own brand of socialism, detached from the "social" aspect, which allowed him to speak without making it necessary for him to act. As Mayoux says,[13] "he was never to live in the irreversible time-continuum of personal, responsible action. He knew action only as a spectacle, and one can hardly wonder that he found it a rather meaningless one."

The "spectacle" comports *distance*, the distance that Jim established when he left the University in 1904, between his own image and the progress of history in Ireland. At the time when he should have been fighting, he was acting the Ibsen-like oracular prophet, and resembled Yeats more than he would have liked to admit.

But the risk is great if one stands near the action; he quits the scene. Once out of Dublin, he can speak for Ireland; he will not be asked in Italy to sign manifestos. He managed to set politics outside the here-and-now. In Italy he became briefly interested again in a flamboyant kind of socialism which is vigorously expressed in his letters to Stanislaus; but on close examination, the reasons for his interest in "socialism," although embedded in apparently detached and altruistic reflection, prove to be very subjective and quite selfish. Socialism is primarily a provisional ash-plant, a stick to beat those to whom his hatred still remains faithful; and with this "big word" he dignifies rather petty or at least egocentric sentiments. Thus, the most precise profession of his socialist faith was drawn from him by (as we have shown) the marriage of Gogarty.[14] In such a socialism there is mixed hatred of the Church, of false friends, of conformity, of the money-based society—if there is an ideology, it is largely negative and emotively-founded.

It is also his way of affirming that he is a "modern" man, and of justifying the choices he has made; it can be seen, for example, that to be a socialist generally means to be opposed to marriage. His understanding with the Berlitz director in Trieste, Artifoni, is largely due to the fact that they were both "socialists," so much so that Joyce's union

[12] *Letters*, vol. II, p. 190, 13 Nov. 1906. (To Stannie, from Rome.)
[13] *Les Lettres Françaises*, no. 863, Feb. 1961, p. 2.
[14] *Letters*, vol. II, p. 88, 2 May 1905, already quoted.

with Nora was considered no bar to his appointment as teacher.

However, apart from his anticonformism, Joyce went through two years of Italian-style socialism, regularly sending reports and commentaries to Stanislaus, who was not at that time wholly convinced of his brother's political good faith, or of that of the Italians, and who still had a liking for compromise. Stannie suspected Jim of humanitarianism, hence of moralising; in fact Joyce's interest in the evolution of ideas around him was not purely philanthropic at all, he simply felt a complete antipathy for the Italian middle-class:

> You seem unable to share my detestation of the stupid, dishonest, tyrannical and cowardly burgher class. The people are brutalised and cunning. But at least they are capable of some honesty in these countries: or, at least, they will move because it is their interest to do so.[15]

It is clear that Joyce did not hesitate to recognise that action was necessary. He followed closely the political debates in Italy. He went to the Parliament or to meetings, as an artist, for the same reason that he still went to Mass—that taste for ceremony or eloquence which, when he was in Dublin, caused him to attend indifferently meetings of the Ivy League or of Sinn Fein, to listen to their speakers and to study from life the artifices of rhetoric. He also participated intellectually, however, and if he comments on the form, the matter is important to him as well; his judgement is cold and objective, as ever, and one can sense that he was moved by the speaker's style, while still standing at a distance from the reality:

> I am following with interest the struggle between the various socialist parties here, at the Congress. Labriola spoke yesterday, the paper says, with extraordinarily rapid eloquence for two hours and a half. He reminds me somewhat of Griffith. He attacked the intellectuals and the parliamentary socialists. He belongs or is leader of the sindacalists. They are trades-unionists or rather trade-unionists with a definite anti-social programme. Their weapons are unions and strikes . . . They do not desire . . . powers which, they say, only serve in the end to support the middle-class government. They assert that they are the true socialists because they wish the future social order to proceed equally from the overthrow of the entire present social organisation and from the automatic emergence of the proletariat in trades-unions and guilds and the like. Their objection to parliamentarianism seems to me well-founded but, if as all classes of socialists agree, a general European war, an international war, has become an im-

[15]*Letters*, vol. II, p. 158, 6 Sept. 1906.

possibility I do not see how a general international strike or even a general national strike is a possibility. The Italian army is not directed against the Austrian army so much as against the Italian people. Of course the sinda-calists are anti-militarists but I don't see how it saves them from the logical conclusion of revolution.[16]

It is clear that Joyce is trying to show Stanislaus that he is aware of what goes on outside, even if all he achieves in the end is a kind of objective lethargy. Joyce is both interested in social movements and weary of them before he starts; after all, his sense of reality is sharp enough for him to have treated in this letter the problems of a whole generation which was to turn its experience into romantic realism, in literature throughout the world. Joyce's few words point-ing out the inevitable crash and the illusory bait of peace are alone a worthy commentary on all the books by the "Men of Good Will."

He followed Irish politics as closely as possible, impatiently asking Aunt Josephine, after Stannie had left, to send him the *United Irishman,* Griffith's newspaper, *Sinn Fein,* and the *Irish Independent.* Arthur Griffith's position pleased him largely because he was "the first person in Ireland to revive the separatist idea on modern lines nine years ago . . . and wants to make Ireland commercially autonomous."[17] Griffith was also anti-clerical, which could not but make him more acceptable to Joyce.

> You ask me what I would substitute for parliamentary agitation in Ire-land. I think that the *Sinn Fein* policy would be more effective. Of course I see that its success would be to substitute Irish for English capital, but no-one, I suppose, denies that capitalism is a stage of progress. The Irish proletariat has yet to be created. A feudal peasantry exists, . . . but this would with a national revival or with a definite preponderance of England surely disappear. I quite agree with you that Griffith is afraid of the priests —and he has every reason to be so. But, possibly, they are also a little afraid of him too. After all, he is holding out some secular liberty to the people and the Church doesn't approve of that. I quite see, of course, that the Church is still, as it was in the time of Adrian IV, the enemy of Ireland.[18]

On the other hand, Joyce, with his scrupulous integrity, disapproved of all compromise, especially of the cowardly acts Griffith let himself fall into, such as offering the hospitality of his columns to the writings of

[16]*Letters,* vol. II, p. 174, 9 Oct. 1906.
[17]*Ibid.,* p. 167, 25 Sept. 1906.
[18]*Ibid.,* p. 187, 6 Nov. 1906.

Gogarty, who published antisemitic articles (a characteristic later transferred to Mr. Deasy in the "Nestor" episode); Gogarty fed people "the old pap of racial hatred, whereas anyone can see that if the Irish question exists, it exists for the Irish proletariat chiefly."[19] The daring of Joyce's thought at this time is astonishing, and he is well in advance of the Irish who wanted freedom in his grasp of social problems. His hatred for the Church enlightens or inspires him. It is especially true that his lucidity of mind serves to excuse him from any participation in the history of his country; and if his socialism has any positive political meaning, it has such insofar as he wishes himself to be an *international* man. The fact that an international association of workers seemed to him an impossibility is here irrelevant, since his main aim was to dissociate himself from Irish national and patriotic movements: "If the Irish programme did not insist on the Irish language I suppose I could call myself a nationalist. As it is, I am content to recognise myself an exile."[20]

Then Joyce returns to his point of departure, the myth of Parnell, for him a sufficient proof that all nationalist action is doomed to failure. He foresees that if Sinn Fein succeeds Griffith too will have his Healy, and names him: the "happy traitor," Gogarty. His action, like Ibsen's, is "a virtual intellectual strike," with "Gogarty and Yeats and Colm the blacklegs of literature."

From 1907 onwards material difficulties became so great that Joyce had scarcely the time to read or write. He found politics boring; and when "the Anarchist" had nowhere to house the "madonna and infant" (for he still could mock himself), he no longer made speeches about it.[21] Furthermore, as he had foreseen, the Italians were becoming restive; on 14 November 1906, the bank where he worked shook to the cries of "Bomba! Bomba!" from an excited crowd. "Nice country!" murmured Joyce in fright.[22] The violence of the crowd and the predominance of misery soon put an end to his socialism which had been really a mask for the "inner heroism" that was threatened with extinction. It was difficult, as he tells Stannie, to be a writer and a bank clerk and at the same time generously broadminded:

> The interest I took in socialism and the rest has left me . . . I look at God
> and his theatre through the eyes of my fellow-clerks so that nothing sur-

[19] *Ibid.*, p. 167, 25 Sept. 1906.
[20] *Ibid.*, p. 187.
[21] *Ibid.*, p. 206, 10 Jan. 1907.
[22] *Ibid.*, p. 194.

prises, moves, excites or disgusts me . . . Yet I have certain ideas I would like to give form to. . . . these ideas or instincts or intuitions or impulses may be purely personal. I have no wish to codify myself as anarchist or socialist or revolutionary.[23]

How could a man who refused to be deceived by the size of the gap between idealism and the brutal facts feel any desire to establish his art in such a no-man's-land full of dangerous explosive? Joyce had not yet reached the stage of laughing at them, but he was already aware of the consequences of national situations. The war came as no surprise to him, for this reason. It was a logical conclusion. This is why, some twenty years later, he was to say to Stanislaus, provoking the other's hostility, with regard to his opposition to Fascism, "Don't talk to me about politics, I'm only interested in style."[24]

If the fate of Ireland were mentioned now, Jim's reaction was to proclaim himself an "artist" and "observer." In *Dubliners*, the anniversary of Parnell's death is celebrated; the past is no longer threatening. In *Finnegans Wake*, without wishing to be a prophet, Joyce foretells the miseries of the Second World War; the work proves to the writer that "politics" is an empty word and at its best a form of world-wide constraint.

When Joyce began work again, giving a personal form to his writing, it was not the colonised and underdeveloped Ireland that he presented; it was his own Ireland, projected into art and thus immobilised for ever as it was, so that it might appear living and moving. His two socialist years were only an altruistic interlude, for in reality he had already chosen the "redeeming selfishness" of the artist before he even left

[23] *Ibid.*, p. 217, 1 March 1907. Cf. Also p. 206:—"rushing off to WORK. Scene: draughty little stone-flagged room, chest of drawers to left, on which are the remians of lunch, in the centre, a small table on which are *writing materials* (*He* never forgot them) and a saltcellar: in the background, small-sized bed. A young man with snivelling nose sits at the little table: on the bed sit a madonna and plaintive infant. . . . Title of above: *The Anarchist.*"

[24] He openly took no interest, in fact; when Italy entered the war in 1915, he described the meeting of Victor Emmanuel, who was a small man, and the Kaiser, who was almost dumb, in these terms:—"It's a duel between a man who can't be seen at twenty paces and another who can't be heard at the same distance." In 1915 he wrote to his friend Francini, "My political faith can be expressed in a word: Monarchies, constitutional or unconstitutional, disgust me . . . Republics are slippers for everyone's feet. Temporal power is gone and good riddance. What else is left? . . . Monarchy by divine right? Do you believe in the Sun of the Future?" (That is, do you believe in socialism? The Sun of the Future was a phrase from the Italian Socialist anthem.) Ellmann, *op.cit.*, p. 394.

Dublin in 1904, when he wrote the atuobiographical essay that was already called *Portrait of the Artist,* with its romantic tones full of hesitation.

But as one reads through the few pages of this piece, the tone becomes elevated, the choice is made definitely, and at the end there is no hesitation. The break with the right-thinking people, which he was already advocating in *Day of the Rabblement,* is complete; his creative egoism would always keep him from any enslavement to social remorse. His true hero is no longer Parnell here, but Ibsen, whose easy comfort and solitude he envies, as being ideal conditions for creation. Public heroism looks fine from a distance, but Joyce has chosen his "inner heroism."

IX. The 1904 Portrait

Introduction

The youthful Joyce, the student in *Stephen Hero* for instance, was scarcely liable to illusions: when his friends and contemporaries went to be killed in 1916, he was writing *Ulysses* and demonstrating his lack of belief in progress, resistance, violence, or political sacrifices. This scepticism of his is illustrated in the brutal episode where Stephen Hero replies to a man who wants him to sign an appeal for world peace, "If we must have a Jesus, let him at least be a legitimate one." This is not a refusal made because of "involvement," but rather a refusal of all involvement; one has to admit, not necessarily approve of, the inevitable. "I didn't make the world," says Stephen; it was the person who did make the world who invented war, so God ought to sign the appeal. Although this may be a play on ideas, the artist can be seen making the declaration that he is the hero he wishes to be: he will sign nothing but his own works. The heroism lies in his refusal to be afraid of other people. His model is not Parnell but Ibsen; he had written to the latter on his seventy-fifth birthday, in March 1901, admiring his complete indifference to the regulations of art, to friends, to all shibboleths, praising him as one who walked "in the light of his own inner heroism." A letter to Stannie from Pola ends thus: "I am sure however that the whole structure of heroism is, and always was, a damned lie and that there cannot be any substitute for the individual passion as the motive power of everything—art and philosophy included."[1]

Joyce distinguishes the military type of heroism which he deplores from that inner heroism which is the motive power of all art.

The fact of signing anything was so important to Joyce that in later life he refused to sign anything that was not of himself, as though he had decided once and for all not to give any foothold, any power over him, to that world whose creation seemed to him a source of nothing but unhapppiness and error. His words, "It was not I, but God or someone else, who made it all," are an instinctive and passionately felt refusal to take on any responsibility; they are his reply as an accused person who refuses to accept his guilt. From January 1904 onwards, he begins to cultivate detachment; he sends to the editors of the review *Dana* a long, difficult and allusive piece, deeply strong and violent, summing up his adolescent experience; the very fact that he chose the autobiographical form shows that he felt himself to have reached the end of the time of idealism.

A Flamboyant Autobiography

"The features of infancy are not commonly reproduced in the adolescent portrait for, so capricious are we, that we cannot or will not conceive the past in any other than its iron memorial aspect. Yet the past assuredly implies a fluid succession of presents, the development of an entity of which our actual present is a phase only. Our world, again, recognises its acquaintance chiefly by the characters of beard and inches and is, for the most part, estranged from those of its members who seek through some art, by some process of the mind as yet untabulated, to liberate from the personalised lumps of matter that which is their individualising rhythm, the first or formal relation of their parts. But for such as these a portrait is not an identificative paper but rather the curve of an emotion.

"Use of reason is by popular judgment antedated by some seven years and so it is not easy to set down the exact age at which the natural sensibility of the subject of this portrait awoke to the ideas of eternal damnation, the necessity of penitence and the efficacy of prayer. His training had early developed a very lively sense of spiritual obligations

[1] *Letters*, vol. II, p. 81, 7 Feb. 1905.

at the expense of what is called 'common sense.' He ran through his measure like a spendthrift saint, astonishing many by ejaculatory fervours, offending many by airs of the cloister. One day in a wood near Malahide a labourer had marvelled to see a boy of fifteen praying in an ecstasy of Oriental posture. It was indeed a long time before this boy understood the nature of that most marketable goodness which makes it possible to give comfortable assent to propositions without ordering one's life in accordance with them. The digestive value of religion he never appreciated and he chose, as more fitting his case, those poorer humbler orders in which a confessor did not seem anxious to reveal himself, in theory at least, a man of the world. In spite, however, of continued shocks, which drove him from breathless flights of zeal shamefully inwards, he was still soothed by devotional exercises when he entered the University.

"About this period the enigma of a manner was put up to all comers to protect the crisis. He was quick enough now to see that he must disentangle his affairs in secrecy and reserve had ever been a light penance. His reluctance to debate scandal, to seem curious of others, aided him in his real indictment and was not without a satisfactory flavour of the heroic. It was part of that ineradicable egoism of which he was afterward redeemer that he imagined converging to him the deeds and thoughts of the microcosm. Is the mind of boyhood medieval that it is so divining of intrigue? Field sports (or their correspondents in the world of mentality) are perhaps the most effective cure, but for this fantastic idealist, eluding the grunting booted apparition with a bound, the mimic hunt was no less ludicrous than unequal in a ground chosen to his disadvantage. But behind the rapidly indurating shield the sensitive answered: Let the pack of enmities come tumbling and sniffing to the highlands after their game. There was his ground and he flung them disdain from flashing antlers. There was evident self-flattery in the image but a danger of complacence too. Wherefore, neglecting the wheezier bayings in that chorus which no leagues of distance could make musical, he began loftily diagnosis of the younglings. His judgment was exquisite, deliberate, sharp; his sentence sculptural. These young men saw in the sudden death of a dull French novelist[2] the hand of Emmanuel God with us; they admired Gladstone, physical science, and the tragedies of Shakespeare; and they believed in the adjustment of Catholic teaching to everyday needs, in the Church diplomatic. In their relations among themselves and towards their superiors they dis-

[2] Emile Zola.

played a nervous and (wherever there was question of authority) a very English liberalism. He remarked half-admiring, half-reproving demeanour of a class, implicitly pledged to abstinences towards others among whom (the fame went) wild living was not unknown. Though the union of faith and fatherland was ever sacred in that world of easily inflammable enthusiams a couplet from Davis, accusing the least docile of tempers, never failed of its applause and the memory of McManus was hardly less revered than that of Cardinal Cullen. They had many reasons to respect authority; and even if a student were forbidden to go to *Othello* ('There are some coarse expressions in it' he was told) what a little cross was that? Was it not rather an evidence of watchful care and interest, and were they not assured that in their future lives this care would continue, this interest be maintained? The exercise of authority might be sometimes (rarely) questionable, its intention, never. Who therefore readier than these young men to acknowledge gratefully the sallies of some genial professor or the surliness of some door-porter, who more solicitous to cherish in every way and to advance in person the honour of Alma Mater? For his part he was at the difficult age, dispossessed and necessitous, sensible of all that was ignoble in such manners who, in revery at least, had been acquainted with nobility. An earnest Jesuit had prescribed a clerkship in Guinness's: and doubtless the clerk-designate of a brewery would not have had scorn and pity only for an admirable community had it not been that he desired (in the language of the schoolmen) an arduous good. It was impossible that he should find solace in societies for the encouragement of thought among laymen or any other than bodily comfort in the warm sodality amid so many foolish or grotesque virginities. Moreover, it was impossible that a temperament ever trembling towards its ecstasy should submit to acquiesce, that a soul should decree servitude for its portion over which the image of beauty had fallen as a mantle. One night in early spring, standing at the foot of the staircase in the library, he said to his friend 'I have left the Church.' And as they walked home through the streets arm-in-arm he told, in words that seemed an echo of their closing, how he had left it through the gates of Assisi.

"Extravagance followed. The simple history of the Poverello was soon out of mind and he established himself in the maddest of companies, Joachim Abbas, Bruno the Nolan, Michael Sendivogius, all the hierarchs of initiation cast their spells upon him. He descended among the hells of Swedenborg and abased himself in the gloom of Saint John of the Cross. His heaven was suddenly illuminated by a horde of stars, the signatures of all nature, the soul remembering ancient days. Like an

alchemist he bent upon his handiwork, bringing together the mysterious elements, separating the subtle from the gross. For the artist the
rhythms of phrase and period, the symbols of word and allusion, were
paramount things. And was it any wonder that out of this marvelous life,
wherein he had annihilated and rebuilt experience, laboured and despaired, he came forth at last with a single purpose—to reunite the
children of the spirit, jealous and long-divided, to reunite them against
fraud and principality. A thousand eternities were to be reaffirmed,
divine knowledge was to be re-established. Alas for fatuity! as easily
might he have summoned a regiment of the winds. They pleaded their
natural pieties—social limitations, inherited apathy of race, an adoring
mother, the Christian fable. Their treasons were venial only. Wherever
the social monster permitted they would hazard the extremes of
heterodoxy, reason of an imaginative determinant in ethics, of anarchy
(the folk), of blue triangles, of the fish-gods, proclaiming in a fervent
moment the necessity for action. His revenge was a phrase and insola-
tion. He lumped the emancipates together—Venomous Butter—and
set away from the sloppy neighbourhood.

"Isolation, he had once written, is the first principle of artistic
economy but traditional and individual revelations were at that time
pressing their claims and self-communion had been but shyly welcomed. But in the intervals of friendships (for he had outridden three)
he had known the sisterhood of meditative hours and now the hope
began to grow up within him of finding among them that serene emotion, that certitude which among men he had not found. An impulse
had led him forth in the dark season to silent and lonely places where
the mists hung streamerwise among the trees; and as he had passed
there amid the subduing night, in the secret fall of leaves, the fragrant
rain, the mesh of vapours moon-transpierced, he had imagined an admonition of the frailty of all things. In summer it had led him seaward.
Wandering over the arid, grassy hills or along the strand, avowedly in
quest of shellfish, he had grown almost impatient of the day. Waders,
into whose childish or girlish hair, girlish or childish dresses, the very
wilfulness of the sea had entered—even they had not fascinated. But as
day had waned it had been pleasant to watch the far last figures islanded
in distant pools; and as evening deepened the grey glow above the sea
he had gone out, out among the shallow waters, the holy joys of solitude
uplifting him, singing passionately to the tide. Sceptically, cynically,
mystically, he had sought for an absolute satisfaction and now little by
little he began to be conscious of the beauty of mortal conditions. He
remembered a sentence in Augustine—'It was manifested unto me that

those things be good which yet are corrupted; which neither if they were supremely good, nor unless they were good could be corrupted: for had they been supremely good they would have been incorruptible but if they were not good there would be nothing in them which could be corrupted.' A philosophy of reconcilement . . . possible . . . as eve . . . The . . . of the . . . at lef . . . ber . . . lit up with dolphin lights but [3] the lights in the chambers of the heart were unextinguished, nay, burning as for espousal.

"Dearest of mortals! In spite of tributary verses and of the comedy of meetings here and in the foolish society of sleep the fountain of being (it seemed) had been interfused. Years before, in boyhood, the energy of sin opening a world before him, he had been made aware of thee. The yellow gaslamps arising in his troubled vision, against an autumnal sky, gleaming mysteriously there before that violent altar—the groups gathered at the doorways arranged as for some rite—the glimpses of revel and fantasmal mirth—the vague face of some welcomer seeming to awaken from a slumber of centuries under his gaze—the blind confusion (iniquity! iniquity!) suddenly overtaking him—in all that ardent adventure of lust didst thou not even then communicate? Beneficent one! (the shrewdness of love was in the title) thou camest timely, as a witch to the agony of the self-devourer, an envoy from the fair courts of life. How could he thank thee for that enrichment of soul by thee consummated? Mastery of art had been achieved in irony; asceticism of intellect had been a mood of indignant pride: but who had revealed him to himself but thou alone? In ways of tenderness, simple, intuitive tenderness, thy love had made to arise in him the central torrents of life. Thou hadst put thine arms about him and, intimately prisoned as thou hadst been, in the soft stir of thy bosom, the raptures of silence, the murmured words, thy heart had spoken to his heart. Thy disposition could refine and direct his passion, holding mere beauty at the cunningest angle. Thou wert sacramental, imprinting thine indelible mark, of very visible grace. A litany must honour thee; Lady of the Apple Trees, Kind Wisdom, Sweet Flower of Dusk. In another phase it had been not uncommon to devise dinners in white and purple upon the actuality of stirabout but here, surely, is sturdy or delicate food to hand; no need for devising. His way (abrupt creature!) lies out now to the measurable world and the broad expanses of activity. The blood hurries to gallop in his veins; his nerves accumulate an electric force; he is footed with flame. A kiss: and they leap together, indivisible, upwards, radiant lips

[3]MS. decayed here.

and eyes, bodies, sounding with the triumph of harps! Again, beloved! Again, thou bride! Again, ere life is ours!

"In calmer mood the critic in him could not but remark a strange prelude to the new crowning era in a season of melancholy and unrest. He made up his tale of losses—a dispiriting tale enough even were there no comments. The air of false Christ was manifestly the mask of a physical decrepitude, itself the brand and sign of vulgar ardours; whence ingenuousness, forbearance, sweet amiability and the whole tribe of domestic virtues. Sadly mindful of the worst, the vision of his dead, the vision (far more pitiful) of congenital lives shuffling onwards between yawn and howl, starvelings in mind and body, visions of which came as temporary failure of his olden, sustained manner, darkly beset him. The cloud of difficulties about him allowed only peeps of light; even his rhetoric proclaimed transition. He could convict himself at least of a natural inability to prove everything at once and certain random attempts emboldened him to say to a patron of the fine arts 'What advance upon spiritual goods?' and to a capitalist 'I need two thousand pounds for a project.' He had interpreted for orthodox Greek scholarship the living doctrine of the *Poetics* and, out of the burning bushes of excess, had declaimed to a night policeman on the true status of public women: but there was no budge of those mountains, no perilous cerebration. In a moment of frenzy he called for the elves. Many in our day, it would appear, cannot avoid a choice between sensitiveness and dulness; they recommend themselves by proofs of culture to a like-minded minority or dominate the huger world as lean of meat. But he saw between camps his ground of vantage, opportunities for the mocking devil in an isle twice removed from the mainland, under joint government of Their Intensities and Their Bullockships. His Nego, therefore, written amid a chorus of peddling Jews' gibberish and Gentile clamour, was drawn up valiantly while true believers prophesied fried atheism and was hurled against the obscene hells of our Holy Mother: but, that outburst over, it was urbanity in warfare. Perhaps his state would pension off old tyranny—a mercy no longer hopelessly remote—in virtue of that mature civilization to which (let all allow) it had in some way contributed. Already the messages of citizens were flashed along the wires of the world, already the generous idea had emerged from a thirty years' war in Germany and was directing the councils of the Latins. To those multitudes, not as yet in the wombs of humanity but surely engenderable there, he would give the word: Man and woman, out of you comes the nation that is to come, the lightning of your masses in travail; the competitive order is employed against itself, the aristocracies are supplanted; and amid the general paralysis of an insane society, the confederate will issues in action."

The Choice of Redeemer Egoism

On 7 January 1904, Joyce wrote, in the one day, this first *Portrait of the Artist*, yet he was always saying that it was not his wish to be an artist. Was he to be Rousseau, was he to be James Joyce? This first *Portrait* is his birth certificate as James Joyce, his first signature as as artist, a promise and an engagement—this explains the frenzied haste in which it was composed, the feeling that one must dive into artistic creation as one dives into the sea, doing violence to oneself. The language of this first essay is particularly interesting, as nowhere else in the later works are we so struck by Joyce's own personal speech. The speaking voice here is still in difficulties, anxious, diffuse, painfully forcing out words that are like cries, because for him the sentence is still the battle-field, and until the very last word he whose fate is being decided there knows not the outcome of the battle. In his previous essays of literary and philosophical criticism, there was no feeling of resistance from the material, the sentences followed on from each other and the expression was clearly logical, but here the words trip and stutter, are wreathed in a dubious romantic symbolism, and seem not to be intended for clarity of expression. The language is hesitant, cloaking the speaker's fear, it moves by leaps and bounds, jerkily, it becomes tangled into inextricable knots that are fatal to the sense; the sentence is an instrument of dissimulation, turing in upon itself, and then over-flowing the limits of the paragraphs. Stylistically it could pass for an obscure parody of the decadent late nineteenth-century art, but it is the form taken by the twenty-two-year-old Joyce's metaphysical anguish, the product of his frustrations, his inexpressible aspirations, his apprehension at the choice that lay before him, the choice of following the beaten track or of making his own way. The time had come to choose, but a man cannot make a choice until he has gauged his strength and recognised what he truly wants. Joyce ended this essay as he did, and called it *Portrait of the Artist*, in a last attempt to remain where he was, at the crossroads of possibilities, in the sphere of cowardice and ambiguity. But the future was already manifestly clear; remaining in contradiction and ambiguity for too long renders some choices impossible. Jim was not to be Rousseau; and this essay made him into the artist he was to become.

For if the essay is called *Portrait of the Artist*, it is simply in order to mislead, for there is scarcely a trace of the actual artist in it. A portrait it may be, but it is a pre-Stephen portrait of a nameless artist, or of one who is not yet an artist. It is the portrait of an "imperson," struggling impersonally to bring into the world that being within it that desires to come into fuller existence. While the theme of the *Portrait of the Artist as a Young Man* is that of the search for and formulation of a personal aesthetic, that of this first *Portrait* is merely a preliminary: the artist is *being* sought for, which accounts for the extreme abstraction. There is no individual, no subject yet. The whole piece offers an elaboration and construction of a context in which the living artist might develop and emerge—a text, therefore, which is prior to the existence of the artist, which precedes the creator and is therefore in a state of chaos, yet which contains the promise of creation. At the end the artist will win his identity. In order to write he will have to multiply his contacts with the outside world, to knit a whole network of relationships into which as artist he will fit; and in the course of this exercise the artist begins to find himself, and to disengage himself from the actual writing. Throughout the exercise Joyce experiences more or less clearly the effects of time and space, of connection with others and of the relationship with oneself. Only as a footnote to this adventure of self-construction does the artist think about inventing his tools and formulating the rules of his rhetoric.

The original individual is seen as rhythm, as the relation of part to whole, as the curve of an emotion; he is not a person with a human appearance and characteristics that can be described, but a fluid movement, a consciousness in time.

There may be some influence of Bergson on this declaration of war on material things, this refusal to consider a living being as immobilised in a superficial, permanent form like a passport photograph, with its "distinguishing marks"; to be in the world is not to look like anyone, but to have some continuity, to possess a fusion of moments of experience; it is to progress, to evolve, to *become* something else, and to be able to *will* to undergo change. Human beings are not fixed "lumps of matter," trapped in a space made up of successive days; but they let themselves float or be carried on the stream of time in which past, present, future interpenetrate and overflow one into another. If the time that clock or calendar tell is abolished, the passing of time is measured by experiences; only the seasons remain. As the *Portrait* develops, in its physiological tempo, there is a time of anger, a time of disgust, a time of initiation, a time of trouble—all full phases that project the soul towards the future—and there is a time of prayer, a time of obedience, a time for devotion and the "domestic virtues," all of which are empty phases of suspended animation, pointing back into the past. These two kinds of time are brought together, and from their confrontation springs that Potential Being which assures the artist of his own identity and duration.

The individual mind, in order to become absolutely itself, undergoes a series of negations.

The consciousness is affirmed by a succession of rebellions and of breaking away from things; and we are given here the story of a rebellious soul. As the sensibilities awake they are faced with prohibitions which religion has made into unbreakable taboos. The consciousness registers the idea of punishment: the Church's time is nothing but the threat of eternity coupled with that of damnation. He who at the beginning of the 1914 *Portrait* was already a nascent Prometheus had had the upbringing of a saint. At the age of fifteen he was motivated by religious fervour and the impulse towards mortification; he felt that he must gain salvation by devotion. And in this phase of puberty was decided the first separation that had to be made; tormented by uncleanness, the individual rejects the impurity found in flesh and blood, the impurity that takes refuge in the holy places—God himself is swallowed and digested, religion is a matter of eating and drinking, the priests deal in flesh, and the very Church is the Church Diplomatic; its daily behaviour is guided by compromise, *laisser-faire* and worldliness, although it lays claim to eternity.

For an adolescent so hungry for self-knowledge and -possession, one can only be snatched away from the earth, from material and mediocrity, in one dazzling swoop of flight, or disengaged from it by the ecstasy that ignores the world. The "curve of emotion" reaches up in a dizzying ascent, breathtaking for the soul in its anxiety to flee from impurity. It must rise into the ideal ether. In order to be oneself, one must first be autonomous, and different from the others; one must work, without fearing the difficulty of the task, at the perfection of one's own good. *The wish to be different,* to start with, the act of removing oneself to a distance, and the setting up of opposition to whatever might deny one's existence, these are the first steps towards solitude. "Every apprenticeship", said Rilke to the young poet, "is a cloistered time"; one retires into the enclosure of the self[4] in order to pursue more thoroughly the practice of oneself—but the idealistic adolescent is still a member of the tribe, and the tribe will not let him go so easily. Stephen Dedalus' triple armour of silence, exile and cunning has not yet been wrought. The idealist who indulges in dreams of battle is none the less equipped already for the heroic combat; a mask acts as his shield, and its resistence is constantly increasing. Dissimulation, selfishness and scorn ensure his independence; he rejects "ingenuousness, forbearance, and sweet amiability." Rapidly he reaches the heights where none can follow him, like one of Ibsen's heroes. Under the "false Christ" disguise and the apparent humility lurks triumphant pride.

The "ejaculatory fervours" of innocence in ecstasy are at an end, and henceforth the sentence is to be a sharp, efficient weapon. The young man's critical mind spares neither his predecessors nor his contemporaries. If the form is that of sculpture, it has the weight and rigidity of that mask which "protects the crisis," covers confusion and dictates what expression one is to assume. But, in order to become oneself, it cannot be necessary to pretend to some other identity; the mask cannot be anything but temporary. The mask is offered the ignominious future of clerk in a brewery, but the satanic self behind the mask knows that it is not destined to serve; in the dark it advances towards its *bonum arduum,* which is difficult and noble. It is imperative to follow the path of difficulty, which is the path of all living things; this is in fact a condition of its development, and this path must be followed at all costs and in the face of all obstacles, until the soul is at last strong enough to proclaim its own absolute sovereignty. And then, surrounded by beauty, trembling as it renews its flight towards ecstasy, vibrant with the thrill of freedom at last attained, the slave soul kills its master, the supreme transgression is committed on a spring night when all things are full of the promise of rebirth, the self leaves the Church by the gates of Assisi, and they close behind him. He has escaped from the prison which still holds the physical bodies and the "grotesque virginities" of his contemporaries.

Once the soul has emerged from its cave, it discovers infinite space —its own potentialities. Vertiginous freedom sweeps it along through all the crazy constellations where the soul and the imagination are no longer subject to any laws of gravity. The soul, liberated from petty disciplines, is now moved by strange impulses and explores the forbid-

[4]Cf. "His sufferings have cast him inwards, where for many ages the sad and the wise have elected to be." (Essay on Mangan, in *Critical Writings*, p. 76.)

den zones of heresy and all exotic hells of secret lore. The clerk-designate of a brewery stands before the alchemist's workbench. Mystery
replaces mediocrity, a thousand voices sing the world's praise, and he
who is now a free being shines suddenly with the light of diabolical
revelation. "Read, and know," he cries to the blind; for the fortunate
soul has not yet abandoned the children of the spirit who are subject
to "principalities" and martyrs to the social lie of religious authority.
Follow me, cries the Young Fool, for I know everything. Say NO, and
you too will know everything, being able to decipher the signs whereby
the past reaches forward into the future, that is rooted in time present.
Stephen walks along the shore that bears such signs, in *Ulysses*, and
urges himself to "Grasp the here and now, through which the whole
future plunges into the past."

But he quickly outgrows his noble ambition to be able to offer eternity to other people; society, the family, the faith, the homeland, all
enchain the weak who have accepted passivity, paralysis and impotence. The artist flees from these entanglements, and already his literary expression has become less lapidary. The sculptured mask becomes
more delicate, the sentence acquires musical and symbolic echoes.
Once the time of disgust and the time of insults have passed, there is
no more time to be wasted with other people. The time of fecundity
is on its way, and the young man has resolutely begun to follow the path
of egoism the redeemer; his destiny awaits him within his own heart.
Other people become distant now because he is making a space around
himself, and that solitude is no longer an unhappy one caused by sadness at feeling different from, and abandoned by, others; it is now a
magic space, the highest possible good, the void where the seeds of
creation will be sown. Rilke told the young poet, "Only one thing is
necessary, solitude. The great inner solitude: to go into one's self, and
to meet no-one for hours, this you must achieve."

These lonely hours are feminine. In the empty space the self has
made it seeks out art and aspires to self-communion, guided by the
certainty that only a fusion of this "egocentric space" with the gentle
hours of solitude and reflection will be fruitful. Night becomes the
discreet accomplice of this miraculous masturbation, this self-love, this
ritual sacrifice that brings fertility to the willing victim. An impulse
drives him beyond the dry dunes and beaches to the holy place, the sea,
which in its ebbs and flows reconciles time and eternity. The phases of
the tides, the movements of under-water currents, all mime on a vast
scale the pulses of the living being. The water in its relations with the
shore is like time that beats itself against space. The tides goes out and

the lonely wanderer follows it, follows the current away from the continent, from matter, from *terra firma,* and by his gesture declares his enmity towards that which is permanent. He comes at last to experience the joy and exaltation of achievement, the passion of his blood's song, and the solitude is holy because it gives him to himself.

In one conquering moment he transcends his fears of death and taboos and all the blackmail of threatened punishments which had made him tremble like a child. He is now the master of his own satisfactions and finds his salvation in himself; henceforth the beautiful and the ephemeral are not incompatible. Art is wedded with Death. Achievement is only a kind of interruption, for the rhythm is taken up again and the original impulse drives on to a new manifestation. What in the world he has rejected used to be called evil is now an intentional and essential part of creation and thus good. Joyce was already aware from his reading of Blake that nothing advances except by contraries and that Heaven may marry Hell; Giordano Bruno and Spinoza told him the same, and Saint Augustine came also to his aid in formulating the philosophy of reconciliation. Things which participate in evil are yet good, and death is a condition of life. Reconciliation is the choice of what Sartre, writing on Baudelaire, called "vertiginous freedom," a freedom which involves no fears of being perhaps infinitely in the wrong in a universe entirely run on principles of Right. Joyce was not far here from the reading of Nietzsche, who places the author above all ordinary morality. The glorious self and the shameful self, with their respective inclinations to the heights and the depths, are joined together in the secret places of the heart, and the soul is no longer torn apart.

And now there can emerge all the artist's powers which had previously been repressed and gagged, finding no way of manifesting themselves except the artifice of verse or the senseless images of dreams. At last the flesh can yield and sin be experienced not as a fall but as a necessary progress, as Energy, the only life that can be provided by the body alone. For the first time the subject of the *Portrait* becomes clothed in flesh, and eventually the mask becomes useless. The young man finds love; the marriage ceremony occurs at just the right moment to put an end to the torment he felt it necessary to inflict upon himself. The loneliness he has now outgrown is sacrificed on the altar of liturgical violet and he is initiated into those ardent rites, of knowledge, rebirth, and self-perpetuation by the act.

If the beneficent one is a prostitute, a "sweet flower of dusk," this is because he can thus love a woman while in reality continuing to love only himself. He does not give himself, but takes, keeping himself intact and taking care not to break into the egoism that preserves him for art; the other person does not matter to him. She may be the mediator and divine messenger of life, but she has no name and her features are very vague. She is the place of wisdom, the path to wisdom, the locus where the person at last coincides with himself, the means whereby the miracle is accomplished. Sin is no longer a matter of degradation, causing a fall, nor a matter of abdication and passivity, but is experienced as communion with oneself and with life; it is already the *felix culpa*, the necessary wound that in "Charybdis and Scylla" makes Shakespeare into an artist, and the "phoenix culpa" of *Finnegans Wake*. The movement of life is orgiastic, following the pattern of awaking desire, strong irresistible tension that reaches out beyond the individual, encounter with the other, distribution of energy, and radiant joy in which all discontinuity is dissolved and desire mingles with its satisfaction.

From the Lady of the Apple Trees the young man receives his sacrament. The time of dispersion and of childhood's worries is over now; the torrents of life spring forth, and passion is channeled, directed towards higher things. There are prisons which are gentle and which bring liberation, defeats which are beneficial, eroticism that can purify, a generous love that is not based on self-interest—not the love which procreates another being, but the love that fertilises man as artist. The litany of thanks to the woman who is the living gate to the world, and who enriched his soul by reuniting it with his body, from which it had long been dissociated, is the first piece in which his art concretely manifests itself; sarcasm brought him his technical mastery, and pride gave him the asceticism of the solitary anchorite dedicated to the achievement of himself. His next requirement was to find the creative rhythm, the harmony of parts and whole, the ephemeral form that defines beauty. *Ad pulchritudinem tria requiruntur, integritas, consonantia, claritas.* These three concepts (see below, chapter V) of wholeness, harmony and radiance, which in the *Portrait* define the beautiful object, are not yet clearly worked out in the mind of the creator-to-be.

He is still working on his personal integrity. Wholeness and harmony had been achieved in solitude, but radiance was yet to come. That which was to be the epiphany, the out-standing of the object, as it were, the moment in which time is suspended by the sudden revelation of beauty and the subject illuminated by the aesthetic pleasure provoked, was a shining brightness which was still for one last and supreme moment that of the subject himself, a look of self-knowledge and self-enchantment, a sublimated narcissism where all possibilities were suddenly manifested. Here, a shining Icarus takes his first flight, angelic and androgynous, inspired by a kiss. Intoxicated by his new role as spouse, he soars higher and higher; winged with air and flames of fire, he becomes possessor of unbounded space. But in his haste is already foreshadowed Icarus' fall: he has to try truly to live before falling back into mere existence, "ere life is ours"—or, in other words, before we fall back to matter, solidity, the common everyday condition. Flight implies descent as joy does sadness, exaltation calm, or union separation. The summer of epiphany is followed by the autumn of frustration.

The breath of creation dies down, and again there succeeds a stifling phase of depression. I am not an artist, Joyce would say to Stanislaus, because I still know that the world exists, that is, I still belong to it, and to my people. Solitude may be broken into by the insistent presence of others' unhappiness, pity makes its way into the young man's heart, and he cannot help but hear the howls and yawns of the world as it drags itself along through slavery to death. He is halted by the temptation to become a Moses-figure, devoted to a mission, to saving others before saving himself, which would mean giving up his persevering progress towards himself. It would mean that he who had glimpsed the light should sacrifice himself to the darkness in which the herd groped and strayed. He is still at this stage Dubliner and martyr, not yet having gained the right to be exile and himself. The man who can speak is to make speeches, not poems, and the seeing man is to guide others; Moses is the bearer of another's Truth and Word, not as sovereign but as the servant of One Greater. The flame comes not from within but from the burning bush.

It has to be admitted that this *Portrait of the Artist* represents the curve of an hesitation; the question 'what shall I be?' is asked, but the questioner does not wish for a reply. At the age of twenty-two Joyce was still aware that there was the sovereign way, that of art, and the narrow way of combat; he still admitted to himself, though unwillingly, that he might well take part in the struggle against tyranny, and that iconoclasm could be considered more "moral" than the selfish cultivation of oneself. Thus he gives the cry at the end of this piece, which surprises the critic who has always been accustomed to consider James Joyce as a born artist. A cry of lyricism, of cowardice, or of regret, it comes from a person who is claiming his rights. Is he to be a hero of the barricades or Stephen Hero; must he leave the Catholic religion only to enter that of politics and to make himself the champion of a faith, attacking Pharisees, patrons, capitalists? He refuses, denies all this—NEGO!

In a last recoiling movement, he refuses to commit himself to being the instrument of anyone or anything. His rhetoric betrays the fact that the writer is in a stage of transition, and is to evolve away from impotence and paralysis, for the Word cannot be magical and creative unless it is free. If subjugated, it loses its power and knowledge, fails to convince, is unable to move mountains or to change the world. The man who has sold his soul has no longer any power over words, or any right to them, he is a mere "spokesman" for a cause. The word must be saved, and restored to its prelapsarian purity. Stephen is to be born in exile, direct product of a definitive refusal. He who speaks in loneliness is his own maker, he who does not wish to be anyone but himself; he wishes to become the person he really is. He is the denier.

He evokes again the anger of childhood when confronted with the pack, the Others, the dutiful disciples. The adult who denies rejects both Their idealistic Intensities and Their materialistic Bullockships, both the excess of soul and the excess of matter. The gibberish of Marx and the prayers of the Gentiles cannot touch him, for he is safely out of reach now, away from the crowd. From afar he makes his proclamation, addressing not those who are already present (and consequently already lost), but the free multitudes whom the artist by his work will help to bring to birth when the world has been freed from its chains and the Church put to flight. In a space cleared in the future, a place of clean ripeness, he is to sow the word that is good, to produce a whole crop of beings ready to live to their utmost, beings who keep their own wills in control without any self-abdication.

In a final explosion the artist-to-be denounces, in a fine prophetic frenzy with overtones of Marx and Nietzsche, himself and the masks he has been adopting; under the "false Christ" and "false Marx" disguises is hidden Stephen Dedalus, not yet very sure of himself, hesitant, in search of his own particular rhythm, and as he pours forth the tide of art upon the world, he is slowly forging his soul. This essay, which set out to give us the artist, ends on an appeal to man and woman as potential genitors, and it is only ten years later that the *Portrait of the Artist as a Young Man* gives us the true image of this mythical being; it took this long for aggressive denial to be peacefully succeeded by acquiescence in self-recognition. In this piece we observe the crucial struggle of the adolescent Joyce to break his fetters, for he has not yet attained to that serene irresponsibility which removes the artist from time and topical happening in order to devote him to art. He has already accomplished a revolution, although only in the sphere of morality, and he has made his first breakthrough in realising the existence of his body, its capacity for enjoyment, and his own right to such pleasure.

He now has to expel all official history in favour of his own, to retreat without loss. His claims that he can show others the way are simply a last lie he tells himself, to disguise the fact that the choice has already been made. It is not possible to transform the world by beginning with an island, nor to recommend that all work together if one's own practice is an arrogant individualism; one cannot be both inside and outside. Ambiguity may, however, be maintained provisionally, and the comedy of altrusim played out. *Dubliners* should be reconsidered in the light of this 1904 *Portrait*; it will be seen as a collection of manifestoes, a denunciation of social paralysis coupled with an exhortation to shake it off. *Dubliners* was to produce *Ulysses*, but was still written in a style of critical realism which could have produced quite the opposite.

The artist is not yet there, but allusions bring him intensely into being. He is denounced and announced, as the ego chooses itself. Barely three months later he was sufficiently manifest to take on a name and place at last, thanks to a new event in his life; the determining facter, which eventually oriented his searching, was love. Everything in the early portrait speaks of the need for an encounter and a revelation that the young Joyce then felt, and on June 10th he met Nora. He had to meet her, he was at last ready. She was sufficiently transparent and simple to appear strange and distant; she could strengthen him and deliver him from fear and hesitation. He was at last able to celebrate that marriage of the self, with no unmanning fear of being in the wrong. He felt now that he really had the right to be artist and creator, the right to welcome and to integrate with the mind his own estranged body. Through Nora the true spouse he could proclaim himself as autonomous artist, his own husband and father at last. The period of transition came to an end with the last stammerings of an uncertain and contradictory rhetoric, and the Artist could begin his own portrait; he was now suffi- ciently detached from himself, having willed that distance across which he could look back, and in which the creative act could take place. The written and the speaking voice were no longer confounded together in ambiguous lyricism.

From the 1904 *Portrait* to the 1914 *Portrait*, from the amorphous to the formed work, from distress to confidence, from Nego to Dico, he lived through the genesis of his vocation, in the lonely space of the crisis; this essay is a piece of work by the self operating on the self. In pangs like the pains of childbirth he who was still innocent of the artifice of Dedalus came to art; from his wanderings in the labyrinth of himself, he remembered the dangers he had passed and the exaltation of pride, as material for that aesthetic mutation in which experience became epic. Words no longer suffered from their user's stammer, expression found its own rhythms, and the artist was able to progress from the mask to his own face. Joyce, now reconciled, could claim his artistic identity confidently. Vital emotion found its true and definitive curve. The political mirage constituted a momentary lapse only, the last real temptation.

On 29 March 1904, the first *Portrait of the Artist* was rejected by the review *Dana*, and so Joyce took it up again, worked on it, named the artist, and made it into *Stephen Hero*.

X. Stephen Hero

1904 was the heroic year of all breaks with the past and all new beginnings. Joyce began it with his flamboyant portrait of the artist in search of confirmation and ended it by leaving for Europe with Nora in October. Between these two events he had written, with surprising eagerness and energy, the poems *Chamber Music* and about five hundred pages of a novel; in June, he met Nora; in July, he wrote the first novella of *Dubliners*, "The Sisters," for *The Irish Homestead*; and at the same time as the latter he also wrote the *Holy Office*, which he gave to his friend Constantine Curran, editor of the University newspaper. New plans came thick and fast; he considered being a singer, then an actor, before at last making his decision to be a "voluntary exile." He was twenty-two years old, Dublin had become unbearable to him, and he was creating a new character, the angry man Stephen Dedalus.

In this atmosphere of excitement Joyce began to define his art as a weapon, and his personal aesthetic as a form of moral resistance.

On 7 January 1904 he wrote *Portrait of an Artist* for the review *Dana*, but the editors, John Eglinton and Frederick Ryan, rejected it because of the allusions made in it to sexual experiences. On 29 March 1904, Stannie, who reports the whole sequence of incidents, noted down that Jim had taken up the slender sketch and was turning it into a novel, the title of which had been suggested by Stannie himself, *Stephen Hero*. Joyce had already written eleven chapters, which is a good month's work; only anger could have inspired him to work so fast. Stannie characterises this novel as a mendacious autobiography and a keen satire. The victims of the satire were at this stage simply everyone Joyce knew, and the Catholic Church; the work was obviously a reply to the editors' rejection.

Stephen Hero is first and foremost a novel of heroic revolt. If the *Portrait* is the book of memory, *Stephen Hero* is nearer to the present —it is the book of scorn. In a page of his journal (quoted by Ellmann, p. 152), Stannie tells us a good deal about the nature of Jim's motives and intentions; the date is Jim's birthday, 2 February 1904, and

> Jim is beginning his novel, as he usually begins things, half in anger, to show that in writing about himself he has a subject of more interest than their aimless discussion. I suggested the title "A Portrait of the Artist," and this evening, sitting in the kitchen, Jim told me his idea for the novel. It is to be almost autobiographical, and naturally as it comes from Jim, satirical. He is putting a large number of his acquaintances into it, and those Jesuits whom he has known. I don't think they will like themselves in it. He has not decided on a title, and again I made most of the suggestions. Finally a title of mine was accepted: "Stephen Hero," from Jim's own name in the book, "Stephen Dedalus." The title, like the book, is satirical.

A week later the first chapter was already finished. To take oneself as the subject of one's novel is not simply an act of defiance; Jim saw himself as Stannie saw him, as an exemplary being, the artist who denies Catholicism and the hero who rebels against all authority. Samuel Butler, Shaw, Edmund Gosse, George Moore and Marcelle Tinayre support the renegade, while Ibsen, Hauptmann, Sudermann and Flaubert encourage the genius. Joyce thus joins on to a double tradition, that of the *Bildungsroman*, and that of the Promethean hero, and the prime intention that marks this vibrantly living book throughout is that of satire. He writes his first chapters against his fellows and contemporaries, conceiving of the book as so wilfully aggressive that he feels it necessary to point this out to his victims-to-be; as Ellmann has deduced, the enterprise had to be modified (inevitably) by the form in which it was to be made public.

The victims, designated and forewarned, could not help but react in the way Joyce wished them to; Gogarty in particular felt himself threatened and alternated between flattery and threats of violence. Thus it was that Joyce reached the first stage of his realism, the phase which he used to call "vivisection." He had always wished that every act in his life, like every emotion, should partake of the nature of an experiment;

the provocation of others in order to watch their reactions was an old custom of his. But now for the first time the experiment could be carried out completely; he no longer contented himself with provocation for the purposes of observation, nor with interminable introspection for the purposes of subsequently writing a book; the book was now being written as the experiment proceeded. Experiment and experience, life and literature, became mingled together in a way which he only used again in *Ulysses*. The book and its plan took precedence over the business of living, and Joyce thus adopted a form of exile by duplicity, as it were. The experiment sometimes gave a distorted view of reality because of the proximity of the book, but at the same time gave it that power and striking quality that only actuality can give.

Joyce attacked in particular the Church and all its dependents, more strongly than he ever did again; he wrote "The Sisters" (the story of the death of an old, half-crazed priest who had been related to his mother's family) in order to bring out the "general paralysis and alienation" afflicting Ireland, and he presented it as an objective epiphany without commentary, at the same time as Stephen was attacking the Church with extraordinary virulence:

> He entered the Church in Gardiner Street and . . . arrived in the right wing of the chapel. The chapel was crowded from altar to doors with a well-dressed multitude. Everywhere he saw the same flattered affection for the Jesuits who are in the habit of attaching to their order the souls of thousands of the insecurely respectable middle-class by offering them a refined asylum, a considerate confessional. (*Stephen Hero*, p. 125)

Stephen similarly criticises the profane aspect of the Church, which reminds him of "an insurance-agency," while in "Grace" Joyce shows his Jesuit preacher indirectly as an insurance agent. And he writes delicate love-poems while Stephen is unambiguously pursuing Emma Clery.

Stephen Hero is a book of revenge, as opposed to *Dubliners*, which was written at the same time and intended as a mirror for the consciences of his fellow-citizens; and Joyce feared that he might be unjust or excessively malicious in spite of himself in his descriptions of Dublin life,[1] yet set *Stephen Hero* in a completely different category of literature, the admittedly subjective.

> The only book I know like it is Lermontov's *Hero of our Days*. Of course mine is much longer and Lermontov's hero is an aristocrat and a tired man

[1] *Letters*, vol. II, p. 99, 19 July 1905.

and a brave animal. But there is a likeness in the aim and title and at times in the acid treatment. Lermontov describes at the end of the book a duel between the hero and G—, in which G— is shot and falls over a precipice in the Caucasus. The original of G—, stung by the satire of the writer, challenged Lermontov to a duel. The duel was fought on the brink of a precipice in the Caucasus as described in the book. Lermontov was shot dead and rolled over the precipice. You can imagine the thought that came into my mind. The book impressed me very much. It is much more interesting than any of Turgénieff's.[2]

It is obvious that many different targets are being aimed at: the hero attacks religion, the cult of one's native land, art, love and the petty middle-class ideas of it, in fact all social institutions, in the name of freedom and integrity; he attacks hypocrisy, servility, fear and selfishness, in the name of a new morality of honesty; he attacks all his enemies, in the name of his ."ishly proclaimed pride, and he attacks himself for his idealism and simple-minded enthusiasm. Stephen and the author, Joyce, are constantly in league with each other. Joyce was still far from the detachment which he later recommended as essential for the artist: when Stephen is angry, Joyce adds his own anger, and although he often takes the precaution of differentiating himself from his hero by "he said that . . . ," "he thought that . . . ," "he decided that . . . ," he often removes these oratorical safeguards of the third person and speaks as himself. We then make no distinction between author and hero, because at such times Stephen is no more than a pseudonym:

> These wanderings filled him with deep-seated anger and whenever he encountered a burly black-vested priest taking a stroll of pleasant inspection through these warrens full of swarming and cringing believers he cursed the farce of Irish Catholicism: an island the inhabitants of which entrust their wills and minds to others that they may ensure for themselves a life of spiritual paralysis, an island in which all the power and riches are in the keeping of those whose kingdom is not of this world, an island in which Caesar confesses Christ and Christ confesses Caesar that together they may wax fat upon a starving rabblement. (*Stephen Hero*, pp. 150–1)

Hardly has Stephen said this before Joyce feels obliged to comment upon the hero's tone of expression, as though to justify himself: he has been driven to satire, and

> This mood of indignation which was not guiltless of a certain superficiality was undoubtedly due to the excitement of release and it was hardly countenanced by him before he realised the dangers of being a dema-

---

[2] *Ibid.*, p. 111, late Sept. 1905.

gogue. The attitude which was constitutional with him was a silent self-occupied, contemptuous manner.

At times the third person is a clumsy disguise for the "I" of a speaker who is striving to be honest: "He felt the need to express himself such an urgent need, such a real need, that he was determined no conventions of a society, however plausibly mingling pity with its tyranny, should be allowed to stand in his way."

These affirmations are identical with those made by Jim and recorded by Stannie, to such an extent that one can perceive the embarrassment that Joyce must have felt at being obliged to make use of the "double" as a subterfuge. But he was writing a novel rather than an autobiography, and so had resolutely to let his character speak for himself, Stephen. This substitution went on for two years, as successfully as it could, although it must have constituted a considerable hindrance to Joyce; thus, we see him in this passage shifting from a narrative past tense to a sudden digression in the present which reads rather like a polemic article in which the novel is temporarily forgotten:

> Everyone knows that the Pope cannot govern Italy as he governs Ireland nor is the Tsar as terrible an engine to the tradesmen of St. Petersburg as he is to the little Russian of the Steppes. In fact in many cases the government of an empire is strongest at its borders and it is invariably strongest there in the case when its power at the centre is on the wane. The waves of the rise and fall of empires do not travel with the rapidity of waves of light and it will be perhaps a considerable time before Ireland will be able to understand that the Papacy is no longer going through a period of anabolism. (*Stephen Hero*, p. 152)

All Joyce's thought is amassed in these pages, which have about them nothing of the novel except the monotonous chronological succession of events. The book is an invaluable document for the thought-processes of Joyce coming to grips with the world, Joyce before he discovered that for him the world was *his way of expressing it*, was what he called "style." *Stephen Hero* soon became a blind alley, and an obstacle to the further progress of Joyce's work; there was no real reason for not continuing the journal indefinitely, for remaining attached to and following the history of Ireland, and basically, in spite of his attempts to separate himself from his book, he was realising more and more clearly that it was not a pure piece of work. From one chapter to the next he evolves towards the discovery that great art must be dramatic rather than lyrical, that it must suggest rather than expound, that it must be created from the starting-point of reality. *Stephen Hero* is simply the critical product of a childhood and adolescence spent in Dublin, and in a sense is only Joyce's response to an overwhelming and oppressive environment.

So, what remains of the experiment in romantic satire, one may ask? To begin with, it taught Joyce the value of silence; *Stephen Hero* is incessantly speaking to other people, showing, though without wishing or meaning to do so, that his need to communicate is great and that his rejection of the Church is still recent and unsure. The dialogue hinders the necessary detachment.

Next, revolt in itself is here a sign of optimism; even if Stephen is called hero, ironically, after Dick Turpin[3] (that is, in affectionate mockery), Joyce was beginning to feel a growing mistrust for all heroism other than that personal heroism which consists of not letting oneself be led into the temptation of conversing, bargaining or compromising with the world. Stephen hungers for "truth" as Joyce no longer did after he left Dublin. "Truth" interested him now as little as did politics. His claims to have a mission of moral import, of which he had boasted to Grant Richards, were now also outgrown. He was reversing all his relationships with the outside world, from 1907 onwards: he no longer defined himself as against the world, but the world as in relation to himself, as matter for his work. The "reflection" of *Dubliners* was effaced; henceforth Dublin was no more than the projection of his memory, imagination, and the intellectual order he imposed. "Heroism" had become for him synonymous with foolery. His letters to Stanislaus during the years 1905–7 show that he was gradually disengaging himself from all idealism, including his youthful admiration for Ibsen or Giordano Bruno; he records, for example, that he had with complete indifference taken part in a procession in honour of the Nolan.[4] Everyday life seemed now to require much more strength and patience than the rebellious life ever had. He had been obliged to discover the heroism of the banal.

In September 1907, he decided to move on from *Stephen Hero* to the *Portrait*, a work which was not finished until 1913. On the other hand, he was already planning to turn the novella "Ulysses" into a book.[5]

---

[3]Richard Turpin (1706–39) was a highwayman who died on the gallows, but whose memory survives in popular tales and ballads, such as *Turpin Hero*. This taste for folksongs also led Joyce to choose as hero of his last book Tim Finnegan, hero of an Irish comic ballad.

[4]*Letters*, vol. II, p. 217, 1 March 1907.

[5]"How do you like the name for the story about Hunter?" (*Letters*, vol. II, p. 193.) It was already *Ulysses*, in 1906.

Thus, *Portrait* and *Ulysses* were being planned at the same time, and it was not anger now that was Joyce's source of inspiration. His hero was to be more lonely, less attractive, dirtier and more pedantic than Stephen Dedalus, and much more secretive; on the contrary, the world was to be felt as much less real than it was in the first version. Heroism was replaced by pride and a sombre melancholy, and Joyce took care that the new Stephen should be as indifferent as the early one had been ardent and enthusiastic, even though he thus ran the risk of making him an unsympathetic character. What was to count in the *Portrait* was not so much the artist as the style of his development.

XI. Heroism is Ridiculous

Sport as Mimic Warfare

During his last year at Belvedere College, Joyce began to realise that he was being singled out as an object of their attentions by the "emissaries" of the Irish authorities, and that they were trying to purchase him by offering tempting advantages. Ellmann records humorously that the first of these "peace-offerings" was that of physical good health. The college had had installed a gymnasium with a sergeant-major in charge of it. Joyce was elected secretary, for he liked to show goodwill to the members of the various cliques at this stage. He exerted himself zealously (as he had after his religious conversion) in exercises on the parallel bars, until he realised that sport was a form of self-perfection corresponding to that of the *Spiritual Exercises*; his attitude towards sport changed immediately to one of derision, and he regarded it as yet another "idealistic cure." He reacted in the same fashion to the offers of the Gaelic League, whose ideas were filtering into the school; by the symbolic gesture of wearing the ivy-leaf in his buttonhole on the 7th October, he demonstrated that Parnellism had had its day and that there was still no reason to put one's trust in Ireland; the Gaelic League, like all similar movements, was bound to fall by treachery from within.[1]

[1] He was sixteen when the director suggested to him the possibility of taking orders, which he rejected, as he does in the *Portrait*.

The heroic transposition of this situation is thus expressed, in *Stephen Hero*:

> Field-sports (or their equivalent in the world of mentality) are perhaps the most effective cure and Anglo-Saxon educators favour rather a system of hardy brutality. But for this fantastic idealist, eluding the grunting booted apparition with a bound, the mimic warfare was no less ludicrous than unequal in a ground chosen to his disadvantage. Behind the rapidly indurating shield the sensitive answered: Let the pack of enmities come tumbling and sniffing to my highlands after their game. There was his ground and he flung them disdain from flashing antlers. (*Stephen Hero*, p. 39)

In principle, cultural evolution manifests itself in the transposition of an act into its imitation, into a game. Thus, for example, a hurley match can be seen on a higher level as the transposition of a gladiatorial combat into mimic. The step from act to game is a sign of progress, but if, on the contrary, the game were only a mask for the act, then there would be a relapse from civilisation to the savage state. When Stephen claims to be the priest of the imagination, he has progressed from the rite of the eucharist to its imitation; when Bloom thinks of the eucharist as cannibalism, he is passing back to the real origin of the symbolism. This retrogression constitutes the basic mechanism of the parody: the imitation of the act is taken in the literal and ritual sense, and cannibalism is a parody of the eucharist. Once the distance between art as imitation and the reality imitated is done away with, all acts and gestures become primitive again. Thus Stephen is led to declare that sport is imitation warfare, and hence is equivalent to scarcely disguised warfare. On making this discovery, he also makes a cautious retreat; since others play at war, he will play at self-defence.

Henceforth Stephen, for the purposes of the cause, makes a wilful confusion between sport and brutality, sport and politics; this lies at the origin of the long symbolic scene in chapter V of the *Portrait*, in which the non-involvement of the artist is justified in complex irony at the expense of his athletic friends. Stephen's policy is inertia; and he watches Cranly, Lynch and Davin playing ball. Davin, the supporter of the Gaelic League, becomes more a type than a real person, and against him as representative of an outworn nationalism that is nearer to folklore than to social and economic realities, Stephen expounds his reasons for refusing to join any athletic society with "democratic" ambitions. In his eyes, as in Joyce's, the Celtophiles were idealists, blinded to reality by the charms of an artificially revived past, officially approved by the bishops. *Stephen Hero* sums up clearly what his successor in the *Portrait* was only to bring forth after long and painful confrontations with others:

> The members of (the society) were fierce democrats. The liberty they desired for themselves was mainly a liberty of costume and vocabulary: and Stephen could hardly understand how such a poor scarecrow of liberty could bring serious human beings to their knees in worship. (*Stephen Hero*, p. 66)

Davin has nothing fierce about him; he has the right qualities for the job, he is "a simple person," of peasant origins, an athlete and not very gifted intellectually. He fears ideological confrontations for which he is ill-prepared, and flees from the discussions Stephen tries to start, just as he had fled when, returning across country at night after a match, he had been invited in by a young woman, alone in a farm miles from anywhere, in case she tried to seduce him.

> I'm a simple person, said Davin. You know that. When you told me that night in Harcourt Street those things about your private life, honest to God, Stevie, I was not able to eat my dinner. I was quite bad. I was awake a long time that night. Why did you tell me those things?
>
> —Thanks, said Stephen. You mean I am a monster.
>
> —No, said Davin. But I wish you had not told me.

His simplicity, nationalism and moral prudery are all bound up together:

> Davin knocked the ashes from his pipe.
>
> —Too deep for me, Stevie, he said. But a man's country comes first. Ireland first, Stevie. You can be a poet or a mystic after.
>
> —Do you know what Ireland is? asked Stephen with cold violence. Ireland is the old sow that eats her farrow.[2]
>
> Davin rose from his box and went towards the players, shaking his head sadly. But in a moment his sadness left him and he was hotly disputing with Cranly and the two players who had finished their game. A match of four was arranged, Cranly insisting, however, that his ball should be used. He let it rebound twice or thrice to his hand and struck it strongly and swiftly.

[2]The "old sow" is a bitter and violent transposition of the traditional symbolic figure of Ireland, the "poor old woman." The insult had a tragic history for Joyce, for it first came to him in a moment of revolt after the death of Georgie, his favourite brother. Jim had sung the song of Fergus to calm the dying child (*My Brother's Keeper*, p. 134). In *Ulysses*, Stephen recalls that he had sung this song for his dying mother. Death, revolt, the desperate singing, reactionary nationalism and its poetry, all become emblems of a repellent, murderous Ireland, the monstrous Old Gummy Granny of the "Circe" episode in *Ulysses*, infanticide everywoman.

The players are those who claim to be on the side of the serious aspect of life, and it is the artist, the player *par excellence*, who stays outside their game. The ball soars up, like the football at Clongowes, the greasy leather ball that Stephen would not touch, which moved heavily through the air like a farmyard goose flying; Cranly's ball is the one to choose, perhaps because it is his vision of the world that is predominant in Ireland—the one dictated by the Church.

Sport as the channelling away of a man's energies provides a constant and humorous theme for Joyce: he is less afraid of golf-clubs and hurley-sticks than of the Church. As Hugh Kenner points out,[3] music, sport and religion are the three passions of Dublin, but for Joyce they are *replacement* activities, channelling the forces of body and soul away from their vocation in life. Religion replaces normal relationships with others by servile idolatry; music gives the soul false ecstasies which last only for a little while, and offers formal beauty as a substitute for reality of content; sport encourages the cult of the physical self and aims for the development of brute force. This is why the typical athlete is given a vague and unproductive personality; in the *Portrait* Davin changes, in an epiphany, into an incestuous brother. (Cf. chapter IV, where Stephen chooses his own Judas-figure, "The Choice of Exile.")

The various themes ironically introduced into the *Portrait* by one who did not wish to be deceived by these apparently inoffensive activities return in *Ulysses*, disproportionately exaggerated and much more crudely portrayed—particularly in the "Cyclops" chapter, where war, sport and nationalism are given a style appropriate to their absurdity and brutal nature—while the antagonists Davin and Stephen are replaced by extreme representatives of nationalism and of its opposite, which for Joyce meant humanism. The Citizen is opposed to Bloom as Goliath is to David or Polyphemus to Ulysses, and small triumphs over great—not because the small folk are stronger than the giants, but because those whose muscles and fury are in good condition are unable to overcome a man whose mind is armed with courage and his own truth. Finally, Joyce had a distrust for material victories, feeling them harmful to spiritual development, and this is important to note in connection with his individualism. There is, nevertheless, a contradiction between what Joyce thought of Ireland and the implications of his declaration to George Borach on 21 October 1918:

[3] *Portrait in Perspective*, p. 122.

As an artist, I attach no importance to political conformity . . . The Talmud says at one point, "We Jews are like the olive: we give our best when we are being crushed". . . . Material victory is the death of spiritual preeminence. Today we see in the Greeks of antiquity the most cultured nation. Had the Greek state not perished, what would have become of the Greeks? Colonisers and merchants.[4]

Parody of the Heroic Age

In his dreams and imagination, Bloom is an idealist; in real life, he is a realist, but not embittered by what he sees; he loves Ireland without being a fanatic. He wishes that independence could be achieved, but does not believe that it will automatically bring the Golden Age. Like Joyce, he feels that there has been a degeneration of values since the heroic days of Parnell. The chapter "Eumeus" is partly devoted to Bloom's reminiscences, tending on the one hand to show that history has now entered upon a vulgar phase, and on the other to prove that Joyce had been right to affirm in his notes to *Exiles* that Ireland never forgives her prodigal son.

These thoughts are the outcome of a comparison between two analogous events, the later one of which is merely a degenerate imitation of the other. The first is supposed to belong to the heroic age; yet it is itself but a parody of heroism, in the cyclic process of return and repetition illustrated in this chapter. Events recur, but "with a difference," a difference which is primarily constituted by a degeneration and devaluation of reality; the symbol of this repetition of events at a lower level is that gesture of picking up and returning someone's hat which Bloom has twice in his life executed. He had once picked up Parnell's hat for him. "His hat (Parnell's) was inadvertently knocked off and, as a matter of strict history, Bloom was the man who picked it up in the crush after witnessing the occurrence. . . . . he turned round to the donor and thanked him with perfect *aplomb*, saying: *Thank you, sir*" (*Ulysses*, p. 575).

That same day, 16 June 1904, that Bloom recalls this, he had repeated the gesture for another man, J.H. Menton, a small middle-class lawyer, who belongs to the age of banality. His grudging thanks serve to under-

[4]Ellmann, p. 460.

line the difference between the two incidents. And Bloom deduces that the moral is "History repeating itself with a difference" (*Ulysses*, p. 580). History repeats itself, and people repeat history, with a difference, but in the latter case the disfigurement is intentional. Thus, when Bloom meditates on Parnell's fate, his personality and the incident of the hat, in a monologue within his mind, reported as in indirect speech, he can remain objective and lucid; he feels no desire to romanticise the incident, or, indeed, the whole history of Parnell, and even less does he consider Parnell's death as the world-shaking catastrophe that it was for the Dedalus family. He is cold and factual, like the sociologist or historian, while around him the drinkers in the cabman's shelter discuss the possibility that the leader will return. Bloom sees in their anxiety disguised worry rather than regret:

> Something evidently riled them in his death. Either he petered out too tamely of acute pneumonia just when his various different political arrangements were nearing completion or whether it transpired he owed his death to his having neglected to change his boots and clothes after a wetting when a cold resulted and failing to consult a specialist he being confined to his room till he eventually died of it amid widespread regret before a fortnight was at an end or quite possibly they were distressed to find the job was taken out of their hands. (*Ulysses*, pp. 574–5)

Bloom's view is undoubtedly the right one, that Parnell was an ordinary man, imprudent, mortal, and probably a little intoxicated by the public's adoration. Bloom does not refuse him the natural grandeur expected of all "leaders of men", but sees it rather as measurable physical size—five feet ten or eleven inches in his socks, thinks Bloom, almost a giant, a most imposing figure of a man. Thus Joyce turns the idea of greatness to derision, reducing down to reality the sometimes prosaic elements that go to make up what men call "Greatness."

History, as rehearsed aloud by Bloom for the benefit of Stephen, is the story of his participation in it, raised to a higher level:

> He, Bloom, enjoyed the distinction of being close to Erin's uncrowned king in the flesh when the thing occurred on the historic *fracas* when the fallen leader's—who notoriously stuck to his guns to the last drop even when clothed in the mantle of adultery—(leader's) trusty henchmen . . . etc. (*Ulysses*, p. 580)

A suitable distance having been established between the narrator and his lofty subject, the personal appearance of Parnell is described with ceremony, or at least with admiration: "Though palpably a radically altered man, he was still a commanding figure, though carelessly garbed as usual, with that look of settled purpose which went a long way with the shillyshallyers . . ." *(Ibid.)*

And now Bloom can no longer resist the temptation towards the heroic, and, overcoming his discretion, tells of his own part in the action, how he "sustained a minor injury from a nasty prod of some chap's elbow. . . . some place about the pit of the stomach," and how, in this dramatic situation, Parnell's hat was knocked off, and "Bloom was the man who picked it up . . . meaning to return it to him (and return it to him he did with the utmost celerity) who, panting and hatless and whose thoughts were miles away from his hat at the time, being a gentleman born with a stake in the country . . . what's bred in the bone . . . in the shape of knowing what good form was came at once because he turned round" and thanked him. *(Ibid.)*

The word "glory" recurs throughout this discourse on time past. Unlike the cabmen lingering at the bar and the other lower-class drinkers who comment on the same tale of the history of Parnell in different tones—tones of slightly prurient vulgarity—Bloom does not for a moment believe it possible for Parnell to return, for even if it were true, as some people said, that he was not really dead, he would have nothing to gain from a reappearance; quite the contrary in fact, for the world had changed so much that Parnell in 1904 would be nothing but a pitiful phantom.[5] This is neatly proved by the Irish people's notion of the whole affair a mere thirteen years afterwards; all they remember is the fact of adultery, as though the conversation were being already transposed as history—and no doubt also because no Irishwoman could ever, possibly, have done such a thing (Yeats and Synge were regarded with disfavour, it will be remembered, for having supposed the Irishwoman capable of passionate feelings). A sailor, the kind of Sindbad usually found in such places, informs the company that Kitty O'Shea was Spanish; and all becomes clear to Bloom, who is now "surprised though not astonished by any means." History repeats itself again with a great difference, for it appears to Bloom that Molly is a beauty of the same type as Kitty O'Shea; it follows, although he does not work this analogy out fully, that he should be the captain, husband of the adulterous wife, and that Stephen could be Parnell, although Stephen refuses to go so far. The potential trio strives to exist for a moment, vacillates, and disappears into unreality again.

"Eumeus," the chapter of time returning and of the exile's return,

---

[5] "And the coming back was the worst thing you ever did because it went without saying you would feel out of place as things always moved with the times." (*Ulysses*, p. 577.)

takes place slowly in the cabman's shelter, Fitzharris's bar, which has also its minute place in history.[6] Everything seems to conspire to slow down the passage of time, and it seems that Ulysses is afraid of going back home, since Penelope in this case is the person she is. The style of the episode is more meaningful than its content. The slow, weary, "narrative" tone slows down and hinders progress, and if history repeats itself so often, this is because Ulysses is taking the longest and most roundabout way home to Ithaca, and has anyway the vague intention of replacing himself by a chosen suitor, who happens to be Stephen here. But Stephen is not to be persuaded by Molly or by Kitty O'Shea to return to Ireland's bed; he is provisionally present and firmly held by his disgust for the "differences" of history. Bloom strikes him as a Christ with a difference, and inspires in him some degree of repulsion also. Christ, Parnell, and Ulysses are heroic if they are kept in the time-scale of memory, but if they are brought into time present they are ridiculous.

It might be justifiable to see in this inner circulation of Bloom's thoughts the germ of that "commodius vicus of recirculation" in *Finnegans Wake*, the adaptation of Vico's cyclic theory of history to the purposes of repeating "with a difference" the archetypal tale of Earwicker and his family. It is certain that Joyce's vision of history was bound to coincide sooner or later with parody, since both history and parody are imitations. The invitation of history proceeds to the disguising of an original event, thus to distortion and degradation; a tragic event if repeated may become comical, Parnell renewed becomes Bloom. The next stage must be that of the imitation of the comical, the comedy burlesquing comedy, the parody parodied. This second stage is less satirical and more burlesque, the further it is from the original serious reference. The tone of *Finnegans Wake* is like this, less bitter than that of *Ulysses*. In *Finnegans Wake* Joyce is parodying Joyce parodying Homer, Dante, God and Mankind, and for this reason history, which was a nightmare for Stephen, is nothing more than a dream for H.C.E.

In his Dublin days Joyce, as seen by Stannie, was as brave as a lion. One can only admire the courage he showed in continuing to write in the midst of severe difficulties, in spite of personal and family misfor-

---

[6]The cabman's shelter belongs to the famous Skin-the-Goat, who was, as popular rumour would have it, the accomplice of the Phoenix Park murderers. In fact, as Robert Adams points out in a note, he was not the driver of the murderers' cab, but of a second vehicle which guarded the first.

tunes, Lucia's madness, his own weakening eyesight which made him almost blind, and the frequent painful operations this necessitated. It could be said that this courage was the reverse of the cowardice he displayed when faced with his overwhelming family responsibilities; or that the writing of *Finnegans Wake* was for Joyce an escape from the fact of Lucia's madness; or that by retiring into language he reduced the threat of the Second World War to a distant notion. It could be said that the choice of art implied flight from the idea of death. All these statements are true in a very incomplete fashion, and Joyce had already heard them as reproaches when he was still living in Dublin; he had replied by choosing "to express himself freely." There is a kind of courage which consists of not being ashamed of one's fear, an honest cowardice, much harder to confess to than the normal sins; it is the brave cowardice that Bloom possesses in *Ulysses*. Bloom is a man who is afraid of meeting his wife's lover; in farcical comedies the lover is hidden in the cupboard, and in *Ulysses* Bloom hides in a museum. This inversion of the classic situation illuminates the character both of the fictional person and of the author; the victim is an accomplice of his own executioner, for reasons which will be examined later. To judge from appearances, one would say that there is nothing heroic about Bloom. Yet in Joyce's plan Bloom is the new Ulysses; so is Bloom the Ulysses of the modern world, or is it that in the modern world the place of the hero Ulysses is taken by some mediocre Bloom? Is Joyce mocking the heroic age as such, or is he bitterly denouncing the present decadence?

In a sense, the answers to these questions are given by the parody-equivalents introduced into the "Cyclops" episode. *Ulysses* has two aspects: firstly, from the literary point of view, Joyce is mocking heroism; thus, the stake with which Ulysses blinds Polyphemus is represented by the cigar Bloom is smoking, size is represented by something insignificantly small, and strength by an inoffensive object. On the other hand, Joyce reminds us, the cigar as equated to this stake is not completely negligible; it is possible to be heroic without using violence. This doubling of identity is the basis of double-edged parody also, for if Bloom is a Ulysses, then Ulysses is only a Bloom. Ulysses was a fine talker, and extricated himself from troublesome situations by craftiness as often as by violence. Bloom succeeds Stephen as "conqueror by the word"; his manner of announcing his opinions recalls John Joyce, and his obstinacy in defending certain humanitarian values, even to the point of forgetting to be afraid, ranks him with Giordano Bruno. His horror of bloodshed inspires one aspect of Joyce's paradox on Shakespeare, and in the "Circe" episode Shakespeare acts as the double of both Bloom and Stephen. Shakespeare does not hide himself under the black cloak of Hamlet because the prince is the protagonist of one of the more blood-boltered Elizabethan revenge plays; he is rather Hamlet the victim, the murdered father.

In "Circe," Stephen in his delirium cries out, "here it is I must kill the priest and the king," meaning, of course, a metaphorical murder, a liberation of the psyche by transgression, rather than a real action. Joyce played upon the idea of heroism during the 1914–18 war, and while the Irish rebellion of 1916 was fermenting he mocked all forms of nationalism (including the Zionism his friend Weiss told him about). Joyce did not believe that it would work, and stated with acid wit, worthy of the Citizen in the "Cyclops" chapter, "That's all very well, but believe me, a warship with a captain named Kanalgitter and his aide named Captain Afterduft would be the funniest thing the old Mediterranean has ever seen."[7] The unpleasant side of this remark is due solely to the pleasure Joyce took in punning on proper names.[8] His anti-Zionism marks the limit of Bloom's idealism, though we shall see later that Bloom shows much more confidence in human nature than Joyce ever did; Bloom's reaction to the idea of Zionism is one of scepticism mingled with sympathy:—"Nothing doing. Still an idea behind it" (*Ulysses*, p. 59).

In 1916, however, Joyce found his neutrality severely tried by the deaths of some of his old friends. Francis Skeffington, nicknamed "the hairy Jaysus," was killed by an English officer, and Thomas Kettle, who had enlisted in the English army with the idealistic hope that England might show some gratitude to Ireland, died in France. To Joyce these deaths were tragic proofs of the stupid futility of war; he reacted by briefly relapsing into nostalgic Parnellism, and then reverted to his voluntary exile, confirmed in his disgust at the massacre to which heroism and nationalism always lead, continuing always to preach non-involvement as his policy. In 1916 he wrote a version of the ballad of Mr. Dooley (a popular song written in 1901 by Billy Jerome, after a character invented by Finley Peter Dunne), in which the British Consul-General in Zurich, A.P. Bennett, could read just what he thought of the importance of the war and of patriotic attachment to one's country. It is entitled "Dooleysprudence":

"Who is the man when all the gallant nations run
to war
Goes home to have his dinner by the very first
cablecar

[7]Ellmann, *op. cit.*, p. 400.
[8]For instance, Weiss had a friend, also Jewish, named Schwarz—a circumstance which must have increased the pleasure Joyce took in teasing them, since according to their names they should have been mortal enemies!

And as he eats his canteloup contorts himself
                    with mirth
To read the blatant bulletins of the rulers of
                    the earth?

> It's Mr. Dooley,
> Mr. Dooley,
> The coolest chap our country ever knew
> 'They are out to collar
> The dime and the dollar'
> Says Mr. Dooley-ooley-ooley-oo.

Who is the funny fellow who declines to go to
                    church
Since pope and priest and parson left the poor
                    men in the lurch
And taught their flocks the only way to save all
                    human souls
Was piercing human bodies through with dumdum
                    bullet holes?

> It's Mr. Dooley,
> Mr. Dooley,
> The mildest man our country ever knew
> 'Who will release us
> From Jingo Jesus'
> Prays Mr. Dooley-ooley-ooley-oo.

Who is the tranquil gentlman who won't salute
                    the State
Or serve Nabuchodonosor or the proletariat
But thinks that every son of man has quite
                    enough to do
To paddle down the stream of life his personal
                    canoe?

> It's Mr. Dooley,
> Mr. Dooley,
> The wisest wight our country ever knew
> 'Poor Europe ambles
> Like sheep to shambles'
> Sighs Mr. Dooley-ooley-ooley-oo."

(*Critical Writings*, p. 246)

It must also be pointed out that Joyce was not just an isolated case of introverted egoism; the 1914 war destroyed many other values as well as that of the efficacity of action. As Mayoux puts it

> Joyce's parody constitutes a refusal, like dadaism and surrealism which developed at the same time and in the same place. Penelope and her lovers correspond to the breasts of Tiresias or the moustaches on the Mona Lisa. It is obvious in what spirit the transposition of Bloom and Ulysses is made, and there is a clear resemblance to John Joyce at the end of his good-for-nothing career, answering advertisements. (*James Joyce*, p. 92)

The Parody Epic of a Nation

Bloom the idealist dreams of a happy, well-organised world, governed by love, a society consisting of one single State, comprising "everyone living in the same place," in which man would be in the image of Christ. The city would be called Bloomusalem; the idealistic imagination, Bloom's imagination, is apocalyptic. Opposed to the apocalyptic symbolism is the world of nightmare, of scapegoats, torture, aggressions, disorder and destruction; and both worlds meet in Barney Kiernan's bar, in Dublin, the place Joyce chooses to represent Polyphemus' island.

The giant confers two metaphorical aspects on the "Cyclops" chapter; it deals with violence and cannibalism, both of which for Joyce were expressions of nationalism, and the third morphological characteristic is the theme of gigantic size, which as a psychological form is the product of strong patriotic pride on the part of the citizens or "fierce democrats." In this world of excess Bloom obstinately chooses the middle way, at his own risk. Joyce places a formidable adversary before him, "the Citizen" (in reality Michael Cusack, sporting trainer of the Gaelic League), accompanied by his fierce dog. The latter detail is of importance because in the animal world the dog represents "the pack of enmities," whose human versions Joyce defied, and also because Joyce was as frightened of dogs as he was of thunder; furthermore, from the "Telemachus" episode onwards the dog is an emblematic animal, because of the terror he inspires and because of the name "dog," which provides Joyce with one of his most long-lived wordplays, since "dog" read from right to left gives God. Joyce was often to allow himself similar irreverence when a good opportunity presented itself, and the dog is thus often a "double" of God, who is thereby reduced to the status of an inferior being, as Ulysses is reduced to Bloom. The citizen and his dog are both good patriots: they both speak Irish. Joyce was annoyed by the cultural Revival, the return to local mythological sources, and the deliberate Ossianisation of literature practised by the patriots; he shows here what he thinks of the intellectual aspect of Irish nationalism in his day.

On the other hand, it is impossible to separate the question of nationalism from the economic question; the "Cyclops" chapter gives Joyce his opportunity to show up the uselessness of a political movement that has no ideological content, and the economic alienation of Ireland. He feels nothing but amused scorn for all idealism; it is clear that the citizen and those around him have no trace of idealism, but are rather characterised by hatred, brutality, and the blindness of Polyphemus—all their energy is channelled into racial prejudice and the behaviour it involves. Bloom, on the contrary, believes in the power of love, in compromise, in the possibility of victory by means of discussion; Joyce dissociates himself from Bloom, unable to share his optimism. Bloom sees "science" and "phenomena" everywhere. "Mister Knowall. Teach your grandmother how to milk ducks." In fact, if he had to, Bloom would try to milk the ducks, "reasonably"; but for Joyce, on the other hand, expecting to find justice and good sense in politics is like wishing that ducks were mammiferous. Bloom really has faith in humankind, but, however estimable his opinions are, he remains ridiculous, a constant failure; he provides a further proof, to his own disadvantage, that history consists of modulations of treason and cruelty, and that Ireland is always ready, when not dreaming of fantastic glories impossible to achieve, to slay her own people or to destroy those who try to guide them.

Joyce makes use of many formal procedures in order to bring out these different points of the action; the symbolism is worked out in detail, as will be seen later. But he begins by determining the position of the author with relation to the scenario of the pantomime; in "Cyclops" he sums up the Irish national situation as he wishes to see it, and so his view is necessarily biased. The situation is grotesque and monstrous, the determining factor of his exile, and so it is in his own interest that he should reinforce what had at the level of the *Portrait* been simply romantic criticism with a tendency towards sarcasm; the portrait of the Irishman, as he would see himself if he could see with Joyce's eyes, reaches its highest degree of ridicule. To gain access to the cyclops' world, all one has to do is to take all their verbal claims seriously and literally, and to translate gestures and deeds into images.

This is why the "Cyclops" episode is produced with a vigour that is all the more enjoyable for not showing the usual Joycean signs of effort; the whole impression given is that of an author who is delighted because he can talk about his enemies with the complete conviction that they are wrong and he is right, can be harsh to the unpleasant people and massacre them with his pen, making ink flow instead of blood. This delight is what gives the episode its tension and rapidity: the author can at last give free rein to his dislikes. Joyce provided most of the episodes in *Ulysses* with a symbolic colour, but there is no colour for the "Cyclops," neither red, green, nor orange, because Politics means the art of faithlessness, change, and the mingling of colours; the colour of the tavern is in fact a mixture, like the mixture of the colonised peoples.

Politics is associated with venality in a comical and revengeful epiphany which brings together and juxtaposes like the two sides of a coin the claims of the legendary chiefs of Ireland and the reality of modern Ireland's inescapable economic dependence and alienation; young Alfred Bergan buys drinks, thus:

But he, the young chief of the O'Bergans, could ill brook to be outdone in generous deeds but gave therefor with gracious gesture a testoon of costliest bronze. Thereon embossed in excellent smithwork was seen the image of a queen of regal port, scion of the house of Brunswick,. . . . defender of the faith, Empress of India, even she, who bore rule, . . . the wellbeloved, for they knew and loved her from the rising of the sun to the going down thereof, the pale, the dark, the ruddy and the ethiop." (*Ulysses*, p. 293)

And Joyce, the anonymous accusor, gives free rein to his satirical powers, bringing forth a catalogue of horrors and aggressions in the manner of Voltaire. Murder is disguised as a romantic pantomime, a public execution is conducted like a fair or carnival before our eyes, an epic boxing-match is produced for us; and while the Dubliners dreamily drink and Bloom sucks his cigar, Noman leads a bloodthirsty saraband of inquisitors, hangmen, boxers, segregationists, racial fanatics, and others, and the bar becomes an ark containing specimens of every kind of human cruelty and intolerance.

In the *Odyssey* Ulysses says that he is called "Noman," a trick of language which gives him the power of invisibility, allowing him to exist and not to exist simultaneously. In "Cyclops," however, Bloom keeps his own admitted identity; it is indeed Ulysses who is armed with the stake to put out the giant's one eye, as in the Homeric legend, but this time it is not he who is noman. Joyce is amusing himself here; the problems of Ireland, history and politics, interest and concern him, not for reasons of patriotism, but because, as Stephen said to Cranly, he knows himself to be the "product" of his race and of its history.

Noman is the invisible spectator, the "I" who narrates the epic tale. His spicy language is both best-quality Dublinese in the style of John Joyce and that of James Joyce the accomplished parodist. Being refined out of existence, his presence is all the more discreet too because he says "I"; literally, by assimilating himself *in person* with them, Joyce achieves the supreme absence. This procedure demonstrates the truth of the paradox Edgar Allan Poe had illustrated in *The Purloined Letter*, that by putting the hidden object in the most evident and banal place one hides it best of all. By going to Kiernan's Joyce causes us to forget him so completely that the substitution of the narrator for Ulysses passes unnoticed to begin with. The game is most admirable when, after Bloom-Elijah, the type of Christ, has left, one realises that Everyman has ascended and that it is Noman who observes and comments on the ascension.[9] Does Joyce in the Tavern see with one eye or two, one may ask?

Finally, Noman the "I" is also the artist as type of Nogod, of Blake's "Nobodaddy" whom Joyce transformed into a series of more or less malevolent Divine Absences, the least fearful of which must surely be the "Nobodyatall" of *Finnegans Wake* (p. 73). This "Nobodyatall" is the force of non-being that makes the Dubliners stay in the cave of Cyclops, to be eaten one after another, always idly hoping that someone will come to save them.

In the "Cyclops" episode[10] the parody constitutes an attack not only on a particular vision of the world but also on that vision's style. When Joyce declares:

> The chapter of the *Cyclops* is being lovingly moulded in the way you know. The Fenian is accompanied by a wolfhound who speaks (or curses) in Irish. He unburdens his soul about the Saxo-Angles in the best Fenian style and with colossal vituperativeness alluding to their standard industry. The epic proceeds explanatorily, "He spoke of the English, a noble race,

[9]A curious fact, typical of the malicious pleasure Joyce sometimes takes in his work, is the presence in it of a number of anonymous characters, beginning with the cyclist who picks up Tom Kernan in *Grace*. Angels or artists, creators or evil spirits, they find their most impressive representative is the "man in the macintosh," whose face is never seen and who is eventually designated by the name of his garment. He haunts Bloom until the "Circe" chapter, anonymous, a parodist of the game of masks and of the philosophy of clothes.

[10]See Vivian Mercier, *The Irish Comic Tradition*, (Oxford, 1962), pp. 210–36, on Joyce and the Irish satirical tradition.

rulers of the waves, who sit on thrones of alabaster, silent as the deathless gods."[11]

he is bringing his satire to bear on the language of the Homeric, epic point of view.

This is done by making use of a vocabulary in which the great, large words are reserved for the expression of size and quantity, and applied to grotesque and unworthy objects, or by using a ridiculous idea as the second term of an Homeric comparison: thus, the nostrils of the Cyclopean Citizen are compared to larks' nests and his eyes to large cauliflowers. The vulgarity is used to explode the epic nobility. The "Cyclops" episode itself is an epic reduced in size and reduced to the absurd. Without leaving the bar, except for Bloom's departure, we can witness a whole series of scenes, like cinematographic projections of excerpts from popular epic, interpolated into Noman's narration of a simple incident, Bloom's clash with the Citizen. By means of a series of interruptions as capricious as anything in *Tristram Shandy*, one oscillates between a fantastic time past and a still more incredible present, as though Joyce were also mocking the purely ornamental descriptive side of these epics. Every detail serves as pretext for some superb description, since the epic is, after all, nothing less than the transposition of an adventure happening to one individual who is supposed to represent the entire country. The epic hero's sword is sacred, and so is the citizen's handkerchief or the biscuit box.

The Cyclops is the true master of the place, and of Dublin, filling all with his huge, bloodthirsty presence. Similarly, in the half-light, as Joyce does all he can to maintain the comic confusion, it is possible to mistake Bloom for Ulysses until the moment when it becomes obvious that he is not; and similarly the Cyclops is more than just the Citizen. He is the Executioner-god, a complex figure that resembles some blasphemous political trinity. He is marked out as God the father by his symbolic animal the dog and by his methods of judgement, and he is associated with two sinister acolytes, the hangman Rumbold (who is invoked by one of the drinkers, and whose presence allows the insertion of an imaginary scene of execution) and the Empress of India. The fact that the citizen is a Fenian and Rumbold an official Fenian-slayer simply emphasises, by this apparent incompatibility, what Joyce thinks of poli-

[11] *Letters*, vol. I, p. 126, 19 June 1919, written to Budgen. In *Ulysses* this becomes, "They're not European, says the citizen. I was in Europe with Kevin Egan of Paris. You wouldn't see a trace of them or their language anywhere in Europe except in a *cabinet d'aisance.*" (*Ulysses*, p. 313)

tics, views which he also expresses directly through Bloom: that those who have power, from whatever source, will inevitably abuse it. Harsh justice, abuse of power and fanaticism have found a worthy spokesman, ready for action.

This abode of muscular patriotism is chosen by Joyce to correspond to the island where so many of Ulysses' companions perished. The list of correspondences[12] for this chapter gives: Tavern: Barney Kiernan's bar in Little Britain Street. One has only just come out of the nearby Ormond, the Sirens' bar, the home of fantasy and illusions of happiness. The Tavern where the Citizen holds forth so peremptorily on politics, dreaming of past glory and future vengeance, is opposed to the Ormond, where Dublin's menfolk act as Casanovas. The longing for an heroic life, either in the eyes of history or in the eyes of the siren women, is the same. Time: 5 P.M. Joe Hynes is returning from a gathering of horse-dealers; he is the man who, in "Ivy Day," had recited the long poem on the death of Parnell. His presence makes the bar echo with the strains of ridiculous patriotic songs like *Hear, O Erin*; the Ivy Leaguers were considered to be liberals. The Citizen's virulent nationalism is ultra-reactionary; he buys drinks for a group of his fellow-citizens whom the reader has already met in *Ulysses* or in *Dubliners*, parasites like Lenehan, alcoholics like Bob Doran, or idlers like O'Molloy. They all share the mediocrity, passivity and selfishness of insignificant people, willing to make up for their insignificance by harshness and cruelty.

The muscle constitutes the Organ corresponding to this chapter because politics is an affair of brute strength. The Homeric similarities are pointed out from the beginning, and everyone drinks. The drink befuddles the Dubliners' brains to such an extent that they believe that Fenianism will save Ireland; this disgusts Joyce, for those who have come through all the testing and returned safely, like Bloom or Joyce or Ulysses, always choose cunning and a purely personal diplomacy and dissimulation as their policy. Bloom marks himself out as a victim for the hostility of these fanatical politicians by ordering a cigar instead of a drink, and by forgetting to buy a round for the others, an antisocial

[12]This table is reproduced in *A James Joyce Miscellany, Second Series*, ed. Magalaner, p. 49; it was made by Joyce and entrusted by him to Herbert Gorman in about 1920; in 1938, Stuart Gilbert had a copy of it which he used in working on his book, *James Joyce's Ulysses*. Joyce was most unwilling for this document to become publicly known, and accused Gorman of having allowed Random House to copy it. These five type-written pages, glued into a strip about three feet long, contain the exact layout of *Ulysses* and its thematic structure, all traces of which were so carefully hidden in the public work.

omission which puts the Citizen into a gigantic rage, a rage which is increased by Bloom's daring to enter his cave and fill it with smoke, and by his behaviour with the stake. Bloom says, "You don't grasp my point." Joyce deliberately chose Kiernan's bar for this scene; there are times when he writes for his fellow-citizens, and when his taste for the realities and circumstances of Dublin is fully indulged. The "Cyclops" is one of the most authentically Dubliner chapters, a fact which is all the more remarkable because, as Budgen pointed out, this episode dealing with politics shows that Joyce had absolutely no national consciousness.

Ireland, for him, meant Dublin. Everything outside its walls was scarcely worth writing a line about. His mixture of hatred and love for the City literally excluded all nationalism; he applies his usual individualism to the reality before him, a circumstance which explains his impatience with the "Irish Dubliners." The bar was a sanctuary for aggressiveness and an arena for rebellious boasters. Stuart Gilbert has given a valuable description of it[13]; the owner had the bizarre hobby of collecting objects that had been produced as evidence in criminal trials, ropes that had been used to tie up criminals, glasses famous hangmen had drunk from, and so on. The establishment still existed in 1939. It is likely that Joyce overheard more than one epiphany there when the worthy Dubliners might be heard discussing hanging—not from the point of view of justice or with any consideration for the condemned man, but from the point of view of the last feat the hanged man accomplishes, that erection which forms the subject of so long a discussion between the drinkers in the bar and the Herr Professor Luitpold Blumenduft, a subject which also returns in the "Circe" episode in more gruesomely real guise.

The Citizen is all the more disconcerting because he is in fact relatively cultured; apart from the few scraps of Gaelic with which he lards his speech (alternating with coarseness like "To hell with the bloody brutal Sassenachs and their *patois*"), he also knows a good deal about the glorious history of Ireland, and praises its past in sad, grotesque lyric phrases.

> *Raimeis*, says the citizen. There's no-one as blind as the fellow that won't see, if you know what that means. Where are our missing twenty millions of Irish should be here today instead of four, our lost tribes? And our

[13]Stuart Gilbert, *op. cit.*, p. 255. See also *Envoy*, no. 1, (Dublin, 1949), articles by Roger McHugh, "A Visit to Barney Kiernan's," and "Hangmen and Divine Assistance."

... wool that was sold in Rome in the time of Juvenal and our flax and our damask from the looms of Antrim and our Limerick lace, our tanneries and our white flint glass down there by Ballybough and our Huguenot poplin that we have since Jacquard de Lyon and our woven silk and our Foxford tweeds and ivory raised point from the Carmelite convent in New Ross, nothing like it in the whole wide world! Where are the Greek merchants that came through the pillars of Hercules, the Gibraltar now grabbed by the foe of mankind, with gold and Tyrian purple to sell in Wexford at the fair of Carmen? (*Ulysses*, p. 319)

This specimen of a Gaelic history lesson is probably just as authentic as the sermons on hell in the *Portrait*. The citizen exhorts his hearers to read Tacitus, Ptolemy, and even Giraldus Cambrensis. In the course of this public-house lecture, with its Irish chorus, Lenehan, John Wyse Nolan, Alf Bergan, Bob Doran, and Joe Hynes, with its antichorus Bloom, the citizen abuses the *Irish Independent* (a low newspaper which had forgotten that it had been started by Parnell) and freemasonry exemplified in the person of Bloom; he gives passionate disquisitions upon the Invincibles, the rebellion years, the unfortunate martyrs who were hanged, Wolfe Tone, Robert Emmet, Thomas Moore, the Sinn Fein, and, logically enough, the Irish language. He ends by giving a direct history lesson in the style of nationalist propaganda, like a good Minister for Culture. The charm of all this resides in the evocation of emotive words and the useless tears that are shed over an age of past glory, in the unholy setting of the bar, before an audience who can hardly be raised to any enthusiasm except by alcohol. The speech is so near to the possible, or to the real and actual, that it is simply the personality of the Citizen which allows the transition to parody to take place.

On the other hand, there is no ambiguity when the dog speaks. Garryowen indirectly inherits the task of mocking by his own speech the literary forms of nationalism, and in particular the traditional Irish *genres* such as the Gaelic satirical poem. His poem is quoted in an article from one of the Gaelic League journals, which is in fact a parody of the journalistic style peculiar to members of the Irish Revival, a style which could best be described as eminently satisfied. The words of Owen Garry, the nationalist hound, are used to show how great a store of intellectual capital is possessed by the new Ireland; the anonymous narrator discusses learnedly a problem of comparative linguistics which needs no commentary. The pedantry, the pompous "university" style, and the affected modesty of the researcher bringing to light his scientific or literary discoveries are all cut to pieces by the dog's claws. Nevertheless, in order to satisfy possible critics, no-one is actually named; the eminent professors and experts on phonetics or philology are not named, because they are "legion."[14]

> All those who are interested in the spread of human culture among the lower animals (and their name is legion) should make a point of not missing the really marvellous exhibition of cynanthropy given by the famous old Irish red wolfdog setter ... Our greatest living phonetic expert (wild horses shall not drag it from us!) has left no stone unturned in his efforts to delucidate and compare the verse recited and has found it bears a *striking* resemblance (the italics are ours) to the ranns of ancient Celtic bards. ... We subjoin a specimen which has been rendered into English by an eminent scholar whose name for the moment we are not at liberty to disclose ... (*Ulysses*, p. 305)

The dog's verses follow, with the direction "to be spoken somewhat slowly and indistinctly in a tone suggestive of suppressed rancour"; the growled or grunted poem is the equivalent of the Celtic verses, and the dog's "rann," or rune, disposes in a single mouthful of all the Gaelic ideology, the vague, rancorous and reactionary muttering that feeds on outdated words and catchphrases. Joyce takes pleasure, as one might have expected, in letting the dog have his say; as a Europeanised intellectual he was deeply opposed to the poetic and anti-intellectual side of the Gaelic Revivalists, which he associated with the unenlightened fanaticism of the "rabblement." The clever dog embodies both of these aspects. Adams points out that the dog is a real Dublin dog, the companion of Old Giltrap, and perhaps also owes something to a performing dog of the same name who was making successful appearances in 1904 at the Tivoli.[15]

Joyce's irreverent catalogues are particularly abundant in the "Cyclops" chapter, and their use is partially justified by the intentional enlargement which the style demands.

In the beginning there was the tradition, with its Rabelaisian lists and its Homeric accumulations, constituting on the one hand a witty game

[14]Legion may of course be just another name for Noman; or this may be what Joyce does *not* say, in order to imply it all the more effectively. Unfortunately, it seems that "eminent professors" are still just as rare in Ireland, to judge by a recent leaflet published by the Corradh na Gaeilge, which has to call upon an American professor, of Irish immigrant descent, for the support of the national identity by means of the language.

[15]R. Adams, *Surface and Symbol*, pp. 107ff.

with words, a taking of pleasure in the lavish outpouring of the resources of vocabulary, a special feast to satisfy the author's pride in
being such a word-rich man; and on the other a kind of challenge issued
to reality, which is limited by its nature and which the author wishes
to emulate, if not to surpass. There is also in the mind of the maker of
lists and catalogues the wishful attempt to create artificially and visually
an impression of fullness, crowding riches and abundance. There is,
finally, the need sometimes felt to replace the quality of a superlative
thing or person by *quantity,* since there is no word adequate to express
the rarety of the object.

For Joyce, verbal accumulation comes under the second of these
headings: the quantity of the names enumerated creates a feeling of
swarming crowds, like the heros of Ireland, the "members of the
clergy," the "twelve tribes of Iar," "the fashionable international world
... at the wedding" (*Ulysses,* p. 325). The handkerchief the Citizen uses
"to swab himself dry" becomes "the muchtreasured and intricately
embroidered ancient Irish face-cloth," bearing on it all the natural and
legendary beauties of Ireland, all the romantic places, the Green Hills
of Tallaght, the brewery of Messrs. Arthur Guinness, Son and Company
(Limited), Isolde's tower, Jury's Hotel, the three birthplaces of the first
duke of Wellington, and many more picturesque or fictitious places
which Joyce enumerates in the tones of a "Museyland" official, enthusiastic, sentimental, yet also specialising in the guide's jargon that
tourists expect. All this ancient green beauty is inscribed, by a miracle
of the miniaturist's art, within the four corners of the "snotrag," for the
world to admire. Legendary Ireland and its riches fit into one handkerchief.

"The bard's noserag" (*Ulysses,* p. 9) had been another cloth, vulgar
in another sense, unfolded for Mulligan to wipe his razor on it; Stephen's flag is snotgreen ("but with a difference," as Bloom would say),
but it is only the dirty and decaying handkerchief that belongs to a
penniless student. The bard is both too poor and too lucid to embroider
upon Reality.

Satire in Joyce's work is never cruel; it never *directly* attacks human
values, or even the Dubliners, for when Joyce denounces the mental
illnesses of Ireland he is speaking in the name of spiritual health, and
very far from joking. On the other hand, Ireland's economic problems
seem to call for less delicate handling. The "Cyclops" chapter is one of
those in which Joyce has really allowed himself to advance to the attack
by creating the necessary *mental distance* first. One can see the serious

problems which preoccupied him in his exile in Trieste, here transposed into different terms; he saw the real Irish problem in Marxist
terms of alienation, and loathed what he called the "empty boasts" of
that vainglorious nation.[16]

His technique consists of, superficially, a disfigurement of style, which
is raised up to the epic level when he wants to parody the nostalgic
megalomania or the mental blindness of the Irish, and then deflated and
flattened down again to the level of reality. Satire is lodged somewhere
in between historical reality and the wilful lies of language. It has here
the full Latin meaning of *Satura:* the over-plentiful supply of non-
productive citizens, the variety of coarse vegetables and cabbage-stalks,
the growing impoverishment of the people, all this is associated with
that ecclesiastical Irish stew, not very nourishing, composed of deacons,
sub-deacons, mitred abbots, priors, superiors, monks of every order,
friars of every kind, with all the saints and martyrs, virgins and confessors.

There is much blessing and cursing in the "Cyclops" chapter; and
there are many priests to be fed, so many, who all pray together, that
it is difficult not to be overwhelmed and lost among their black robes.
Perhaps more people are needed to officiate, in order that all voices
may be heard. "A Nation Once Again," sung by the Irish Caruso-
Garibaldi, is applauded by the nation in question in the person of its
high ecclesiastical notables, "as well as representatives of the press and
the bar and the other learned professions."

Again, when the chapter begins with an evocation of the market-
gardening and vegetable riches of Ireland, this is simply Joyce's way of
emphasising the dreams of greatness in which his idealistic compatriots
indulged, proud despite everything of being "descended from kings";
and the more he adopts the epic tone and multiplies the adjectives, the
more he makes it implicitly clear that in reality there is not enough food
to feed the whole nation. The past may be a feast worthy of the gods,

[16]See the lecture he gave in Italian, at the People's University in Trieste, in *Critical
Writings*, p. 209. It is dated 1907, and deals with Ireland as land of saints and scholars:
—"I do not see the purpose of . . . the empty boasts that the art of miniature in the ancient
Irish books such as the *Book of Kells*, the *Yellow Book of Lecan*, the *Book of the Dun
Cow*, which date back to a time when England was an uncivilised country, is almost as
old as the Chinese, and that Ireland made and exported to Europe its own fabrics for
several generations before the first Fleming arrived in London to teach the English how
to make bread. If an appeal to the past in this manner were valid, the fellahin of Cairo
would have all the right in the world to disdain to act as porters for English tourists." Cf.
Ulysses, p. 141, "Kingdoms of this world. The masters of the Mediterranean are fellaheen
today."

but the present is no more than a potato or two.[17] Joyce invites his reader to a veritable marriage-feast, but conducts the feast with the malicious humour of a Cervantes; every dish is described and praised until it is transformed into something else, and we never actually taste it. The egg turns into an oblong precious stone, agate or amber, of varying dimensions. When we hear the cackling, roaring, lowing, bleating, bellowing, rumbling, grunting, champing, chewing of the various animals for the feast, we feel that a royal welcome is being prepared; but then Garryowen "lets a grouse out of him," and we see that there is really nothing there but the empty biscuit tin.

In the portrait of the heroically-sized Citizen we recognise an exaggerated type of Davin, and the enlargement process has here been reduced to the most simple technique, the use of adjectives like "large," "vast," and "massive." "The figure seated on a large boulder at the foot of a round tower was that of a broadshouldered deepchested stronglimbed frankeyed redhaired freely freckled shaggybearded widemouthed largenosed longheaded deepvoiced barekneed brawnyhanded hairylegged ruddyfaced sinewyarmed hero" (*Ulysses*, p. 289).

The "hero" is here only an ordinary man seen through a telescope. The moral portrait of the citizen shows us a one-eyed ogre, a typical ogre thirsting for drink like Polyphemus, angry and frustrated because Ulysses-Bloom is not going to buy him one. In the *Odyssey* Polyphemus is the victim of someone smaller than himself. He is the Champion of the Cause, a legendary figure to the ordinary Dubliner:

> So we turned into Barney Kiernan's and there sure enough was the citizen up in the corner having a great confab with himself and that bloody mangy mongrel, Garryowen, and he waiting for what the sky would drop in the way of drink.
> —There he is, says I, in his gloryhole, with his cruiskeen lawn and his load of papers, working for the cause. (*Ulysses*, p. 289).

The "cause" and the "legend" become indistinguishable, in the halfHebrew, half-Homeric setting of mythology, where Goliath and Cyclops are brothers of Cuchulain and Conchubar, Gaelic heroes whose exploits Yeats was re-telling.[18] The Cyclops-Citizen is Everybrute as

---

[17]Old Gummy Granny (*Ulysses*, p. 528) has "the deathflower of the potato blight on her breast."

[18]In *Deirdre* (1907), *The Green Helmet* (1910), etc. It was against Yeats and his romantic idealisation of the Poor Old Woman in *Cathleen ni Houlihan* (1902) that Joyce set his toothless old Ireland, slayer of young men, asking not for money but pleading thus:—"If any one would give me help he must give me himself, he must give me all . . . It is a hard

Bloom may be Everyman. Cuchulain may be noble, but Goliath certainly is not, and it is the small men like Alf Bergan, Bob Doran, or Bloom who act the part of David. Joyce detested violence, whatever its motives. He invents a fictitious genealogy, mixing into it:

Saints: St. Brandan;

Noble Heroes: Cuchulain, Wolfe Tone;

Giants: Goliath;

True Irishmen: MacMahon;

Honorary Irishmen: Patrick Shakespeare, Brian Confucius, Murtagh Gutenberg, Patrick Velasquez;

Emperors: Caesar, Napoleon;

Gods or Prophets: Buddha, Mahomet;

Scientists: Volta, Paracelsus, Benjamin Franklin;

Legendary Characters: Tom Thumb, The Last of the Mohicans, The Man who Broke the Bank at Monte Carlo.

It contains a hundred "false" or "honorary" Celts, borrowed from high and low throughout history and literature, after the usual practice of oppressed minorities who feel the need to assemble an impressive collection of ancestors, even if they are not necessarily authentic.

From the discussions which arouse the Cyclops to anger it can be deduced that patriotism is synonymous with all intolerance and fanaticism. The Citizen is a good nationalist but a bad man, because he can only see with the one eye, that of the fanatical Irishman thirsting for independence; his other eye, the ordinary human one, is closed, so much so that he "cannot see" Bloom, because he is "an Israelite." Joyce develops at length the paradox of his attitude of apparently humanitarian protest towards the cruelty of the English, a cruelty specially blessed by the Anglican Church,[19] but his own attitudes are just as sadistic and fanatical to anyone who is not as convinced and intolerant a nationalist as he. Every ideal, as it is turned into an institution, becomes a religion,

service they take that help me. Many that are red-cheeked now will be pale-cheeked; . . . many a child will be born and there will be no father at its christening to give it a name. They that have red cheeks will have pale cheeks for my sake, and for all that, they will think they are well paid." (Yeats, *Collected Plays*, London, 1960, pp. 84ff.) This scene was supposed to take place in 1798, the tragic year of the uprising and execution of Wolfe Tone.

[19]"I'll tell you what about it, says the citizen, Hell upon earth it is. Read the revelations that's going on in the papers about flogging on the training ships at Portsmouth. A fellow writes that calls himself *Disgusted One*.

So he starts telling us about corporal punishment and about the crew of tars and officers and rear-admirals drawn up in cocked hats and the parson with his protestant bible to witness punishment and a young lad brought out, howling for his ma, and they tie him down on the buttend of a gun."(*Ulysses*, p. 322.)

and a murderous one. The end is an ironical apotheosis in which Bloom, whom the Citizen had called a Judas, is called up to God the Father in heaven, as a type of Elijah; as the type of Jesus, he is the only non-violent hero, and the Citizen, without realising it, is stoning the emissary of his own God, like Polyphemus throwing rocks into the sea. He has to slay the sacriligious talker who would replace the Gaelic heritage by the half-breed Levitical tribe in which Mendelssohn, Marx, Spinoza and Jesus are cousins because God is their "Uncle":

> —Where is he till I murder him?
> . . . Hold on, citizen, says Joe. Stop.
> Begob he drew his hand and made a swipe and let fly. Mercy of God the sun was in his eyes or he'd have left him for dead. (*Ulysses*, p. 336)

The weapon of the revenger is an empty biscuit tin, and all the crumbs (of the Host, as it were) have already been devoured by the Citizen's dog. The sun blinds the Citizen, and illuminates the figure of Bloom, the man who believes only in love as a force beyond nationalism.

The citizen does not realise how right he is when he says that there is something of Christ in that Jew, Bloom. Garryowen, the cynanthropic citizen, whose personality as dog is inseparable from that of his chauvinistic master,[20] swears in Irish; both growl, foam at the mouth and show their teeth with all the eloquence of bloodthirsty hostility. When the master stops for breath, the dog takes up the same theme: a "bloody old mongrel, growling and grousing," he reminds us, as if it were necessary, that Joyce detested dogs almost as much as he detested war and any other form of violence; the "bloody old towser" is full of obvious hostility to any unsatisfactory Irishman. "Come in, come in, he won't eat you," says the citizen to Bloom, and Ulysses comes in, nervously entering the Cyclops' cave, to realise that the dog is as anti-Semite as his master:

> So they started talking about capital punishment and of course Bloom comes out with the why and the wherefore and all the codology of the business and the old dog smelling him all the time I'm told those Jewies does have a sort of a queer odour coming off them for dogs about I don't know what all. . . . (*Ulysses*, p. 298)

---

[20]In fact, he is only a temporary master, because in politics, one changes masters as easily as one changes shirts. The dog really belongs to "old Giltrap."

Bloom is an idealist who believes it possible to train dogs by kindness, and if one judged by this characteristic alone one would be inclined to believe that in politics Joyce dissociated himself from Bloom. Like Bloom he was a pacifist, but much less optimistic. All Bloom's simple, altruistic, humanitarian speeches in this political chapter are from the start reduced to the level of the ridiculous, by means of an elementary literary trick; he speaks in the tones of measured good sense and believes that his audience share his views, but in the eyes of the others Bloom is merely a "cod," a joke, and no-one listens to him seriously. As fish and as lamb, therefore, Bloom's language is much too Christian for the Citizen. The latter as adversary is infuriated by his "but don't you see?" and "but on the other hand." Bloom is made a "cod" as much as Stephen is "dog," and the Dubliners seem to derive the same ironical pleasure from insinuating that Bloom is not so much a man as a "half and half ," a creature neither fish nor flesh. Bloom as Christ, although neither he nor his fellow-citizens recognise this, feels a tolerant sympathy for all animals, including dogs; he even believes that they can be "trained by kindness." His faith in canine nature is by no means shared by Stephen, who, in "Proteus," sees a mutant dog whose ancestors rather disquietingly include a leopard, a panther, a fox and a piece of carrion flesh. This dog-god frightens him so much that he brandishes his ashplant at it.

On the beach of eternity Stephen meets this living, mutant dog, and a dead dog too, signifying the mutability of God who hides himself in the skins of many different creatures and goes round nosing at their remains. In the tavern of Time Bloom, armed only with his charity, confronts the militant and fanatical God whose word is an indistinct rune (rann). He makes advances of friendship to Garryowen, who shows his teeth in a growl; but Bloom the Cod has nonetheless feelings of sympathy for Emmanuel-as-Dog, in a curious reversal of the usual relations between the pitiful Jesus (who appealed to Joyce) and the pitiless Father.

"You know, Budgen, I am not a bloodyminded man," Joyce would often say, "so that the phrase became a kind of refrain or motto."[21] He also used to say that the slaughter of the suitors had always seemed to him an act unworthy and untypical of Ulysses, because he could not bear the idea of an "Ithaca" episode in the Homeric style or in the style of the fifth act of *Hamlet*, which Stephen calls a "bloodboltered shambles." "Ithaca," which was written in 1921, after the First World War

---

[21]Frank Budgen, *The Making of Ulysses* (London, 1934), p. 263.

and its real slaughter, wears a peaceful aspect but does not spare the
suitors anything except violent death: Bloom's catechism eliminates
them by its demonstration of non-violence. Nevertheless, there are
moments when self-defence is necessary; Bloom is almost overwhelmed
by the Citizen's extreme vituperation. His obstinate pacifism provokes
hatred; equity, a virtue he likes to think he possesses, has no place in
the Cyclops' world, where one must be on one side or the other but
cannot be in the middle. The Fenian's threats are a parody of Christ's
words, "He who is not with me is against me"; and according to this
maxim it is enough to stand opposite Bloom, or for him to disapprove
of the citizen, for him to be at once loathed and shut out from the
others' company. Bloom represents the *via media*, the golden mean,
and he threatens all nationalist values with the cold fishy stare of the
cod. He is constantly adopting "equitable" positions or outlooks, and
thus sets himself apart from the rest of the world, at a constant distance
away from all, yet not out of their reach. He gives other people more
and more reasons to be aggrieved against him, and firstly, in the sphere
most important to the Cyclops, he antagonises them over the question
of sport and its importance:

> So off they started about Irish sport and shomeen games the like of the
> lawn tennis and about hurley and putting the stone and racy of the soil and
> building up a nation once again and all of that. And of course Bloom had
> to have his say too about if a fellow had a rower's heart violent exercise was
> bad. (*Ulysses*, p. 310)

Opposite Bloom is young Bergan, champion of the noble sport, all the
more belligerent in his words because he is small and an Irishman; his
god is the boxer Myler Keogh, the idol of Dublin, but Bloom does not
worship the boxer.

The second stage is the opposition of Dublin and Bloom over the
affair of the anonymous postcard sent to Denis Breen, whose wife used
to be so friendly with Bloom—a card bearing the enigmatic obscene
message U.P. Bloom's opponent this time is the citizen:

> Pity about her, says the citizen. Or any other woman marries a half and
> half.
> —How half and half? says Bloom. Do you mean he . . .
> —Half and half I mean, says the citizen. A fellow that's neither fish nor
> flesh. (*Ulysses*, p. 314)

The third case involves Irish justice and "the high sanhedrim of the twelve tribes of Iar":

> —The strangers, says the citizen. Our own fault. We let them come in. We brought them. The adulteress and her paramour brought the Saxon robbers here.
> —Decree *nisi*, says J. J.
> And Bloom letting on to be interested in nothing, a spider's web in the corner behind the barrel, and the citizen scowling after him and the old dog at his feet looking up to know who to bite and when.
> —A dishonoured wife, says the citizen, that's what's the cause of all our misfortune. (*Ulysses*, p. 317)

Bloom is guilty of having an adulterous wife; this is a slight extension of Mr. Deasy's idea.[22]

The discussion becomes more profound, as the great questions of political morality are introduced: "Persecution, says he, all the history of the world is full of it. Perpetuating national hatred among nations" (*Ulysses*, p. 324). Bloom has gone beyond the pale, for here moderation is a crime; he dares to doubt the absolutely unique virtues of the Irish, and he even insinuates that violence is natural to mankind instead of being the exclusive property of the English: "But, says Bloom, isn't discipline the same everywhere? I mean wouldn't it be the same here if you put force against force?" (*Ulysses*, p. 323). He must be ejected at once, for such subversive thought. It seems, moreover, that Bloom had provided Griffith with some ideas, and this, of course, is unpardonable, for a Jew to tell an independent Dubliner what to do! "Let us muck out of it ourselves," chorus the nationalists, who spurn the idea of foreign aid. Only John Wyse Nolan (perhaps because of his name) and Martin Cunningham (alias Shakespeare) protest in Bloom's favour, thus:

> And after all, says John Wyse, why can't a jew love his country like the next fellow?
> . . . That's the new Messiah for Ireland! says the citizen. Island of saints and sages!
> —Well, they're still waiting for their redeemer, says Martin. For that matter so are we. (*Ulysses*, p. 330)

---

[22] *Ulysses*, p. 37:—"For a woman who was no better than she should be, Helen, . . . ten years the Greeks made war on Troy. A faithless wife first brought the strangers to our shore . . . A woman too brought Parnell low."

And then Bloom commits the worst possible offence by reminding the ostentatious anti-Semite that Christ was a Jew. "By Jesus," cries the citizen, "I'll brain that bloody jewman for using the holy name. By Jesus, I'll crucify him so I will" (*Ulysses*, p. 335).

Joyce brings this episode to an end by mingling the Homeric myth with allusion to the Christian myth, making the *Odyssey* illustrate the words from the Sermon on the Mount, in St. Matthew's Gospel, "Beware of false prophets who come to you in sheep's clothing, for within they are ravening wolves." The Citizen defines Bloom as "a wolf in sheep's clothing" (*Ulysses*, p. 331). The trial is over, and all the expected business attended to, when Joyce makes the judge prick up his ears and by a final joke show his presence in the episode: Ulysses had escaped from the Cyclops' cave under the belly of a sheep, and so here Bloom finds, in a distant and comical fashion, his typological vocation; his real charity is suspected of concealing the blackest duplicity, and he is associated with the wolf, crueller even than the dog.

Bloom's own view is expressed thus to the confused Stephen in the "Eumeus" episode, for "People could put up with being bitten by a wolf but what properly riled them was a bite from a sheep. The most vulnerable point too of tender Achilles, your God was a Jew, because mostly they appeared to imagine he came from Carrick-on-Shannon or somewhere about in the county Sligo" (*Ulysses*, p. 500).

The Execution of the Young Rebel is an entertaining and instructive show for the good people of Ireland. "The last farewell was affecting in the extreme. From the belfries far and near the funereal deathbell tolled. . . . deafening claps of thunder and dazzling flashes of lightning. . . . assembled multitude which numbered at the lowest computation five hundred thousand persons" (*Ulysses*, p. 300).

A grandiose panorama worthy of the majestic spectacle is evoked. Bloom tries to explain "what I mean." We were with Bloom in Barney Kiernan's, seeing and listening to him; we are there in the same embarrassing situation as Bloom, hearing the Citizen's threats, but in the twinkling of an eye, the time it takes to swallow a mouthful of beer, Joyce has set up an immense stage in that imaginary space which their mutual hostility and opposition has created between Bloom and the Citizen. While Polyphemus is recovering his breath, Joyce improvises a film-like dream upon the appropriate theme of the "Hero of the Cause." It opens in the style of a journalist endeavouring to communicate the incommunicable quality of a supremely moving occasion. Not being an artist, he has to have recourse to the humiliating procedure of claiming to be "rendered speechless" by the inexpressible gravity of the occasion; and is then replaced by an abler commentator, with a gift for pompous rhetoric, an artificial, prosaic Milton.

When sufficient fullness and dignity of tone have been achieved, the journalist is recalled; he is a smart fellow who knows how to flatter, and enumerates the distinguished people present, beginning with the High Commissioner (in person, too!), the municipal band, the Little Sisters of the Poor and their orphan charges, etc. Everyone is there, representatives of order, rejoicing, charity, authority (Their Excellencies *in person*), all the most municipal powers. The noise and the music go to five-hundred thousand heads, and a certain confusion occurs; the last farewell is forgotten in favour of immediate amusement. The "Friends of the Emerald Isle" inadvertently begin murdering each other. After a great deal of bloodshed, the hangman steps on to the scaffold with his usual majestic simplicity and modesty, wearing his favourite flower, the phallic *Gladiolus Cruentus*. The signal for prayer is given, and an admirable example of Christian humility is offered by the priest who kneels in a puddle of rainwater to administer the last sacraments.

And there is water everywhere; five hundred thousand people shed some tears each, and remember that the chief character is to be put to death. The ritual sacrifice proceeds. The condemned man is noble and generous; he has bequeathed his intestines to the amalgamated cats' and dogs' home, thus showing that he would favour a universal reconciliation of dogs and cats everywhere, for whom he gives his intestines. There are cutting instruments supplied by Sheffield, two "commodious milkjugs" to receive the victim's blood, perhaps for the preparation of sausages or black-pudding for the cats and dogs, and the blood-pots, as seems only right in Joyce, are milkjugs really. "It's sad though, all the same," as Skeffington remarked to Jim after the death of the latter's brother. Five hundred thousand tender hearts are comforted by the marriage of the hero's betrothed, for Joyce appreciates the importance of the heart, even in the imposing breast of the implacable lieutenant-colonel, "he who had blown a considerable number of sepoys from the cannonmouth without flinching."

The hero's Irish fiancée gives her hand (with the agreement of the five hundred thousand worthy spectators) to a noble young Oxford graduate, "noted for his chivalry towards the fair sex." The marriage is blessed by the Church, everyone weeps with joy and admiration to witness the delicacy of the Englishmen's sentiments, and the whole episode comes to the correct happy ending. It is forbidden to believe

in the purity of democracy; and this tragedy is aimed at the Sean
O'Casey type of revolutionary.

For Joyce the reality is simply the Citizen, abusing "the Saxon" as he
abuses the Jew, without the least notion of ideology in his head. The
horrible, blood-soaked scene of the execution is treated as an opportunity for expressing noble sentiments, as a fairground, as a theatrical
performance involving romantic love and reconciliation through the
blood of the young rebel. Even the hangman appreciates the moving,
ceremonial aspect of his performance, and he wears a flower in his
button-hole. It is all very edifying.

It happens that the hangman's name, Rumbold, is one that was very
familiar to Joyce, and that his satire of the cannibal crowd furnished a
pretext for a personal revenge. Joyce hated bloodshed; but he believed
in the power of satire, which in the time of the ancient Irish bards had
been considered capable of wounding or even of killing. Thus Joyce
executes the hangman who dispatches the young rebel. We know how
much he allowed himself to cheat and rearrange in his books, and how
he recognised no frontier between his art and his life, not separating his
writing, which was alone and always with him, from his external conversations and contacts with others. Between the matter of life and the
words he used, between the lines of a work that had been long in
preparation, everyday vicissitudes could at any moment insert themselves, and could remain, unforeseen but eternal.

Thus, if one reads these episodes in the usual manner of a reader who
opens a book expecting light on the works of the imagination and on
aesthetic construction, one may well fail to observe that Joyce himself
is here protesting, gesticulating, and leading his own life as Joyce; while
one is tempted to seek always for Ulysses behind Bloom, one misses
Joyce, ironic and angry, moving back and forth between Bloom and
Ulysses. Joyce wrote the "Cyclops," at the right time according to his
creative plan,[23] and took great care with the correspondences to the
Odyssey. The Dublin Polyphemus, however, exists alongside a Swiss
Polyphemus with whom Joyce had long and troublesome relations,
ending in lawsuits which took up all the time not devoted to the "Cyclops" and to the duties of friendship. The real Cyclops is an unpleasant
fellow-citizen of Joyce's, the Consul General, Bennett. While Bloom
speaks for the eternal Joyce, and for that which is Ulysses in Everyman,
he is also speaking as a friend and representative of Joyce in 1918. The

[23]He wrote the eighteen episodes *in their Homeric order*, remaining remarkably faithful to the form.

"Cyclops" chapter acts as the weapon, the stake, to a furious, Odyssean Joyce, spearing his English enemy with his pen. Rumbold the hangman bears the same name as the British representative in Berne who would not deign to take Joyce's part against the British representative in Zurich at the time of the epic lawsuit against Carr; he was a martinet and amateur actor who became cast for the part of Judas when, as treasurer of the local English Players, Joyce was unjustly asked to pay a sum of money which Rumbold considered due.

The Carr affair[24] was at this stage of his life one of the most important events for Joyce; he seems to have arranged the whole business against himself, like a theatrical show, in order to have real proof of the antago-nism felt by the authorities against him as champion of Art. He had already experienced the Treacherous Friend and his betrayal; he had suffered the miseries of unrequited love, whether he wanted to or not; he had, at least in part, failed in his combat with the Church, since some of the most delightfully symbolic incidents in it had been provoked by Stannie; and he had enthusiastically conducted his war against romantic and reactionary artists. Now he had to find some pretext for arousing the consular administration, and the shade of the Minister of Foreign Affairs, behind whom, to Joyce's great delight, could be discerned the whole of the British Empire and all its history of colonisation. Carr's breeches, which cost Joyce and the English Players so much, well de-served the Homeric kick which Joyce gave them and their subsequent celebration throughout his works, right up to *Finnegans Wake*.

The "evil ones" were punished, Rumbold being sent to Poland and Bennett transferred to Panama, and Joyce believed, or wanted to make himself believe, that he had had something to do with it. Temporal punishment not being adequate, he inflicted on them the eternal pun-ishment that he reserved for his most deadly enemies, and threw them to the reader, his Minotaur. Rumbold became an illiterate hangman, executioner of Gann and Smith (originally employees of the Consul General), and finally makes an illustrious appearance with his friend Carr in the "Circe" episode, as a uniformed brute and poet-slayer. The struggle between Rumbold and Joyce, symbolising the clash between the intellectual feebleness of governments and the superiority of genius, is nicely illustrated by the hangman's comical letter:—"i have a special nack of putting the noose once in he can't get out hoping to be favoured i remain, honoured sir, my terms is five guinnese. H. Rum-bold, Master Barber" (*Ulysses*, p. 297). Money impels the master barber

---

[24]See Ellmann, pp. 439–41, for details.

to take up the pen, an instrument with which he is obviously not at ease. Joyce also emphasises H. Rumbold's complete lack of any sadism, and thus makes the whole business much more sinister; there is no trace of humane feeling in the professional's exercise of his craft, he is simply a technician and nothing more. This seems half-way between Villiers de l'Isle Adam's "Le Convive de la Dernière Heure" and the maniac inventor of Kafka's "Penitential Colony." For Joyce, Rumbold is one of the "barbarians," of those who coldly and unfeelingly practice their cruelty, and such is his scorn for this type, that he describes the man as a grotesque illiterate, a skilled hangman. In effect, there had been a clash between Joyce and Carr, whom he had engaged as an actor; it concerned a sordid matter of money, and Joyce was apparently in the wrong, but as things took their course he behaved in so provoking and unjust a manner that Carr at last lost his temper and threatened to wring Joyce's neck. This was all the latter had been waiting for, and he took the threat literally, probably with malicious delight.

At the beginning of 1910 the revolutionary actions of the Sinn Fein movement became a matter of international importance. Joyce, feeling his art to be threatened by any historical change or progress, since he defined himself by his opposition to the world as it was, remained on the defensive. Budgen suggested that England was wasting troops by maintaining a foothold in Ireland and would do better to economise by granting the Irish political autonomy. Joyce replied, "Ireland is what she is. . . . and therefore I am what I am because of the relations that have existed between England and Ireland. Tell me why you think I ought to wish to change the conditions that gave Ireland and me a shape and a destiny?"[25] This was not a joke; and in fact this remark sums up the paradox of Joyce's political attitude; he was more progressive than the Fenian revolutionaries in 1904, when no-one in Ireland knew what Marx meant, yet from 1918 onwards he became admittedly a reactionary.

His work is inspired by contradiction, and it was the general paralysis of Ireland that drove him to write, as it was the primitive condition of the people that sent him out towards Europe. Similarly, his atheism was not that of an agnostic, but was a form of counter-Catholicism, a furious, rabid Catholicism, and his "socialism" was simply an anti-chauvinism. If Ireland became a democratic layman's-land, then he would have to change the structure of the work he had conceived as counter-creation.

[25]Budgen, *op. cit.*, p. 155.

of patriotism offered by Bloom in the cabmen's shelter. Bloom's version of patriotism is a democratic Utopianism:

> I want to see everyone, concluded he, all creeds and classes *pro rata* having a comfortable tidysized income in no niggard fashion either, something in the neighbourhood of £300 per annum. That's the vital issue at stake and it's feasible and would be provocative of friendlier intercourse between man and man. At least that's my idea for what it's worth. I call that patriotism. (*Ulysses*, p. 569)

Then he adds, for the benefit of Stephen to whom the words have no meaning, "if you work." You have every bit as much right to live by your pen in pursuit of your philosophy as the peasant has," he says, but it is clear that Mr. Bloom's egalitarian notions can only be shocking to Stephen, for whom "living in Ireland" is synonymous with death, and who loathes the peasant for his backwardness and servitude. To have as much right as a peasant is simply to have a claim to be buried in the communal grave. And Stephen does not want "to live by his pen," it is not an instrument to earn one's bread but a means of creating oneself a country. Writing is the place of both exile and repatriation, and this is why Stephen declares "I suspect that Ireland must be important because it belongs to me" (*Ulysses*, p. 570). This private and personal conception of one's country proves to be beyond Bloom's understanding, and Stephen, having made the exceptional step of breaking his rule of silence, returns to his inner exile, and leaves Bloom alone (though unconscious of his solitude) in a country that does not want him. "Let us change the subject," pronounces Stephen, meaning "Let us leave each other."

XII. The Abolition of Words

The Parnell Affair as Excuse for Political Disengagement

Joyce claimed *Dubliners* as a work of redemption and of moral import:

> I believe that in composing my chapter of moral history in exactly the way I have composed it I have taken the first step towards the spiritual liberation of my country. Reflect for a moment on the history of the literature of Ireland as it stands at present written in the English language before you condemn this genial illusion of mine which, after all, has at least served me in the office of a candlestick during the writing of the book.[1]

These novellas were to give the people of Dublin the opportunity of discovering the origin and effects of their alienation. It seems that for a while Joyce believed himself to have an Ibsen-like mission to denounce all national lies, a belief which constituted his own personal and vital lie; *Dubliners* is in fact an antiportrait, a series of images to which Joyce opposes the positive features of his own personality. It is almost necessary to read this collection, not starting from the author and proceeding towards the work, but starting from the description of the Irish national malady and its symptoms and proceeding towards the reconstruction of the author's problems.

To begin with, it must be emphasised that Joyce wrote these novellas between 1904 and 1905, although the temptation facing reader or critic

[1] *Letters*, vol. I, pp. 62–3. To Grant Richards, 1906.

would be to date them ten or fifteen years earlier; when he wrote "Ivy Day in the Committee Room," he was indirectly giving expression to an idealism that was most laudable no doubt, but which was then some years out of date, for to dream of the heroic Parnell in 1904 was historically unpardonable. If one had admired Parnell, by 1904 it was time to rally in support of Griffith or Padraic Pearse.

But it was necessary for Ireland to be still the ungrateful old woman who kills her children, for otherwise Joyce might have felt obliged to fight for her cause. How fortunate that it was the Church and his country that killed Parnell, for this *felix culpa* on the part of Ireland ensured the work of Joyce and its character. A reading of "Ivy Day" will show to what extent Joyce was able to convince himself, by deforming the real situation, by simply stopping artificially the historical process of development.

The little world, half sordid, half sentimental, of those who meet on Ivy Day, the 6th of October, in commemoration of Parnell, is, unknown to those taking part, the scene of a sorry farce, which Joyce uses to provide himself with justification for his rejection of such things.

The same arguments justify Stephen's withdrawal in *Portrait,* and are taken up again in the "Wandering Rocks" episode of *Ulysses.*

Stephen did not mince his rancorous words when Davin urged him to "be one of us." No-one, he said, "has given up to you his life and his youth and his affections. . . . but you sold him to the enemy." Parnell's fate is both the excuse and the reason for refusing any political involvement, which is Stephen's answer to any "appeal." Joyce, while he shared Stephen's idealism and rancour, added to it a touch of "scepticism" (carefully distinguished from "cynicism"). While he was writing the "Cyclops" episode, he had many discussions with Frank Budgen, an Englishman whose liberal views were the result of good sense rather than of sympathy, and the most frequent subjects of discussion were the Irish vocation for treachery, the problems of Home Rule, and the British Empire. Joyce used to worry about what his fellow-countrymen would think, though in a spirit of solidarity which, it must be admitted, was with him a secondary or minor consideration.[2] In the order of precedence—for Joyce the artist must always come first—he did not wish to harm, or to believe, anyone, but would not hinder others in their beliefs or practice. They might pray or slay as they wished, and Joyce

[2]"It is the work of a sceptic, but I don't want it to appear the work of a cynic. I don't want to hurt or offend those of my countrymen who are devoting their lives to a cause they feel to be necessary and just." (Budgen, *op. cit.,* p. 156.)

wrote. He felt that it might be he who would save Ireland. The Irish nation as seen by Joyce is present between the chapters of "The Wandering Rocks" and "Cyclops" as shapeless crowds, who are apparently moving but completely inert within; Bloom calls them "puppets," and it is true that they only respond to outside stimuli or to the pressure of rather petty needs. From "Ivy Day" to "The Wandering Rocks" Joyce is justifying his obstinate exile.

Political Ignominy—"Ivy Day"

This was Joyce's favourite of his own novellas; if "Cyclops" satirises the disproportionately vast ambition of Irish nationalism, then inversely "Ivy Day," written in 1905, satirises the Irish political situation, which derived its meaning and relative proportion from the presence of an invisible giant, present and alive in people's minds. This, it could be said, is the Lilliputian method of satire at work, reducing everything by reference to a superior, larger being. On this 6 October, a group of Dubliners from various social strata assemble in Wicklow Street to make their preparations for a municipal election, and the day is the anniversary of Parnell's death. Some of the agents, assembling at the end of a rainy day, have remembered this and wear an ivy leaf behind their lapel. The ivy is perennially green, but memory is less lasting; this 6 October soon appears as a day of forgetfulness, of shame or of inconvenient recollections. The agents discuss local politics, and their conversation bears witness to the disintegration of political and moral values that has come about since the Leader's death. The rain matches both the mourning of the past and the sadness of the present, while the imagery that lights up the darker corners of this evening and its events only accentuates the shadows.

In the small bare room, the ancient caretaker fans a fire which is in danger of being choked by ashes; and the commemoration begins under the auspices of a dying fire, guarded by a weeping old man. The Phoenix would find it difficult to arise from these ashes, and despite the direct allusion to resurrection in the poem recited at the end ("They had their way: they laid him low./ But Erin, list, his spirit may/ Rise, like the Phoenix from the flames,/ When breaks the dawning of the day"), it is clear that there is no faith now, and that no-one really wishes to revive the spirit of Parnell, for he would be too intransigent and too honest to suit anyone in this new generation, except perhaps (this is the Triestine, socialist Joyce speaking) the workers. But the workers would have very little chance in competition with the two parties capable of financing election campaigns, the nationalist party in whose favour the conservative candidate has stood down, and the unnamed party of Mr. Tierney, for which the O'Connors, Croftons, Henchys, and Lyons are working. It is Joe Hynes who speaks up for the working classes, in Marxist terms which suggest that all the virtues have taken refuge among the proletariat:

> —The working-man, said Mr. Hynes, gets all kicks and no halfpence. But it's labour produces everything. The working-man is not looking for fat jobs for his sons and nephews and cousins. The working-man is not going to drag the honour of Dublin in the mud to please a German monarch.
> —How's that? said the old man.
> —Don't you know they want to present an address of welcome to Edward Rex if he comes here next year? What do we want kowtowing to a foreign king?

We shall see that Joe Hynes, "a tall, slender young man with a light brown moustache," who looks like Joyce, is a "loyalist"; as his friend O'Connor says, "poor Joe is a decent skin." He clearly has a sense of humour, a certain firmness, and real loyalty to Parnell and to the socialist creed. If Parnell were alive, say Hynes, O'Connor and old Jack, things would be different now; and old Jack says, "Musha, God be with them times! There was some life in it then." And this is true; then, Parnell was God. But the door opens and a little man bustles in, hurries to the fire, "rubbing his hands as if he intended to produce a spark from them," and Mr. Henchy has arrived. It can be seen that he does not like Hynes, or the working class, or the "hillsiders and fenians" whom he confuses together and insults in a most conventional fashion: "Some of these hillsiders and fenians are a bit too clever if you ask me, said Mr. Henchy. Do you know what my private and candid opinion is about some of those little jokers? I believe half of them are in the pay of the Castle" (that is, of the English government).

In the half-light there come and go various representatives of the alienation from which Dublin suffers, the most typical being the indefiable person, "resembling a poor clergyman or a poor actor," whose face has "the appearance of damp yellow cheese," and whose voice is "discreet, indulgent, velvety." It eventually turns out that he is a poor, unbeneficed priest, "travelling on his own account." Everything rings false in this devalued world, except the elementary desires: everyone is thirsty and impatiently awaits the arrival of the promised bottles of stout. Here can be observed the beginnings of that downgrading technique Joyce was to use so freely in *Ulysses;* just as the princess Nausicaa is replaced by a lame schoolgirl, the times of Parnell and his glory are cheapened by the succeeding age. The ambitions of Ireland are limited to the consumption of alcohol, and Mr. Henchy, the most active and unscrupulous of the Dubliners present, burlesques the rise of a citizen to the highest bourgeois honours thus:— "You must owe the City Fathers money nowadays if you want to be made Lord Mayor . . . Would I do for the job? . . . . Driving out of the Mansion House, in all my vermin, with Jack here standing up behind me in a powdered wig, eh? . . . And I'll make Father Keon my private chaplain. We'll have a family party."

Henchy has a sense of humour that springs from his awareness of the country's degradation. This is not a source of grief to him, however; on the contrary, he exploits it. He knows how to make use of circumstances as best he can, for purely selfish ends. He is the anti-idealist, who sees politics as nothing more than a business proposition. The well-told joke may make his audience forget the date of this day which for Henchy has been profitably employed; but pettiness is apparent in all his jokes and actions. Everything that is done or said is appallingly trivial, even when it is not a matter of vulgar sentiments or cowardice; the assembled agents carry out their campaign, not for a beloved or trusted leader, but for "Tricky Dicky," who is known for his untrustworthiness, and who "only wants to get some job or other." The agents are not deceived by him, because there is no question of politics in the business for them; they have simply taken temporary jobs as agents, in order to pay some urgent debt, and all that counts is that they should be paid. As they wait, because the trickster "with those little pig's eyes" for whom they work is in no hurry to honour his debts, they fall back upon the drink, which they have also been awaiting with growing impatience.

The scene is indeed far from the majesty of Ireland's "uncrowned King." The imaginary presence of Parnell embarrasses them, and the behaviour of these men who live with the times expresses their embarrassment or their excessive joviality. This meeting is quite a close parody of an "heroic" political gathering; but these Dubliners have assembled at a time when politics is the exact opposite of heroism; Mr. Henchy pretends to act energetically, bustling about, talking loudly, calling for more light and warmth. There can be little honesty and less dignity when the deified leader is replaced by a mean little man whose father was a money-lender and pawnbroker. Worst of all, this downfall is accompanied by a renewal of treachery; there is no longer such a thing as individual honour, and soon there will be no national honour left either. The only subject which evokes any reaction from the agents' guilty consciences is the possibility of King Edward's projected visit to Ireland.

The tone changes abruptly from the sordid to the slanderous. The comedy acts as a disguise for unscrupulousness; for Henchy, for example, the king is not a symbolic figure and his visit ought not to be treated sentimentally, but accepted for what it is, an opportunity to revive the Irish economy. "The King's coming here will mean an influx of money into this country. The citizens of Dublin will benefit by it." We are no longer concerned with freedom, but with profit; "It's capital we want." Mr. Henchy takes no account of any sense of honour, for, after all, "Parnell is dead." This is of course true, but here it sounds like a repetition of the treachery, a denial of all he stood for. "Look at all the money there is in the country if we only worked the old industries, the mills, the ship-building yards and factories." Mr. Henchy knows where his interests lie, and Ireland needs money. The citizens, the ratepayers, everyone concerned would benefit, if this "jolly fine, decent fellow," Edward VII, came to Dublin.

Some of those present feel that they must, rather inconveniently, raise objections; Mr. Lyons points out that "King Edward's life, you know, is not the very . . ." But Henchy will not have any moralising in political matters, and judiciously recommends that they "Let bygones by bygones"; he reminds them that Edward is a human being, which is true, and that he likes his amusements like the rest of them:— "he's just an ordinary knockabout like you and me." Basically, what can they find in him to complain about? He is a "man of the world,"[3] and if he were not English, he would have all the qualities of a good Irishman: "He's fond of his glass of grog and he's a bit of a rake, perhaps, and he's a good sportsman. Damn it, can't we Irish play fair?" This is a good example of the impeccable logic of treachery. Mr. Lyons is not fully convinced by the argument, though: "That's all very fine. . . . But look at the case of Parnell now," he says.

But Mr. Henchy replies, "Where's the analogy between the two cases?" In the name of what does Mr. Lyons claim that one can compare Edward with Parnell? But there is no answer; Henchy pretends not to understand "the connection," and with the skill of all those who practise the political trade, he changes the subject, ignoring the contra-

[3]Like the Jesuits in "Grace," who are "men of the world like ourselves."

dictions of the doubtful morality involved and acting the part of the generous, forgiving man who reconciles opposing views. Everything falls back into the chaos of degeneracy and lies again. "Don't let us stir up any bad blood," says Mr. O'Connor with subtle hypocrisy, quietening his own conscience by this act of reconciliation. "We all respect him now that he's dead and gone," he adds, meaning that Parnell no longer frightens us, though while he was alive his frankness and honesty hindered and embarrassed us because we were cowards. This is what Bloom thought also, in the cabmen's shelter. Even the conservatives forgive the adulterer, now that he is dead, and respect him "because he was a gentleman." Parnell, of course, as gentleman is not of the same species as Edward, "a man of the world" and "a jolly, fine, decent fellow, and no damn nonsense about him."

"Parnell is dead," and nothing need hinder Ireland from welcoming the English king. And so, who *is* worthy to revive the flame, and who is not unworthy to wear the ivy leaf? Not the younger generation, to judge by old Jack's son, who is at the worst stages of degeneracy; if he is forced to get himself a job, "he drinks it all." Another proof is offered by the boy who brings the bottles of stout; Mr. Henchy offers him a drink, much against old Jack's will, and as Jack gives the boy a bottle, he asks him how old he is, as though trying to recall him to sense and health before it is too late. But the lad already knows whom to heed and whom to respect, not the distressed old father but the tempter Henchy; "That's the way it begins," says the old man, but in fact that is how it ends. They suddenly remember that today is the anniversary of Parnell's death, and feel slightly embarrassed by this. Parnell exists so little that when the need to communicate is felt, they do not know quite what to do, not having thought of preparing any ceremony. Hynes, who had vanished during the discussion, as though Joyce had obscurely wished to keep him from being a witness to this deadly wake, now returns, and the vague Parnell wake that takes place has this in common with the wake for Finnegan the mason: that if the shade of Parnell has made even a timid appearance in people's minds, they have hastened to reduce it again to its customary impotence, and similarly the guests at the wake persuade Tim Finnegan, whom the scent of whiskey has recalled to life, to lie down again. Parnell, however, resembles Hamlet's father much more than he resembles Finnegan; and whatever they do to exorcise him, he remains firmly ensconced in the individual conscience.

At the end, Joyce's intention is to evoke more concretely the death of the Leader, because the presence of their eternally absent King is so strongly felt by all the characters, *as it was felt by Joyce himself,* as a perpetual reproach and remorse for their decadent state. Through a paradox which represents the highest achievement of his deceptively realistic art in *Dubliners,* Joyce is, in the writing of "Ivy Day," doubly present; he is every Irishman, and thereby guilty of the murder of Parnell, and he also *is* Parnell, invisible but present behind every line and every word, to such an extent that one can sense his irony informing everything that is said. It is all written down in the characters' uneasy consciences. Mr. Henchy shamelessly invites Joe Hynes to recite "that thing you wrote," as though to demonstrate that the break between living present and dead past is complete, and that Parnell henceforth belongs to literature rather than to history.

The poem is ambiguous; what the metaphor actually alludes to and what it makes manifest can be interpreted on many levels, some of them liable to become mutually contradictory, and we must examine all of these levels and not just the apparently literary one which is the first to be perceived. The thematic tension thus established acts upon the reader's mind, making him sensitive to the smallest variations in tone; and "The Death of Parnell" is seen to be a poem of several different degrees of irony. To begin with, there is the literal irony of reciting a poem of grief and indignation to an audience that remains completely cold and unmoved. Then, by its relationship with this audience, the poem acquires an aggressive tone, because Parnell died betrayed by people whose description ("modern hypocrites," "coward hounds") identifies them with the audience, who are complacently listening to the poem; they behave as though they were not the people being criticised in the poem, as though they had nothing to do with it, and applaud their own condemnation. Next, the irony becomes historical too; the contrast is established between the message of hope which the poet cries prayerfully towards the future and the reality of this future, made concrete as the moment in which the poem is being read —and the hope is seen to be both vain and ridiculous.

His spirit may / Rise, like the Phoenix from the flames, / When breaks the dawning of the day," cries the poet, and on this echo of the Psalms, the fire in the grate goes out. Erin is compared to an Eastern queen who sees all the hopes of her life perish on the pyre where her dead king is burned: — "He lies slain by the coward hounds / He raised to glory from the mire; / And Erin's hopes and Erin's dreams / Perish upon her monarch's pyre. / / In palace, cabin, or in cot / The Irish heart where'er it be / Is bowed with woe—for he is gone/ Who would have wrought her destiny./ He would have had his Erin famed,/ The green flag gloriously unfurled,/ Her statesmen, bards, and warriors raised/ Before the nations of the world./ He dreamed (alas, 'twas but a dream!)/ Of Liberty: but as he strove/ To clutch that idol, treachery/ Sundered him from the thing he loved."

Yet in reality Erin had taken great delight in raising that pyre and in burning her "hopes and dreams," for fear that they might come true.

Insensibly the distance grows, between Parnell's death, theatrically deplored as a great loss, and the real indifference of his so-called followers; between the tragedy of the hero's death and the meanness of the chorus who bewail it; between the swollen rhetoric of the lamentations that are recited, and the actual paucity of the Dubliners' vocabulary; between the dead dream and the living nightmare; and as it grows, the irony is further modified. Read before an innocent audience it would simply be an expression of some puerile optimism; but, to a guilty audience, it denounces their crimes clearly and candidly. Hynes reciting the Death of Parnell is like the actors in *Hamlet* acting out the murder of a king before the king's murderer; the whole tragedy is in Claudius' silence. Similarly, when Hynes finishes his poem, there is a silence, lasting for a moment while everyone hastens to adjust his mind to the consciousness of guilt and to decide on the appropriate behaviour to adopt; this moment of mutual admission of guilt is broken by their applause, for the guilty have found their line of defence, and their reply to the indirect accusation. They choose the role of spectators, excusing themselves thus from any responsibility, and they congratulate the poet on his mastery of the art.

Yet there was that moment in which Parnell almost began to exist again, that silence which he occupied so fully that he almost returned to them; and in that silence, that moment, was produced their awareness of the discord between the last verse and its echo in time present, in actuality as they knew it. It was not the silence of shamefaced reluctance to speak, but the silence in which the dishonourable Dubliner was faced with the image of the honourable man who was to exist when Parnell returned, when freedom ruled, in the psalmist's ideal future.

"And on that day may Erin well/ Pledge in the cup she lifts to Joy/ One grief—the memory of Parnell." Each knows that the memory of Parnell is only a form of remorse, and each lifts the bitter drink of guilty conscience to his lips, but no toast is drunk to freedom, because they are soon to drink to King Edward. All the themes which could have led to tragedy have been turned aside into farce.

Parnell as a Sign of Death for Ireland

The memory of Parnell has two completely different meanings. For some people Parnell means freedom, honour, and dreams of greatness—a positive sign. But for others, far from being the liberator, Parnell is the persecutor of the bad conscience, the oppressor, the negative sign of dishonour. Each of these two tendencies divides again into two contraries, which rule each other out. For the positive Parnellists there is no hope for the future, no resurrection; the younger generation is degenerate and alien; one is a Parnellist in spite of everything, desperately, without really believing.[4] For the negative Parnellists, Parnell no longer exists; but he still exists in one's own mind to some degree, and one cannot extirpate him completely; one still believes a little. Thus, as a result of these two tendencies, Parnell, is a more dangerous dead man than people had realised; not only is he dead, but also he continues to exist in men's memories as a force of inertia, deadening and rendering powerless their deeds.

Joyce feels it necessary to prove that Parnell signifies death for every Irishman; he is the sign of death for the country. There is no place for the powers of life between the territories of these two forces of inertia. The memory of Parnell stifles both eloquence and hypocrisy, and the true language of degenerate Ireland is silence, for the word is dead, poisoned by lies. Yet in the deadly silence is heard unanimous applause; "even Mr. Lyons clapped," and this gesture is a silent admission of shared guilt, complicity, and shame. Each man indulges his longing for spiritual purity, irrevocably lost, although he would never openly admit it; and this applause is a troubled equivalent of confession. But here there is no forgiveness; Parnell may be compared to the Phoenix, but he will not rise again.

He has become a legendary hero, a character in a poem. Mr. Henchy cries, "Isn't that fine? What?" It is indeed fine, and the audience reacts to the artistic beauty. What pleases them is not the substance but the form; by misdirecting their attention towards the form Henchy causes the poem to be criticised as a work of art, and not as a message. In fact, if the poem were to have any value, it would only have the value of the

[4]It must be emphasised that all this takes place in the social circles John Joyce used to frequent; and that there was still an amount of hope living, maintained by intellectuals such as de Valera, Pearse, or Griffith.

message, for the poetical wrapping is of very dubious quality. Thus Henchy misdirects and loses the message.

"Mr. Crofton said that it was a very fine piece of writing" is the last sentence of the novella; and he has the last word in the story just as in the political reality he was to have the last word, saying in effect that 6 October had lost all its power as appeal or rallying-cry. The last word, in all senses, is the word that finishes, and puts an end to things. The poetic myth is dead, the human legend gone, and a whole code of living values come to an end. Parnell no longer speaks, but is spoken about; he has become simply a subject for a bad poem.

When Mr. Crofton has said that the poem was well written, the day, and the story, have ended, but the working of the irony continues: the poem was probably written by Joyce himself. It is believed to be a version of *Et Tu Healy*, which Joyce wrote in 1891. This is a third degree of irony, in which tragedy becomes swallowed up in the grotesque. Parnell had to be dethroned more subtly than by mere denial, and Joyce was always an expert at dethroning myths. A hero, however great, who inspires such unfortunate and tasteless verse, cannot help but suffer from it. The irony has probably a secret source, in that the boy Joyce was probably not entirely innocent in writing his poem; in spite of his youth, he may well have realised that he also was guilty of treachery, a treachery against values he knew. Would it not have been possible for him to write a formally correct poem, and to forget to some extent the subject in the effort to complete a difficult exercise?

One may well conjecture, from one's knowledge of Joyce, whether the nine-year-old Jim had not already discovered how to turn his emotions into art. The only difference would be that at the age of nine one might have some scruples about using a man's death for the making of a poem, but at the age of twenty-five one would be less strict. John Joyce, who never read a line of his son's later work, was delighted with the nine-year-old boy's poem, and, recognising his talent, had it printed and widely distributed. Even as the boy Jim received the congratulations of friends, he must have felt that he was building his nest of self-esteem and pleasure on his subject's coffin. Thus the boy committed the sin of which he was later to accuse all bad artists, that of compromising the virtue of his art by subordinating it to others' use, to political bombast; he was as guilty as those "coward, caitiff hands" whom he denounced, having made Parnell the object of an egoistic exercise, a source of praise and self-satisfaction.

Therefore, Parnell was, for more reasons than one, a sign of remorse to Joyce. It may well be that one of his intentions in "Ivy Day" is to denounce himself as he denounces the others, and to admit his own cowardice by associating himself with them as actor and not merely spectator of their comedy of guilt. It is not claimed that Joyce was such a masochist that he felt the need to flagellate himself (with ivy) for his misdeeds; but it should be pointed out that he was so lucid on the subject of himself that he would never let himself be caught out, or be shown to be in the wrong, even in his first youthful essays; we see, as we read "Ivy Day," that Jim could never have been Stephen Dedalus. The only heroic period in his life occurred at a time when his "second consciousness," the sense which warned him as soon as he was about to take himself seriously, was already functioning fully. To some extent the purpose of "Ivy Day" is a double one: the symbolic ivyleaf reveals and catalyses the acids that eat into the characters' souls, and is also cathartic. Joyce is purging himself of a bad intention and of a bad poem. But at the end, he refines still further the irony, with a vague feeling of guilt still; he admits that the poem is of no more worth than the man who declaims it, but this admission costs very little, and is hardly a damaging one to make.

His creative conscience redeems the act of bad faith which he has made through his concern for moral contrition, by the constant use of irony. It may be objected that the reader does not know that Joyce is prompting Hynes, but on the other hand one must remember that the author himself always said that he had invented nothing, and that he wished readers to take the trouble of tracing him to his hiding places in the work.

Dublin Citizens—Beingless Beings

The "Wandering Rocks" chapter[5] is divided into eighteen sections plus the final procession, which mimic chaotically the eighteen divisions of 16 June 1904. Ulysses had had to choose between passing between Scylla and Charybdis, and passing between the Moving Rocks, which clashed together like vast jaws in the middle of the sea; Jason had passed through them safely, only losing the point of the bow, but the Argo had

[5]Its correspondences are: Art, mechanics; Symbol, the citizens; Place, the streets; Organ, the blood; Technique, the labyrinth.

been a magic ship. Everything takes place as though millions of blind, mindless globules, circulating in the veins, driven by some alien power, knew that they were nourishing an organism which was their enemy. The British Empire absorbs the strength of Ireland. Ulysses had chosen to pass through Charybdis and Scylla, avoiding the other way; and so it is clear that Ireland is engaged on the most dangerous crossing.

The inert citizens whom the current bears along Dublin's arteries are saluted or blessed by those who represent Caesar and Christ. That which is Caesar's and that which is God's, this same wandering crowd is guarded on both sides by two authorities whose complicity is manifest; their aims and their methods of procedure are clearly defined. Joyce had drawn in red on a map of Dublin the itineraries of Lord Dudley, the viceroy, and Father Conmee, calculating virtually to the minute how long these journeys would take; space in this labyrinth is composed of moving units, and in its motion represents Joyce's conception of history. We have here a petrified civilisation, the sclerotic arteries of a body politic in which the human particles circulate.

The labyrinth starts with Father Conmee, the superior of Clongowes, and ends with the viceregal cavalcade; the noise and show of the latter calls forth characteristic gestures from a number of representatives of the City. Simon Dedalus bows low (*Ulysses*, p. 247), the Reverend Hugh C. Love "makes obeisance," a sad grey head continues gazing at its chessboard—for John Howard Parnell, brother of the dead King, has the sinister habit of playing this symbolic game. The viceroy must be the most non-existent character in *Ulysses;* Joyce leads him in full regalia all round the city, but he is always seen from afar, and is really only the symbol of riches, authority, and the lack of real government. He is only there because of the injustice of history, and is therefore not granted any human characteristic; even the most wretched components of the crowd are more closely looked at than he. The viceroy is like gold in the mud of the streets. Father Conmee, "the best Rector Clongowes ever had," is the figure of the indigenous authority, always the same—benevolent and without malice—but absolutely blind to the very real sufferings of his flock. His dreamy thoughts are reported to the reader, and show fully the skilful Jesuit tolerance. His high preoccupations end in bathos:

> Father Conmee thought of the souls of black and brown and yellow men and of his sermon of saint Peter Claver S.J. and the African mission and of the propagation of the faith and of the millions of black and brown and

yellow souls that had not received the baptism of water. . . . . But they were God's souls created by God. It seemed to Father Conmee a pity that they should all be lost, a waste, if one might say. (*Ulysses*, p. 217)

The same inappropriate economy recurs again and again: one can save millions of African souls, while letting millions of Irish bodies die of hunger; *requiescant in pace*, they will be all right, being baptised already. Father Conmee's benevolence smacks a little too much of the comfortable refectory.

"It was idyllic: and Father Conmee reflected on the providence of the Creator who had made turf to be in bogs where men might dig it out and bring it to town and hamlet to make fires in the houses of poor people" (*Ulysses*, p. 216).

He dreams of "old times," of his beloved little book *Old Times in the Barony*, of marrying "a bride and a bridegroom, noble to noble," of the Nones which he should have read before lunch, "but lady Maxwell had come," of Mrs. M'Guiness who is "like Mary, queen of Scots, something." And on the other side of the Liffey and of the chapter, we have William Humble, earl of Dudley.

Between these two worlds wanders Stephen. He stops in front of a jeweller's window, where the jewels in the showtrays are covered with a thick layer of dust. "And you who wrest old images from the burial earth!" (*Ulysses*, p. 238). Stephen's only riches are words and images, "cold specks of fire" wrested from the earth, and waiting to be given new life by the poet.

But the poet is still caught in the world where energy comes from factory and powerhouse and the beings are "beingless":

> Stop! Throb always without you and the throb always within. Your heart you sing of. I between them. Where? Between two roaring worlds where they swirl, I. Shatter them, one and both. But stun myself too in the blow. Shatter me, you who can. Bawd and butcher, were the words. I say! Not yet awhile. A look around. (*Ulysses*, p. 236).

In the end, it is Stephen who decides to shatter the world of theology and its false lights, in the house of Circe.

Stephen continues, "the handle of the ash clacking against his shoulderblade," as though to give himself some personal, mechanical energy. He has long considered his fellow-citizens as "beingless beings"; and the problem of how a living man could be non-existent, like a dead man, had preoccupied him when he was building his biography of Shakespeare on the theory of being a ghost by means of death, absence, or by being forgotten. But the first time that he had analysed the meaning of the gradual effacing of a person, even to the forgetting of his name, was in the *Portrait,* and the process was for him directly connected with Parnell.

The Abolition of Names

The first diminution of the power of the Word is connected with a nervous crisis experienced by the boy Stephen. Parnell becomes simply a name and a date in history books, and the boy experiences for the first time the phenomenon of "loss by effacing"; it is not a case of ordinary forgetting, of lack of memory, or the traumatic shock of a real death. In fact, Stephen has not yet any close knowledge of the latter, and it is not until much later that he acquires such knowledge. This transformation of Parnell into a vague phantom is much more important, both for the child Stephen and for the nascent artist within him, as well as for the form his art is from the beginning destined to take. It may be possible to see here the origin of one of Joyce's most important attitudes to his work, both in theory and in practice, the gradual disappearance of the author:

> He recalled only names. Dante, Parnell, Clane, Clongowes. A little boy had been taught geography by an old woman who kept two brushes in her wardrobe. Then he had been sent away from home to a college, he had made his first communion and eaten slim jim out of his cricket cap and watched the firelight leaping and dancing on the wall of a little bedroom in the infirmary and dreamed of being dead. (*Portrait,* p. 93)

The experience is reported in the *Portrait* as it occurs to Stephen's thoughts some years after the death of Parnell, on the occasion of a trip to Cork, his father's birthplace.

> But he had not died then. Parnell had died. He had not died but he had faded out like a film in the sun. He had been lost or had wandered out of existence for he no longer existed. How strange to think of him passing out of existence in such a way, not by death but by fading out in the sun or by being lost and forgotten somewhere in the universe! (*Ibid.*)

Parnell is only a name now, and behind that name there is death; but it is not so simple as that, for it is not merely a matter of Parnell's being dead and buried, for his name also is dead; and the death of that name had caused the boy Stephen also to "wander out of existence." In earlier days, at the mere mention of Parnell's name, Ireland was in turmoil, in action; the name was magic, calling the soul of Ireland to its awakening; as old Jack says, in 'Ivy Day', "there was some life in it then."

In the past, Parnell was alive, present, and the Word was all-powerful; today his name has no power, but has become a mere ordinary word. Hearing this name which has lost its magic so completely, Stephen discovers both the potentialities of the Word's existence and the changes a human being undergoes in Time, and the manifestation of all this in language. He discovers that the Word itself may be mortal, may be reduced to a mere sound, closed, self-contained, and with no more significance than its literal meaning. God is not he who is, but he who speaks, whose word is the infinite space of all men's dreams. Physical death is not a mystery, but the phenomena of language and its changes are the most striking enigma to Stephen; this is because he has wandered out of existence, out of the immediate concrete universe, which is no longer familiar to him. In Cork, he is suffering from a neurosis which makes him seriously doubt his own existence, and there is no more an echo when he speaks. When he was a child, he would think to himself, "I am Stephen," and the world would respond; when he was ill, Parnell died. But now this necessary exchange between the self and the outside world is interrupted:

> Nothing moved him or spoke to him from the real world unless he heard in it an echo of the infuriated cries within him. . . . . Wearied and dejected by his father's voice, he could scarcely recognise as his own thoughts, and repeated slowly to himself:
>
> —I am Stephen Dedalus. I am walking beside my father whose name is Simon Dedalus. We are in Cork, in Ireland. Cork is a city. Our room is in the Victoria Hotel . . . Simon and Stephen and Victoria. Names. *(Ibid.)*

This loss of reality is the first death that the nascent artist suffers. He has to disengage himself from that order of things in which he echoes others, and to establish a different order in which it is he who speaks and the world that echoes him. When Parnell was alive, the boy Stephen had managed to coincide with the world, by the facile process of identifying himself with Parnell. Without clearly realising it, he wanted to be the chief, the man who speaks first and who has the last word. As long as he did not speak in his own name he was more dead than alive, alienated, a stranger, because "to be Stephen" had no meaning until the phrase was made to denote a real entity. In Cork, he can hear only his father's voice. The father refuses to acknowledge time; he mingles past and present in a fictitious immortality, fearing to be other than the man he used to be. The father's voice here is the voice of death, and the father fears his son, because the son's existence recalls him to present reality. In this unreal world, Stephen is not at home either, because he is everywhere rejected, and his father denies him.

Stephen is absent because he is no longer the small boy he used to be *allowed* to be. All names are false, because Victoria, Simon, Stephen, when simply juxtaposed, have no real meaning; they cannot form a whole or another name, they are simply objects and sounds, noises. The young man cannot recognise or respond to anything, because the significant Word, to which all others were related, has disappeared. No other charm can replace it, neither that of the father nor that of Victoria (seen as the empress, the mother, or the enemy, for all these meanings are relevant); Mr. Dedalus and Stephen are staying at the Victoria Hotel for a good reason, and the allusion is not lost on the young man. To say, in such a void, "I am Stephen Dedalus," is simply to register the fact that one has moved one's tongue and exhaled, that one has experienced the metaphysical anguish of one's non-existence, and that one knows that no-one has listened.

The young man must recognise himself in order to exist; he must be able to speak his name in a world which will respond. He must be reborn in the place he chooses, which will assuredly not be Cork, his father's birthplace, and he must create himself a world whose echoes he can control, a world from which he may be absent without being dead or abolished, a world where he will be free from the effects of time and change. The birth of Stephen as an artist conscious of his vocation takes place to the accompaniment of the sound of waves and the music within him, as his name, shouted into the air, is a word of such power that it can call up "a winged form flying above the waves," the symbol of the legendary artist, of Daedalus (*Portrait*, p. 169).

Thus, the death of Parnell had a treble repercussion upon Joyce's work: it marked his own childhood with the horror of History; it later became a moment in the development of the artist's "temperament," representing the time of abolition necessary before the second birth; and discreetly but with surprising force, it pointed out Joyce's awareness from an early age of the mysteries of language.

By the experience of the power of a word, and of its subsequent disappearance, Joyce was able to establish that the relationship between word and reality, between sound and sense, depended as much on the hearer as on the speaker. The symbol, i.e., the fullness of sense that comes after the actual noise, is fragile, and it is not sufficient merely to speak; in order to exist one must also be received, listened to, understood. On the spiritual level, this means that God, if he is not listened to, is lost; he becomes a mere sound, a "noise in the street." God or the artist is at the mercy of the listener, and is only the interpretation that the latter gives him.

On the sexual level, which in Joyce's thought must always be present in all metaphysical meditation, the fragility of the symbol and of the fullness of meaning signifies that the man to whom woman does not respond is a mere nothing, scarcely extant at all. If the word Bloom is not listened to by Molly, it becomes worthless. On the aesthetic level, this thinking makes Joyce will all his speaking to be intelligible, since he is so acutely conscious of the need to be read and well, correctly, read. It eventually brings him to the attempt to save his work from death through inaudibility, gradually reducing the distance between the word and its appeal to the senses, and trying, particularly in *Finnegans Wake*, to create a *full* kind of writing—a language that would be immediately understood and meaningful.

Part Three: The Choice of Heresy

XIII. Non Serviam

Introduction

The five chapters of the *Portrait* follow the two axes of the artist's development, Quest and Rebellion. They are at first separate, but become identified from chapter IV onwards; during the first three chapters, Stephen is still the object of the world around him, that forms and influences him. He allows this to happen, despite the anguish it causes him and the rebellious instincts that are germinating within him, but his main feeling is one of discomfort—he is not where he ought to be, and he is not yet the person he ought to be. Throughout various hesitations, this feeling lasts, inspired by the mysterious incidents that mark out his childhood and adolescence, until he makes the decision not to obey or serve, repudiating the judgement of others which had previously exerted such pressure on him. He proclaims himself artist, and is treated as a heretic; but he no longer responds to the call of authority.

The Epiphany at Work

The first chapter is constructed in imitation of the way a small child constructs his world; it consists of a series of scenes in the raw state, juxtaposed, and their power is such that they imprint their forms on the child's mind before he is old enough to interpret them, to give them the meanings they obviously have for the adults around him. They have certain characteristics which repetition brings to his notice, and he reacts in an idiosyncratic fashion, because he is peculiarly sensitive to words, to the transposition of events into language; he reacts so strongly that words and sounds begin to seem, more so than any other sense-perceptions, the intermediaries, or perhaps even the recipients, of hidden meanings.

The first two pages of *Portrait* are made up of the connection between and synthesising of two main scenes, accompanied by the child's observations of the people around him. His immediate circle is composed of father, mother, uncle Charles, and Dante. The Vance family, with Eileen, live in another house. His first experience of the outside world introduces music, dance, and poetry, is therefore presented as quite agreeable, but ends on a violent note of epiphany.

> When they were grown up he was going to marry Eileen. He hid under the table. His mother said:
> —O, Stephen will apologize.
> Dante said:
> —O, if not, the eagles will come and pull out his eyes.
> Pull out his eyes,
> Apologize,
> Apologize,
> Pull out his eyes.
> Apologize,
> Pull out his eyes,
> Pull out his eyes,
> Apologize.

The child learns fear, dissimulation, and the potential cruelty of adults.

The origin of the scene lies in a real event of Joyce's childhood; in 1891, at Bray, he had committed his first offence against the adult world, as represented by Mrs. Conway (Dante), and was threatened with hellfire if he continued to visit the Protestant Vances. At the age of nine, Jim was no longer impressed by such a disproportionate threat, but he remembered the form of the episode, and it provided him with this epiphany:[1]

> Bray: in the parlour of the house in Martello Terrace.
> Mr. Vance—(comes in with a stick) . . . O, you know, he'll have to apologize, Mrs. Joyce.

[1] First epiphany in the Buffalo MS. *Workshop*, p. 11.

Mrs. Joyce—O yes . . . Do you hear that, Jim?

Mr. Vance—Or else—if he doesn't—the eagles'll come and pull out his eyes.

Mrs. Joyce—O, but I'm sure he will apologize.

Joyce—(under the table, to himself) Apologize, Pull out his eyes, Pull out his eyes, Apologize.

The pattern imprints itself on Stephen's mind for more serious reasons, and Joyce makes use of all its thematic possibilities. The incident becomes archetypal, with its monitory voice of the avenger, armed with his stick, with the treason of the mother, and the choice the accuser offers between two deaths: submit and renounce, or be blinded. That is, suicide or execution. One must give oneself the lie and lose the right to speak, or by refusing to change what one has said, lose the right to see. This dramatic choice between mendacity and darkness, before which the mother, at any rate, does not hesitate, introduces the theme of the fear of punishment along with other motifs which are bound to recur later. Punishment, the putting out of eyes, escape by evasion, the pleasant sound of the threats made in rhyme, all recur throughout the work. Joyce hears it all, being hidden under the table.

The child whom the adults torture and interrogate makes his reply by not answering them. He chooses himself, and speaks for himself alone. In this first speech, masochism is blended with parody, making the child forget the real cruelty by directing his attention to the play of words and sounds. Under his table he discovers the power of the spoken sound, and transforms his fear and shame into rudimentary art; against the stick he adopts *exile* under the table; against his mother's betrayal, he arms himself with *silence;* and against the fear of being blinded, he creates, utilising that fear, a relationship with himself, using the craft and *cunning* of art. The artist's motto is already sketched out here, in a rudimentary form: silence, flight, and word-play.

It has been pointed out that in Stephen's experience, Mr. Vance's stick is no longer present; but in *Portrait*, Mr. Vance is replaced by Dante. The stick is lost, but in its place are the two brushes, standing for Ireland, the one with a maroon velvet back for Michael Davitt and the other with a green velvet back for Parnell, which Dante (Mrs. Riordan) keeps in her press. Furthermore, Mr. Vance had been a Protestant, but with Dante in his place, the threat is made by the Church.[2] The conflict between the artist and the Church begins, and all because of a girl. Desire becomes introverted and associated with the forbidden;

---

[2]Ellmann, *James Joyce*, pp. 25–6.

at one stroke, the sacred, the forbidden, the beautiful, and suffering as pleasurable are associated for the young artist. This moment is probably the first shock his consciousness receives, the moment whose forms and modulations recur throughout his work. The age at which mental forms become fixed and symbols established ends with the need to apologize, to obtain forgiveness, and the threat of being blinded by the eagles.[3]

In the child's mind the experience crystallises all these seemingly disparate elements, converging in one terrible threat. He makes them into a kind of imaginary mosaic, whose complementary constituents eventually come together in a coherent whole; he reorganises the series of events, ignoring their chronological succession, and draws from them a set of obscure associations and laws of causality. If Stephen wishes to possess Eileen (or any other E.) then the eagles will come (or any other aggressor armed with a pointed weapon aimed at his eyes). This is the first statement. Other elements are added to this, disturbing because they seem really to have no direct connection with the threat: Dante is kind, and rewards Stephen when he brings her pieces of tissue paper, thus she can be both kind and unkind. Again, she has two brushes, symbolic objects which introduce Stephen into the world of politics and are related to that of the sacred. His mother puts down an oilsheet when he wets the bed; she smells pleasant, and plays the piano for him to dance. It is she who says, "O, Stephen will apologize". The mother is thus associated with the small child's enjoyable guilt; she smells good, but she judges her son and finds him guilty; she exerts gentle but stern pressure on him, and has the power to make him dance to her tune. The father, on the other hand, has no part in the world of threats, although it was he who began the story of the artist, telling what had happened "once upon a time" to the "baby tuckoo," whom Stephen believes to be himself.

The whole of the first chapter develops around these themes, which are contained in embryo in its first part. For the child, it is a time when the hostile world surrounds and outstrips him, when at school he discovers how different he is, while in the adult world similar antagonisms divide people into hostile groups. The distribution of the scenes, their length, their order in the general structure of the chapter, are all designed to show the relative importance of things in this world. As Grant H. Redford has pointed out,[4] more than half of the first chapter is

---

[3]Cf. Morris Beja, *The Wooden Sword*, in *James Joyce Quarterly*, vol. II, no. 1, Fall 1964, pp. 33ff.

[4]Redford, *The Role of Structure in Joyce's Portrait*, in *Modern Fiction Studies*, IV, Spring 1958, pp. 21–30.

concerned with religion and politics as factors of destruction, troubling the harmony of the family, the adults' dignity, and the order of justice. The Christmas dinner is one single scene, sixteen pages long. Between the first scene with its eagles and apology, and the Christmas dinner scene, the second long section is set at the boy's school; it represents a completely strange society, with laws and threats of its own, but everything about it is more complex than things were at home. Stephen is mocked, humiliated, alone, bullied, punished; he falls ill; he has no idea of the answers to the loaded questions which other, apparently initiated boys ask him, and cannot solve the riddles proposed by his companion in the infirmary. He has not yet worked out what he must think in order to be acceptable to the others. He feels vaguely guilty as their victim. Bewildered by their looks and jokes, he cannot decipher the signs which are present and clear to everyone else.

The fear of being blinded moulds the pattern of the child's behaviour up to the time when he makes his definitive break with those who had made the threat. The direct image of the eagles is transmuted into other, equivalent, images, sometimes less direct and more metaphorical, sometimes less mythical. The eagles have many descendents in *Portrait,* and take on many forms, as does the fear that drives him to dissimulation and the necessity to justify himself.

The eagles still have some epic grandeur, but the bird who succeeds to their place is distinctly less noble, although he is still the castigator; Heron, a school-mate who has the name, appearance, and even the attitude of a bird of prey, is the next who wishes to force Stephen into submission. The irony of the choice is clear, and related to the procedures of blackmail, since the blinding threatened is no longer physical but spiritual, and is meant to follow, instead of replacing, the humiliating act. Indeed, Stephen has already dedicated himself to the truth, so that for him to accept the conventions of moralising hypocrites would be to choose deliberately the blindness of the rabblement. But to refuse means to be beaten. This time he is not in danger from the eagles' beaks, but from the symbolic weapon brandished by Heron, a weapon worthy to figure in the Cyclops' armoury.

It is in fact a cabbage stump, which serves to attach their hostile behaviour, which they pretend has an intellectual motive, firmly to the Irish soil, which, as we know, produces nothing but cabbages and potatoes. The detail is intentional, for the episode had its origin in a scuffle between Joyce (at the age of twelve) and one Albrecht Connolly, in which however a stick took the place of the cabbage stump.[5] There were not to be any real eagles after all in the artist's life. But on several dramatic occasions he is blinded, by tears, whenever he is shown as the victim of unjust accusations, or of his own difference from the others; he breaks his spectacles on the cinder-path at school, and everything goes hazy; it becomes impossible for him to read the letters on the blackboard, although he tries his best. The scene that takes place now corresponds to the Christmas dinner episode by its violence, and by its importance in the formation of the artist's soul; after the disintegration of the family, the Christian religion and morality are the next to have their authority demolished, by a blow from a ferula. Father Dolan, the prefect of studies, is responsible for administering corporal punishment; Stephen has only just made the discovery that the Jesuits are as imperfect as other men, susceptible to anger and roughness, touched by flattery, when he finds himself suddenly accused of lying and cheating: Father Dolan claims that he broke his glasses on purpose. The world of justice collapses at once; the accusation is followed by no production of proof but by immediate condemnation and the sentence is carried out on the spot. Stephen, already half-blinded and staggering with fear, feels his eyes burn with tears of pain at the blows of the ferula. He learns perforce to recognise injustice, and at the same time sees the cruelty of which religion can be capable, a cruelty which can go so far as to be sadism:

> And as he knelt, calming the last sobs in his throat and feeling the burning tingling pain pressed into his sides, he thought of the hands which he had held out in the air with the palms up and of the firm touch of the prefect of studies when he had steadied the shaking fingers. (*Portrait*, p. 51)

This firm touch, this assured pursuance of injustice, horrifies him more than the physical pain does. A whole page expresses the horror he feels at Father Dolan's cruelty. It echoes the poem about the eagles, but here the conscience is more alert, the rhythm long, repetitive, like a panting breath, the plaint of the victim; its theme, like that of a psalm, is "it was unfair and cruel". He had done nothing, he had always worked well, commendably well, and been obedient, and had yet been punished. "It was cruel and unfair to make him kneel". The people responsible might well regret having done it, but all the same, "it was unfair and cruel".

[5]Ellmann, *op.cit.*, p. 40.

Five or six times the trapped consciousness returns to this event, as though ritually repeating a killing by means of drama; as the mind grasps all its implications, revolt takes on a ritual pattern. Through the power of events, the ferula becomes a symbol of the fearsome blind act itself, and turns into more than a simple memory. Stephen is as sensitive to words as he is to sensations, and the instrument, the "bat," has a name which becomes charged with all the emotion attendant upon the incident; fear, rebellion, blindness, and pain become associated with the master and his gesture as much as with the word "bat"; it can also signify the cricket bat, and thus sport in general, which completely fails to have any attraction for the intellectual Stephen. Later, this association becomes extended, and by contamination, as it were, everything representative or reminiscent of spiritual blindness recalls for Stephen the black sleeve of the soutane and the sound of the ferula. Bat is also the animal that lives in darkness and shuns the light; and by this tortuous route the theme of the unjust priest's spiritual blindness is transformed, by the time Stephen reaches adolescence, into the theme of the woman's soul, blinded by prejudice.

Chapter III of the *Portrait* begins on a December evening. "It would be a gloomy secret night," and the youth would follow a devious course, until his feet led him round a dark corner into the ill-famed part of town. This dark and sinful night exists only in Stephen's dreams, while he is imprisoned in the schoolroom; in reality, he has before him a scribbling-pad, and in his soul not the ardent darkness of the houses of pleasure but the "cold darkness" of satiety and indifference.

Everything is cold, with the chill of "the worshippers who stood bareheaded, four deep, outside the church" on Sunday mornings (*Portrait*, p. 104), with the chill of his thoughts; "his mind wound itself in and out of the curious questions proposed to it. . . . Is baptism with a mineral water valid?" (*Portrait*, p. 106). The rector arrives to prepare the pupils for the coming retreat, and while he gazes "keenly at his listeners out of his dark stern eyes. In the silence their dark fire kindled the dusk into a tawny glow" (*Portrait*, p. 108). The evening which might have ended in the yellow glow of the bordello is to end, for Stephen, in the hell that has been awaiting him.

The whole chapter is shot with redness or darkness from the fires of hell. The twilight of the days of retreat is dull and menacing, announcing the end of a world which God cannot tolerate any longer. "Rain was falling on the chapel, on the garden, on the college. It would rain for ever, noiselessly. The water would rise inch by inch, covering the grass and shrubs, covering the trees and houses, covering the monuments and the mountain tops. All life would be choked off, noiselessly" (*Portrait*, p. 117).

It might be; but it does not happen. The last sermon is reached, and "they lie in exterior darkness. For, remember, the fire of hell gives forth no light" (*Portrait*, p. 120). If the sermons on hell take up so much space in the *Portrait*, this is not in order to frighten the reader, nor yet to justify Stephen's fear and subsequent surrender, for Joyce could have given a sufficient impression of hell in a few pages. But he felt the need to fill the centre of the book with four genuine sermons, taken bodily from Saint Ignatius Loyola's *Spiritual Exercises* and from Pinamonti's *Inferno Aperto* of 1735. Joyce grants twenty-six pages of his personal kingdom to the terrifying words of the preacher, as though to yield his due to the God who is so greedy for the recovery of souls; the tithe, a tenth of the two hundred and fifty-two pages of the *Portrait*, the midmost circle of its spiritual gyres, is sacrificed to the word of the enemy, in honour of "a great soldier of God," a "conqueror". "Ten thousand souls won for God in a single month!" "A great saint, and a man of letters," says the preacher, in praise of Saint Ignatius.

Elizabeth F. Boyd has shown[6] that the sermons are faithful to their original: Joyce hardly even took the liberty of condensing, and did so very honestly when it seemed necessary. Is this his way of submitting, or does he perhaps admire the fanatical priestly turn of mind? Joyce would not be Joyce, however, if he had not left his own trademark somewhere in all those pages which he has virtually plagiarised from the meditations and exercises of seventeeth-century Jesuits in Italy; his condensation, which, according to Elizabeth Boyd, consists mainly of omitting quotations from Scripture, merely intensifies the impression of *darkness;* it is impossible to see in hell, as in Dublin at night. The darkness of hell is scarcely an original theme, but Joyce emphasises it for a very good reason; for its relevance to the eyes and their punishment. As in every place of spiritual misfortune, there are in hell substitutes for the eagles that eat living eyes; Joyce introduces subtly, in the dark and monotonous world of the sermons, slight signs of his own wounded presence. Into Pinamonti's list of the parts of the body that burn eternally, Joyce puts "the tender eyes flaming like molten balls" (*Portrait*, p. 122), which the Jesuit had inadvertently omitted. He also insists at length on the stench of hell, which corresponds to Dublin, and this can be counted as his other personal addition.

We know that since 1907 Joyce had been having trouble with his

[6]In *Modern Language Notes*, LXXV, Nov. 1960, pp. 561–71.

eyes, but does this authorise us to read into the work a pathetic admission of the fact? Should one take the precautions of biographical pseudo-criticism and point out that Joyce was almost blind, as Milton was completely? It is easy to discuss the work of a genius and to diminish its value by calling it a "blind man's writing" or "a deaf man's music". For Joyce the most important thing was to apprehend the whole world *as completely as possible*, but he was surrounded by the taboos of the Church; "Thou shalt not see" is a mutilation of the freedom to think for oneself, and "I see" means "I understand". In the Trieste Notebook (*Workshop*, p. 96) Joyce lists the distinguishing characteristics of various real or fictitious people, as they are transformed from life to work; Dedalus has a very long list, which is particularly interesting because of the forty-odd characteristics attributed to him only a third are directly used in the work. The last of these, not used as such in either *Portrait* or *Ulysses*, is as follows:—"He desired to be not a man of letters but a spirit expressing itself through language because shut off from the visible arts by an inheritance of servitude and from music by the vigour of the mind."

We can see how conscious Joyce was of his choice of art. Language is the matter of an art that wishes to free itself from servitude, and instinctively Joyce places more confidence in the light of the mind than in the light of day. His mind is not to be blinded; yet it is still possible for him to lose his sight or at least the ability to look at things. The fundamental equation is always "think straight/see clearly," the first term being Joyce's essential ambition and the second acting as a metaphor or auxiliary of meaning to the second. To this equation Joyce opposes "think in cowardly, insincere fashion/be unable to see a thing," and in the same way makes use of the second term to illustrate the effort the masters make to turn their charges away from what for the artist is Truth. Those who use their sticks to blind or to intimidate the enslaved also need those sticks to guide their faltering steps because they are blind. Their blindness is not physical or the result of disease, but comes from a cataract of the mind which they do not recognise. Joyce makes them walk uncertainly in the ways of the mind, and the stick as weapon to threaten others' eyes becomes stuck in the mud—instead of pointing towards heaven and light as Joyce's did or towards the lamp as Stephen's ashplant did—in the "Circe" episode. For there are two ways of holding a walking stick: it may point down to the earth or it can be brandished and whirled in a fashion doubtless ridiculous but nonetheless heroic.

The mind's weakness reveals itself immediately in language, and it is always in the linguistic arena that the combats take place in which

Stephen comes to grips with the orators of mendacity. The wars are fought over language itself, the vehicle of all power and all life. Art is the expression of free thought; and it becomes clear that the final combat of freedom against paralysis, of sight against blindness, or of power against inhibition, takes the form of a battle of words—and the conqueror is master of the world.

The Recurrent Accusation

The first time, it came as a surprise to the child to be accused unjustly; but this happens again and again, and the recurring accusation is accompanied by a similarity in terminology which makes it difficult to tell where guilt begins and injustice ends. In fact, from the time when the small boy hid under the table, he started to learn dissimulation, either concrete (in the form of physically hiding under the bedclothes, for example) or psychological, presenting to the world the impenetrable surface of "the enigma of a manner," a solemn mask which was sometimes identical with what it hid and sometimes completely different. In any case, Stephen was living in a secret world, gropingly in search of himself—and this was probably what brought him the hostile opposition of the majority. This may be interpreted as the necessary and typical "absence" of the poet as child, but he was innocent to begin with. He was confident and trusting when he entered Clongowes, and the others finally managed to destroy this innocence and trust. He does the right things, he tries to please and to give the right answers, and then Father Dolan punishes him, although he has done nothing wrong. His innocence is troubled and rather disgusted by this; the accusation rests on nothing but a suspicion, after all; Father Dolan says "I see schemer in your face". This is not the first time this has been said to him, either, for when he was ill the prefect had come to see him:— "He was not foxing. And he felt the prefect's hand on his forehead". Father Dolan's expression becomes the ironic refrain characterising one of the artist's typical attitudes; Father Dolan's name for it is "that trick," and Stephen later calls it "cunning".

The scene in *Portrait* is intentionally dramatic; it also exists in two comic versions, the one earlier than *Portrait* and the other much later. In *Stephen Hero*, Stephen cannot help calling his mother's confessor "a jack in the box"; the mechanical and repetitious movement of the puppet corresponds to Father Dolan's prophecy: he will be in tomorrow and tomorrow and tomorrow. That this is comic is confirmed by the scene in 'Circe', at the other end of the work, in which Father Dolan rises up really like a puppet, with the crack of a ferula, in Stephen's fevered memory. The accusation recurs almost mechanically, and calls forth an equally mechanical response. When Heron accuses Stephen of being a "sly dog" and a hypocrite, Stephen's "face mirrored his rival's false smile" (*Portrait*, p. 78); he has entered upon the way of simulation.

Stephen's early life follows two rhythms, which seem to exclude him; the rhythm of the past, as used in the story, "once upon a time," relegates the boy's own existence to mythical unreality. He who sets up his own personal time and rhythm by a fabulous and non-historical genesis cannot avoid disturbing or preventing the establishment of his own consciousness in the real present. Stephen is not "you," but "another"; a series of imperatives, "Apologize, submit, obey," blindly enslave the child's mind, unused as it is to resistance, annihilating the will to be oneself and even depriving him of the freedom to exercise a perfectly normal faculty.

The Other, the adult, is at the beginning of it all; and the Other is not pleased with Stephen; in his oddness, his difference, he seems to be the predestined victim of the adults' anger. Far from being a god, or even what Justius in *Finnegans Wake* calls "some god in the manger," the child has the choice between being a docile dog in the manger or a "bard," an "egoarch" who goes his own way in complete isolation and no longer obeys the Superego at all. When Stephen bends over the mirror Mulligan offers him, at the beginning of *Ulysses*, he is still obeying orders: "Look at yourself, you dreadful bard" is an ironical order, recalling the first order the priest gave him, "look at yourself and admit your guilt". Stephen knows from his earliest childhood that he is caught in the gaze of others, "As he and others see me" (*Ulysses*, p. 10).

The questions the other children ask him mark out the place he is to occupy in the miniature universe of the school. At Clongowes, one gains some measure of identity, but only as "the self others see". The feelings of separation and of self-recognition develop as his answer to the questions, "What is your name? (Answer: Stephen Dedalus") and "What is your father?" (Answer: "A gentleman"). Stephen is no longer his mother's little Stephen. He has become other people's Dedalus, and Dedalus is a funny name. "What kind of a name is that?" asks his first tormentor. Son of a father who is not a magistrate and of a mother who kisses him goodnight, Stephen seems marked out as a butt for general sarcasm, as the circle of guilt closes round him again. His father should be a magistrate, but is not, and his mother kisses him before he goes to bed. The child's trial is indefinitely repeated and prolonged, ending always with a death sentence, either by drowning for sexual offences or by burning at the stake for heresy. He attracts suspicion because his name is Dedalus,[7] the pseudonym of the Artist, which in profane language is the synonym of the Heretic. Not only does he fail to be the person he should be, but also he has great difficulties in becoming the person he will need to be later. As it is pointed out in *Finnegans Wake*, the process of development is also ruled by imperatives; orthodoxy and security are to be found in "the howtosayto itiswhatis hemustwhomust worden schall" (p. 223).

To please his father, he must be a sportsman and a gentleman, for

while his mind had been pursuing its intangible phantoms and turning in irresolution from such pursuit he had heard about him the constant voices of his father and of his masters, urging him to be a gentleman above all things and urging him to be a good catholic above all things. These voices had now come to be hollow sounding in his ears. When the gymnasium had been opened he had heard another voice urging him to be strong and manly and healthy and when the movement towards national revival had begun to be felt in the college yet another voice had bidden him be true to his country and help to raise up her language and tradition. In the profane world, as he foresaw, a worldly voice would bid him raise up his father's fallen state by his labours and, meanwhile, the voice of his school comrades urged him to be a decent fellow, to shield others from blame. (*Portrait*, p. 84)

Everyone expects him to choose one of these courses that are open to a respectable young man; but Stepehen revolts. He is different, and always has been; he "gives them ear, only for a time" and continues to pursue his phantoms.

The rebellion takes place first in his imaginary world, and is soon joined by a feeling of predestination. A great number of facts converge, to bring about a revelation, particularly his strange name and his feeling of being always an outsider, exemplified at the children's party where, "though he tried to share their merriment, he felt himself a gloomy figure" (*Portrait*, p. 68). Silent and watchful, he has no wish to join in

[7]In *Stephen Hero*, Joyce was still intentionally keeping to the odder spelling, "Daedalus".

the games. He longs to meet in the real world "the unsubstantial image which his soul so constantly beheld"; chapter II represents the time of discontent and of quest, inspired by "a premonition which led him on" (*Portrait*, p. 65). He seeks everywhere, wandering and exploring among the docks and strange alleyways, far from other people. This knowledge that he is different from others sometimes seems like guilt, for he obliged to admit that he *looks* different: his face betrays him, as it were. He turns this into a proof that he is destined for exceptional greatness. In the outside world, he appears to submit, he makes the appropriate gestures, but in the inner world he is in search of his supremacy. This is particularly manifest in his relationship with the Church; the double servility of one who is obedient to an institution that is itself in submission to another superior hierarchy is satirised in the 'Telemachus' episode of *Ulysses*. If everyone in Ireland lives in the watchful sight of God and of his servants, then Stephen, the first person, can be nothing but the slave of a slave or the servant of a servant.

> He went over to it (the shaving-bowl), held it in his hands awhile, feeling its coolness, smelling the clammy slaver of the lather in which the brush was stuck. So I carried the boat of incense then at Clongowes. I am another now and yet the same. A servant too. A server of a servant.
> ... After all, I should think you are able to free yourself. You are your own master, it seems to me (says the Englishman Haines).
> —I am the servant of two masters, Stephen said, an English and an Italian. (*Ulysses*, pp. 15ff)

Still the same, or, to be more precise, still in the same place and in the same situation, in Dublin, hence in prison; also, still within himself, now more than ever before, Stephen is slowly approaching his centre.

Ironically, it is the false priest Mulligan who states his identity: for Stephen is a bard, one of the wandering, anti-clerical poets who enchanted or revolted the Ireland of the Middle Ages. "Look at yourself, you dreadful bard," cries the mocker, holding out a mirror. And Stephen obediently bends over the mirror held by the enemy; he is offered his own image. He used to be a villain; today he is "this dogsbody". "Who chose this face for me? This dogsbody to rid of vermin," he thinks. In *Finnegans Wake* (p. 193), Justius holds the mirror out to Mercius that he may see his scandalous heirloom, his clock-face handed down from one to another, saying, "Look! do you see your dial in the rocking-glass?"

In the course of the episode in Chapter II of *Portrait* where Stephen plays a part in the Whitsuntide play at school, the first trial of the Artist as heretical and deliberately perverse takes place.

When Bloom lights a fire for Stephen, in the 'Ithaca' episode of *Ulysses,* Stephen recalls to mind all the fires that have been lit for him throughout his life. Some had been lit by his father, when the family still had a home; but his back was turned to them, because already he was meditating treason. Others had been fires for the burning of heretics, lit by the servants of God, or by their servants. Nothing could be more humiliating than to be struck by the slave of a slave,[8] and this is the experience that Stephen can never forget, the experience that confirmed him as a martyr of Art, forced back against the barbed wire fence of life. "Struggling and kicking under the cuts of the cane and the blows of the knotty stump Stephen was borne back against a barbed wire fence" (*Portrait,* p. 82).

Two scenes take place simultaneously, juxtaposed by Stephen's memory and by his habit of living the present moment while keeping himself at a distance from it, as though simultaneously to experience it and to watch himself experiencing it. In the present tense, Dedalus is "a model youth. He doesn't smoke and he doesn't go to bazaars and he doesn't flirt and he doesn't damn anything or damn all." This is the sarcastically saintly portrait his rival Heron gives of Stephen. But this little saint is really a "sly dog"; Heron has just seen "her," and she is "deucedly pretty". Stephen stands revealed. The scene proceeds in parody of a judicial trial, in which the accused makes his confession, while Stephen's imagination simultaneously recalls the original trial, which had been much more serious. The method of capture is the same, making use of surprise as a weapon of aggression and catching Stephen off his guard. "Mr. Tate, the English master, pointed his finger at him and said bluntly: This fellow has heresy in his essay" (*Portrait,* p. 79). The boy has said that the soul is deprived of the possibility of ever approaching the Creator; he feels so distant from everyone that this impossibility could apply to any other relationship, and not only to that of the soul and its Creator. The accusation of heresy is felt to be a general accusation: he is not only heretical from the theological point of view, but also because he is *different,* again:

[8]Cf. *Finnegans Wake,* p. 233: "But leaving codhead's mitre and the heron's plumes sinistrant to the server of servants and rex regums and making a bolderdash for lubberty of speech . . ."

A hush fell on the class. Mr. Tate did not break it but dug with his hand between his thighs while his heavily starched linen creaked about his neck and wrists. Stephen did not look up. It was a raw spring morning and his eyes were still smarting and weak. He was conscious of failure and of detection, of the squalor of his own mind and home, and felt against his neck the raw edge of his turned and jagged collar. *(Ibid.)*

The accusing finger marks him out for public mockery and revenge, in a way that excludes him from the community; he is "this fellow," and feels this designation as a painful insult, as painful as his weak and smarting eyes and as his consciousness of misery. It is spring, but not for Stephen. The master's linen is impeccable, the pupil's collar is sufficient sign that he does not belong to the same world of prosperity. And Stephen makes no protest; he is "detected," and admits that he is poor and weak, and thus heretical too:

—Here. It's about the Creator and the soul. Rrm . . . rrm . . . rrm . . . Ah! *without a possibility of ever approaching nearer.* That's heresy.
Stephen murmured:
—I meant *without a possibility of ever reaching.*
It was a submission and Mr. Tate, appeased, folded up the essay and passed it across to him, saying:
—O . . . Ah! *ever reaching.* That's another story. *(Ibid.)*

But this act of submission does not finish the incident. Tate has thrown him to the rabblement. Although absolved by the Jesuit after his public submission and humiliation, he is again attacked, this time for non-conformity, and this time he reacts more strongly.

Heresy as Heroism

In the world of theology, Stephen knows he is on the point of committing fraud. The docile pupil becomes an heresiarch when God is replaced by poetry. The ancient trial within the trial continues, and is echoed during the scene in the street; the inquisitors this time are fellow-pupils of his at Clongowes, led by Heron, who "cleft the air before him with a thin cane"; he and his two acolytes—the judge and his assessors—are armed with weapons that replace the eagles' beaks.

This time, the conversation leads on to books and writers. Stephen masters the irritation he feels at hearing the dunce and the idler of the class boasting about all the books in their fathers' bookcases at home. But when Heron declares that Tennyson is the greatest poet, Stephen forgets his prudence and bursts forth in defence of Byron's claim to that title.

—In any case Byron was a heretic and immoral too.
—I don't care what he was! cried Stephen hotly.
—You don't care whether he was a heretic or not? said Nash.
—What do you know about it? shouted Stephen. (*Portrait*, p. 81)

This passionate Stephen has nothing in common with the timid one who murmured his reply to Mr. Tate. Nothing makes him retreat, neither Heron's stick whipping his legs, nor the blows from the cabbage stump, nor the barbed wire. Stephen, who fears physical pain, when put to the torture adopts the heroic attitude of Giordano Bruno: "Admit that Byron was no good.—No.—Admit.—No.—Admit.—No. No." And while in the past the younger Stephen, blinded by tears, had moved on, the adolescent Stephen admits that he is not a saint, and that she is, after all, pretty. As he indifferently makes this hypocritical admission, he recalls to mind the earlier heroic refusal to admit, when he took the part of Byron whom he resembled. For Byron's sake he would have let them kill him.

But there are some confessions which do not involve the soul; this is why Stephen can recite, "only from his lips," the *Confiteor*. It costs him nothing to do so, for he is not betraying the way to his soul or its secrets to the eye of the heron or of the master, but is on the contrary decoying the inquisitor to another place where he, Stephen, is not.

—So you may as well admit, Heron went on. . . .
He scarcely resented what had seemed to him a silly indelicateness for he knew that the adventure in his mind stood in no danger from these words: and his face mirrored his rival's false smile.
—Admit! repeated Heron, striking him again with his cane across the calf of the leg.
The stroke was playful but not so lightly given as the first one had been. Stephen felt the skin tingle and glow slightly and almost painlessly; and, bowing submissively, as if to meet his companion's jesting mood, began to recite the *Confiteor*. The episode ended well, for both Heron and Wallis laughed indulgently at the irreverence. (*Portrait*, p. 78)

As ever, the imitation threat is threefold: blows from the stick, blinding, censure. But the artist feels his fear of the stick only as a secondary emotion, since the real misfortune would be a lack of creative power in the world of art. The three punishments are always inflicted by three types of executioner, women (as type of the mother or of Our Lady), the priest's acolytes who proceed to the imaginary business of blinding him, and the priests themselves, who seek to paralyse the living Word. The presence of one of these redoubtable figures indicates that the others cannot be far away. If the priest appears, the mother will be near at hand; when Stephen's eyes are in danger, the woman's ghost will not be far off. The height of the art of inflicting suffering is reached when all three aggressors appear at the same time—the case at the end of Chapter V, where, to Stephen's detriment, E. C. and Father Moran seem to have concluded some surreptitious pact. Joyce attributes similar characteristics to these three types of aggressor by a projection of his own feelings on the subject.

The consciousness of one's own guilt, if repressed, leads to symptomatic difficulties in communication: voices become disagreeably harsh, and hesitate, punctuated by dry, humourless laughter; speech is abruptly interrupted and broken up, or becomes deliberately allusive, as though to confuse and befool the victim, until he is tracked down to his lair. Eyes give lying glances, gestures are condemnatory and equivocal, and all this is an example of Joyce's special brand of "rearrangement"—but also of his utilisation of *all* perceptible signs given—as being capable of reinterpretation. As he points out himself, in the analysis of the epiphany in Chapter V, the revealing things are those which are hidden in the spaces and interstices of speech. The words are at liberty to some degree, though always closely watched, but generally people forget to take equal care of the silences and tones of voice involved.

In the case of an inquirer, the true questions are the silent ones read between the lines of those actually asked aloud. The replies received are accepted sarcastically because they are given *voluntarily;* the inquisitor believes that truth is only obtained by violent means. Beneath the "urbane," "amiable," or "tolerant" tones of Heron, beneath Mr. Tate's laughter, is hidden the brutality that in the time of childhood was open and unconcealed. The inquisitors and their accomplices act out the different stages of the Question with interrogation, flagellation, impalement, the cleaving of the air, the lighting of little symbolic fires for the stake, and so forth. And the motivation behind this appears through gestures that escape from the conscious control of the mind:

it shows itself to have strong sexual overtones, and thus Joyce takes pleasure in turning the accusation back upon the accusers, denouncing their frustration and jealous resentment, for what they would accomplish they dare not. Stephen, Shem, the artist, are those who seek to fulfil their desires: "We thought, would and did". At the end of the *Portrait* is a subtly comical incident which contains all Stephen's rancour and jealousy within itself:

> Other wrangle with little round head rogue's eye Ghezzi. This time about Bruno the Nolan . . . He said Bruno was a terrible heretic. I said he was terribly burned. He agreed to this with some sorrow. Then gave me recipe for what he calls *risotto alla bergamasca*. When he pronounces a soft O he protrudes his full carnal lips as if he kissed the vowel. Has he? And could he repent? Yes, he could: and cry two round rogue's tears, one from each eye. (*Portrait*, p. 248)

The little Italian inquisitor likes his food, and Joyce's art transforms this liking into a substitute-sin for lechery. One cooks the heretic, and one eats risotto. Bruno, whom Joyce has already quoted in *Day of the Rabblement*, is assuredly the symbolic person of whom he is most fond. He burns him yet again in Bloom's yellow robe, in the "Circe" episode, remembering his discussions with Father Ghezzi, his Italian master at University College, which supplied him with the material quoted from the end of *Portrait*.[9] Joyce jokingly turns him into an Irishman by the name of Browne & Nolan (a Dublin bookseller), in *Finnegans Wake* and nicknames him Nayman, the man who says No. As Justus, the Jesuit brother in *Finnegans Wake*, puts it, the language of the accusation is either "oblique," setting up a tribunal from which the third-person victim may try to escape, or "imperative," thus direct. "Stand forth, Nayman of Noland (for no longer will I follow you obliquelike through the inspired form of the third person singular and the moods and hesitenties of the deponent . . .) . . . let us pry. . . . Cur, quicquid, ubi quando, quomodo, quoties, quibus auxiliis?" (*Finnegans Wake*, pp. 187–8).

The same assembly, convoked to answer for an offence committed by this "man of Noland," echoes throughout *Finnegans Wake*, followed by the eternal questionnaire of the confessor. He who lives in the enclosed space of his own soul, repelling all assaults on it, is henceforth not only the crafty man with a mask, but also the still more cunning "twiminds," capable of self-discovery by concealment and of building his own king-

---

[9]Ellmann, *op. cit.*, pp. 60–1. Charles Ghezzi, S.J., introduced Joyce to Dante and d'Annunzio.

dom on the foundations of his soul: "You have become of twosome twiminds hidden and discovered, nay condemned fool, anarch, egoarch, hiresiarch, you have reared your disunited kingdom on the vacuum of your own most intensely doubtful soul" (*Finnegans Wake*, p. 188). The ambivalence represented by Shem and Shaun is the consequence of all the aggression the artist has had to face, to which he has responded by creating his own clandestine thought living in the limitless silence and space of his imagination. It leads on to Nayman's land, where the enemy can no longer pursue him.

It was this concealed thought which was accidentally surprised when the young Stephen was still clumsily seeking the way of Art, and clashed with his teacher on the question of heresy. It must be pointed out that Stephen first lets the adversary gain some advantage over him *because of something he, Stephen, has written.* The transgression is always the same, both sexual and intellectual from earliest childhood: it is an attempt at self-satisfaction, folllowed by an idiosyncratic disfigurement of the Word; or it is twisting theology for one's own personal use, which is forbidden. It is also the act of taking a song (the song of the green rose) and making it one's own by changing its form, as on the first day the artist as "hiresiarch," or as "baby tuckoo," makes his nest in the words of another, making use of the divine Logos until he has truly found his own voice. The act of writing is always dangerous for a pupil of the Jesuits, since it is automatically adding to creation and should rightfully belong to the Master. The use of the pen is the equivalent of the "egoarch" 's gesture, and for the artist this seems to be an invitation to rival the Creator—it seems as though God is tempting him by obliging the young man to write only A.M.D.G. This Creator is also a Tempter.

"Imitate My works" he seems to say; do as I do or I forbid you to write; be my servant or you will suffer for it. The adolescent has the choice between an alienated, insincere pen, and an heretical pen. The provocation proves too strong, for to alienate one's writing deliberately is to renounce one's very self. Self-esteem and a regard for freedom of thought and of speech are inflamed by the words "Thou shalt not . . ." By imitating the Creator the young man prepares himself for action with the gift of practical irony and a cynicism consisting of complete readiness to reap all the benefit he can from the enemy.

Just before he met Nora, Joyce was at the end of his patience and of his financial tether, and was planning to join a troupe of travelling actors. Stanislaus tells us that he intended to adopt the pseudonym Gordon Brown, a translation of Giordano Bruno, whom he admired as intensely as he did Ibsen at the time. Bruno had, apart from the glory of the rebel, the added glory of martyrdom, and it seems that Joyce was consciously preparing himself for a similar role in 1903, when he wrote a review of J. Lewis McIntyre's book on Bruno for the *Daily Express* of 30 October 1903. For Joyce, Bruno's life was to be read as an heroic fable: he was a Dominican (and not a Jesuit, which was a point in his favour), a daring "commentator of old philosophies," who invented the theory of the coincidence of opposites which Joyce was to use in *Finnegans Wake*, a writer of polemic, and burned on the Campo dei Fiori; and "through all these modes and accidents. . . . [he] remains a consistent spiritual unity".[10] His philosophy delighted Joyce by its daring contradictions: rationalist and mystic, theistic and pantheistic, he attempts "to reconcile the matter and form of the Scolastics"—which redoubtable terms in his system, being called rather body and soul, almost entirely lose their metaphysical character. This reconciliation resembles Joyce's own attempt to confound, if not to conciliate, body and soul to such an extent that the two terms may become interchangeable, an attempt which we shall later endeavour to examine. One can understand the young man's ardent worship of the hero who did not hesitate to suffer death for the "vindication of the freedom of intuition," although, it must be admitted, Joyce had no such death-wish. His heroism was prudent, and his defence mechanism consisted of moving to a safe distance; he defends his own truth to the very end, and from the summit of the mountain he shares with Ibsen and Nietzsche he violently attacks the world of "puppets" and of hypocrisy.

Heresy as Acting a Part

If Stephen is heretical, he discovers his heresy to be a source of new attitudes to take and of renewed inspiration; he acts the part, and others are taken in by his acting. He investigates all the potentialities of the part, undergoing an apprenticeship in hypocrisy by acting out the parts of accuser and accused. Since he is accused of scheming and playing a part, he extracts whatever profit he can from the ambiguous situation. Like Joyce, he is good at acting, and on the night of the Whitsuntide play he begins to play the hypocrite intentionally. As ever, he is at the

[10] *Critical Writings*, p. 133.

centre of a world from which he longs to escape; as ever he watches, through the window, the spectacle to which he is a stranger. It remains alien to him. That evening the school is transformed into a theatre; the house of the Jesuits turns into a theatre for profane rejoicing, although it still keeps some of the signs of its normal functions. The Blessed Sacrament has been removed from the tabernacle, and the space before the altar is arranged for a gymnastic display. Sport and its instruments —clubs, dumbbells, and so on—fiill the holy place. The sacristy and the chapel are thronged with children in stage costumes.

Everyone is taking part in a huge theological farce, from which God is totally absent; in the bustle of the celebrations, He is quite forgotten. In a dark corner, a large old lady in black pays her devotions to a pink-dressed little girl with long golden hair, who looks like the ideal E.C. It is really little Bertie Tallon. Stephen's memory, always very sensitive to encounters in time present, is painfully over-excited, for he sees a parody of his own romantic feelings going on before his eyes, as Bertie-E. C., the boy-girl, is a mere mockery of the complexity of E. C.'s provocative absence/presence. She cannot be grasped, mentally or physically. "The excited prefect was hustling the boys through the vestry like a flock of geese," and all these staccato movements, this disorder, the jokes people are making, create one of the types of festive atmosphere to which Stephen's response is always one of melancholy and, if possible, of flight. Nothing makes him sadder nor more lonely than the jokes and games of others.

This evening time and space are falsified for the purposes of the celebration, and thus are doubly alienating; this is imitation reality. Things are deconsecrated on two different planes, and Stephen is stripped of the self-identification which he has been accustomed to maintain by his consciousness of being *different*. Usually, he feels that he is walking through a ghostly, theatrical world as the only spectator of a play whose characters are ignorant of their own play-acting; he alone is in contact with reality. This evening, however, the unconscious puppets dress up voluntarily as puppets. And Stephen himself has been given a part to play in this representation of unreality. This is the reason for his desperate feeling of being dragged into their world of dissimulation and absence, and his despair is aggravated by the fact that his usual refuge is also being profaned: the imaginary world of travels, dreams, and secret meetings is invaded by ghosts. For the others this is an entertainment, a game, but for Stephen it is an intolerable invasion, an act of aggression. The others disguise themselves, but he is stripped; the mascarade unmasks him.

The others play and pretend, while Stephen lives in a nightmare, for the enemy is imitating him and stealing his personal pose, usurping his act. He who longed "to meet in the real world the unsubstantial image which his soul so constantly beheld" is surrounded on all sides by images, and is present at a de-romanticised performance of his own dreams; the poet's ship rests at anchor. The scene is set for the dreams to be carried out; he is fascinated by ships about to depart, and

> The light spread upwards from the glass roof making the theatre seem a festive ark, anchored among the hulks of houses, her frail cables of lanterns looping her to her moorings. A side door of the theatre opened suddenly and a shaft of light flew across the grass plots. (*Portrait*, p. 75)

Methodically and artificially, the atmosphere favourable to a soaring flight is created: under the influence of the music and of incommunicable emotions, he takes off and soars high, borne on the waves of sound, and like Icarus he falls. An explosion brings him abruptly back to the reality of the theatre: "Then a noise like dwarf artillery broke the movement. It was the clapping that greeted the entry of the dumbbell team on the stage."(*Ibid.*)

Again, he falls a prey to the false charms of imagination, as in the distance a speck of pink light glows in the night, with the promise perhaps of Dante's celestial rose. He smells a faint aromatic odour, and at once the Virgin and her mystic nard are present to his mind.

> As he walked towards it he became aware of a faint aromatic odour. Two boys were standing in the shelter of a doorway, smoking, and before he reached them he had recognized Heron by his voice.
> —Here comes the noble Dedalus! cried a high throaty voice. Welcome to our trusty friend! (*Ibid.*)

This is the voice of the Shakespearean villain, covering treason with flattery. The trap is closing. Stephen has fallen into the hands of the enemy. And this time the theatre moves inwards; the play of memory and of alienation takes place in that invisible but real sphere of space and time extending between the two actors Stephen and Heron, and in this sphere it is what is not said that creates the strange vocal vibration. Wallis, who is Heron's friend, accomplice, and shadow, is the uninformed spectator before whom Heron and Stephen become partners in mystification, playing their parts in time present while they live out their real relationship behind their masks in secrecy, upon another stage that is also cruel, but strange and silent. The present is only the covering of that past they share, and Wallis is excluded from this without realising it. Heron and Stephen speak their lines as the present demands it, but the past is rising from its grave as they do so. In fact there is a lie, and a truth also, in the relationship between Stephen and Heron. In the present, the lie and nothing else is manifested in their words; Heron begins the theatrical dialogue in the conventional way, that is, in the apostrophic style which the other traitor, Mulligan, was also to adopt, and Heron's awareness of his treachery is expressed by his theatrical manner of speech. In the area beyond the words a scene is enacted whose protagonists are still Stephen and Heron, but their roles ara exactly reversed:

> I was just telling my friend Wallis what a lark it would be tonight if you took off the rector in the part of the school-master. It would be a ripping good joke. . . . Go on, Dedalus, he urged, you can take him off rippingly. He that will not hear the churcha let him be to theea as the heathena and the publicana. (*Ibid.*)

Stephen is asked to imitate, that is, to substitute himself for another, to act the part of his own master and to pronounce condemnation against himself—to be the inquisitor of his own heresy.

He decides to go along with the game of hypocrisy: having played the part of a saintly and virtuous hypocrite whom Heron was determined to unmask, he now accepts the role of mimicking the authorities and by playing the clown to obtain some silence, some relief from the rather painful questions Heron is so skilful at asking. Heron instinctively knows the chink in Stephen's armour is that he hates allusions to his father. Heron associates the pretty girl with the presence in the hall of Stephen's "governor":

> We saw her, Wallis, didn't we? And deucedly pretty she is too. And inquisitive! "And what part does Stephen take, Mr. Dedalus?" "And will Stephen not sing, Mr. Dedalus?" Your governor was staring at her through that eyeglass of his for all he was worth so that I think the old man has found you out too. (*Portrait*, p. 77)

The figure of his father in Chapter II of *Portrait* evokes for Stephen thoughts of complicity with the Jesuits and of the humiliation caused him by the family's social downfall. The ambivalence of his feelings of shame (since he is both ashamed of his father and ashamed to face his father) is his secret weakness, and it is further complicated by the girl's presence, because it is tacitly understood between father and son that it is the father who is successful with the ladies, while the son is not interested in such matters. By his imitation of the rector, Stephen distracts his adversaries' attention from the question.

One immediate consequence of the theatrical performance is that for the first time the notion of being closely *watched*, as though by a prison guard or even a voyeur—the boy's feeling that his every move is watched by disapproving or inquisitorial eyes—becomes *concrete*. Not only does Stephen visualise this state as concrete, but also the event in question provides him with a reasonably exact metaphor to describe his isolated position in the world. In his imagination, everything becomes organised around the idea of the entertainment that is in progress, and its music serves as background to his personal reactions; the traps, the pitfalls and seductions, everything that awaits him in real life, seems concentrated in this one experience, and what he sees projected on to the stage is an image of his own destiny. For Stephen, as he crouches in a corner watching the others moving about, this evening is the time of memory: all his past returns, humiliations, and temptations are resurrected and mingle with the present, rising like a tide of emotion (anger or tenderness) in his soul. And then the tide is brought to a standstill:

> All day he had imagined a new meeting with her for he knew that she was to come to the play. The old restless moodiness had again filled his breast as it had done on the night of the party, but had not found an outlet in verse. The growth and knowledge of two years of boyhood stood between then and now, forbidding such an outlet. (*Portrait*, p. 77)

This evening he realises that all his emotions and his expression of them are imaginary and artificial; all grows cold at the contact with reality, but in his thoughts, he is still with her.

> She was sitting there among the others perhaps waiting for him to appear. He tried to recall her appearance but could not. He could remember only that she had worn a shawl about her head like a cowl and that her dark eyes had invited and unnerved him. He wondered had he been in her thoughts as she had been in his. (*Portrait*, p. 83)

In reality, he knows that he can only be happy when far from all other calls, out of reach, alone in the company of his phantoms. In the darkness, waiting to go on stage, he yields to the image of "her serious alluring eyes"; "for one rare moment" he feels truly "clothed in the real apparel of boyhood". For that moment he is a youth like the others, and when the world begins to spin in time to his emotions' rhythm, he lets himself be tempted. And not for the first time, either. There has already been the one festive evening that involved powerful temptation, but then the voice within him—though as yet nameless and unidentified— was the stronger. "He heard what her eyes said to him from beneath their cowl and knew that in some dim past, whether in life or revery, he had heard their tale before. . . . Yet a voice within him spoke above the noise of his dancing heart, asking him would he take her gift to which he had only to stretch out his hand" (*Portrait*, p. 69).

He had not stretched out his hand. Both yesterday and tomorrow the young man stays in his place, refusing to pursue the fleeing shape, which only flees in order to provoke him to follow, because he knows that his heart is not the most reliable adviser. The pursuit the girl offers is fruitless and his soul's death is hidden in the charms of "her fine dress and sash and long black stockings," forever promising but never giving. Before the age of traps and decoys is over, Stephen is to yield two or three more times to the charm of the dream, but he never goes as far as the gesture, as far as the final flight, ecstasy, and betrothal when dealing with his imagination. He is to be constantly tempted to accept self-surrender (just for a moment) in order to gain the right to stretch out his hand to Her. At this Whitsun play, in the presence of all his enemies, he reaches the very edge of alienation; he *lends* himself without giving, adopts disguises, and responds to orders and to subtle lures to the point of dizziness and bewilderment, as though wishing to explore the gloomy cage prepared for him and to taste the bait set out. He ventures so far into the darkness that he suddenly has to turn and flee, and it is not the spirit of Byron that brings him aid, but the sordid nature of reality, destroying the magic of the theatre and breaking the spell of his alienation. The illusion has been brief; the artist knows that the trappings of the festive entertainment mean death to him.

When on stage, disguised and playing the part of the grotesque pedagogue (a role which he might later be called to play in real life), he visualizes what the world would be like if he accepted: grotesque, the cynosure of all eyes, himself posturing in front of "the void of faces," into which at the very most he might be able to project some vaguely desirable image of himself. This vision immediately brings him back to his senses.

The Satanic Progression

From the moment that Stephen decides not to be anyone but himself, not even to pretend to be otherwise, he breaks with the world in which he only has a place if he plays the correct part: he rejects his obligations towards country, Church, and family, to which he no longer feels he belongs. Until his vocation is revealed to him, until he meets the image which he has been awaiting since childhood, the "harbinger of life's course," he feels *different*, he feels that he is not as he should be; and until he has his vision of the girl on the beach, which confirms for him his artistic vocation, he knows that he is not so much different from the world of tradition as completely alien to it. All its contexts are foreign to him, and he must build up his own homeland—his own tradition and faith—in harmony with his nature. He is not at home in Ireland. Continued service of what he no longer believes in would be worse than submission; it would be a denial of himself.

The Satanic progression consists of a number of negative steps. The first chapters of the *Portrait* show Stephen in search of his identity and of his place in the various social structures. From the beginning he is called Baby Tuckoo, the cuckoo who is born in another bird's nest, and he sadly begins to realise this after he has tried and failed to order and embellish the world of his family; he feels that he is not of the same blood as them. He has tried, to the point of hypocrisy, to make himself a niche somewhere by obedience, then by disobedience. He has tried to compensate for reality by his dreams; he has sought his own life through piety, then through immorality. And each time his failure has brought him increased anger and weariness.

If he is none of those things which the voices of the world around encourage him to be (neither a gentleman, nor a good Catholic, nor a decent fellow, nor strong, manly, and healthy), this is because he is unable to recognize anything in the narrow space in which he is trapped with these voices. His senses, like his mind, are irritated—attacked by a reality which memory makes more substantial. A painful or disturbing experience, by repetition, leaves an impression which becomes part of him. Reality has an unbearable way of encroaching on his sensibilities, and he can neither serve nor desist without finding his very soul invaded and transformed by the world outside. If he serves Ireland, he knows that he will lose that which makes him different, and that he will begin to resemble his country. This hyper-adaptability, the sign of extreme sensibility, almost of neurosis, is the beginning of his rebellion; it also is the reason for the intensely subjective form of the *Portrait*, which is written in the language of confrontation. *Non Serviam* is less a refusal than a declaration of resistance, which is why he begins with a reappropriation of reality after his rebirth as artist.

His identity is revealed under circumstances which, taken together as a whole, form a counterpoint to the world in which he was mistakenly staying: the network of images which he always interpreted as signifying his condemnation or as representing his own distress is now, in the Satanic world, transposed, the same symbols having a different meaning. All that was ill-omened in the common world has a beneficent counterpart in the parallel world. Instead of the eagles, Stephen sees rising in the sun the hawk-like man who is Daedalus the artificer. Instead of the bat, symbolising the spiritual darkness of womankind, he sees the "strange and beautiful seabird". The water that he loathes becomes wedded to the sky and to the sea-banks where he is finally consecrated as artist. Everything happens as though there were another side to reality, and on that other side a different reality, the realm of the imagination, the world of art with which the artist maintains a reciprocal relationship of creation and exchange; and in that world action has a constructive and liberating aspect, because Stephen believes in it, and sees himself in evolution there, without having to see himself in chains.

In fact, if life and art are separate and opposed—as they are in vulgar minds—the one being hard "reality" and the other a mere luxury of the idle mind, Stephen and his antagonists behave in such a way that the relationship between the serious and the playful, between the responsible and the irresponsible (which in the course of their conversations seems negatively established, and loaded against Stephen), becomes, by means of a very subtle and simple piece of pantomime, immediately reversed in his favour. While Stephen is investigating the direction of his own development, searching constantly and never satisfied by the first step, taking the greatest care to avoid errors and lies, his friends Lynch, Cranly, and Davin each perch fearfully in his own particular religion. Their submission to the imperatives of society (Lynch represents worldly success), country (Davin stands for nationalism and patriotism), and religion (Cranly is the right-thinking Catholic) is complete. Stephen and his doubts annoy and trouble them. The three anti-Stephens refuse to doubt, because they are afraid of the spiraling insecurity doubt might bring them; they do not doubt intellectually because their critical minds have been relegated to the use of Another. But they are less happy and less satisfied than their self-esteem would suggest, for each one is dissimulating to the best of his ability the fact that there is a great gulf fixed between *necessary* belief and spontaneous disbelief.

To maintain such a dissimulation necessitates an act of faith—of such bad faith that all three betray themselves to Stephen by their attitudes, which range from open hostility to the rare impulses of friendship. Stephen disturbs them and threatens their peaceful existence by his wish *to be loyal to his doubts,* a requirement which he puts before that of loyalty to his faith. Blind faith, says the Satanic Stephen, is worth nothing, and only by questioning the motives and the very nature of fidelity and loyalty can one build an honest relationship for one's soul with the world. If you do not wish to leave, says Cranly, you must not think that you are obliged to do so, nor need you consider yourself as a heretic or an outlaw; but he cannot see that Stephen is doing his utmost in order to be considered a heretic, and that he is even confiding his most tendentious thoughts to adversaries carefully chosen for their appropriateness. Cranly is well known for his orthodoxy and for his filial devotion, and so Stephen chooses him to hear how he, Stephen, would rather cause his mother to suffer than endanger the integrity of his own consciousness.

> —Do you believe in the eucharist? Cranly asked.
> —I do not, Stephen said.
> —Do you disbelieve it then?
> —I neither believe in it nor disbelieve in it, Stephen answered.
> —Many persons have doubts, even religious persons, yet they overcome them or put them aside, Cranly said. Are your doubts on that point too strong?
> —I do not wish to overcome them, Stephen answered. (*Portrait,* p. 239)

Lynch is well known for his extreme poverty, and so to him Stephen speaks of pure beauty: " 'What do you mean', Lynch asked surlily, 'by prating about beauty and the imagination in this miserable Godforsaken island? No wonder the artist retired within or behind his handiwork after having perpetrated this country' " (*Portrait,* p. 215). This sounds like the voice of Stannie, echoing the voice of Jim.

Lynch, Davin, and Cranly are in league against Stephen's "analyses" and speeches, as Stephen circles skilfully about them, showing up the aggressiveness of their real natures.

Ironically, these three believe in the necessity of silence, exile, and cunning, although they do not compromise themselves by admitting as much; when Stephen speaks to them, pouring forth his thoughts and his griefs, although his pretext for so doing is that he needs to try one last time to communicate with others—to confide in them, and to break down the isolation of separate souls—he is in fact plotting his own expulsion and making use of others for his own ends. When he finally announces to the world in general that he is going to keep silent, to practise cunning, and to leave forever, he is in fact taking pride in ostentatiously flaunting his own cleverness, a cleverness almost too clever for itself, indeed, for until the very last moment Stephen is still quite ready to heed his country's call.

He fears nothing so much as unexpected sympathy, and everything might have been different if he had found one person to listen to him and to welcome him innocently and sincerely. The man who says, "Look, I am going to kill myself," wants to be stopped, as the person who says "Well, I'm going now" wants people to restrain him and keep him in their company. Stephen wants someone to hold him back, someone who will really love him, yet he knows that he exists within the reality of Dublin, that he has chosen the way of refusal, and that no-one will stretch out a hand towards him. To be honest many people will be relieved to see him go: already their looks are shut, like their doors, their backs already turned; his beloved looks straight through him, greeting the man standing next to him, and no-one really wants him. Were it not for the obscure prestige conferred on him by his skill with language and by his apparent knowledge of secrets, no-one would try patiently to understand him or to hold him back. Stephen's gravity, his pride, and his loyalty to himself are so great that any real dialogue is impossible. Finally, it is important to examine the type of doubt he has chosen: there are two kinds of doubt, the first being the Cartesian type, which questions all received knowledge and information in order to reconstruct the world upon a foundation of clear and distinct ideas. It makes a clean sweep to begin with, and is then replaced by progressive affirmations. But Stephen's doubt is completely and absolutely negative; he has no intention of replacing one faith by another, since he refuses to serve any set of beliefs. There is nothing stable about the artistic condition, since its essential characteristics are rebellion and being different, and therefore one must always doubt, doubting even the doubt itself, in order to build, as it says in *Finnegans Wake*, on the vacuum of one's own intensely doubtful soul.

Der Geist der Stets verneint: Goethe's expression from *Faust* is quoted in 'Humanism,' a review dated 1903, in which Joyce violently attacks that pragmatism which claims to be the spirit of civilisation and which is contrasted with the benighted barbarian who believes in the Absolute. For Joyce, "pragmatism" equals "common sense," which is just another name for stupidity, for the death of real thought.[11] It is clear, when one recalls the manifest hypocrisy that originally inspired English pragmatism, that Joyce has chosen the most advantageous point from which to attack: William James was the president of the Society for Psychical Research until 1914, and it was considered correct to take an interest in the occult while rejecting any concern for immortality. The soul was replaced by "spirit". Joyce's disgust for spiritualism and theosophy corresponds to his disgust for the moral timidity and intellectual cowardice of those who claimed to have aspirations to spiritual freedom—who escaped from the arms of the Church only to entangle themselves in the veils of Isis.

Against this false revolt Joyce chose the way of permanent refusal, agreeing to be he who says No despite the consequences, even if it means his life. For one can achieve autonomy only by opposition, and without opposition one only changes from slavery to slavery. This is why Joyce chose to admire Giordano Bruno, who "through all these modes and accidents . . . remains a constant spiritual unity". Heresy is to be preferred to death, replies Stephen to Cranly's inquisitorial probing, "and I am not afraid to make a mistake, even a great mistake, a lifelong mistake, and perhaps as long as eternity too".

In fact, as we shall see from the analysis of Chapter V, Davin, Lynch, and Cranly have long been betraying or deserting Stephen; his exile is less a flight from his enemies than a concrete expression of his actual situation as pariah. For Stephen art is a vocation, and the response to that call should involve his whole being, yet that response can only take on its full meaning after a long process of development, leading to eventual maturity. He has made the response, but has scarcely yet begun to become an artist; he is still at the stage of defining his motives and of seeking a direction for his flight.

"Art" to those who politely surround it with veils of prudent ignorance and lack understanding, is a kind of mental magic, difficult to imagine. The artist is supposed to demonstrate his art by performing some sort of miracle, by producing some instant verbal manifestation, or an essay on aesthetics. Somehow, in the vague imagination of the dean, the Jesuit comfortably installed in the place of the absent living God, there is an idea that the artist is like a rival preacher, who manipu-

---

[11] *Critical Writings*, p. 135.

lates his ideas of the beautiful as the priest handles matters of dogma, following a logical rule laid down by a superior authority. " 'You are an artist, are you not, Mr. Dedalus?' said the dean, glancing up and blinking his pale eyes. 'The object of the artist is the creation of the beautiful. What the beautiful is is another question' " (*Portrait*, p. 185). And he asks, "When may we expect to have something from you on the esthetic question?" Donovan, the respectable, successful student, echoes this with "I hear you are writing some essays about esthetics".

Stephen protests that "I stumble on an idea once a fortnight if I am lucky". Art is only a call to create: it can only be defined and set down in formulae after the completion of the work, and at the beginning there are only certain very elementary principles, which act simply as temporary props. The Jesuit, like Stephen's fellow-pupils, treats art a priori as the profane form of an intellectual system whose sacred and dogmatic form is religion, and whose concrete form in life is sport—like every game, it involves only the player, but not the whole man. In a word, it is not "serious". Davin, Lynch, and Cranly do not take Stephen seriously as artist at all: art is his hobby, and he is an interesting, slightly eccentric fellow. His success is partly due to his reputation and partly due to the fascination of his hobby for others—just like any other acrobat or performing juggler. But it is clear to the others that his hobby, which absorbs him so much, has nothing to do with real life. In real life one does not play such games, take such risks; one does not, and cannot, earn one's living with words. Lynch, the chosen partner in a painful dialogue on aesthetics, speaks for Ireland when he says, "If I am to listen to your esthetic philosophy give me at least another cigarette. I don't care about it. I don't even care about women. Damn you and damn everything. I want a job of five hundred a year. You can't get me one" (*Portrait*, p. 207).

Conclusion

The Satanic progression leads to doubt as the only attitude consonant with reason.

Stephen refuses the Eucharist because of its symbolic power: he is not worried about the miracle of transubstantiation as the orthodox conceive of it. He alludes to a pseudo-transubstantiation which is not miraculous, but whose operation is pseudo-scientific; the host is still a symbol, but not of the body of Christ which it is *in potentia*. On the contrary it symbolises the Church's "twenty centuries of authority and veneration". Stephen declares, half-joking, that what he fears is the chemical action that this symbol of servitude and submission may have on his soul.

Rather than make his spirit submit, he deliberately chooses heresy; and this very choice is in some sort an act of homage to the system in which he refuses to believe, since he still stands in the traditional ideology of Catholicism. His liberation is precisely a refusal of Catholicism, a "*nego,*" a negative act, and not an affirmation or a replacement: "What kind of liberation would that be," he asks, "to forsake an absurdity which is logical and coherent and to embrace one which is illogical and incoherent?" (*Portrait,* p. 243). The coherence and harmony of Catholicism gratify the artist in him, but the impossibility of individuality in Catholicism nauseates him. His mind is wrapped in the cowl of a heretic monk, and he joins the company of all the rationalists and doubting philosophers of the Middle Ages. From *Portrait* onwards, his mind is filled with friendly figures—modern artists and mediaeval sceptics—such as William of Occam who rejects the idea of miracles and replaces it by the necessity of an act of faith quite separate from reason, and who at the same time declares that no society is superior to the actual individuals composing it.[12]

He admires in particular Scotus Eriugena, who champions the primacy of reason in cases of conflict with the authority of the Fathers because authority is only fossilised reason, whereas reason is the living source of authority; authority is only the truth as grasped by reason and set down by the Fathers in their writings. One must begin by believing in God's authority, but in order to understand what one believes, it is necessary to appeal to reason, so that one may compare God's authority with that of men. Reason is thus both source and limit of the faith, and only God is infallible. Therefore, Joyce refuses the intellectual obedience the Jesuits demand, which is set out in Saint Ignatius' *Ratio Studiorum:* Loyola imposes strict Thomism and absolutely rejects all other theories, especially the philosophy of Averroes. The rigidity of faith thus imposed is contrasted with the smoothness and adaptability of their methods of persuasion as described in the *Spiritual Exercises* and as put

---

[12]For Joyce's heresies, see J. Mitchell Morse, *The Sympathetic Alien* (London, 1959), particularly chapter V, 'Jesuit Bark and Bitter Bite'.

into practice by Father Purdon in 'Grace'. Absolute submission is achieved by making the effort to believe that "what to us seems white is black, if the hierarchical Church tells us that it is black".[13]

Joyce's struggle against obedience extends from *Dubliners* to the great quarrel between the Mookse and the Gripes in *Finnegans Wake*.

[13]Para. 365 of the Rules for accommodating one's thoughts with the Church.

XIV. From Hell to Hell

It is not his revolt against the Church that finally ranges Stephen on the side of sin and of experience, but rather the failure of all his attempts to beautify the world around him and to improve the lot of his family. An artistic despair leads him into the hidden ways of the imagination, deeper and deeper into the guilt that resides in his private world. The laughable difference between his ambitions towards purity and beauty, and the sordid dirt of reality around him, brings him to the state of taking pride in his sins: the world humiliates him, unjustly, although he once had the privilege of being clothed in the magical garments of beauty. He suffers his misery, not as a social condition or a fact of family life, but as a personal downfall and degeneracy. He enters on a phase of fury and madness, directed against himself (for lack of any immediate adversary), and "his life becomes a tissue of subterfuge and falsehood" (*Portrait*, p. 99). He takes a morbid pleasure in disfiguring everything he sees, and calls up in his dreams innocent faces transfigured by lecherous cunning, their eyes shining with brutish joy. Everything has to fall, and to crawl, since he must. He wanders about at night, and the Eden-like visions he used to have, of little closed and virginal gardens, of soft lights and of Mercedes, of the rose-trees and of loving words, are now vanished, leaving only an echo of the idealistic past. Now he stalks through dark muddy streets like a beast after its prey. Nothing can hinder the feelings of exaltation he derives from his self-destruction. He enjoys his hell because, like Satan banished from Paradise, he has decided that hell shall be his heaven; the supreme perversion consists of making wrong into one's good, the source of one's pride, and of deriving a monstrous glory from one's shame.

Dreaming of the blest encounter with a pure, womanly figure, which used to be his only dream, he wanders in "a maze of narrow and dirty streets" (*Portrait*, p. 100). He embarks, unforeseen, on one of those exotic journeys which had always been a temptation to him: once his heart had danced like a cork to the rhythm of E. C.'s movements, and another time he had walked by the docks and wondered at the vast number of corks dancing on the water. . . .

The Hell Within: Delight in Disgust

As soon as he enters this noisy, dirty part of town, he is struck by its exotic appearance: "He walked onward, . . . wondering whether he had strayed into the quarter of the Jews". This is Joyce's way of introducing the Oriental revery which continues later in the mind of Bloom. The yellow gas-flames burn as though before an altar; the women and girls in long gowns are leisurely and perfumed, because this is how Stephen, conventionally enough, imagines the desirable woman. He wanders, and loses himself, in order to find himself somewhere completely different, in the yellow light of the pre-Christian world. He observes himself to be "in another world: he had awakened from a slumber of centuries," and he who awakes in this warm, scented and permissive world is not called Stephen. He is rebaptised for the occasion with the ritual nickname of Willie, in parody of the ceremonies of rebirth into another world—of initiation into the mysteries. Willie sees, on the other side of the Catholic Hell, the innocent hell of satisfaction; the labyrinth of delirious guilt has led him to the entrance to an unknown labyrinth, one gentle, gay, and peopled by women, where the pink-gowned phantom does not flee, but embraces him, "gaily and gravely". This is a peaceful and silent hell, where all cries die away, and the world is warm and gay, calm and grave. Stephen weeps with joy at his deliverance; *She* has come at last! Not Mercedes, nor Eileen nor E. C., but *She* whom he had already hymned in the first version of the *Portait* in 1904, parodying with tender solemnity the litany of the Virgin.

It was too much for him. He closed his eyes, surrendering himself to her, body and mind, conscious of nothing in the world but the dark pressure of her softly parting lips. They pressed upon his brain as upon his lips as though they were the vehicle of a vague speech; and between them he felt an unknown and timid pressure, darker than the swoon of sin, softer than sound or odour. (*Portrait*, p. 101)

This redemption by the sin committed with another, in whose sin he too has sinned,[1] is, for the artist, accompanied by the discovery of a language: the lips that press upon his own lips press also upon his brain, as though to teach him the inarticulate and vague language of the body. But the adjective used here is already a sign that this language is inadequate, that a vague language is merely the shadow of a full and living tongue, and that future failure is already pointed out in advance. It is not in this world that Stephen is to find life awaiting him; he thought that the world in which he awoke was the right one, but in fact he had awakened inside the nightmare of evil. The waking was only a dream, and the faultless world an illusion.

Stephen only once experiences this liberating ecstasy. It was too beautiful; he was, after all, only a passerby in this third world. It is not possible to escape from the hellish reality of the second world or from its invasion of the first—vulnerable and personal—world of the guilty conscience. Willie was happy, but Stephen may not pass from one world to the other with impunity; the imagination is indeed powerful, but the superego condemns all attempts to escape. Henceforth, when he makes incursions into forbidden territory, he does so as a Christian, accompanied by his avenging conscience and possessed by destructive masochism; the prostitutes' calls have no effect on his body but on "his sin-loving soul," and by means of "their soft, perfumed flesh" he reconstitutes his own unhappiness and disgust. The voyage of delirium has not led far. He savours the dirt and vulgarity of this artificial paradise as a discipline. "The other world," on his return to it at the beginning of Chapter III, bears its true name of "the squalid quarter of the brothels," and is now truly Hell, including circles that grow progressively narrower and darker. He ventures into them with fear and joy, although he had not been afraid the first time. He goes not in search of deliverance but towards his own damnation, expecting that the prosti-

[1]This is the definition of temptation given by the Maynooth Catechism, and adopted by Stephen in his discourse on Shakespeare in 'Charybdis and Scylla'.

tutes' flesh will call to his soul, for his flesh is not excited any more and it is his soul that experiences the deadly pleasures.

Basically, Stephen is deceived; the warmth that seemed to promise a flame of joy hardens and grows cold, and all the lights go out. The altar that should have been the place for the celebration of a creative transubstantiation is in fact "a clothless table," stained by "a ring of porter froth". Language remains vague; there are no secrets; the sordid hero of these adventures becomes similiar to the kind of individual he would wish to avoid. He is not going to become an artist with the help of prostituted flesh; the third world only brings him to the desert of his fleshly being and to "a cold lucid indifference." Even terror—that religious sentiment so necessary for the achievement of exaltation—even the fear of self-loss or self-lessening which springs from a healthy self-esteem, must vanish in this world where the women are neither sufficiently terrifying nor sufficiently retiring.

> At his first violent sin he had felt a wave of vitality pass out of him and had feared to find his body or his soul maimed by the excess. Instead the vital wave had carried him on its bosom out of himself and back again when it receded: and no part of body or soul had been maimed but a dark peace had been established between them. (*Portrait,* p. 103)

This peace is the peace of chaos and death, for in Stephen's case peace is unfavourable to creation, insofar as the latter is only begun by the sparking off of a mechanical process of aggression followed by a defence-reaction. Stephen finds out that mortal sin means immediate death in this life. Pride leads him on to multiply his wrong by new sin, from day to day; he punishes himself, repeating an action which is henceforth dreary and unmeaning, through pride and the memory of the first moment of glory. Like Satan he is obstinately determined to make evil his destiny, and to judge God as incapable of pardoning him. "His pride in his own sin, his loveless awe of God, told him that his offence was too grievous to be atoned for in whole or in part by a false homage to the All-seeing and All-knowing" (*Portrait,* p. 104).

Transgression is accompanied each time by a loss of reality which is the very reverse of the mystic's ecstasy, and is the sign of alienation. When Stephen yields to the motherly embrace of the prostitute ("he wanted to be held firmly in her arms, to be caressed slowly, slowly, slowly. In her arms he felt that he had suddenly become strong and fearless"), he becomes "conscious of nothing in the world" but the pressure of her lips.

Earlier, when he had tried to appease the fierce longings of his heart, he had found that "everything else was idle and alien". He is so encircled by sin that he and it form a narrow, closed universe with no escape. His body is caught in that embrace in which he abdicates all will of his own, yet still his soul explores the strange, cold world of damnation, finding an almost aesthetic joy in this sinuous progress. There is no need for an accuser now, for in a completely detached manner Stephen watches himself proceed towards Hell, shame and fear replaced by a scorn for the innocence of others and a pleasant hypocrisy. He finds order and harmony in this darkness; music, the necessary accompaniment of his inner life, bears "his weary mind outward to its verge and inward to its centre" (*Portrait*, p. 103). The images in the psalms of prophecy soothe him, and the rhythm of Latin lulls his conscience. Rounded, happy arms delight his flesh no longer, but long sinuous phrases now caress his soul. The Puritan already makes the sinner's reasoning yield, and impurity cannot be a source of joy.

This thinking goes as far as to separate body and soul. The flesh continues its sad orgies while the soul takes its strange, arid pleasure "in following up to the end the doctrines of the church and penetrating into obscure silences only to hear and feel the more deeply his own condemnation". This joy which takes its source from Nelly the prostitute is too facile to be accepted. Stephen says, in fact, that he can only love the inaccessible, the eternally desirable, the blessed and untouchable virgin. A fierce passion for her brings him from defeat to exasperation, towards the true altar of love where "spikenard, myrrh and frankincense" burn. Nelly's scent is but a vulgar imitation of Our Lady's perfumes.

Again Stephen enters the world of prophetic images. Mercedes is now Mary, and he is again her knight, but the third world has made a breach in his imagination: reality is seen as a dark and infernal trinity, the three worlds communicating in one vast psychological chaos, for now sin has introduced its scent of guilt everywhere, overflowing the consciousness and affecting even the sense-perceptions. "He tried to think how it could be. But the dusk, deepening in the schoolroom, covered over his thoughts". "His mind wound itself in and out of the curious questions proposed to it," as Stephen, the snake in the grass, prepares for sacrifice. He is to be offered a specially made Hell of his own quite different from this.

The Style of the Troubled Conscience

The almost complete bodily transposition of a retreat sermon,[2] which breaks in upon Stephen's consciousness with its images of stereotyped terror, is a forerunner of episodes in *Ulysses:* the style is that of objective reality in order to mark its strangeness to—and difference from—the subject. By using a piece of completely foreign prose, Joyce suppresses the central awareness of Stephen's consciousness for the length of the sermon. This on the one hand gives Hell a much more autonomous (and thus more concrete) existence, and on the other confers upon this horrible world enough strength of its own for it to invade Stephen's consciousness and cause bewilderment and alienation. Joyce would cheerfully mock that vulnerability which he shared with Stephen: he once wrote the following limerick in a letter to Ezra Pound (9 April 1917):

> There once was a lounger named Stephen
> Whose youth was most odd and uneven—
> He throve on the smell
> Of a horrible hell
> That a Hottentot wouldn't believe in.

Even though the Hottentot would not believe in it, Stephen wished to do so—at least for the time it took to burn himself sufficiently so that he might keep the image of it as both a proof of the cruelty of the Church and a psychological stimulant for himself. It is necessary to have been afraid if one is to know what bravery is.

It has been said that *Portrait* can be read as a succession of conflicts between dream and reality.[3] In fact there is no neat dividing line between Stephen's dream-experiences and his encounters with reality, but such a distinction exists in *Ulysses,* where the 'Circe' episode is definitely hallucinatory. There is only one reality in *Portrait,* which is lived out on different levels by the young man whose consciousness and imagination are undergoing modifications ranging from the imperceptible to the violent as he passes through the crises that mark his spiritual evolution. The world outside seems more or less substantial as Stephen's own state varies. It is important to point out that it is the effects of sin

[2]See Elizabeth Boyd, *art. cit; L'Inferno Aperto* of Giovanni Pietro Pinamonti (first published 1688, first translated into English 1715); and Kevin Sullivan, *Joyce among the Jesuits,* pp. 125–8.
[3]Hugh Kenner, *Dublin's Joyce* (London, 1955).

and of the religious terror following it which break the boundaries of objective reality and the protection of subjectivity—and to such an extent that reality, as Stephen transforms it into his imaginary hell, overflows and invades the outer world. The ugliness of reality rose in its sordid tide within Stephen's soul, while the ugliness of that soul seemed to him to contaminate the universe. This is all the more striking because the two movements towards interpretation follow each other: at the end of Chapter II, Stephen has given up trying to introduce some order and beauty into the chaotic life of his family and, as though impelled by a need for vengeance and satisfaction, goes off to seek the desired communion in the disorder of the senses. Being a stranger and outcast in his own family, he is "adopted" by a prostitute, who is, of course, part of the new communion.

"By day and by night he moved among distorted images of the outer world". He moves in a world which he distorts, and the reader is moved into a reality which never gives any impression of being real. More exactly, the reader is ushered into the mental circumvolutions of an extremely subjective person. It is neither Life nor the City that Joyce describes through Stephen, but rather the claim that Stephen himself makes at the end of the book of "I go to encounter for the millionth time the reality of experience and to forge in the smithy of my soul the uncreated conscience of my race." This may serve as the best definition of that "neo-realism" of which *Portrait* is the subjective application. What Stephen encounters is reality as experience, and what he brings back to his "smithy" for the forging of the conscience of his race will be the negotiations of himself with this reality.

This is as much as to say that Joyce reconstitutes Dublin here, the Dublin of the *Portrait* being Stephen's Dublin, while the town in *Ulysses* is that of Bloom. The two towns may be superimposed, but they are quite different. Chapter III is thus doubly important, because on the one hand reality takes its revenge on the mind which had distorted it, and on the other it is already possible to see a fully developed technique of rendering the real as subjective and more inward, a technique which is used so completely in *Ulysses;* the author is adept at using language to move or change the centre of reality to inner or outer regions of the consciousness.

At the beginning of Chapter III Stephen is frequenting the world of sensual satisfactions, slipping under the ban of the Church. In this world, the body does the talking and gives the orders to such an extent that each part of Stephen's body seems possessed of a strange autonomy, while his soul is reduced to howling wordlessly like a beast. His feet carry him into the labyrinth of the forbidden district; his blood revolts; "the inarticulate cries and the unspoken brutal words rushed forth from his brain"; his lips refuse to bend down to a kiss; his belly counsels him to stuff himself full of stew.

Joyce gives us the portrait of a man possessed, and even if Stephen is not conscious of actual devils, he feels himself gripped by terrifying forces. He hears the buzzing of a crowd in his ears at strange times. When he undertakes the deconsecration of reality by means of the savage desires and monstrous lusts of his dreams, he believes himself to be acting with free will: "He bore cynically with the shameful details of his secret riots in which he exulted to defile with patience whatever image had attracted his eyes". His response to the dirtiness of the real world is a taking of pleasure in foulness; he wallows in lechery that leaves no respite. What he had voluntarily begun escapes from his control before he realises it, and he leads himself on with hopes of the encounter of which he dreamed—yet he is now separated from it by a horrible reality. Reality is already a totally subjective concept; he is a prey to "some dark presence moving irresistibly upon him from the darkness, a presence subtle and murmurous as a flood filling him wholly with itself". The shifting, murmurous tide of the outside world (against which he had wanted to raise a dam of elegance and order) has become his very thought, and its uncontrollable proliferations surround and penetrate his inner world. This demonic infiltration is directly opposed to the blessed visitation of his soul by the angel of beauty. He is still beyond all clarity of conscience—he is always the product of the Church and of its system of threats and rewards. The Church has such a hold over him that it imposes its own vision upon Stephen while he is in a state of mortal sin. The hell described by Father Arnall (borrowed, as we have already seen, from the Italian Jesuits) is received into Stephen's soul, and he is carried back to his childhood by seeing "the figure of his old master, so strangely re-arisen" from the past; he remembers the ditch he fell in, the little cemetery where he had dreamed of being buried, the firelight on the walls of the infirmary, and the now-disappeared innocent boy also rises again, to be set by Father Arnall in his right place in the majestic order of Time as controlled by God. The events between the successive sermons and their various effects on Stephen are expressed by subtle modifications of the forms of language. "During these few days I intend to put before you some thoughts concerning the four last things. They are, as you know from your catechism, death, judgement, hell, and heaven," says the preacher in giving the programme of the retreat, accompanying it by many invocations of

God, the saints, and the angels on behalf of all the sinners present.

For Stephen this signals terror. A thick fog darkens his mind. Outside reality is dull, dark, and motionless—as though everything were already dead. "And that was life," thinks Stephen, meaning the life of a beast, of an inert body and materially-oriented soul, congealing in thick grease. He who had until this very day been capable of sustaining a living relationship with words finds himself lost, and even incapable of coherence. "The letters of the name of Dublin lay heavily upon his mind," for all is in decomposition.

The following day brings him death and judgement, and he is powerless; he no longer hears Father Arnall's words, but another voice, his own voice, whispers death and despair into his soul, repeating the sermon to him and imagining the death of the body. "Into the grave with it! Nail it down into a wooden box, the corpse". This is himself, horrified with fear for his own safety. Suddenly his imagination outstrips the preacher's harsh tones, and in a frenzy of self-hatred continues, "Thrust it out of men's sight into a long hole in the ground . . . to rot, to feed the mass of its creeping worms and to be devoured by scuttling plump-bellied rats" (*Portrait*, p. 112). Then Stephen lets the supreme judge speak directly as he drives the unjust, the hypocrites, the accursed, far from him.

The preacher recalls to him that "death is the end of us all," and that "death and judgement . . . are the dark portals that close our earthly existence, the portals that open into the unknown and the unseen, portals through which every soul must pass, unaided save by its good works". It seems to Stephen as though these portals of darkness leading to the unknown are opening for him. "Now it was God's turn". All the great apparatus and the great solemn cry of the judge impress Stephen, and he is as captivated by the sonority of the phrase as by the epic evocation of Apocalypse. His soul responds to "the arch-angelical trumpet" that blows "the brazen death of time". The wind of the last day blows and scatters the jewel-eyed harlots, who flee before the hurricane, shrieking like mice; this is not in the sermon, but it is the second response of Stephen's audio-visual imagination, of that perpetual overflowing of creative force which is—did he but realise it—the very sign of how impossible it is for him to surrender his mind or soul to others.

These sermons, filling his soul with shame and terror, inspire an extraordinary series of imaginary visions: he is soon to discover that sin and fear are better spiritual stimulants for the poet's imagination than virtue and piety are. One need only compare Stephen repentant to Stephen terrified to realise that for him hell is the monotony of good conscience. The world of dreams and of created life pours all its strangeness into his humbled mind, and produces a weird vision, inspired perhaps by de Quincey's dreams of Easter redemption. Stephen sees himself standing in a wide landscape where sea and sky gently mingle, where God does not exist because he is too severe and cannot pardon even the error of two children, Stephen and Emma; but She, the Virgin, who is not offended unites the guilty children. It may be God's turn now, but Stephen is manifestly trying to rid himself of the shackles of this excessively great presence. He is already attempting to draw near the delicate sensual pleasures that emanate from the musical, shining beauty of the Virgin. This vision is succeeded by another in which a flood covers all the trees, houses, monuments, and mountains, rising as Stephen likes to imagine it, but with a touch of the baroque about it in order to deprive God of his conventional, ordinary flood. "All life would be choked off, noiselessly: birds, men, elephants, pigs, children".

It is, of course, possible not to stop at this one detail in the mass of hallucinations recorded; but it seems to be a sign from Joyce, in this rapid foolish enumeration, that already the sinner is beginning to fall back towards the pleasure of such baroque sights and images, before he has even achieved redemption. Finally, Father Arnall devotes several minutes to the description of the abode of the damned, with the slow precision of a mathematics lesson in over seven long, rhythmical paragraphs. This hell is a model of organisation for physical and mental torture, a model of order and elegance in sadism, and thus could not fail to captivate Stephen's still rebellious mind. He is almost subjugated by the musical harmony, the dark glow, the balance between the parts and the whole which make that world an evil masterpiece. But, well proportioned as it is, and beautiful as a temple, this hell introduces Stephen to another with the sinister grace of a ballet. The one is a monument and the other a kind of pantomime, early predecessor of the hallucinations in the house of Circe; maddened, the inner speech acts out God's judgement for itself—for a moment—and the contrast between majesty and illusion makes the parody:

> God had called him. Yes? What? Yes? His flesh shrank together as it felt the approach of the ravenous tongues of flames, dried up as it felt about it the swirl of stifling air. He had died. Yes. He was judged. A wave of fire swept through his body: the first. Again a wave. His brain began to glow. Another. His brain was simmering and bubbling within the cracking tenement of his skull. Flames burst forth from his skull like a corolla, shrieking like voices: Hell! Hell! Hell! Hell! Hell! Hell! (*Portrait,* p. 125)

For Stephen, the return to banality is made very seriously: "He had not died". There is still time.

As time goes on, the irony grows heavier; this time the sermon deals with the extension, duration, and eternity of the torments of the damned. And now it is all over, and one has only to confess.

Stephen remains alone with his soul, or rather, alone with his chorus of demons; they enjoy the situation intensely, waiting, spying, amusing themselves by wondering what he will do about his confession. Stephen's hell is not far away; in fact it is his room, where he has committed so many imaginary sins. And all his sins are there, describing the most terrifying and sardonic spirals. Joyce used to say that Art has the gift of tongues, and it is true that everything in *Portrait*, as in *Ulysses*, speaks its own particular language; the language of Stephen's sins reels out its phrases as though trying to stifle him in their long coils. "We knew perfectly well of course that though it was bound to come to the light he would find considerable difficulty in endeavouring to try to induce himself to try to endeavour to ascertain the spiritual plenipotentiary and so we knew of course perfectly well . . ." This is the voice of pride —which fear has not succeeded in reducing to silence. Stephen indeed denies his sins, but cannot avoid hearing their language, which is a travesty of his own.

> He can escape from sadism, but is unable to break loose from masochism; the soul, however free, is marked by the monstrous rhetoric of punishment. Agreed, the hell described is far too realistic not to exist, but Stephen is already transposing it into the personal key. Alone with his soul, like Virgil with Dante, he treads the steps that lead towards the tribunal of his room, "the dark shell of the cave": "He went up to his room after dinner in order to be alone with his soul, and at every step his soul seemed to sigh; at every step his soul mounted with his feet, sighing in the ascent, through a region of viscid gloom" (*Portrait*, p. 136).

For the artist believing in the evocative power of words, the sermons were more than a skilful piece of oratory designed to bring the sinner to his knees. They had an effect on the world outside and on the cave within, touching Stephen on the raw in his imagination, in his spoken language, and in the relationship between his reason and his words. They have affected his actual vision of the world. It is the artist in him that has been put to the torture, for he has been thrown into the appalling circle of Disfigurement, where the world grimaces and the tongue turns against itself, coiling serpent-like about words; yet the thought that is bitten and writhes from the viper's poison is still alive and has not been alienated. In apparent delirium it is ironically triumphant, for we first think that the word really has been punished: as J.-J. Mayoux says, (*op. cit.*, p. 75) "the accused, guilty, condemned and terrified voice of Beckett's Lucky is heard here for the first stammering time".

But, beyond the fever of language, his thought fights against delirium, for his entire life and work are at stake. The viper poisons all his sense-connections with reality, punishing the flesh by inflicting delirium of the senses. Stephen loses contact with the perceptible world, no longer looking at that which is not himself from the heights of his former pride; his sin has smeared a film of dirt over his eyes and lips, and he sees everything through his own disgust. The first separation had been intellectual. At this crisis of spiritual terror, he feels that he is being attacked in his imagination, and out of respect for words he at first yields to the power that uses them. But the world that appears to him is a world of hallucination:

> He feared intensely in spirit and in flesh but, raising his head bravely, he strode into the room firmly. A doorway, a room, the same room, same window. He told himself calmly that those words had absolutely no sense which had seemed to rise murmurously from the dark. He told himself that it was simply his room with the door open. (*Portrait*, p. 136)

The world as seen by a guilty conscience is unrecognisable. Stephen has lost reality—irrecoverably it seems. His ideas of identity are confused and changed, his memory and reason paralysed, and his own room with the door open seems to him the yawning mouth of hell. Yet, paradoxically, the violence which has been done to the young man's imagination is the final step in its liberation, for the artist who has passed through the delirium and confusion can find beyond them another limitless reality. Until now the world had been like a path bordered by two hedges, but after the descent into hell, the boundaries disappear. Now there is no limit between reality and dream, between the law and the forbidden, between the language that is subject to the conventional grammar of communication and the free word.

The long, winding phrases are not meaningless, as Stephen tells himself that they are, but on the contrary form his first free sentence, his first sentence to take no account of tradition. Its meaning exists not only at the level of the words, but also in its movement and rhythm; it projects and develops its meaning in a new allusive dimension beyond what is actually said—a fresh and as yet untouched field of significance. The demons who wish to break up his thought and cloud his senses are in fact not those whom he has believed them to be. He is in the process of discovering that the world is not solely what it appears to be—that its meaning cannot be expressed logically—and this discovery costs him considerable mental anguish. Nietzsche used to say that "I fear that we cannot rid ourselves of the notion of God, because we still believe in grammar"; it is this belief in grammar that is slowly dying in these convulsions of language and of Stephen's mind. The sentence he has heard terrifies him, because it is so different, such a departure, from the act of contrition which he remembers from the recent service in chapel. It has imprinted itself on his memory like a geometric line, its sincere repetition banishing all doubt:

      —O my God!—
      —O my God!—
      —I am heartily sorry—
      —I am heartily sorry—
      —for having offended Thee—
      —for having offended Thee—
      —and I detest my sins—
      —and I detest my sins—
      —above every other evil—
      —above every other evil—
      —because they displease Thee, my God—
      —because they displease Thee, my God—
      —Who art so deserving—
      —Who art so deserving—
      —of all my love—
      —of all my love—
      —and I firmly purpose—
      —and I firmly purpose—
      —by Thy holy grace—
      —by Thy holy grace—
      —never more to offend Thee—
      —never more to offend Thee—
      —and to amend my life—
      —and to amend my life—

This beautiful regular construction of prayer that echoes itself is contrasted with the insinuating, horizontally proceeding thought that is still in search of its own way; here is born the language that secretes and bears in it its own meaning, which is to print that meaning upon reality. Language as reality recreates the world from its echo; it questions itself and it answers. It *is* the same window, but it is also the other room and the other window, opening out on to the infinite spaces of creation.

The Illusion of Beginning a New Life

Instead of the eloquent and exact hell of the spiritual exercises, Stephen has his own particular hell in which to wander. The encounter with the demons was a hard one: never had Stephen been so disarmed and helpless, never had Joyce delivered his hero up to the forces of Ireland so completely, nor refined himself as author so thoroughly out of existence. Stephen finds himself in a dark wood, and like Dante he passes through an agony of fear and encounters various wild beasts.

The damnation which Stephen lives through in his nightmares is like a first draught of History. The young man is given no help, not even the indirect aid of irony; the terror, fear, and contrition are sincere, and it seems as though Stephen will eventually be broken. For the first time he addresses the Virgin not as a delightfully disturbing figure of womanhood but as a beloved mother, as She who intercedes for him, and his own voice exhorts him to "Confess! Admit! Kneel!" Father Dolan is replaced by the feeling of shame, and Stephen vomits in the washstand that used to go "suck". To submit, confessing his sins and accepting the responsibility and the punishment, seems the only remedy; it must wait no longer. He decides to repent.

During the armistice which follows his submission to fear, the young man begins to reflect on the same question that preoccupies Adam in Book X of *Paradise Lost*, namely, how is it that a sin can be so swiftly committed, yet forgiveness be so difficult to obtain? And why should man have to pay the price of death for his humanity?

Why should there be such a difference between the eternity of Hell and the brevity of the sin? "Even once was a mortal sin. It could happen in an instant. But how so quickly? By seeing or by thinking of seeing. The eyes see the thing, without having wished first to see. Then in an instant it happens" (*Portrait*, p. 139). In his new innocence, the repentant Stephen asks these dangerous questions, which while they threaten his purified soul are also already orienting him towards his second conversion of becoming a priest of the imagination. In his analysis of the fatal process, in fact, he is already discussing the origin of sin in terms of an epiphany: man looks, and suddenly beauty is manifested. This in

embryo is his aesthetic theory, although still in the imperfect stage of
being bound up with the emotions.

Reflecting on the nature of desire, Stephen regains his soul and wins
it for the cause of art, but his body is still definitely subject to doubt, to
the source of uncontrollable impulses. The artist is to set up his art at
a distance from his own body, in the world of images, and far from the
ideas of "good and evil which excite desire and loathing" (*Portrait*, p.
207). The serpent must be slain, for

> It must understand when it desires in one instant and then prolongs its
> own desire instant after instant, sinfully. It feels and understands and
> desires. What a horrible thing! Who made it to be like that, a bestial part
> of the body able to understand bestially and desire bestially? . . . His soul
> sickened at the thought of a torpid snaky life feeding itself out of the tender
> marrow of his life and fattening upon the slime of lust. (*Portrait*, p. 140)

Stephen goes to confess his sins; the journey through Dublin is another test for his fallen pride, for the streets are ill-lit, the surroundings
sordid, the people he sees wretched and poor, and an old woman points
out the way to the chapel for him with a shaking, withered hand. In the
church, the candles on the high altar have been extinguished. The
priest, faceless in his Dublin-brown Capuchin cowl, enters his den and
lurks there hidden. Stephen goes to confess, hiding himself behind the
armrest. He repents. He is so ashamed he wants to run away, but God
is about to pardon him. He is sincere in making his confession, in feeling
ashamed, and in longing for forgiveness. He even goes so far as to
imagine that the ugliness of Dublin hides a spiritual splendour which
is visible to God, if not to the artist. But Joyce still inserts his usual
warning signs—not because Stephen is a hypocrite, but because Joyce
is indirectly pointing out that this genuine repentance is only an admission of guilt obtained under pressure by means of the sermons. His
awareness of the setting as a whole and of the detail of the sordid
surroundings, the misery, the harsh voices, the smells of fish, beer, and
damp sawdust all affect him. All his senses humiliate him, but he accepts
this as part of the punishment. All the agitation in his spirit is caused
not by genuine repentance but rather by those feelings of shame which
are in fact the mask for his selfish pride; he would rather have committed any crime whatsoever than "say it in words". Yet again, images,
language, and his own pride draw the young man towards the una-
shamed freedom of art.

This time God wins, although only conditionally. Stephen repents, "because God was merciful to poor sinners who were truly sorry," and he insists, reverting to his childish guiltiness, in order that God will look at him, "It was true . . . God could see that he was sorry. He would tell all his sins". He settles his accounts with God, entering into a relationship of passionate exchange with him. Almost amazed at having succeeded in making his confession, he feels happy, pure, and holy; his soul is so light that he feels "it would be beautiful to die" at that moment. "It was beautiful to live in grace a life of peace and virtue," too. It would be perhaps too beautiful, and only a dream: "In a dream he fell asleep. In a dream he rose and saw that it was morning. In a waking dream he went through the quiet morning towards the college" (*Portrait*, p. 146). The morning confirms that it was not just a dream; the great victory is that the past is finally past, that one is ready to begin a new life.

> He knelt there sinless and timid; and he would hold upon his tongue the host and God would enter his purified body.
> —*In vitam aeternam. Amen.*
> Another life! A life of grace and virtue and happiness! It was true. It was not a dream from which he would wake. The past was past.
> —*Corpus Domini nostri.*
> The ciborium had come to him. (*Portrait*, pp. 146–7)

Henceforth, he need only organise his everyday life with that sense for order which characterises all the ritual forms, all the dogmata and beliefs of the Church. His days become models of organisation, worthy of the infernal hierarchy itself.

"He drove his soul daily through an increasing circle of works of supererogation" (*Portrait*, p. 148). At the beginning of Chapter IV, Stephen, as he enters this circle after having been saved, becomes a missionary, and, in imitation of Saint Ignatius whose arm used to grow weary from the number of baptisms he performed, Stephen heaps up prayers and penances on behalf of the souls in purgatory. His fervent activity, organised in a rigorously ritualistic pattern, is yet strangely temporal in its attachments. He prays at unusual times of day, as though he could rival eternity: "Every part of his day, divided by what he regarded now as the duties of his station in life, circled about its own centre of spiritual energy. His life seemed to have drawn near to eternity". (*Ibid.*) His belief is naïve and ironically honest, for in fact he is fighting the blackmail that had threatened him with hell by promulgating the blackmail of redemption. He feels, however, vaguely defrauded already. The preacher says that if you do wrong, you are judged in an instant, yet even if Stephen strives night and day towards sanctity, there is no guarantee that he will ever have any right to enter Paradise. He feels that God's justice is very skilfully arranged, and appeals to it as hidden threat rather than as possible reward. His persevering holiness, in that case, has no more meaning. Already, symptoms of rational thought can be observed in his faith:

> He believed . . . all the more, and with trepidation, because of the divine gloom and silence wherein dwelt the unseen Paraclete, Whose symbols were a dove and a mighty wind, to sin against Whom was a sin beyond forgiveness, the eternal mysterious secret Being to Whom, as God, the priests offered up mass once a year, robed in the scarlet of the tongues of fire. (*Portrait*, p. 149)

The Holy Ghost is invisible, and Stephen has always sought the invisible, though in the hope of seeing it become manifest one day. Here can be seen again one of the themes of heresy: God remains too distant and unapproachable. Time becomes disagreeably apt again, through inclining dangerously towards the past. The circular repetition of ritual, the eternal beginning again, the renewal of humiliation—all this seems a projection of hell's order into this world, which one is nevertheless always purifying in turn by one's devotions. The past may be past and absolved now, but unfortunately one still has to reckon with the present which is not yet past. Stephen begins a reckless course of prayer against sin, which leaves him breathless and teaches him that sin is indestructible and that life automatically and ceaselessly revives guilt. In order to have one's accounts clear with God, one would have to be constantly confessing; the past is always present.

> Often when he had confessed his doubts and scruples—some momentary inattention at prayer, a movement of trivial anger in his soul, or a subtle wilfulness in speech or act—he was bidden by his confessor to name some sin of his past life before absolution was given him. He named it with humility and shame and repented of it once more. (*Portrait*, p. 153)

By repetition, humility turns into humiliation, and the dream turns into an endless nightmare. Even the rhythm of indirect speech recalls the inflexions of the demonic sentences that haunted him during his religious crisis:

It humiliated and shamed him to think that he would never be freed from it wholly, however holily he might live or whatever virtues or perfections he might attain. A restless feeling of guilt would always be present with him: he would confess and repent and be absolved, confess and repent again and be absolved again, fruitlessly. *(Ibid.)*

The Satanic spirit regains its superior position quite openly now. Just as the time of sensual joys had been ephemeral, so the time of sanctity comes to an abrupt end. Within the person of the sanctified Stephen there begins to act his other self, he who is delighted by candid, passionate speech, who is more attracted by language than by the Word of the Lord; his artistic self, banished during the religious crisis, now returns. This self had loved Our Lady, for the pleasure of being able to recite *"Quasi cedrus exaltata sum in Libanon,"* because the musical qualities of it soothed his conscience; this self had become intoxicated by *images*, and had been mistaken about the nature of its own motives; this self had admitted that "the glories of Mary held his soul captive" (*Portrait*, p. 104), without explaining that it was their form, rather than their object the Blessed Virgin, that actually fascinated him. And how could the poet accustom himself to a long monotony emptied of these and other invocations? Stephen is still unaware of the needs of his artistic self, but even at the height of his zeal his sensibilities give him warning.

The rosaries, too, which he said constantly—for he carried his beads loose in his trousers' pockets that he might tell them as he walked the streets—transformed themselves into coronals of flowers of such vague unearthly texture that they seemed to him as hueless and odourless as they were nameless. (*Portrait*, p. 148)

The ecstasy of his new life lasts as short a time as did the life of Willie, who went before in an earlier attempt to find the way out of the labyrinth of desires. It seems that Stephen cannot find peace in an existence which is half of life and half of death; the first *vita nuova*, following the first voyage to another world, had informed his body, but at the price of his soul. The second offers him his soul in exchange for his body. But his soul remembers profane joys, and tries by a kind of cheating to return to the complete life, for "the imagery of the canticles was interwoven with the communicant's prayers". Again, voices murmur within him, and for the third time he is called, for the third time he cries out in protest.

Hardly has he begun to have doubts about the radical amendment of his life, hardly has the devil begun to besiege his inner citadel, when, in the second section of Chapter IV (the chapter of eventually revealed vocation), he sees the Jesuits come and offer him their occult power, saying, "Have you ever felt that you had a vocation?" The question is ambiguous because the director is a Jesuit, and because in his own way Stephen is very much a Jesuit too; the reply would only echo the ambiguity if the priest had not added, "I mean, have you ever felt within yourself, in your soul, a desire to join the order?"

Images, gestures, and dialogue make three different kinds of sign to Stephen: what is said, what is done, and what Stephen himself sees by disfigurement of the present or by recollection of the past. These three modes form the structure of the scene of three concentric psychological circles, which encircle the chosen but timid victim, the reticent Stephen. The first speech is adressed directly to him, in order to seduce him; it deals with clothes, with advantages, and supernatural power and with being chosen by God. The technique of persuasion by words is perfect, the tone of delivery grave but cordial. The voice hides the real intention while it lays the ground work. It stops, then resumes, its tranquil progress in a cordial and grave manner.

It digresses in order to lull and hypnotise. It speaks in a "low discreet accent"—and moves to the attack. While the Jesuit is calculating his next move, Joyce surprises him; since Joyce paid a great deal of attention to the silent speech of the voice, naturally the sound of the words struck him as revealing more than the actual meaning of the phrases did, and this caused him to insist upon the "speech within, or below, what is said". (The spoken word is often no more than the echo of an outside situation.) The tone rises, "a strong note of pride reinforcing the gravity of the priest's voice," the address becomes more lyrical and exclamatory; the priest's voice is now echoed by the voice of Satan, promising that to enter the order means to possess "secret knowledge and secret power". The director is a magus, protected by divine decree; one remembers the theme of simony, the key theme of the first novellas in *Dubliners.* The priest makes his appeal, and Stephen hears him, but *cannot see* anything, darkness being most convenient for secrets. He cannot read the expression on the director's face, for the latter is standing in the embrasure of the window with "his back to the light".

The second address is indirect, and here Stephen is alert for the smallest gesture the other may make, in order to decipher its exact meaning, which will explain the motives not expressed in words:

leaning an elbow on the brown crossblind, and, as he spoke and smiled, slowly dangling and looping the cord of the other blind. Stephen stood before him, following for a moment with his eyes the waning of the long summer daylight above the roofs or the slow deft movements of the priestly fingers. (*Portrait*, p. 154)

Here Joyce does not hesitate to make the symbolic intention clear; there is no digression, no reference to any previously introduced motif (except for that of the colour brown that stands for Dublin), and no distance between the given fact and its meaning. The symbol is nakedly clear, as though Joyce had not wished to bring in any sign of non-communication, and as though he had wished the meaningful brutality of the images to agree with the director's spiritual maltreatment of Stephen. The Jesuit's ambition shows manifestly through the gentleness of his words; the skeleton beneath the soutane is visible, and the will for power can no longer be hidden under a show of piety.

The scene is now set for the passion of Stephen, even the cross is there. The light is outside, and the hangman's knot awaits him indoors. First, the victim must be "fascinated," hypnotised into agreement, as "The priest let the blindcord fall to one side and, uniting his hands, leaned his chin gravely upon them, communing with himself" (*Portrait*, p. 157). His body is invisible. Where he stands, the only communication possible is communion with one's own pride, in ghostly image.

He held open the heavy hall door and gave his hand as if already to a companion in the spiritual life. . . . Smiling at the trivial air [Stephen], raised his eyes to the priest's face and, seeing in it a mirthless reflection of the sunken day, detached his hand slowly which had acquiesced faintly in the companionship. (*Portrait*, p. 160)

The dark charm is broken by the passage of four real "companions," four young men walking arm-in-arm. Their trivial music lays no claim to the power of invocations since their officiating priest is only the chief of a gang of young men, but he leads his flock along briskly to the strains of an accordeon.

The third speech is Stephen's long, difficult, and guarded monologue to himself. He pursues his thoughts intensely, while his mouth utters only laconic or insignificant replies and his face tries only to reflect the "complacent smile" of the priest which he cannot actually see.

Standing face to face "in the shadow," a ghost and his reflection exchange, in low voices, monstrous phrases inspired by pride: in Ireland, all souls are in the hands of phantoms of the Holy Ghost. One has "the power to bind and to loose," the power of life and death over every being, the right to imprison lives, to curse souls, to turn God himself into a piece of bread! Even God can be contained in the ciborium, reduced to manageable, edible proportions. Stephen says nothing, Joyce makes no comment, but when Stephen chooses to be "a priest of the eternal imagination," he does so in order to reestablish the purity of the artist and of his calling. He takes, that is, the ordinary bread of everyday experience and transforms it into the radiant body of life, not of "eternal, everlasting life," but of "everliving" life; he who absorbs the divinity into himself is still only mortal, while he who takes part in the creation of beauty does not *eat* life, because for him it is not dead.

Two spectres present themselves to the eye of Stephen's imagination in the form of imaginary doubles of himself as a priest. A man is transformed by his ordination:

> He had seen himself, a young and silent-mannered priest, entering a confessional swiftly, ascending the altarsteps, incensing, genuflecting, accomplishing the vague acts of the priesthood which pleased him by reason of their semblance of reality and of their distance from it. (*Portrait*, p. 158)

He is attracted by the *simulation,* by the imitation of reality; yet his respect for reality is so great that he prefers not to have any magic power to transform it. He does not wish to change reality but rather to transubstantiate his vision of reality—to bring it from the world of the imagination into literary creation. The work is not reality, but springs from the union of reality with the poetic imagination: "He shrank from the dignity of celebrant because it displeased him to imagine that all the vague pomp should end in his own person or that the ritual should assign to him so clear and final an office".

The priestly power would destroy the mystery, which is the object of Stephen's love. Its very unreality tempts him for a moment towards this vague existence of which he has dreamed. Its lack of contact with the real is fascinating: behind the golden dalmatic, behind the amice, behind the mask and the borrowed words, behind the curtain of the confessional, behind life, lies death garbed in the "spiritual life," "grave, and ordered and passionless" as the "mirthless mask reflecting a sunken day from the threshold of the college". The priest cannot juggle with the mysteries of life, but rather life touches even the masks to some degree. At night—in the solitude where no living being throws any light on the dead face—the spectre is nothing but an old and powerless garment.

> The Reverend Stephen Dedalus, S.J.
> His name in that new life leaped into characters before his eyes and to it there followed a mental sensation of an undefined face or colour of a face. The colour faded and became strong like a changing glow of pallid brick red. . . . The face was eyeless and sour-favoured and devout, shot with pink tinges of suffocated anger. Was it not a mental spectre of the face of one of the Jesuits whom some of the boys called Lantern Jaws and others Foxy Campbell? (*Portrait*, p. 161)

The portrait of the artist as a Jesuit is very revealing: a shapeless, eyeless face, animated only by by either pride or anger. Stephen knows that the foxy one is afraid, that he who puts on an act needs his audience to be deceived, because he only lives when he is acting before them and being seen. Anger is simply a cover for distress: if the Jesuit is *not* terrifying, if the community do not kneel, then the priest is reduced to the status of his garments; he may still be a consecrated priest and a priest forever, but it is in the sight of men rather than in the sight of God that the priest wants to be seen and recognised.

The mirthless mask reflecting a sunken day from the threshold of the college lingers in Stephen's troubled mind, but it is a powerless image, not only now in the present, but also in the recent past which had at the time exercised such magic power over him—it has become retrospectively impotent. Stephen crosses the bridge over the stream of the Tolka, with the director's voice echoing vainly in his memory; "the exhortation he had listened to," instead of producing some magical effect, "had already fallen into an idle formal tale". The words of it have no power: "the wisdom of the priest's appeal did not touch him to the quick," for the voice of death can hardly be expected to have any strong effect on his living soul—"his soul was not there to hear and greet it" (*Portrait*, p. 162).

The image of the Virgin is dead too, in her shrine "perched fowlwise on a pole". *(Ibid.)* The cedar of Lebanon, the spikenard, cinnamon, and incense are gone. In the alley where the Dedalus family lives the predominant scent is "the faint sour stink of rotted cabbages," the poor man's vegetable, the food of humiliation. Its stump once served to beat the boy Stephen, and its smell is like that of rotting flesh; yet for all that Stephen can still smile "to think that it was this disorder, the misrule and confusion of his father's house and the stagnation of vegetable life, which was to win the day in his soul". *(Ibid.)* Vegetable life and starvation, famine rations, almost death, are his choice, for it is at least death in the context of a *real* disorder—a death not very far removed from a possible life. To illustrate this, we have the solitary farm hand, who makes Stephen laugh to recall his method of working, "considering in turn the four points of the sky and then regretfully plunging his spade in the earth". Agreed, that man is wretched and alone, and has to work hard on thankless earth, but at least he can dream of horizons.

Stephen's brothers and sisters, assembled in the kitchen for the last time before yet another forced change of address, have certainly not had enough to eat, but the soft light of evening shows "in their faces no sign of rancour" and no trace of the redness of pride. Stephen sits down with them, rather than in the refectory of the house of the dead. Tomorrow they will have to move house again, for the family home has no stable resting place, but they can still sing together, and it is like "the voice of Nature herself". With deep distress, sadly and remorsefully, Stephen joins in the song; they have not asked him to make his communion, but the artist responds to the appeal of life, however wretched it may be.

As their voices echo with the overtones of weariness ("even before they set out on life's journey they seemed weary already of the way"), Stephen brings out from the treasures of his memory a sentence from Newman, transforming the note of weariness into musical rhythm. On the day following his choice of poverty, of chance, and of the brightness of reality, he takes the last step away from his "guardians," from those who had wished him to be "subject to them and serve their ends". Another glorious future seems to offer itself, "the university!" His refusal to serve anything other than "the end he had been born to serve" helps to separate him definitively from his past; the break with his father had become complete when the latter had betrayed his son by becoming an accomplice of the rector at Clongowes; and his mother is also growing more distant from him because of her hostility to the university. The break occurs silently, and Stephen is now no longer bound to anyone or anything. The voice of Cardinal Newman echoes at the end of this scene of temptation, speaking to Stephen not as convert but as writer (cf. the end of chapter I of *Portrait*).

Three Antidotes to the Claims of an Ordered Existence

The first three chapters of *Portrait* show Stephen faced by temptations and resisting them, first with the instinctive resistance born of panic, and later in an increasingly lucid and organised fashion. At the end of the book Stephen explains to Cranly that as the soul awakes it is surrounded by nets and fetters, and that the awakening, if it ever takes place, only begins to happen in the second age, that is, in adolescence. There has been a long period first when Ireland was still trying to seduce the boy into staying with her. He receives violent treatment only in the rare cases when he is not already obediently bound and gagged.

The first manoeuvres are insidious, as though the powers of the enemy were disguising and decorating themselves in order to captivate their prey with the lace and black stockings of young girls, the gold and ivory of the Virgin, the intoxicating scent of incense, dance, caress, and spectacle. Dublin is hidden in cloud and haze, "like a scene on some vague arras" (*Portrait*, p. 167). All forces are brought into action to subdue this young man, whose sensual imagination has since childhood delighted in "certain soft and delicate stuffs used in their making" (i.e., of women's clothes), which "brought always to his mind a delicate and sinful perfume" (*Portrait*, p. 155). He is attracted, as with open arms and beating heart he seeks to grasp transient beauty. Only one thing restrains him: the fact that very early in his life he had cast a glance behind the veil, which for him removed the element of mystery. He knows that glittering beauty conceals a trap.

Simultaneously, there come three appeals urging him to live in Ireland; all three make themselves heard in the same place, in the school which has been transformed into a theatre for the occasion, as Stephen is preparing to play the part of the ridiculous schoolmaster. Inquisitively, he observes a young Jesuit, who is the sort of man he might one day be, on a visit to the college, with his small curly head, freshly shaven face, spotless soutane and spotless shoes—the perfect example of the order, of the men who know how to live well. Order, cleanliness, elegance, all the pleasures of the kind of life which Stephen tried and failed to construct for his family are still within his reach. Yet it seems to him that the young priest's mocking smile means something other than devotion. "He tried to read for himself the legend of the priest's mocking smile" (*Portrait*, p. 84), but this is a book which, however fascinating its pages may be, he has read before. His memory takes him back to the days before he entered Clongowes. His father had said "that you could always tell a jesuit by the style of his clothes". The present superimposes its own images, and the young man feels that there is in fact some resemblance between his father and the elegant smiling priest.

The sacristy and the ministry of the Church are both being profaned, so much so that the holy place also comes to resemble the noisy, dirty home of the Dedalus family, from which he is trying to escape. The air becomes impregnated with the harsh smells of gas and grease. Scarcely have the noise and ugliness of church and home become thus identified, when the third appeal comes to him; in the silence of his imagination, across the crowded audience, he perceives "her eyes," and momentarily responds to their call.

If he is not to be seduced by the promise of order, he is still somewhat susceptible to the power of love. But this power is limited to an ephemeral breath of romantic sensuality, inspired by books, and leaving him with

> nothing . . . save that which seemed to him an echo or a prophecy of his own state. It was only amid soft-worded phrases or within rose-soft stuffs that he dared conceive of the soul or body of a woman moving with tender life. (*Portrait*, p. 155)

This courtly terminology is effectively devalued as soon as he actually touches "the brittle texture of a woman's stocking". The delicate words have nothing to say for prostitutes, and are never heard by the beloved except in the fulfilling of certain ritual formalities and in defining the speaker's place in society. "For one rare moment"—when in fancy dress for the college play—he participates as an actor in the artificial situation which he normally avoids; he goes into its "dim scenery," and notices with surprise that the play has "suddenly assumed a life of its own". Perhaps Dublin too is only a play which passes from apparent lifelessness to life and meaning if one accepts to act in it? But the question dies unanswered when the curtain falls, when it is clear that it was only make-believe: "on the lines which he had fancied the moorings of an ark a few lanterns swung in the night breeze, flickering cheerlessly". And Stephen rushes out, like the little boy in *Dubliners* who dreamed of bearing his chalice safely through the midst of his enemies, past his waiting family, past the Jesuits, and "begins to walk at breakneck speed down the hill" (*Portrait*, p. 86). Obscurely, but profoundly, he feels that he has been given a warning and he struggles against temptation, forging three weapons for himself, the most immediate being that of *flight*, of physical escape. When "She," Reality disguised, approaches him he looks, is fascinated, is about to hold out his hand to her, but at the last moment on impulse he takes flight instead; putting his hands in his pockets, he turns his back, or he simply takes to his heels.

The second weapon is that of *counterpoison*—of choosing some drug which will attenuate or eliminate the hallucinatory effects of the scented incense—and it is chemically composed of different odours, each with its peculiar effect. Together, they influence the memory, dissipating the dangerous vapours. The third weapon is much the strongest and most "natural," consisting of an *automatic self-defence mechanism*, of which Stephen himself is not consciously in control, but which is automatically activated in case of danger, particularly at the approach of the sirens. The first reaction is intended to disenchant the eyes, the second to bring about a catharsis of all the senses, and the third is the defence mechanism of the soul itself, which Stephen calls simply "power": He is ignorant of its nature but familiar with its manifestations: "A power, akin to that which had often made anger or resentment fall from him, brought his steps to rest" (*Portrait*, p. 86). If one observes this power at work, however, it will soon become clear that it is simply the first form taken by the artist's own special "power".

The youthful Stephen is attracted by two beings, one of whom is visible and real and the other of whom is as yet unknown and awaited. The attraction is both provoked by another person and improved upon by the dreams that Stephen's romantic reading inspires. The longing for this "someone" makes him "wander up and down day after day as if he really sought someone that eluded him" (*Portrait*, p. 67), although he has no idea who it might be. The charming glances of "She," who both as little girl and as young woman is indeed real (although she is unique and unreal in being "She," the essence and ideal of womanhood), bring him firmly back to the city, with its groups and cliques. "She" wants to make him dance to her tune and wishes to make him take part in the games at the children's party, where the others are romping noisily and cheerfully in their fancy dress. She tries—"flattering, taunting, searching, exciting his heart"—to draw him out from his isolation. The crucial test takes place in a symbolic and typical setting and in a very tense atmosphere; the incident itself, or something very like it, has happened before, and is to occur several times more before the artist definitively makes his escape; the tone of the whole scene and the way that it weighs on the young man's conscience are expressed in a paragraph which, beginning in realism, creates a strange world of unreality.

"It was the last tram. The lank brown horses knew it and shook their bells to the clear night in admonition" (*Portrait*, p. 69). The conductor chats to the driver, the night is silent, and there is nothing extraordinary about that. But these occurrences are filtered through Stephen's troubled eyes and mind; the phrases come and go as though dictated by his wandering thoughts, first hesitant and then turning again to complete the inevitable circle. "No sound. . . . the lank brown horses . . . shook their bells." A wordless act occurs in this place, where silence is only broken by the sound of warning bells, the first form of that silence which the artist has chosen as his refuge, and instead of words there is the language of gesture and movement accompanying the dance of seduction: "she came up to his step . . . and went down to hers again," making Stephen's heart dance "upon her movements like a cork upon a tide".

The comparison is deliberate. Stephen's heart is like a cork on the tides of emotion, dancing in just the same way as when he strolled along the docks in Dublin watching the ships prepare to leave. He too is destined to leave, of course, but not to be a trifling piece of rubbish floating wherever the tide carries it; when he leaves, he will be in complete control of his departure and of his journey. If someone tries to make him dance to his tune, this is enough to inspire Stephen to escape. The dance is one of the more subtle motifs accompanying the theme of music in the *Portrait:* the music is taken over by the personality or by the brain, while, on the other hand, the dance is always a movement initiated by someone else—and is all the more alienating because it cannot be performed alone but requires one or more partners. In the figurative sense, the dance is a pleasure which brings one closer to other people, but in actuality, Joyce makes it the symbol of movement forced upon one, of artificial pleasure, of the offer of a way of life which is not chosen, and this is what dancing signifies from the very beginning, from the sailors' hornpipe that baby tuckoo dances. It is opposed to the theme of escape. It is too incarnate a dream to satisfy one who yearns for exotic mysteries. Everything, even the leanness of the horses and the rails of the tram, contains a warning.

Just as the dance is contrasted with the free flight of Stephen's soul, so the predestinate inevitability of the rails is contrasted with the free departures of birds, ships, and poets. The tramlines, a mere fossilised and deadly version of the real journey, offer the traveller only a wretchedly shrunken route which permits of no deviation. With its driver, its bells, and its empty seats strewn with a few coloured tickets, it belongs to the subjugated world where sinister pawn-tickets and tram-tickets pile up like consecrated wafers in the ciborium—to the world that lets itself obediently be driven or led along. To yield, even though against his will, is something which, he feels, he must have done thousands of times before. "Yet a voice within him spoke above the noise of his dancing heart, asking him would he take her gift to which he had only to stretch out his hand". What stops him is the sudden recurrence of a childhood memory, of Eileen who ran away from him, laughing and expecting him to chase her. She wants Stephen to catch her because *she* wants to catch *him*, and as Stephen knows, that *"she"* means all those who catch or want to capture him. And so he says nothing, but simply goes away; this first act of refusal is motivated by both an instinct for self-preservation and a schizoid reaction which, on feeling it impossible to communicate, needs to invent a refusal as justification. He retires into his solitude again, and makes a rather pitiful lie into a proud truth for himself.

He confirms this by a second gesture, which appears mechancial but is not: he tears his ticket into shreds, as though to mean that he will go no further, that he will not communicate, that he will not marry. "I could easily catch hold of her," he thinks, "I could hold her and kiss her". But he does neither of these things, because he knows that he is truly unable to welcome her, to open his heart to her, and he knows that she wants him to catch hold of her. If he yielded here, he would not have made a conquest, he would simply have obeyed and done what was expected of him. His flight and escape are seen ambiguously; flight seems a resistance, but it is also a disguise for cowardice. He flees from her again after the play at Belvedere, although he found enjoyment in knowing that she was present in the dark hall. He is still fleeing from her when he is an undergraduate, still desiring her and still spying on her movements. Unlike Stephen, hero, who went boldly to the attack without mincing his words, this young man hides his feelings and represses his desires; at the most he betrays his emotions by blushing, but always remains silent before her. And when she goes away, he writes in his solitude.

Flight may not always be a sufficient safety-measure; it is also necessary to purge oneself of the intoxication that scents can cause. Stephen succeeds in this by composing an antidote from a mixture of all the unpleasant smells possible:

The first sight of the filthy cowyard at Stradbrook with its foul green puddles and clots of liquid dung and steaming bran troughs sickened Stephen's heart. The cattle which had seemed so beautiful in the country on sunny days revolted him and he could not even look at the milk they yielded. (*Portrait*, pp. 63–64)

To the mixture he adds the strange and medicinal smells of Clongowes, which he associates with sickness and death, and the smell of horses' stale and rotten straw. Dizzily balanced on the edge of the possible, forever oscillating between dream and reality, he needs from time to time to purge his imagination. The mingled smells of rotten straw, urine, carrion, and foul green mud are not merely nauseous to the mind—they are accompanied also by visions of a sort to recall the dreamer sharply to his senses. In feverish moments when Stephen feels that his imagination is about to take off and sail away in its ark, or to leap out into space, maddened by pride, hope, and desire that "send up vapours of maddening incense before the eyes of his mind," he can always drive the madness away quickly by means of reality in this form. The stench completes the process which flight had begun, and in this sense it is good. "It is a good odour to breathe" (*Portrait*, p. 87). Stephen cures himself in the dark lane where the smell is strong.

To Stephen, the reality of Dublin is like a lane that leads from the morgue into stench and darkness; life extends along it between death and decomposition. This method of curing the soul by means of the stench of Dublin could be characterised as psychosomatic.

The passage from concrete reality to imaginary creation is a constant process in the formation of the artist as such, for his soul and body seem to be composed of one and the same unique sensitive substance. Sense-perception and mental response are two nearly interchangeable forms of dialogue with reality, and what Stephen feels is expressed as the incarnate word of his soul. By association, olfactory, auditory and other sensations—following the soul's development—become equivalent to actual messages, and this explains the importance attributed to material detail, since it becomes charged with subjective spiritual meaning. Thus, for instance, certain childhood experiences of the artist have gradually assumed a value which they never had to begin with. Stephen would have liked to share the life of the milkman driving on his rounds every evening, when he still found the nomadic aspect of the job attractive, but the beauties of a milkman's life were soon spoiled for him by unpleasant, intruding reality and by the interpretation by his memory of that reality in abstract terms. The memory brings about various *rapprochements* which eventually usher the entire outside world into Stephen's consciousness; the smell that breaks the illusion is not necessarily that of the dunghill, for it gains itself an autonomous existence.

It becomes less the odour of any particular matter than the imaginary smell of a whole town, wished for, breathed, and virtually invented by one person who requires the world to smell unpleasant because it is unpleasant to him. As an abstract smell, it is present to the artist—who in fact believes that he is perceiving it *in reality*— every time that he feels threatened by the pervasive corruption of the town. This experience is the very reverse of the Proustian experience, which is produced by a present whose sensible qualities are not altered by time; the taste of a *madeleine* remains objectively the same. Joyce proceeds by analogy and not by identity, and concludes from similarity of appearance to similarity of meaning. Thus, the experience of the cowshed and its attributes is repeated under other circumstances, and grows more and more charged with the meaning of all the differences within the similarities. Disgust is the manifestation of being physically distant, while moral distance is expressed by indifference.

The "bad" smells, like sins, attract as much as they repel, and Stephen in flight seems a worthy forerunner of Leopold Bloom.

The adoption of an attitude of indifference is at first considered to be a mysterious "power" which knocks the passions out of action as soon as there is any danger that they might flare up. Nothing can last— neither hate, nor love, nor anger; for Stephen these are simply empty words, which he has heard repeated but has never been able to use himself; they are an ephemeral disguise for the soul, as the costume and powdered hair had been for the small boy playing the part of the schoolteacher, and their names belong to the vocabulary of stage, pulpit, or literature. This indifference in fact originates in former attempts of his to defend himself from the surrounding world as it advanced in decadence and degradation; because he was "angry . . . with the change of fortune which was reshaping the world about him into a vision of squalor and insincerity" (*Portrait*, p. 67), he detached himself from these things, patiently observing ugliness "and tasting its mortifying flavour in secret". From henceforth, he lets no feeling reach his heart; even the warmth he felt once during his conversion, after meditating on "the great mystery of love," and the intuition of ecstasy are forbidden, for "he had been forewarned of the dangers of spiritual exaltation" (*Portrait*, p. 150).

All feeling must lead to some involvement, and Stephen has decided to remain on the fringe of society. No provocation can hold him back, in the toils of anger or resentment, in unwanted involvement. Already, the earlier Stephen, the Hero, was refusing all forms of love, remaining totally indifferent to the accusations of everyone, maintaining "that a vaguely inactive pity from those who upheld a system of mutual servile association towards those who accepted it was only a play upon emotions as characteristic of the egoist as of the man of sentiment" (*Stephen Hero*, p. 132).

The same metaphors in *Portrait* express what had been so dogmatic originally; in fact the "detachment" is so sharp and decisive that in the usual confused fashion Stephen feels the effects of it in his own body. A very precise separation exists between the inside and the outside, emphasised in the progress of the person's growth, "as if his very body were being divested with ease of some outer skin or peel". At the time of the most violent crisis—the most relevant to his artistic pride and integrity—Stephen takes cognisance of the strangeness, the extent, of his faculty of detachment:

> While he was still repeating the *Confiteor* amid the indulgent laughter of his hearers and while the scenes of that malignant episode were still passing sharply and swiftly before his mind he wondered why he bore no malice now to those who had tormented him. He had not forgotten a whit of their cowardice and cruelty but the memory of it called forth no anger from him. All the descriptions of fierce love and hatred which he had met in books had seemed to him therefore unreal. Even that night as he stumbled homewards along Jones's Road he had felt that some power was divesting him of that sudden-woven anger as easily as a fruit is divested of its soft ripe peel. (*Portrait*, pp.82–3)

This "power" is the creative power, still in embryo; the reverse, and the indication, of the artist's power is a kind of impotence of the affections. Love, hatred, anger, have no hold over him, and only the soaring feelings of his imagination are real: the feelings of self-love, of inspiration, of the profane joy excited by an encounter with a messenger of life. The artist only achieves happiness alone or in the company of his own phantasms.

This retirement is associated in the realm of the senses with cold, with ice, and with the moon, not by an ordinary facile symbolism, but because Joyce is very careful in the preparation of his "instants of revelation". On the one hand, he plays with the idea of contrasting Stephen's psychological chills with the fires of hell, yet without giving in the *Portrait* the origin of this chilliness. It was described thus in *Stephen Hero:*

> It was, in fact, the very fervour of Stephen's former religious life which sharpened for him now the pains of his solitary position and at the same time hardened into a less pliable, a less appeasable enmity molten rages and glowing transports on which the emotions of helplessness and loneliness and despair had first acted as chilling influences. (*Stephen Hero*, pp. 152–3)

On the other hand, the sterile and lonely coldness of the young man who is cutting himself off from the world and stripping himself of every passion, yet who has not yet found his own kingdom in exchange, is to be replaced by the joyous and fruitful separateness of the artist, when he is deified as Thoth, the moon-god, for whom words can replace reality.

The antidotes to the claims of an ordered, but dead, existence constitute the artist's second weapon—that of separation or of exile by retiring into the self. Stephen has already discovered remedies; he remains a peaceful spectator. His psychic armoury of remedies and antidotes is largely dependent upon his indirect contact with reality, that is, his way of approaching reality through words and appearances, and thus of transforming it by the very mode of his approach. Stephen is preparing his departure and its appearance very carefully, because he intends it to have a precise meaning as an heroic challenge and statement of defiance; Chapter V consists of a series of mental battles in which he creates and defeats the enemy. Like Thoth in Plato's *Phaedrus*, he offers to judges he himself has chosen his inventions, intentions and ideas, and they are rejected. The rejection of Stephen appears to be the fault of other people, but in reality he has already withdrawn from them and has voluntarily played the role of scapegoat. As a man who is really and essentially an outsider, he pretends to be still "inside," in order to make his chosen course of exile appear a necessity demanded and enforced by those inside. Dublin is hell: therefore he must leave, but this is simply a transposition of the truth. It is *necessary* for Dublin to be Stephen's Hell.

Dublin as Hell

Dublin's Hell, like Dante's eighth circle, is crammed with seducers, flatterers, simoniacs, false prophets, dealers and traffickers, hypocrites, untrustworthy advisers, falsifiers and forgers; it is the home of "fraud," the term Stephen Hero applies most constantly to the world around him. Distortion, venality of values, simulation, and deceit are denounced in Chapter V.

It begins with a frugal family breakfast, minutely realistic and sordid, according to Joyce's intentions at the time of writing *Dubliners*. There are traces of misery and wretchedness everywhere, pools of pig-swill, evidences of poverty such as pawn-tickets, disorder and grumbling from his sisters. "A university student is so dirty that his mother has to wash him," yet, the evening before, he had attained to the ecstatic rose of his imaginary paradise. When examined more closely, the family scene proves to be the point of departure—in space and time—for Stephen's last season in hell; exactly the same schema of alienation and defensive withdrawal is to be found in the first chapter of *Ulysses*, where his feelings eventually coalesce into a manifest will to leave and never come back. The same schema begins the *Inferno*, with its realisation after a troubled night under the eaves of forest or city, that one must at all costs surmount the hill where virtue is to be found. Chapter V is as profoundly allegorical as Dante's cantos. Every detail is guilty of duplicity, insofar as its reality makes it unbearable to Stephen; the play of symbolism in this passage is double, for while the interplay of correspondences is Joyce's conscious work, the emotive significance of reality only takes on its full complement of meaning in Stephen's reactions to the aggressive ugliness of the world, which follows him and pervades every morsel of his life. As at the beginning of the first chapter the child lived through his relationships with others in growing disquiet, so now relationships with others and with the world outside are experienced in bitterness and humiliation; the ugly and the hideous are repeated over and over again, "his father's whistle, his mother's mutterings, the screech of an unseen maniac". All the apparatus for mental torture is installed before the day dawns, down to the box of blue and white pawn-tickets, derisively marked in the Virgin's colours to represent a Church betraying its flocks to the English, a box "speckled with louse marks," the poor grave and coffin of the family's ambitions, and the white enamelled basin where the mother washes her son's ears and scolds him. The sordidness extends throughout the world and time and reaches back to his childhood, as Stephen's life assumes the yellowish hue of "the dark pool of the jar. The yellow dripping had been scooped out like a boghole and the pool underneath it brought back to his memory the dark turf-coloured water of the bath in Clongowes" (*Portrait*, p. 173).

In *Dubliners*, Joyce intended to make a clinical study of that Dublin disease which in his youth he had diagnosed as syphilis. The word recurs constantly in his conversations with Stannie in 1904. In the book, the name of the disease has disappeared, but it is replaced by an aetiological table of symptoms, the two main ones being paralysis and a particular form of mental alienation. All the characters are more or less afflicted by these ills, or else suffer because they live in close proximity to someone who is. Given the nature of the disease, the outcome can only be fatal. *Dubliners* begins with the tale of a dead man, and ends with "The Dead," whose ironical message is that Dublin and the whole of Ireland are frozen to the marrow, and that the only people present are the dead who are not still living but not yet forgotten.

In the *Portrait*, Joyce has changed the nature of his metaphor; disease, after all, is a human matter, even if it destroys, and one cannot but feel compassion for the afflicted. This time he goes further, with less of the rhetorical and slightly pompous overacting which, as a young medical student, he had found necessary to counterbalance with macabre humour. Ireland, acting as theatre or grove of Academe for Stephen's progress, is much more intensely present than was the vague, hardly suggested, grey-brown labyrinth of the novellas. Its harbour, rivers, alleyways, country roads, parks, and beaches are all on display, and space takes a passive though portentous part in history. Dublin and its environs become consecrated places—theatres or temples which house performances or parodies of the Mass—and whose design obsessively repeats the form which space took in the earliest gaze of the future artist; everywhere the road, the first road, recurs.

Stephen has two different visions of the city: as a vague theatrical décor, "a scene on some vague arras, old as man's weariness," it is hung up as a backcloth for his dreams, and as seen from afar by the artist it is a picture in a history book. Seen at close quarters by the young rebel, its sad grey streets close him round as he walks through them in horror; in chapter V of the *Portrait*, Dublin and its inhabitants seem the continuation in reality of that hell which the sermons had caused to gape in Stephen's imagination. The ghostly, colourless, demon-haunted city upon which Stephen exercises his will as an exile is as carefully and precisely worked as a mediaeval artist's hell; he stands out against the hideous harmony of its people and objects. Stephen is caught in Dublin and Dublin is absorbed by Stephen in a reciprocal relationship leaving no room for objectivity. It is a dehumanised world which can transform itself without warning into a refuge or a zoo where men become like animals (*vid.infra*, in Ch. V, "The Bestiary"), where appearances hide error, lies, impotence, and the connivance of his contemporaries in a complicity which excludes him. Whether their conspiracy be real or imaginary, or in fact provoked by Stephen himself, is of no consequence; what matters is that Stephen makes out of it a work of his own, by which the threat of hellfire is turned to account as justifying the legitimacy of his attitude. Heresy thus becomes charged with different values; the artist's deviations are salutary processes, and his literal or metaphorical wanderings are already a way of separating himself from that space which contains Dublin.

The style of Dedalus' hell suggests decadent, violent, and melancholy visions. The style and its metaphors are a commentary, not on reality but on Stephen's states of mind, for since his encounter in the previous chapter with the incarnate image of beauty made from life he is in a state of flux, and is undergoing metamorphosis. He is no longer simply a victim of the provincial mores and atmosphere of Dublin, for now he feels himself summoned to an angelic state of being. The irony of multiple identity appears in the metamorphoses of the city, which parallel his own; the colonnade of the library serves as the temple during his deification as Thoth. The space which the small boy of the first chapter came to know by crawling about in it now stretches vast in every direction round his wings. And already Dublin is no longer only the cage, Ireland is something more than Crete; if Stephen still meets the cow it is no longer on the road but in an immense zoo, and if he still hides under the table, it has grown much larger. The hiding-place the eagles threaten is now coterminous with the whole of Stephen's limitless mental universe.

From Personal Hell to New World

Beyond and below all surfaces, reality is perceived by Stephen simultaneously as a magical world, a prison, a lunatic asylum, an hospitable refuge, and an unhealthy spot haunted by the ghosts of saints and philosophers, and inhabited by consumptive, perverted, miserable creatures, by priests made from ashes—by large numbers of young people with their backs turned to the threshold of life. Great currents of agitation are felt, not as of normal movement onwards to the future, but rather the hysterical trampling of men and women tightly imprisoned and in danger of suffocation, yet who choose to die rather than to risk the vertiginous freedom of the world outside. The violence is all the more dramatic because the damned fulfil the part of demons, tormenting each other. Stephen's personal hell was at least less destructive, since he was in fact punished; but punishment of oneself is an irrevocable condemnation to the silence of death. One can at least protest against ill-treatment inflicted by another; excess of pain or fear frees Stephen, giving rise to his strong opposition to injustice, while his soul refuses responsibility for the vagaries of his body. On the contrary, however, Irishmen of the Cranly or Lynch type are their own executioners: they appear to him sometimes like beings possessed by devils, their faces twisted with hatred and fury, because they have let Dublin engulf them; having no courage to escape, they have yielded and given in to the temptation of submission.

Their fidelity to religion has led them to be morbidly disloyal to themselves, or at least this is how Stephen interprets what he sees. The people around him are no longer the sick men of *Dubliners*, but men degraded by their superstitions, by their submission to a theological witch-doctor, by their complete lack of power in the formation of their own destinies. Just as in a modern capitalist world social transformation, following upon lack of active participation in life, manifests itself in terms of amoral and apolitical human gestures, and in what Lukacs calls "reification," similarly in the world of Ireland man has become a mere spectator, and reality is the property of that "great old swindler," God. The child's feeling of loneliness becomes a feeling of separation from everything, after his experiences in hell; this separation is elevated to the status of the artist's personal law as he revolts against those who would only admit him to their society upon his abolishing his individuality.

After the spiritual crisis, separation is first experienced as a sin and then as a distinction—the young man, realising that he has been dispossessed of his inheritance, claims his share of the universe. In the theological order of things, his share was hell. And so he adopts it, making God his rival rather than his master. Everything can be made to fit into his infernal point of view: sin becomes an act of independence leading to self-knowledge, and the final challenge to God lies in the recognition that although He may have created the physical being the birth of the soul is the work of the person himself, of each individual—a slow, dark and painful birth, contemporaneous with the moral experience of evil. The rose to which Dante attains after a long upward flight opens "sin by sin" within the artist's conscience. The first three chapters end with a fall into hell, followed by an ascension, then by a deception, that of the false paradises that Stephen believes himself to have reached, before the moment when it is finally granted to him to perceive his own world.

The earthly rose and the heavenly rose, the wild rose on the little green place, all wither, as do the red and white roses of the English war in which Stephen cannot truly take part (in Chapter I): the white rose of his penitent heart, the mass of white flowers on the altar, the pale and silent flames of death, cold and dead roses, the roses that turn into wreaths which are insubstantial garlands of prayer, the vague unearthly rosaries, and the "rose-soft stuffs" that in his imagination clothe the "body of a woman moving with tender life". All these disappear as the scarlet rose of triumphant beauty opens in the strange light where the soul swoons, ravished into a new, fantastic world. Henceforth, he knows "the hidden way"; he need not search anywhere but in himself, and as a visitor he can calmly return to hell and question the damned. Now that all his questions about his own destiny have been answered, he can leave his long inner monologue, and go out to inspect the traps which he has escaped from and the animals still struggling in them. At this point he speaks, more fully and openly than ever before or again; Dublin and his contemporaries have turned into the first circle of his exile, and experience—or rather "adventure"—has begun.

On the beach where his transfiguration takes place, Stephen is a type of Albion or of Swedenberg's "bird-man," "heavenly man, animated in all his limbs by angelic life-fluid". A longing for experience can be heard in his inner resolutions, a Blake-like exaltation of human wisdom; he resolves not to receive wisdom from the hypocritical mouth of another, but will acquire it for himself, living in his own fashion.[4]

Stephen refuses to fit into that order of things in which life obeys a set, ritualistic timetable and human behaviour is subject to moral laws.

[4]Dante meets Ulysses in the eighth circle of hell, the place of the fraudulent, and Ulysses says, "Neither my fondness for my son, nor my aged sire's distress, nor the affection due which should have rejoiced Penelope's heart, availed to overpower within me my eagerness to win experience of the world, and of the virtues and vices of mankind. . . . O brothers, I cried, bethink you of your origin; ye were not created to live the life of brutes, but to pursue virtue and intelligence". (*Inferno*, canto 26.)

"He was destined to acquire his own wisdom or to gather that of others among the ambushes of the world": this passage determines all Stephen's (and Joyce's) morality and conduct. Thus Stephen clearly formulates the necessity of the fall as an experience inaugurating the age of wisdom, a moral law which was to be developed and even turned into an imperative in *Ulysses*. Stephen *wishes* to be Icarus; having been the wondrous artificer of his own destiny, he wills his fall because it is a human experience, and because the hawk-like man is more man than hawk, he wills his exile for the sake of the hope of return (or despair of return) it involves—like Dante.[5]

The bird is at any rate destined to know cage and bars; Stephen is no optimist, and the world is indeed full of ambushes, but if one is going to fall into a trap, let it be from the greatest height possible. Stephen refuses the inferior traps of hell, fear, family and Church, because he who is born in Ireland is born inside these traps, and unless he escapes he will never know the taste of freedom, nor the smell of wild flowers. If one has to be captured in the end, one should at least choose for one's capture to follow the full mastery of one's fears and one's vertigo. There are traps like coffins, and Stephen rejects these; there are sins as living traps, and these he accepts: "The snares of the world were its ways of sin. He would fall. He had not yet fallen but he would fall silently, in an instant." He is afraid of falling, of leaving, of actually living. In Chapter V, he is Dedalus the artificer, preparing his flight, and in his resoluteness he acts the part of father to himself. But as he takes flight the voice heard is the voice of Icarus; foreknowledge of the fall existed before the preparations for flight were completed. As soon as he chooses the assurance of time instead of the promise of a proud eternity, he has foreknowledge of his Icarian fall. He is already impressed by the irony of the situation, and smiles to imagine himself alternately as the doubter, the god of writing, or the migratory bird.

Joyce's most subtle transposition is surely that which turns the Augustinian theory of the *felix culpa* into a theory of sin as an instrument of art. For Saint Augustine, Adam's sin is "happy," insofar as it already contains within itself the promise of the Redemption, and, in effect, God creates only good, since evil is by definition nothing but non-good. As darkness is only absence of light, so evil is the absence, loss, or lack of good. Being—all that is—is good. Joyce's intellectual manoeuvre con-

[5]See Ellmann, *op. cit.*, p. 371.

sists of suppressing certain points in this argument, so that he only keeps those which are relevant to his theory, or rather to his heresy, of creation; thus, sin is an act which may be criminal or anti-social, but which cannot be "bad"—on the contrary, it is an act whose consequences are good. This transition from morals to aesthetics takes place in the silences between the sophisms in *Portrait* and under cover of some very transparent word-play in *Finnegans Wake*. In *Portrait*, Stephen foresees, desires, and yet fears the eventuality of the fall. In *Ulysses*, the voice of Icarus is ironic, and the appeal to the father *(Pater, ait)* still a sign of dependence. In *Finnegans Wake*, the Gripes declares with pride, "My tumble is my own," a formula which is all the more Satanic because he seems to have willed not only his rise, but also and more specially his fall. The connections between these two, the complementary and contradictory brothers, are in such a "transfusion" that it is difficult to tell which of them is the chief—the "arthoudux". Originally, the artist is on the side of Cain and Satan, because they are inventors and artificers. Cain the pariah defies Abel, saying, "I Cain but are you able".[6] It is Cain's crime that founds the City of Mankind, for Cain and his sons built the first town. Fratricide is the origin of town-dwelling, in fact, and one can see how Joyce, as a city man who despised the country, would feel himself naturally on the side of the founder. Sin is indeed the foundation of art. From now on, cunning is the virtue of the forger who fabricates an anti-world, thus resolving the apparent contradiction between the myths of Jacob and Esau and of Cain and Abel, where Joyce seems to cast himself in the opposing roles of Jacob and Cain, the elder and the younger brother. In fact, Jacob, like Cain, is an ancestor of Ulysses; he has no hesitation in cheating for gain, and, disguised in a goatskin, impersonates his brother.

The sympathy Joyce feels for the freely-thinking man dominates his idea of exile—which is simply a necessary condition for the exercise of free thought—well expressed in the phrase from *Finnegans Wake*, "ex nickylow male come mickelmassed bonum," in which Saint Augustine is parodied, and through him the idealistic Stephen in *Ulysses* who was so susceptible to the magic of beautiful optimistic phrases. Here Nick the devil is in favour of Mick the angel, and from the former's baseness grows much good.

Similarly the idea of original sin, that is of sin as naturally ingrained in humanity from the very beginning, becomes the concept of sin as essential to the commencement of the work of art. For this, Joyce

[6] *Finnegans Wake*, pp. 63, 416, 419.

borrows from John Scotus Eriugena[7] the theory of the division of the human individual, and refashions it for his own uses: what had been theological heresy becomes aesthetic theory of the artist's nature, and at the same time that the young man is gleaning some notions from Aquinas, he also takes from the *De Divisione Naturae* (written c.867) what he needs for the support of his theory of the artist's ambiguity. Eriugena says that humanity was separated into two sexes by Adam's sin; Adam had already fallen before he was tempted, for if he had not acquiesced in the error he would not have been pervious to temptation. Thus punishment and separation come into the world. Man exiles himself from the spiritual Paradise of communion with God, before his banishment from Eden. This process corresponds to the double time of Stephen's expulsion. Eve is created during Adam's sleep, because for Eriugena sleep is a sign of the relaxation presaging the dullness of the soul which ceases to contemplate the Creator. Woman only appears when man has ceased to be fully vigilant; sleep is both cause and effect of sin. Humanity is created by the division of one sole being into a masculine and a feminine principle, and similarly the artist is born from the division of mankind into masculine and feminine—so much so that sexuality and narcissism, homosexuality and heterosexuality, are all creative manifestations of the single being who is drawing always towards his inner unity. In the works of Joyce the form this takes is that of the hermaphrodite, and Stephen is its manifest imaginative example at the moment of his dream-visit by an angel announcing the appearance of a new creation.

This duality returns as a major theme in *Finnegans Wake*, by way of its equivalent theme, the duplicity of the cheating twin, Shem, who is Shame and Sham too. Shaun claims to be solely himself, whether he is called Justius or the Mookse, but Shem, or Mercius, is divided, "of twosome twyminds, hidden and discovered"; he is twice twoman.

Conclusion: The Reply to Hell

The experience of reality is confirmed by various discoveries: to begin with, for him who lives in the Catholic world of Dublin there is no

---

[7]Scotus Eriugena was born in Ireland, taught in Paris around the year 874, and was the first great mediaeval philosopher.

alternative to submission except the adoption of heresy, with its inevitable accompaniment of punishment. Stephen then carries out the Satanic operation of making Hell his starting-point and creating a world for himself. Hell becomes the outside world, although the Church had tried to install it firmly *within* his consciousness by means of that conviction of guilt which Stephen calls "agenbite of inwit" in *Ulysses*. The free world is, on the contrary, situated in the universe of dreams and isolation; in the sphere of Art the young man encounters harmless images of the Beautiful in a beatific state of absolute solitude. Hell is urban, chaotic, dirty, and wretched, while the inner space is as vast as the sea and sky stretching to the horizon, but in order to reach it one has to have passed through hell, as Stephen passes through Dublin before reaching the sea. He rejects the worldly images offered to him by society as soon as he discovers their dangerous meanings, and goes to seek his reality elsewhere—where his solitude is not seen as a separation from other people but as an absolute, where he can identify and recognise himself, where he can even accept to take a name.

Here he finds the second lesson which contact with reality can teach: the power and mystery of language. The misery of the first age of his life, his time at Clongowes, was due to his feelings that he was somehow "strange" and "different," to his suspicions that he did not belong to this world, society, or even family. It was accentuated by his intuitions of the enigmatic and his clashes with other people's words. The whole story of the artist's growth and development can be seen as an exploration of the relationships between language and reality, from word to word, from mystery to revelation. From the beginning, all experience passes through the medium of words. The artist's development corresponds to his initiation, first into the use of words in speech and then into the mystery of writing; in the same way his knowledge of himself is bound up with his relationship to the proper names he encounters, and his knowledge of the world is a function of his acquisition of a vocabulary unfamiliar to him.

XV. The Discovery of Language

Prolegomena

From the first words the boy learns, language appears to him a mysterious way of expressing the world, which is the property of the authorities and of the adults, who know its secret and its use. What strikes him most is the ambivalence of the magic power possessed by words. Language is divided into two categories: the one maleficent and sacred, the other profane and evocative of beauty; the one connected with sex and religion, the other with art and sensuality. As soon as he is conscious of the world, Stephen does not hesitate to view both himself and it through the *word*, which becomes for him the desirable good, the door through which one must pass. By his nature he is already the rival of the Demiurge, long before he reaches the formulation of his *Non Serviam* whereby he announces himself as unique proprietor of the true word.

The Mystery of Words

At the beginning of the book of the artist, everything is presented in words—in a few pages, the first questions are asked, as though Joyce were showing us genesis through the eyes of an innocent consciousness, where imagination replaces thought and words resuscitate images. The material world presents itself to the senses as form, colour, and sound, and in it Stephen learns of what Joyce calls "strangeness" and "difference"—terms constantly repeated. He experiences strangeness in his own body, and difference by means of the names and words which stand for different places and other people. Language is situated between the self and the world; words define the "otherness" of that world, its nature and its horizons.

Language also has infinitely varied virtues and functions, as well as its relationships with material objects, which fascinate the creative artist-to-be; there are some words which do not seem to refer to any concrete visible entity, names which have no image corresponding to them, and thus the imagination in its attempts to correlate word and object finds unlimited freedom: somewhere, there might be a green rose.

Words exist which mean two radically different things, like "belt," which is a blow from a fist, or an article of clothing; the child senses the existence of multiple meanings.

There are words which are not polite like "backside," and there are odd, unpleasant words like "suck," the sound of sinks or lavatories emptying. In this case, Stephen discovers that there is some unexplained relationship between the words and the traces they leave in the individual mind, through memory. Such words exert a power which is not simply nominative—but actually perceptible—upon the physical person. They make him feel hot, or cold, or damp; they are very near to the status of objects.

There are words, such as "simony" and "politics," which are dangerous and powerful, although they seem to have no immediate connection with concrete reality and are used by the adult world as starting-points for accusations and acts of violence.

There are expressions and phrases as lovely as music which belong to the world of pure beauty. From childhood onwards, he instinctively relates every beautiful object to literature, even the useful sentences designed for writing practice; they are turned away from their original function by the boy who is later to fall in love with the hymns in praise of Our Lady: "And there were nice sentences in Doctor Cornwell's Spelling Book. They were like poetry but they were only sentences to learn the spelling from" (*Portrait*, p. 10).

Inversely, he abstracts whatever is good and warm and bright from its context in reality and assimilates it to the more welcoming and reassuring world of the book: "It was nice and warm to see the lights in the castle. It was like something in a book." *(Ibid.)*

Finally, there are universal verities which depend upon laws known to everyone but the boy Stephen. They are imposed, in dramatic form, by majority opinion: "all the fellows said" that Kickham would be captain of the third line. All the boys call Simon Moonan "McGlade's suck," yet to Stephen this is an ugly sound, with a different meaning. The young sensualist feels different and strange in the world of this community with its specific language and customs: "All the boys seemed to him very strange. They had all fathers and mothers and different clothes and voices" (*Portrait*, p. 13). All the boys know the right answers, except Stephen, and he alone feels out of place, both socially and geographically: "He could not learn the names of places in America. Still they were all different places that had different names. They were all in different countries and the countries were in continents and the continents were in the world and the world was in the universe" (*Portrait*, p. 15).

His reaction is to set himself in the middle of the world, and by writing it out he states his name and place; the famous column of writing on the flyleaf of his geography book, "in his writing," is the very image of the world as seen by the artist, "himself, his name and where he was". The universe consists of a whole series of concentric places, verging on the one living individual:

Stephen Dedalus
Class of Elements
Clongowes Wood College
Sallins
County Kildare
Ireland
Europe
The World
The Universe

Stephen may read this up or down; he discovers his own finite nature as related to the infinity of the universe by the instinctive use of an image of order similar to that of the mediaeval world, in which the ladder is replaced by the circle; without realising it, the boy Stephen has established the diagrammatic pattern of Joyce's work. His vision of the world is still a spatial one, for the child seeks to be at the centre, to place himself objectively and in relation to everything else. Where the universe stops, he imagines a thin line beyond which is God. The progression of language has led him from "Stephen Dedalus" to an uncomfortable God who is not a father-figure.

The discovery is an intellectual one; only God can think of everything. Thus, in his childhood, the artist-to-be begins his dialogue with the rival creator, He who can think the whole world, and whose name is significant of the same thing in every language. When Stephen declares that "God was God's name," he comes to grips with the greatest mystery—that of the difference or identity of a being in relation to language. God is in fact the only example of a proper name which is independent of language; a proper name is not to be translated, whatever country it is in or whatever its intention. In Dublin or Paris, Dedalus is Dedalus, but while God is called God in English, he changes his name into the language of the person addressing him. The name as a unit does not belong to any one language. God is not a concept, but he is both singular and universal. And so there is a name which is not a word but a being, that being responding to a multitude of names without thereby suffering any change.

It is not surprising that the concept of the name as proper noun should be one of the first to concern this child whose own name predestines him: Dedalus is "a funny name," and seems strange, like the name of someone else, in whom Stephen does not recognize himself. His feeling of alienation only disappears when he eventually feels that this name designates him personally, when he becomes this person and brings the new Daedalus and himself to coincide. But, on the contrary, "though there were different names for God in all the different languages in the world and God understood what all the people who prayed said in their different languages, still God remained always the same God and God's real name was God." To be everywhere oneself, be both the name and the person, and not to "bear a name" which turns one into an object for other people is to be quite beyond experience, out of reach of history and of that other mystery which in the next paragraph the child learns to call "politics," beyond those things which at this stage of his development he perceives spatially.

Between Stephen and an invisible God there arises a relationship of complicity regarding that Universe whose infinity thought cannot contain; in a sense, it is because Stephen is incapable of envisaging the universe which he imagines as larger than his mind can grasp that he finds it necessary to imagine the One who can both imagine and comprehend it. His wish to imagine the whole leads him to the thought of God, and thence to the desire to *be* God—to have the power to see everything, everywhere, without being seen; this mental journey is represented by the time that passes between childhood and the self-deification and -elevation on the beach at Sandymount. There is on

Stephen's part an innocent but skilful attempt to rehabilitate God, in his final affirmation that "God's real name was God," as much as to say that all God's names are foreign words, and that God has no other name but that which man chooses to give him. Thus, his "real name" is the name Stephen chooses to give him in his (Stephen's) native tongue. In this way, he manages to obliterate to some degree the terrifying "difference" which the discovery of concrete space has made him feel. Some comfort can be found in the Name which is spoken everywhere, which even the universe cannot surpass. This first meditation expresses indirectly what is to evolve as a major axis and theme of Stephen's thought in *Ulysses:* the contrasting structure of the inside and the outside. The child's uneasiness springs largely from the contradiction upon which his existence is based, namely, that he is spatially and in fact inside the world formed by his class, the College, the County Kildare, while subjectively—by his awareness of his difference—he is outside it. God manages to be both inside and outside. These feelings are at the origin of the artist's vocation insofar as it is a choice of the outward appearances of the world. The failure of thought to encompass infinity is compensated for by the triumph of the word that can utter the name of the infinite.

This extreme sensitivity to language is the seed of the artistic consciousness; the mystery of words is present at the origin of *Dubliners* as it is at the artist's birth. For Joyce, all experience of reality must filter through language, or rather is lived through language in that inner space of the consciousness where the world takes place like a narrative; words are more present than things. To be conscious of a strangeness in regard to reality is the first step towards the transposition of existence into language, towards seeing in words the qualities and the mystery of objects. It might almost be said that this "otherness" does not arise from any relationship with other people, for here the "other person" is the language itself, and with it Stephen erects a complex of emotional and sensual relations. He loves or fears words as he would love or fear actual people, even going so far as to adopt the necessary artifice of making his native language into a foreign tongue; he does this, it seems, in order to guarantee being sufficiently distant from it for his feelings of being different to encourage his desires. It is necessary for the words to be the property of others, of the English or of the Church, for him to feel the exaltation of conquest and the guilt of the expatriate; everywhere, language is the property of others before he appropriates it for himself, and even at school the other pupils use a special vocabulary which he cannot decipher.

Stephen's situation at Clongowes is that of the outsider or stranger who is involved by chance in the life of a community, in usages and happenings whose meanings he does not know. Two series of incidents —separated by the scene in which the word "politics" becomes charged before his frightened eyes with shouting, weeping, and the breaking of the family order—illustrate visually the child's condition as outsider, as one who is different. Each time the scene begins with a panoramic view of all the others in a crowd, strenuously active, responding to the common language which they share, and then reverts to the solitary figure, silently watching from a distance. The first time, we see a sports field: "the wide playgrounds were swarming with boys. All were shouting . . ." and "on the fringe of his line," the small, weak Stephen tries to avoid the crowding players. He does not take part in physical exercises, he remains outside the physical world, and is unable to answer such elementary questions as "Do you kiss your mother before you go to bed?" In this interrogation his own body, his familiar gestures, and his secret acts of tenderness are exposed to the mockery of the others, and seem to him to be declared wrong: what had seemed quite natural at home now seems suddenly forbidden and even shameful. The concept of sacredness is conveyed to him in its negative form, and he finds that he is in a state of sin.

The second incident contains the same schema and proceeds at the same pace, but now it is the guilty soul rather than the body that is on trial; the structure of the two passages is parallel. The group knows the facts, and Stephen, on the outer edge of the group, leans forward to hear. The joking atmosphere of the first episode has changed to a more painful one, for this time truly holy things have been profaned. Again, Stephen is among the others, but not *with* them; his fear is caused by his ignorance. The others know what this crime means: "—You know the altar wine they keep in the press in the sacristy—Yes.—Well, they drank that and it was found out who did it by the smell. And that's why they ran away, if you want to know" (*Portrait*, p. 40). In both of these cases, the denunciation is made by Wells, who acts the part of detective or spy, and who accused Stephen of kissing his mother goodnight; he seems very well informed about the crime in the sacristy.

Stephen did not steal the altar wine, and it is no crime to kiss one's mother goodnight, yet he feels doubly guilty. His very innocence, when brought face to face with that knowledge of evil which Wells represents, seems wrong. Then the boy Athy appears, the same who had been his companion in the infirmary and who had asked him riddles. And Athy makes the revelation still more terrifying, with an impressive sense of the theatrical. Calmly, amid a general hush, he reveals the height of the crime that has been committed. In the sacristy, they were not drinking the wine, they were "smugging. And that's why". And they were not in the sacristy, but in the lavatories. This disclosure sets off in Stephen's worried mind a series of questions and associations of ideas expressing guilt and hysteria, in a tumult of confusion mixing up his own problems with his own as yet nameless sensual experiences and the acts committted by others with their appalling consequences. This is all bound up with words and phrases which have long mystified him, and takes place in a series of enclosed spaces, as though sin were to become crystallised in a space particularly reserved for the purpose or evocative of it. For the reader, the superimposition of these enclosed spaces in which successive revelations take place may be only a consequence of Joyce's concern for harmony which makes the *Portrait* a succession of scenes and the expression of the pursuit of one visionary Time.

Joyce doubtless intended to imitate more or less ironically the liturgical progress of the Mass or to recall great Biblical and Evangelical events; there is necessarily a return to original sin when one enters into the mechanism of wrongdoing inspired by desire, followed by punishment, the whole renewing the fall of Satan or of Adam. One is thrown down (like the boy Stephen, who was pushed into the filthy ditch where the rats lived) or driven out (expulsion or flogging being the alternative punishments offered to those who were "smugging"). Feelings of awe and mystery give rise to ideas of consecration, of investing the atmosphere with holiness; both sacredness and profaneness are associated with the various initiatory rites undergone by the child, and sexual ritual, ceremonial washing, and purification—the concept of those places which it is dangerous for the profane to enter—all imprint their traditional pattern on his troubled mind. The real places which serve as temples are such that their juxtaposition may cause mockery; the same "faint sickness of awe" grips him at the thought of the dark silent sacristy: "It was not the chapel but still you had to speak under your breath. It was a holy place. . . . A strange and holy place" (*Portrait*, p. 41), as when he thinks of the boys misbehaving in the lavatories. ("By thinking of things you could understand them," he feels.) Why were they in the lavatories? Perhaps "because it was a place where some fellows wrote things for cod". The graffiti on the lavatory doors are like hieroglyphics to him, the words and drawings enigmatic, and this impresses them on his mind: "there was a drawing in red pencil of a bearded man in a Roman dress with a brick in each hand and under-

neath was the name of the drawing: *Balbus was building a wall.* . . .
It had a funny face but it was very like a man with a beard. And on the
wall of another closet there was written in backhand in beautiful writing: *Julius Caesar wrote the Calico Belly"* (*Portrait*, p. 43).

The association of such a vulgar word with a great man's name and
with the idea of writing is very disturbing. These apparently mad
phrases become part of the little store of unexplained expressions which
Stephen has been accumulating, waiting for them to reveal their secret
meaning. Along pathways opened in his mind by terror and worry,
Julius Caesar and Balbus join another complex of images with words,
those of the *Domus Aurea* and *Turris Eburnea*, which Stephen is just
beginning to decipher.

The investigation proceeds as follows: "They were caught smuggling,"
and Stephen looks at the other boys' faces. "But they were all looking
across the playground. He wanted to ask somebody about it. What did
that mean about the smugging in the square?" (*Portrait*, p. 42). The
guilty boys are Simon Moonan, who has "nice clothes" and owns "a ball
of creamy sweets," the reputed "suck" (i.e., favourite) of one of the
Jesuit masters, and Boyle, whom they call "Lady Boyle" because he is
so preoccupied with cleaning his hands and fingernails. Boyle's hands
remind Stephen of Eileen's "long thin cool white hands," and lead him
into strange confusion. Hands capture his awakened imagination, turning into deliverers of life's sensations: there are the thin white hands of
Eileen, the little Protestant girl who was the immediately forbidden
object of his first affections, because of whom the eagles threatened to
pull out his eyes; there are the hands of the boy Boyle; there are desirable, gentle, feminine hands, unlike those of Athy which are bony and
ink-stained; there are hands as white and pure as the ivory which Stephen suddenly associates with them, by bringing into contact two metaphors, one of which originates in a silly joke. Boyle is nicknamed
"Tusker" because he had once said that an elephant had two tuskers
instead of two tusks. This foolish schoolboy joke is connected with the
metaphor of "Tower of Ivory," and Eileen, whose image suddenly occurs to him, brings with her the memory of his guilty desire, which adds
itself to the complex net of evolving meanings in his mind.

Domus Aurea makes him think how "her fair hair had streamed out
behind her like gold in the sun," and the riddle is solved. But strangely
solved, for the litanies of the pure and precious Virgin, like a house or
a garden enclosed, have been pulled down into the profane meadow
where the provocative little girl runs laughing. Stephen's triumphant
conclusion from this discovery is a profane form of the religious act: "by

thinking about things you could understand them". This insistence on thinking things out sets off what later becomes the epiphany: Stephen triumphs because by taking the mystery into his inner world he has been able to reach the truth. To begin with, he had questioned the others and examined their faces, but found no answer. His own meditation has brought out the meanings he sought, and shown him the power of thought to extract meaning from reality.

The inquiry continues with another question on the actual place where the boys were caught misbehaving. What surprises Stephen is the strangeness of their action, and even more the choice of a place so unsuited to behaviour which for him is associated with his mother's perfume and with happy evenings at home. Gradually he feels drawn into the forbidden world, by his involuntary collusion with it: he kisses his mother, he likes Eileen's hands, he is sensitive to the mysterious atmosphere of the sacristy, altogether he may unconsciously have committed a multitude of sins. His fear is at any rate nourished in his unhappy silence by the ideas of the odd (queer, funny, strange) and of the double game (cod, joke); from fear he moves on to obscurely trying to justify his fear, and from the feeling that it is all very queer he passes to the mental identification of women's hands with the hands of Father Gleeson, who is to flog those who have done wrong: softness and cruelty, whiteness and violence, go together.

> But Mr. Gleeson had round shiny cuffs and clean white wrists and fattish white hands and the nails of them were long and pointed. Perhaps he pared them too like Lady Boyle. But they were terribly long and pointed nails. So long and cruel they were, though the white fattish hands were not cruel but gentle. (*Portrait*, p. 44)

There is something about those hands that stirs a latent masochism in the boy:

> And though he trembled with cold and fright to think of the cruel long nails and of the high whistling sound of the cane and of the chill you felt at the end of your shirt when you undressed yourself yet he felt a feeling of queer quiet pleasure inside him to think of the white fattish hands, clean and strong and gentle. (*Ibid.*)

Everything is confused with the pleasure of anticipated pain, which Stephen takes as the subject of his next curious and chilly meditation. The intuition of sadism is clear, partly because Athy says that "they'll both get it on the vital spot". "He wondered who had to let them down [the pupil's trousers], the master or the boy himself." The cold, the holy terror, and the delicious shivers of fear completely occupy the small boy who dreams of the high whistling sound of the cane coming down, of the nails that must be cruel because they are long. He is moved as though his first fear and his first desire, Eileen and the eagles, were fused together in one ambivalent impression. Beauty, sweetness, and femininity as sources of both pain and strange quiet pleasure are all "thought" by the child without being really experienced in the world of the senses. The world of sacredness insinuates its personal taboos between memory and imagination, Eileen becoming the prototype of every woman who brings both aesthetic delight and dangerous pleasures—the very thought is enough to give him a pleasurable shudder.

The ideas of sin and of beauty suggest reprehensible dreams to the boy; he takes consecrated objects solely and deliberately as a source of perceptible beauty, not of spiritual symbolism, and thus makes another step away from religion and towards his own vocation. In *Dubliners*, this magical process, not unlike that of transubstantiation, is called by its correct name, simony. The young Stephen is guilty of simony insofar as he substitutes temporal values for those of the spirit:

> That must have been a terrible sin, to go in there quietly at night, to open the dark press and steal the flashing gold thing into which God was put on the altar in the middle of flowers and candles at benediction while the incense went up in clouds at both sides as the fellow swung the censer and Dominic Kelly sang the first part by himself in the choir. (*Portrait*, p. 46)

Thus he dreams, savouring the wondrous transgression and the delight it gives to all the senses. And the altar wine, the smell of which makes him feel slightly sick, even though it is transubstantiated, can intoxicate him by the sonorous beauty of its name. The word "wine" does not make him think of Christ, but rather turns his thoughts to the grapes that ripen in Greece. He commits his first simoniac act on the day of his first communion: to the ambivalence between fear and desire, manifest in the choice of the words troubling him, such as "kiss," "suck," "smug," and in the abundance of adjectives signifying passivity, repetition, silence, holiness and mystery, there is added the ambivalence of the communion itself and of its immediate profanation. For physically it is profaned by the disgust aroused by the priest's winy breath as he bends over the child who with closed eyes, open mouth, and tongue slightly out awaits the host; spiritually it is profaned by his escape in imagination to the world of paganism with its grapes in purple clusters, its "houses like white temples" (rather than like ivory towers). The word "wine" suggests aspirations towards adventure which find their first romantic embodiment in Chapter II when Stephen is reading *Monte-Cristo;* Greece is replaced by Marseille and its sunny trellises, while the elusive figure who is the *Domus aurea* and *Turris eburnea* takes the name of Mercedes. The Greek temple is transposed by the dreamer into a "small whitewashed house" near Blackrock.

Thus in the child's imagination a confusion grows up around certain obsessive words, halfway between distress and fascination, which is to prove most fertile for the artist. The effect defines the cause here and the darkness seems to contain hidden light within it; the order of things is exactly the opposite of that of ordinary causality. The words which trouble the schoolboy at Clongowes all belong to the world of sensuality, "kiss," "suck," "smug," "wine," and there would be nothing unusual about that were it not for the fact that through them the child feels that he can be reached by the two worlds of authority, that of his family and that of his teachers, to which he is subject. The words "kiss," "suck," and "smug" change their meanings and functions depending on the time and place in which they are used. The child had already met the words "kiss" and "suck" during his early family life and had instinctively associated them with sensations rather than attributing social significances to them.

"Kiss" was the sound his mother's lips made, associated with dampness and with the motion of bringing two faces near to each other. At school, what had been simple tenderness becomes a question of good and evil; the literal definition of the gesture, "you put your face up like that to say good night and then his mother put her face down," becomes charged with ethical meaning. Among the Jesuits, this movement becomes liable to punishment with a beating.

The word "suck" brings the boy's relationship with his father into the sphere of guilt; it had meant an unpleasant noise made by the dirty water going down the drain in the lavatory of the Wicklow Hotel, where the boy and his father had been staying. "Suck" is also the nickname of Simon Moonan, the favourite of one of the Jesuits; like "kiss," it evokes an image and connections of uncertain but unappealing nature. The water is only slowly absorbed by the hole in the washbasin, and the memory of the sound it made gives the child a fit of shivering; "to remember that . . . made him feel cold and then hot". Between McGlade the Jesuit and Moonan his "suck" there exists a father-and-son relationship comparable to that between Simon and Stephen Dedalus.

In this disgust for all familiar contact, which leads eventually to sensory hallucinations, one can already see the reactions of the young man who in Chapter II rejects his family and denies that he belongs to anyone or anything, and even those of the Stephen who, in *Ulysses*, feels repelled by the soft, strange arm of Bloom that is linked in his. In these first feelings of repulsion the proud, individualistic side of the artist's character asserts itself.

For the artist, relationships between human beings are always covered in a veil of mystery; they can be resolved in disgust, generally speaking, or at the best in a kind of holy horror, while words as images transport him into delightful lands of fantasy, words implying contact bringing him abruptly back to himself. Thus Joyce establishes two worlds: the one is that of poetry, symbolism and the mysterious East, related to that of *The Arabian Nights*,[1] and provides a stage for all the facile and romantic imaginations of which the *fin-de-siècle* was capable, while the other, although real, is really more fantastic. In it Stephen goes his imaginary way from words to images within the visionary universe that is about to grow, overflowing the globe of this earth and reaching the skies, and his connection with reality is transposed into words with growing intensity. No longer does he dream of punishments, nor of the menacing, unpleasant face of Father Dolan, whose threats, imitated from *Macbeth*, are a grotesque metaphor of the eternal recurrence of judgment: "Tomorrow and tomorrow and tomorrow . . . Every day Father Dolan." The prose of reality reflects Stephen's own view; since he is basically the indirect narrator of the *Portrait*, and since everything is seen by him and reported by Joyce who has identified himself with the narrator, the world is to be seen and deciphered through his weak and smarting eyes, which is why his dream-visions have the brightness and strong colouring that reality cannot have. Shortsighted, and without glasses, his eyes often blurred by tears, Stephen disfigures the objective world outside, because although he can hear its sounds clearly he can only perceive its shapes very dimly unless he is extremely close to the object in question. This is exemplified in the portrait of Father Dolan, which is all in grey, vague and approximate: "white-grey not young face, his baldy white-grey head with fluff at the sides of it, the steel rims of his spectacles and his no-coloured eyes looking through the glasses".

[1]Cf. *Scribbledehobble*, ed. Thomas Connolly (Northwestern U.P., 1961), p. 25. 'The Sisters' is equated by Joyce, in these notes on his own writings which he made for later use in *Finnegans Wake*, with the *Arabian* or *Thousand and One Nights*.

This vision is disturbing, not only because of its formulation and details, but also because it constitutes one of the first examples of that faculty the artist's eyes have of taking to pieces and dismembering other people; Stephen sees them as though they were made up of disparate bits, because his sensibility can dissect reality, enlarging or reducing whatever aspects have for him at the moment assumed the value of signs or symbols. For a moment, Dolan's head fills all space. Joyce was to play on the same effect in the novella 'The Sisters,' which opens *Dubliners*. Joyce is still dealing with the mystery of words, and even more with the meanings of gesture and silence.

The Magic of Signal and Silence

There are three versions extant of 'The Sisters,' the first novella in *Dubliners*[2]; it is the least explicit of the stories in the collection and the most important by virtue of its place at the beginning, by the multiplicity of its themes, and by the nature of its subjects, the child narrator and his master, an old priest, who has recently died. It was first written in July 1904, for George Russell (AE), who offered Joyce a pound to write "something simple, rural, live-making, pathetic,"[3] yet even the first version of the story, for the *Irish Homestead*, caused Joyce to declare to his friend Curran, "I am writing a series of epicleti—ten— for a paper. I have written one. I call the series *Dubliners* to betray the soul of that hemiplegia or paralysis which many consider a city." "Epicleti" (although to be strictly accurate, Joyce should have written "epicleses" in Latin or "epicleseis" in Greek) means an invocation, now dropped from the Roman ritual, in which the Holy Ghost is besought to transform the host into the body and blood of Christ. It is clear that from the outset Joyce's intentions were more profound than Russell's, and that they include an attempt at symbolism.

The three versions of 'The Sisters' show such marked differences in depth that one may wonder whether Joyce did not give Russell a simplified version, rather than the original story. At any rate, his originality in choosing both subject and title for this piece, destined for the readers

---

[2]Cf. Magalaner, *Time of Apprenticeship* (London, 1959), pp. 72–87 and 174–80, comparing the three versions and giving the *Homestead* text in full.

[3]Ellmann, *op. cit.*, p. 169.

of the *Irish Homestead,* must not be overlooked. In fact, he was taking advantage of Russell's hostility to introduce as an apparently realistic piece a novella which in both form and content was equivalent to a full manifesto. Stanislaus was aware of this, since Joyce had confided in him, less pedantically than in his explanation to Curran,

> Don't you think there is a certain resemblance between the mystery of
> the Mass and what I am trying to do? I mean that I am trying. . . . to give
> people some kind of intellectual pleasure or spiritual enjoyment by con-
> verting the bread of everyday life into something that has a permanent
> artistic life of its own.

'The Sisters' is in fact an experimental novella in which the author takes pains to transmute the banal into art; the intellectual pleasure involved is all the greater in that the everyday matter is taken from an area which itself had offered the example of transformation. There was an irony unperceived by the 1904 reader, in the fact that Joyce had chosen a priest to play the part of the powerless magician upon whom the artist confers permanence of life by his art.

Finally, the narrator, who is also the author, is the disciple of a master who hands on to him less religious teaching than vague occult knowledge; its meaning is not revealed during the time that the narration lasts, but in that allusive space which exists for those who can read between the lines of language. Joyce is using here for the first time not only a particular method of symbolism but also an aesthetic of the enigmatic which is related both to word-games and to revelation—a technique which he was to use more and more extensively in his later works.

In *Dubliners,* and until *Ulysses,* the appearance of reality is always preserved—in theory, 'The Sisters' is a realistic work based on an anecdote from real life, the death of a slightly crazy old priest who is a relative of May Murray (in the last version he is also a paralytic). The paralysis is real, but Joyce implicity makes it into a symbol of the general paralysis of Ireland, and from this point onwards every symptom or incident applying to an individual is to be tacitly considered as applying generally to Ireland also. The priest dies, and a small circle of acquaintances comments on his life and death, while his body lies in state and his young disciple observes, in himself and in those around him, strange attitudes that seem to hesitate between pity and a certain repulsion; ambiguous expressions occur in conversation, referring to the past, possibly to some wrong the dead man committed, for "he had his cross to bear". We learn that he suffered from some ill-defined remorse of unknown origin. The narrator is frustrated by his lack of some necessary knowledge: he speaks in the first person, as do the narrators of the next two novellas, which follow and complete 'The Sisters'; he comes and goes—seeking the answers to his questions—between two sealed worlds, that of the family and the magic world into which his old friend Father Flynn had introduced him. But on both sides he is shut out, because he is only allowed a partial knowledge by each and because the man who had initiated him into all the wonders and curiosities of history has departed without giving him the final word that elucidates all.

Father Flynn is twice dead. The narrator only registers the second death, but he had earlier witnessed the first death, that of the spirit. Father Flynn had magic power, since by invoking the name of God he could transmute ordinary substances into divine. The apprentice to whom he wishes to communicate his knowledge studied diligently, but the learning seemed vague and somehow hidden in the world or amongst words. The child of *Dubliners* here resembles the boy in *Portrait* in his anxious effort to pierce through the mystery of "things". In *Dubliners,* Joyce has already established the presence of "things" as a second reality, a disturbing world of phenomena, which is not what it appears to be, but which seems to signify *something else;* it is not the full space that it seems to be, but a place of danger, with gaps through which one may fall and cracks through which evil spirits may emerge. In 'The Sisters,' because of the presence of the dead man, the adults move about carefully on tiptoe, whispering; the child scarcely dares to eat for fear of making too much noise. But in between words and things creep secret meanings and between words there are strange silences. All these gaps in space, all these instances of dead time, arouse the child's curiosity and his fear, because he does not know, or is afraid of finding out, what lies hidden behind the invisible or the unspeakable. The dead man's pupil seeks out the hidden meanings, observing, spying on the adults' movements between reality and conversation, hoping to come suddenly upon the secret of the transubstantiation of reality, if it be possible.

In fact the first version, the shortest, made the child simply the witness of a life that had ended, and made no provision for the development of the sub-historical motif of the complex relations between the priest and the child, which are the very essence of the story in the final version. Everything constituting the originality of the novella was added later, including the theme of paralysis. In the first version, for no apparent reason, the priest dies exhausted and half-mad. The child learns from the notice of his death that Father Flynn had been sixty-five years old, and thinks that he had looked much older and that he had seemed to lead so empty and regular a life that there was no reason why he should not have lived for as long as he wanted. All the strange links between the boy and his mentor are left unsaid; the narrator merely mentions that Father Flynn had a low opinion of women, their devotedness and servility, perhaps because his own sisters were so stupid, and the only remark which indicates the meaning with which Joyce was to fill the final version is the phrase, quite anodyne in its context, "Perhaps he considered me more intelligent and for this reason would speak with me a little". These few words become characteristic of a whole system of teaching later on.

The motif of the journey to Persia, the dreams and hallucinations, the apparition of Father Flynn's head, are not mentioned, nor are the symbolically-charged themes which are to be relevant not only for this novella but also for the whole collection and for all the techniques of Joyce's symbolism in his work. He says nothing of the whole system of gestures that imitate ceremonies of the Church, like the dead man's dream-confession, and in particular the discreet but revealing pattern of refusals and mental blockages undergone by the child's mind in its rejection of the master's religion. In the first version, the sisters and the aunt indulge in the traditional harmless gossip, transforming the death into an interesting and to some extent troublesome event, affecting mainly the departed, since the survivors seem to feel very little distress. The final revelation takes up all the intensity of feeling: Father Flynn had once broken a chalice, and "of course, they say it was all right, that it contained nothing, I mean. But still," it had turned his brain. And the conversation ends on the pious wish, "God rest his soul," which gives the novella a sardonic final note. The whole piece gives the impression of mediocrity, platitude, and absence of the sacred, rather than of the deconsecration suggested in version three and emphasised by Eliza's grotesque simplicity: "We done all we could. . . . we wouldn't see him want anything while he was in it". The central character of the first version, the dead man, appears as an ecentric who from his youth had shown signs of psychosis which took the form of fits of dumbness. He suffers from loneliness in the first version, but in version three it is only auxiliary to the real trouble, that of the overwhelming irony provided by the difference between his omnipotence as priest and his personal weakness and "scruples".

The sisters have a more central part to play in the first version, and it is easier to see why they give the story its title: as a pair of stupid and dull-witted people, they form a sharp contrast with their brother who had dreamed of power and had failed in his attempt to reach a higher scale of being. They win because they can continue to live in complete triviality without any scruples or intelligence; Nannie, who is deaf (this is not explicitly stated in version three, but the aunt makes signs to her rather than speaking), used to read the newspaper to him, has been doing so for years, and can read tolerably well, but she always calls it the *Freeman's General* instead of the *Freeman's Journal.* This mistake is attributed to Eliza in version three, along with many other mistakes in speech. What is comedy in the first version becomes strange because of the lack of any explanation in the third version. Deafness is indicated by the silence of the aunt and of Nannie, but this dumbness is part of the general silence which is scarcely permitted to be broken by the occasional sigh or half-finished sentence, and thus it becomes part also of the general immobility where death, paralysis, and the power of words hold the imagination prisoner. Eliza is obviously the tutelary genius of the place.

In the first version, she is actually seen behind the counter of the umbrella shop with its vague sign reading "Drapery"; in version three, she is found in the house at various symbolic moments, being, in fact, the only member of the Flynn family to speak. Nannie expresses herself by grimaces, and "poor James" only spoke to the boy, and hardly at all to his sisters. He was nothing but a body to feed and clothe, as far as they were concerned. Only the child knew that he was not simply a pitiful burden. But Eliza's mistakes in grammar are not only signs of humble birth, of low social rank in Irishtown, as they are in the first version; the author has chosen them in order to make them part of the two patterns underlying the whole story—the theme of paralysis and the theme which could be characterised as the contrast between the weak profane word and the mighty magic and sacred word. Eliza mangles her English grammar and pronunciation, while "poor James" was able to teach the child Latin as spoken in Rome. If Flynn suffers from physical and spiritual paralysis, the sisters suffer from that intellectual paralysis which Joyce considered to be the national malady of Ireland; thus, Eliza tells the aunt what a good heart the dead man had: "But still and all he kept on saying that before the summer was over he'd go out for a drive one fine day just to see the old house again where we were all born down in Irishtown. . . . If we could only get one of them new-fangled carriages that makes no noise that Father O'Rourke told him about, them with the rheumatic wheels, for the day cheap . . ." The confusion between "rheuma" and "pneuma" is a special play on words, for Joyce is anxious to point out the simple-minded materialism and the total lack of "spirit" which characterise the two sisters.

The Homestead version is clumsy and over-explicit, while the novella in its present form is a tissue of insinuations and allusions; comparison of the two shows that Joyce passes from plain realism to a form rich in mystery, leaving a heady strong perfume behind like that of the flowers in the dead man's room. He does this by suppressing all commentary and all references to an already known reality; he sets all the events in an absolute time present, and although the novella is written in the past tense, it has no explanatory roots in any time past. Thus the sisters Eliza and Nannie have most equivocal attitudes and parts to play in version three: Nannie looks and behaves like a servant, and as the child sees her in a series of brief mimed scenes where nothing is said she seems to be both puzzling and designated, at least in the author's mind, for the fulfilment of some sacred duties about which we know nothing. There is some obscure connection between Nannie and the child, just as there is a complexity of other almost magical bonds between him and the other characters. The indefinable link of animosity between him and old Cotter in version three, for example, is partially defined by the contrast with the child's secret alliance with the priest, and is harshly explained and illumined in the first version. In the original, all antipathies, rivalries, and scorn are explained along with their motives, as they are in traditional stories, but here there is nothing left at the end but the heavy gesture and language of the inexpressible.

The narrator is inspired by feelings of aversion or of self-esteem which he knows and recognises, but the child in version three is swept along by a tide of vague emotions which overwhelms him and causes him to have disturbing dreams, whose strangeness seems prophetic of further hidden depths. The narrator in the first version is presented at the beginning as being devoured by morbid curiosity and awaiting his friend's death with an intensity that touches on desire; but the death-throes of Father Flynn in version three fill the child with holy terror which is intimately connected with the master's spiritual domination over him. Yet to start with, this terror seems no more than a kind of superstitious communion involving the mystery of death such as any sensitive child might experience. The relationship of possession is inverted: it is the child who prides himself on being the only friend and confidant the priest has, and who thus feels entitled to be the first to know of his death—his friend's death *belongs* to him, as it were, and he hates old Cotter for depriving him of the first news.

This wish for power is less explicit in version three, where Cotter has a relatively reduced role to play; he is still the adversary, but he is accepted into the clan of the child's family, while the ghostly presence of the priest invades all consciousness and fiendishly takes hold of the child's mind. The only characteristic detail of the first version that was both banal and meaningful has disappeared in the final reworking, and in the removal and replacement of this theme can be seen the key traits of Joyce's art; the first paragraph of the first version is pervaded by the strange presence of what the child calls "Providence". The intention is probably, though not manifestly, anti-theistic, but the word "Providence," repeated four times in the first ten lines of the story of a priest's death, does seem to suggest some intention of glossing over the idea of God by the use of a word which can mean "God" or "Chance," or even "accomplice daimon," according to circumstances. "Night after night I had passed the house," at the same time each evening, as though by chance. This sort of providence plays with its subject, bringing him into the street beneath the lighted window, that he might observe it and wonder when the other was going to die, and then mockingly arranges for him to be at the other side of town the night the man actually died.

This might be simply coincidence, but the narrator's impatience and vigilance indicate how ambiguous his time of waiting is. The child wishes for Flynn's death, although we are only told the reason why in version three. In the first version there seems to be nothing more than a rather unpleasant rivalry between the child and old Cotter; the latter expresses himself in a paragraph which is charged with meaning but isolated in the context of that version to such an extent that it is difficult to grasp its psychological continuity there. The child dislikes old Cotter because he is boring and because he was the first to hear the news; he is cross because he has been "beaten to it," and had been sure that "he would die at night". One could speculate indefinitely on the reasons for this displeasure; the wish to be the first person told may represent a kind of perverse communion, or jealous love, but Joyce says nothing more. Only in version three is a clear rivalry established between Cotter and Flynn as antagonists, as well as between the narrator and Flynn against Cotter.

Providence disappears from the final version, and in its place Joyce introduces—rather than the extravagances of chance—the enigmatic power of words, which come to be more important than the priest's actual death.

It is no longer a matter of the child's unexplained intuition, the presentiment that "he would die at night," which had directed all his watchful attention towards the nighttime; now the actual *cause* of death becomes obsessive, in a form of emphasis on the power of words, which governs all the subsequent development of the story. Father Flynn exercises this power, and old Cotter is his main adversary contesting his right to this power. The priest had in fact announced his own coming death, and everything took shape around that fatal sentence: "He had often said to me: 'I am not long for this world,' and I had thought his words idle. Now I knew they were true".

The window which the child has "studied" for days is more than a window; it is also the mirror that reflects the candles lighted for the dead. The child waits for death to confer on it a special value by its arrival and imprint, wondering whether a word has more power than an object, whether it exists more than the object itself, and he repeats the word "paralysis" during the three evenings of his vigil like a magic formula. The boy muttering "paralysis, paralysis" gently under his breath probably senses that he is the possessor of extremely powerful instruments which he does not know how to use, but by repeating the words he can share, perhaps actively, in the fate of the dying man.

This is the first lesson that Joyce teaches his reader, and it is also the narrator's own experience. The key to the whole work can be found in the first lines of the first novella of *Dubliners*. The repetition of the word "paralysis" has become a maleficent act, and made the word into one of those incantatory expressions which are strange because they are incomprehensible. The actual word seems to be the name of some fiendish, wicked being: "It filled me with fear, and yet I longed to be nearer to it and to look upon its deadly work".

This terrible power of the word is immediately associated with evil and guilt; the child insinuates, by means of his verbal imagination, that the priest is possessed by some demonic being who had come to him because of a sin he had committed. The demon, which the child confuses with its name, "paralysis," and then makes objective by calling "it," is a creature that fascinates. The attraction, mingled with fear and curiosity, shows that there is already a strong bond and deep understanding between pupil and master. The logical consequence of the boy's ambiguous wait for his master's death is this experimenting with the sorcery inherent in language.

As though to strengthen the impression of black magic, the author associates two other words with paralysis, which are signs of intellectual and spiritual deviation: "it had always sounded strangely in my ears, like the word gnomon in the Euclid and the word simony in the Catechism". In 'The Sisters,' Father Flynn is called simoniac by his pupil, when the latter receives his confession in a dream. There are in fact several simoniacs in the story; Flynn and Cotter are each in his fashion types of Simon Magus who lived at the time when Jesus was curing the paralytics and cripples, and who offered the apostles money for their secret in order to act as a miraculous healer for profit. He it was who began the trade in spiritual values; all collusion between spiritual and temporal is sinful, being a use of the Word for forbidden purposes and a contamination of real life. Father Flynn and old Cotter are both initiates of certain mysteries, and they torment the child's mind with fear and temptation; there is, indeed, probably an ironical intention in the parallel suggested between the operations of the distillery and the process of transubstantiation.

As Magalaner suggests,[4] in the final version the priest has become the representative of a paralysed religion towards which he tries to entice the child. Only in this version does the uncle declare, ambiguously, that the priest had "had a great wish for him"; the initiation would cost something (and this is the sin of simony). Magalaner deduces this from the interesting modifications undergone by the text: in the first version the aunt, out of the goodness of her heart, brings Flynn the snuff, "High Toast," and he gravely bows his head to thank her, while in the third version the child brings the snuff as a gift from his aunt, "and this present would have roused him from his stupefied doze. It was always I who emptied the packet into his black snuff-box . . ." Joyce obviously intends to show here both exchange and simony, but to say that the priest is the simoniac is to reverse the meaning of the word; the child is the buyer and thus the sinner, while the priest is simply his master in guilt. Besides, all he has to offer is an empty chalice, and it seems as though the parade of the Church's ceremonies and vestments conceals the lack of a true vocation; this idea gradually becomes clear as the story progresses.

Old Cotter is the master of another strange language, but the child soon grows bored by it; Cotter's alchemy is not efficacious like Flynn's, and at the most it can only promise a banal intoxication. Cotter is simply a minor rival of the true sorcerer. "When we knew him first he used to be rather interesting, talking of faints and worms; but I soon grew tired of him and his endless stories about the distillery." Father Flynn takes Cotter's place, with his paralysis which is just as fascinating as these strange "faints," which turn out to be only a technical term of the

[4]*Op. cit.*, pp. 76–8.

brewing trade. Father Flynn is destined for the worms in reality, for he will soon be dead, while for Cotter they are just a name for beer-pipes. Father Flynn was possessed of many secrets, while Cotter was interesting to begin with and then boring, because the mysteries of the distillery are soon plumbed; Flynn could reveal the complexity hidden in apparent simplicity:

> Sometimes he had amused himself by putting difficult questions to me, asking me what one should do in certain circumstances or whether such and such sins were mortal or venial or only imperfections. His questions showed me how complex and mysterious were certain institutions of the Church which I had always regarded as the simplest acts.

The child seems to have received a very mixed instruction, which in its entirety appears to have no coherence at all; he has been told "about the catacombs and about Napoleon Bonaparte, . . . the meaning of the different ceremonies of the Mass and of the different vestments worn by the priest". Death, sin, Napoleon, and the eucharist are all tangled together; the sacred knowledge reaches such vast proportions that the boy "was not surprised when he told me that the fathers of the Church had written books as thick as the *Post Office Directory* . . . elucidating all these intricate questions". By this irony both the Book and the Word are deprived of their sanctity, being reduced to volume and size rather than being appreciated for their content. Napoleon's incongruous appearance in this catalogue is only explained by his reappearance in *Portrait,* under similar circumstances: on the same day that Lady Boyle commits his mysterious sin, Stephen fearfully recounts to himself the various strange things he has encountered at different stages of his initiation, and the more or less forgiveable breaches of respect to the Deity which one could commit. The wine which is stolen from the sacristy reminds him of the day of his first communion, which should have been a holy day for him, but appears, as far as he can recall, to have been the day that he first committed simony, for as soon as he was admitted to the holy place he appropriated and transformed its secret for his own personal pleasure in a very subtle complex way.

The beauty of the word "wine" had suggested to him the image of grape-clusters, associated in his mind with the image of the dream-woman who offered a bunch of muscatels to Stephen in his disguise as Monte-Cristo. He resists the temptation haughtily, not because he is a hero but because all the pleasure lies in the fact of actually being tempted. The wine is profaned by the temptress, but also by Stephen's disgust which finally makes it clear that he has no real faith in the holy ceremony: "the faint smell of the rector's breath had made him feel a sick feeling on the morning of his first communion". The moment when he opens his mouth to receive the host is not the moment of ecstasy or of quiet contemplation, but of nausea, and this is why one of the articles of most people's faith—"the day of your first communion was the happiest day of your life"—seems very surprising to him.

It is as though on that day Stephen passed two doors at once through the power of words: the door of the Church which would henceforth admit him as an adult, and the threshold of art. This takes place under the majestic auspices of Napoleon, who for the masters at Clongowes is less the great emperor than the good Catholic:

> Once a lot of generals had asked Napoleon what was the happiest day of his life. They thought he would say the day he won some great battle or the day he was made an emperor. But he said:
> —Gentlemen, the happiest day of my life was the day on which I made my first holy communion. (*Portrait*, p. 47)

It is difficult to see what business Napoleon and Julius Caesar have at Clongowes, in those feverish pages that represent Stephen's thoughts at the time of the great crime committed by the two "suckers" Moonan and Boyle.[5] And why does Stephen in his masochistic dreams define the theft of a monstrance, "the flashing gold thing" (i.e., the violation of the House of Gold, the seizing and possession of Eileen or of E.C.), as the most abominable crime possible?

> It was a strange and a great sin even to touch it. He thought of it with deep awe; a terrible and strange sin: it thrilled him to think of it in the silence when the pens scraped lightly. . . . to drink the altar wine . . . was a sin too: but it was not terrible and strange. (*Ibid.*)

This curious differentiation of the two acts of profanation subtly takes up again the theme of woman as dangerous, while the solitary rebellion of the simoniac announces that the artist is present.

In Joyce's works, emperors make strange appearances to small troubled boys; they are romantic figures, solitary, victorious, and with a great power of attraction—heroes who have succeeded in winning the

---

[5]Hugh Kenner, in *Dublin's Joyce*, suggests that at the level of *Portrait* names are to be interpreted as having hidden meanings; thus, Simon Moonan, as well as being a simoniac, would be a moony being, cold, pale, feminine, and Boyle "boylan" with forbidden desires.

supreme and quasi-divine power. But some emperors are different from others: on the lavatory wall Stephen deciphers the strange graffito, "Julius Caesar wrote the Calico Belly". He prefers the Roman to the Corsican, if only because of the former's Caesarian birth, and for his crossing of the Rubicon. The Calico Belly is of course the *Bellum Gallicum*, which represents yet another victory, as both commander and writer, making Stephen doubly jealous.

In 'The Sisters' the whole story of resistance to religion is mimed and murmured, according to the established pattern of profane imitation of the rites. The theme of communion is probably the most notable addition which Joyce made to the first version; the whole of this paragraph was originally missing:

> In the little room downstairs we found Eliza seated in his arm-chair in state. I groped my way to my usual chair in the corner while Nannie went to the sideboard and brought out a decanter of sherry and some wineglasses. She set these on the table and invited us to take a little glass of wine. Then, at her sister's bidding, she filled out the sherry into the glasses and passed them to us.

The chair, the pulpit where the master used to perform his communion and transubstantiation, is now occupied by Eliza. The two sisters are usurping even the forms of his magic. Powerless and dumb, the child witnesses the third death of his master, a post-mortem death by sacrilege. The sisters innocently share the dead man's functions, one taking his chair while the other unconsciously imitates the gestures of communion. Nannie insists that the boy take some cream crackers but he refuses, because he says he is afraid of making too much noise eating them. In fact, his refusal is like Stephen Dedalus' refusal of the grapes, and later of Bloom's kindly offers: he does not wish to participate. Nannie is disappointed. Everyone falls silent: "we all gazed at the empty fireplace". The scene of refusal and absence ends thus on a far-reaching level of symbolism; Joyce often uses this symbol of the absence of fire to indicate absence of life, and similarly, the silences are much longer than the speeches in 'The Sisters'. Again, when Nannie takes the boy and his aunt to the coffin, the boy "pretends to pray," but is troubled and distracted by the slippers, worn and trodden down unevenly, which he can see when he kneels behind Nannie.

The motif of simony is connected with that of the gnomon; the former governs the inner workings of the spirit while the latter throws its shadows varyingly over time and space. There is no break in the harmony of the symbolism, for every detail is connected to the central theme of language. Thus, the child only believes in Father Flynn's death when he reads the card pinned up outside the closed shop; he knew about it already, but only the written text assures him completely that it has happened. He comes out of the half-light where he had lived with the priest and steps into the sunlight: "I walked away slowly along the sunny side of the street". The gnomon is the spike whose shadow tells the time on a sundial; the play of night and day, of sun and shadow, their variations, indicated by concrete objects, are important as archetypal symbolism in 'The Sisters': "I found it strange that neither I nor the day seemed in mourning mood and I felt even annoyed at discovering in myself a sensation of freedom as if I had been freed from something by his death."

In the *Homestead* version, Joyce insisted on what a fine day it was, but made no move to connect this with the obviously present psychological problems; it could be taken as simply a detail by a carefully realistic writer. In *Dubliners,* the allusion is made more exact because the necessity is not to show some cosmic mourning in mediaeval style but to point out that the narrator has suddenly discovered that Flynn's death is not entirely displeasing to him. Flynn had laid claim to his soul in order to initiate it into dark sources of power, but now his disappearance has allowed it to return into the light—although he has left in the soul certain traces of something unknown, which will be more clearly revealed in dreams.

The death takes place at night, as foreseen; the narrator hardly dares believe in it. Joyce brings into play the mechanisms of belief and faith, or rather of conviction and belief, in order to emphasise the hold that the master of language has over the child's mind. The boy has received information, sometimes amounting to education, from two rival masters, who in reality were making use of him as the object of their disagreement. Old Cotter, the distiller, dislikes Father Flynn, probably on account of some matter of Dublin morality never fully explained, which he expresses solely by the vague disapproval which annoys the narrator so much: "No, I wouldn't say he was exactly . . . but there was something queer . . . there was something uncanny about him. I'll tell you my opinion. . . ."

Cotter announces the priest's death, indirectly, and by the simple use of the past tense; it is a calculated effect. The boy at once meets it with a silent resistance, which is already the prototype of Stephen Dedalus' cunning silence: "Old Cotter looked at me for a while. I felt that his little beady black eyes were examining me, but I would not satisfy them by looking up from my plate. He returned to his pipe and finally spat rudely into the grate."

"I wouldn't like children of mine," he said, "to have too much to say to a man like that".

Cotter doubtless felt rather annoyed to see that his former admirer was now bored by him, and this would explain his increased opposition to the Magus Flynn; he brings the news of his death on purpose to see the effect it will have on the apprentice, what his face will betray of his feelings. While the child gorges himself on stirabout and refuses to let Cotter's "little beady black eyes" have any effect on him, Cotter and the uncle discuss the absent corpse in detail. Old Cotter has "his own theory" to the extent that it was "one of those . . . peculiar cases," but he will not expound his theory before the child. The difference between Flynn and Cotter is that while Flynn did not hesitate to communicate the most important and difficult secrets to the child, Cotter always stops halfway through a word, excluding the child from the world of knowledge and power. His theory begins with the statement, "I wouldn't like children of mine to have too much to say to a man like that," and continues with "it's bad for children". It is clear that he suspects Flynn of saying things which are bad for children to hear and know.

The uncle approves of his argument; he says that he is always telling his "Rosicrucian" nephew to take exercise and daily cold baths. The joke has a wider application than the uncle realises, with its teasing allusion to Rosicrucianism adding to the general impression of blasphemy and the occult. No-one explains anything to the child; he stands in front of mystery, frustrated and angry, examining the distiller's words to see if he can find the formula which must be hidden in his unfinished sentences and in his silences. The boy's dreams are also additions to the original text; they represent the beginning of a new use of dreams—more symbolic and hallucinatory than psychological—which for Joyce was connected with the sense of "being separate" which the waking mind feels, and with the waking dreams of travel and departure and the sleeping dreams of prophecy. They are a way of revelation by images.

At night the priest's head appears to him, and the child hides under the bedclothes (an attitude in which we later find Stephen too) and tries to exorcise it by thinking about Christmas. But the head pursues the child under the bedclothes, further even than into the imagination, into the realms of solitary vice. The master is no longer there; "he's gone to a better world," as his sisters say, and left behind only his dead body, a grotesque, soulless object handled and moved about by the sisters.

The child learns in detail what they have done to him, and the women agree that he "makes such a beautiful corpse". He has become simply "poor James," an object belonging completely to those whom he used to despise, the sisters, with their smug satisfaction at their own charitable works: "we done all we could . . . we wouldn't see him want". They too are quite relieved now that he has "gone". Eliza sighs, "Ah, poor James!"

> She stopped, as if she were communing with the past, and then said shrewdly:
> "Mind you, I noticed there was something queer coming over him latterly. Whenever I'd bring his soup in to him there, I'd find him with his breviary fallen to the floor, lying back in the chair and his mouth open".

They sip their sherry in silence, in a toast to death past and present, and the sherry loosens their tongues. They make their communion, as the gossip verges on confidential matters, and at last the child is slightly, though sinisterly, illuminated by the strange words in which they denounce James's wrongdoing. The old chapel is heavy with silence and the apocalypse is near; first come the evil omens, the holy book profaned, the mouth gaping open as though emptied of the holy word.

" 'He was too scrupulous always,' she said. 'The duties of the priesthood was too much for him. And then his life was, you might say, crossed.' 'Yes,' said my aunt. 'He was a disappointed man. You could see that.' "

The victim is transformed into a criminal; he committed a sin and his paralysis was the punishment for it. Father Flynn was "a disappointed man" and the magic would not work for him, or rather it turned out to be maleficent.

> The grey face still followed me. It murmured; and I understood that it desired to confess something. I felt my soul receding into some pleasant and vicious region; and there again I found it waiting for me. It began to confess to me in a murmuring voice and I wondered why it smiled continually and why the lips were so moist with spittle.

The head is a witness, an accomplice, a whisperer with wet lips; the child at last guesses from it that he has been taught something more or something other than the mysteries of the Church; he is followed by the head for having let himself be used by Father Flynn. No-one will ever know what the smiling head confessed, because the secret of the confessional is kept. But the world of mystery has been entered by the dark portal of dreams under the bedclothes, and in this world of uncertain boundaries people become things; the child encounters an evil object, the head which is an "it," murmuring low and sinister things. The secret of old Cotter's silences is explained; Cotter still lives in a world in which one *does not say* harmful, secret things out loud, and he avoids spreading possible contagion by the spoken word. Flynn's compulsive confession is contrasted with the prudent allusiveness of his profane rival.

> As I walked along in the sun I remembered old Cotter's words and tried to remember what had happened afterwards in the dream. I remembered that I had noticed long velvet curtains and a swinging lamp of antique fashion. I felt that I had been very far away, in some land where the customs were strange—in Persia, I thought. . . . But I could not remember the end of my dream.

The child is not guilty, although he knows himself to be the accomplice of some magic that ends he knows not how. Flynn has spirited him away to Persia in the night to hear unimaginable tales. Cotter has not expounded his theory, and the child has not been able to finish his dream—or else he has done so, but has forgotten what he did in Persia with Flynn, who had all the answers, but who is dead, and the answers with him. Henceforth the child will have to extract the hidden meanings by himself. "It was that chalice he broke. . . . That was the beginning of it. Of course, they say it was all right, that it contained nothing, I mean. But still. . . . Poor James was so nervous, God be merciful to him!"

An empty object is "not important"; but perhaps its very absence of contents is in itself a sign, perhaps its breaking was the concrete symbol of a more serious break, perhaps the magus-priest had discovered the secret that God did not exist. Since breaking the chalice, he lives alone in his confessional, waiting for death to come and paralyse his body, for his soul has already been killed. In the darkness, he waits for his confessional to turn into his coffin, he waits with his eyes wide open, mocking himself and confessing to himself his secret sin. Father Flynn is too scrupulous to communicate it to anyone else; he is also slightly mad. "There he was, sitting up by himself in the dark in his confession-box, wide-awake and laughing-like softly to himself." There is something diabolical here, perhaps the smile of the "maleficent being" that possessed him. The confession becomes an initiation as soon as, in the dream, the child responds, gradually letting himself be seduced, listening, and eventually also smiling.

Beside the coffin, he suddenly fancies that the old priest is smiling, "but no. . . . I saw that he was not smiling. There he lay, solemn and copious, vested as for the altar, his large hands loosely retaining a chalice". In the first version, the dead priest is holding a rosary in his hands,[6] and in the intermediary version his hands "loosely retain a cross". In the *Dubliners* version, a chalice has been put between his hands, and this is yet another grotesque sign of spiritual absence on the part of the sisters: they seem to have deliberately chosen this sinister object, as though they had to turn the drama into macabre farce. While Eliza is reporting on the scandalous nature of her brother's madness—"and what do you think but there he was . . ."—the maleficent presence insinuates itself among them: "She stopped suddenly as if to listen. I too listened; but there was no sound in the house: and I knew that the old priest was lying still in his coffin as we had seen him, solemn and truculent in death, an idle chalice on his breast".

"An idle chalice" seems to close with an echo the whole pattern of symbols that were empty; the words of the priest had been as vain and powerless as his idle chalice, signifying spiritual death and vanity.

Joyce would not have been capable of giving his own name to a priest without some ironical purpose. This unfortunate James had ventured upon a great enterprise, and had failed, but Joyce was not to be disappointed. The duties of the Artist towards the Eucharist were not too heavy for him to bear. In art there are answers to the questions. The child would not drop the chalice full of the Holy Blood, the Word full of its Meaning, precisely because it *was* full; the creative Word is never thought of as being powerless or absent. The empty chalices, the prayers to One who is Absent, are those that bring death, because no-one is there to make any response, but the chalice of James Joyce is like the horn of plenty, the inexhaustible, full Word, and the Word is an unalterable eucharist because in Joyce's world words make alliances with each other and not with Someone Else. In reality there is no silence: the word that speaks to mankind of reality cannot die, but must be always heard and understood.

The writer is never alone, and the book is neither a coffin nor a confessional. Nor is it in the exotic Orient that he is to make his discoveries, but in the ordinary matter of everyday life; this is where he is to make his voyages of revelation, as Stephen Dedalus does. The artist is to seek Araby within himself, and this is the implied conclusion of the novella; it is echoed by 'Araby,' the story of an evening's failure. Its hero is the same angry small boy, who lives in the house of a recently deceased priest with his aunt and uncle; a "confused adoration" for the

[6]Magalaner, *op. cit.*, p. 85.

sister of his friend Mangan turns him into a courtly lover, and for her sake all the street noises and the sounds of the market—the vulgar and harsh voices of "drunken men and bargaining women"—converge "in a single sensation of life: I imagined that I bore my chalice safely through a throng of foes". Her name brings to his lips strange prayers and praises which he does not himself understand. For her sake he decides to go to the bazaar "Araby," whose name "called to me through the silence in which my soul luxuriated and cast an Eastern enchantment over me".

With an amused care for details, Joyce transposes the setting of 'The Sisters' into North Richmond Street, and the quest begins again on a more romantic level; there is even a very un-Edenic apple tree in the garden, and near it, under a bush, a rusty bicycle-pump, which recalls the motif of "pneumatic wheels" in 'The Sisters,' and is destined to be turned into an emblem for A. E.'s spiritualist interests in *Ulysses*. The Eastern enchantment recurs, but leads this time to a desert Araby which has lost its charms, guarded by two great urns that are heavy with "a silence like that which pervades a church after a service".

The Initiator, Master of Fearful Mysteries

The model of the master who initiates into mystery and simony appears in its first guise, rather crudely, in an epiphany (no. 22 in the Buffalo MS.), which is later reproduced in *Stephen Hero* (p. 244). Joyce had in fact really encountered the terrifying person who here fascinates the sensitive child during a short visit to Mullingar in July, 1900. The beggar in the epiphany is simply a vulgar bully who exerts an influence, which has nothing to do with his situation, upon the two children whom he addresses.

> In Mullingar: an evening in autumn.
> The Lame Beggar—(gripping his stick) It was you called out after me yesterday.
> The Two Children—(gazing at him) No, sir.
> The Lame Beggar—O, yes it was, though . . . (moving his stick up and down) But mind what I'm telling you. . . . D'ye see that stick?
> The Two Children—Yes, sir.
> The Lame Beggar—Well, if ye call out after me any more I'll cut ye open

with that stick, I'll cut the livers out o'ye . . . (explains himself) . . . D'ye hear me? I'll cut ye open. I'll cut the livers and lights out o'ye.

The plain threat, which recalls on a realistic level the epiphany of the eagles, is almost at once complicated by the addition of symbolic characteristics, and the aggressive language is supported by visual signs. Thus the stick to cut out livers, like the beaks that pull out eyes, suggests the image of a torture that is related to both castration and blinding—not in the literal sense of physical violence but as immediately comprehensible metaphors for attempts to curtail the threatened person's autonomy, his freedom to see and to form judgements. Joyce tones down the character's apparent brutality, but portrays him in such a way that his appearance produces an equally strong, but more mysterious, terror. Even when paralysed or disarmed he can terrify by mime, gesture, and a torrent of words which essentially resemble the antics of the devils in Stephen Dedalus' imaginary hell. In fact, without saying so explicitly, Joyce makes his initiators paralysing, "maleficent beings". Through the conversation of the stranger in 'An Encounter' it is possible to guess at the ambiguous nature of Father Flynn's friendship with his disciple. They both maintain a peculiar relationship with language, being either paralytic or wanderer; the master who seems to hold the secrets of power is a sick man or a tramp. If he inspires horror and pity as he intimidates his audience, it is because he is not the master of his own knowledge but rather its slave, apparently fascinated by his own thought. The words are stronger than the person who speaks them, and this state of alienation is perceived at once by the child, who feels obscurely that there is some connection between what is said and the reduced circumstances of the speaker.

'An Encounter,' the novella following 'The Sisters,' turns in centripetal spirals around a person who seems disagreeably familiar, an unknown man whose slow, ceremonious movements remind us of Beckett's slow-moving, solitary old men. This "queer old josser" seems to have many characteristics in common with Father Flynn from the point of view of his appearance, and the obsessive repetition of exterior details creates the impression that they both belong to a kind of secret community; the unpleasant nature of the signs which seem to indicate this suggests that their activities are equally dubious and sinister.

The various people who take it upon themselves to initiate the boy in strange and indirect ways are all characterised by the same symbolic attributes: faded green and grey are the colours of spiritual anomaly, just as browns and yellows stand for dreary, dusty Dublin. These unhealthy souls inhabit unhealthy bodies, whose skin is grey, as Father Dolan was grey. "It may have been these constant showers of snuff which gave his ancient priestly garments their green faded look," thinks Father Flynn's disciple, and the concrete explanation seems valid, although on further reflection one finds its meaning ambiguous. If the snuff does in fact stain and fade the cloth, it is still true that the child attributes this fading and spoiling to excessive and clumsy use of the present he has given to the simoniac. The man in 'An Encounter' is also dressed in this lifeless green.

> He came along by the bank slowly. He walked with one hand upon his hip and in the other hand he held a stick with which he tapped the turf lightly. He was shabbily dressed in a suit of greenish-black and wore what we used to call a jerry hat with a high crown. He seemed to be fairly old, for his moustache was ashen-grey.

The slowness of his movements ("He walked towards us very slowly, always tapping the ground with his stick, so slowly that I thought he was looking for something in the grass"), like Father Flynn's clumsiness with his hands, is a bad sign; these strange beings have a rhythm of life which betrays both a lack of vitality verging on extinction and an absorption in zones of consciousness so far from the surface that they can only emerge with great difficulty to the everyday world. They emerge like sea-monsters rising to the surface in order to grasp their prey and drag it down again to the depths. When they first arise, they have some difficulty in speaking, and a detail both comical and repugnant occurs in both novellas—that of the smile without words which appears when the initiate has made some innocent remark which betraying his igno-rance: "When he smiled he used to uncover his big discoloured teeth and let his tongue lie upon his lower lip—a habit which had made me feel uneasy in the beginning of our acquaintance before I knew him well".

The sight is repellant, but the child grows accustomed to it, after first registering distrust. Joyce is evidently toying with this notion of disgust, because we find that he uses the vision again in 'An Encounter,' this time without the reassuring comment, as "The man, however, only smiled. I saw that he had great gaps in his mouth between his yellow teeth". This remark immediately follows the man's insinuating words that "there were some of Lord Lytton's works which boys couldn't read"; the man is setting himself up as the guardian of forbidden rites or mysteries. What follows now takes place for the boy on two different levels: on the one, he takes note of a series of alarming attitudes and actions on the man's part, for instance, that he shivers several times, and that "he gave the impression that he was repeating something which he had learned by heart or that, magnetized by some words of his own speech, his mind was slowly circling round and round in the same orbit".

He excuses himself for a minute or so and walks to the edge of the field, where he remains for a few moments, doing something odd. The other level on which things happen is that of the monologue, with its varied themes composing a complicated mystery which the boy cannot understand; it fills him with terror until he can manage to break the spell and escape. "Saying that I was obliged to go, I bade him good-day. I went up the slope calmly but my heart was beating quickly with fear that he would seize me by the ankles."

The young narrator of the encounter is prepared, by his temperament and by his education, to listen to the strange old man's revelations; at school, he belongs to a band of "reluctant Indians," who play wild games through fear of seeming over-studious or "lacking in robustness". Like Stephen Dedalus, he is conscious of being superior to his companions, and also like Stephen, he dreams of adventure, travel, and discovery. The themes of the exotic and of liberation are linked with a complementary theme extending the field of the romantic imagination, then abruptly narrowing it again; the boy wanders along the Liffey watching the cargoes being unloaded, vaguely hoping to see any sailors with green eyes, for he has a confused notion that green is the appropriate colour for such adventurers:

> When we landed we watched the discharging of the graceful three-master which we had observed from the other quay. Some bystander said that she was a Norwegian vessel. I went to the stern and tried to decipher the legend upon it but, failing to do so, I came back and examined the foreign sailors to see had any of them green eyes, for I had some confused notion . . .

Because the boat has no name, it remains a part of the world of dreams, and the voyage is impossible. The narrator and his companion, a non-reluctant Red Indian, imagine what it would be like to run away to sea, and then return into the reality of Dublin and its filthy streets again. Adventure awaits them not on the high seas, but in the person of a fairly old man with an ashen-grey moustache who first subjects them to interrogation, as Father Flynn used to do, in order to sound out the intelligence and cultural standing of his audience:

He asked us whether we had read the poetry of Thomas Moore or the
works of Sir Walter Scott and Lord Lytton. I pretended that I had read
every book he mentioned, so that in the end he said:
"Ah, I can see that you are a bookworm like myself. Now," he added,
pointing to Mahony, who was regarding us with open eyes, "he is different;
he goes in for games."
He said he had all Sir Walter Scott's works and all Lord Lytton's works
at home and never tired of reading them.

This might be merely the banal, friendly interest taken by an adult
in talking to children, but it opposes reading to sport, and again puts the
narrator on the side of words rather than of action. He finds that the
unknown man considers him as an equal, or at least as someone with
intelligence and inclinations similar to his own, and he tries to take
advantage of this; wishing to be one of those who know, he is ready to
betray Mahony the player of games, "because I was afraid the man
would think I was as stupid as Mahony". Thus, by the indirect means
of the cult of the intelligence, he concludes a tacit and mysterious pact
with the unknown; and once he is thus guilty through pride the unknown can get him into its clutches, drawing him on towards more
profane and esoteric considerations. The stranger turns to the subject
of love, speaking "as if he were telling us something secret which he did
not wish others to overhear". He talks about the nice soft hair and the
soft white hands of girls, and the narrator is disturbed because he thinks
of girls in much the same way and his sensual imagination coincides so
nearly with the old man's. It was noble to be his accomplice in matters
of culture, but to be so closely associated with him in these forbidden
dreams is troubling; the boy feels paralysed by this complicity and falls
silent, keeping his eyes lowered as if to avoid some hypnotism or enchantment, making use of the same tactical resources as Stephen—
refusal, silence, and cunning. When Mahony, who has been watching
the stranger's abnormal behaviour, exclaims, "I say! Look what he's
doing!" the narrator reacts by proposing a magical means of escape,
namely that of disguise: "In case he asks us for our names, let you be
Murphy and I'll be Smith". This instinctive camouflage, the invention
of a false identity, is an implicit admission of the awed fear which
reaches its height after another speech by the man, this time on a
subject stranger than the beauty of girls. The boy involuntarily looks up
at the man, who has transferred the concept of adventure into the zone
of homosexual sadism, where the child cannot follow him. "I. . . . involuntarily glanced at his face. As I did so I met the gaze of a pair of

bottle-green eyes peering at me from under a twitching forehead. I turned my eyes away again."

Thus the adventure ends, with the vision in a field near Dublin of those green eyes that should have promised adventure, escape, and freedom. Books, the beauty of girls, and freedom of desire are all sharply transposed from the intoxicating world of the narrator's dream-explorations into the morbid emptiness where Stephen is later to confront the demons of his own lusts. For the narrator, it is as though his original guilt, his decision to play truant from school in order to realise his dreams, had predestined him to this encounter with perversity. His awareness of having done wrong begins to confuse his sense of values, so that reading becomes equated with the pleasures of the flesh, both being performed in secret, far from the world of school.

A symbolic interpretation of these first two novellas would see these incidents as encounters of the apprentice intellectual with the spirit of simony, taking place in magic settings in which both art and religion are, in their oral and literal manifestations, held up to mockery. The *wrong* use of the spirit, of the sacred word, of the imagination's power, is concealed beneath the actual words, is insinuated between the really spoken word and the message implied, poisoning silence with its hellish breath; it follows one into one's hiding-place, even under the bed-clothes, while in an atmosphere of foulness the master sorcerer lures his pupil on to share a secret shame, and even if the apprentice resists the temptation to self-destruction, he does not escape scot-free. He is very near to letting himself be taken over as soon as the temptations begin; only Flynn's death frees him, in 'The Sisters,' and in 'An Encounter' he owes his safety to his turn of speed and to the presence of Murphy-Mahony. He almost gave the necessary response, and he left his name behind like the hero of a fairy-tale, because at this stage the narrator is not yet armed; subsequent encounters will cause him to begin evolving a system of defence, however, and the successor to the child of *Dubliners,* who is the artist of the *Portrait,* will turn more and more resolutely away from evil teaching, replacing the feelings of uneasy complicity by distrust, and then gradually by open aversion.

The presence of the masters whose task it is to initiate Stephen is less explicitly oppressive; their power is not so great as that of the earlier masters, but the path of the conscience between curiosity and guilt is the same.

Joyce brings about the initiation of the schoolboy in *Portrait* through a series of confrontations with the Enemy, of the green eyes or impure soul, which take place in identical conditions; it will be noticed that Flynn makes a ghostly reappearance in Stephen's life, as trainer and misleader, and that his relations with his disciple are still the same, except for a superficial modification which Joyce skilfully turns into a source of comedy, or rather of a shadow of comedy. The worried child who appears in the first stories of *Dubliners*, whose real name we do not know because he says "I" and calls himself "Smith," is simply the first incarnation of the artist in the process of formation.

Father Flynn is reincarnated in Chapter II of the *Portrait*, in the person of Uncle Charles. The critics have been puzzled by this strange old man who smokes his "villainous awful tobacco" at the beginning of the chapter in which the artist passes from troubled but romantic child-hood to an intoxicated adolescence where the flesh takes over from the word. Uncle Charles smokes his tobacco on the first day of that division of time that ends for Stephen in the arms of a young woman with a gay, grave face. Father Flynn has changed only his name, and now presides over his pupil Stephen as he sows his wild oats. Everything begins again, with hallucinatory similarity; Uncle Charles goes for his morning smoke to a shed at the bottom of the garden, with the same passionate devo-tion as the priest had gone towards his only remaining pleasure, prayer. The old man goes out to his shed as though to church, with hair carefully brushed and wearing his tall hat. He celebrates the office in his own fashion in the shed, which is both his chapel and his "sounding-box"; "every morning he hummed contentedly one of his favourite songs: *O, twine me a bower* or *Blue Eyes and Golden Hair*," while the blue and gold of Our Lady or the gold of Eileen's hair fill his nephew's mind.
Uncles Charles feeds his nephew:

> He would seize a handful of grapes and sawdust or three or four Ameri-can apples and thrust them generously into his grandnephew's hand.
> . . . On Stephen's feigning reluctance to take them, he would frown and say:
> —Take them, sir. Do you hear me, sir? They're good for your bowels.
> (*Portrait*, p. 61)

We have here a quasi-comical transposition of the friendship between the paralysed priest and his young friend; the uncle feeds the body as the priest feeds the soul. The uncle has a double, who is the ghost of Father Flynn, of the lame beggar of the epiphany, and of the unknown man of 'An Encounter'; he is an old friend of Stephen's father named

Mike Flynn. He too takes care of his pupil's body. Stephen is thus the disciple of two masters—or rather of one master with a double identity, Charles-Mike Flynn. As though by sheer chance, Flynn the trainer is an athlete who is no longer able to run: "When the morning practice was over the trainer would make his comments and sometimes illustrate them by shuffling along for a yard or so comically in an old pair of blue canvas shoes" (*Portrait*, p. 61).

He is as helpless as his predecessors, he too having the dull gaze of one whose life has been a failure:

> Stephen often glanced at his trainer's flabby stubble-covered face, as it bent over the long stained fingers through which he rolled his cigarette, and with pity at the mild lustreless blue eyes which would look up suddenly from the task and gaze vaguely into the blue distance while the long swollen fingers ceased their rolling and grains and fibres of tobacco fell back into the pouch. *(Ibid.)*

Mike and Charles share between them the attributes and heritage of the Reverend father, one of them dropping fibres of tobacco as Flynn dropped snuff when his hands no longer obeyed him, the other having inherited the red handkerchief and the deprecatory manner. "Perhaps he prayed for the souls in purgatory or for the grace of a happy death or perhaps he prayed that God might send him back a part of the big fortune he had squandered in Cork" (*Portrait*, p. 62). What Mike and Charles indirectly teach the boy is equally mysterious, and concerns the sources of the adult world's power: they discuss sport and politics, Ireland and Munster. Stephen, like the boy in 'The Sisters,' listens avidly, believing himself to be preparing for some kind of mission in "that world". "The hour when he too would take part in the life of that world seemed drawing near and in secret he began to make ready for the great part which he felt awaited him the nature of which he only dimly apprehended."

This "great part" seems reminiscent of Father Flynn's "great wish" for the boy. The child is still blindly serving his masters' purposes, but not for long. In fact, while the hour is "drawing near," for what he believes to be his destined *re-entry* into the world, he is already unconsciously preparing his hasty departure: "his evenings were his own". After the day's lessons at school, Stephen is his own master, and the teaching he gives himself is in effect a sort of counterpoison; he opposes the handful of grapes and sawdust which his uncle gives him to the muscatels on their "sunny trellises" outside the white house where

Mercedes lives; and if at the end of his heroic romantic dream he refuses
the grapes she offers him, this is because the Avenging Monte-Cristo-
Stephen has already been to the end of the book and knows all the
adventures. He has realised that the long-awaited "hour" is merely a
trap; he has learned from the gallant count that Mercedes is in league
with his enemy, society, and that the attraction she possesses as rose-
protected-by-whitewashed-walls is simply a baited trap disguised by a
refusal. Mercedes is a sister of the gentle, sweet E. C.

The Shaping of the Young Artist's Consciousness

The methods of initiation determine the form of the initiate's responses:
at Mullingar in 1900 the lame beggar hobbles on the scene with his
threatening stick to spread violence and sadism in Joyce's world. He is
to be found in *Stephen Hero* as he was in reality; but Stephen's reaction
("The recollection of the beggar's sharp eyes struck a fine chord of
terror in the youth," *Stephen Hero*, p. 246) is less simply motivated than
it seems. His terror is both a natural reaction of self-preservation and
a source of extreme disquiet, for the child or young man is not frightened merely by the threat or the blow, but in particular by the Beggar's
look and by what he reads in that look. Stephen Hero explains that he
had never seen so malevolent a look; it transmitted a greedy, evil
power, and the eyes flashed a message of death, as though the anonymous individual before him wanted not only to exercise vengeance in
the shape of physical violence, but also to subdue his soul. Fear "strikes
a fine chord" from Stephen's sensibilities, as it were from the vocal
cords of his conscience. The threat of those eyes calls forth a response
which at once animates a whole pattern of intellectual reflexes, the
expression of which is the beginning of the work. The hostility of real
life sets the creative process in motion.
      This phenomenon is of capital importance in the ontology of Joyce's
work: the first motive behind the necessity to write and to be an artist
is not purely the manifestation of a desire to create for the sake of
creating and thereby to experience a divine feeling of omnipotence,
but, on the contrary, the creative impulse is caused by a painful encounter with real life, illustrating the hostility of life and its intentions of
altering the hero's subjective nature. This is why Joyce's art begins with
the *Nego* of the 1904 *Portrait;* this negative beginning sets up the

creator as anti-self of the supreme Creator. The young man responds to aggression by defiant challenge. What he is to construct will have its roots in an already extant construction, but one which had automatically and a priori excluded him as autonomous individual. The creative act, at first defensive, becomes offensive later, since it is not sufficient simply to have repelled the aggressor; and fear becomes a desirable possession because it excites the rebellious imagination. Hence, the artist finds it necessary to arouse and provoke the aggression against which he is to write.

The consequences of this basic attitude are felt at the level at which the aesthetic vocation is determined as well as at the level where that vocation is consecrated into technical terms; the choice of the forms and instruments for creation, the choice of one's direction, are gradually accompanied by a strategic procedure of recovery. "The others" had wished to prevent him from speaking, and so he had beaten a retreat into silence, so that his thought, by refusing to manifest itself in the outside world, might offer them no opportunity to seize or condemn it. Behind that silence, with only the speech of the enemy echoing there, the artist confers with himself, making his own laws and working out a plan for reconquest in this war about words.

Guilt is redeemed after the twofold discovery that while the innocent is unjustly punished the punishment is in fact deserved on a secret level of the personality where, often unknown to the aggressors, a forbidden activity is taking place which leads to the "solitary vice" of writing. The child's response to accusations and threats had been fear and flight, but the young man finally finds the weapon which will allow him to offer some opposition to the adversaries; he learns how to handle this weapon in the hostile world—in order to turn it against those who taught him its use. Morally, this weapon is his awareness of transgression, which he turns into deliberate transgression, and concretely it is his writing or else the pen, the instrument of writing. Joyce has a tendency to situate intellectual or spiritual conflicts in the outside world by representing them objectively in scenes which sometimes resemble pantomime, in which actual objects are used to symbolise the complex adoption of an attitude. Thus the pen, both literally and metaphorically, is the weapon of the writer-to-be. It is made abstract before being made concrete. Contrariwise, the real girl is transformed, first into the image of a girl and secondly into a word that is evocative of her, for the purposes of creation. In real life, writing and the girl are incompatible, for while the former manifests the need for spiritual autonomy felt by the person who wishes to write, the latter marks him out for the perilous attention of the eagles and of all their human substitutes, priests, parents, and social imperatives.

In the situation of the artist of the *Portrait*, growing up as he does in Catholic Ireland, to choose writing means to choose a solitude in which it is the purpose of art to replace all absent humanity, including the girl. In other words, solitary dreaming and writing poems in one's room provides a satisfaction which is equivalent to that of masturbation on the sexual level, and this form of individualism is accompanied by feelings of unambiguous shame. This is the explanation of the self-styled Smith's feelings, when he senses that the sadistic homosexual has found him out, and when he is led into strange pleasures by the shade of Father Flynn. It also explains the ambiguity of the warning signal that sounds in Stephen's mind after meeting the lame beggar; it becomes clear that he is not merely impressed by the man's peculiar appearance, but that he also painfully "recognises" the other, with an obscure and nauseating feeling that he also resembles him.

When the two boys in *Dubliners* meet the strange man, Mahony says "he's a queer old josser!" and watches him, because he does not understand the situation, because the old man is completely different from him; the narrator, fascinated and horrified, does not raise his eyes, because he knows without having to look, and is discovering with fear that he and this disturbing person have something in common. Similarly, in 'The Sisters,' the child meets the heavy grey face of the paralytic in the darkened zone where the fraudulent soul wanders, and under the blankets, drawn round him like the curtains of the confessional, he receives the phantom's secrets, as it murmurs them softly; then a feeble smile spreads over his face too, "as if to absolve the simoniac of his sin". In the mirror-situation of the dream, under the heavy hangings of debauchery, confessor and penitent make their communion in a shared smile, a shared complicity in sin. The apprentice confessor recognises the image of his own erotic dreams in the simoniac's fantasies, in his ghostly appearance.

In *Portrait*, Stephen's dreams of terror are more precise. After Boyle and Moonan have been caught "smugging," for which they must receive a flogging, Stephen indulges in masochistic imagining of the actual punishment, and it is noteworthy that he is more deeply excited by the idea of the beating than by the thought of the crime itself. But his dream-meditation on Gleeson, his soft white hands and his cane, is rudely interrupted by the only too real ferula of Father Dolan, who cares little for any considerations of aesthetic appreciation of sounds.

The pain is too strong and too humiliating for any sublimation of sensations to occur. If masochistic romanticism almost inspired the boy to homosexual exaltation, the ferula destroys all such impulses before they can develop further. "A hot burning tingling stinging blow like the loud crack of a broken stick made his trembling hand crumple together like a leaf in the fire" (*Portrait*, p. 50).

Stephen's first experience of sado-masochism occurs while he is still struggling with the confusions of childhood. He soon leaves behind him the possibility of flamboyant perversity, and by his escape he shows his refusal to form part of any masochistic relationship; he leaves this to be inherited by Bloom in *Ulysses*. In fact, from the moment of his encounter with those "no-coloured eyes," Stephen has already made his refusal, and like a little Bruno of Nola passing through the flames has refused to let bodily pain force a prayer from his lips. Now he is safe, his spirit unbroken, and what Father Dolan has taught him is not the secret and perverse joy of masochism but rather a rebellious hatred for all injustice and sadism.

> But it was unfair and cruel. The prefect of studies was a priest but that was cruel and unfair. And his white-grey face and the no-coloured eyes behind the steel-rimmed spectacles were cruel looking because he had steadied the hand first with his firm soft fingers and that was to hit it better and louder. (*Portrait*, p. 52)

This time, the eagles nearly did pull out his eyes, for Stephen was afraid: he shut his eyes as the ferula was raised, and he heard the swish of the soutane sleeve. His eyes were "scalded with tears," but he "held back the cry that scalded his throat". The metaphor of blinding is moderated, but the injustice is the same; the ferula is soon to be succeeded by Vincent Heron's walking-stick, punishing Stephen under the pretext that he has been concealing a love-affair under a show of virtuous behaviour. Again the stick is brandished at the conclusion of a series of experiences which link his secret thoughts, desires, and troubles of the flesh closely to the clear ideas of his developing aesthetic.

If the heretic refuses to catch the girl, despite her coquettish provocations, it is because he is on the contrary choosing to involve himself in the world of freedom of thought, and his response to repression is creation. "She" may run away from him, but he keeps in his imagination the memory of her disturbing presence, and from it grows the work of art.

Thus art is considered from the beginning as an expression of resistance to the world. The sense of the forbidden is at the root of that inspiration which gradually confers on the "unsubstantial image" the sense of his soul constantly beholding a form closer to reality; similarly, his anger—caused by "the change of fortune which was reshaping the world about him into a vision of squalor and insincerity"—makes him wander restlessly along the quays of Dublin, where the movement, the bales of merchandise, and the ships being loaded suggest to him "vastness and strangeness," the beauty of "the bright sky and the sun-warmed trellises of the wineshops". His mind exercised by bitter thoughts, his wanderings are but the concrete form of the wanderings his soul takes in its search for something unknown but ardently awaited, something or someone that must come, sooner or later. Yet there are still familiar and accessible objects; thus the voice within him asks whether he will stretch out his hand to accept the living gift offered to him in the person of a charming girl. It would be possible to catch hold of her; nobody is looking. He could kiss her without running any risk. But he does neither, as though her presence were too disquietingly real, as though his desire did not wish to be satisfied, but wished rather to continue desiring, stimulated by the fear that someone might be looking.

What he wants is the impossible, the absent image or woman, because in this quest what matters is not so much the object sought and dreamed of, but the changes the young man undergoes and the interesting emotions aroused in his soul by the search. In a short scene, following that of Stephen's temptation on the steps of the tram, Joyce finally describes the first creative act of the artist-to-be, with very slight irony veiling the symbolic importance of the moment. Every detail has its place in a vast process which is to become archetypal:

> The next day he sat at his table in the bare upper room for many hours. Before him lay a new pen, a new bottle of ink and a new emerald exercise. From force of habit he had written at the top of the first page the initial letters of the jesuit motto: A.M.D.G. On the first line of the page appeared the title of the verses he was trying to write: To E——C——." (*Portrait*, p. 70)

Everything is new, as though the author intended that the world and the artist's soul should be in communion for the moment prior to genesis; and the room's emptiness is reminiscent of the setting of the retreat, which was also designed to take part in his waiting. The exercise book is emerald green, the colour symbolising dynamic creation in *Portrait*, the same colour as the hieroglyph of seaweed on the thigh of the girl on the beach who appears to him as "an envoy from the fair courts of life," and the same colour as the *Tabula Smaragdina*, attributed to the Egyptian god Hermes-Thoth, the inventor of writing, who appears to Stephen to confirm and consecrate him in his artistic vocation. But even as Thoth is invoked here, the world of reality is still present, and will not forgo its prey; neither will the God of the Jesuits so easily let his creature free. "From force of habit" Stephen writes down the A.M.D.G. which consecrates whatever is written to the glory of God, and naïvely writes underneath the sacred dedication the profane dedication "To E—— C——," because "he knew it was right to begin so for he had seen similar titles in the collected poems of Lord Byron." Thus Byron, as Stephen's spiritual ally, presides over his entry into literature as he had over the boy's first steps in heresy.

There are three stages to the creative process, and their nature is already very informative about the artist's character: first, he lets himself drift away into a revery in which all concrete details disappear because they are "common and insignificant"; the tram, the horses, Stephen and the girl all disappear and are replaced by the impression left by his emotions. In this romantic evocation everything is vague; Stephen's technique is far removed from Joyce's realism and fairly near to decadent symbolism, expressing the passive sweetness of a delicate masochism. "Some undefined sorrow was hidden in the hearts of the protagonists as they stood in silence beneath the leafless trees and when the moment of farewell had come the kiss, which had been withheld by one, was given by both" (*Portrait*, p. 71). At this stage of the artist's development, art still expresses itself, as Joyce amusedly emphasises, through the insipid romanticism of the *fin-de-siècle*. The helpless melancholy, the disembodied love, and the purple style all connect the youthful Stephen with the decadent contemporary English writers; the voice of Walter Pater sounds throughout the young poet's imagination, and it seems to be his idea of the intensity of "some passionate humour, intuition or idea," concentrated in one single instant that leads Stephen on his search for emotions to formulate the epiphany. He shares with the symbolists of his time—with Arthur Symons, and even with Hopkins—his feeling of the inconstancy of real objects, whose only permanence is due to their fixation in language.

At Stephen's age, Joyce probably felt in much the same way, as we can gather from a veiled allusion, in Stanislaus' *Dublin Diary*, to the conclusion of Pater's book, *The Renaissance*: "Jim says that his ambition in life is to burn with a hard gem-like flame". Jim said this, no doubt,

without pointing out that this pleasing expression was taken from Pater's "To burn always with this hard gem-like flame is success in Life".
Similarly, the first commandment of the Epicurean gospel, "Be perfect
in regard to what is here and now" (*Marius*, ch. IX), is repeated on the
beach of Sandymount in *Ulysses*.

The piece written for E. C. is typical of that "luminous silent stasis"
which, according to Stephen, Galvani called "the enchantment of the
heart" and Shelley likened to a fading coal (*Portrait*, p. 213). The page
may be read as an episode of a *Bildungsroman*, as the description of one
instant of the years of apprenticeship, in which the artist-to-be is shown
at the precious moment of transmuting the real into poetry; he is caught
in the very act of systematically destroying reality, and, as J. J. Mayoux
describes it, with relation to the liberation of imagination and language
in the mind of the young rebel,

> at this moment there is put into operation a new dispensation in which
> the narrator-self, the artist's present incarnation, moves off on his own
> orbit, and, losing contact without apparently being aware of so doing,
> proceeds without any outside support or foundation in reality. The author
> suggests and points out this abolition of frontiers by suppressing transitions
> and signals when his hero takes flight, suspending his contact with the
> perceptible world and passing into the state of dream.[7]

Everything happens on the very edge of consciousness, on the margin
of the exercise book, in the space left for dialectical criticism. Stephen
is not yet lucid enough to be master of his own identity; his passions are
those of an adult, but his actions are still a child's. God, whom he invokes
on the written page, is on the point of extinguishing his inspiration, for
if God is present, then once again Stephen is prevented from embracing
E. without shame or hindrance. What Stephen wants is to capture E.
in the lawless world of the imagination. "Nobody is looking," he thought
to himself, as she made his heart dance "like a cork upon a tide," but
someone had been looking, and that look had been enough to stop him
from catching hold of her and kissing her. That someone was the sceptic, half-paralysed self of the Jesuits' pupil, and in the tram he had
simply been prudent and unhappy, not a poet.

Now that he is alone, "nobody is looking" except his own secret,
unalienated self, which is still growing but already on the threshold of
mastery, not the pupil self but the artist self who writes "To E—— C
——" under the "A.M.D.G." like a challenge; it is he who wishes to

[7]Mayoux, *Joyce*, p. 75.

grasp "the beauty that has not yet come into the world," for that beauty has not yet fallen into the clutches of the guardian-God, is not subject to conventional morality, and is not liable to say after having tempted him, "O . . . you're . . . very . . . wick . . . ed"; it is the beauty that can be apprehended in silence.

This diagrammatic passage which represents an important moment in the young man's development, a complete moment which can be detached from the whole, can only be grasped in its singularity, appearing thus as an exemplary experience, appropriate for the illustration of a number of traditional themes such as those of alienation, the feeling of loneliness, the quest for literary form, the transmutation of emotions, and the process of creation through reminiscence. One then sees Stephen as a version of Wordsworth rather than of Byron. But in fact, if this incident is not an isolated one (and it is only circumstantially autonomous), then it can be interpreted as being lived on two different time-scales, the time-scale of reality and that of dream.

In reality, it concerns a piece of writing inspired by a young man's wilful failure to make contact with a young woman, after a banal episode of adolescent shyness. In the imaginary time-scale, it is nothing less than the reproduction by life of the first act in the book of the artist, for in *Portrait* a double growth takes place, developing parallel and reciprocally. The consciousness develops and watches itself develop, following the pattern of spontaneous growth, and at the same time is constantly being modified by encounters with a reality which is at first presented as the mysterious "road" along which the self travels in search of the image of itself—the consciousness expands. Its aim is the realisation of itself in the full maturity which will come when the consciousness is able to comprehend and embrace reality to the highest degree. The world is already there at the first moment, but the "baby tuckoo" can only perceive fragmented aspects of it, is unable to understand or interpret. The figures who are present at this moment are replaced by other, equivalent figures, while "baby tuckoo" changes his name without changing his identity; the successive images of the self which have to be outstripped and surpassed in order to reach the final image are shown in a series of happenings which have their echoes at a higher level of consciousness. Gradually the strange idols grow larger, and hollow, and turn into increasingly complex signs, while reality becomes more elaborate and the self moves about within a network of associations of figures and values, with relation to which it defines its own essence. The original situation is repeated, firstly in such a way that the nascent self might believe it to be definitive; at every step it expects to find itself again threatened, mocked at, and abandoned.

The road goes on, and the self evolves, until the time comes to break the repetition of that first moment and to leave once and for all the time and place of "this moocow"; Stephen turns off, and no longer defines himself as "baby tuckoo," but as an opposed being, a self in search of its own time and place, longing to set itself up in its own personal reality.

And now begins the double kind of time in which his encounter with E. C. takes place: an intermediary time of waiting before the apocalyptic time, when the searching self finds the image of itself into which it wishes to transform itself for eternity, that final realisation of the Artist-Self.

While the reader remains on the time-scale of chronological and psychological evolution, he is already, without knowing it, caught in the "simultaneous time" of Joyce's writing. If Byron appears here, he does so becuse he is awaiting Stephen later on. If E. C. moves up and down, offering and then fleeing, it is because she is the Unattainable, the shining and ephemeral image; Stephen wishes to convince himself that it is only a symbol or at least a bait, hiding the most terrible dangers in its smile and its curls. The emotion aroused by the incident is a premonitory echo of those which are to attack the young man in the episode of the Whitsun play. The same polarisation of attraction and repulsion and the same typical figures recur, tracing out a spiritual pattern which becomes definitively impressed upon the young man's mind. It is as though in the space of loneliness between the newly written page and his mother's mirror Stephen had acted out, like an actor at rehearsal, an imitation or a priori projection of his own destiny before time had brought it into concrete existence.

The real woman allures in order to deceive and disappoint; she plays the game of being a woman without permitting the gesture which would give the game some semblance of reality—a petty and banal deception. The powerful creative emotions Stephen draws from her, as he masks his rebellion with an appearance of timidity, Joyce ironically takes seriously. The creation ends on an act of narcissism. The woman of his dreams is silent and accessible. To write in order to change the world is a way of cheating God by imitating him, a way of criticising the order of his creation and of choosing protective self-love as against his glory. The motto of the Jesuits, nailed down by its four full-stops, is opposed to the vague, floating, mysterious evocation of the woman's name. In the act of writing, both the real woman and the dream woman fade away; only the trace of a kiss remains. The poet embraces himself, and the new pen accomplishes what he had not done, yet always dreamed of doing before—it creates a world with no cow, woman, father, hangman-God, with no trams or taboos, no rails and no noise, no fear, mockery, sin or punishment. In this new world, Stephen is at liberty to go up or down the steps; the ascent from reality to the realisation of the self is to transform the "tranquil watcher of the scene before him" into an actor who leaps forward into ecstasy that carries him far from the theatre and its masks into the world where he can write his own lines and be the author of his life:

> He left the stage quickly and rid himself of his mummery and passed out through the chapel into the college garden. Now that the play was over his nerves cried for some further adventure. He hurried onwards as if to overtake it. (*Portrait*, p. 86)

This whole story of temptation, of noble refusal, and of proud imagining sounds ironical when one considers the disproportionate relationship between the incidents and Stephen's magnificent reactions. This disproportion emphasises both the real and the figurative theatricality.

Basically, the erotic dreaming which persists from childhood to adolescence serves as a pretext for Stephen to make those grandiloquent responses which feed his vanity and console his self-esteem. The true sign of his vocation is to be found in his love and fear of words; the woman is simply a routine temptation, an object of worship, or an excuse. It must not be forgotten that the world Stephen invents is empty, motionless, pale and disembodied, reduced to a vague emotion. Stephen is not Joyce, he has not even the strength of Wilde; he is more like Ernest Dowson. His art, in its hostility towards reality, is an art of escapism and flight; he has not yet reached the concept of exile as critical realism.

She whom Stephen awaits must come to him in the real world; Mercedes is only a puppet in a dream. Yet Stephen seems to have carefully organised obstacles to any real meeting: "He did not know where to seek it or how, but a premonition which led him on told him that this image would, without any overt act of his, encounter him" (*Portrait*, p. 65). It, in fact, must come to him, which in Ireland is impossible. Until the end Stephen stays in his place, waiting for "her" to give herself, and thus dissimulating his own fear of taking. Until he actually leaves, he is haunted by the dream of being transfigured in her sight: "He would fade into something impalpable under her eyes and then in a moment he would be transfigured". (*Ibid.*)

He longs thus to be metamorphosed; but she will never come to the trysting-place. Stephen himself has to go to encounter himself, replacing the girl and materialising the image which his soul had so constantly beheld into the form of artistic inspiration; the artist gives himself poetry and writing in the place of the beloved.

As he bears this image of woman within him, Stephen is several times "transfigured" despite himself, in comic and trivial fashion: one day he is mistaken for "Josephine," and another day his own father denatures him by calling him a "bitch". He retires more and more from the dance; he takes less and less part in the games, and especially the sports, of others. Cowled in the bedclothes, he is safe and sheltered, priest of the enclosed world, imitating both E. C. and the confessor; he invents a substitute world for himself in which everything is replaced by words, of liquid joy and ecstatic flight, all in that *fin-de-siècle* atmosphere that Joyce can counterfeit so well.

The Imagination Inspired by Strange Words

Following up the quest for meanings which had begun in *Dubliners*, the *Portrait* appears largely as a study of the magic or poetic connection between language and reality; Stephen discovers on many levels the creative power of language to modify or define reality, until at last his vocation is revealed as also determining and determined by words and names.

Portrait itself was Joyce's formal reply to society, to a society which was torn in pieces and abandoned to the disorder of history; the book has a logic and continuity, a harmony of parts and whole which makes it a book of order despite the chaotic and fragmented matter from which it is made. Similarly, Stephen's mind responds to the collapse of national and spiritual values which he must unfortunately witness by seeking in himself rather than in the outside world to set up a logical interpretation which may unify the disorder of mental images and of emotions which society or other people have left in his memory. He struggles inwardly to find the general pattern into which he can fit all the disparate scraps of reality, so that he may then find the place that is rightly his. As he begins his quest for the meanings of reality, he finds himself in possession of two different types of element: on the one hand he knows a story that his father told him, and in which he seems himself trapped. Simultaneously, on the other hand he finds himself a prey to sensations and emotions which form a context for the story, yet he cannot grasp the logical connections between his father's text and its context. All his efforts in the first chapter are towards a reconstruction of the world from these disparate pieces; the problem to be answered is "What is the relationship between sense-data and intellectual data?" What part is the child to play in the world at whose centre he stands?

The story of the artist begins like a legend or nursery-tale, as though Joyce wished to set the *Portrait* objectively in the long line of parodies of literary genres, and subjectively, for Stephen's consciousness, in an atmosphere of the marvellous, in which anything may happen (especially metamorphoses, which are to be expected in stories where animals and men rub shoulders). If there is parody, one cannot help thinking that this Portrait of an Artist who is later so often defined in terms of rivalry with God or Jesus begins with a reminiscence of Genesis: the book begins not with an action or an objective presence but with a story written inside another story. This beginning of life by the word is a subtle sign of the artist's promised vocation.

> Once upon a time and a very good time it was there was a moocow coming down along the road and this moocow . . . met a nicens little boy named baby tuckoo. . . .
> His father told him that story: his father looked at him through a glass: he had a hairy face.

The little boy that the cow meets on the road is called "baby tuckoo"; he has not yet achieved the first person, "I," but is the third person here, and then later the generalised second person. Perhaps because the hero of the story has a name borrowed from baby-talk, the child does not hesitate to recognise himself: "He was baby tuckoo. The moocow came down the road where Betty Byrne lived: she sold lemon platt". This little boy has already a multiplicity of meaning.

The identification of the conscious self with "baby tuckoo" takes place in three stages, in an order which is to become archetypal: the awareness of the presence of the father watching him precedes the feeling of being the "baby tuckoo". He is born into his own awareness in this strange situation where his father has put him, small and gentle, standing before the cow on the road. He begins to feel that he is "tuckoo," and that he is now out in the world. (In this world, as previously in the cradle, there is nothing that happens to him.) He is also, like the cuckoo, in someone else's nest, namely, his father's. He passes now, abruptly and without any transition, from the uncompleted story to song, from narrative to words in rhythm. Again, a kind of disfigurement takes place, from "O, the wild rose blossoms" to "O, the green wothe botheth". "He sang that song. That was his song." The first act of baby tuckoo is to begin singing his own song. His personality affirms itself on the aesthetic level by the transformation of the poem someone else teaches him; he makes it his own. This appropriation by deforming or modulating the material is the first act of one who is to be a priest of the imagination, who is to love the canticles and the Mass for their formal beauty.

Then comes the first sexual experience, of warmth, cold, wetness. The mother appears and her first act as mother is to put down a rubber sheet —a gesture characteristic of the good housekeeper anxious to protect the bedclothes, but also a silent reproach to the child.

> When you wet the bed first it is warm then it gets cold. His mother put on the oilsheet. That had the queer smell. His mother had a nicer smell than his father. She played on the piano the sailor's hornpipe for him to dance. He danced:
> Tralala lala,
> Tralala tralaladdy . . .

He sings, dances, and he belongs to a middle-class family for whom the piano is a sign of social status rather than of culture. What matters at this stage is the order of the child's acquisitions, which determines his approach to the world. His discovery of the world begins with the story of baby tuckoo as told by his father. He starts from this tale— guessing that he is the hero of it despite himself—from the context of distress, guilt (he must apologise), and fear (if not, the eagles will come and pull out his eyes), from the presence of people who attract him by some quality they possess (Eileen with the golden hair, Dante with her two brushes, one green and one maroon, his father with his hairy face and his monocle), and tries to grasp the world as a unified and harmonious whole.

His only relatively positive experience at this age is the discovery that language is much more tractable than reality; it is possible to imagine unlimitedly, and by changing the position of the words in a sentence to invent a green rose, to think it fully, while in the world it is impossible to change the place of things or of people because the differences are definitive. Eileen is Protestant and not Catholic; her father and mother are not Stephen's.

To give this brief episode a symbolic interpretation, it seems that, if it is the father who comments on his son's introduction into the world, it is the mother who brings to it the ideas of sin and of sensuality. Sin, wetness, warmth and cold, the queer smell, all make "you" into a child who is ashamed of his body and who is made conscious of this by the occult presence of his mother and of the "queer smell". Yet he will be sensitive also to the mysteries of the senses.

Then there is music, which forms part of the network of mistrust; the mother plays the piano to make the child dance. Later on, and especially in *Ulysses*, it will become clear that music and the piano are methods of sentimental distraction employed by the powers of authority to soothe Ireland's fears and to make her docilely obedient. All the pianos played in Joyce's work are strumming the melancholy music of Ireland's alienation (for instance, in the 'Sirens' chapter), and to it is opposed the inner music that accompanies the "ejaculatory fervours," swoons and trances of the developing soul, and particularly the great cries of deliverance which mark out, as we shall see, the crucial moments of the artist's soul in gestation.

The first narrative and its attendant sensations are fixed by Stephen in his memory and sensibility, forming an immutable kernel of feeling unaffected by time; the present always contains for him some trace of this complex of emotions which the imagination is seeking to interpret. Stephen has no rest until he finally succeeds in making words and meanings coincide in a whole; his intellectual procedure is methodical. Each time that he re-encounters a word or sensation which belonged to that first state, he at once seeks to get it into both the past schema and the pattern which is at that instant in formation. This tension and pursuit of meanings is only resolved at the end of the first chapter, at the end of Stephen's first childhood, when he has understood by painful experience the meanings and laws of the world in which he has been placed.

The next stage of his exploration of reality beyond language is marked out by noises and rhythms, as on the sports field at Clongowes Wood he discovers the noisy, *different* existence of his fellows' bodies. The animal and violent presence of the "rude feet" is only to him a demonstration of his own physical weakness and smallness, and is not exorcised until the triumphant disembodiment of Chapter IV, when, on the beach after the macabre sight of his companions' wet, naked bodies, and their vain cries to him, "the mere sight of that medley of wet nakedness chilled him to the bone". He feels the pleasure of "his mild proud sovereignty," of his "fluid and impersonal mood," and he feels his own eternity shine forth in his strange name Dedalus as he emerges from "the mists of childhood and boyhood". His soul soars above the world and his body becomes a breath "commingled with the element of the spirit".

But at Clongowes he is still far from this soaring flight that brings him into eternal conjunction with the Cretan inventor, and when Nasty Roche says that Stephen Dedalus is a queer name, he falls back defenceless, rejected like an object from that queer world where he feigns to run in order to appear like the others; he must run, he must take part in the games, and all actions are dictated from without. At school he suffers from the disturbing lack of connection he finds between the significant and the signified; it is difficult to see the meaning of this quatrain, which serves for spelling practice:

> Wolsey died in Leicester Abbey
> Where the abbots buried him.
> Canker is a disease of plants,
> Cancer one of animals.

These are "nice sentences," like poetry, but they lead nowhere. What place can they have in the intellectual harmony which Stephen hopes exists beyond the intelligible?

It is not surprising that this whole chapter is written in the form of an indirect inner monologue, alternating, though with no transitions, with a series of sense-data recorded by the subject; his dreams and fantasies on time past and time future are interrupted by the uneasiness of time present, although Stephen only takes a purely detached and mechanical part in the latter.

His isolation is expressed physically by the distance which really separates him from the other pupils, and mentally by the secret meditation which he pursues alone on the nature of things and the hidden power of words. He has formal obstacles to pass such as the problem of the relationships between words like "suck" and "kiss," and the people whom the words affect. All the impressions superimposed on his feverish memory fix themselves upon a totally senseless image which brings with it a further cluster of unpleasant associations, connected with ugly words like "suck"; the memory of the white lavatory basin and the sound the water made make him feel hot and cold by turns. He remembers the taps which gave hot and cold water, "and he could see the names printed on the cocks". These new elements extend the domain of mystery, as the ideas of whiteness, heat and cold, and the names of the taps become associated with the sound of the basin.

Everything is distorted by the fever which fosters these strange feelings and projects them into the enclosed world of Clongowes, with its damp, cold corridors and its lighted gas-jets chirping softly. During the arithmetic lesson his face is first hot ("red"), because he is the champion of the white rose team, whose supremacy is threatened, and then cool and white. Red roses, white roses, and white face make him think of the wild rose on the little green place: "but you could not have a green rose. But perhaps somewhere in the world you could." Thus body and memory, past and present, here and elsewhere, heat and cold, the little song of the gas burning and the sound of the lavatory emptying all weave a network of associations—dominated by the distant figure of the father and by Stephen's own distress and uneasiness. The combative reality of the war of the roses disturbs his dream of beauty and the image of what has never existed, but he continues to accumulate information and to travel on towards the discovery of the meanings hidden behind words.

All strange words bring disorder, brutality, and alienation into this world where Stephen is still groping his way by means of the sense, and all the associated sensations eventually take on a significant form, after long and intense reflection.

"By thinking of things you could understand them": this is the conclusion, formulated like an intellectual law, to which he comes after the meaning of "Tower of Ivory" and "House of Gold" is suddenly revealed to him. The first question had been: "How can a woman be a tower of ivory or a house of gold?"—a question as difficult and important as that about the green rose. Yet it says in the litany of the Virgin that she is truly *Turris eburnea.* For Stephen, the mystery of analogy is made clear by means of a sensory experience, and similarly every metaphor and symbol henceforth will unite the concrete reality and the unreal. Flesh and spirit are made one, as in literary creation, but the revelation, despite its nature, is not a pleasant one, for hardly has Eileen been identified with the words that sing her praises when she escapes from him. And anyhow, she has been forbidden to him.

The excitement caused in the imagination by the sound of words ends on a note of sadness and mourning for lost reality. The loss is involuntary when it concerns Eileen or her replacement, the image of Mercedes in the rose garden, and voluntary when the key word "foetus" drives the young man's imagination down into the hells of his guilty conscience. Soon the process of separation is completed in such a way that beauty and satisfaction are attributed to language alone, while unhappiness, loneliness, and separation are consequences of the original and ever-renewed experience of being driven out of paradise, which is the discovery that beautiful, soft, white things are forbidden.

Driven forth from reality, the imagination invents a world which is at first poor and primitive, but which becomes gradually more and more grandiose, and in it the artist moves towards his meeting—no longer with Mercedes but with the image of Beauty.

After the sailor's hornpipe and the threat of the eagles, music, dance, and religious terror become the attributes of all authority, disguising its hostility, and at first Stephen accepts all this, although fearing it. In Chapter II, the father is replaced by Uncle Charles, and the boy hears songs in celebration of the forbidden female figure, *Blue Eyes and Golden Hair,* he is made to run round the track in the park and to kneel down in church: he is put again into an alienating situation, and this time organises his resistance from within. The "cave" in which he takes refuge is on the parlour table, built by himself from transfers and coloured paper; he learns prudence, and no longer says that he will marry Eileen, but in his dreams goes to Mercedes.

This is the beginning of the world of dream, and of the creative imagination. Guilt no longer exists at the level of words, but in thought. It has already marked the dreamer's conscience to some extent, for Baby Tuckoo might have married Eileen, but the price was too high. The boy associates the desire to possess with the dreadful fate of being blinded, and from now on there is no more thought of marriage: fear of the spouse is all too clear in the choice of the character whose heroism is designed to hide Stephen's weakness. Monte-Cristo, the "dark avenger," inspires the proud refusals which dissimulate Stephen's despairing inhibition; repudiating the fruits of fascination for alleged reasons of honour, he says to Mercedes, "Madam, I never eat muscatel grapes," and in this noble yet comical fashion he acts out scenes from the novel, thoroughly mingled with personally meaningful elements.

The muscatel grapes may be interpreted as referring to the altar wine, but they are nearer to the exotic fruits which occupy the Dublin child's greedy imagination, and may also comport a slight ironic reference to sexual desire. After all, the grapes from Greece which Mercedes offers do belong to the category of dangerous fruit, like Eve's apple and the melon offered by an Eastern figure in a dream in *Ulysses,* representing Molly's hips. On a more banal level, which was doubtless all the original was, the detail is supposed to emphasise the noble abnegation of the hero, whose model in real life was often tormented by dreams of vast and exotic banquets. In *Stephen Hero* the muscatels are not offered by Emma but by a student called Whelan who is the orator of the Debating Society, a suave, well-fed young man who, according to a marginal note of Joyce's, had once offered him grapes, whereupon Stephen had uttered the appropriate words. In any case, the refusal is a refusal of the good things of life; not touching E. C., not taking her hand, not wishing to possess her, and not admitting to oneself the primary motive for one's flight constitute the negative form of what is later presented as the artist's positive decision. Joyce is discreetly showing that Stephen's self-protection is of a rather hypocritical nature; yet the youth has to justify to himself this constant withdrawal, when his heart *dances* at her slightest movement. The heart's *dance* is simply another enchantment caused by the mother-figure. And his heart is like a cork on the yellowish waters that will never bear him off to the lands of which he dreams.

> He passed unchallenged among the docks and along the quays wondering at the multitude of corks that lay bobbing on the surface of the water in a thick yellow scum. . . . The vastness and strangeness of the life suggested to him by the bales of merchandise stocked along the walls or swung aloft out of the holds of steamers wakened again in him the unrest which had sent him wandering in the evening from garden to garden in search of Mercedes. (*Portrait*, p. 66)

Not eating the grapes, not catching hold of E. C., is in fact an adoption of the interdict in order to impose it upon oneself by saying "I shall not eat the grapes"; it is again the proud inversion process which is at the root of all actions for the artist in his rebellion.

The revelation of his vocation is for Stephen closely associated with his entry into the world of words; with Thoth as his patron, he knows that he is henceforth dedicated to art. He spends the rest of his time in Dublin exploring this new world and in performing experiments, as though to measure the extent of his power, of the hold language has over reality. His entry into this world is hailed in gently comical fashion by the fervent, naïve exclamation, "The university!" (*Portrait*, p. 165). He has just broken his last emotional link with the "sentries who had stood as guardians of his boyhood and had sought to keep him among them that he might be subject to them and serve their ends." (*Ibid.*) For the sake of the University, that land of his dreams where beautiful words abound, he has just silently broken with his mother, because she was opposed to his plans, and the novice student realises this "dimly and without regret". He even feels a sort of pleasure on entering this new life, for the antagonism which he encounters has become so necessary to him as a source of inspiration; he achieves the University not only for himself, but also against his mother, and this act takes on meaning from that opposition which defines and confirms it: "Yet her mistrust pricked him more keenly than his father's pride and he thought coldly how he had watched the faith which was fading down in his soul ageing and strengthening in her eyes." *(Ibid.)*

In fact, this breaking of relations obscurely satisfies his plans: it is necessary for him to be able to have some grudges against his mother, as Joyce tried to have and to express against May Joyce, in order not to be held back by any considerations of duty. And thus he feels an obscure satisfaction with "her disloyalty". The University, or rather his dream of the University, develops in exactly the same way as his dreams of Mercedes or of the "image of beauty" had done, and the sensual exaltation, the passionate transference of the whole to the inner world, show how cut off he now is from reality. His joy foreshadows the moment of revelation that is to come to him on the beach, as soon as he has registered at the Faculty. He has already had, many times and in the same form, the feeling that "a new adventure was about to be opened to him." The actual object which moves the "long slow waves" in his soul is only a pretext, for all that is permanent is his certainty of having been chosen, of having received a call. "The University" is the magic word which gives him access to culture, which for him seems to reduce itself to literature for the sake of beautiful cadences:

> It was an elfin prelude, endless and formless; and, as it grew wilder and faster, the flames leaping out of time, he seemed to hear from under the boughs and grasses wild creatures racing, their feet pattering like rain upon the leaves. Their feet passed in pattering tumult over his mind, the feet of hares and rabbits, the feet of harts and hinds and antelopes, until he heard them no more and remembered only a proud cadence from Newman. *(Ibid.)*

The University means the right to open the treasury of language and to enjoy it. He passes triumphantly from the key word to the phrase in which magic and music are contained. From now on, Newman, Ibsen, Cavalcanti, or Ben Jonson accompany him in his wanderings, and life passes on to the rhythm of phrases borrowed from one or another of them—until the day when he is again dispossessed by a single word from the dean of studies. This word is "funnel," and the dean uses it just after Stephen has risked a pretentious allusion to Newman. But Stephen, the master of the noble rhythms and silver-veined prose of great English writers, is not acquainted with the word "funnel"; at home, in Dublin, it is called a "tundish". He extracts himself from the difficulty with an ostentatious pirouette, saying, "It is called a tundish in Lower Drumcondra, where they speak the best English". But, just as during the monstrous disquiet of puberty he had seen words empty themselves of all meaning before his eyes, now the distress caused to him by his ignorance of this word excludes him abruptly and cruelly from the banquet of culture, as he has already felt himself excluded also from the banquet of life. "The little word seemed to have turned a rapier point of his sensitiveness against this courteous and vigilant foe. He felt with a smart of dejection that the man to whom he was speaking was a countryman of Ben Jonson" (*Portrait*, p. 189).

At that moment Stephen the bard awakens within Stephen the schoolboy; he realises that this acquired language will always be foreign to him. All its joys are fradulent and humiliating; he can have no peace in practising his art in a borrowed language. His thought at this moment determines later the whole of Joyce's revolution: "I have not made or accepted its words. My voice holds them at bay. My soul frets in the shadow of his language." *(Ibid.)*

At the end of *Portrait* all Stephen's intellectual activity is pressed into service for the construction of an aesthetic system for a work that is to come. But words are out of season for the moment, until the artist has acquired sufficient stature to "make" his own language. Neither in reality nor in literature is Stephen to find his other world; when we lose sight of him at the end of *Ulysses*, he is on his way towards a new language, borne along by the phrase which has passed beyond the bounds of vocabulary and syntax, "the heaventree of stars hung with humid nightblue fruit".

Thus the ultimate transgression is to be a challenge to language itself, since at the end it appears as the last and most subtle net that holds back the artist's soul.

The creative heresy becomes linguistic heresy.

The Contribution of the Church

Joyce says that he left the Church in 1898, at the age of sixteen, like Stephen in *Portrait;* but if he rejected the intellectual and social tyranny which it was imposing upon Ireland, he yet remained faithful to certain forms and images which thus took on both profane and universal significance for him. Thus, Jesus becomes the type of the hero who is abandoned and betrayed by his father, just as Parnell is the hero betrayed by his country; the figure of the Virgin, inseparable from that of woman, becomes of central importance to his mythology of creation. The rites and ceremonies of religion are models of beauty in their harmony and order. It can be seen how truly Joyce had steeled his soul "in the school of old Aquinas," as he puts it in *The Holy Office.*

At Clongowes Wood and then at Belvedere College Joyce received a Jesuit education following the rules laid down by Saint Ignatius Loyola. At Belvedere he discovered Saint Thomas, and at the same time, at the age of about sixteen, he also discovered his own agnosticism, and his idol Ibsen; scarcely had he begun to doubt the Faith when he found in Ibsen's ethics a moral and artistic replacement. At University College, he read Giordano Bruno with great enthusiasm, and D'Annunzio, to whom Stephen Hero owes a great deal.[8] He pointed out in *Day of the Rabblement* (1901) that literature had changed since Flaubert, Jakobsen, and D'Annunzio. His reading followed such a pattern that as the Irish literary revival was flourishing in Dublin with Yeats and the Abbey Theatre, he was discovering the French symbolists, reading Verlaine and Rimbaud, Arthur Symons' *The Symbolist Movement in Literature*, Flaubert—and Danish and Norwegian literature by way of Ibsen and Strindberg in the theatre, Björnson, and in particular Jakobsen. At the age of eighteen, the poles of reference of his critical intelligence were *Madame Bovary* and *Il Fuoco*, representing respectively the realism that has no fear of reality (he accused George Moore of distorting it) and the symbolism that has no fear of decadent ecstasies. On the other hand, he disliked Yeats' reactionary dabblings in folklore and fairy-tale, although he admired him as a writer.

His tastes were clearly defined: literature was for him divided into two forms of expression, the one being of moral and reformative bias, modern and ideologically open, related to the humanist grandeur of Ibsen and to Flaubert's refusal to make mankind heroic. The other was purely decorative, consisted of pellucid rhythmic prose or of poetry, suitable for the outpourings of the soul but by no means universal. It was the language which the individual spoke within himself, the language of love and its emotions. The object of love was a distant, mysterious woman, the type of whom was, according to D'Annunzio, the Mona Lisa, or perhaps the image of the poet's own soul. Yet this flamboyant

[8]In *The Workshop of Daedalus* there are interesting extracts from *Le Vergini delle Rocce* and *Il Fuoco*, pp. 269–79; Stelio and Stephen speak the same symbolic language, so much so that whole passages of *Il Fuoco* could be reproduced in *Portrait* without remark.

art, inspired by love, must always be peripheral; the writer may adopt it to express the emotions and torments of his heart, but it is not meant to be offered to the public.

In 1903 Joyce went to Paris as all these influences were maturing together in his imagination; there three further experiences were to confirm and define his points of reference. These were first, his reading of Aristotle, the *De Anima*, the *Metaphysica* and the *Poetica*; secondly, the temptation to be absorbed by the warm, scented, luxurious life of the noisy streets and to appease the hungers of his troubled flesh there; and thirdly, his reading of various French authors, in particular Dujardin's *Les Lauriers sont Coupés*. Joyce was systematically plowing his way through European literature. This intellectual conjunction has the same triple aspect which later determines the aesthetic propounded by Stephen, with its wish to unify and order the world through a universal deductive system, its desire to participate physically in life in order to draw one's emotions from it, and its adoption of narrative techniques which unite symbolism and realism. (For Dujardin, the symbol grows in the fruitful earth of reality.)

Through Aristotle's "psychology" (as he calls the *De Anima*, telling Stannie that he is "up to his neck" in it) Joyce rediscovered Saint Thomas, from whom he had been temporarily distracted by the study of Bruno, and this time Saint Thomas was less the master of Jesuitical casuistry than the philosopher of genius who had given the European vision of the world its form for several centuries. Ibsen was still his moral guide, the critic of a decadent society whose slavish victim Joyce at this stage still was. But from now on no-one else was to mark him any more; he had been given everything he wanted.[9] In 1904 he was master of the cultural heritage, both Catholic and heretic, of which he had nearly deprived himself. He believed in nothing, as he often had occasion to declare, whether religion or science. But his imagination was animated by reading Vico, for example, and his mind was only able to create freely within and against the fixed, total forms of the mediaeval Summa. Dynamism and permanence, the movement of history in its limited fixed space, set their unavoidable dialectic like a seal upon his

---

[9]He continued to read very widely until the age of thirty-five, when his attacks of iritis became so severe that he had to ask his friends to read to him. He read the Russians, Tolstoy, Dostoievsky, Pushkin, etc., and in no prescribed order Renan, Lombroso, Marx, Fogazzaro, Anatole France, Paul Bourget, while his knowledge of Proust was superficial and gathered from others. Later he read Freud and Jung, who gave him little or nothing but feelings of scorn or irritation which led him to use them sometimes as figures of caricature. Only Vico, whom he read about 1922–3, gave him any intellectual pleasure, and that because the *Scienza Nuova* seemed to confirm his own ideas of history.

divided imagination. This is why his work is propelled by the constantly renewed statement of oppositions, insoluble without the world of mediation, which is the work in which they are reflected.

Joyce's created universe is basically a summa of all the intellectual, psychological, and spiritual ambiguities dividing early twentieth-century Irish man: ephemeral, contradictory man caught between a mental Middle Ages and the modernity of the present, both petty and great, ridiculous and lost in a world which now opens out into space, into relativity and the indefinite; his awareness is humiliated, yet he recalls a smaller, ordered, limited world, as Bloom—abandoned in a city which treats him as an outcast—still recalls the times when life had a meaning and when he knew what he would find at the end of the day.

Much has been said about Joyce as a Catholic, and in his lifetime those about him, though not his intimate friends, predicted that he would probably return to the Church.[10] In fact, he rejected its dogma, refused to pay allegiance to its spiritual power, but kept to the exterior forms which make a ritual art of the Catholic faith. His sensibilities were impregnated by its liturgy, and he who rose up against the authority of the spirit did not deny the influence of the letter. It is true that the fascinatory power of Catholicism can be gauged by its occult and provocative presence in his work; the progress of the *Portrait*, as we shall see, mimics the itinerary of the soul towards full communion with the divine. Stephen's efforts to solve the mysteries of the world and of the part he is to play in it map out a path which is in itself already the form of the *Portrait*, and indeed of *Ulysses* too. He proceeds towards a reorganisation of the world within his own mental patterns and forms, and in the isolation of his own inner self he formulates a new order, a world whose coherence consoles him for and constitutes a revenge upon the treacherous circumstances of the outside world. As his task progresses, he realises that this setting in order can never be completed, that it must be pursued *ad infinitum*, and that only the verbal trace of the work so far accomplished remains. In effect, the paradox of endless books like *Portrait* or *Ulysses* is that the author's artistic plan and his vision of reality are contradictory; the need for order, which he inherits

[10]"It has become a fashion with some of my brother's critics (among them his friend Italo Svevo) to represent him as a man pining for the ancient Church he had abandoned, and at a loss for moral support without the religion in which he was bred. Nothing could be farther from the truth. I am convinced that there was never any crisis of BELIEF. The vigour of life within him drove him out of the Church. . . . something of the pomp and ceremony with which the legend of Jesus is told impressed him profoundly; but on almost all points of first importance, his attitude towards Catholicism was more like that of the gargoyles outside the Church than of the saints within it." (*My Brother's Keeper*, p. 130.)

from the Catholic culture whose forms are outworn for him, clashes with a modern vision of the world of the present day.

The contrast between the age-old forms which had stood for a world whose disintegration the author had witnessed in his childhood, a world which he had voluntarily quitted, and the amorphous world which was being evolved from the ugliness and violence of his youth, as grasped by his critical intelligence, started Joyce on his career of parody. If through love of beauty he wished to conserve order, it was necessary to impose the latter by force or by cunning upon a reality which no longer responded to such criteria. The consciousness of this discrepancy was first expressed as the longing for a beauty that existed only as an idealistic dream impossible to find in the world, and this longing might suggest to the artist the idea of flight and escape into a dream-world, that is, the choice of a poetic genre with no connection with reality; on the other hand he might achieve a compromise between formless material and disaffected form, the conjunction of which would necessarily cause the reader to become aware of the discrepancy and thus to measure and judge time past by time present and vice versa.

It is impossible not to sense the irony and the distress which are dogging Stephen as *Ulysses* opens, inaugurated by the enemy, by Buck Mulligan, the grimacing false priest who intones *Introibo ad altare Dei*. This modern Odyssey begins with a blasphemous celebration of the Mass, and Stephen, in rejecting the comfort of the closed worlds of Greece or Ireland which he evokes so sardonically, shows that the epic age, with its reliance on a positive feeling of totality, is for him completely dead. Mulligan the praiser of Hellenism and of security is only a cruel and foolish figure passing aimlessly through history, while the artist, like Bloom, stakes his soul on the game, determined to continue his quest beyond the known world to another world which he is to construct as an autonomous totality: the world of art.

Ulysses consists of two journeys, Stephen's and Bloom's. Only chance brings these two Dubliners together, for they have nothing in common; chance, and the author's strange will towards order, wishing to make one unique work out of many books, bring it about that the arbitrary, absurd, and providential meeting of Stephen with Bloom, and by way of Bloom with Molly too, should give the overall meaning to the work, The figure of the Trinity is thus the ruling image of *Ulysses*, although it is not to be interpreted with any theological orthodoxy; the three human beings are not the symbol of the divine mystery, and indeed, if one were to seek to establish any such correspondence, God would be a ridiculous and unproductive father, despised by an ambitious son, and the Virgin would be a very perverse Madonna. Thus the meeting at night in Eccles Street, however promising one might find the name (that of a street in an attractive but socially degenerated district of Dublin) is not successfully accomplished, and possesses a formal meaning only because of the presence of a myth which has lost all spiritual content and meaning.

Stephen explains to Cranly, in Chapter V of *Portra* that Catholicism is "an absurdity which is logical and coherent".

It could be said that in *Ulysses* in particular, Joyce is recovering the coherence and mocking the absurdity, for example, by making the centre of *Ulysses* a simulacrum of the obscene and blasphemous Black Mass. Finally, throughout his evolution through the work, Stephen takes great pleasure in his skill in manipulating Thomism as an intellectual rapier. But it is only an instrument, for all that: he cares less about spiritual exercises than about the intellectual gymnastics which he practises in front of his contemporaries, as he sketches out his own aesthetic conceptions by means of a series of questions which he models on Saint Thomas' *Quaestiones Quodlibetales*. Similarly Joyce, when pursuing the operative ideas of his aesthetic, noted down these questions in his Paris notebook, failing to conceal their scholastic origins by their humorous formulation:

> Question: Why are not excrements, children, and lice works of art?
> Answer: Excrements, children, and lice are human products—human dispositions of sensible matter. The process by which they are produced is natural and non-artistic; their end is not an aesthetic end; therefore they are not works of art.
> Question: Can a photograph be a work of art?
> Answer: A photograph is a disposition of sensible matter and may be so disposed for an aesthetic end but it is not a human disposition of sensible matter. Therefore it is not a work of art.
> Question: If a man hacking in fury at a block of wood make there an image of a cow (say) has he made a work of art?
> Answer: The image of a cow made by a man hacking in fury at a block of wood is a human disposition of sensible matter but it is not a human disposition of sensible matter for an aesthetic end. Therefore it is not a work of art.
> Question: Are houses, clothes, furniture, etc., works of art?
> Answer: Houses, clothes, furniture, etc., are not necessarily works of art. They are human dispositions of sensible matter. When they are disposed for an aesthetic end they are works of art. (*Critical Writings*, p. 146)

In *Portrait*, Stephen takes a secret pleasure in making use of Saint Thomas's moral philosophy for the propagation of his aesthetic ideas, a pleasure which Joyce in the studious solitude of the Bibliothèque Sainte-Geneviève had no need to share.

All the definitions of the beautiful, of comedy and tragedy, of the lyric, epic, and dramatic forms which Joyce makes, are merely complex gropings on the part of a mind seeking its own way, one almost too accustomed to abstract scholastic research. His own true poetics were to be the result of a succession of personal clashes with life. What he retained from his years of Thomist studies was not the contents of the *Summa Theologica,* but rather the idea and the necessity which presided over the conception of that *Summa,* the vision of the world as an ordered cosmos in which everything has its place and every being its function, where every detail takes on its meaning both in its individual singularity and in its participation in an harmonious whole.

Conclusion: Priest of the Imagination

Only in September 1907 did Joyce decide finally on the form to be taken by his novel *Stephen Hero* on which he had been working for three years; the combination of one particular determining event in his life, with his need to reorganise the amorphous episodic material of the work, led him at last to the discovery which was to be the basis of his aesthetic. Henceforth art, religion, and physical gestation were to coincide in his mind, as he had been vaguely wishing them to do for some time, and this coinciding was to dictate the form most naturally appropriate to his subject. He told Stannie, who noted it down on 8 September, that the *Portrait* was to begin with Stephen's first experiences at school, and to comprise five long chapters. In a way, chance had crystallised the form of his poetic, although its component parts had always been present in his mind, without his hitherto having attempted to combine them together. He must have needed time before daring to channel processes for the purposes of literary creation which his past and his youthful loyalties had made sacred—in particular the mystery of motherhood.

His own mother had died in 1903, and from her he had derived his notions of conception as a venerable and tragic mystery. He accused himself of having caused her death by his abandonment of the faith at

the age of sixteen. The motherhood of Our Lady never ceased to preoc-
cupy him, and this theme was soon joined by that of embryology, the
study of which he began at the time of Nora's first pregnancy in 1905
and which provided him with some discreet effects in the composition
of 'A Little Cloud'.

In July 1907 he went into hospital for some weeks with rheumatism
of the joints, and on 26 July Nora gave birth to Lucia Anne in the same
hospital. During the time of this birth, and his and Nora's subsequent
months of sickness and his own convalescence, Joyce meditated on the
parallel between artistic conception and gestation and their human
equivalent. He thought that while confined to bed like Nora he must
experience the same feelings as an expectant mother. In the period
preparatory to writing, the artist seemed to him to resemble a mother
—or more exactly to resemble the Virgin Mother—since the imagination is impregnated, as was Our Lady, by no outside human intervention. Such was the strength of this comparison that it became an integral
part of Joyce's thought and personality rather than a mere ephemeral
and artificial borrowing or purely aesthetic statement. Joyce sincerely
lived in this relationship to his work. Five years later he was to write
to Nora from Dublin, where he was having difficulties with George
Roberts over the publication of *Dubliners*, "thinking of the book I
have written, the child which I have carried for years and years in the
womb of the imagination as you carried in your womb the children
you love, and of how I had fed it day after day out of my brain and
memory . . ."[11]

This feminine nature of the artist seems a normal state of affairs to
him, yet it does not stop him from thinking of himself from 1907 onwards as both mother and son, the latter being his favourite role in his
relations with Nora. In effect, he *is* her son, as he is the rebellious son
of Mother Church, guiltily fearing the gratitude which must make him
all his life a prisoner of this relationship; before the birth of the work
he defines the birth of the artist. His body is born of woman but his soul,
as Stephen puts it in *Portrait* (p. 203), "has a slow and dark birth, more
mysterious than the birth of the body". Joyce began to think of an
embryology of the soul as the new form for his book. The metaphor
became the principle of the work's structure.

By his discovery of this original metaphor permitting him to unify the
Portrait as it progressed through the development which dictated its
movement and rhythm, Joyce was able to satisfy at the same time his

[11] *Letters*, vol. II, p. 308, 23 Aug. 1912.

need to reconstitute in his work an order comparable to that which he admired in religion and its rituals. He no longer had any religious belief, but his artistic sensibility still longed for the ceremonies and gestures of the Mass, and to some extent was jealous of its integration of all the myths into an harmonious whole, closing upon itself in the perfection of the Word and able to open out upon the world, able even to divide itself into father and son without breaking the unity of the One.

Theology and aesthetics, art and life, realism and symbolism, were now sufficiently close to one another in the artist's imagination for fruitful connections and exchanges to be made between them; Joyce was now able to define an aesthetic system whose centre was not the world but rather the place where the artist encounters reality.

Furthermore, the *Portrait* was to have that closed, protected, foreseeable form which *Stephen Hero* had lacked, causing the young man in that first version to experience greater and more painful contact with the world. Thanks to the metaphor of the incarnation of the word, the "education" aspect of *Stephen Hero* was replaced by one of "revelation," by the notion of the almost mystic vocation of the very consciousness itself.

This is why Stephen, after his birth into the world of art, is able to express his personal theory in terms of *development*.

As a parallel to the concept of the creative process, Stephen defines "the phenomena of artistic conception, artistic gestation, and artistic reproduction," showing clearly that the characters created by the artist and projected by him into literary form receive life from the creator's own life force and not by any outside intervention: "in the virgin womb of the imagination the word was made flesh". The progress from the lyric form to the epic form is described lengthily to Lynch in Chapter V; the form of a work is given by the artist's emotional connection with others:

> The simplest epical form is seen emerging out of lyrical literature when the artist prolongs and broods upon himself as the centre of an epical event and this form progresses till the centre of emotional gravity is equi-distant from the artist himself and from others. The narrative is no longer purely personal. The personality of the artist passes into the narration itself, flowing round and round the persona and the action like a vital sea. . . . The dramatic form is reached when the vitality which has flowed and eddied round each person fills every person with such vital force that he or she assumes a proper and intangible aesthetic life. The personality of the artist, at first a cry or a cadence or a mood and then a fluid and lambent narrative, finally refines itself out of existence, impersonalizes itself, so to speak. The

aesthetic image in the dramatic form is life purified in and re-projected from the human imagination. The mystery of aesthetic, like that of material creation, is accomplished. (*Portrait*, p. 214–15)

This definition is expressed in a language which is no longer borrowed from that of Saint Thomas because, as Stephen explains, from the moment when it is a matter of defining not the object or the notion of the beautiful but rather the creator as subject, he "requires a new terminology and a new personal experience". When he expounds his philosophy of aesthetics, his soul is detached from his body, and as he says to Lynch, "we are just now in a mental world". He has in fact reached the fifth stage of the spirit.

The five stages of the soul's development follow faithfully the pattern worked out by Joyce.

It must first be emphasised that the form of the *Portrait* consists of a sort of literary game, since the structural metaphor is of double reference; on the one hand, it represents a psycho-physiological development, and on the other, the entire book is a metaphor of the aesthetic whose eventual formulation permitted the book's creation. It is a moving picture of the artist's soul on its journey between art and life.

Joyce did not tell Stanislaus why this gestation should take place in five stages, but it may be supposed, as a recent article has suggested,[12] that they correspond to the five degrees in the ladder of perfection or chain of being which is found throughout the cosmic vision of both the middle Ages and the Renaissance; the descending hierarchy (which constituted the foundations of psychology and ethics as they were then thought of, being the heritage of Aristotle and Galen as Saint Augustine and Saint Thomas had adapted them and as the scholastic system had handed them on) was perfectly suited in fact to the needs of the Joyce whose soul had been formed in the school of old Aquinas and who had spent 1903 in Paris studying Aristotle. He shows the effects of this in his life and in the *Portrait*.

This applied theology, developed along the lines of an experimental method, defined the complex relations between body and soul, thought and emotion, the sexes, races, and temperaments, the nature of diseases, etc., all within that sphere or microcosm that is human nature, man. A series of parallels or correspondences is established between man and the universe in such a way that creation is perfect. Man's place

[12]Sidney Fesbach, 'A Slow and Dark Birth,' article in *James Joyce Quarterly*, Vol. IV, No. 4, Summer 1967, pp. 289–300.

is at the middle of the ladder; God is enthroned at the top. At the next lowest step come the angels, then men (with women slightly below them), and below men is the animal kingdom, with the vegetable kingdom below that. As one moves from bottom to top, naturally awareness, freedom, and the use of reason appear, and increase as one ascends further; it was agreed that man desired to tend towards the heights, that is, towards the angelic condition, and that his reason by way of his will could bring him near to it.[13] Similarly, it was thought that man was tempted down, towards the animal condition, passing through woman, who represents sexuality, since the nature of woman bordered on that of the animal just as the nature of man bordered on that of the angelic. Stephen tends not only towards the angelic state, but also beyond to divine status.

The combination of this ambition with the idea of a growth proceeding from the original primitive moment of the embryo obliges him to set out from the very bottom of the ladder, from the vegetable state.[14] The progress from one degree to the next is saluted by a loud cry in *Portrait*; the soul leaps forward at five moments of spiritual epiphany, torn in common from the artist's physical self almost in spite of him, as though Joyce wished to emphasise that aspect of being chosen which marks out one who is a poet less by choice than by nature or by supernatural decision—one whose vocation is analogous to that of a priest. The first cry is wrenched from him by the blows from Father Dolan's ferula: "in shame and rage he felt the scalding cry come from his throat and the scalding tears falling out of his eyes and down his flaming cheeks" (*Portrait*, p. 51). Until now he has been as passive and subdued as a plant, but he is wrenched from the vegetable state by the experience of injustice. A whole image cluster of leaves and fire accompanies this moment, as though to emphasise the hell to which he is delivered who has as yet only the awareness and sensibilities of an artist: "A hot burning stinging tingling blow like the loud crack of a broken stick made his trembling hand crumple together like a leaf in the fire"

[13]For the problems of the concept of the soul, body, and spirit, and the tradition of the ladder of perfection, see the excellent studies of Geoffrey Bullough, *Mirror of Minds*, (London, 1962), A. O. Lovejoy, *The Great Chain of Being* (Cambridge, Mass., 1936), and more generally the studies of Mircea Eliade on the Sacred and Profane, and on Shamanism; Maud Bodkin, *Archetypal Patterns in Poetry*; and Northrop Frye, *Anatomy of Criticism*.

[14]The same hierarchic pattern inspires the vision of developing humanity described by Asia in Shelley's *Prometheus Unbound*, but the ironic system involving a falling back which Joyce uses is the very opposite of what he called Shelley's "Schwärmerei of a young jew".

(*Portrait*, pp. 50–1). The same pattern recurs in Chapter II where Stephen is "like some baffled prowling beast," unable to speak and a prey to demons: "The inarticulate cries and the unspoken brutal words rushed forth from his brain to force a passage. . . . the cry that he had strangled for so long in his throat issued from his lips. It broke from him like a wail of despair from a hell of sufferers" (*Portrait*, p. 100).

When Stephen reaches the human condition, language is given back to him, but not the courage to use its words: "To say it in words! His soul, stifling and helpless, would cease to be. . . . he repeated the *Confiteor* in fright" (*Portrait*, pp. 143–4). The language of man expresses his awareness of his sins. It is no longer fright or horror that guides him in Chapter IV to the angelic height, but the fortunate desire to accomplish his self in heaven: "His throat ached with a desire to cry aloud. . . . to cry piercingly of his deliverance to the winds. . . . An instant of wild flight had delivered him and the cry of triumph which his lips withheld cleft his brain" (*Portrait*, p. 170).

"His soul had arisen from the grave of boyhood," from the cerecloths which are the shame and humiliation caused by the possession of a body. This time "the flame in his blood" is not that of hell, but inspires a longing to wander to the ends of the earth. Everything takes place in the world of the imagination, in a visionary world worthy of Blake, whom Stephen Dedalus constantly read and absorbed: "A wild angel had appeared to him, the angel of mortal youth and beauty," and "her image had passed into his soul for ever".[15] Henceforth the angel of life confirms him in his artistic vocation: beauty, youth, and death are united in this apparition which precedes his deification, and from this moment on the real relationship between words and the soul replaces that of the body and the world. His last cry celebrates his ecstatic ascension: "In the womb of the imagination the word is made flesh". The quality of the cries uttered at these five moments of separation, these five provisional births, corresponds to the progress made by language passing from the inarticulate groan to poetry by way of obscene exclamation and prayer.

Thus one is present at the birth of the soul that is to overcome all the ethical and material obstacles in its way: successively, physical pain and the shock of injustice, then sexual desire and disgust for the flesh, then

[15]"Soul" is used 172 times in *Portrait*, but "body" only 57 times and "flesh" only 22, according to L. Hancock, *Word Index to James Joyce's A Portrait* (Southern Illinois U.P, 1967).

the tortures of hell and the sermon, the vision of the beautiful object and the swooning of the body, and finally ecstasy with no sensual contact, not even those of sight. One observes the progressive articulation of language. At the end, Stephen's soul is the "form," in the Aristotelian sense of the word, of the novel, the "form of forms," as Stephen himself says in *Ulysses*. This "spiritualisation," this play of the spirit at incarnation, is made in imitation of the Christian myth.[16] This view is not new to Joyce, for he was making use of the pattern already in the 1904 *Portrait*, and in an article of the previous year dealing with the philosophy of Giordano Bruno it was still this progress of the artist that he admired: "Inwards from the material universe . . . his opportunity for spiritual activity, he passes, and from heroic enthusiasm to enthusiasm to unite himself with God" (*Critical Writings*, p. 134).

Stephen indeed does not attain union with God, but it is in himself that he finds "that which is strong and suddenly rapturous" which the mystics call God. This essay on Bruno contains an interesting remark to the effect that he is "the father of what is called modern philosophy". To be "modern," it seems from what follows, is to make the attempt "to reconcile the matter and form of the scholastics"—terms which in his system, under the appellation of body and soul, almost entirely lose their metaphysical character. If in this Bruno is "modern," Joyce remains a Thomist in his incapacity to reconcile matter and form in reality; what he eventually did was to substitute form for matter.

Furthermore, the gestation of the soul takes place in Aristotelian fashion, insofar as every mystic explosion or birth consists of the "actualisation" of a possible or potential; each chapter is firstly a mode of the artist's development, as he rejects a number of possibilities in order to choose what Aristotle calls the "actualisation" of one possible. It may well be that Joyce also had in mind the theory of the "movements" of the soul, of the three functions—physical, mental and spiritual—through which the soul operates. These three functions correspond to the triple division of the universe into vegetative principle, sensitive principle, and rational principle. Through the first principle man participates in inanimate nature, by, for example, his unconscious functions such as digestion and growth.[17] A corresponding state for Stephen exists in the first part of his life, the time of home and school, when the

[16]Robert J. Andreach has recently suggested in *Studies in Structure: Stages of the Spiritual Life in Four Modern Authors* that the novel was constituted by following in reverse the fivefold division of the spiritual life.
[17]Aristotle, *De Anima*, 415 a–b.

imagery which predominates is a vegetable one of roses, holly, ivy, crumpled and withered leaves; and this would find confirmation in Stephen's remark to himself after his refusal of the Jesuit Father's offer: "this disorder, the misrule and confusion of his father's house and the stagnation of vegetable life . . . was to win the day".

Thus also, in *Finnegans Wake*, Shaun says of Shem, "He's weird, I tell you, and middayevil down to his vegetable soul" (*Finnegans Wake*, p. 423). Man shares his sensibilities with the animals, and from this principle depend all the senses, whose task it is to transmit messages to the brain, where there reside the three faculties of common sense, imagination, and memory.[18] And as Fesbach points out *(art.cit.)* these correspondences can be found in *Portrait*: the trip to Cork is a journey through a town of the memory, and Stephen's animal nature is more than evident, disfiguring all reality by means of its mad visions resuscitated by the sight of the word "foetus" carved on a student's desk. Finally, the rational principle connects man with the angelic nature and manifests itself in two forces, the understanding and the will; the last three chapters show the gradual conquest of the inner world by Stephen's rational will, as he climbs the ladder of angelic being.

This process of integrating the action into a higher form, which by its meaning also participates in the action, makes the *Portrait* into an embryo *Ulysses* also. The action is sublimed on to a spiritual level, although this is disguised by the intensely subjective atmosphere which emanates from the personality of the rebel artist; yet this sublimation keeps the book within the theological world, although not committing it in any way thereto. The mental landscape and the real landscape are intensely opposed to each other, being presented by way of the only substance whose existence is both affirmed and made increasingly concrete—language. In fact, as the artist's spiritual evolution proceeds, Dublin becomes more imprecise and distant as the inner world extends and is given material status by the words which Stephen uses to define it; in Chapter IV, the youth who had once been afraid of words has become the master of "a lucid supple periodic prose," and he draws a phrase out of his treasury to name the world. He says, "A day of dappled seaborne clouds," and like the child in 'The Sisters,' who exercised his occult power by repeating the word "paralysis" to himself, Stephen repeats the phrase gently, and his surroundings respond harmoniously:

[18] *Ibid.*, 414 b, 427 b.

"The phrase and the day and the scene harmonized in a chord. Words" (*Portrait*, p. 166).

The "glowing sensible world" that is expressed "through the prism of a language many-coloured and richly storied" is rendered subject to his word; the sumptuous world outside is only a setting for the inner world where the poet's thought contemplates his "individual emotions". He does not of course abolish the world that is expressed through colours, sounds, and shapes, but goes beyond it to reach the kingdom of his own soul where all this is replaced by words. As he explains to Lynch a little later, "sound and shape and colour are the prison gates of our soul" which must be left behind in order to express from the gross earth an image of beauty. In other words, for Stephen in *Portrait*, for the young aesthete, reality is an obstacle to be cleared, to be left behind, to be replaced by a metaphor suggested by analogy. The whole structure of *Portrait* is inspired by the analogy with the history of a poet's soul; and in this sense *Portrait*, like *Ulysses*, is mythopoeic: the subject dictates the form precisely because it consists of the search for that form. The equation of balance is here more perfectly achieved, more organic, than in *Ulysses*, because in the latter the framework of the *Odyssey* remains artificial, and is only integrated with the whole by means of the parody.

The same process of incorporating an as yet incomplete aesthetic into the work which illustrates the principles of that aesthetic is taken up again in *Ulysses* on a different level. In effect, if in *Portrait* the birth of the soul is analogous to the birth of the work, in *Ulysses* the subject is no longer the birth of the artist but rather his impregnation for the purposes of artistic creation. This is why the dominant theological figure in *Portrait* is Our Lady and the symbolic scene appropriate is the Visitation, while in *Ulysses* the Artist exercising his powers suggests rather an analogy with God the Father and God the Son.

It must be recalled that this is only a matter of a structure which gives the work its form in time, just as the *Odyssey* is only the scarcely visible temporal infrastructure in *Ulysses*; these five great moments do not contradict in any way the views of Hugh Kenner, whose theory is that *Portrait* is a lyrical work of three hundred pages in length, consisting of "the simplest verbal vesture" of the "instant of emotion" in which Stephen emerges winged above the waters, soaring up to follow Thoth the hawk-man.[19] "The lyric image of a growing dream" follows the plot and the romantic emotions of the Count of Monte-Cristo, that mythical

[19]Hugh Kenner, *Dublin's Joyce* (London, 1955), pp. 118ff.

avenger who returns from exile (as, indeed, does Ulysses himself, to take revenge), who haunts the imagination of the boy Stephen. Kenner sees the order of the five chapters as the ironical progress of a successful effort to attain a balanced and peaceful life in the world of Dublin; scarcely has this been achieved, in an ecstasy of peace, when everything again is brought into question, surpassed, and destroyed in the soaring madness of the artist's vocation. The chapters with odd numbers, he says, I, III, and V, end on notes of peaceful comfort, of "truth" and "the good life," thought of in terms of white pudding, sausages, and peace. Thus, Chapter III ends:

> On the dresser was a plate of sausages and white pudding and on the shelf there were eggs. They would be for the breakfast in the morning after the communion in the college chapel. White pudding and eggs and sausages and cups of tea. How simple and beautiful was life after all And life lay all before him. (*Portrait*, p. 146)

He is calm, as he is at the end of chapter I:

> The air was soft and grey and mild and evening was coming. There was the smell of evening in the air, the smell of the fields in the country where they digged up turnips to peel them and eat them when they went out for a walk to Major Barton's, the smell there was in the little wood beyond the pavilion where the gallnuts were. (*Portrait*, p. 59)

Here his submission to the duty of living assumes an ideal form. The even-numbered Chapters II and IV end with crazy explosions of emotion, far from the home and the table set with food, from the kitchen and the dawn of innocence. On the lonely sands at twilight,

> He turned landward and ran towards the shore and, running up the sloping beach, reckless of the sharp shingle, found a sandy nook amid a ring of tufted sandknolls and lay down there that the peace and silence of the evening might still the riot of his blood. (*Portrait*, p. 172)

> —Heavenly God! cried Stephen's soul, in an outburst of profane joy.
> He turned away from her suddenly and set off across the strand. His cheeks were aflame; his body was aglow; his limbs were trembling. On and on and on and on he strode, far out over the sands, singing wildly to the sea, crying to greet the advent of the life that had cried to him. (*Ibid.*, p. 171)

Kenner condemns the vicious quality of this joy by making it parallel to that described at the end of Chapter II:

> Her round arms held him firmly to her and he, seeing her face lifted to him in serious calm and feeling the warm calm rise and fall of her breast, all but burst into hysterical weeping. Tears of joy and relief shone in his delighted eyes and his lips parted though they would not speak.
>
> She passed her tinkling hand through his hair, calling him a little rascal.
>
> (*Portrait*, p. 101)

Although this analysis of the novel's structure is not wrong, its viewpoint is doubly false: the end of Chapter V offers an evident contrast to the counterpoint of this vision, since it does not end in a state of equilibrium as do Chapters I and III, but on a note of final challenge and defiance, Icarian indeed, but scarcely submissive or reconciled. Kenner finds himself faced with the necessity to consider the last forty pages as unfortunate and misplaced, since, as he says, it would be necessary for "his equilibrium in Chapter V, though good enough to give him a sense of unusual integrity in University College," to be maintained by "prolonging the college context for the rest of his life". But it is clear that Stephen will not remain a University man for long. Kenner sees this as a fault in construction which Joyce attempts to disguise for the purposes of symmetry by the trick of introducing the seven pages of Stephen's journal as an appendix leading up to the declaration—"Welcome, O life!"

On the other hand, Kenner's theory also supposes a falsification of Stephen's quest, because to diminish the importance of the ecstatic finale to Chapter III by comparing it to the ending of Chapter II is as good as to say that the vision of the bird-like girl is equal in quality to the encounter with the young prostitute—an affirmation scarcely worthy of serious consideration. It is true that Stephen's swooning, *fin-de-siècle* emotions manifest themselves in much the same way on both occasions, but he is not to be deluded as to the negligible value of fleshly contacts: this is simply a substitute and simulacrum for the joy which he expects to appear one day.

It is nevertheless true, as Kenner says, that the theme of the three odd-numbered chapters can be summed up as "the revolt of the self against authority," while the two even-numbered chapters concern the clash between Dublin and the dream, the whole being given unity by the one project, the encounter with the alter ego, which finds its consummation in the double vision of Stephen as Saint Stephen and as

Daedalus' son. This valuable statement of themes is easily brought into agreement with the idea of structure leased on gestation, if one rejects the static plan which Kenner suggests.

The *Portrait* is first and foremost a history, the story of a process of becoming, and not a simple pattern of alternating high and low. There is symmetry rather than equivalence between the different episodes; the progression is clear, comparable to the modifications in the life of a man who discovers himself to have a vocation for the Church, for the soul arrives at its goal by gradually divesting itself of its temporal garments and detaching itself from the things of the flesh. This of course does not mean that Stephen is a saint or a disembodied angel, but it is his mind which gradually turns away from questioning the world by means of sense perceptions and evolves until it can question only its own mental categories. The body does not let itself be forgotten; indeed it speaks a language only too clear to the artist, who is basically never quite sure that he really wishes to be an exile. It will be seen later on that he has to make considerable efforts to take up his Byronic act again. The sausages and white pudding and the wife by the fireside constitute a setting not without charms of its own.

Finally, it is quite true that Stephen's flights of imagination and emotion are written in a style which parodies Walter Pater and his followers; a style not lacking in a few satirical touches which mockingly mirror the elaborate casualness of Oscar Wilde, as the dreamer meditates solemnly on the portrait of the typical "decadent poet," as though he were the subject of a Beardsley engraving. The *fin-de-siècle* vocabulary tacitly underlines the puerile side of Stephen's affectations, with its "weary, swooning, ecstasy, aflame, aglow, wild, angel, etc." Stephen's purple rhetoric can only mean that Joyce is smiling as he relates the spiritual adventures of a young man of the previous generation, passionately attached to the symbolists, a reader of Rimbaud (in *Stephen Hero*) and a rebellious pupil of Irish Jesuits.[20] The cadences of a passage like, "radiant his eyes and wild his breath and tremulous and wild and radiant his windswept face," the accumulation of the adjectives, and the ternary composition ("windswept face") are too close an echo of Swinburne for there not to be an intention of parody. The stylistic exercise is interrupted by the comic chorus of the bathers, whose familiarity seems to furnish a trivial commentary to the Icarian fall:

[20]According to Hancock, *op. cit.*, the word "weary" occurs 22 times in *Portrait*.

Again! Again! Again! A voice from beyond the world was calling.
—Hello, Stephanos!
—Here comes the Dedalus!
—Ao! . . . Eh, give it over, Dwyer, I'm telling you, or I'll give you a stuff in the kisser for yourself. . . . Ao!
—Good man, Towser! Duck him!
—Come along, Dedalus! Bous Stephanoumenos! Bous Stephaneforos!
—Duck him! Guzzle him now, Towser!
—Help! Help! . . . Ao! (*Portrait*, p. 168)

The parody of a generation's style which apes its own emotions is resumed more fully and completely in the 'Oxen of the Sun' episode in *Ulysses*, and extends into an imitation of the successive voices of English literature throughout the ages, associated again with the metaphorical use of embryology. For it is a specific characteristic of Joyce's imagination that he should identify all history, even that of art, with an organic and anthropomorphic growth, while also evoking by profane allusions the great movements of the mystic life. The aspects of autobiography and poetic unite together in this *Portrait* of an artist's soul.

Part Four: Exile as Recovery

XVI. The Choice of Exile

Introduction

"My mind rejects the whole present social order and Christianity—home, the recognised virtues, classes of life, and religious doctrines," wrote Joyce to Nora in August 1904, as he was preparing to leave Ireland and go into voluntary exile.[1] His feeling of being different, which had been until then an excuse for participating by opposition and for defining himself within what he called the "classes of life," had become more precise, no doubt because the presence of Nora made it possible for him to envisage "a more concrete separation". Joyce was about to pass from the condition of rebel to that of exile, from his state of guerrilla war against the Church as the dominating power within society to a state of open war against the whole of society and the individuals composing it. Gradually he was to enlarge both the circles in which he was caught and the very concept of exile itself; already he had made a virtue of his heresy and now he was to make his exile into an imaginary citizenship.

Thus the transition is made from the unhappy Dublin consciousness to a universal consciousness; for as he moves away from a particular place and circumstances, he gains a vaster world in which to set his

[1] *Letters*, vol. II, p. 48, 29 August 1904. He also says, "I cannot enter the social order except as a vagabond. I started to study medicine three times, law once, music once. A week ago I was arranging to go away as a travelling actor".

works. Exile is no longer simply a separation from a world which he finds intolerable and which will not tolerate him, but becomes over the years an *absolute* exile mindful of its origins, though quite detached from them. His art naturally follows the lines of this progress; while the artist in *Portrait* puts himself in the position of an exile without leaving Dublin and continues a dialogue which demonstrates constantly both the difference and the presence, he is no longer present at all in *Ulysses* except in appearance. In fact the exile is effective even if he happens by chance to find himself again in the country he has denied, as shown by the disappearance of the dialogue—which is replaced by long monologues, occasionally interrupted by swift ironical sallies from the citadel of the self. Exile is the very form of Stephen's soul and of Bloom's life in *Ulysses*; we shall study the chapter of Joyce's life which begins in 1904, at the stage of his work which begins with *Portrait*, and marks the transformation of the passive feeling of being in exile into the decision to take up a deliberate physical exile.

The Metaphor of Exile

From the very beginning of the work, Joyce indirectly gives the impression that the world, family, and society all were able to begin without Stephen. The brief episodes of discovery are written from the point of view of the outer world, and only gradually do they move in to consider the subject, the watcher. Everything is seen by this subject, but such is his feeling of alienation, and so great is the power of the world of objects, that he sees himself as "he" rather than as "I". It is not the subject who occupies the centre of the stage here, yet it is he who speaks. "He was baby tuckoo . . . he sang that song. . . . he hid under the table". This foreignness of the "I" with regard to himself is marked not only by the use of the third person, who is the self's way of imagining himself, but also by the transposition of the situation into visual metaphor. His look can be a way of opening the world to him, but it is much more strongly a parapet behind which he can shelter from the group, from the others.

The development of the artist's inner reality—of what Joyce calls his soul—takes place on two parallel planes, each with its own rhythm, throughout his life. One consists of the incessant progress of an inner reflection along an imaginary line which remains the same from childhood to maturity, the knowledge of a self which is within a world yet which has such an acute awareness of so being that it experiences at the same time a feeling of *not*-belonging. On the very edge of this world, it balances on the clearly defined line separating it from a completely different world into which the slightest shock might precipitate it. This ambiguous feeling is so strongly present that Joyce translates it into concrete terms: it literally informs Stephen's vision of the world or of himself, projecting the pattern of circle and circumference on all his relations with others and with himself.

Being *inside* corresponds to the situation of the child in the adult world; he thinks that it is necessary to be like the grown-ups or the masters, and feels vaguely guilty of not belonging. His situation with regard to his contemporaries is one of "being on the edge"; thus, at Clongowes, in the miniature society swarming with boys obedient to the masters' calls, Stephen "kept on the edge of his line, out of sight of his prefect". Now and then he makes a few token movements in order not to be accused of laziness or of refusing to act like the others. And while they run about shouting, he thinks. He is on the edge, ready to overbalance into their world if prudence so counsels; and in a fraudulent solitude he becomes acquainted with himself. His inner life now develops uninterruptedly and he awaits only himself. There are still many points of contact or of impact with the world outside, but when the soul has to take cognisance of the outside, it simply makes use of it as a landmark in its navigation towards the self, away from the Circes and Charybdis. Thus while apparently submitting, Stephen moves about "within" as he does "on the edge," and contrives to lose nothing more than provisional states or versions of himself this way. The others are always "the fellows" or "they," and Stephen is present, fascinated but terrified, passive, as he is on the famous evening when the word "politics" becomes meaningful to him.

On that occasion, he is only a reflection of Mr. Casey's and his father's feelings, and he blushes, laughs, weeps or trembles in imitation of them, without speaking or understanding. Similarly, on the occasion of the sacrilege committed in the sacristy or the misdoings in the lavatory, he listens to the others' conversations, he "bends forward his head to hear," he looks at their faces in search of enlightenment, but he does not speak. He loses himself in reminiscences inspired by a holy awe and terror while the "fellows were talking together in little groups here and there on the playground". But he is still outside. The only time that he had been "with" someone, it had ended with an abrupt separation; he had stood beside Eileen, he had been near to another human being, near enough to establish a pleasant if disturbing contact. She had put her hand into his pocket and he had touched her hand. Then she had run away laughing.

At this stage Stephen is painfully aware of the smallness of his body, the weakness of his eyes, and the strength, brutality, and violence of the world in which the voices of prefects, parents, and other pupils resound. The silence which he keeps is not yet the chosen silence which serves as a weapon; it is rather the dumbness of the worried or shy person. When he speaks, he does so in answer to loaded questions; already, he feels the need for flight and escape. But he has not yet thought of any crafty methods; he simply tries to make himself inconspicuous. He hopes to escape from Father Dolan, the symbol of injustice and enmity, by keeping out of his way: "It was best to hide out of the way because when you were small and young you could often escape that way". To hide physically is the counterpart of the dissimulation which as a young man he is to use as a much more efficacious weapon.

The feeling of being on the edge of the group comes from what Stephen calls an obscure "foreknowledge"; from his childhood he has felt himself to be living in a time which opens on to the future, a time of waiting. He watches time present, and every action in it seems futile or ridiculous; instinctively he chooses the role of spectator, but since he is in the present, he feigns participation in order to dissimulate his spiritual absence from the group. Life appears to him not as an "existence" but rather as a "destiny," a time to be lived through which will only assume its proper meaning at the end, at the right time. The vocabulary of the inner discourse which he addresses to himself shows the evolution of his inward experience. In the first chapter all his reflections centre on the mystery of the present, which he seeks to solve with the aid of memory; this time is the time of questions and of appearances. He is constantly asking "why?" but receives no reply except by referring to his own impressions or memories; who was right? how could a woman be a house of gold? why was he opposed to the priests? And he thinks of the evening in the infirmary, of Mr. Casey in the crowd, of the dark silent sacristy. "He remembered the summer evening he had been there". He thinks, wonders, evokes, and fears. Time past makes no reply, and he makes very little progress in time present. He remains as much a stranger to society as he was when he had not grasped the meaning of a single word.

From Chapter II onwards he starts to await "the hour when he too would take part in the life of that world" which he dimly perceives by way of the words which he doggedly repeats like a man driving nails into a wall; he has had the first annunciatory intuition. "In secret he began to make ready for the great part which he felt awaited him the nature of which he only dimly apprehended." This stage of presentiments is divided into two: the communal time he spends with the masters who guide and lead him, and his own private time. Thus we see him during the holidays at Blackrock, guarded by two initiators who train him, the one in physical exercises and the other in spiritual exercises as though in semi-parody of the Jesuit training. Uncle Charles takes him out shopping, and Stephen feels ill at ease in the old man's company. In the chapel "Stephen knelt at his side respecting, though he did not share, his piety". Similarly, he submits to the attentions of the old runner Mike Flynn and goes through the required motions, although his heart is not in it. As he "ran round the track in the style Mike Flynn favoured, his head high lifted, his knees well lifted and his hands held straight down by his sides," he would think of the pitiful character that Mike really was, and of his failed life. Old age and death are in wait for Flynn, who as Joyce briefly tells us in passing, goes into hospital in September. Yet Flynn, like Uncle Charles and like the Jesuits, is there for the purpose of teaching the boy how to live. He lives in his own private world, and the "long train of adventures" begins which is destined to lead him from hero to anti-hero to himself at last.

To start with there is a model, "the Count of Monte Cristo," "strange and terrible," not a living person, but a figure out of a book. Such is the strength of Stephen's imagination that it inspires him even in his escapes into the dream world; he first builds up on the parlour table "the wonderful island cave" and "the bright picture of Marseille" springs to mind. But this easily made artificiality cannot satisfy him; he needs to rediscover the "vision". The reality of dream cannot bear the presence of the concrete reality. In his imagination he lives through adventures as marvellous as those in the book, until he sees at last "an image of himself, grown older and sadder, standing in a moonlit garden" (*Portrait*, p. 63).

Monte Cristo, the dark avenger, is one of the heroes who act to mask the soul which is not yet fully born.

In the *Portrait of the Artist* there is no one portrait of the artist, and in fact, no portrait at all. This is because the artist whom Stephen awaits with impatience because he is to furnish him at last with his true face and the form of his destiny has still not really appeared, even at the end of the book. Yet perhaps the portrait is simply the sum of those images of himself which Stephen tries out, considers, and finally rejects. The word "portrait" may make the reader forget that this book is not concerned with the physical or moral portrait of an artist, nor with the play of reciprocity as is *The Portrait of Dorian Gray*, but rather with the "portrait" of a soul. The term would be inadequate if the title were only to be taken as a figure of rhetoric, but "a portrait of the artist as a young man" implies the complex relationship of the artist to his art, the progress of which he is able to follow by taking himself as his model and point of reference. The art, and the artist as creator, develop along parallel lines: the young man watches himself in the process of becoming an artist, and it is the image of his artistic power that he incorporates in his work; thus, he will only know himself when he has finished his book or his painting, and even then it is not a fixed image of himself that he will grasp, but rather an awareness of the promises and potentialities of his imagination. Nothing can be more difficult and deceptive than this attempt to describe oneself while conducting a search for that self. This is why Joyce noted down under the heading "Dedalus" in his Trieste notebook: "He felt the growing pains of his soul in the painful process of life. He shrank from limning the features of his soul for he feared that no everlasting image of beauty could shine through an immature being."[2]

These two characteristics do not occur in the text, but they form an exact definition of the difficulties which Stephen and Joyce reciprocally encountered. An incomplete soul is indeed nothing but a succession of faceless hesitations and impulses. The masks which Stephen adopts because he is not yet himself are provisional faces—what Joyce calls "images" of the artist-to-be. We never "see" Stephen, although he has occasion to look several times in a real mirror, because this book is concerned with deciphering the history of a creator rather than painting the portrait of a man. The growth of his soul is essentially connected with the double phenomenon of vital evolution; on the one hand, as James used to say to Stanislaus,[3] a man is the result of his experiences in childhood and adolescence, and on the other hand, the gradual conquest of the artist's being is represented or commented on by the evolution of his relationship with language. Joyce provides a symbol for this second process in the name of Stephen, "DEDALUS". At one stage, difficult for us to imagine though it now may be, Joyce was thinking of calling the main character "Daly"—a name of no particular resonance,

---

[2] *Workshop*, p. 95.
[3] Stanislaus composed the biography of James, *My Brother's Keeper*, by following the stages of growth chosen to correspond with that of a plant.

but one which, unlike Dedalus, does sound Irish. The choice of "Dedalus" is thus a sign that the book is not simply a realistic biography or autobiography, that it forms part of a work which tends towards myth by way of a carefully established symbolism. It is true that the name "Dedalus" is an odd one, as Nasty Roche says, and it would in fact be unlikely for the bearer of such a name to affirm his authentic Irish descent, were it not that the author's intention to transpose the sum of experience on to an aesthetic and moral level is manifest.

Before discovering the prophetic value of his name Stephen wanders through reality and imagination, lingering over the portraits of certain chosen heroes whom he considers, though without really believing as such, as reflections of himself. He does not yet know who he is able to be, who he should be; he only knows what he does not wish to be. His experiences are negative ones and he proceeds in unconsciously Aristotelian fashion by the elimination of possibles towards the moment when his image will be manifested as epiphany, in a vision neither expected nor anticipated. As he progresses on his quest for the meaning of life, his heroes and masks change, their choice being dictated by the situation in which he finds himself caught; his substitute figures are not models for admiration and imitation. He tends to identify himself with a series of heroes—Parnell, Jesus, Byron, Bruno—not because he wishes to be a hero, but because to some extent these men resemble him in their passion for individual integrity, going in some cases as far as martyrdom itself.

The succession of the poses he adopts represents the amount of spiritual progress made: first there was Parnell, whose death marked his early childhood and led him to question the authority of the Church and of the Jesuits, and then there was Byron; but as we have seen the Parnell phase was relatively short, because Stephen had no intention of playing a part in history. Then there was Monte Cristo, who avenged for Stephen his failure with Eileen, offering him the image of the repentant Mercedes so that he might act the part of the scornful great lord—and here Stephen began to pass from reality to fiction, for Monte Cristo does not really exist. As he brooded on proud vengeances, "a strange unrest crept into his blood" and the shade of the Count faded, while the image of Mercedes remained, sister-image to "the unsubstantial image which his soul so constantly beheld," and which "he wanted to meet in the real world". The real world alternates with that of the dream, enticing and deceiving; his feverish dreams about Mercedes are followed by meetings with "her" in which he discovers the joy of his own solitude and during which he takes great care to remain cold and unmoved.

The magnificence of Monte Cristo is set up like an ironical mirror to the episode of the Whitsun play, in which the boy is obliged to play in reality the part of the ridiculous schoolmaster. This, however, is the last time that Stephen accepts a part in the comedy of reality. His feeling that life is awaiting him elsewhere makes all constraint intolerable, and moreover, he has been betrayed by his father, who had previously made banality reasonably bearable and lively. Henceforth, he has no wish to play; he wants to live, as Stephen Hero had been accustomed to say in more violent terms.

> The toy life which the Jesuits permit these docile young men to live is what I call a stationary march. The marionette life which the Jesuit himself lives as a dispenser of illumination and rectitude is another variety of the stationary march. (*Stephen Hero*, p. 191)

As soon as Stephen has consciously separated himself from the world and begun to make his soul voluntarily that of an exile, forging himself weapons of attack and defence, in the "suspended time" of his true birth and emergence from his bonds and veils, he no longer accepts with the same resignation as before the masks he is called upon to wear and the parts he is supposed to play. His last act as a docile young man occurs at the Whitsun play, his last submission to the comedy one must act at school. But in that theatre the separation between the two worlds shows up with the clarity of an epiphany, and the inanity of the speech Stephen makes to a hall full of invisible faces and anonymous people only emphasises this—especially since the speech is not even composed by him.

By his rejection of the stage costume he rejects all the parts offered to him, keeping in his memory alone the images of the robes he might have worn; thus, he imagines himself as a Jesuit and gives himself the secret pleasure of winning the heart of the girl whom in reality he does not want. He sees himself in the cowl of a perverse monk, a profaner of the cloister, an heretical Franciscan, deciding to serve and then renouncing his servitude, weaving a subtle net of sophisms like Gherardino da Borgo San Donnino, whispering in the girl's ear alone. Free but naked, he plays with the idea of assuming the robes which symbolise the alienation and emasculation which others wish him to adopt as his soul's garment. He tries them on; he mocks; he sees himself as monk, judge, Florentine. And that secret laugh shows that he is becoming mature, that he has outgrown the season of torments, fears, and melancholy, and entered upon that of irony and cynicism.

As though to emphasise the change in Stephen's soul, Joyce gives Monte Cristo an unworthy successor in the person of Claude Melnotte, the sentimental hero of a bad play by Bulwer Lytton. As Magalaner has shown,[4] the brief allusion to this character whose "soft speeches" rise to the lips of the boy as he dreams is intended to replace Monte Cristo's heroic role and to destroy that former idol by degrading it; Mercedes is still there, but the voice heard in the night is that of Melnotte, a man of no birth or honour, a gardener's son. The theme is the same, the haughty disdain of the lady whom the hero is to win in the end, but Bulwer Lytton treats the story in a different way from Dumas. Melnotte wins the lady after many years, true, but by unheroically saving her father from bankruptcy. He too is blessed by Fortune: an unexpected inheritance of wealth makes him worthy of Pauline's love, while wars and travels give him the necessary polish. He so far resembles Edmond Dantès, but the tale of the avenger is retold on a lower level here by a prolix early-Victorian writer. He is to Monte Cristo as Gerty McDowell is to Nausicaa. Both of these patient and eventually successful lovers correspond to a certain form of desire on the part of the "vagabond of the soul": the lover gains his reward, acts magnanimously towards the unworthy beloved, finds strength and maturity in exile.

The Dedalus family—thanks to Stephen's prize money, which allows him for a very short time to acquire the good things of this world, love included—go to see *The Lady of Lyons*, the play in which Claude is the hero. The young man must have been struck by Melnotte's romantic speeches and by their apparent similarity (in expression) to his own longings,[5] but Melnotte's final ambition shows him up as one of the sentimental *petits-bourgeois* whom Joyce and Stephen both detested so much. The goal of so many labours, the reward of so many hardships, is Pauline; yet for Stephen, Pauline would be the height of misfortune and no reward. What he awaits, in his comparative ignorance of woman, is a unique image of beauty, never before seen in this world—a Beatrice profane but pure, visible but inaccessible. Melnotte and Mercedes arouse in him "a tender premonition . . . of the tryst he had looked forward to and. . . . of the holy encounter at which weakness and timidity and inexperience were to fall from him."

And he does indeed wander by chance into "another world," where

---

[4]Magalaner and Kain, *Joyce, The Man, The Work, The Reputation* (London, 1956), pp. 112–9, 325–6.

[5]For example, the lines quoted in Magalaner, *op. cit.*, p. 118: "Wealth! wealth, my mother!—wealth to the mind—wealth to the heart—high thoughts—bright dreams—the hope of fame—the ambition to be worthier to love Pauline."

the gas flames burn as though before an altar, where Mercedes has the plump shape and gay, gentle, real voice of a prostitute he meets. Perhaps this is the long-awaited image at last in the flesh? At any rate, he now feels "strong and fearless and sure of himself". Yet this is not the world he had desired. The fear and shyness from which her perfumed arms free him are only the fears of the flesh, and Stephen does not become Dedalus here. He has simply had one of those negative experiences which cause him to progress by way of error to the truth.

All these dreams are reduced to ashes by the retreat and its sermons. The repentant Stephen replaces the wild roses, the trellises and gardens of Marseille with the scent of his own purified heart, "like perfume streaming upwards from a heart of white rose". Everything now is white, as by opposition to the dark avenger and the night scenes lit by gently tempting gleams: white pudding, white roses, white purified heart. "In the morning light the pale flames of the candles among the white flowers were clear and silent as his own soul." On his knees, he awaits—not the figure of his dreams, not the prostitute, but—"corpus Domini Nostri," and this is a dream that will last. "The ciborium had come to him," and at the end of the labyrinth of eroticism is the Body of the Lord. Stephen returns to order, but the order is that of the Jesuits, offering him the chance to wear their robes. He sees in his mind's eye a possible Stephen, the Jesuit; but unfortunately, although he can clearly decipher the name of the Stephen in this new life, "the Reverend Stephen Dedalus, S. J.," he cannot see the face—or rather, the name evokes only "the mental sensation of an undefined face or colour of a face". Behind the name the artist's imagination refuses to put a face or a soul; there is nothing but a patch of "pallid brick red," and, worse still, it is eyeless and "shot with pink tinges of suffocated anger".

This is a mask which will not do; he chooses rather to fall, to accept disorder and stagnation; he rejects the false spiritual life and the angelic pose. And Newman's prose brings him consolation with a beautiful expression inspired by Virgil, "like the voice of Nature herself". Still the rhythm of words, be they Christian or pagan, calms his soul.

In the long smooth cadences of language, "the rhythmic rise and fall of words" spoken, the movement of the tides, an ancient music full of names and memories, calls him at last to the discovery of himself. He is not destined to be political hero or romantic martyr; the other world is timeless and unbounded, and has begun "slowly climbing the air" towards it. Suddenly the name of Stephen takes on timeless meaning and shows forth Daedalus the fabulous artificer. Stephen's soul is born here, stripped of its material bonds and rising to the sun. The experience is so strongly fantastic that during the time of this flight Stephen is completely metamorphosed. In the soaring stylistic flight, incredulity halts, out of breath, and we hear the inarticulate cry of the bird, following the jerky, ejaculatory parody of the Icarian fall; yet although this cry has more beauty than the other inarticulate cries, including those of the rutting beast, it is still not a poem: "His throat ached with a desire to cry aloud, the cry of a hawk or eagle on high. . . . This was the call of life to his soul . . . not the inhuman voice that had called him to the pale service of the altar" (*Portrait*, pp. 169–70).

This cry is no doubt symbolic; but all the same, only the grotesque image of Thoth is able to make these apparitions credible. This final splendid hallucinatory metaphor is the last in a series of expressions, voluntary or otherwise, of the feeling of being in exile; the series has comprised the distancing of exterior things, the refusal to dance, to join in the game, or to enter into orders, shyness, weakness, and fear —all these "grave-clothes" of the soul, and the quest for "the other world". Now, "where was he? He was alone". In this ecstatic loneliness, away from all company, "unheeded, happy, and near to the wild heart of life," in "a waste of wild air," in this happy exile and solitary paradise, the image of the girl enters his soul and marks it forever. She stands there like a bird, with her ivory thighs and golden hair, childish and virginal, resembling Eileen, but alone, motionless, and tranquil, without shame or wantonness. In this desert, beyond "all the ways of error and glory," he encounters the "wild angel, the angel of mortal youth and beauty," and in the world deserted by language, in an ecstasy which no word breaks, there sounds the silent call, the sign of life.

The bird-girl has a mythical presence which no other creature in *Portrait* has, seeming "like one whom magic had changed into the likeness of a strange and beautiful seabird"; yet she is concrete, real, in the coloured flesh, and is thus truly the angel of life, far removed from the spectral misty world into which Stephen must fall again before his departure. Yet after this airy flight, even falling is sweet. The young man lies upon "the earth that had borne him," while his adventure continues in yet another world, "uncertain as under sea, traversed by cloudy shapes and beings," and in his dream unfurl the shining petals of a flower of light that floods all heaven, as though to show that Dante has found his Beatrice.

With awakening returns reality, and the last glance the new initiate gives to this world shows him the new moon rising, and distant pools. Immediately the scene changes to the opening of Chapter V: "He drained his third cup of watery tea to the dregs . . . staring into the dark pool of the jar" (*Portrait*, p. 173).

Now Stephen is ready for the painful but necessary exile which must be his. Soon he will assume the ancient insignia of the scribe-god Thoth. The long stay that he makes after his revelation constitutes a detailed preparation of his soul for its destiny of exile and writing.

In order concretely to express his exile, Stephen offers himself now as scapegoat to all and affirms his identity as god of writing against all. In chapter V he chooses his Judas-figures.

Joyce only finished *Portrait* after 1909, having rewritten the first three chapters after the summer of 1907. The causes for the interruption were material: it was difficult to earn a living, Stanislaus sometimes refused to feed the whole family by himself, and Joyce often squandered his money on drink. All this was accompanied by his bitterness at encountering as many obstacles as he did to the publication of *Dubliners*. The year 1908 was a particularly stormy one for the little group of exiled Dubliners, and Nora was tending to side with Stannie against Jim. To be truthful, Joyce was grieved because he was not recognised and hailed as a great writer in Ireland. He was also grieved, although without being able to admit as much, by being far away from Dublin; he was constantly harrying Aunt Josephine to be his regular Dublin correspondent and to send him all the newspapers, books, and magazines that she could which were concerned with Ireland. From 1906 onwards his former companions, Eugene Skeffington, Oliver Gogarty, and Tom Kettle had become notable personalities on the political and social fronts, while Joyce, in desperation, was changing from one bank to another, without, however, changing his job. He also was preoccupied by the historical evolution of Ireland, despite his affectation of a critical objectivity and his justification of his policy of non-involvement by referring to the faults in Griffith's ideology.

His distress and jealousy are amusingly summed up in a letter he wrote to Stanislaus:

> Eglinton was sure I would come back begging to Dublin and J.J.B. that I would become a drunkard and Cosgrave that I would become a nymphomaniac. Alas, gentlemen, I have become a bank clerk, and, now that I think of it, bad as it is, it's more than either of my three prophets could do. (November 13, 1906)

And so he fled to Rome, or rather he tried to escape from Joyce the bank clerk. He was also escaping from Trieste, the scene of his unhappiness and of his peccadilloes—yet also the kindly city where he had friends to look after him—in which he felt ashamed of himself. Making the move towards escape is a habit of his, but one can see that this time the place of exile was chosen as a punishment; in Rome he would feel really alien, a complete stranger, caught in the deleterious surroundings of the Church which he had left so proudly. His stay in Rome was to some extent an imitation return to Dublin, and the road leading him to Rome led him also to that return, as he at last became aware of the meanings of his exile. To begin with, he would admit that Ireland's presence was indispensable to him, while also recognising the ambiguity of his feelings towards it; for, like every exile, he had had good reasons to flee, yet he still retained a glowing image of the country he had lost. And he told Stannie that he felt ashamed when in his presence anyone attacked his "poverty-stricken country".

On the other hand, Rome represented for him, in the fashion of an epiphany, a theme which was to provide him with plenty of food for thought: the presence of the past and the traces of long-dead generations, to which his imagination and sensitivity strongly responded. Rome, like Dublin, was a great Catholic city that had lost its splendour. Joyce's mind became obsessed by metaphors, as he saw himself haunted by the Dubliners as Rome was haunted by its dead, and he eventually recognised that these dead (his mother, Dublin, the Church, the new intelligentsia) had a disturbing way of insinuating themselves into the minds of the living. In Rome he began to write 'The Dead,' the most nostalgic, the most connected with Dublin, and basically the most realistic of his novellas; he stated his appreciation of Ireland's hospitality, yet at the end the snow covers all Ireland in its winding-sheet. Rome was to be the place of exile chosen by Richard Rowan, that tortured double of Joyce whose painful return to Dublin after nine years' absence reproduces the miseries felt by Joyce during his stay of several months in 1909. But before returning, it was necessary to prepare oneself to face the prophets of doom.

In Dublin Joyce met all his traitors again, from Gogarty (whom he could never forgive for his riches, for his blasphemous talents, for his literary charlatanism, nor for his selfish coarseness as manifested throughout the time that they shared the accomodation of the Martello tower), by way of Byrne, Cosgrave, and Skeffington the feminist, to the latest comer Thomas Kettle. This last-named had just written an article on *Chamber Music*; appearing in the *Freeman's Journal*, it heaped him with praises, while remaining rather unpleasant and somewhat ambiguous, and served as a model for the extract from a review read by Robert

Hand in *Exiles*.[6] Joyce thanked Kettle at the time, however, and seven years later made him into one of the Judas-figures too. In Kettle, as in Cosgrave, he had "the faith of a master in the disciple who will betray him". He had also had a lesson in bad journalistic writing, as we can still see in the 'Eolus' episode of *Ulysses*.

Throughout the year 1908 and the spring of 1909 Joyce was more than ever turning towards Ireland, and preparing to return there. Back in Trieste, he applied himself especially to journalism, producing a series of articles in Italian for the *Piccolo della Sera*; they deal with aspects of Irish history, literature, and politics, but in reality these three headings serve as camouflage for one subject only: the old theme of betrayal, varied according to the circumstances. These articles are very valuable for throwing some light on Joyce's thought in the years 1908–9. They allow him to confront his treacherous "friends," for the moral slough in which he found himself at this time provided much scope for his enemies' mockery. He needed to make a triumphant return in order to dazzle friends and enemies, even if he did so with the blatancy of a Gallaher. As a journalist, he wrote for the pleasure of airing the talents about which he often boasted, and in order to let Dublin know that he had "arrived". He wrote especially to flourish the "weapon of his art," the best example of which is to be found in the long essay on Oscar Wilde which appeared on the 24 March 1909, *Il Poeta di Salome*. The pretext for this essay was the performance in Trieste of Strauss' opera *Salome*, and from this Joyce elaborated a portrait of the poet in which there occur a number of his favourite ideas on art, the artist, and the "rabblement". Necessity makes him adopt, although with some reti-

---

[6]Compare these two passages, the first by Thomas Kettle, the second from *Exiles*:

"Those who remember University College life of five years back will have many memories of Mr. Joyce. Wilful, fastidious, a lover of elfish paradoxes, he was to the men of his time the very voice and embodiment of the literary spirit. . . . There is no trace of the folklore, folk dialect, or even the national feeling that have coloured the work of practically every writer in contemporary Ireland. Neither is there any sense of that modern point of view which consumes all life in the language of problems. It is clear, delicate, distinguished playing with harps, with wood birds, with Paul Verlaine."

"Not the least vital of the problems which confront our country is the problem of her attitude towards those of her children who, having left her in her hour of need, have been called back to her now on the eve of her longawaited victory, to her whom in loneliness and exile they have at last learned to love. In exile, we have said, but here we must distinguish. There is an economic and there is a spiritual exile. There are those who left her to seek the bread by which men live and there are others, nay, her most favoured children, who left her to seek in other lands that food of the spirit by which a nation of human beings is sustained in life. Those who recall the intellectual life of Dublin of a decade since will have many memories of Mr. Rowan. Something of that fierce indignation which lacerated the heart. . . ."

cence, the defence of a man for whom he felt very little sympathy (partly, perhaps, because Wilde was nobly born and thus closer to Gogarty than to Joyce, and particularly because Joyce had an instinctive, although suppressed, repugnance for homosexuality).[7]

The whole of Joyce's study is oddly constructed on two lines which interweave and cross. Thus, he begins by reciting the list of names Wilde bore, and in which he took such pride, in order to mock the poet's "youthful haughtiness," yet adds at once, "His name symbolises him; Oscar, in the amorphous Celtic *Odyssey*, nephew of King Fingal and the only son of Ossian, was treacherously killed by the hand of his host as he sat at table" (*Critical Writings*, p. 201). Joyce continues as he has begun, aiming his darts at all the institutions, conventions, and personalities constituting the "choir of the just"; his claws scratch at "a pompous professor named Ruskin," Lady Wilde—the revolutionary Irish mother who felt that Dublin Castle should be destroyed—the cult of the sunflower, decadent Anglo-Saxon youth, and especially the "court jesters to the English," those eminent Irishmen who have pandered to London taste, from Sheridan to Bernard Shaw. In *Ulysses*, Stephen refuses to act the jester for the Englishman Haines, and in silence perseveres with his Wildean theory on *Hamlet*, with its paradoxes and deductions that appeal to no-one. He intends to impart it to the Irish National Library and to no-one else. Hardly has he accused Wilde before he begins his rehabilitation; the antipathy Joyce feels for the Apostle of Beauty is dissipated as soon as that Apostle becomes the victim of an Icarian (or Joycean) fall. He is then admitted into the company of martyrs, because "his fall was greeted by a howl of puritanical joy". The lesson which Joyce draws from Wilde's sad story is in fact a defence of his own case; Wilde, he explains, was "hunted from house to house" for crimes against public morality (as homosexual and later penitent Catholic, Wilde could only be a pitiful version of Parnell), but the truth was that "Far from being a perverted monster . . . he is the logical and inescapable product of the Anglo-Saxon college and university system, with its secrecy and restrictions" (*Critical Writings*, p. 204). This is not only true, but also useful to Joyce's argument; he is in fact the logical and inescapable product of the Irish system, and the narrowness of Jesuit education, as suffered by some exceptional souls, can but

---

[7]His characters with homosexual tendencies always have a troubled mind, from the main characters in *Exiles* to the Shakespeare whom Stephen discusses in *Ulysses*, and whom Joyce never much liked.

lead to rebellion and atheism. This accusation is followed by a very perspicacious analysis of what Joyce calls "the pulse" of Wilde's art—in effect an exposition of the pulse of Joyce's own art, the sense of sin.

He deceived himself into believing that he was the bearer of good news of neo-paganism to an enslaved people. His own distinctive qualities, the qualities, perhaps, of his race—keenness, generosity, and a sexless intellect —he placed at the service of a theory of beauty which, according to him, was to bring back the Golden Age and the joy of the world's youth. But if some truth adheres to his subjective interpretations of Aristotle, to his restless thought that proceeds by sophisms rather than syllogisms, to his assimilations of natures as foreign to his as the delinquent is to the humble, at its very base is the truth inherent in the soul of Catholicism: that man cannot reach the divine heart except through that sense of separation and loss called sin. (*Critical Writings*, pp. 204–5)

One might think this to be a piece of self-analysis by Joyce. "Man cannot reach the divine heart." Joyce has here taken up a phrase used by Yeats in *The Tables of the Law*, a novella which he admired and knew by heart. But in the place of God he puts the Creation. The necessity of separation and of "sin" for creation makes him at last offer himself as scapegoat, and he sets out for Dublin in July 1909 in order to be exiled anew.

The pharmakos or scapegoat, archetypal victim, is neither innocent nor guilty.[8] He is innocent insofar as whatever happens to him is much more serious than any crime he might have committed, and guilty because he lives in a guilty world; he takes on his meaning as a manifestation of that society's guilt. Society projects or deposits upon him all that is sick or evil in itself, and then drives him away in order to achieve purification for itself. As simultaneously innocent and guilty, the pharmakos shows up the irony and incongruity of life; the archetype of this absurd irony is Christ, who is shut out from human society because of his innocence, or perhaps in spite of it. Prometheus and Job are also victims of this dialectic of injustice. The movement from a statement of innocence to a statement of guilt leads the character (and the subsequent work he creates) from a primarily human situation to a destiny which surpasses the human condition and attains the status of myth. Thus, the history of the artist begins realistically and ends in Chapter V in an openly mythical atmosphere containing reminiscences of ritual sacrifices and slain gods.

Shut out from the society of men, the hero-victim is accepted and

[8]See Northrop Frye, *Anatomy of Criticism*, pp. 41–2.

welcomed into the world to which in reality he belongs; for Christ, there is a return to the divine, for archetypal figures like Hercules, there is a welcome into the company of the gods. For Stephen, there is the world of art. But no-one can enter this other world without having successfully undergone its tests and trials; the Egyptian Book of the Dead shows the dead man being interrogated rather than judged, before he is accepted. There is thus a double and almost simultaneous movement in the myth of the scapegoat, and his expulsion from one society is followed by his reception into another. The theme of the flight from the land of Egypt is also the theme of the journey across the desert to the Promised Land. Stephen's exile has also a double meaning, for it is necessary for it to be both positive and negative, voluntary and involuntary, flight and quest. It is necessary for him to be driven out and for his condemnation to serve as a test which, if successfully passed, confers the right to salvation. In Chapter V the presence of Stephen crystallises all those oppositions which are represented almost allegorically by a series of individuals—and the moral and metaphysical code which is the basis of society is manifested in all its obstinate rigidity, which is seen as a response to the presence of this "foreign body".

Conversely, Stephen defines his position and its difference by separating himself from every allegiance to this code of values. Such detachment raises the victim from the lowest position to the highest in mythology generally, from execution to deification. In this sense, Stephen may well be both Icarus and Daedalus, for after all the fall of Icarus is only another representation for the death of the son. From this mythical point of view which Joyce has chosen, Chapter V should be read on several different levels, like *Ulysses*; the anagogic level is here the spiritual plane, and Stephen an imitation of reincarnation of Christ facing the crowd and the Pharisees who desire his death. On another level, he is transformed into Thoth, the god of writing. The multiplicity of aggressive figures (whom he voluntarily calls up, as we shall see) corresponds to the pack of hounds eagerly pursuing their prey, the stag with flashing antlers; this situation, a favourite of Joyce's in his youth, is transformed into a ritual dismemberment of the sacrificial body. Parnell, Osiris, Orpheus, Pentheus, and Jesus are all mutilated, wounded, and slain anew in Stephen, and the consequences of this execution are double. First, the society that has committed the murder is strengthened by the sacrifice. Thus, ironically, Joyce's exile or Stephen's flight brings about a consolidation of Ireland by removing the agitator that questioned its organisation and put it in jeopardy; this consolidation also confirms the exile in his conviction that he has made a necessary choice. Society cannot help being troubled, too, by some pangs of conscience, and Stephen is able very skilfully to make his "treacherous" friends feel uncomfortable about this.

He is followed by no-one, yet everyone listens to him, and in some minds he even manages to sow some seeds of doubt. It must finally be emphasised that here, as in all myths of ritual sacrifice, the spiritual world is to be distinguished as a reality distinct from the physical world. The physical world is often represented by means of animal imagery, corresponding to the cruelty attributed to society; the crowd as seen by the victim is Hydra or Leviathan, or Spenser's Blatant Beast. Similarly, in the Bible, the lamb is delivered to the wolves, and the society of devils is represented by Egypt or Babylon, whose kings are monsters or ferocious beasts like Nebuchadnezzar. It is not surprising that Dublin becomes the animal city for Stephen as soon as he has recognised himself as Thoth. The creatures whom he meets reveal their beastly nature —as one would expect from the connotations of the myth. But the *Portrait* is not a religious allegory, and the myth is only a deconsecrated structure from which Joyce draws as much effect as possible, binding realism together with dream and symbolism; if Stephen is not a type of the artist as god like Thoth, then the animal appearance of the world is merely a projection of his imagination, feverishly inflamed by the desire to leave and the fear of leaving. The theme of the fall, upon which Hugh Kenner places so much emphasis in an attempt to rehabilitate Joyce the Catholic,[9] is indeed present in *Portrait*, but its full meaning depends on its ambivalence. Stephen is not an artist but a decadent aesthete. It is necessary to lose one world in order to gain another, as Waith says,[10] and the *Portrait* defines the conditions of creation for one particular writer named Stephen Dedalus.

The young man cannot take a step in this world without becoming involved in a fundamental antagonism. His close friends, his masters, his fellow-pupils, his brothers and sisters, all despite themselves turn into messengers of death, a ghostly multitude that is in opposition to the image of the girl. Chapter V is a chronicle of Stephen's encounters with representative figures who speak on behalf of all the possible existences in Dublin, and a record of their failures. In fact, Stephen passes from

[9]See 'The Portrait in Perspective,' in *James Joyce, Two Decades of Criticism*, ed. Sean Givens, pp. 132–74; Kenner concludes from the affirmation that the central theme of the book is that of sin that Stephen's Icarian fall is proof of his being not an artist but a decadent aesthete.

[10]Eugene M. Waith, 'The Calling of Stephen Dedalus,' in *College English* XVII, p. 257, February 1957.

one to the other, bearing his challenge and hoping to produce exciting effects from it; it is necessary for him to be driven out or declared heretical, and if this does not occur he has to interpret his encounters in such a way that his departure still seems necessary and unavoidable. He well knows how to choose the friends in opposition to whom he may seek a contact with others which he does not, in fact, desire; his hand is seeking for another hand that will not draw back, his voice longing for an ear that will not be closed, and his eyes constantly scan the faces that pass by, spying on their deceitful glints and almost pleased when they find only dead, weary, shifty, or lying eyes looking back. Voices are cold or harsh or cutting—or perhaps they only appear so because it is necessary that they should.

And when Stephen declares to the dean who is squatting in front of the hearth that "I am sure I could not light a fire," he is confessing to a much more mortifying lack of ability and power than one realises. He cannot light a flame in other people; no-one likes him. The only flames that burn for him are those of the pyre that burnt Giordano Bruno, the patron upon whom he calls before his flight in order to strengthen him in his heresy. There are two main reasons for his choice of adversaries: on the one hand, he is conducting the process of separation methodically, and has to reject all more or less pure forms of idealism, which he does by conversing with their specific representatives, and on the other he is an instrument of revenge directed by Joyce against his former friends, even those who held no grudges against him. He who does not completely approve of Joyce is automatically a traitor; and thus J. F. Byrne becomes Cranly, Vincent Cosgrave is Lynch, George Clancy produces Davin, and Skeffington is McCann. Only Gogarty is kept back for some greater destiny, after having appeared as Goggins and then as Doherty at the time of Stephen Hero. One meets again even the priest as seducer of Nora, and three less specific character-types, the Jesuit Father, the mother, and the flirtatious young woman.

The Judas-Figures: Their Models and Functions

The original of Cranly was Joyce's friend John Francis Byrne, nicknamed "The Great Inquisitor".

Byrne was the least intelligent of Joyce's friends and yet the one to whom he seems most attached; this attraction is remarkable for what it tells us about Joyce, for the close, silent nature and aspect of Byrne fascinated the curious Joyce, who felt the power of silence to be limitless if one assumes that it hides words. "The nightshade of his friend's listlessness seemed to be diffusing in the air around him a tenuous and deadly exhalation" (*Portrait*, p. 178).

Stanislaus, with the penetrating lucidity of one who plays second fiddle, and who can observe without being observed, understood at once what was hidden behind the silence and the "intense face":

> J. F. Byrne is a man who never thinks until someone begins to speak to him. Then he deliberates behind an impenetrable mask like a . . . bishop's face, and one is given to understand great mental activity. Having spoken, he pretends to infallibility. The more subtle the conversation becomes, the more brutally he speaks. He is fond of the words "bloody" and "flamin' ". (*Dublin Diary*, 3 April 1904)

Stannie by his very objectivity had captured the essence of Byrne; and Jim adopted most of his notes for his own purposes in his Pola notebook (quoted in *Workshop*, p. 89). In the Trieste notebook he added, "He hears confessions without giving absolution: a guilty priest," and "He asked me if I would deflower a virgin".

The intensity is simply a mask for complete lack of thought, for thought has been replaced by ready-made dogma. Cranly-Byrne has submitted to the Church's imperatives because he has nothing of his own to say; he is nothing but an empty mind, unable to make any response to the excitements and demands of others' thoughts. He can only receive and listen; he cannot even say Amen, because he is not the priest of the divinity to which he has sacrificed his individual thought. And this is the man whom Joyce chooses to receive his confidences, to share his spiritual torments. He probably took a secret pleasure in shocking this impassible visage, especially because of its resemblance to a bishop; as he acted the part of the renegade he doubtless found satisfaction for his imagination in watching the powerless Byrne. Stannie notes that "the thing about Byrne, according to Jim, is that he is so daringly commonplace". This commonplace, brutal speaker is the defender of the Christian virtues, the champion of the home, and in particular of the love owed to one's mother. Nevertheless, he must have possessed some real qualities; his loyalty was such that Joyce, when betrayed by Cosgrave, quite spontaneously took refuge in Byrne's house. He was renowned for frankness, and he lived at that time in 7, Eccles Street; the fact that

Bloom lives in Byrne's house may represent a discreet gesture of gratitude on Joyce's part.

J. F. Byrne wrote an autobiography which, innocently or otherwise, is called *Silent Years: Autobiography with Memoirs of James Joyce and Our Ireland*.[11] The manically detailed material descriptions, interrupted on occasion by maudlin reminiscence and presented in a total incoherence, render comment superfluous; it can be understood that all Byrne-Cranly's wisdom was manifested in his silence. It is delightful to discover the true story of the dean and the fire (*Silent Years*, pp. 33–7), for it presents in epiphany fashion the difference between the Promethean artist and the faded priest at the beginning of Chapter V. Historically, Byrne takes the part of Stephen and Father Darlington that of the dean; Byrne has here the dull eyes of limited intelligence and it is Father Darlington who can see clearly into his puerile behaviour. Byrne insists heavily, unaware of the ironical reversal of roles which Joyce was to make, on aspects of the situation which in fact make him look a fool: "The dean says, 'Pon my word, Mister Byrne, there's quite an art in lighting a fire, is there not?' And all I said in reply was an emphatic assent, 'Yes, sir, there certainly is'."

J. F. Byrne must always have regretted the impulse which led him to tell Joyce in 1902 this banal incident in which Father Darlington played such an illustrious part; he certainly always considered himself morally responsible for the transformation of the venerable gentleman into a pitiful bat-like figure. Twenty years later he visited Joyce in Paris in order to reproach him for this breach of confidence. He tells us that Joyce begged his pardon, but does not say in what tone of voice he did so.

The place occupied by Cranly was greatly reduced between *Stephen Hero* and *Portrait*. In the former work, he is subjected to systematic denunciation: he is stupid, crafty, hypocritical, ignorant, "testing everything by its food value," and yet a great admirer of Stephen. In *Portrait*, he acquires a certain mystery; he is not fully exposed to our gaze. There is no aesthetic side to him, and many characteristics of his would be quite obscure if Joyce had not made some vague allusions to his peasant birth and upbringing. This is, in fact, only done at the end of the book, in Stephen's journal, and by an allusion to Wicklow in a conversation with Lynch. Joyce had a deep contempt for rural Ireland; with the exception of Connaught (for the sake of Galway, where Nora was born), the country had as little attraction for him as it has for Gabriel Conroy

[11]See extracts quoted in *Workshop*, pp. 139ff., 180ff.

in 'The Dead'. He loathed the obscurantism, the superstition, and the submissiveness of the peasants, and could only feel disgust for those whose view of life was limited by hams and harvests.[12] The fact that Cranly is a peasant is very suitable for one who is to play the part of defender of the faith; the superstition and materialism of country life are in themselves an indication of the little worth Stephen sees in his adversary. The mystic roses and perfumes are for the poet, and the pig-styes for the Catholic believer.

Cranly is strong but heavy and dull. In Dublin, his speciality is the improvement of young clerks by means of evening classes; his will to power and influence can only be exercised in a brutal way, and in the town he feels out of place. His appearance and his vulgar accent cannot help but be displeasing to Stephen who dislikes anything rustic or provincial. He comes from "Wickla," as he often says in *Stephen Hero*, from "behind a bushel of Wicklow bran," as Stephen puts it in his anger at seeing Cranly insinuate himself into E. C.'s favour.

Cranly's impressive and deliberate air is only a camouflage for his peasant origin; he only becomes at all lively and interested when the conversation turns to pigs, hams, and kindred subjects.

Byrne considered Joyce's conversations as "Terpsichorean conversational antics," he says; and it is indeed necessary to read *Silent Years* in order to appreciate the difference between the silence of a Byrne (signifying lack of thought) and that of a Joyce (which is the cunning disguise of living thought). In *Portrait*, Cranly is associated in Stephen's mind with dark ideas; behind the mask, which is that of a fanatic, a bishop, or a decollated Saint John, Stephen deciphers fear, betrayal, death, and even hell. And for all this the poet is attracted to this brutal and militant guardian of the faith whose heart conceals a motherly tenderness.

Throughout a series of painful scenes, dialogues, and experiences, the nickname "Great Inquisitor" begins to partake of the nature of an epiphany. Cranly's aggressiveness is all the more disturbing because he is the defender of the beauties of home and family life; this mixture of roughness and sentimentality seems to remind us of the cruelty and the love of music conventionally attributed to the S.S. Stephen himself only escapes from his violence by a double and rather confusing manoeuvre: he has a double or understudy in the person of Temple, a simple-minded young man who looks foreign (which annoys those around him)

---

[12]Yet in Italy he would defend the wretched Irish peasant, as we can see, for instance, from the article 'Ireland at the Bar,' which appeared in the *Piccolo della Sera* in September 1907.

and who is quite intelligent (which is an even worse offence).[13] He makes some remark of surprise about one of the priests whose vocation had come late in life, and who had abandoned his wife and children after his conversion, and this remark sparks off Cranly's anger:

> Cranly seized him rudely by the neck and shook him, saying:
> —You flaming floundering fool! I'll take my dying bible there isn't a bigger bloody ape, do you know, than you in the whole flaming bloody world! (*Portrait*, p. 199)

Temple, an inferior version of Stephen, prides himself on a candour which is meant to be modelled on that of Rousseau.

> —Blast him, curse him! said Cranly broadly. Don't talk to him at all. Sure, you might as well be talking, do you know, to a flaming chamber-pot as talking to Temple. Go home, Temple. For God's sake, go home. (*Portrait*, p. 200)

The choice of words (blast him, curse him . . . for God's sake) is deliberately ambiguous; Stephen does not fail to observe Cranly's lack of spiritual balance. His threats to Temple are indirectly aimed at Stephen, "the mind of man independent," and the individual mind for which he stands, for everything that the candid, clumsy Temple says can be translated into the more skilful language of Stephen too. Cranly is ferociously pure—for him every man is a swine—and his obsession with the pigs, together with his obvious intellectual insufficiency, causes him to see everywhere men as swine, and to criticise the simple youthful curiosity manifested by Temple; he interprets everything the latter says as though it were obscenity or blasphemy:

> Temple turned back to Stephen and asked:
> —Do you believe in the law of heredity?
> —Are you drunk or what are you or what are you trying to say? asked Cranly, facing round on him with an expression of wonder. (*Portrait*, p. 230)

Stephen knows that Cranly has a strange way of commemorating defunct friendships, and is ready to see himself as the subject of the next epitaph, "A flaring flaming bloody idiot!" He looks at Cranly's face, distorted by hatred, and seeks with curious anxiety for some sign of his

---

[13]Temple is founded on the medical student John Elwood, with his feverish face and slow, clumsy walk. "He has a long head like a gipsy, Jim says. He is reported to be the best chemist in the medical school." (*Dublin Diary*, p. 36.)

friendship. To him Stephen confides his spiritual troubles and his clashes with his family, as though he were choosing a judge to condemn him; Cranly is incapable of love except in the form of hatred, and his violent passion for woman as wife and mother makes him liable to the worst brutalities of hysterical sanctity. Every word that relates to love as physical maddens him with rage, for to him love is the enemy to flesh. His aggressive reactions are abnormally strong here. This would be sufficient to ensure for Stephen the form of excommunication which he wants to provoke, but this is not all. On the one hand, Stephen has found out that Cranly is his rival for "her" favours, and thus feels guilty. "She passed out from the porch of the library and bowed across Stephen in reply to Cranly's greeting. He also? Was there not a slight flush on Cranly's cheek? Or had it come forth at Temple's words? The light had waned. He could not see" (*Portrait*, p. 232).

On the other hand, he has a vague presentiment that something more dark and suspect attracts Cranly to him:

> Stephen, remembering swiftly how he had told Cranly of all the tumults and unrest and longings in his soul, day after day and night by night, only to be answered by his friend's listening silence, would have told himself that it was the face of a guilty priest who heard confessions of those whom he had not power to absolve but that he felt again in memory the gaze of its dark womanish eyes.
>
> Through this image he had a glimpse of a strange dark cavern of speculation but at once turned away from it, feeling that it was not yet the hour to enter it. (*Portrait*, p. 178)

From then on, Stephen tries occasionally to understand the secret of Cranly's loneliness, his refusal to exchange confidences with his friend, and his look of a guilty priest enjoying a confession.

The part Cranly plays, his affectation of a fatherly, emotional superiority, and Stephen's identification of his friend with an image which is both feminine and ecclesiastical, all these things cause Stephen to feel a certain emotion when the other touches him:

> Cranly seized his arm and steered him round so as to lead him back towards Leeson Park. He laughed almost slyly and pressed Stephen's arm with an elder's affection.
> —Cunning indeed! he said. Is it you? You poor poet, you!
> —And you made me confess to you, Stephen said, thrilled by his touch, as I have confessed to you so many other things, have I not?
> —Yes, my child, Cranly said, still gaily. (*Portrait*, p. 247)

Even the turn taken by their discussion of love sounds harsh and somehow false:

—Have you never loved anyone? Cranly asked.
—Do you mean women?
—I am not speaking of that, Cranly said in a colder tone. I ask you if you ever felt love towards anyone or anything? (*Portrait*, p. 240)

This may be the speech of a guilty priest, but is already a forerunner of the speech of the disciple to the master he will betray, the speech of Robert Hand in *Exiles*.

Cranly, now grave again, slowed his pace and said:
—Alone, quite alone. You have no fear of that. And you know what that word means? Not only to be separate from all others but to have not even one friend.
—I will take the risk, said Stephen.
—And not to have any one person, Cranly said, who would be more than a friend, more even than the noblest and truest friend a man ever had.
His words seemed to have struck some deep chord in his own nature. Had he spoken of himself, of himself as he was or wished to be? (*Portrait*, p. 247)

Finally, Cranly is a mediocre character, as is suggested by Stanislaus, and by Maurice in *Stephen Hero*, upon whom Stephen wishes at all costs to confer some mysterious quality which will make him a fit audience for genius.

Between *Stephen Hero* and *Portrait*, the character of Cranly acquires a new dimension which can best be gauged by considering the disappearance of the whole mechanism of psychological, or rather phenomenological, analysis which is applied to his rather disagreeable behaviour in the first version. Laconic, masked, and disfigured by Stephen's gaze, he becomes disturbing and inspires an instinctive but nameless mistrust. His cruel nature appears in enigmatic form in the last chapter, when he asks a riddle which Stephen hears and writes down on 30 March, a riddle like an epiphany: "A mother let her child fall into the Nile. Still harping on the mother. A crocodile seized the child. Mother asked it back. Crocodile said all right if she told him what he was going to do with it, eat it or not eat it" (*Portrait*, p. 250).

In Stephen's imagination this crocodile becomes a monstrous equivalent for the old sow that eats her farrow and of every kind of threat to the freedom and the life of the soul that is born in Ireland; he both thinks and speaks of this several times. Joyce's artistic intention becomes clearer if one compares the notes in his Pola notebook (mainly borrowed from Stannie's diary) which served for the creation of the character in *Stephen Hero*, and his notes made in Trieste; the Byrne described in the former is indeed an "immoral plebeian," a ridiculous and pretentious fellow realistically expounded. The person he becomes for the purposes of art in the Trieste notebook is a perverse creature of symbolic depth; he is something more than himself. Joyce insists on his role of usurper and on his relationship to the powers of religion, and especially on his vulgarity and lack of culture.

In the Pola notebook he is:

> Features of the Middle Age: a pale, square, large-boned face, an aquiline nose with wide nostrils rather low in his face, a tight-shut lifeless mouth, full of prejudice, brown eyes set wide apart under short thick eyebrows and a long narrow forehead with short coarse black hair brushed up off it resting on his temples like a iron crown.
> The Grand Byrne.
> Wicklow.
> Brutal, "bloody," "flamin'."
> Thomas Squaretoes.
> Talking like a pint.
> Deprecate eke so.
> Did that bloody boat the Seaqueen ever start?
> Immoral plebeian.
> His Intensity the Sea-Green Incorruptible.
> to make me drink
> Stannie takes off his hat.

In the Trieste notebook (1907–9), the notes which Joyce used in the composition of *Portrait*:

> He hears confessions without giving absolution: a guilty priest.
> His silence means that he has an answer to what puzzles me.
> His speech has neither the rare phrases of Elizabethan English nor the quaintly turned versions of Irish idioms which I have heard with Clancy. I hear in its drawl an echo of the Dublin quays, given back by the decaying seaport from which he comes, and in its energy an echo of the flat emphasis of Wicklow pulpits.
> He asked me if I would deflower a virgin.
> He has one epitaph for all dead friendships: A Sugar.
> He spoke to me as: my dear man.
> On the steps of the National Library he dislodged an old fig-seed from a rotten tooth.
> He said that I was reared in the lap of luxury.[14]

[14] *Workshop*, pp. 89 and 92–3.

In *Portrait*, Cranly's complete inanity is translated as epiphany in an icy silence, and a series of visions confirms Stephen's intuition of his intellectual loneliness, ending thus: "Stephen watched his face for some moments in silence. A cold sadness was there. He had spoken of himself, of his own loneliness which he feared. 'Of whom are you speaking?' Stephen asked at length. Cranly did not answer" (*Portrait*, p. 247).

In *Stephen Hero*, the diagnosis had been more frank and more simple: Cranly had been a proud, selfish man wanting to exercise some power over another, both flattered and disturbed by the inexplicable fact of Stephen's friendship with him. All his petty and hurtful behaviour was designed to camouflage the intellectual nullity of which he was so conscious beside the brilliant poet Stephen. And why did Stephen choose such companions? Partly, it seems, because at the beginning he was taken in, as Joyce was, by the appearance of wisdom, and partly because Joyce was attracted by mediocre people who would be passive and easy to subjugate, because his wish was to expound his ideas rather than to discuss them. Furthermore, Byrne, Clancy, and Cosgrave were of low social origin, and with them Joyce did not feel inferior or socially uneasy, for they might take his poverty-stricken clothing for artistic costume. Joyce was acquainted with young men from higher social levels who were more intelligent and cultured, and who esteemed him considerably; Skeffington, Gogarty, or Eugene Sheehy would have been more likely to discuss ideas freely with him, but Joyce suffered because his self-esteem was hampered by class barriers here. Only Gogarty, who for a while superficially affected Bohemian life, was admitted to some intimacy, before Joyce realised the artificiality of his affectations.

The original of Davin, George Clancy, is one of the few friends Joyce had at University College and who did not betray him—perhaps because, as chance would have it, he never met him again after college. Only Davin (who is Madden in *Stephen Hero*) calls Stephen by his Christian name, and even affectionately calls him Stevie sometimes. He is a peaceful Hercules who belongs to the Gaelic Sporting Association founded by Michael Cusack in 1884 and who supports every movement in favour of the Gaelic with sincere enthusiasm and a complete lack of ideology. Joyce detested the hefty Cusack and his violent, unintelligent behaviour; the movement could only seem to him a caricature of intelligent nationalism. He felt it better to pay heed to the type of nationalism represented by Thomas Kettle, which, although Catholic, was at least open-minded about Ireland as part of Europe, than to listen to Citizen Cusack's disturbing racialist speeches on the need to revive the nation by means of its healthy, sporting younger generation—speeches which today would sound disagreeably Fascist. Yet Davin is the only person for whom Stephen feels affection without any mistrust; he is "flattered by his confidence and won over to sympathy by the speaker's simple accent". Unlike Lynch and Cranly, Davin also confides in Stephen, and it seems that at last this may be a real and happy friendship. But the innocent and friendly Clancy was unable to understand Joyce's violent hostility to the game of hurley.

In *Portrait*, Davin is saddened by Stephen's attitude and mistakes his meaning when he mocks the brandishers of hurley sticks; what Stephen is saying, in effect, is that if there must be an armed revolution, then it should at least be an effective one. And Joyce proved to be quite a good prophet in those years 1913–14, apparently foreseeing the absurd massacres of Easter 1916, when the disorganisation and lack of preparation of the various small clandestine groups brought Irish nationalism to a pointless and bloody, though heroic, failure, and achieved nothing but the creation of further myths to replace those of Parnell or, for others, of the Fenians. To Davin, the refusal to practise some sport and to learn the Gaelic is a rejection of one's origins: " 'Then be one of us,' said Davin. 'Why don't you learn Irish? Why did you drop out of the league class after the first lesson?' " (*Portrait*, p. 202). (Here can be felt some of Joyce's annoyance with people like Padraic Pearse, the idealistic teacher of mathematics, who proclaimed the Republic in 1916 and who taught the Gaelic while insulting and deprecating the English language.)

The conversation that follows is like a dialogue between two deaf men, for Stephen and Davin define "the Irishman" in diametrically opposed fashions. What Stephen says here is what Joyce was to say all his life, and what he was to say to Budgen in Zurich, at the time of *Ulysses*, in just the same form. It is the formulation in reactionary terms of a defeatist and alienist policy for the sake of purely subjective and personal good. It hardly differs from what Stephen says here as truth:

> A tide began to surge beneath the calm surface of Stephen's friendliness.
> —This race and this country and this life produced me, he said. I shall express myself as I am.
> —Try to be one of us, repeated Davin. In heart you are an Irishman but your pride is too powerful. (*Portrait*, p. 202)

What Davin says is quite true, although the words he uses are bound to make Stephen rebel. It is indeed true that he, like Joyce, is deeply an Irishman; but he does not wish to be a ridiculous or shameful Irishman. Shortly he is to define himself as product of Ireland by an opposition which is a kind of fidelity, or of angry recognition of the mark Ireland has left upon him. Davin too is a product of Ireland in the opposite sense: he is completely brainwashed by the vague mental forms of University College, and his language might be that of a Jesuit when he says, "You're a terrible man, Stevie, always alone," taking the short pipe from his mouth.

The misunderstanding is all the more serious because it has other, secret sources; these are added by Joyce, who fits Davin into a whole complex of antagonisms, some evident and others not, in order to weave all Stephen's grievances and grudges into one inextricable fabric whose place is between the consciousness and its expression in words and the obscure unconscious or dissimulated motives behind it. Thus, just as Cranly with his touch and his womanish eyes is connected with a vague suspicion of homosexuality, Davin the pure is connected with a sexual problem of a different order: he belongs to what Stephen Daedalus used to call the brotherhood of the "grotesque and absurd virginities". At least, this is what Stephen deduces from the narrator's virtuous behaviour in the story which Davin tells him; the latter intends not to boast of his amorous conquest but rather to display a puritanical indignation. One night, after a hurley match, he walked home across country, and stopped at a cottage to ask for a drink of water, and

> a young woman opened the door and brought me out a big mug of milk. She was undressed as if she was going to bed when I knocked and she had her hair hanging and by something in the look of her eyes . . . I thought that she must be carrying a child. She kept me in talk a long while at the door, and I thought it strange because her breast and her shoulders were bare. She asked me was I tired and would I like to stop the night there. (*Portrait*, p. 182)

But Davin who has toward Irish myth and legend "the same attitude as towards the Roman catholic religion, the attitude of a dull-witted loyal serf," does not go in: "I thanked her and went on my way again, all in a fever. At the first bend of the road I looked back and she was standing at the door. The last words of Davin's story sang in his [Stephen's] memory. . . ." (*Ibid.*)

What Stephen thinks is expressed by a series of images drawn from the past and superimposed; their ambiguity is made clear less by the commentary Stephen himself makes on them than by the meanings which are called up by an imagery which has already been used under different circumstances. The story told by the "peasant student" as he walks through the "dark narrow streets of the poorer jews" (where Stephen had eagerly sought a kind of liberation) evokes even in that place of sad and weary eroticism an image of woman "reflected in other figures of the peasant women whom he had seen standing in the doorways at Clane," the image of a woman "calling the stranger to her bed," because the Irish soul, even when lit feebly by its vacillating conscience, must plunge back into darkness and loneliness. The prostitution of the "soul" suggested by the peasant woman's behaviour is even more humiliating than that of the soulless woman. This bat-like behaviour, frightened and wavering in the light, is that of the Irish soul faced with life —that of the obscure race that lives on potatoes. The woman who gives herself to the stranger is also E. C. whispering her "innocent transgressions" to the priest, and she is Ireland, milking her cows that the English may have milk; she is innocence in guilt. The bat, obviously an emblem of blindness, has already been used as a comparison in the terrifying evocation of Father Dolan. Thus the Church, woman, sexuality, and prostitution mingle in Stephen's mind, and discourage him—not because of any Puritanism in his nature, but because of his pride. The woman did not choose Davin; she would give herself impartially to any stranger if he were sufficiently young and attractive. The images of virtue, truth, beauty, and virginity tempt the poet who loves light and handsome lines, but woman is venal and vulgar; he repeats this to himself, as a short epiphany-like episode comes to illustrate his disgust: " 'Buy that lovely bunch. Will you, gentleman?' The blue flowers which she lifted towards him and her young blue eyes seemed to him at that instant images of guilelessness, and he halted till the image had vanished and he saw only her ragged dress and damp coarse hair and hoydenish face" (*Portrait*, p. 183).

In any case, she cannot tell the genius from "a tourist from England or a student of Trinity"; women are neither nationalist nor Catholic when they act naturally. They are blind and alone and sad.

These are the retarded creatures that live on the dark roads of the country in Ireland, or the dregs of the urban population. In Davin's anecdote Stephen finds again one of Joyce's favourite themes, the backwardness of the Irish peasant. And he sees in his friend's eyes "the terror of soul of a starving Irish village in which the curfew was still a nightly fear."

This is a terror which Stephen, like Joyce, also feels strongly, for in the last analysis Joyce was frightened by the fact that the Irishman was excluded from the world because of the degenerate nature of his race, as well as by his inability sufficienty to modernise his mental world to permit him any meaningful contact with Europe. Stephen Daedalus had expressed himself venomously on the subject: "The [English] intelligence of an English city is not perhaps at a very high level but at least it is higher than the mental swamp of the Irish peasant" (*Stephen Hero*, p. 59).

But in *Portrait* everything, beginning with Stephen himself, is raised to the level of archetype. The peasant becomes a devilish being, whom a note in Stephen's journal (14 April) describes as his deadly enemy, the mythical ancestor of his race, the anti-Dedalus who cannot even imagine the world around him but who has not yet progressed beyond a vaguely Ptolemaic conception of it. The old man spits and says, "Ah, there must be terrible queer creatures at the latter end of the world". For him, the world has two ends, that where his hut stands, and "the other," which has little or no interest for the ancestor of "a race of clodhoppers". The Old Man of the Mountain and the Woman as Bat are the retarded deities of this dead world. Stephen is haunted by him, as he is in *Ulysses* by the ghost of his mother. "I fear him. I fear his red-rimmed horny eyes. It is with him I must struggle all through this night till day come, till he or I lie dead, gripping him by the sinewy throat till . . ." (*Portrait*, p. 252).

But what can Stephen do? He feels incapable of bringing about a Copernican revolution in such a backward world, and the power of the Church is too strong: all those who wish to bring enlightenment are heretics. Ireland remains the poor, submissive old peasant woman who serves the young men with milk in *Ulysses*. But one may still wonder whether this is the whole truth, or whether Stephen does not find rather facile justifications in confusing the Church with Peasant Superstition; it may well be that what he detests is not so much the primitive Catholic peasantry as the Gaelic mind, with its "unwieldy tales," "upon which no individual mind had ever drawn out a line of beauty". What is missing in this world of dark roads is a form that will be familiar and ritualised: the reassuring, immutable, and harmonious architecture of the mediaeval world, of culture, and the lighted thoroughfare bearing towns and signs of the past.

Eventually, the awkward friendship between Stephen and Davin concludes on a troubled and painful note, with the vision aroused in Stephen's mind by their encounter with a dwarfish, monkey-faced man called The Captain, who is as fond of Sir Walter Scott's novels as was the pervert in 'An Encounter,' in *Dubliners*. The story goes that he is "come of an incestuous love," and this idea calls up in Stephen's mind the image of a melancholy couple, Davin with his sister, embracing without joy or passion. Stephen recognises his friend's strong caressing hand, and wonders why he should have had such thoughts. "Had Davin's simplicity and innocence stung him more secretly?" The phrase would remain obscure to the reader were it not that all these vague impulses of a mind attracted by perverse and ignoble thoughts take on meaning (although purely retrospective) through the much more explicit psychological investigations of *Exiles*. There the need to befoul and to be befouled, ill-explained in the romantic and adolescent context of *Portrait*, is expressed in all its brutality, and what Richard says reveals latent homosexuality and masochism in Stephen's emotions, as a later analysis will show.

Francis Skeffington was a character who seemed to have stepped straight out of some Victorian London or Oxford;[15] he was the type of the "vaguely anti-everything" rebel, as Francis Newman, the Cardinal's agnostic brother, used to say of himself. Idealist, iconoclast, feminist, vegetarian, pacifist, he was opposed to every institution; he wore golfing breeches because he wished to protest against conventional clothes, a beard because after Parnell it was no longer the done thing; he was a naïf but daring agitator, whose prestige may well have detracted from Joyce's somewhat. It would annoy Joyce to find himself in company with a rebel more radical than himself. But, fortunately, Skeffington still had some religious belief, and was blindly confident in politics. This enabled Joyce to make from him the enthusiastic, aggressive, and self-sufficient MacCann who wishes (as he did in real life) to make Stephen sign a petition approving of the czar's apparently pacific designs. Nothing could be more opportune for Stephen, the ceremonious and sceptical, than this militant fervour which so often goes astray and furnishes material for mockery.

"MacCann began to speak with fluent energy of the Tsar's rescript, of Stead, of general disarmament arbitration in cases of international disputes, of the signs of the times, of the new humanity and the new gospel of life which would make it the business of the community to secure as cheaply as possible the greatest possible happiness of the greatest possible number" (*Portrait*, p. 196). His reported speech

[15]He added the name of his wife, Hannah Sheehy, to his own. Sheehy-Skeffington was shot by a mad English officer in 1916, as he was attempting to stop a group of revolutionaries from pillaging.

sounds very like Bloom's proclamations of the new Bloomusalem in 'Circe' or his political speeches in 'Eumeus'—to which Stephen responds with the same cool irony. MacCann-Skeffington had all the vigour of the fanatic and was easily provoked to insults; thus, Stephen is called "reactionary," which is not entirely untrue, and "minor poet," which is unfair. In real life, Joyce and Skeffington maintained a respectful discord between them,[16] and Joyce had had to seek out some murky conspiracy in order to implicate in it, for his own purposes, the innocent "Hairy Jaysus". When, in 1903, the latter had suggested that Joyce give some French lessons at the University, Joyce personally conveyed his refusal to the dean Darlington, convinced, or feigning to be so, that the Church was seeking to seduce or compromise him by offering him such propositions. Thus Skeffington too could be a Judas-figure.

Because Byrne represented immovable, passive power, and because he had never done Joyce any direct wrong, he was designated to be the apostle and defender of mother-love, which Joyce—although always wishing to receive it from someone—feared and always associated with death. His friend Vincent Cosgrave, however, sinned greatly against Joyce; he accompanied him on debauches when at the University, was an indefatigable disciple, always free and easy, always available, intelligent, and (as far as we can tell from Ellmann and Stanislaus) always conscious of himself as a failure. He lived on Joyce's intellectual "unconsidered trifles," and was the perfect friend according to Joyce's definition. Because he was weak and ill-treated, his real liking for Joyce led him to oppose the others, in particular Byrne the favourite, and to wish either to possess his friend fully or, if this were not possible, to destroy him. He is both pitiful and dangerous, playing the part of the small traitor in both Joyce's and Stephen's life. More masochistic than sadistic, he has neither Cranly's brutality nor the resource of silence as mask; he is a small unfortunate Iago, unable to overcome his own weakness, an ideal Judas-type. If Joyce and Stephen are capable of pity, Lynch and Cosgrave are incapable of generosity. This was what was to kill Cosgrave, but not before he had injected some of his poison into Joyce's heart too. As he appears in Stannie's diary, he is unstable, intelligent, and sardonic, but with a low mind—the opposite of Byrne, who is infinitely less intelligent and more crafty but also less vile. He commits real acts of cowardice, in particular that which earned him the name

[16]They had had printed together, at their own expense, the articles which they had written for, and had censored by, the College—Joyce's *Day of the Rabblement* and an essay by Skeffington claiming equal University rights for women.

of Lynch. He always walked with his hands in his pockets when following Joyce on his wanderings. In the Trieste notebook, Joyce wrote "His
hands are usually in his trousers' pockets. They were in his trousers'
pockets when I was knocked down on S. Stephen's Green." So
they were when Stephen had a similar experience in Nighttown, in
Ulysses;[17] as though he knew in advance that both would repeat the
myth of Judas' kiss, Joyce was not deceived by Cosgrave's ambiguous
behaviour, attributing it to the misery of his imprisoned soul. In the
Trieste notebook he wrote a symbolic portrait of Cosgrave, repeated
word for word in *Portrait of the Artist*, expressing his scorn and pity for
this condemned man:

> The long slender flattened skull beneath the long pointed cap brought
> before Stephen's mind the image of a hooded reptile. The eyes, too, were
> reptile-like in glint and gaze, Yet at that instant, humbled and alert in their
> look, they were lit by one tiny human point, the window of a shrivelled
> soul, poignant and self-embittered. (*Portrait*, p. 205)

In his notebook, Joyce wrote after the image of the serpent ashamed
of his serpent-nature, "He is a self-consumer," a phrase which seems
tragic in its implications.

The young Joyce *knew* all this, as did Stephen, and took it into account when adopting an attitude of indulgence towards his friend the
serpent. Lynch has not the strength of will to live. Cosgrave's temporal
punishment was to be nicknamed "Lynch," after the mayor of Galway
who hanged his own son, and Joyce was to act more fiercely when his
resentment was not tempered by pity. Cosgrave was a double-sided
personality in whom good and bad were close companions; while he was
spreading the news of Giorgio's birth with the words "Mother and
bastard both doing well," he was also writing a charming letter of
congratulations to Joyce, offering to help him read over *Stephen Hero*
and asking, "Meanwhile why in the name of J.—Lynch. Anything but
that." For Joyce, it was merely a spark of wit, but for Cosgrave it was
a lasting mark of his own treachery, a treachery which found more
scope in which to exercise itself when Jim returned to Dublin. Stephen
creates his Judas by naming him Lynch.[18] Joyce did not know that
Cosgrave had attempted to gain Nora's favours, after Jim had met her.
She had given him no encouragement, but (and this shows again his

[17]See Ellmann, p. 156.
[18]In 'Circe,' "Exit Judas—et laqueo se suspendit." Cosgrave drowned himself in the
Thames in 1927.

unhappy, unbalanced nature) he had confided the "affair" to Stannie in strict secrecy, feeling unable, no doubt, to bear his guilt without going through an indirect form of confession. In life, he was destined to be the slave rather than the disciple of this master, who unbendingly pursued his own doctrine. Stephen's behaviour towards Lynch is quite different from his behaviour when with Cranly; the relationship of domination is almost reversed, for while Stephen follows Cranly and waits for him, it is Lynch, who, apart from a few gestures of irritation, follows Stephen: "Stephen turned towards his companion and looked at him for a moment boldly in the eyes. Lynch, recovering from his laughter, answered his look from his humbled eyes." *(Ibid.)*

Lynch is the champion of pornography, of the aesthetic of the ugly. His vocabulary is dirty, his habits betraying inhibition and pointless revolt. To him Stephen expounds his aesthetic theory, choosing as though to please himself an audience with sufficient sensibility to understand him, but one who is too materialistic and unhappy to be convinced. Their dialogues become comical by their contrast: when Stephen says,

> To speak of these things and to try to understand their nature and, having understood it, to try slowly and humbly and constantly to express, to press out again, from the gross earth or what it brings forth, from sound and shape and colour which are the prison gates of our soul, an image of the beauty we have come to understand—that is art

the poor and envious Lynch says things like "To think that that yellow pancake-eating excrement can get a good job, and I have to smoke cheap cigarettes!" *(Portrait,* p. 211).

Cosgrave's favourite colour was yellow, probably by chance (unless, given the time in which the book is set, 1898–1903, it is meant to be an allusion to the yellow favoured by aesthetes like Aubrey Beardsley), and Joyce takes pleasure in this craze for yellow, because for him the spectrum from yellowish to brown was emblematic of decomposition and treachery. Cosgrave had also confided to Joyce that in childhood he had once eaten cow-dung, and this experience—hardly surprising to us after Freud's discoveries—takes on an ironical significance when it is recalled that even in childhood Stephen's experiences were already of an artistic or moral order, and that the sight of cow-dung made him sick. Everything fits neatly together to make Lynch into the complete "anti-artist". He says, "Please remember, though I did eat a cake of cowdung once, that I admire only beauty".

From Lynch's actions we see how forbidden desires are satisfied in the most alienating fashion: Lynch, who loves only beauty, manages to soil everything he sees or hears by his inevitable masochism, and his relationships with living things are obscene or excremental. When confronted with the statue of Venus he scribbles his name across its "hypotenuse";[19] it is clear that he is imprisoned irremediably in his Irish soul.

Sound and shape and colour are doors to the soul, but they are condemned in Ireland where the soul is to be forbidden even the purest pleasures. Even nature is sparing of sounds and colours, and in grey monotony seems to be on the side of mankind, making the fine phrase *Pulchra sunt quae visa placent* seem as out of place as possible in the setting, in Dublin: "A crude grey light, mirrored in the sluggish water and a smell of wet branches over their heads seemed to war against the course of Stephen's thought" (*Portrait*, p. 206).

Lynch is sensitive to the unfavourable surroundings, with more impatience than Stephen:

> A long dray laden with old iron came round the corner of Sir Patrick Dun's hospital covering the end of Stephen's speech with the harsh roar of jangled and rattling metal. Lynch closed his ears and gave out oath after oath till the dray had passed. Then he turned on his heel rudely. Stephen turned also and waited for a few moments till his companion's ill-humour had had its vent. (*Portrait*, p. 209)

The artist is better able than Lynch to bear the ironical offensive of reality, because the latter is only sensitive to the murderous irony of life; while Stephen talks of beauty, music, and harmony, Lynch's world suddenly explodes into ugliness and hideous noise. Stephen can make use of the dissonance to emphasise what he was saying about *consonantia*, but Lynch—because of his refusal to choose art as means of escape—is imprisoned by that refusal and has to undergo the horror without being able to laugh at it or turn it to account.

Cosgrave did not have his hands in his pockets when Nora came on the scene. Eventually, in 1909, he was able to realise briefly his old secret dream, to dispossess and wound the master, Joyce. Cosgrave

---

[19]Lynch says, "I told you that one day I wrote my name in pencil on the backside of the Venus of Praxiteles in the Museum" (*Portrait*, p. 205). Compare the thoughts of Bloom in the Museum: "Beauty: it curves, curves are beauty. Shapely goddesses, Venus, Juno: curves the world admires. Can see them library museum standing in the round hall, naked goddesses. Aids to digestion. They don't care what man looks. All to see. . . . They have no. Never looked. I'll look today. . . . Bend down let something fall see if she." (*Ulysses*, p. 173.)

boasted that he had taken Joyce's place with Nora on the nights when she did not meet Jim.

Joyce owed a good deal to this Judas, even the exaltation of his love for Nora and the enrichment of his art on deeper levels—as we shall see in examining *Exiles*.

Last Hesitations

The last four pages or so of *Portrait* make a clean break technically with everything that has gone before them, just as Stephen is in the process of making his final break with Dublin. He signifies his exiled condition by withdrawing into the depths of himself, into his own conscience with its turmoil of doubts, of dreams whose meaning he is trying to find, of visions of reality whose hidden significance he is studying. Joyce thought it ridiculous of Stannie to keep a diary; indeed, it would be more accurate to see these brief notes, often syntactically disjointed and fragmentary, as resembling the working notebooks in which Joyce recorded, dating them as he did so, his dreams, epiphanies, and reflections on problems of aesthetics. His state of mind is, nevertheless, ambiguous, and he is anxious not to conceal this from himself. Between his long conversation with the solemn Cranly on 22 March and his final decision to leave, on 27 April, five weeks pass in material and spiritual preparation, but also in grave hesitations. As long as Stephen continues to test the autonomy of his thought and imagination, he is aware of vague forces of resistance within himself, especially his attachment (which, though tenuous, is still real) to his mother, and the physical attraction he still feels towards the girl. He makes one last effort to combat these feelings within him, defending himself with every weapon he has. The 5 and 6 April are days of temptation: "Wild spring. Scudding clouds. O life! . . . Eyes of girls among the leaves. Girls demure and romping." The temptation is still there; and at once resistance is organised, in a fashion both comical and touching.On 6 April, Stephen must have confided his distress and his crazy hopes to Lynch. Perhaps she remembers the past. . . . but Stephen the sophist replies that the past is consumed in the present and that the present is living only because it brings forth the future. Lynch contributes to the deconsecration of myth by one of his habitual vulgarities, which would destroy any romanticism. "If Lynch be right, statues of women should always be fully draped, one hand of the woman feeling regretfully her own hinder parts" (*Portrait*, p. 251).

At last, in the evening, the lonely artist comes to the aid of the troubled adolescent, opportunely recalling to him one of his favourite ambitions: "I desire to press in my arms the loveliness which has not yet come into the world." *(Ibid.)* The same thing takes place on 15 and 16 April, when a real meeting with "her"—in which she has appeared dangerously encouraging for once—drives Stephen to take refuge in "the white arms of roads, their promise of close embraces," the spell of voices in the air and that of ships "shaking the wings of their exultant and terrible youth". In Stephen's expression of his doubt, "Yes, I liked her today. A little or much? Don't know. I liked her and it seems a new feeling to me. Then, in that case, all the rest, all that I thought I thought and all that I felt I felt, all the rest before now, in fact . . ." (*Portrait*, p. 252). One can recognise the troubled circling which characterised his thought and mind at the time of his conversion. It is not easy to be a mere young man having to wrench himself from the clinging arms of the mother and the beloved. On 26 April, the mother disappears from the story, in circumstances whose domestic symbolism is somewhat striking; yet all the same she is his last witness, and Stephen needs her to prepare his belongings for departure. Bearing in mind the glorious mythology that inspires the young poet, one could say that here Mrs. Dedalus plays the part of Daedalus himself, arranging his pitiful rags ("my new secondhand clothes") as the other had prepared his son's wings, and, like the fabled artificer, giving the rebellious son plenty of useful advice which he receives with indifference. "Mother is putting my new secondhand clothes in order. She prays now, she says, that I may learn in my own life and away from home and friends what the heart is. . . ." *(Ibid.)*

This mother has the same sadly devoted attitude, the same obstinate faith as May Joyce—virtues Jim constantly put to the test. It is now necessary for him to deny at last this family and this mother, in order to become the creator, the father, of his race.

The Artist does not wish to be "man born of woman"; if, in the grotesque imagery Joyce borrowed from Leo Taxil, the pigeon impregnated the Virgin Mother,[20] the artist's soul is impregnated on a similarly lofty plane by a similar apparition, that of the bird-girl. The time of gestation is now complete; the Artist is born in the spring, on the evening of March 21, as though he had been called upon to manifest his creative powers by choosing this day for his birth, like those vegeta-

[20]See Magalaner, *Time of Apprenticeship* (London, 1959), pp. 50–70.

tion gods whose seasonal cults Frazer describes in *The Golden Bough*. "*March 21, night*. Free. Soul free and fancy free. Let the dead bury the dead. Ay. And let the dead marry the dead" (*Portrait*, p. 248).

But birth is not the same as the ripening to maturity; here it is simply a difficult annihilation of the first, physical birth. Stephen's diary is a symmetrical counterpart to the fable of the first act of submission and of the entry into the world where he had to face the "moocow"; it is a declaration, more densely and intensely personal, that he has now recovered all that was his, the belongings of which he had been previously dispossessed; it declares that he is independent, that he is breaking away from all the people who had presided over his former state of alienation. He emerges from death into life. He repudiates his mother as giver of death rather than of life. But the ironical implication here is that one cannot really leave one's mother, any more than one can really leave the Church; *they* do not leave *him*.

Stephen does not talk like a self-centered, gently suffering aesthete, but more like a man who is being torn in two different directions by his loyalties. Joyce is bringing about a transition in time; the time of confession has been left behind, with its narrative of past errors and transgressions, the Story of the Artist is over. The present is only living because it brings forth the future, as Stephen declares on 6 April, and we are borne with Stephen far from time past to hover high above the present and to see, faintly dawning in the distance, time future. This will be the time of the living, the time of that which has not yet come into the world, the time of terrifying detachment and solitude.

On 27 April, Stephen takes wing, with an anguished cry of ill-omen; as he leaves, he invokes the father with the prophetic words of an Icarus who has been given full freedom. Harry Levin rightly points out that by calling upon Daedalus Stephen also invokes Icarus, and thus darkly offers himself to his fatal destiny and to a replacement father-son relationship.

It will be seen that this appeal has many meanings; having cut every bond and finally come forth from the womb, Stephen rises with a cry into the real life that is the substance of art. Creation is to be his time-scale and the work of art his field of activity. Already he foreshadows new, vital structures for the future; the universe of artistic creation excludes the woman, and is born from the artificer. It is necessary for him to invent a father.[21]

In Ovid's *Metamorphoses*, from which Joyce took the epigraph for

[21]Harry Levin, *James Joyce, A Critical Introduction* (London, 1960), p. 62.

this book, *"Et ignotas animum dimittit in artes"* (VIII, 188), Daedalus, weary of his long exile in Crete, was filled with longing for his native land, but found himself enclosed by the sea. "Though he may block escape by land and sea," he said, "yet the sky is open, and that way we shall go. Though Minos rules over all, he does not rule the air." Thereupon, "he set his mind at work upon the arts unknown and changed nature".[22] He made wings for himself and for Icarus and both flew away like gods.

On the evening of 21 March, Stephen records that he is "soul free and fancy free"; that very morning, he had freed his artistic imagination, letting himself freely interpret reality by way of a symbolism personal to himself which was his way of changing nature. He had brought about a metamorphosis by the artifice of analogy, thinking about Cranly and the latter's parents, who had been the subject of a long note the previous day; he had called up their appearances to his mind's eye and described them in broad, realistic strokes:

> Can see him. Strong farmer type. Pepper and salt suit. Square feet. Unkempt, grizzled beard. Probably attends coursing matches. Pays his dues regularly but not plentifully to Father Dwyer of Larras. Sometimes talks to girls after nightfall. But his mother? Very young or very old? Hardly the first. If so, Cranly would not have spoken as he did. Old, then. Probably, and neglected. (*Portrait*, p. 248)

Stephen is free as soon as he has made his decision to be master of the skies, spurning the earth and sea which are so often in *Portrait* associated with woman, the mother, and the powers that he repudiates. His imagination knows no further obstacles and he is sure that he has no more obligations towards objective reality. The farmer and his wife are transformed by art into Elizabeth and Zacchary; Stephen enters the vast world of correspondences where the soul can stride over superficialities and centuries with the aid of mythology and the links it establishes. For the belly bacon and dried figs which are Cranly's principal diet, one may "read locusts and wild honey". Stephen is beginning to use the techniques of *Ulysses*. He continues to explore knowledge; on 22 March the journey from one world to another is accomplished, without any comment, simply by means of juxtaposition: *"March 22.* In company with Lynch followed a sizeable hospital nurse. Lynch's idea.

[22]Joyce changes the original line by putting it in the *first* person.

Dislike it. Two lean greyhounds walking after a heifer" (*Portrait*, p. 248).

The greedy, food-centred dreams that come to Bloom as he follows the neighbours' maid are sketched out in a couple of lines:

> The ferreteyed porkbutcher folded the sausages he had snipped off with blotchy fingers, sausagepink. Sound meat there like a stallfed heifer. . . . To catch up and walk behind her if she went slowly, behind her moving hams. (*Ulysses*, p. 59)

From day to day the style of these notes oscillates between the free and experimental art of Daedalus and the foolish ambitious dreams of Icarus. He is the father who wishes to return to his native land by means of his art's inventions, and he is the son carried away towards the sun by the impulse of his pride. Stephen is very keenly aware of the possible duality of his destiny. He hesitates, repudiates the present, fears the future. And all the while his mind is turned towards "her"; out of the twenty-two notes, seven concern waiting for her, with urgent, sad, jealous questioning, with the temptation potentially present always accompanied by the fear of temptation. His departure is neither calm nor confident as Joyce's had been. He sets out, terrified that he is to repeat the fall of Icarus in his own person, having the previous day spoken with the voice of Daedalus: "Welcome, O life! I go to encounter for the millionth time the reality of experience and to forge in the smithy of my soul the uncreated conscience of my race" (*Portrait*, p. 253).

Daedalus in the plan and the intelligence, he is Icarus in his doubt; yet he is not condemned for this, as some critics such as Hugh Kenner seem to believe. Harry Levin concludes his study by declaring that Stephen appeals here to a father other than Simon Dedalus or the Church: "His wings take him from the fatherland. The labyrinth leads toward a father," alluding to the myth of Bloom as father-substitute.[23] But in fact, Stephen will have no father but himself. The father-son relationship that *is* meaningful to him is that which he discusses with his mother, and records in his diary on 24 March with deliberately casual impertinence, the "relations between Jesus and Papa". "Papa" here is God the Father, and Stephen's cry of appeal—"old father"—is the warning cry of the Christ to his father.

[23]Levin, *op. cit.*

He knows already that he must be both Father and Son, that he must be the Son in order that the Father's plans (that is, those of the Artist) may be fulfilled.

It is customary to refer, in order to support the theory of the Icarian fall, to what Stephen says in *Ulysses* when he is back in Dublin again: "Fabulous artificer, the hawklike man. You flew. Whereto? Newhaven-Dieppe, steerage passenger. Paris and back. Lapwing. Icarus. *Pater, ait.* Seabedabbled, fallen, weltering. Lapwing you are. Lapwing he" *(Ulysses,* p. 206).

This is not an humiliated confession made by Stephen, but an address to him which he ironically imagines his adversaries making in their malevolence. The context shows that interpretation of the passage should be connected with the evocation of "strange names" and their possibly prophetic references: John Eglinton, whose real name is Magee, has just remarked rather strongly, "You make good use of the name. Your own name is strange enough. I suppose it explains your fantastical humour". Stephen says nothing, but thinks of the mysteries of such sounds. The fallen bird has the unusual name of "lapwing," and Stephen becomes obsessed by the word, repeating it at intervals throughout his reflections on treachery. In fact, two legends are super-imposed in Ovid's *Metamorphoses,* as in Stephen's memory, and he confuses them through the juxtaposition of the name Icarus and the word "lapwing". Ovid tells us that while Daedalus was burying his unfortunate son, a twittering lapwing put its head out of a muddy ditch nearby, flapped its wings, and chirped for joy. This bird, at the time the only one of its kind, was in fact the nephew of Daedalus who had been transformed thus by Minerva after his uncle's crime. For this gifted nephew, sent as an apprentice to his uncle, had invented the compass and the saw; Daedalus, angry and jealous, had pushed him off the roof of Minerva's citadel and spread the rumour of his accidental death, but Pallas, pitying the young man, had caught him in his fall, dressed him in feathers, and turned him into this bird.

Joyce could not be unaware that the story of the lapwing occurs immediately after that of Icarus. Furthermore, it stands as a reversed version of the story of Icarus; it is basically the same as the myth of the clever son and the stupid son (perhaps a distant version of the tale of Esau and Jacob), and Daedalus' jealousy is a characteristically Greek notion involving the elimination of the rival as a matter of course. The beloved son falls, stripped of his wings, while the adopted nephew is thrown down but finds wings from his fall. This may be variously inter-preted: Joyce may have meant that Stephen's fall was not as catastrophic as his adversaries insinuate, but that Minerva was watching over him. It may be a metaphorical reference to the declaration that Stephen has just made that the errors of genius are the portals of discovery. But it is most probably that we have here a "paganised" version of the theme of that hangman-God who condemns his son to suffering and then watches him as he lives through it, or of the treachery of the Dublin intellectuals who rejoice at the Death of Icarus without realising that Lapwing is still there.

Yet Joyce's plan was quite definitely to make a portrait of the Artist, of an Artist, *as a young man;* this means that what interests him will be the obstacles to be overcome, the failures, setbacks, mistakes, disasters. This does not mean to say that Stephen will never be an artist, but that Joyce *does not follow him as far as his success.* This is because as soon as Stephen reaches a stage where he can create—as soon as the testing time is over—he will have reached a phase of his development where he can no longer be the object of Joyce's consideration, for he himself will be one who watches others and in so doing observes himself. For the moment, he has not progressed beyond the stage of self-inspection or finished writing the complicated book of his life and mastering its motifs; all experiences outside Dublin await him still. It would be wrong to assume that because in the sequel the main role is given to Bloom, Stephen has drowned in his own selfish pride and is never likely to amount to anything more than a wandering beggar. He is still experimenting in *Ulysses,* making experiments and having experiences which would have been forbidden to him before his fall, before he went away to Paris. He had at least acquired there a type of ironical permit to misbehave himself "*à la française*".

In *Ulysses,* freed from his allegiance to family and Church, he is preparing to do combat with other idols, with the lies of language and with false "literature," that are still standing; he is very near his goal. And it seems most likely that after *Ulysses* there would be nothing more for Stephen Dedalus to do but to prepare himself for the final accolade of his life, for the ultimate experience, which would consecrate his vocation—be it success or failure—which would finally and completely detach him from himself. This was the kind of thing that happened to Joyce in 1904. After *Ulysses* there would be no "sequel" to the history of Stephen, for he was no longer of interest to Joyce, because: (1) Joyce's art could only display itself fully and to advantage when being sharpened on something resistant; (2) Joyce did not wish to play with romanticism and narrate "a brilliant career"; and (3) Stephen becomes too simple and too much himself as soon as he drives away temptation and puts Art first, because Joyce preferred to deal with the moment of ambiguity. It is certain that the *Portrait of the Artist as a Young Man* consists of a series of approximations to reality, but that Stephen is always present on several simultaneous levels of consciousness, which are not co-incident with one another. Stephen does not know exactly whether it is the artist, the young man, or the image of himself that he is saving by his flight. All the difficulty (and hence the interest) of *Portrait* lay in the necessity to create a form appropriate to this process of "observation in progress".

For Joyce, the work of art after *Portrait* must create its own norm. The style of *Dubliners*, for instance, had the faded insipidities and the obsessive monotony of everyday life in that dead Dublin. Stephen had to follow a soul in search of itself, one still unacquainted with itself, and so *Portrait* had to accept the garment of a borrowed language, since the artist who has not yet demonstrated his originality is of necessity an imitator of contemporary forms and fashions. This explains the expression of Stephen's thought, so characteristic of the turn of the century, his flaccid poses which contrast with the strength needed to make his decisions and carry them out, the flourishes and luxuriant ornamentation of the language of the emotions. The reality, which does not have to be sought for, is naturally sordid. Hence the beginning of *Portrait*, in particular the first chapter, was much more "realistic" and "modern" in its ellipses and it its existential intuitions, even in its historical accuracy, than was Chapter IV, for example. At the beginning the observer's awareness still had the spontaneity and freshness of one who has had no contact yet with books, and was grasping events and things in their raw state with no intermediaries.

In Chapter V, Stephen is on stage. Occasionally we glimpse the distance which he is maintaining between his own soul and his apparently serious involvement with and concern for other people. In the Diary his own reality is able to appear, restoring the balance somewhat.

A success story with Stephen as the main character would be too close a copy of Joyce's own, and he had no desire to practise that form of flirtation with oneself which generally constitutes the successful man's autobiography.[24] Joyce now transfers his interest to Bloom, because

---

[24]"Fragments from a diary, no form for a triumph," we are told by Tindall, *A Reader's Guide to James Joyce* (London, 1959), "are a form for disorder and despair. . . . Joyce chose this significant form to suggest his solipsist's condition: all in pieces, all coherence gone, at loose ends at last. . . . This feeble ending, the very form for Stephen, shows what he lacks. To become more than diarist the 'artist' must have not only a forger's cunning but

Bloom is a Dubliner trapped and ill-at-ease in Dublin, a man who is inwardly "complete" and what Joyce used to call "all-round"—a profoundly human figure, but unable to live. Bloom fascinates Joyce because he belongs to those who are unjustly punished, who sail their way between life and death, never able to land anywhere. Rejected by Dublin because he is too much alive to fit in with the other dead, he cannot live *within* himself because he is not sufficiently strong as a man. He is a "displaced" person unable to take refuge either in the pub or in art, having no real faith or home, while Stephen in *Ulysses* is only apparently homeless, for in reality he is his own refuge and special sanctuary. He belongs to himself, and is not alone within.

humanity and love. Stephen gets away, but he does not know himself or all mankind as the artist must" (pp. 68–9). Thus Tindall reduces the entire *Portrait* to what he calls a simple moral idea: that Joyce condemns pride. Kenner sees the end of *Portrait* as representing Joyce's own indecisive hesitation at not knowing how to get rid of Stephen, yet says that he was already planning his downfall prior to *Ulysses*—whence, says Kenner (in *Portrait in Perspective*), the impossibility of knowing whether to take Stephen seriously or not. Kenner is quite sure that Stephen will never be an artist, but in that case why should Joyce give us this disturbing diary of his? Tindall accuses him of being completely self-centred and assures us that "a man in love with himself keeps a diary".

XVII. Exile of the Soul

The Fall Treated as a Game

Ugliness of the outside world as an objective discovery is all the more serious an experience for the young man because he had desperately sought to build himself an inner world which would be protected against "the sordid tide of life without him"—an imaginary and delightfully exotic world of harmony and pleasure, a world which is disintegrating from within and collapsing. His disgust with himself is caused by the same disorders which had made him flee before, and the inner tides that flow over his barriers are full of the same floating filth as is "life without him". If his difference, which constitutes his only hope of salvation, does not even exist at the level of this filth, then dreams and reality are submerged in one single foul tide and Stephen's heart dances on the same dirty waters as the hearts of the wandering dumb animals of Dublin. The crisis of adolescence is so violent for Stephen that in his mind religion, sensuality, disgust, and the mysteries of reproduction all crystallise into symbolic meanings centring on the terror aroused by the idea of physical contact and the consequences of an embrace. From this crystallisation there results a series of attitudes of flight—disguised as literature—as Joyce by way of Stephen tries to restore the flesh to its proper worth, designating the body as experimental space for art's creation and associating the idea, necessary because it opens the gates of experience, of the soul's liberation with that of sin.

He unscrupulously takes over the theological theme of the *felix culpa* for use in his own sacrilegious scheme, praising impurity as a necessary aid to spiritual growth. Adam's sin, from the theological point of view, is only "happy" because it necessitates the redemption of man and justifies the coming of Christ; for Joyce, the "happiness' consequent upon sin is the birth of the Artist, a birth seen as the fruit of sublimed sin. "Unfolding itself sin by sin," the soul moves towards experience; does it thus become more open to live as it commits more and more sins? Joyce himself did not follow this road of experience through sin very far. Once the soul had become capable of flying with its own wings, the flesh appeared unnecessary. The *felix culpa* is transposed in its aesthetic form into the world where the work of art comes to birth; "errors are the portals of discovery".[1] Again we glimpse here that confusion between Art and attack upon Religion which makes (as it always does in Joyce's work, at first unconsciously and then more and more definitively) all writing the space in which is carried out that experimentation which tends to deify the Word; thus all work is born from a *felix culpa*, and *Finnegans Wake* is the greatest sin of that "culprit," who in *Finnegans Wake* is the last name borne by one who in the *Portrait* was called Heretic. Thus the Artist proceeds from sin to sin, from transgression to flight, committing the sin of writing and then trying to disculpate himself by another piece of writing, playing the game of putting himself on trial and accusing himself, until in the end he becomes Shem the author, the pen-wielder, and masturbator, glorying in his nature as "phoenix culprit".

Until 1914, Joyce-Stephen used to insist upon the delightful necessity of *sharing the sin*, because he felt afraid and ashamed, and needed to be punished for his sin, and also because he felt the need to make another person feel fear and shame—to punish another as well as himself. But after a serious crisis which was to find expression in *Exiles* Joyce found that he no longer needed any witness or accomplice in sin other than himself, and decided to perform his transgressions alone in order to reap all their benefits alone. Just as he had eliminated the auxiliary brother on his way from *Stephen Hero* to *Portrait*, now, after *Exiles*, he could eliminate all feminine assistance. He had first "opened up the soul" of this chosen Other (in fact, Nora) by the agency of sin in common in order to discover and remove her secrets; and now he could recreate female characters without having to refer to the original model. Now,

[1]In *Ulysses*, Stephen says "A man of genius makes no mistakes. His . . . errors are the portals of discovery". This is Yeats' phrase transposed into Joyce's language, a phrase the latter often quoted as a summary of the Catholic attitude towards the state of "separation".

he knew more about women than "the devil's grandmother".

Joyce's art was an attempt to recover possessions, such as life, woman as wife or companion, freedom of his own speech, independence, and the wherewithal to write, which he felt he had been deprived of in the theological world from the very beginning. He bent all his energies to the achievement of this recovery, having first made a long and thorough study of the thief and of the possibilities of deceiving him. The Despoiler is the Maker and Master of the stolen world, and the young man cannot expect any help from law or other people; he can only try to rob the One who has robbed him. Being himself a stolen object, he must first escape from this world of concealment and operate from without. As we have seen, the *Portrait* is an account of the realisation of this primary deprivation, followed by the decision to recover the self and its rights, and the execution of the first part of this plan—the emergence under the aegis of Thoth, god of writing. The second stage would be the recovery of reality by means of writing, which is an instrument for the substitution of one world for another, and the re-placement world would be fabricated by the use of a language specially invented by the artist.

Stephen tries by means of art to win "another world," a world beyond the circles of Dublin and of the Church; writing then becomes for him a kind of repatriation, a way of being in Dublin without actually being there. Similarly, by writing he tries to find again the soul-mate of his dreams who has haunted him since childhood but who has always been forbidden or inaccessible. But he notices that if any woman does accept him and agree to follow him, she brings within her the ghostly presence of the Enemy, and the Third Person is surreptitiously and undesirably present again. One can practice the ultimate subterfuge of making this Other, this Maker, into another version of oneself, hence into an accomplice, a witness, an invited guest. Or one can decide that it is He who is the alienated one. In the latter case, one can then decide to stop living in hiding and to come out, to turn life into a pantomime and the conjugal relationship into a theatrical space where He is no longer the prompter but a mere spectator forced to keep silent.

In the *Portrait*, as soon as desire is first experienced (the episode ending with a piteous flight and the hiding under the table), woman and poetry are linked in traumatic fashion in the artist's imagination; naturally dependent one upon the other, they are also mutually exclusive. The poet is inspired by emotions of love, but the act and practice of writing presuppose the absence of the beloved object. The form of relations existing between the young man and the girl is analogous to that between the artist and theology; the young man is conscious of attraction and analogy, but he also knows that the girl always withdraws or hides, as God withdraws himself from the sinner. The very act of formulating one's desire (which the girl herself has coquettishly provoked) causes her to take flight. Thus she is replaced by poetry, as the artist substitutes the act of spiritual creation for the physical act of love. Art can only thrive in a free atmosphere, but love involves binding and submission, which is why these two possible modes of existence are incompatible, at least in the world of Dublin: for art and love to be reconcilable it would be necessary for the woman to accept marriage with one who was as clearly as possible destined to accomplish an Icarian fall, and thereby to agree to follow him into exile and into that fall.

Now, by definition, woman is associated with the Church (as tower of ivory and house of gold, is identified with it), as the artist is identified with Thoth, the winged god of writing. The woman's vocation is symbolised by a closed garden or house, while that of the artist writes its words and signs across infinite space. This is why Joyce illustrates the impossible union of the spirit which is open to the world with the flesh which is not by the episodes of parody in Stephen's love-life in *Portrait* and by caricature of the "modern" young woman in *Stephen Hero* and in *Dubliners*. He shows that, whatever the fashions or times of love, the woman will only offer herself conditionally to the artist, although she will give herself without reserve to the priest. He further shows that with the gift of her body she wishes to capture the poet's soul and spirit, and that, in short, she offers ephemeral *"nourritures terrestres"* for which he is to abandon his infinities and eternities of the imagination. Woman is not life, even if her body as it moves about may give this illusion. In *Portrait* Joyce defines and clarifies the metaphors which he is to attribute later to woman in *Exiles* and in *Ulysses*, and exposes her false lures of romanticism and feminism. Considerations of aesthetics and freedom are his pretext, but they serve as a cover for his scorn and distrust for any woman who claims the type of honour due to the Church, to Our Lady, or to a man.

This gives us certain comedy scenes whose mocking intentions do not always conceal some humourlessness in the author—for in love as in politics, Joyce was capable of bad faith. Until Anna Livia, his portraits of women are far from appealing or charming: he sees woman as a mixture of two simplified aspects, the one attracting and the other repelling, her arms held out in welcome but also to grasp and hold, her flesh welcoming in order to bury and absorb. She is the contradiction to the artist's decision to fly away. Her fascination resides in what Joyce calls "the mystery of the body," which is simply the anatomical and physiological difference, unimaginable to the masculine mind. Joyce was doubtless inspired to his rare love-affairs by the writer's professional jealousy or curiosity towards the unknown or ungraspable.

According to all appearances, the image of woman is stereotyped, belonging to the class which Joyce, borrowing the expression from Goethe's *Faust,* called the *"Ewigweibliche"*—the eternal feminine. To Joyce, woman is a natural, familiar, concrete object, and as the typical woman-object constantly escapes him, causing the eternal masculine rage. He genuinely feels rage, but he is also able to detach himself from it sufficiently to draw comical effects from it in *Portrait* and in *Ulysses.* By her animal or mineral nature, woman can stand for pure beauty, and by her *difference,* by vagueness and aloofness, she may become partially divine, so that her distant image becomes the icon before which Joyce likes to prostrate himself. In both cases, he can make use of her, tranquilly assured that she has no inner self or personality or individual opinions which might hinder this utilisation. Woman, he feels, is merely superficiality; within, apart from maternal instincts and "simplicity," there prevails a foggy darkness like an Irish winter night. It is noteworthy that Joyce envisages the "awakening" of the girl as the process of becoming aware in adolescence of the disturbing presence of the flesh. She is an attractive object of pleasure, or a symbol of the inaccessible—of indulgence—but as an individual the woman does not exist for Joyce, for he notices her only if she appears, born out of his imagination, to take her place harmoniously in his mythological scheme, and if she remains sufficiently distant to preserve the illusion and to leave the artist's proud solitude undamaged. The eyes of the soul as channels for love are one of the causes of the ontogenesis of the artist, and Joyce maintained a very complex imaginary set of relationships with his wife. Their union acted as a kind of theatre in which he could try out and rehearse episodes of his work.

Love as Play

His stormy and passionate correspondence with Nora is founded on an extravagant eroticism (intentionally extravagant) and on equally exaggerated anguishes and raptures. Nora was able to play all the parts demanded of her, whether Jesus or Judas or Nora or May Joyce.

For Joyce, writing was always the appropriate field for the expression of anything, however mad it might seem; like Stephen at Sandymount, he used his letters as means to an end in his attempt to surpass reality and its limitations. In writing, everything is possible, yet nothing can be made actual. Joyce has left two valuable accounts, concerning two infidelities which had no real consequences for his own genuine love, of the passionate dreaming which he could accomplish in writing. These brief affairs are important because of the imprint they have left on his work, and to his careful analysis of them we owe the themes of Bloom and Shakespeare as Don Juan, and the character of Martha Clifford in *Ulysses*. These infidelities seem surprising when we recall that the man who committed them declared to his friend and pupil from Trieste, Ettore Schmitz (Italo Svevo), on his return from Dublin in 1912, "What is certain is that I am more virtuous than all that lot—I, who am a real monogamist and have never loved but once in my life."[2]

But from time to time Joyce needed to stir up griefs in his soul. He never went back to Dublin after 1912; he no longer questioned Nora's faithfulness to him, and thus tormented her less. After eight years of frankness they had told each other all that needed to be told. Joyce thus adopted the resources of venial infidelity, which was enough to give him a new source of guilt, now that he had plenty of excuses and justifications. His courtship of Amalia Popper between 1912 and 1916, and his similar game with Marthe Fleischmann between December 1918 and March 1919, had the same reasons and the same repercussions for Joyce; yet he remained a "Platonic" lover, limiting his passion to excited and dramatic speeches and staying faithful both to Nora and to the virginal myth.

The two episodes occurred opportunely, bringing their contribution to the work in progress. Amalia is observed, followed, and described, like E. C. at the end of *Portrait*, while Joyce watches himself watching her. But what for Stephen becomes a bitter feeling of betrayal, a belief that he has been deceived by his friend Cranly, is experienced by Joyce with incomparable lightness of style and power of ironic observation. He used to keep a notebook which he entitled *Giacomo Joyce*, in which he recorded his feelings while playing the part of Casanova, and this notebook by Giacomo (James) is a masterpiece of burlesque on the theme of love as already described by the author of *Ulysses*. Everything in it is fine and delicate, expressed in a bare, stripped style which forms

²Ellmann, *James Joyce*, p. 349. See also pp. 353 ff., 462 ff.

a direct contrast to the depressions or exaltations of *Portrait*; the romantic is parodied, as Amalia is described in terms which recall the prostitute Zoe in 'Circe,' different genres are examined and Joyce makes his
impressionistic notes on situations.[3] Amalia seems to have freed Joyce
the ironical man, who did not dare to juggle with language or with his
own feelings. Never had his talents for expression, so freely exercised
in his letters to Stannie, sparkled with such comedy and flourish; he is
conscious of playing a part, much more so than he is with Nora. Like
a good actor, he lets himself believe in the game he is playing, but never
forgets that he is someone's "double"; for Amalia, the young Jewish girl,
daughter of Leopoldo Popper, a gentle, slightly ridiculous Triestine
businessman, he plays at being a ridiculous and gently jealous Casanova.
He tries to seduce her, but with a clumsiness and lack of success which
recall Stephen, but unlike that languishing hero, he finds some pleasure
and amusement in the absurdity of his own conduct:

> Cobweb handwriting, traced long and fine with quiet disdain and resig-
> nation: a young person of quality.
> I launch forth on an easy wave of tepid speech; Swedenborg, the Pseudo-
> Areopagite, Miguel de Molinos, Joachim Abbas. The wave is spent. Her
> classmate, retwisting her twisted body, purrs in boneless Viennese Italian:
> *Che coltura!* The long eyelids beat and lift: a burning needleprick stings
> and quivers in the velvet iris.[4]
>
> *A gentle creature.* At midnight, after music, all the way up the via San
> Michele, these words were spoken softly. Easy now, Jamesy! Did you never
> walk the streets of Dublin at night sobbing another name?[5]

Amalia was nothing for him but a young woman whose image and
attitudes inspired him because she was one of those distant, emotionally
disturbing Southern women whose prototype was Mercedes; her Semitic features were inherited by Molly Bloom, but the soul of Nora and
the psychology of Everywoman as seen by Joyce are hidden behind the
pretty mask.

---

[3] For instance, "She raises her arms in an effort to hook at the nape of the neck a gown
of black veiling. She cannot: no, she cannot. She moves backwards towards me mutely.
I raise my arms to help her: her arms fall. I hold the websoft edges of her gown and
drawing them out to hook them I see through the opening of the black veil her little body
sheathed in an orange shift. It slips into ribbons of moorings at her shoulders and falls
slowly: a little smooth naked body shimmering with silvery scales. It slips slowly over the
slender buttocks of smooth polished silver and over their furrow, a tarnished silver
shadow.... Fingers, cold and calm and moving...." (Ellmann, *op. cit.*, pp. 354–5, quoted
from *Giacomo Joyce*.)

[4] *Giacomo Joyce*, ed. Ellmann (New York, 1968), p. 1.

[5] Ellmann, *James Joyce*, p. 354.

In these beautiful foolish notes, as in some of the later letters to Marthe Fleischmann, Joyce's secret self is speaking, manifesting that strange passion for Jewish women which made him also mistake Marthe for a Jewess:

> Would you like me to tell you something?
> My first impression of you.
> Here it is.
> You were dressed in black, wearing a big hat with waving feathers. The colour suited you very well. And I thought: a pretty animal.
> Because there was something frank and almost shameless in your allure. Then, as I watched you, I noticed the softness and regularity of your features, and the gentleness of your eyes. And I thought: a Jewess. If I am wrong, you must not be offended. Jesus Christ put on his human body: in the womb of a Jewish woman.[6]

This Joyce is God's enemy, who by his loves and his writing contests the rights of the master of pain and death over his victims. "But bend and hear: a voice. A sparrow under the wheels of Juggernaut, shaking shaker of the earth. Please, mister God, big mister God! Goodbye, big World! *Aber das ist eine Schweinerei!*"[7]

He writes to Marthe in December 1918, "Every morning I opened the paper and was afraid I might read your name in the death announcements! I would open it always in anguish, very, *very* slowly. I thought: she will go away—she who has looked at me with pity—perhaps with tenderness. . . . You are not afraid of death—but I am!"[8]

The young woman is to him a rare and fragile bird whose weakness moves him; she is able to turn into an angel, or to become woman in her fullness as mother of all men, as earth and flower, as hedgerow blossom or mystic rose:

> Once more in her chair by the window, happy words on her tongue, happy laughter. A bird twittering after storm, happy that its little foolish life has fluttered out of reach of the clutching fingers of an epileptic lord and giver of life, twittering happily, twittering and chirping happily.[9]

Again, he writes to Marthe on 2 February 1919, "And through the

---

[6] *Letters*, vol. II, pp. 431–2. The original is in French, here translated by Christopher Middleton. The presentation, as a prose-poem, shows that Joyce is fully conscious of the game that he is playing and is using the vertical form to convey the impression of hasty, passionate speech.

[7] *Giacomo*, p. 7.

[8] *Letters*, vol. II, p. 434 (original in French).

[9] *Giacomo*, p. 11.

night of the bitterness of my soul the kisses of your lips fell upon my heart—soft as rosepetals, gentle as dew. O rosa mistica, ora pro me!"[10]

But still he is the same Joyce, dreaming of the one unique Nora, the same artist with his fear of God dreaming of the unique image of beauty which he has created; and the image has now come out from the books and walks about in the world, as though reassuring him that what he has created is truly alive. Marthe, whom he had first noticed by chance in a Zurich street, was to begin with a person who bore a striking resemblance to the bird-girl seen on the beach. There was also the constant fascination felt by the male for the mystery of a body different from his own, be it Marthe's, Nora's, or Gretta Conroy's. "Perhaps you understand the mystery of your body when you look at yourself in the mirror, where the wild light in your eyes comes from; the colour of your hair?"[11]

In Ireland at the beginning of the century there were "modern" young women like the Sheehy girls who combined with a natural Irish charm all the right middle-class virtues and a fervent idealism in matters of politics. Jim and Stannie were often invited to their social evenings, where could be found all the up-and-coming young men (especially those who might be advantageous marriages for the Sheehy daughters). The two brothers proved susceptible to their surroundings, falling quietly and shyly in love with the Misses Sheehy, in a manner worthy of Claude Melnotte. Jim's talents for singing, mime, dancing, piano-playing, and general foolery were much appreciated by the company; but it is hardly the artist's place to act the jester for the ladies because he is too poor and ill-dressed to play the gallant. To be an artist in that context was to be a curious eccentric, a Bohemian. Joyce felt no such care for the equality of the sexes as did his friend Skeffington, who even adopted his wife's surname as part of his own.

The emancipation of woman was a theme dear to Ibsen, but in his sense it was a complete, spiritual emancipation—a dangerous undertaking leading the woman who refused to compromise into exile and death. The emancipation of Irish woman was a middle-class myth, and was in practice strictly limited to the recognition of intellectual equality, which constituted no threat to social and religious conventions. A Maggie Sheehy would not have broken off all relationships with her family to follow such a clownish fellow as Joyce; he in his turn would

[10]*Letters*, vol. II, p. 436 (original in German).
[11]*Letters*, vol. II, p. 432.

not have known what to make of a wife who laid down the law about Goethe without ever having read him, or of a Gaelic militant of brutal idealism like Molly Ivors, whose oratorical address to Gabriel Conroy shows a perfect mixture of masculine fanaticism and feminine perversity. There is no room for such a woman and her imperious demands in Joyce's world, and this is why he distinguishes so sharply between modern woman and eternal feminism. Modern woman, who frightened Jim despite her boyish sensual charms, is only present in *Stephen Hero,* which she permeates completely; in this first version of *Portrait* the artist's sexual problems take up nearly as much space and attention as his crises of revolt and rebellion. The "hero" appears as a proud, ridiculous, somewhat obsessed adolescent who tries to act the part of a conquering hero and who loses a great deal of his own prestige as a result of grotesque emotional disturbances. Angrily, he pursues, attacks, loses, and retrieves the girl who is the object of his distress.

Emma Clery is a real live girl in *Stephen Hero;* she is nubile, attractive, and aware of her charms. She flaunts her attractions—always within the permitted limits—and dances gracefully on the very edge of the forbidden. She is the Siren of Dublin, making the young men sing to her tune, enticing them to imaginary voyages which she will not share. Mortal and of the earth, she takes pleasure in teasing and in keeping the young men at a distance; she feeds on incense and compliments with double meanings, flattery, tea and little cakes, and eventually on wedding cake. She is visible, real, flesh and blood, and her lively, languishing eyes seem anxious to confide in one; but no confidences are vouchsafed. She provokes and flatters, making a great show of her intellectual ornaments, her intellectual charms; she is, in short, a fashionable young woman who prides herself on being patriotic, disguising her desire to be courted as a desire to share in progressive idealism with the young man:

>—Are you a believer in the emancipation of women too? she asked.
>—To be sure! said Stephen.
>—Well, I'm glad to hear you say that, at any rate. I didn't think you were in favour of women.
>—O, I am very liberal. (*Stephen Hero,* p. 158)

Leaning on Stephen's arm just a little more than is absolutely necessary, she gravely makes her little speech, and Stephen replies, lowering his tone of voice. The conversation runs along two different lines, and the speakers follow it, rivalling each other in duplicity. Emma acts the innocent and Stephen the experienced villain and seducer, and each knows that the other is lying—yet one can only play with fire if one's partner holds his breath. Stephen is polite and Emma charming, but Stephen is making his replies to the perverse Emma hidden behind the virtuous Emma, while Emma-the-perverse hears him and Emma-the-virtuous answers. She affects girlish innocence: so Stephen believes in the emancipation of women? Oh, so he is not a mysogynist, then? But her body cannot lie as well as her words can; she does not blush, and her eyes shine, when Stephen demonstrates his liberal free-thinking views. The play-acting of attraction between the sexes is constantly being denounced in *Stephen Hero*, which dates from the time when Joyce was feeling humiliated by his position as a failed Don Juan in a social set where he felt out of place and inferior. Stephen wonders what Emma can really be, with her pretentions to total spirituality and her obviously material and fleshly person:

> —I love the Irish music, she said a few minutes afterwards, inclining herself towards him with an air of oblivion, it is so soul-stirring.
> Stephen said nothing. He remembered almost every word she had said from the first time he had met her and he strove to recall any word which revealed the presence of a spiritual principle in her worthy of so significant a name as soul. (*Stephen Hero*, p. 161)

The inanity and falsity of the character of Emma sparked off that revolt which was to lead Joyce towards Molly Bloom; the weapons Molly uses in seduction are frankly and openly sensual—she has also a genuine, if naïve, taste for poetry.

The heroic Stephen has to continue with the experiment, hoping against hope to oblige Emma one day to recognise truths which to him seem evident. Since she claims to be modern and emancipated, he appears to say, let her prove it to me; here is her chance. He may indeed be able to call her bluff and teach her truly to "live". A comedy of manners takes place which shows Stephen as infinitely more romantic and less experienced than he is in *Portrait*; his ideas on women are comparable to his ideas on art, but take no account of social or historical reality, or even of psychological probability. He who is so prudent when concerned with an essay on aesthetics shows himself to be most imprudent when the essay is a practical exercise in life; in both cases, the main thing is to be free and for this one needs only to open the window to

life and let in fresh air. Open the window and Stephen, as a good
disciple of Ibsen should, will come to bring about your spiritual liberation. Emma can savour the homage he offers without compromising
herself as long as he confines himself to erotic allusion.

> —You know I was delighted to see you. I had to jump up and rush out.
> I couldn't have sat there another minute . . . I said, here is a human
> creature at last. . . .
> —You strange boy! she said. You mustn't go running about like
> that . . .
> —We are both young, aren't we?
> —Yes, Stephen.
> —We feel full of desire.
> —Desire? . . .
> —I knew (your) stride.
> —Stride?
> —I saw a young woman walking. (*Stephen Hero*, p. 202)

Emma no longer affects indifference; her eyes shine, but Stephen
makes a melodramatic proposal to her, in the manner of Richard Rowan, offering her the prospect of mutual spiritual liberation, and she
says he must be mad, "Tonight when you are going to bed remember
me and go to your window. I will be in the garden. Open the window
and call my name and ask me to come in. Then come down and let me
in. We will live one night together—one night, Emma, alone together
and in the morning we will say goodbye" (*Stephen Hero*, p. 203).
He is not mad, simply very cunning, for his offer is unacceptable.
Joyce would not have made it, but Stephen does so because he expects
and even desires to be refused. The whole of this strategy is intended
to strip the myths away from love, so that it may appear in a more
despicable light to one who does not wish to assume the responsibilities
of loving yet who wished always for the pleasures of love. Stephen's
specious reasoning is too clumsy and over-simplified to be convincing,
and so Joyce changed the tale of Emma completely when he came to
Portrait, refining it and enriching it with his most valued theme: Emma
is no longer a woman who refuses her womanliness for reasons of social
self-defence, but becomes the temptress and traitress, the women who
flirts with God and his priests. The evolution, from Emma to E. C., in
two versions of the theme of conditional and unconditional gifts is a
proof of the progress Joyce's art had made in the replacement of the
heavily theorising commentary by the discreet but more effective allu-

sion. What Stephen says to Lynch—"I like a woman to give herself. I like to receive. . . . These people count it a sin to sell holy things for money. But surely what they call the temple of the Holy Ghost should not be bargained for! Isn't that simony?" (*Stephen Hero*, p. 207)—is childish and crude when compared with the fascinating description of the temptress: "She was dancing towards him and, as she came, her eyes were a little averted and a faint glow was on her cheek. At the pause in the chain of hands her hand had lain in his an instant, a soft merchandise" (*Portrait*, p. 219).

The hand is offered to him who will pay the price. If only she really were a figure of complete purity, he thinks, if only the ban on approaching her had some sacred motive instead of being selfishly materialistic. "And if he had judged her harshly? If her life were a simple rosary of hours, her life simple and strange as a bird's life, gay in the morning, restless all day, tired at sundown? Her heart simple and wilful as a bird's heart?" (*Portrait*, p. 216).

If the woman's heart is a bird's heart, how can it beat either constantly or innocently? If it can, then one must believe in the existence of the blessed and immaculate Virgin. Stephen no longer knows what to think; E. C.'s eyes say one thing and her body another; her voice and her words say different things. He cannot grasp her real nature. The word "body" may indeed be simply the verbal dress of the word "soul," but it is more likely that the word "soul" is a disguise for the feelings of shame the body inspires—as Stephen Hero had already sensed in his own flesh. What if the scent of Emma's body were the spikenard and myrrh which draw the poor sinner to the love of Our Lady?

> He submitted himself to the perfumes of her body and strove to locate a spiritual principle in it: but he could not. She seemed to conform to the Catholic belief. . . . By all outward signs he was compelled to esteem her holy. But he could not so stultify himself as to misread the gleam in her eyes as holy or to interpret the rise and fall of her bosom as a movement of a sacred intention. (*Stephen Hero*, p. 161)

This investigation of Stephen's is comical; but in *Portrait* the denunciation of Emma is transferred to the symbolic plane, and she becomes an integral part of the feelings of separation which exist between man and woman, between flesh and spirit. Associated with the theme of exile, she is also a source of creation, for the artist who finds it painful not to be her master, growing weary of her "ardent ways," eventually creates a poem, the villanelle of the Temptress, to fill up the vacant place.

The composition of the only known work of Stephen Dedalus occupies the centre of the last chapter in *Portrait*; the symmetrical structure of this chapter, in its general outlines, constitutes part of an immense symbolic plan. In it aesthetics are worked out and maturity approached, the dialectics of exile and departure are considered, and its form and proportions are illustrative of the *Portrait*'s final phase. The four divisions of it correspond to and echo each other; the first and third sections are longest and consist of a peripatetic exposition of Stephen's views. They concern rather tense and aggressive phases in which Stephen confronts other people and in which his vocation as artist and martyr is confirmed. In the first section, the young man successively confronts or flees from his family, the political idealists, Davin, the dean, the vulgar group of his fellow-students, and Cranly, and he eventually expounds his aesthetic in detail to Lynch, reaching at last the steps of the library where he sees and observes, though does not approach, the beloved. After a shower, the girl students flutter away, and the morning ends on an unanswered question about "her heart simple and wilful as a bird's heart?"

Interpolated here is the episode of the visitation that comes to the poet's soul that night, followed by an account of the composition of the villanelle and its full text. Upon these six verses the world of imagination —the world in which Stephen had been alone—closes. And again, suddenly, we return to the scene of the shower the previous morning; today, the third part begins with a question which echoes the other which had been left unanswered at the end of the first section, "What birds were they?" Again, Stephen is thinking in questions, on the steps of the library. But this time, the birds are not girls, but symbolic birds, real birds in fact, the swallows with "their dark darting quivering bodies flying clearly against the sky. . . . circling about a temple of air" (*Portrait*, p. 224).

The air becomes holy and Stephen sees himself as a worried augur taking the auspices; he thinks too of Thoth, and smiles at "the god's image for it made him think of a bottle-nosed judge in a wig, putting commas into a document which he held at arm's length" (*Portrait*, p. 225).

This is the beginning of his second morning of detachment from others. It resembles and corresponds to the previous one, but is still full of the night's visitation and of poetic turns of phrase; the imaginary is constantly invading the real. This time, by way of his companions, Stephen breaks off relations with the Church and with the family, and explains at length to Cranly not his artistic credo, but his morality and his personal profession of faith in art. The conversation ends in silence with a feeling of loneliness and of cold sadness. "Cranly did not answer."

After this come the pages of the diary Stephen keeps before his departure, corresponding to the inner dialogue with his soul which had taken place on the night of the villanelle.

Thus, the poem, inspired by an encounter with "her," is written into a world of correspondences and of symmetries in time. "An enchantment of the heart! The night had been enchanted. In a dream or vision he had known the ecstasy of seraphic life. Was it an instant of enchantment only or long hours and years and ages?" (*Portrait*, p. 216).

Music presides over the inspiration of this young man who is so like Joyce, this writer of lyric poems generally inspired by impulses of love. His ecstasy is described in terms of unhesitatingly romantic and Christian imagery. The inspiration is spiritual and pure, poetry and purity being inseparable. The young poet awakes, and all is beginning, delightful birth from night, cool waters, dawn, and the breath of the seraphim. Space has no existence in the enchanted moment, and all substance is dissolved in "cloud on cloud of vague circumstance"; the object of the dream is but "confused form". The poet's body is an emotion, pure of all flesh, and his being is angelic. His androgynous soul receives all sensations and his imagination is impregnated by the breath of inspiration, for his spirit has received "the white flame" within it. As the sleeper uneasily travels towards awakening, the reflection of "the instant of inspiration" becomes transformed and more precise: first a point of light flashes forth, evolving into confused form and then into a "rose and ardent light". This rose and ardent light is "her heart, strange that no man had known or would know," and a seraphic canticle celebrates the praises of E. C.'s heart.

This is not the first time that Stephen has had a vision of the celestial rose. Once before, on the beach, life had sent him a messenger, a wild angel who had ravished his soul to heaven. Then he had fallen asleep and dreamed his ascension into the infinitely unfolding space of the celestial rose, alone in a vaporous, dim, other world—in a romantic fusion of all elements, leaving the angelic bird-girl behind him, forgotten somewhere between earth and sea. But that time, when he awoke, able only to remember that he had been in another world, he had written nothing. The dream had ended with the great rose opening, and with a painful return to reality. Perhaps this time "the word was made flesh," because the angel Gabriel himself had entered into Stephen's soul, and possibly because Joyce needed his adoration for Our Lady to aid him in writing his ardent and tender poems. The poetic conception and gestation follow the usual pattern; hardly have the sublime heights been reached when the fall comes. Hardly has the poem "sent forth its rays of rhyme," when the process of destruction begins, and the flesh reclaims its precedence over the soul.

In the same flamboyant fashion Joyce describes the burning of the other world: "its rays burned up the world, consumed the hearts of men and angels: the rays from . . . her wilful heart". And the words come to his lips. If woman is on high, the home is here below, and if the incense does rise, the censer is only the earth, "a swinging swaying censer, a ball of incense, an ellipsoidal fall". If the censer is likely to arouse symbolist recollections, the curve described by it is an allusion to a ridiculous physics lesson in the previous chapter which had been riddled with surreptitious obscene remarks. "The dull white light spread itself east and west, covering the world, covering the rose-light in his heart," like the shroud, or the snow, that covers all Ireland at the end of 'The Dead'. The heart falls silent and tries to hide its confusion in the body, which is in a plain, ordinary room, with a "naked window," where the cold morning light is gathering; a distant bell re-establishes the idea of time and of its mechanically regular rhythm. The ecstasy cannot resist the onslaught of harsh, naked reality. The candle has gone out; and Stephen writes in "small neat letters" on a piece of rough cardboard a condensed account of his flight through the infinite. Then, with "his soul all dewy wet," he replaces the night's dream by a critical meditation, evoking a visit which had proceeded in a manner similar to that of his Visitation, but without its ecstasy; it is repeated, but in grotesque mode:

> The lumps of knotted flock under his head reminded him of the lumps of knotted horsehair in the sofa of her parlour on which he used to sit, smiling or serious, asking himself why he had come, displeased with her and with himself, confounded by the print of the Sacred Heart above the untenanted sideboard. (*Portrait*, p. 218)

As he wakes up, he hastens to write, *"fearing to lose all"*. The origins of the work of art are connected with the fear of loss, with writing as compensation and replacement for one who is absent, and the artist's first relationship with his work is a transposition of the impossible relationship between the young man and the inaccessible temptress. He calms and appeases his feelings by means of the verses written *for her*. And because she has withdrawn her delicate, venal palm from his greedy hand, he must rub his own hands to make them capable of feeling again. He declares the androgynous nature of his creative self and impregnates his own imagination.

Joyce gives us the key to his code in two words: "heart" and "soul";

they may be used indifferently for man or woman, but "heart" occurs more often in connection with the poet, while "soul" is attributed rather to the female source of inspiration. "Heart" is almost always equated with "flesh," and the "heart's cry" with the cry of desire. "Soul" is associated with "nakedness," meaning the real body of woman, clothed in the veil of shame; confession is a spiritual undressing just as literary composition is a demonstration of virility. The rivalry between the priest of the Church and the priest of the imagination is seen essentially in their respective power over words, for the servant of the Church has only a vicarious existence as a borrower of the divine Word, while the poet is a creator. This explains Stephen's scorn for E. C. and "her paramour, a priested peasant". He feels that he can do more with words than the latter could, for "He had done well to leave her to flirt with her priest, to toy with a church which was the scullery-maid of christendom" (*Portrait*, p. 220).

There was very little of the Casanova in Joyce's character, and his pride was satisfied by the exercise of his power with words. At the end of his work, "heart" and especially "heart of hearts" (the secret being and the source of life) become, in *Finnegans Wake* (p. 188), "art of arts," where the loss of the initial letters is very meaningful.

Stephen's revolt is all the more vital in that it is undertaken in the name of life and of art, but an order of precedence exists in the urgent imperatives; the young man is still struggling with his rival for the sake of life and for "enchanted days," and his heart's cry is but the sublimation of a more elementary appeal which uses poetry as dissimulation, rhythm as replacement, and music to disguise its frustration. The poetic visitation had, after all, ended on a very prosaic note of pollution: "the earth was like a swinging swaying censer, a ball of incense, an ellipsoidal fall. The rhythm died out at once; the cry of his heart was broken." We find a small ironic vocabulary-list of unhappy eroticism here, its terms borrowed from the romantic or theological vocabularies and used, seriously by Stephen in his moments of ecstasy, but ironically by Joyce as he describes them. In *Portrait*, the irony is somewhat masked by the play of symbols, but, on the contrary, in *Finnegans Wake* it is so provocatively present as to be almost exhibitionist.

But the "eucharist" style is not blasphemous, for its irony is not directed against the Creator; it represents Joyce's secret self-flagellation —his attempt to exorcise his very real taste for lyrical outpourings.

Conclusion: Joyce as Decadent Poet

In fact, Stephen's poem, which is underestimated and decried by critics accustomed by the subtle ironies of *Ulysses,* is a "real" poem, very different from the sinister lamentation for the death of Parnell found in *Dubliners;* it could take its place with no incongruity in the collection *Chamber Music,* and it appears with similar form, entitled 'Nightpiece,' but completely dissimilar content in *Pomes Penyeach.* The faith which pervades the villanelle is driven out, and the piece becomes a hymn to sin "as the bleak incense surges, cloud on cloud,/Voidward from the adoring/Waste of souls". The imagery of 'Nightpiece' is entirely negative, as though in deliberate Satanic game: "hosts of seraphim stand quiet in moonless gloom". But as the last poem in *Pomes Penyeach,* 'A Prayer,' shows, the weariness and trouble of these verses are not simulated emotions; their impulses were the lively movements of youth and their cries of love were caused by genuine feeling. After the age of thirty, Joyce experimented and practised with his emotions, seeking images of woman such as that of Amalia; but he no longer felt those ecstatic moments of creation which he had experienced, and of which he had been ashamed in 1907. He repudiated *Chamber Music* just before it was printed, finding it insincere and sentimental (both qualities unworthy of the author of *Portrait*), and he condemned its "feudal terminology" which, it must be admitted, he used as lavishly as Stephen ever did.[12] "Feudal" is used to mean "courtly," but with the added suggestion of the languishing, *fin-de-siècle* courtliness. The cadences of Swinburne and the languours of Dowson are found, with a certain Elizabethan note of sensuality, in the villanelle. Melancholy questioning is a favourite feature of these poems;[13] and the vocabulary is (no doubt excessively) decadent, yet it suits the message of the villanelle perfectly. Following in the tradition of a Christianised Renaissance (very fashionable since Pater popularised it), the author reproaches an invisible lady for tempting men's burning hearts and for demanding from these fallen angels tributes of love which are never requited.[14]

The figure of the temptress is both pagan and Christian, and corresponds to some degree, as recent studies have shown, with She whom

[12]Compare the self-criticism in *Finnegans Wake* (p. 164): "We now romp through a period of pure lyricism of shamebred music . . . evidenced by such words in distress as *I cream for thee, Sweet Margareen.*"

[13]Cf. *Chamber Music,* III, VIII.

[14]See references in *Workshop,* pp. 255–63.

Robert Graves calls the "triple muse," woman as goddess of heaven, earth, and hell, the first one, the creator and the destroyer, or, in Judaeo-Christian mythology, Eve, Mary, and Lilith. Joyce's typology, however, turns most often on the opposition between innocence and guilt, between the mother and the spouse of man-the-child; when the source of pure and seraphic inspiration had dried up, Stephen reverted to the erotic imagination, tempered as it was by a confusion of roles. The eyes speak the language of sensuality, but the nakedness of woman enfolds the man with a motherly gentleness: "Her eyes, dark and with a look of languor, were opening to his eyes. Her nakedness yielded to him, radiant, warm, odorous and lavish-limbed, enfolded him like a shining cloud, enfolded him like water with a liquid life" (*Portrait*, p. 223).

This is the secret voice of Joyce speaking to Nora. And the poetic language is simply "symbol of the element of mystery". He seems to suggest that poetry, unlike other literary forms which are less near to spontaneity, may be born from the spiritual and sensual communion of man and woman, provided that woman be absent, but consenting.

In *Portrait* Emma, being too real, disappears and turns into E. C. the symbol, and Stephen's transports and raptures are more convincing thereby, because the poet is still in the imaginary, permissive world, within his silence, while E. C. is surrounded by hypocritical interdicts and transgressions. Nothing is said, but all is carried out in mime.

The Temptress returns, tempted and afraid, always the same—refusing to admit that she is desirable and desired—leading men on by her looks and then fleeing from them, "coming up to his step" on the tram and "forgetting to go down". Fear and shame win the day, and the eyes that "seemed about to trust him" never do so; he will never know whether she has really lived. She gives herself up wholly to her confessor, "looking at him out of dove's eyes, toying with the pages of her Irish phrase-book". Father Moran murmurs, "The ladies are with us. The best helpers the language has". Yet the language of those languishing eyes was surely not the Gaelic; the national language is the modest veil of this extra-confessional confession, which acts as the go-between to a profane communion. Stephen is not deceived; she prefers the hypocritical charms of an outdated and therefore harmless language to the verses of a modern poet. She unveils her soul to a false magician, a Shaun, but withdraws and hides from the true priest of the eternal imagination. She is formed for the song of life, and she yields to the dirges of death and its blackmail.

He had told himself bitterly as he walked through the streets that she was a figure of the womanhood of her country, a bat-like soul waking to the consciousness of itself in darkness and secrecy and loneliness, tarrying awhile, loveless and sinless, with her mild lover and leaving him to whisper of innocent transgressions in the latticed ear of a priest. (*Portrait*, p. 220)

E. C. becomes the charming and refined figure of Irish womanhood, incapable of embracing except in the sight of the priest, loveless and sinless, sharing her mystery between the timid lover and the hidden priest, loaning (after the contract has been duly drawn up) to the one her body and to the other opening her soul. In real life, Joyce always wished to be both the lover and the confessor, and to have no watcher other than himself; but there must always be a watcher. Thus there develops a *ménage à trois*, a subtle and sacrilegious adultery, a pattern of the relationship between the man and the woman which becomes indispensable to Joyce and which he uses in all the imaginary conjugal situations in his work. Between man and woman a third person always insinuates, who may be a dead person or a "phantom by absence," but who is never eradicated. Joyce both needed and feared a rival; and this rival is all the more dangerous because his lack of real presence in the flesh makes him somehow holy to the woman, and his insubstantial nature permits him to insinuate himself into her very "soul". This infidelity of the soul causes the greatest suffering precisely because the imagination cannot be controlled: what is she thinking? of whom? is she thinking of me at this moment? wonders Stephen, in the desperate, crazy hope that the union which is forbidden in the flesh may somehow be consummated in the imagination, in the dream. Joyce attributes to Stephen the torments of his own imagination, which he had experienced ever since his first years with Nora, when they had frequently been separated.

While his soul had passed from ecstasy to languor where had she been? Might it be, in the mysterious ways of spiritual life, that her soul at those same moments had been conscious of his homage? It might be.
A glow of desire kindled again his soul and fired and fulfilled all his body. Conscious of his desire she was waking from odorous sleep, the temptress of the villanelle. (*Portrait*, pp. 222–3)

As ever, it is in the womb of the imagination that both Stephen and Joyce achieve their most ardent ecstasies. For such is the impression left on his ways of thinking by the Church that he cannot feel desire of the flesh except when aware of such desire as transgression and when threatened by sacramental reprisals such as excommunication; yet, on the other hand, possession seems both dangerous (since it leads to marriage and to submission) and ridiculous (since the true virginity has been taken by the Lord, in the terms of a strongly eroticised feudalism). But the flesh is precisely what this Other cannot know, and thus it is in an eroticism of the flesh that man may hope to exist without a rival. This satisfaction is immediately snatched from him, though, because the woman at once takes the story of her "innocent transgressions" to "the latticed ear of a priest". And at once the paradise-for-two is destroyed; in this paradise, man has to share everything with his rival. There is still Hell; only through sin, which forces the woman to confess to man that she is a corporeal being too, only when the man succeeds in resuscitating a certain animality, can he share a nature from which the Other is debarred and fully excluded.

In the sharing of humiliation there can be established that complicity which Joyce would have called love if the word "love" had had any meaning for him. In reality, "love" only exists in the distorted forms of compassion and of inquisitive jealousy. There is no direct communion, for every embrace is a challenge and an expression of defiance to the Watcher. All life begins with and from its first sin, and is therefore always troubled or wilfully guilty, and never pure.

Because of Joyce's deep-seated, puritanical moralising turn of mind, marking the flesh out as a forbidden and disgusting object, he could only see a Godless communion as possible in a context of mutual degradation or befouling. The jealous ambition that obsesses him is to master "the dark shame of [her] womanhood," and this theme of the shame that invades all ardent ways, this feeling of exasperated frustration, is all too familiar to the husbands who have been betrayed by an unreal (and unfortunately immortal) rival, in 'The Dead,' in *Exiles*, in *Ulysses*.

The theme of exile and of betrayal, more complex than the simple exile of the Artist who is driven out of society for not being like the others, ends all of Joyce's books. Every social exile or expatriation is accompanied by a deeper and more painful separation, that of flesh from spirit, from the garden enclosed of the Song of Songs which is forever forbidden, like the Promised Land which Moses was only allowed to see from a distance.

To be admitted into the "heart of hearts" was the supreme desire, one which Joyce never achieved. As Richard Rowan in *Exiles* understands, the true virginity is that of the soul, and it can only be given once; there has always been "someone" there before him. This "someone" who usurps the happiness of the couple may have been a former lover, long since dead, yet whose memory is still green—this is the case in 'The Dead,' in *Exiles*, and in Nora's own life. But the predecessor, be he the ghost of an earlier romantic love or the Holy Ghost, dispossesses the present lover, and in every embrace the man feels that the traces of the other are still there. An immediate and physical fidelity cannot effectively efface the primary betrayal.

These a priori connections set the typical couple of Joyce's writings in a distorted situation and start off a cycle of betrayals which become inescapable. The presence of a third person leads to jealousy, voyeurism, and a kind of homosexuality.

XVIII. The Notion of Exile Within

"Love" is one of the words which Joyce distrusted, because it belonged to the emotive vocabulary of notary's clerks and petty, mediocre business employees of Dublin like Chandler in 'A Little Cloud' and Doran in 'The Boarding House'. This middle-class and Anglo-Saxon distrust of woman would surprise us in a devoted admirer of Ibsen, if Joyce had not left throughout his work clues and allusions which enable us to guess at the reasons for his antipathy; he expresses himself perhaps most clearly in his biographical essay on William Blake:

> Like many other men of great genius, Blake was not attracted to cultured and refined women. Either he preferred to drawing-room graces and an easy and broad culture (if you will allow me to borrow a commonplace from theatrical jargon) the simple woman, of hazy and sensual mentality, or, in his unlimited egoism, he wanted the soul of his beloved to be entirely a slow and painful creation of his own, freeing and purifying daily under his very eyes, the demon (as he says) hidden in the cloud. (*Critical Writings*, p. 217)

The distinction between cultivated woman and simple woman also guided Joyce in making his choice. The "simple woman" is able to be "the beloved" for "the genius," a term by which Joyce designated Shakespeare, Blake, and by implication himself. And she is so because her soul is made of a vague, docile stuff to which the genius can give its form. Assuredly the cultivated woman of the early 1900's would not be so malleable; the suffragettes, the militant ladies of the Gaelic League, the heroines like Maud Gonne or the women of letters like Lady Gregory would have no attraction for the proud but timid genius. The Countess Markievicz, the revolutionary Amazon who in 1909 lent her lawns to the young soldiers for a drill ground, appears in the person of the forceful, attractive ladies of society who accuse Bloom of obscenities in 'Circe'. Ellmann attributes Joyce's dislike for using the word "love" in describing his own feelings to prudence and egocentricity, but his refusal seems rather due to respect for Nora and for the "proper" meaning of the word, "a penny-novelette word," as he says to Stannie. What Jim gives to Nora is "life," in its natural honesty and fullness; he admires, honours, and desires her—and when he humbly repeats to her that she has "the most beautiful and simple soul in the world," he does so because for him she is unique and perfect. He explains this to her clearly, so that she may see herself as he sees her: "Why should I not call you what in my heart I continually call you? What is it that prevents me unless it be that no word is tender enough to be your name."

Nora was a simple woman of hazy sensual mentality like Gretta Conroy and like Bertha, Richard Rowan's young wife. With no education, ideas, or pretentions, she could be mentally moulded to suit the liking of the man who dominated her. Her presence did not disturb his solitude. At first, Joyce was only attracted by her physical appearance: a young Irish redhead with blue eyes, met by chance, she was merely an image to him. But Our Lady too is only an icon raised by the worship of a cult to the rank of divinity; similarly, Joyce was to make Nora an object of worship, the incarnation of powers and forces that both attracted and repelled him. Having no firm belief in herself, she was able to lend herself to these metamorphoses, which she considered to be the follies natural to a genius. For Joyce, Nora is Ireland and the Church; he has for the Church a respect based on fear and for Ireland a jealous love, both of which he transferred to Nora. At the same time, he often pretended to submit to her severity and authority, provoking her to exercise them. He provoked the storm and then bowed to it. He would offend her as he would offend the powers that he hated, but would never go to the limit because basically, and beyond all revolt, he was subject to her. He would inflict humiliations upon her, but much more upon himself. Wishing to leave her, he would be afraid of losing her, and while unfaithful himself would accuse her of infidelity. All his own ambiguities find free play and catharsis in this intimate play-acting. Like Ireland and like the Church, she belongs to him, yet he does not admit that he may belong to her. And this admittedly adolescent game was to last until the maturity of *Finnegans Wake* was achieved—when Joyce was no longer conversing with Ireland and the Church, but with his own work and his art.

The Simple Woman

No other woman could have fulfilled the part of Nora as humble yet obstinate queen of Joyce's heart, adoring and supporting him until his death; when she was nineteen she did not hesitate to break all the laws of her world and of her conscience, and all Jim's life she respected his irreligion. She was gifted for what Joyce called "life," being completely herself and accepting this as simply as she accepted him. Ellmann sees her as a simple provincial girl, newly arrived from the country, suddenly meeting a "gentleman," but, in fact, her life had been in its own way rather similar to Jim's. At nineteen, the sum of her experiences was depressingly negative: a large family, a degenerate, drunken father, sadistic and tyrannical uncles, frustration of emotions, and a demoralising initiation by a vicious priest into the mysteries of sex. Her independent temperament and appetite for life—which would have made her into a romantic rebel if she had had middle-class aspirations and education of any sort—expressed themselves by transgressions and acts of disobedience such as going out with a Protestant, partly in order to annoy the uncles and at the risk of a sound thrashing, and of roaming about the streets of Galway dressed as a man. These show less tendency to perversion than a despair at feeling herself condemned by her femininity to a slavish existence. Jim, in the same conditions of oppression, had been able to stand aloof by the very fact, of course, of being a man. There was very little hope for a provincial girl of nineteen in the restless but blind society of 1904 Ireland.

A letter from Jim to Stanislaus, written from Pola on 3 December 1904, tells Nora's life-story; among other revelations is the fact that Nora's "awakening" closely resembled that of E. C., except for the fact that Nora's soul was not like a bat. The Father Moran whom she knew was also more enterprising:

> Papa had a shop but drank all the buns and loaves like a man. The
> mother's family . . . intervened. Sequestration of Papa. Uncle Michael

supports Mrs. and the children, while Papa bakes and drinks in a distant part of Connacht. . . . Her uncles are worthy men as you shall hear. When she was sixteen a curate in Galway took a liking to her: tea at the presbytery, little chats, familiarity. He was a nice young man with black curly hairs on his head. One night at tea he took her on his lap and said he liked her.[1]

The most curious detail must be that of her first love, which is the same as that of Gretta Conroy and of Molly (Mulvey is a Protestant, and his name is given to the young man who was once Molly's lover), and the same as Stephen's forbidden love for Eileen.

> She used to go with Mulvey (he was a Protestant) and walk about the roads with him at times. Says she didn't love him and simply went to pass the time. She was opposed at home and this made her persist. Her uncle got on the track. Every night he would be at home before her. "Well, my girl, out again with your Protestant." Forbade her to go any more. She went. When she came home, uncle was there before her. Her mother was ordered out of the room. . . . and uncle proceeded to thrash her with a big walking-stick. She fell on the floor fainting and clinging about his knees. At this time she was nineteen! Pretty little story, eh?

Nora's tranquil ignorance was for Joyce both a stimulant and an ironical game to be played: "she cares nothing for my art," he remarks with no great bitterness. He was not seeking an intellectual, feminist companion to act as rival and critic, but a friend and companion for body and soul—a woman who would make a true man, a father, of him, and who would understand him. He would not ask her, "Will you marry me?" but rather, "Are you the one who will understand me?" Nora followed him, understood, and held him in her hand like a pebble, as he says in a letter of December 1909, "I thought I heard my country calling to me or her eyes being turned towards me expectantly. But O, my love, there was something else I thought of. I thought of one who held me in her hand like a pebble, from whose love and in whose company I have still to learn the secrets of life. I thought of you, dearest, you are more to me than the world."

In 1914, after living with Nora for ten years, Joyce wrote *Exiles*, that cathartic play in which he sums up and examines his experience as man and as artist, revealing the double lesson which he had learned from living (alone) with someone: that in the most closely knit couple, each person is still inaccessibly alone; that doubt cannot be resolved; that constant suffering is nourished by this relationship; that the beloved's

[1] *Letters*, vol. II, p. 72.

different nature cannot be grasped, and that this unique something about her which one longs to possess always escapes one because Someone Else, be he man or God, has always been there first. On the other hand, there is certainly some shared experience in the stuff of everyday life together, the acceptance of the unhappiness one feels at not being able to *be* the other person, and at one's inability to give or receive fully. There is the experience of having undergone troubles together, and that of sins committed together, for from *Portrait* onwards the principle of the sharing of sin is the main basis of Joyce's ideas on eroticism. This is what Joyce timidly and secretly calls "love," and this communion with Nora which lasted throughout his life is something which he scarcely dares mention in his work—as though he who would never hear a word said against Nora, who would not let a coarse word be said in front of her because he felt so much distress on her account, had not been willing to make her an object of curiosity to the world of his readers, nor even to risk letting her walk the same Dublin streets as Bloom and Stephen.

Thus it is that Nora, who is secretly present in *Ulysses*, only reappears in *Finnegans Wake*, as the river whose waters are mingled with all rivers. Joyce had learnt early in his life that what man wants to be and what he is do not coincide, for a censorship has sundered Reality and Dream forever. What man desires—purity for himself, the virginity of the other person, and the complete freedom to give and receive—is impossible to fulfil. By writing *Exiles*, Joyce destroys dream with reality. The longing for an innocent, prelapsarian world, natural and living without animality, is as impossible to accomplish as is the aspiration towards holiness. All that man can know is impurity even in the heart of purity: Bertha's doubtful virtue, the sadomasochism of Joyce himself and of all his *personae*, Richard Rowan, Robert Hand, Shakespeare, Bloom, and H. C. E.; everyone encounters evil and is tempted to succumb to it.

Joyce tells us how men who wish to fly are condemned to fall, being born after the fall, how they wound and punish themselves, *willing* their vulnerability, how the fall provides the ambiguous pleasure of dizziness and terror combined with punishment as ridiculous act. One can desire to be Daedalus, and one can be proud to be Daedalus, but in being Icarus there is an enjoyable feeling of terror, and the two go together. One might almost believe that man makes himself wings in order to fall from a greater height. An amazing complicity exists between Joyce and Nora, revealing in the raw state his process of creation. Scenes and whole dramas take place, to be transferred later into the book, altered, and played through again in a lower key; in real life the tone remains serious, but the episode passes into the book by way of irony. An experience lived by Joyce on a solemn note may be lived through again by Bloom on a grotesque note. How and why the separation takes place between life and its parody is the problem.

At what point does Joyce cease to feed the work with his own substance, and at what point does the work become, even if fraudulently, the theatre of satisfactions for the imagination? Joyce is as near to Stephen as to Bloom; a Stephen who yielded to the thousand charms of E. C. would have had to flee from the tracks left by Father Moran, just as Bloom has to avoid Boylan, and as Joyce himself would flee from the ghosts of dead lovers or the figures of lying suitors.

His letters reveal the continuity between life and writing. As Ellmann emphasises in his introduction to the second volume, Joyce wished to keep all letters he wrote or received, not out of sentimentalism or for the sake of being indiscreet, but because he defined himself as a writer completely. This did not prevent him from writing with no concern for the production of a work of art, with a sometimes brutal plainness of speech. But however plain they are, his letters are signed Joyce as much as his other work is, and as an artist he was conscious of the documentary value they would have for future readers. They are, marginally but still essentially, a part of his collected writing, and reveal many secrets of the genesis of the work, but above all they reveal their author's ambiguous nature—a mixture of pride and of vulnerability which he was well able to make use of for the benefit of his creation. From the very beginning, Joyce imposed upon his life an order which his artistic vocation had shaped and necessitated: art was to be first and everything else subordinated to it.

In his letters to Stanislaus, written in 1904 and 1905, Joyce establishes the vital principles of an aesthetic system which is openly intended as a rival, and a successful rival, to theology and which draws much of its meaning and depth from this rivalry; thus, the artist, preceding man and challenging God, devotes the whole world, body and soul, to the purposes of his work. He may go so far as to integrate the details of his sexual life into art, since the latter is now substituted for religion and its rites. In such a context, the individual personality of Nora has scarcely any room for, or any right to, originality; she has to fit into a situation which has already been foreseen as necessary by the artist. She has to play the parts and carry out the functions which are required and imposed on her. This imposition explains their occasional quarrels and their constant oscillation between harmony and separation; Nora's relative docility, lending itself to alternations of morbid eroticism and spiritual exaltation (both of which were necessary for the sustaining of Joyce's creative impulses), sometimes rebelled against the methodical selfishness of such a "crazy lover". Their relationship would then take on the appearance of a parody-version of the dialectics of master and slave: if Nora-the-object leaves, then the master responds by threatening to leave her, according to the classical schema of Daedalus the proud. In 1922, Joyce was still the trembling, if tyrannical, worshipper of the beloved that he had been in 1904, the year of the hegira. She left, against his wishes, taking the children to Galway, and when he begged her to return, answered dryly that she might. Declaring that he could not live without her, he promised her a fur coat, a food allowance, he appealed to her compassion, he fainted in Miss Beach's shop, but if she remained obstinate, then: "we must part forever, though it will break my heart". The flattery—"How glad I am to hear you are looking younger!"—is not disinterested, for he wants something in exchange, "O my dearest, if you would only turn to me even now and read that terrible book which has now broken the heart in my breast and take me to yourself alone to do with me what you will!" This was to be the perpetual quarrel, the perpetual blackmail, between Joyce and Nora: if you read *Ulysses* I am your devoted servant, if not, you are "my queen," but I choose art rather than you. *Exiles* expresses an identical mixture of supplications, threats, dependence, idolatry and pride.

The sixty letters written to Nora between 1904 and 1909 are full of the same tortured amorous intensity, and in them there must surely be found the most valuable revelations to anyone studying the work of Joyce. One already knew that Stephen Dedalus was the image of Joyce in his youth, but the letters reveal that Bloom is even nearer to Joyce the "simple-minded," who attributes to Bloom his sexual and amorous experiences, within and without marriage; that the 'Circe' episode is the dramatisation of masturbations and masochistic play rehearsed with Nora; and that Molly has inherited much of Nora's frankness. A great many of the themes in *Ulysses* originate in the extraordinary complicity of this couple. Nora's letters, written with the illogical and natural simplicity which Joyce characterised as "feminine" in the style in which Molly thinks the 'Penelope' episode, show that she participated in this game which made her Jim's accomplice against the world without realising its implications other than the physical; she never read anything he wrote, and she would humour him when they were together at home, but her complaisance stopped there. Joyce stands alone at the centre of his work, integrating life into his creation, unknown to those who live in the outside world. He was transforming experience into literary substance and in obedience to the dictates of his imagination and its needs would turn Nora into "queen" or his mother—into the symbolic figure of Ireland or the grotesque and sadistic monster Bella-Bello who apes the Church.

In reality, only Joyce knew who he truly was; he would only show himself in his "nakedness" (a favourite word) to the woman who was unable to estimate or appreciate his genius. To others, as he used to say, he gave nothing but his pride. In the last analysis, what mattered to Joyce was the necessity of maintaining, within a conjugal-type existence, a situation of separation which would enable him to feel himself condemned to exile despite the privileged relationship in which he stood. Life with another person must be for the artist a planned form of exile still.

The Artist's Wife as Mother Church: Nora as Epitome of Exile

Joyce's letters to Nora are first of all expressions of simple feelings, saying that Joyce loves Nora, that Joyce hates the Church, and that the Church prevents him from loving her simply. Joyce had, in his life as in his art, a passion for honesty—to say everything, to see everything, explain, open and free all things—combined with a childish nostalgia for innocence. This honesty is, of course, the honesty which consists in remaining faithful to oneself, and the honesty of others as it may not actually exist but as it is sensed beyond all betrayals and beyond its absence. The dream of innocence is even harder to achieve, and thus more wondrous. Innocence is as unapproachable as the Blessed Virgin Mary in the flesh is for Stephen, or the Promised Land for Bloom, and it is lost in advance, its very essence being that it is the name for the feeling of loss and of alteration that the soul experiences.

These feelings of separation and dispossession are at the root of the desire to create, for one creates in order to retrieve and to recover what was lost; Joyce sees this as a necessary dialectic and by no means accidental. It is because Ireland is alienated and alienating that he has become what he is, and this superstition of his own being becomes henceforth the unalterable formulation of a law which must be applied and justified in everything; to possess one must have been dispossessed, and in order to rise one must have fallen. The creative act is only resuscitated in the vertigo of the fall and serves as a defence, a reply, a protest. Thus the artist discovers his affinities with the figure of Moses, whose career seems to Joyce to prefigure a destiny similar to his own; as he glimpses the highest good it withdraws from him always. And it is the fate of humanity to discover good only by also discovering evil; there is a choice only between blindness and ignorance, or knowledge and separation.

Those who are innocent enough to reach the promised land are incapable of appreciating it, like the two old maids who climb to the top of Nelson's pillar to have a bird's-eye view over the city, but are so terrified by the height that they decide to sit down and eat their lunch, oblivious of the sights they came to see; they prefer their earthbound condition to the airy height. Or, to put it another way, one has to choose between the dizziness of horizons and the limited routine of daily life. Joyce illustrates this by parody in the little episode entitled 'A Pisgah Sight of Palestine' in *Ulysses*; the sight of the promised land is only given just before the death of Moses, before the "birth of the soul," or Stephen's discovery of himself. One awakes in the situation of a bat or of a dog sleeping by the fire, still bearing the marks of prenatal dream, and, as soon as one opens one's eyes, one is guilty, because one has begun seeing. As Anna Livia says, "It's something fails us. First we feel. Then we fall" (*Finnegans Wake*, p. 627).

"A sense of her innocence moved him almost to pity her, an innocence he had never understood till he had come to the knowledge of it through sin, an innocence which she too had not understood while she was innocent or before the strange humiliation of her nature had first come upon her" (*Portrait*, p. 222). The association of life with sin is obviously a determining one. Awareness is always awareness of humiliation. The discovery of nature, that is, of the body, is always tragic. Joyce felt such horror for the flesh that only by disposing of it or relegating it from his imagination could he attain inspiration; the soaring flight which reveals Stephen to himself in Chapter IV of *Portrait* is begun by an abolition of the flesh, since in fact it is only the flesh which is caught in the nets which Ireland has thrown about him: "He remembered in what dread he stood of the mystery of his own body". It is the sickly and weak and perishable flesh that makes the alienating suggestions. However romantic the language of the revelation, it is nonetheless the *exact* expression of Joyce's concept of the space in which creation takes place; there has to be separation of body and soul:

What were they now but cerements shaken from the body of death—the fear he had walked in night and day, the incertitude that had ringed him round, the shame that had abased him within and without—cerements, the linens of the grave?

His soul had arisen from the grave of boyhood, spurning her grave-clothes. (*Portrait*, p. 170)

As for woman and mortal life, woman is only "a necessary evil"; like everything that seduces and then dispossesses one, like everything mysterious and alluring, sacred and impenetrable, desirable but dangerous —she is a trap, the most refined type of trap, the bait which the Church holds out, the means by which the punishment comes. Yet she is also the one with whom one enters "the gates of all the ways of error and glory"; she is both life and death. As the face of the Church she can scold and then absolve, and before her man is but a little boy, like Bloom.[2] Her soul, the image of Ireland, flits heavily about in the gloom of chapels and beats its bat-wings against the lattices of the confessional. She is mother and feeds a child; she is the artist's rival and prefers the child to the book. And for these very reasons the artist needs her: so that she may renew by her presence his consciousness of guilt which is productive of creation; so that she may sharpen his desire for loneliness and secrecy. Exile caused by guilt is the limitless space of the imagination, the alibi for transgression by writing; far from Dublin by himself, Joyce would have found it difficult to keep up his feeling of having been victimised and his need to cry out or to create as a means of defence. This is why he never separated himself from the woman who embodied the idea of separation; it may, in fact, be added that Nora was particularly suited for the allegorical role of the Artist's Wife, as a charming embodiment of the idea of solitude. Joyce must have taken a malicious pleasure in his knowledge that Nora would never read what he wrote. Furthermore, "the priest of the eternal imagination" never confesses, he only hears the confession of the penitent woman before him; Joyce knew Nora's secrets, having obstinately and systematically extracted them from her in the usual fashion of a jealous man, but Nora must have complained that she hardly knew the man who shared her bed and who affected Bloom's sleeping position.

To experience exile even within the most lasting union is to set oneself constantly into the most favourable situation for artistic inspiration. The rehearsal of one's reasons for leaving is one of the essential

---

[2]"The childman weary, the manchild in the womb." (*Ulysses*, p. 870.)

motivators of Joyce's imagination, for it is thus that he has to renew the primal transgression which marked him out as artist by vocation. But if it is relatively easy to commit a sexual transgression, repetition of the sin tends to blunt the accompanying distress. So, Joyce invents a whole labyrinth of treacheries, of such complexity that no Ariadne's thread will ever bring him out. He perpetuates his infidelity to Nora by his writing, and accuses her of infidelity, although he has neither proof nor confession. He simply decides once and for all that he has not been "the first"; he makes his books form an enclosed space for him, but Nora often threatens to invade this privacy. And without confiding in anyone, he makes life into a stage where he "rehearses" the work of art.

The normal realistic procedure is to repeat what is going on outside, but Joyce, on the contrary, provokes minimal incidents and then notes down the results. The game is a dangerous one, and a time comes when the scene-setter—having been driven away from life by the cruelty of reality—has to take refuge in an art which no longer tries to experiment on living matter, and this is what happened as his daughter Lucia grew up. After *Ulysses*, the flesh and its true pathology impose their ineluctable demands upon one who had boasted of being a fearless vivisector. The author of *Finnegans Wake* is afraid of life, and no longer plays at being afraid of the Church, nor does he now invent private hells set in houses of ill-fame. The all-too-real closing of Lucia's mind turned the relationship of life and art from "Life as stage for Art" into "Art as painful mockery of Reality" for Joyce.

To Leave Without Leaving: Nora as Erin

Because the relationship between the world's hostility and the creative impulse is all-important for Joyce, he sometimes provokes the world into betraying him in order to feel victimised. The world is experienced as the aggressor, and everyone else is enemy or accomplice through inability to see, to understand. As soon as Joyce feels himself to be alone in an unhealthy world, he also feels threatened by the other people's sickness. To remain by himself would be a denial of his human nature, but to go back to the others would be to risk death by suffocation. It seems that Nora saved him from this choice, but it would be inaccurate to say that she reconciled him with the world; rather she gave him the

courage to accept a necessary exile. Into that exile he took the very
things that he had wished to reject, because he needed Dublin and
needed the family cell, and all the attributes of them which caused him
pain.

In the alphabetical notebook he kept in Trieste he recorded little
ironical epiphanies which revealed to him the nature of those near to
him, *as he sees them* rather than as they are. Under the letter N the
portrait of Nora is sketched in four strokes which speak volumes for the
artist's ironic lucidity:

> Wherever thou art shall be Erin to me.
> She said to me: Woman-Killer! That's what you are!
> She speaks as often of her innocence as I do of my guilt.
> She wears limber stays.

Alone, Joyce is not bored; he lives with his Alter Ego, developing his
duality into a creative duplicity, playing with his self a game whose only
rule is that everything is allowed except being one. Obsessions, instead
of inhibiting, are fruitful, as Joyce ventures into romanticism or pain;
while the self lives its mortal life out and gives itself up to passion,
terror, guilt—everything that can bind or involve it—the artist watches
over it, making notes, and already writing the work. Joyce gives himself
to Nora and crowns her his queen, but at the same time he is writing
Ulysses, into which the actual Nora cannot penetrate. Jim believes
himself betrayed and weeps with grief before his friend Byrne, but
already within himself Jim is composing *Exiles*. Similarly, beneath the
intensely serious tone of the letters he writes as "the crazy lover" can
be perceived his fundamental detachment; the mechanism of creative
irony is set in motion as soon as he takes up the pen. "Shem the Penman" cannot avoid being double when even his instrument is a symbol
of magical masturbation. He who writes, writes down himself first of all,
for all to read.

This is the fashion in which Joyce writes to Nora; before even writing
to Nora, what he writes is to himself. Merely reading the letters makes
this clear. Already the act of writing puts one in a situation where one
is guilty, and in order that Nora may scold him, he writes *to* Nora rather
than *for* Nora. He writes in order to watch *himself*, to please or to hurt
himself, and in this solipsist game Nora is simply an object for his desires
to play with; in his game with Nora, the toys are God and his command-
ments that say "Thou Shalt Not". It is necessary to have all the cunning
of Shem and Shaun together to manage to commit a sin and then to

accuse someone else—if it was not you it was your Shemblable.[3] And in this sense Bloom may be seen as Joyce's "freer," the embodiment of his mad frustrations and of all his masochistic dreams. Bloom the brother and freer of Joyce is in appearance the character least like him, and in reality (or at least in the dreamed reality) the nearest to him.

It is necessary thus for Nora to be and not to be a saint, to be and not to be Molly. Joyce loves her more than anything in the world, but he fears her too, because of his need to live in a world full of imaginary obstacles. She is Our Lady the Virgin so that Joyce may feel sufficiently guilty; she is the subject of constant doubt so that he may imagine himself deceived by her; she takes on the aspect of Molly in order that Joyce may be Bloom. And he loves her precisely because she will lend herself to this complexity of myth, but also because fundamentally he knows that she never does more than *lend* herself. The reflection in her eyes is always that of Joyce, so much so that when they embrace he finds himself involuntarily acting out his part in his relationship with Ireland, his feeling of being befouled by Dublin and his wish to befoul it—all the ambiguous feelings illustrated in powerful metaphorical terms in the first chapter of *Ulysses*. He feels foul because he has been befouled, for in every murder it is the victim who must feel guilty, in every sin it is the one who is ill-treated who must feel ashamed, and the aggressor has his triumph in his pride. Thus, at the beginning, Jim's attitude to Nora reproduces his situation in Dublin, the relationship with one person reflecting relationships with all others; in Dublin he would behave scandalously, polluting the temples of society with his drunkenness. And if he vomited, it was not simply a result of having drunk too much; it was done because Dublin was literally sickening to him.

Dublin was the object of an unhappy love-hate relationship which provoked Joyce to the most painful masochism, and he transferred these feelings to Nora in order to accumulate the grief and pain which acted as stimuli to him. The drunkenness, like his writing, is a sin voluntarily committed against Nora, against the maternal image that she stands for, against Ireland. It may be wondered to what extent the author of *Finnegans Wake* (with its rehabilitation of the father who is still an object of scorn in *Ulysses*) made his communion with the drink that had been such a consolation to John Joyce, and, further, how responsible alcoholic dreams and delirium may have been for the logorrhoea of his later writing. When Joyce said of Dublin, "Have I ever left

[3]"He feels he ought to be as asamed of me as me to be ashunned of him . . . my shemblable! My freer!" (*Finnegans Wake*, p. 489.)

it?" he knew quite well that he had only left that place which on maps is marked Dublin; far away from it, he was recreating his own inner Dublin with Nora. For him, Nora was doubly valuable as the image of all that he loved and of all that he found constraining. She had the legendary charm of Erin, and for this aspect of Nora-Erin he would write poems and sing old songs. She had risen up into his life like a vision of pure beauty, and in a sense had given wings to his flight, just as the vision of the girl on the beach had given wings to Stephen's soul. "I want to go back to my love," he says, "my life, my star, my little strange-eyed Ireland!"[4]

Eroticism as Perversion of Catholic Worship

Joyce used to reconstitute in his relationship with Nora that pattern of morbid fascination followed by flight which he had rejected (or so he believed) at puberty upon discovering the terrifying delights of the flesh, when he had left the Church. But he could never shake off the Church's imagery, nor, in particular, its interdicts. Nora could be disguised as Our Lady, as E. C., as a prostitute, or she might be a pure maiden listening to the litanies of her worshipper, or a vague disembodied figure confessing her "innocent transgressions" to Joyce, or a shameless welcoming woman, receiving the shame and the remorse of her tormented visitor.[5] The bracelet which Joyce had made for her as an admission of his guilt and pledge of love, of love declared like an act of faith, looks very like the rosary used by devotees of the Virgin. Joyce is always guilty of something, of making unjust accusations or of filthy dreaming or (like H. C. E.) of imaginary attempts upon Nora's virtue— all these are necessary preliminaries to the game of confession and absolution.

[4] *Letters*, vol. II, p. 276, 16 December 1909, from Dublin.
[5] "Tonight I have an idea madder than usual. I feel I would like to be flogged by you. I would like to see your eyes blazing with anger.

I wonder is there some madness in me. Or is love madness? One moment I see you like a virgin or madonna, the next moment I see you shameless, insolent, half naked and obscene! What do you think of me at all? Are you disgusted with me? . . .

Are you too, then, like me, one moment high as the stars, the next lower than the lowest wretches? I have *enormous* belief in the power of a simple honourable soul. You are that, are you not, Nora?" (Letter of 2 Sept. 1909.)

If by means of Nora Joyce was able to free the artist in himself, he was far from having freed the fleshly man, because it is not possible to be converted to paganism, even if one thinks that one has rejected the Church. Although in his intimate self he would dream of euphoric freedom, his flesh was still soaked in Catholicism to such an extent that pleasure could only be achieved if tribute were paid. He has to break every interdict in order to achieve pleasure, because it is only as one falls that one feels a longing for one's lost wings, for their delicious loss, and only in befouling oneself can one evoke the idea of purity. Joyce feels not so much free as vertiginously unchained, and guilty.

Nora was chosen as his companion in his fall, since the important thing was the necessity of sharing sin. Communication takes place at the level of perversity, where Joyce could be with Nora in a way that Bloom could never be with Molly. In isolation, Molly and Bloom ruminate on their dissatisfaction. Joyce speaks Bloom's language to Nora in order to draw her into the complexity of the game—to make her his accomplice in dialogue and experiment. First he has to discover and define his limits, and this search is expressed in words because for Joyce writing is of prime importance and even the embrace must come second to the expression, the *writing*, of his desire. He goes to the very edge of the human kingdom, to the brink of the animal realm, as though to establish an aesthetic of ugliness and of risk.

He exalts foulness in an attempt to pass from innocence to shame and to feel, transmuted into words, the pleasant horror of transgression.

> Do not be offended at what I wrote. You thank me for the beautiful name I gave you. Yes, dear, it is a nice name, "My beautiful wild flower of the hedges!" . . . You see I am a little of a poet still. I am giving you a lovely book for a present too: and it is a poet's present for the woman he loves. *But*, side by side and inside this spiritual love I have for you there is also a wild beast-like craving for every inch of your body, for every secret and shameful part of it. (letter of 1 Dec. 1909)

There is also the pleasure derived from being really "wicked," but this pleasure rarely goes as far as sensual enjoyment before turning tail and rushing headlong to confession. For there is also pleasure in confession and absolution. And all this is only possible if Nora consents to play her part in the game too.

Nora was exactly the right companion for this eternally guilty man; instinctively she knew that the real Joyce, proud but vulnerable, was a man who needed to be looked at, who needed to be scolded, in order to be able to create. "I am an enemy of the ignobleness and slavishness of people. . . . Can you not see the simplicity which is at the back of all my disguises. . . . No human being has ever stood so close to my soul as you stand" (letter of 29 Aug. 1904).

Joyce expects that Nora should be able to see through him and his disguises; the women he knew before her were "pure daughters of Ireland who raised their skirts to step over" Joyce the bemired drunkard who wallowed in the part in which he had cast himself—that of a Stephen who staggers along with no Bloom to guide him. The Satanic pose was indeed a transparent artifice, but nonetheless it frightened the pure ladies, like Mary Sheehy, who, saying in her emancipated way, "You're very wicked," received the answer, "I try to be"; she doubtless understood this to be a remark dictated by false modesty, though in fact it was the simple truth. In this admission, Joyce showed real humility; but he wished to appear evil rather than to be actually wicked; his heart was not in it, and satanism was a luxury whose success depended upon financial freedom and independence far out of Joyce's reach. A. E. called him "a presumptuous beggar".

Joyce was such a good actor that he sometimes seemed about to be deceived by his own act and to believe himself really wicked, when a glance from Nora would recall him to order. She was not to be deceived by appearances, and Jim hardly dared believe in them; she called him a "saint," both delighting and disturbing him. He wanted to feel sure that she was not deceiving him or confusing him with anyone else, and so he scrupulously enumerated his wrongdoings, his disguises, his impostures, so that nothing might prevent Nora from seeing him as he was. Her eyes replaced his "spiritual account-book," and in the strange fascination of their first weeks together, he told her everything about himself, drawing up the list of his deeds and recounting all his crimes in detail, while she listened and offered him a myriad reflections of himself, so that in bending over her he could see himself as she saw him. Sometimes he would feel that the reflection was that of someone else, that eyes might betray, and this would so disturb him that he could have no peace until he had reconstituted in the mirror the true portrait of the artist. Later, he would often ask his wife, "Who am I?"—not because he did not know who he was, but because he needed to be completely accepted. If his blue-eyed queen would honour him as he was, then life and the whole world belonged to him. "What do you think of me at all? . . . I gave others my pride and joy. To you I give my sin, my folly, my weakness and sadness," he wrote to her in August 1909.

In Pola, in 1905, when Nora was pregnant, Jim out of work, both of

them cold and hungry, she grew bored and told him that he was a great
waster of paper.

> Nora says I have a saint's face. Myself I think I have the face of a
> debauchee. But I am no longer so . . .
> We have had quarrels—funny affairs. Nora says they were lovers' quar-
> rels and says I am very childish. She says I have a beautiful character. She
> calls me simple-minded Jim. . . . Nora has conceived, I think, and I wish
> her to live as healthily as possible. (letter of 28 Dec. 1904)

Absolution restores the heretic to innocence. Nora strips Jim's soul
bare, and (curiously enough) uses the same vocabulary as he, saying that
he has "a beautiful character" and "a saint's face," and that he is "simple-minded," especially when he believes himself to be very bad. And
he in his turn gradually strips bare the womanly part of her nature,
instructing her in recklessness, indecency, shameless acts and obscenity, leading her from the innocent perversity to the conscious perversity which brings pleasure. For some years he maintained a garden
of erotic delights with her, designed with craft to cause shuddering or
sublime disturbances to the mind of the unwary. Jim and Nora played
out their mystery in which all desires were satisfied, the desire to sin,
to profane the holy, to be innocently guilty or covered in shame, to
savour the sin and desire the punishment, to lose oneself and to be born
again—in short, giving oneself the illusion of falling, in order to experience really the vertigo of the fall.

He demanded all and she refused him nothing, even the most secret
thoughts, even her past life, the purest of her soul and the most impure
of her body; he must needs envelop all of her; Nora as flower, Nora as
queen, sow, prostitute, mother, and child, for the purer she was, the
greater the amorous deconsecration, and the more youthful she was,
the greater the sin. On 22 August 1909 he wrote to her:

> Dear love How sick, sick, sick I am of Dublin! It is the city of failure, of
> rancour and of unhappiness. I long to be out of it. I think always of you.
> When I go to bed at night it is a kind of torture for me. I will not write
> on this page what fills my mind, the very madness of desire. . . . Give
> yourself to me, dearest, all, all when we meet. All that is holy, hidden from
> others, you must give to me freely. I wish to be lord of your body and soul.

Why should Joyce hate the priests if not for having stolen from him
the possibility of the supreme sin, or the uncle, if not for being his rival
in incest? Joyce's jealousy is less a proprietary sentiment than the feel-

ings of the "strange lover," as he calls himself; he wishes always to be the greatest culprit.

According to the desire he feels to create *himself* in the image of his wishes, to represent himself as he wishes to be (as father and master or as child and slave, as Shakespeare or as Bloom), and according to the part he happens to be playing in real life at the time (be it Stephen or Bloom or H. C. E.), he sees Nora as the mother insulted and repudiated, or as Molly, or as the eternal Anna Livia. This explains why the Nora of his secret fantasies is rarely the real Nora or anything like her. It seems that Joyce would have wished, in order to desire Nora, that she should be the exact opposite of herself, as we can see from his dream-fantasy in which she appears as a brutal, crimson-faced giantess, precursor of the monstrous Bella-Bello Cohen. "I am your child as I told you and you must be severe with me, my little mother. Punish me as much as you like. I would be delighted to feel my flesh tingling under your hand . . . I would love to be whipped by you, Nora love!" (letter of ?13 Dec. 1909).

He goes on to explain exactly how, and imagines her beating him in a paroxysm of rage for some small, dirty, childish misdeed. He seems to be discovering the sinister pleasures of torture, and we hear the cries of Bloom, grotesquely echoing the cry of Stephen, tormented by his lubricious demons in *Portrait*.

The executioner Bello is a cruel nurse, who closes the circle of castigators which began with the mother and her denunciation and led on to the Church as source of punishment, to "Dio boia" and to Nora.

> *Bloom:* (Fainting.) Don't tear my . . .
> *Bello:* (Savagely.) The nosering, the pliers, the bastinado, the hanging hook, the knout I'll make you kiss while the flutes play like the Nubian slave of old. . . . (He twists her arm. Bloom squeaks, turning turtle.)
> *Bloom:* Don't be cruel, nurse! Don't!
> *Bello:* (Twisting.) Another!
> *Bloom:* (Screams.) O, it's hell itself! Every nerve in my body aches like mad! (*Ulysses*, p. 491)

It is clear that here Bella-Bello Cohen is a fearful figure representing the Church, simultaneously man by means of the threatening priests and woman as madam of an establishment in which Irishmen seek some illegitimate consolation.

The origin of Bloom's androgynous nature can be found in the complex relationships which Joyce invents. Profanation frees one to all the delights of multiplicity, as the liberated body realises the metamorphoses of which it has dreamed. Jim strips Nora of her impenetrability until she has no secrets left—even in her "solitary" actions—thus she ceases to be a different being, ceases to be imprisoned in her own loneliness. Jim approaches the mystery of her being so closely that the continuity established between the two of them allows him to move freely from masculine to feminine and vice versa. The pleasure he takes in treating Nora as an object and as his victim is only preliminary, for there can be no "virtue triumphant," as in Sade, if the victim remains obstinately innocent. Yet there is one point at which, with the clarity of an epiphany, Nora as subject takes over before Jim's eyes from Nora the object, and the "melancholy music" of shame is heard. Joyce grasps his own human nature as something basically destructive, uncontrolled and brutal, and he takes Nora, not in delight but in sympathy, in pain shared and communicated.

> Ah not lust, dearest, not the wild brutal madness I have written to you these last days and nights. . . . is what drew me to you then and holds me to you now. No, dearest, not that at all but a most tender, adoring, pitiful love for your youth and girlhood and weakness. . . . my faithful darling . . . my sweet-eyed schoolgirl.[6]

The moment of satisfaction is also the moment of his self-inflicted punishment; the sight of Nora defenceless shocks him out of his detached "otherness," and at that moment he *is* Nora, not in the union of the flesh which would make them into an ephemeral being, Norajim, for in such physical enjoyment is separation, but in the moment of the true espousals, when the spiritual marriage is celebrated.

On returning to that level of life at which they are different people again, Jim can be observed playing the part of confessor so that Nora may act as the penitent. He longs for an ideal, past "holiness," and manifests his wish to enjoy the sweetness of absolution. Sometimes they exchange roles, giving a spice of perversity to their wrong: "I remember. . . . in the tumult of our embraces you used a certain word. It was a word of provocation, of invitation and I can see your face over me (you were *over* me that night) as you murmured it. There was madness in *your* eyes too and as for me if hell had been waiting for me the moment

---

[6]*Letters*, vol. II, p. 272.

after I could not have held back from you."[7]

The greater the shame, the sweeter the redemption, yet the shame itself is also sweet. It is a mistake to confuse Joyce's erotic cycle with a repetition of the myth of Adam and Eve. In paradise, Jim and Nora can avoid shame; they hide nothing from each other, in body or in soul. The naked soul is incapable of guilt; if one sins and then does not let any feeling of guilt hide the wrong that one has done, one renders the act harmless and takes away its maleficent powers. The soul's garment is the lie; thus, one ought to say everything honestly. But can there be an innocent honesty, or an innocence which is not dangerous? Joyce thinks not, and if Nora gives herself so freely to him, he feels that this may be an indication of wantonness, and that she might easily give herself to someone else. Suspicion is a poison whose taste he enjoys, voluntarily and involuntarily, in sado-masochistic fashion. The fear is reasonable, after all, since only a chosen love of a unique woman for a unique man could reassure Jim fully that Nora had never murmured to anyone else, "What is it, dear?", leaning over him in the darkness that her "tranquil, saint-like eyes" might drink in the fever in the beloved's eyes, exciting him. He must simply assure himself of the truth or untruth of this, and this is what he did in 1909. At least, this is what he tried to do; he was not concerned particularly for Nora's virginity, but for whether she were telling him the truth or not—one might almost think that the ideal situation for him would be to find that she had some past sin on her conscience, that it might act as a further bond between them. "Sweetheart, answer me. Even if I learn that you too have sinned perhaps it would bind me even closer to you. In any case I love you. I have written and said things to you that my pride would *never again* allow me to say to any woman" (letter of 3 Dec. 1909).

If there can be a "natural" eroticism, it must be that which is not confined by prohibitions; in this love without restriction they find life, and their embraces act out the seasons and changes of that life. In one of his very earliest letters to Nora, Jim had written, "When you come next leave sulks at home—also stays." If there are no stays, there will be no "paralysis," bodies may touch and flesh live "naturally". One cannot help recalling the rhetorical speeches of Robert Hand in *Exiles*.

The soul, once rid of its stays, of its inhibitions, is naturally tempted to veer unreasonably in the opposite direction; at the moment when it risks all, when it is in danger of losing control, it feels itself to be truly

[7] *Letters*, vol. II, p. 243.

valuable. Nothing refines the soul so much as a potentially dangerous situation, as Stephen realises when he flirts with temptation in order to test his powers of resistance. There is a moment of anguished delight reached by way of disorder and dislocation, when one no longer recognises oneself, intoxicated by the feeling of being inhuman yet fearing the descent into complete animality. This too, says Joyce, is part of love. "My little silent Nora . . . I want you to read over and over all I have written to you. Some of it is ugly, obscene and bestial, some of it is pure and holy and spiritual: all of it is myself. And I think you see now what I feel towards you" (letter of 7 Sept. 1909).

He tries to demonstrate his proposition that in order to be a saint a man must have been a swine first, and asks whether it is possible to be both. From the 'Circe' episode in *Ulysses*, it would seem that any ascent other than an imaginary one is impossible. But Bloom is alone; with Nora, Joyce no longer feared self-loss, and if she existed, hell did not. He knew that he could always return from his metamorphoses, back to human shape, and that even as a swine he was still human to her. There could still be times of ambiguous delight, but the illusion of innocence could be restored immediately, by means of that free conscience which disarmed evil of its malice and harmful powers. They were saved by their fidelity to themselves and to each other, and by Nora's open generosity; for only a sexual loneliness is degrading. God is absent, or is made absent, from the garden where they taste their forbidden fruit; they tempt each other, and act the part of victim in turn, causing each other to fall and then forgiving each other again; no supernatural power forbids their secret marriage. "My darling Nora, I am panting with eagerness to get your replies to these filthy letters of mine. . . . I love you, Nora, and it seems that this too is part of my love. Forgive me! Forgive me!" (letter of 3 Dec. 1909).

All is possible if the other person will give absolution. Jim can fall and crawl to such an extent that his own follies amaze him, but Nora's glance will restore and purify him always; she makes merry over this, like the washerwomen in *Finnegans Wake*. And Nora when besmirched by his love is even more worthy an object of love. When Jim asks, "Am I not a swine?" he expects her to answer, "You're just a child," and then all is well. She wills herself to be shameless and symbolically nubile for him, and in his gratitude he venerates her like the holy figure of Our Lady. The little girl prostituting herself becomes the queen, and Jim prostrate before her becomes her sovereign; he crowns the woman who is his redemption. They stand facing each other like two innocent children, and then like Stephen and the bird-girl. And when their desire flames up from the fuel of sin, they have already reconstituted a sanctuary, with new prohibitions to profane, and the game begins anew. They have restored a new kind of sacrosanctity; and even if Jim has some disgusting habits, and if Nora's drawers are not always clean, the dirt is not impure, nor the stain one of guilt. The desire for life becomes identified with the desire for knowledge, whose lowest manifestations are voyeurism and curiosity, whose highest is simplicity.

It is perhaps in art, Nora dearest, that you and I will find a solace for our own love. I would wish you to be surrounded by everything that is fine and beautiful and noble in art. You are not, as you say, a poor uneducated girl. You are my bride, darling, and all I can give you of pleasure and joy in this life I wish to give you. Nora darling, let our love as it is now never end. You understand now your strange erring wilful jealous lover, do you not, dearest? . . . He loves you, believe that always. He has never had a particle of love for anyone but you. It is you who have opened a deep chasm in his life. . . .
You have been to my young manhood what the idea of the Blessed Virgin was to my boyhood. O tell me, my sweet love, that you are satisfied with me now. One word of praise from you fills me with joy, a soft rose-like joy. Our children (much as I love them) *must not* come between us. If they are good and noble-natured it is because of *us*, dear. We met and joined our bodies and souls freely and nobly and our children are the fruit of our bodies.
Good night my dearest girl, my little Galway bride, my tender love from Ireland. How I would love to surprise you sleeping now! There is a place I would like to kiss you now, a *strange* place, Nora. *Not* on the lips, Nora. Do you know where? (letter of 31 Aug. 1909)

As they grew older, the work became more of a rival to Nora, who for her part was unable to replace Jim by art; there is a discreet regret in her words to a friend, "my husband is a saint," although what Jim was experiencing was probably satiety rather than mystic sanctity. He now knew more than "the devil's grandmother," and he had a great deal still to write. So life went on and he played with the myths of the fall and the redemption which he had learned, which he had exorcised, and which he was consequently now able to parody. But Nora still ruled over him in secret: Molly tires and Anna Livia passes, but Jim at the age of forty still worships as he did at twenty. In April 1922 he writes, "My darling, my love, my queen. . . . Your image is always in my heart."

In general the reader thinks of the identity of Bloom with Joyce in terms of "exile" and proceeds no further, but to see thus far is simply to see Bloom as the typical Jew of the Dispersion, and to ignore his individual personality as Bloom. (The antisemitic reader who would explain all Bloom's failings and weaknesses by his Jewish origins would not dream of making the comparison, but would reason thus: Bloom is a swine because he is a Jew. Neither Joyce nor I are Jews, etc.)

We cannot imagine Bloom at the end of the day meeting a youthful, Irish Molly with calm eyes instead of creeping furtively into the old bed with creaking springs. Bloom is the secret Joyce, the Joyce who hides and denies himself—who fears himself and does not know himself well. Despite Bloom's Jewishness, he is really the emanation of unsuccessfully exorcised Catholicism. Joyce understands the worst in Bloom's nature so well, because it was not foreign to him. Bloom is not Joyce, but he is the dream-self projected into the daily nightmare and waking dream that is Dublin in *Ulysses*. Bloom is too far away from reality to be able to accomplish that necessary ironical separation which is what saves Joyce from himself, and he gradually sinks into a loneliness peopled only by the ghosts of his desires and fears; Bloom loses himself. Joyce, changing his identity by means of a game with therapeutic intention, can find himself again, everywhere the same.

But between himself and the other, the Bloom-self, whom he does not wish to be, he sets a pile of books. If Bloom is an ashamed Joyce, confessing without removing his mask, Joyce was in reality a Bloom with the art of self-mockery as an added quality, an ironical Bloom.

XIX. *Exiles*, or the Discovery of Creative Doubt

The play *Exiles* resembles *Stephen Hero* by its intermediary situation between art and life; like the first version of the *Portrait* it is closer to real life than to art, and is the fruit of research and experiment in psychology rather than in aesthetics. Both works seem to have been intended as preparations for more finished, polished works and at the same time to serve as a kind of journal for Joyce, who stands very close to the hero or artist who lives through the fruitful experiences described. This explains the serious tones of Stephen Hero and of Richard Rowan, which sometimes verge on the ridiculous, and the ironical distance which their successors maintain between life and their own emotions. These two works, imperfect by reason of the elements in them not yet decanted or distilled into art, are made up of a mass of thoughts and emotions noted down over many years and essentially important and secret, as though Joyce had had to write a first version of his books before being able to make of them a free creation, separate from himself. The writing of both *Exiles* and *Stephen Hero* required a distancing rather than an organising process, and as he was writing them, he was creating in a much more objective and skilful fashion other works of perfectly accomplished art. As we read of the fervours and the troubles of Stephen Hero, we tend to forget that he is a contemporary of those Dubliners whose life is caught and itemised in a symbolic network already worthy of *Portrait*, a predecessor of stylistic revolution.

As we read *Exiles*, the emotional sum of five crucial years in the life of Jim and Nora, we forget that he has made the *Portrait* already and that since 1907 he has been planning *Ulysses*. Yet *Exiles* is the thematic embryo of *Ulysses*; all the main themes are sketched out there, and some examined in reasonable depth, beginning with the theme of exile, which gives the play its name. Richard Rowan follows in the footsteps of Stephen and Leopold Bloom. In this difficult play, almost inaccessible to the general public because of its dense, morbid ambiguities, Joyce deals with the complex problems of doubt, jealousy, and conjugal loneliness, and with the fundamental paradoxes of *Ulysses*, the ideas of masochism as creative force, of deliberately courting pain, of the delicious torment of the cuckold, the recovery of all forms of separation and exile as the conquest of the necessary place of creation, the inner space, and finally the theme of the unjust cruelty of God, executioner of humankind and of Himself in the person of His Son.

Love and friendship, the forms of union possible between human beings, are reduced to tragic myths whose central figure is Christ; to be betrayed and abandoned is the fate awaiting those who venture into the double loneliness of the couple. Every relationship is ruled by ambivalence. The parallel between the two types of relationship is established around the desire to possess the other, less by respecting him than by depriving him of the qualities, such as strength or beauty, which one admires in him; the master is betrayed by his disciple, who carries out his dispossession for and by love. In the *Portrait*, Joyce had already adopted for Stephen's use the certainty that Stannie felt in real life: the artist's false friends will always seek to profit by his intelligence and steal his ideas.

In *Exiles* Robert Hand wishes to possess his friend, but this cannot be accomplished in the flesh because love between man and man is impossible without degradation; hence it must find spiritual satisfaction. Thus, Robert seeks to possess Richard's mind, and not only his mind but also the imprint made by his admirable personality upon those close to him, who are so subject to him that everyone says that Richard has "made" their souls to his own liking. Bertha is a creation of Richard's, and by desiring Bertha, Robert may claim that it is Richard that he loves in her. He may claim this at any rate, for Joyce is not deceived by such homosexual oversimplifications and rationalisations, even if they do provide him with subtle effects. At the end, if Robert does love Bertha through love for Richard, the result is still sufficiently ambiguous to allow for all possible doubt.

In this play Joyce reaches the limit, the boundary, where behaviour changes its meaning and the serious turns to the grotesque. The hypothesis of Judas' purity is an attractive one; but in this middle-class, ordinary, non-divine world, the net result is still cuckoldry and hypocrisy after all. The glorious complicity of Christ offering himself for the kiss he knows will betray him, transposed into the setting of Dublin, becomes masochism or paranoia. Richard is closer to Bloom than to Jesus, but he does not know this. On the contrary, Joyce already knows the masks and the devious complacency of the betrayed husband; the antagonist of *Exiles* is hardly attractive or pitiable because he is too coldly aware of his contradictory impulses and because he plays them out in a way that will probably cause his wife suffering.

Bloom in the same situation, favouring Molly's adultery to the extent that he will bring her chosen lover home for her, does not try to dictate the course of the game. He does not aim at some other man by way of Molly, he does not desire thus to acquire a master, but in the person of Stephen the poet he sees another, younger, more brilliant Leopold Bloom; he has a genuine love for Molly, which has no equivalent in the feelings of Richard Rowan, for the artist of *Exiles* loves none but himself, as Joyce frankly tells us in the notes he wrote as commentary on the play about 1913. Bertha is far from enjoying the triumphant liberty which Molly has. Richard is the projection, haughty, aloof, and still very like the heroic figure of Parnell, of Joyce outraged and tormented by jealousy, while Bloom is the man Joyce can be in his weakness and in his erotic fantasies. Both are born from an experience of life which, after its exposition as a theorem in *Exiles*, becomes the principle of an aesthetic which develops from the definition of the artist's being and function in its relationship with creation.

Discovering the Fruits of Doubt

In his years in Dublin Joyce was unfamiliar with doubt—or at least with that doubt which questioned the reality of his "artistic temperament," of what Stanislaus called his "genius". During the long, annoying years of negotiations before the printing of his books, he never doubted for a moment the perfection of his craft and the authenticity of his vocation. In September 1905 he wrote to Stanislaus,

It is possible that the delusion I have with regard to my power to write will be killed by adverse circumstances. But the delusion which will never leave me is that I am an artist by temperament. Newman and Renan, for example, are excellent writers but they seem to have very little of the temperament I mean. Whereas Rimbaud, who is hardly a writer at all, has it. Of course Renan is an artist and must have the temperament but it is balanced by the temperament of a philologist. Newman must have it too but balanced by the temperament of a saint.

His departure a year earlier had been an act put on for the benefit of the public, a scene of heroic defiance, announcing that he was voluntarily going into exile and attempting to hide from his family, and particularly from John Joyce, that he was not going alone.

His first letters to Stanislaus from Pola and Trieste in 1905 and from Rome in 1906 show that he is constantly preoccupied with emphasising to all and sundry the victorious aspect of his departure, while badgering Stannie alone for material aid:

> I have come to accept my present situation as a voluntary exile—is it not so? This seems to me important both because I am likely to generate out of it a sufficiently personal future to satisfy Curran's heart and also because it supplies me with the note on which I propose to bring my novel to a close.[1]

He takes advantage of every circumstance, and if life has perhaps preceded art by action, he recovers it by skilful reformulation; by such tricks he creates the illusion that he is the sovereign master of his destiny, interpreting everything, however accidental, as an episode in the history of the artist's gestation. His lack of stability and his refusal to adapt or settle down, which caused him to be constantly on the move —from the Berlitz school in Trieste to a bank in Rome and back to Trieste, and so on—show that his departure was not an emigration towards a better standard of material life but a spiritual exile, setting the object of his thoughts at a distance from him in order to exercise his imagination the more easily. Dublin and its inhabitants remained central in his thoughts. Wherever he happened to be was not his home, but merely a temporary stopping-place. Despite his wish to be a citizen of Europe, all that he writes in his first years of absence is destined for the Dublin reader.

He seizes the first honourable excuse to go back to see what impression he has made at home, and to dazzle his former friends, the "provin-

[1] *Letters*, vol. II, pp. 83–4.

cials," a little. When he arrived in Dublin in 1909, with his Italian journalist's identity card, he was acting the return of Gallaher for the benefit of the impressionable little Chandlers. He came as a visitor (for there could be no question of interrupting the heroic pose he had adopted), even taking pleasure in appearing in the unexpected role of business man, handling Triestine capital in the most up-to-date commercial enterprise. And then, suddenly, life caught him by surprise. There had been many treacheries, maintained over the years, many traitors like Gogarty, and Joyce knew how to work the mechanism of these relationships, and how to draw discordant music from them. But this time he was attacked in a sensitive area, caught off his guard: he was told that Nora had been unfaithful to him while they were still in Dublin. At once, the prestige of exile disappears, the hero is cast down and transformed into a victim; this descent into the banal makes him ridiculous. Joyce's suffering was genuine, but the vertigo caused by the fall must have been delightful.

Scarcely had he taken cognisance of this wound, before he began discovering the infinite possibilities for artistic exploitation of the role of cuckold; depending on the verbal expression of the situation, one can be grotesque or tragic, abandoned like Charles Bovary (whom Joyce mentions in his notes on *Exiles*) or like Christ, or like both. Grief appeared at just the right time for use in the enrichment and humanising of the theme of exile; to be distant physically would be too nobly, superficially aloof. Joyce finds the necessary depth for the theme in this treachery of Cosgrave's; he can move the notion of exile into the inner world and make it into a spiritual exile. He has also found a successor to the infamous curate, a friend who has betrayed him. He does not hesitate, but doubts; he seems, indeed, to have given free rein to his passions at this time, as though fearing that they might evaporate and deprive him of interesting and useful emotions.

J. F. Byrne recalls how Jim came to his house in tears, seeking refuge, because Vincent Cosgrave, that prototype of the long succession of Judas-figures in his work, had been boasting of his successes in courting Nora in 1904. Jim, reassured at last with great difficulty, wrote to Nora the most passionate letters of his life, his feelings exalted by his doubt into a paroxysm (whose verbal formulae he carefully notes) and the movement of swelling pride is followed by a fall, declining into humble homage at the feet of the outraged "queen". He writes letters full of reproach, she grows indignant, he repents, she declares that she is tired of him, he offers himself to her for punishment, claiming that he deserves the worst possible torment. A bonfire of unbridled sensuality results, kindled by the thought of punishment being inflicted at the hands of one who is the gentle Holy Virgin for him. He claims that, thanks to this dreadful incident, he has rediscovered the purity and nakedness of their souls, as it must now be transmitted to their bodies.

> What can come between us now? We have suffered and been tried. Every veil of shame or diffidence seems to have fallen from us. Will we not see in each other's eyes the hours and hours of happiness that are waiting for us?
> Adorn your body for me, dearest. Be beautiful and happy and loving and provoking, full of memories, full of cravings, when we meet. Do you remember the three adjectives I have used in *The Dead* in speaking of your body. They are these: "musical and strange and perfumed". My jealousy is still smouldering in my heart. Your love for me must be fierce and violent to make me forget *utterly*. (letter of 22 Aug. 1909)

Certain passages of the letters are plagiarised by Richard, five years later—which proves yet again that Joyce is an artist above everything, considering himself as object rather than subject. To hear him, one might indeed believe that nothing *could* come between them now, but in the space of a few months Joyce has finished acting the enraged spouse and assumes the role of the naughty little boy who adores his mother. He takes pleasure in this situation, this condition of child-like weakness, and incites Nora to behave as though omniscient and all-forgiving:

> Darling, when I go back now I want you always to be patient with me. You will find, dear, that I *am not a bad man.* I am a poor impulsive sinful generous selfish jealous dissatisfied kind-natured poet but I am not a bad deceitful person. Try to shelter me, dearest, from the storms of the world. ... I am *sure*, darling, in your heart of hearts you must think I am a poor silly boy. You proud little ignorant saucy dear warm-hearted girl how is it that I cannot impress you with my magnificent poses as I do other people? You see through me, you cunning little blue-eyed rogue, and smile to yourself knowing that I am an impostor and still you love me. (letter of 23 Dec. 1909, from Dublin)

Hardly has he found calm again, when suffering reappears as temptation. Since Nora is faithful and generous to him, he must seek material for his jealousy elsewhere in the past, where no reassurance is possible and where there is no evidence but the tomb of a long-dead Platonic lover. This time the theatre of his martyrdom is Galway, where Nora lived in her childhood before she met Joyce. If Vincent Cosgrave were a possible or likely rival, the jealous imagination that examines past history knows no bounds. It is hurt by anything and everything; and in his torments Joyce becomes almost ridiculous: a young girl's glance confounds him completely, and he disputes possession of Nora's image with a young policeman from Galway:

> Darling, I am in a most dreadful state of excitement at present. All day I have been in the middle of the bustling Xmas crowd down at the cinematograph. There was a young constable there on special duty. When it was over I took him upstairs to give him a drink and found he was from Galway and his sisters were at the Presentation Convent with you. He was amazed to hear where Nora Barnacle had ended. He said he remembered you in Galway, a handsome girl with curls and a proud walk. My God, Nora, how I suffered! Yet I could not stop talking to him. . . . I wondered did my darling, my love, my dearest, my queen ever turn her young eyes towards him. I *had* to speak to him because he came from Galway but O how I suffered. . . . O, darling, I am so jealous of the past and yet I bite my nails with excitement whenever I see anybody from the strange dying western city in which my love, my beautiful wild flower of the hedges, passed her young laughing girlish years. (letter of 24 Dec. 1909)

The Pleasures of Doubt

During this time, Nora had stayed behind in Trieste, where Stanislaus was looking after her. It would scarcely be surprising if his attentions had been closer and his care less fraternal than Jim expected, and the latter suffered the torments of a husband deceived by his friend and of Hamlet the father betrayed by Claudius. Nora made it obvious that Stannie had caused her displeasure. Joyce probably never had any proof of his brother's treachery, but it was at this time that the concept of Shem and Shaun, the rival brothers of *Finnegans Wake*, began to take shape. Once his sadness had passed, and once he had offered to Nora the little golden chain, a symbol of reconciliation, upon which he had had engraved "Love is unhappy when love is away," Joyce could begin again the delightful game of doubt and uncertainty (see Ellmann, pp. 297 ff.). Joyce was basically a complaisant type, the sort of man who likes to show off his wife's attractions to others and to know that they desire her; in Trieste he long received visits from a Venetian journalist,

Roberto Prezioso, who served as one of the models for Robert Hand, and whose name occurs in the list of Bertha's attributes, "Garter: precious, Prezioso, Bodkin, music, palegreen," in Joyce's notes to *Exiles*.

The Prezioso affair is typical—Prezioso found Nora very attractive and said as much—giving Jim the pleasure that Bloom found in showing Stephen suggestive and tempting photographs of Molly. But when Prezioso, like Robert, wished to make further acquaintance with her beauty, Jim outraged but secretly delighted, publicly slapped his face and brought him to tears. Prezioso wept, Jim wept, Nora wept, as Richard and Bertha weep too. Joyce knew only too well how to unleash floods of emotional tears. The sight of Prezioso in tears impressed to such an extent a Joyce who was himself easily moved to tears or outcries that he made his Robert Hand a man of both aggressive virility and humbled sensibilities. For years afterwards he would relive the whole scene in his dreams. He had created this entire intolerable situation himself, and its outcome could not fail to be intolerable to one of the friends involved; having shown himself guilty of masochism, he had also demonstrated an unjust sadism towards Prezioso. All this happened in Trieste between 1911 and 1912.

Since his experiments with doubt had suggested to Joyce that being hurt might be a source of creative power, he manipulated this necessary factor in 1912, when Nora and Lucia visited Galway; he became violently impatient and jealous of the dead lover, again accusing Nora of imaginary infidelity yet hastening to join her, unable to live without her:

> I can neither sleep nor think. . . . Last night I was afraid to lie down. I thought I would die in sleep. I wakened Georgie three times for fear of being alone. It is a monstrous thing to say that you seem to forget me in five days and to forget the beautiful days of our love. I leave Trieste tonight as I am afraid to stay here. . . . I shall arrive in Dublin on Monday. If you have forgotten I have not. I shall go *alone* to meet and walk with the image of her whom I remember. . . . What are Dublin and Galway compared with our memories? (letter of 12 July 1912)

Scarcely had he arrived before he was revenging himself in a fashion worthy of Richard Rowan: making a macabre visit to the cemetery where his rival lay disarmed. He wrote to Stannie, "I cycled to Oughterard on Sunday and visited the graveyard of *The Dead*. It is exactly as I imagined it."[2]

---

[2] *Letters*, vol. II, p. 300; in his work, Joyce replaces the name Oughterard by that of Rahoon, for reasons of euphony.

These cruel fantasies would be grotesque, were Joyce not secretly searching for a formulation through repetition of significant patterns, which from now on all fit into his preparatory thinking for *Ulysses*; the alarm of the summer of 1909 is used to crystallise transpersonal ideas into serious and comical forms. Throughout his emotional experiments Joyce is forming and sketching in the exile of a Bloom, accomplice of his own misfortune, and the biography of a Shakespeare as told by Stephen in *Ulysses*; all this returns at last to the primal idea—the myth of the One Before that is the source of the creative impulse.

In a theological world, God is The First One: He has preceded the artist by His Creation, and He has preceded the man by the hold He has established, by means of His priests, over the soul of woman. For the proud man the creative act itself is an act of challenge and defiance to God, and the sanctification of woman is less a form of extreme love and devotion than an intention to challenge God by deconsecrating the incarnate symbol of Our Lady's virginity. Rape, which is still a matter of blasphemy in *Exiles*, becomes a matter of parody in *Ulysses*, where Bloom breaks off the mythical combat with The Other because he is no creator: he further renounces almost completely his claims on Molly's body, which as intermediary might have caused him some unpleasant encounters. On the contrary, Richard takes great pains to organise his morbid meetings with Robert, choosing him as adversary and as his own representative. Not the Muse but the wound he receives inspires the poet; creation and destruction, possession and dispossession are inseparable.

In *Exiles* Joyce expresses himself most openly as Satanic double of God, in the person of Richard Rowan. His notes,[3] almost all concerned with Bertha, are directly inspired by Joyce's relations with Nora and with God as Predecessor, He who is jokingly nicknamed in *Finnegans Wake* "Huges Caput Earlyfouler"; in this name can be recognised Hugh (Boylan), the word "huge," and Hugh C. Love, the Jesuit in Circe's black mass; Caput the head and Kaputt, the broken; and the "earlyfouler," father and initiator, he who was there first.

Nora, like Gretta Conroy, had told Jim of a youthful romantic affair she had had with a young Irishman, Michael Bodkin, who had died of tuberculosis; the figure of Bodkin had thus become the centre of the first circle of Joyce's jealousy. The absent presence of this innocent rival

[3]Written in a blue notebook now in the library of Buffalo University, they were published by Viking Press, New York, in 1951, and by Jonathan Cape, London, in 1952, in their respective editions of *Exiles*.

could serve as the pretext for a skilful deployment of masochism, for one cannot kill or absolve a dead man or "God". This posthumous adultery is a sentence which cannot be reversed, for it is impressed upon an innocent memory, and this is what constitutes a cruel delight for Joyce's imagination: that there was Another! Even though the love between Michael and Nora was only a brief Platonic affair, Joyce could never *know*, and this made their love of much more use to him than the horrible incident involving Cosgrave in 1909; on the latter occasion Joyce had finally discovered the truth and had it established before witnesses, and the emotion had been a living one, but it was now dead. Yet the invisible and silent Michael is like the Holy Ghost; the memory of a world in which Joyce did not exist is alive in Nora's mind, and this kind of pre-natal death fascinates him. It seems as though he had been betrayed in advance; he maintains this idea which excludes him from life, savouring it as the most refined possible form of exile. He still contradicts it too, by means of the proud argument which makes him eventually victorious over every rival; he is living while Bodkin is dead, but he is also immortal because he is an artist. This feeling of dominating time present and time future is expressed in his notes to *Exiles* in these terms: "Bodkin died. Kearns died. In the convent they called her the man-killer: (woman-killer was one of her names for me.) I live in soul and body." "She" is Nora or Bertha, or both of them together, she is both the giver and taker of life.

> She is the earth, dark, formless, mother, made beautiful by the moonlit night, darkly conscious of her instincts. Shelley whom she has held in her womb or grave rises: the part of Richard which neither love nor life can do away with; the part for which she loves him: the part she must try to kill, never be able to kill and rejoice at her impotence. (Notes to *Exiles*, p. 167)

"Shelley" is Joyce's name for the creative power within him, that which makes his greatness and cannot be destroyed. His clarity of vision was exercised to the utmost in his estimation of the mystery he knew himself to be for Nora; he knew himself to be born of her love for him, and that that love threatened him with death, if he were to allow himself to be simply the spouse of the beloved woman. Nora is wife and mother of her lord and master, though she does not know this; she is Mary because he is Jesus. "Her tears are of worship, Magdalen seeing the rearisen Lord in the garden where he had been laid in the tomb." *(Ibid.)* Joyce follows the analogy through, going so far as ironically to choose Rome as the place of exile, mingling together Shelley, Jesus, the poem, and the Church. "Rome is the strange world and strange life to which Richard brings her." *(Ibid.)*

Jealousy lurks beneath this interplay of voluntary coincidences; in Nora's memory the tomb of Shelley had recalled that of Michael, and she had wept, as she had wept over the inglorious tomb of Rahoon. In death she embraces Bodkin: "She weeps over Rahoon too, over him whom her love has killed, the dark boy whom, as the earth, she embraces in death and disintegration. He is her buried life, her past."

The dark-haired Irish boy is dead for her, and in death and memory now they are inseparably united. Joyce, or his double Richard, only possesses her in this life and this present time. What would have happened if the other had lived? Joyce feels, impossibly though on a very deep level, displaced and replaced by the other one. He is grieved by the thought that perhaps she did not "choose" him in the absolute sense, that perhaps her life for her was already over when Michael died. In another sense, this feeling is the same as that which caused Stephen to fail in his attempt to love God: he could not bear the idea of the blind, all-demanding love of God, and, similarly, Nora's almost incomprehensible love was both moving and hurtful to Joyce. She had not chosen him; God had not chosen Stephen; and in *Exiles* Bertha has not chosen Richard—he says that she was too young and too ignorant to know what she was doing. This kind of love is too much like blind Catholic faith; Joyce was never able to resist the desire to test it, the need to try and to burden it almost to destruction, and to give Nora a "freedom" which might guarantee that it was he and not another in his place whom she really wanted.

This creative jealousy, this suffering allied to art, is accompanied by an even more subtle inversion of roles, for the jealous man is tempted by the prospect of being a cuckold, and his reasons are perversely argued; as Joyce explains in a note, it is not a matter of deriving pleasure from suffering, but of desiring to be united with the betrayer, through the physical possession of the same woman. Joyce is attracted to God through woman, and Richard Rowan goes so far as to confess that, like a priest, he feels vicariously the emotions proper to adultery, possessing Bertha through the flesh of his friend Robert. To touch without touching and to sin without sinning is skilfully worked out, but he has to go still further: he wishes to be the Other, to be both the dispossessor and the dispossessed. "The bodily possession of Bertha by Robert, repeated often, would certainly bring into almost carnal contact the two men. . . . To be united, that is carnally through the person and body of Bertha as they cannot, without dissatisfaction and degradation, be united carnally man to man" (Notes to *Exiles*, p. 172). God is he who interferes; he prepares the meetings, and then disappears, leaving us nothing but the role of spectators.

When Stephen attributes to the artist the place of God, the creator refined out of existence, he is attempting to transmute this notion of God as *voyeur* into a realistic "objectivity". God in his corner, an exile through choice, is the supreme *voyeur*, he who enjoys by proxy. And for this reason Joyce carefully emphasises in his notes that the liberation of Bertha is not a disinterested gesture made for the young woman's benefit, but rather the height of Richard's egoism; his only ambition is the accomplishment of himself, and this description seems as valid for Joyce as for Richard:

> Richard must not appear as a champion of woman's rights. His language at times must be nearer to that of Schopenhauer against women and he must show at times a deep contempt for the long-haired, short-legged sex. He is in fact fighting for his own hand, for his own emotional dignity and liberation in which Bertha, no less and no more than Beatrice or any other woman is coinvolved. (Notes to *Exiles*, p. 169)

In fact, all the action of the play pivots round the personality of Richard, which is defined against that of Robert and through the person of Bertha. The young woman is only the nebulous matter in which the two men wander, seeking their free selves and each other. In this strange navigation the woman's body is both water, earth, and moon, life and death, fecundity and sterility, purely elementary; her mind is "a grey seamist amid which common objects—hillsides, the masts of ships, and barren islands—loom with strange and yet recognisable outlines". She is simply a passage, the *vas naturale*, says Joyce, quoting the Fathers of the Church. Obviously Bertha only exists as a means of sexual communication.

The real interest of the play lies in the struggle which takes place under the surface between Robert and Richard, in "three cat and mouse acts". Joyce defines it as "a rough and tumble between the Marquis de Sade and Freiherr von Sacher-Masoch". The outcome is unforeseeable because woman is unpredictable. And if "the new Ireland cannot contain both," if Robert has to go into exile, we do not know, and neither does Joyce, whether "her thoughts will follow him into exile as those of her sister-in-love Isolde follow Tristan". He who remains behind is the masochist, the artist, the provoker, and Robert is the one who leaves. Again Joyce surprises us, for we should expect, seeing the distribution of the roles and knowing that Richard represents the author, that it would be the artist who went into exile and was compared with Tristan. But, on the contrary, Tristan is the strong man, the journalist, and already, by his lack of scruples and of true greatness, a first version of Ulysses. *Exiles* would then be, as *Ulysses* is for the *Odyssey*, a parody of exile and return—the real exile being, of course, to return to Ireland.

Arrangement of the Two Couples in Exiles

Given Joyce's real intention, one can appreciate the bewilderment of the spectators to whom he exhibited this series of moves between two pairs of characters.

The subject appears to be the rivalry of two former friends for the favours of Bertha, but in fact the real couple is formed by the two men, their relationship defined by analogy with that of Jesus and Judas. Robert is fully qualified to play the part of the traitor: "Robert is glad to have in Richard a personality to whom he can pay the tribute of complete admiration . . . this he mistakes for reverence" (Notes to *Exiles*, p. 175).

Hatred and love mingle gently in the heart of this man who is humiliated by the object of his admiration. Richard's way of abandoning himself to Robert has also a rather unchristian air about it. "Richard accepts Robert's homage for Bertha as by so doing he robs it from Bertha's countrywomen and revenges himself and his forbidden love upon them" (Notes to *Exiles*, p. 172).

In other words, Richard feels such resentment, such a dislike for the Irish woman enmeshed in the taboos of her Church, that he would not hesitate to divert Robert by the offer or the sacrifice of Bertha, as though in order to demonstrate the superiority of illicit love. Consideration of the excessive nature of this attitude would suggest that Joyce himself must have been more concerned with pride and self-love than with the love of another, and this to an abnormal degree. It seems that the dominant sentiment was the need for vengeance, to such an extent that one wonders where the real love for Nora began and where the intention of challenging society and its God ended. The mixed and impure nature of his motives is a permanent characteristic which helps to determine the orientation of the work, and in *Exiles*, which is so near to reality, Joyce allows the maximum of ambiguity to pervade all the characters' relationships. All Joyce's efforts, and Richard's too, are directed towards the accomplishment of his destiny, and to this end he feels that he must sacrifice any weakness caused by love for another. His concept of Christ as a lonely man, without a woman, pitiless and solitary, explains the apparently unlikely comparison made between Him and the frigid, aloof hero of *Exiles*.

In the first act, Richard Rowan the artist returns from Rome (where Shelley and Byron had chosen their exile), accompanied by his twenty-eight-year-old mistress Bertha, a young woman with grey eyes, and by their illegitimate son Archie. Nine years ago, in 1903, he had fled from Dublin for the same reasons as Stephen and Joyce had fled: he had no longer been willing to serve something in which he had ceased to believe, namely the social taboos that were then represented by his authoritative and extremely devout mother. She has since died in all the obstinacy of the Irish Catholic faith, without forgiving him for his heresy and immorality, yet although the mother is dead, the bitterness in Richard's heart is still alive. It is clear that the Irish have not killed the fatted calf to celebrate his return, and he is as aware of this as is Joyce, who comments, "Why the title *Exiles*? A nation exacts a penance from those who dared to leave her payable on their return. The elder brother in the fable of the Prodigal Son is Robert Hand. The father took the side of the prodigal. This is probably not the way of the world—certainly not in Ireland" (Notes to *Exiles*, p. 164).

This note manifests the specific form of Joyce's aggressive attitude towards Ireland; as usual, he does not hesitate to modify a myth for his own purposes, and to do so without telling the reader. He alters the myth here, for it is Ireland *the mother* that punishes the prodigal, that wears the mask of the pitiless, obstinate mother-figure.

The first act deals with a joyless return, filled with distrust and deception. Richard and Bertha are awaited by a symmetrical couple, Robert Hand and Beatrice. Robert is the reflection of Richard in a distorting mirror, the failed artist or the successful artist who has a public; he is a journalist and has been negotiating to facilitate Richard's return, has even obtained the promise of a post at the University for him. He is engaged to his cousin Beatrice (a slight suggestion of incest here) who, despite her name, has nothing of the glowing brilliance of her Florentine model. She is a Protestant, and she is like "an abandoned cold temple," yet for nine years she has been Richard's inspiration; he has written for her, and she has faithfully corresponded with him. The second attribute of the Virgin Beatrice is that she teaches the piano and the harmonium, but this does not mean that she is to be seen as the symbol of music, grace, and harmony; on the contrary, she involuntarily sows discord between Richard and Bertha. Thirdly, like Joyce and like Gabriel Conroy in 'The Dead,' she wears glasses; the radiant Beatrice who illuminated Dante is so short-sighted that she has to look at the world by means of these intermediaries. She cannot be in direct contact with the world. The detail is intentionally grotesque in this bourgeois comedy where Joyce pretends to take himself seriously.[4] The first act, in which people should be meeting and finding each other again, is disconcerting; formally, it is arranged like a farce, with one R and one B always on stage, a B or R always threatening to appear, and an R or B making a hasty exit.

Richard sees Beatrice again; he could "see" her well enough when their closeness was a matter of distance, but he admits that they had nothing in common but bitterness. When Bertha meets Robert the lack of equilibrium makes itself more strongly felt; they have not communicated with each other for nine years and have exchanged, by contrast, nothing except a note which Robert sent the previous evening, declaring that he had long desired Bertha and that he intended eventually to possess her. She who has sacrificed everything in order to follow Richard to Rome accepts with a strange passivity his proposal that they meet that very evening. Nine years of spiritual communion have done less for one R-B couple than this brief meeting has done for the other pair.

The two men come face to face in a scene heavily charged with symbolism and symbolic objects; Robert kisses a pebble polished by the sea, the symbol of natural beauty. Robert twice asks Richard for a light, and he drinks alone, while their conversation revolves slowly around past, present, and future. Robert says that he is a disciple and admirer of Richard, and Richard says that he has "the faith of a master in the disciple who will betray him". He denounces his own Judas in order to assume the crown of thorns.

In his notes, Joyce supposes that every spectator is a Robert who should be wishing he were a Richard in order to belong to Bertha, that is, wishing to be Joyce, Jesus, a priest, or at any rate someone other than himself, if not several others. Every feeling which lays claim to simplicity is a false one. Each of us is an exile to every other, voluntarily and involuntarily, and while appearing to bring about some reconcilia-

---

[4]It may also be taken from *Giacomo Joyce*, p. 1, where Amalia is portrayed as cold, pale, untouchable, somewhat like Beatrice: "her movements are shy and nervous. She uses quizzing-glasses."

tion, each of us is blindly groping for the space which constitutes the difference and the separation from others—the space within himself or between himself and other people, where he can be alone. Although apparently dealing with a return to the native land, *Exiles* in fact represents a taking stock and a realisation of the impassible barriers that form the boundaries of people and of images of oneself; the "exiles" are four people who are in process of falling and of watching themselves falling, subjectively as Stephen would say, in order to take pleasure in the vertiginous descent from the heights. The fall in *Exiles* still obeys those laws of gravity which are the subject of Bloom's meditations, and the weight of a guilty conscience increases the speed of the fall. In ironical parody of *Paradise Lost* the first act consists of an inclined plane leading towards sin.

In the second act Bertha goes to Robert; the scene of the sin is carefully decorated with faded roses and funereal draperies. The house is the same house where the two Rs used to meet long ago. Robert plays Wagner, and sweetens the air with a scent-spray. It rains, and Richard is on his way with an umbrella, a preventative measure. Robert goes out without an umbrella and is greatly discomfited by the weather; only Bertha has no fear of the rain, symbol of fertility and purity. Because God is there from the beginning, it is Richard who comes first; God comes to prepare the trap and to see that everything is ready for the sacrifice, that the ritual of his own shame be performed in orthodox fashion. He explains to Robert that He knows everything, that He loves Bertha, and that because of this love, He wishes her always to have the freedom to choose and to give herself. He lives in fear of constituting by his existence an obstacle to some greater, more powerful love. But his generosity is not to be considered as pure nobility of soul, for its motives are mixed with a desire to be betrayed by her and by his best friend.

Thus, he has come to offer Robert the freedom he had already offered to Bertha; Robert goes away to consider this offer, and Richard receives Bertha back. Robert and Bertha, forcibly sent by their God into the place of temptation, (although they had believed that they were acting on their own initiative) are in their forced freedom led to their bed by the very man whom they must betray and abolish. God wishes to be disobeyed, and the Fourth Person of God is Satan. Bertha's last words, "Dick, my God, tell me what you wish me to do," are as ambiguous as one could wish, but this time it is the master who betrays and abandons the disciples: "Who am I that I should call myself master of your heart or of any woman's? Bertha, love him, be his, give yourself to him if you desire—or if you can" (*Exiles.* p. 106). Robert and Bertha, paralysed by this freedom, discover with anguish that it is productive of nothing but loneliness, and they pity each other; Bertha exclaims gently, "O, you poor fellow!" and Robert says, "My poor Bertha!" Strange relationships, both tender and brotherly, develop between them, and Robert seeks to win Bertha over to himself. But the lamp has gone out, and he will not succeed; Bertha belongs to Richard, the priest of the deviant imagination. The three characters have awakened, like Adam and Eve, after imagining but not committing the sin, to the discovery of shame, to the revelation that evil and good do not matter, since one is always punished anyway. Like Adam and Eve, they have been making their first clumsy experiments with a terrible freedom.

Certainty is a snare and a delusion, the creative act can only spring from an act of destruction, and friendship is a mask for treachery, the maternal relationship, and desertion; patriotism leads to exile and religion is but death in disguise (in the play, Beatrice, the living-dead, symbolises dead religions), and truth consists of lies to oneself.

The complexity of *Exiles* is due to the fact that for Joyce it is necessary to demonstrate these truths (which by Joyce's law of ambiguity are also lies), whose nature is such that the characters can only react to them by flight. By way of the master Ibsen, Joyce had heard the voice of Kierkegaard speaking of "despair" and of the "concept of anguish".

Of these four characters who face each other in couples or obliquely, Richard seems to be the one who possesses the truth; he is the admired master and God of the other three. He has made them what they are. All the other characters in the play are only reflections of him. When he left, Beatrice's love for Robert waned because, as she says, "I saw in him a pale reflection of you: then that too faded" (*Exiles*, p. 24). But he has not succeeded in creating them in his own image; these creatures rebel, dispute his authority like the wicked angels, and he cannot overcome them. Yet he can openly enjoy their rebelliousness and disobedience. The Joycean God provokes events. The striking and embarrassing feature of this God is His insecurity: He has no confidence in anyone. He would like to have some confidence in himself and thus not to need the others, but it is clear that he is unable to do so; he is constantly in need of witnesses, of reassurance—of mirrors reflecting his image. The paradox of his nature lies in his wish to be alone, in his decision to go into exile, and in his discovery that his exile was pointless, less geographically than spiritually efficacious, and not an act of defiance but a cowardly flight. He is repeatedly accused: "You left her in her hour of need" —in the proper sense of the words, you left your mother to die alone, you left your country when it was struggling against the English, you deserted your wife in her hour of temptation.

Bertha, in the situation of Jesus in Gethsemane, cries, "Why, then, did you leave me last night?" (*Exiles*, p. 147). The exchange of roles is subtly operated and elaborated by Joyce, according to Richard's conception of himself as God the Father or God the Son. What counts is to emphasise the atmosphere of being "abandoned spiritually," and even, simply, to convince the unbeliever of the reality of things spiritual: "Robert is convinced of the non-existence, of the unreality of the spiritual facts which exist and are real for Richard, the action of the piece should however convince Robert of the existence and reality of Richard's mystical defence of his wife" (Notes to *Exiles*, p. 165). Joyce thus clearly intends to affirm what he calls "the spiritual," a theological vision of the world. But if the world of souls or of forms is real, it then appears as neither divine nor rational nor a unity; it appears as divided and devilish, or at the least heretical, for the master of things spiritual, be he named God or Jesus, is as masochistic as only Satan can be.

All Richard's actions reflect this cruel distortion. He returns only because he has a negative need for other people; he has—like Joyce—to exist, to encounter others, to affirm himself by provoking aggression in others. By leaving Ireland where he was ill at ease, he only replaced a contradiction which he had not perceived to be simply the contradiction between mind and body. He left like Byron and returned like Joyce, for it was the same Richard, made up of a soul and a body ("I live in soul and body"), of two incompatible characters who left and who returned. At the end of the play, Richard knows henceforth that it is impossible to be self-sufficient like a god or hero. By experiencing dependence, he has learned that in order to be a master one must have a disciple, and that Robert was not truly his; that in order to be a man one must have a woman; that in order to create one must have a model; that evil is necessary that good may exist; that in order to be free one must be alienated; and that Beatrice is the absence of Bertha, a bodiless, lifeless spouse, an empty temple. This is what he tries to explain to his son Archie, in the grievous paradox of the tale of the cow-thief: "While you have a thing it can be taken from you. . . . But when you give it, you have given it. . . . It is yours then for ever" (*Exiles*, p. 62).

If you do not wish your goods to be stolen, he explains to the boy, you must give them all away. When you have nothing more, you are no longer in danger of losing anything. This is not just a banal cautionary tale; the symbolic cows that may be stolen represent Bertha, and Richard wishes to give Bertha away so that she cannot be taken from him.

This may be aberration or self-denial or the height of selfish pride, for Richard is both Christ and Satan. Thus adultery takes on ambiguous meanings and becomes a *felix culpa*. Joyce's note is pregnant with consequences: "Richard having first understood the nature of innocence when it had been lost by him fears to believe that Bertha, to understand the chastity of her nature, must first lose it in adultery" (Notes to *Exiles*, p. 168).

Just as Adam and Eve could not appreciate paradise until they had lost it, and just as Stephen's soul opens out its petals sin by sin, in the same way Richard is only innocent when he is guilty and Bertha only chaste when an adultress. This partially explains the discretion surrounding the night Bertha spends with Robert; all that counts is the result of the ordeal. Bertha comes out pure and triumphant from the test of sin imposed upon her, in a nakedness of soul comparable to that of Griselda, and it is of little or no importance whether she did or did not commit the sin, since it is useless not to commit sin. For Richard it was necessary that Bertha should be possessed by Robert for her soul to appear to him in all its virgin beauty. Joyce even envisaged a complicity between Robert and Richard, with the Judas-friend accepting the role of traitor, as though thus to establish more firmly the sadism of one and the masochism of the other:

> In the last act (or the second) Robert can also suggest that he knew from the first that Richard was aware of his conduct and that he himself was being watched and that he persisted because he had to and because he wished to see to what length Richard's silent forbearance would go. (Notes to *Exiles*, p. 173)

If Bertha must be initiated into the nature of chastity by the ordeal of impurity, her chastity must be respected; and so the author, after having led the reader to the scene of adultery like a legal witness, cheats —putting out the lights, pulling the curtains, talking of dreams, and going so far as to contradict in his notes what the actor himself says. For Robert seems to imply discreetly that he has known Bertha in a dream more real than reality, while Joyce in his notes (which, it must be remembered, were only published very recently) claims that the audience is wrong in believing adultery to have taken place. Richard both fears and tries to bring about his adultery, as he himself admits:

> In the very core of my ignoble heart I longed to be betrayed by you and by her—in the dark, in the night—secretly, meanly, craftily. By you, my best friend, and by her. I longed for that passionately and ignobly, to be dishonoured for ever in love and in lust, to be . . . to be for ever a shameful

creature and to build up my soul again out of the ruins of its shame. (*Exiles*, p. 97)

All Joyce's algebra of desire is summed up in this ambiguous equation, the equivalent of which might be found in the works of Kleist, de Sade, or Villiers de l'Isle-Adam. If Bertha really is a victim of her simple virtue, like the Marquise von O or Sara in *Axel*, Richard is a more complex character; like Saint Anthony, he has to face every temptation and to pursue grief and pain to their limits, he has to destroy all in order that a new soul may arise from the defiling of the body. Yet there is also a special pleasure to be taken in the destruction of the body, particularly if the body destroyed is that of another human being. In this lies the whole secret of his pleasure. He desires a desire, no doubt, but the desire for which he longs is that of another man, not his own. And this desire of another man's desire is further strengthened if its object is the woman whom they both desire; this process, akin to voyeurism, and as such well known to Joyce, was to become the great crime of H. C. E., the guilty father in *Finnegans Wake*. It is a particularly subtle form of this perversion, with three main sources: first, there can be no doubt that the sensual feelings of Joyce or of Richard were stimulated by the idea and by images of cuckoldry; second, as an author Joyce is interested in the theme of the deceived husband, which he illustrates by the example of Parnell in his last note to *Exiles*; and third, if Richard wishes to experiment with the pleasures of adultery in imitation of Parnell, he does not wish to risk the possibility of such a scandal as the latter's affair with Mrs. O'Shea caused. He would prefer to adopt the words of Axel, who refuses to consummate his love with Sara in these terms: "Living! Our servants may do that for us". Joyce's note on page 174 is to the same effect. He does not wish to be obliged to play the required comedy, to pretend to love, and so he replaces himself by his best friend, who is also his disciple in the same way that the apostle is the double of Christ and his substitute. Thus, he is the *voyeur*. But the woman whom the friend possesses is Richard's own; hence Richard-Robert deceives and betrays himself! He is simultaneously lover and cuckold, suffers as one and enjoys as the other. Both sadist and masochist, he deceives himself with his own wife, whom he is thus enabled both to despise and to desire more ardently.

Richard provokes the crisis at the moment of the play because it is now that he needs this experience. He is coming to the end of one period of his life, that of the progress towards maturity, of exile and of the beginnings of the work. He had begun by a defiant challenge, and he has come now to a second beginning. He has to return to the place where he has slain his own creatures in a ritual murder which is intended to create out of itself a new situation. At the time of his first exile Bertha had not been free, but unconsciously and blindly she had sacrificed everything to follow him. Richard with subtle frankness recreates the situation as it was when he left, with the same characters, but this time he leaves them completely free to make their choices.

But, once again, he cheats, he abolishes the passage of time and acts as though his son did not exist, as though Bertha were still the nineteen-year-old girl she can never be again. Having set up his situation, the artist in his wish to be God arranges a temptation, and sends his creatures forth into the garden of temptations. In truth, he is hardly inventing here, for he has discovered without much displeasure that Robert has always been in love with Bertha. God realises that the world existed before he created it! Robert as Adam and Bertha as Eve act out the ancient mystery, and Richard acts the part of Satan too; he is the serpent who wishes to make man and woman aware of good and evil, and he has to describe and appreciate innocence. This is what he has tried to do before, with Bertha; when they were in Rome he was unfaithful to her several times, and wanted her to participate in his wrongdoing. He recalls, "I remember the first time . . . I wakened her from sleep and told her. I cried beside her bed; and I pierced her heart" (*Exiles*, p. 93).

Bertha's heart is pierced by a doubly symbolic wound; she appears as a figure of the suffering Christ and Richard is seen in his double role as God the Father and Supremely Wicked Being. Later in the play, Bertha represents Jesus on the Mount of Olives—alone, deserted and desperate —and as Joyce explains in his notes, the actress playing Bertha must give in this scene "a suggestion of hypnosis". She is also wounded with that "deep wound" which Richard claims as his right and which he inflicts upon himself in Act III.

"I was feeding the flame of her innocence with my guilt," adds Richard, and when Robert protests at his cruelty, he replies, "She must know, even if it were to kill her". Richard has after all deceived her *in order to tell her* of his infidelity, with the truly sadistic intention of projecting his own suffering into the mind of another.

It is clear that the danger here was great, but Richard's pride would not allow him to withdraw. He has done a godlike thing ("I tried to give her a new life"), but he has been unable to give her freedom, and this is what he makes one last desperate attempt to do when he sends Bertha to Robert. But Richard is God only in his own mind, and since he is not omniscient he will never know what really happened. God had left man free to make his choice with all its paradoxical implications because God could know everything; there was a prohibition, and God knew from all eternity that it would be broken. Richard, as we shall see, knows without truly knowing; in the will that arranged the trap he is the Father, but in the suffering he is the Son and he forgets his knowledge. The sin is necessary in that it prepares the way for the redeemer to come, and so it may be that Bertha's sin is meant to be a *felix culpa* enabling Richard to be Christ.

This may be the explanation of the dreadful night which Richard spends on the beach, suffering from hallucinations, and which Joyce compares to Christ's night alone on the Mount of Olives. Richard confides to Beatrice that he was pursued by "demons": "The isle is full of voices. Yours also. Otherwise I could not see you, it said".[5] Perhaps this is meant as an image of the world, an island full of voices. "I made the sign of the cross upside down". This night, cathartic as that spent in the house of Circe, has simply revealed to Richard his innate duplicity and the real nature of his desire to re-establish continuity between body and soul, a continuity the lack of which had grieved him, deeply marked as he had been by the Catholic religion.

The core of Richard's and Bertha's distress is that there is something between them which they cannot name, and for which each considers the other responsible: Bertha cries out, "I gave up everything for him," and Richard says, "you drove everyone else from my side—every friend I ever had". Gradually the conflict becomes more sharply defined; the source of the malady lies in the fact that Richard is divided against himself, acutely aware of being a body and a soul which are irreconcilable and the negation of each other. Richard, and after him Beatrice and even Robert, favours the soul and scorns the body. In his horror of the body he is led to despise Bertha and Robert and all that is incarnated, and to elevate to sublime heights the frigid Beatrice whom Joyce shows to be incomplete and inadequate.[6] Richard's attitude towards women is ambiguous, for he does not wish to confuse body with soul; thus, he attributes the soul to Beatrice and the body to Bertha, forbidding either of them any claim to being complete by denying Beatrice's body and

[5]From *Giacomo Joyce* we learn that this phrase was once used by Amalia, in a context such that its reappearance here must be understood as one of Joyce's private jokes; the epiphanic phrase takes on different meanings in different contexts.

[6]Beatrice is twenty-seven years old, while Bertha is twenty-eight. Joyce notes, on p. 163 of *Bertha*, "Robert likens her to the moon because of her dress. Her age is the completion of a lunar rhythm." Beatrice is an incomplete woman because she lacks this one year, because she has never experienced a love-hate relationship, because she is neither wife nor mother, and because she is a Protestant.

Bertha's soul, and thus maintaining them in a state of discontinuity dependent upon him. In this way he divides himself into two unrejoinable halves, inflicting upon himself a wound which he has lovingly and masochistically provoked, and which brings him to his desperate weariness at the end. God at last rests from the wrong that he has done.

On the other hand, he seeks to humiliate and mortify himself in a fashion which represents the height of Satanic pride. He strives to defile his fleshly love by prostituting it to another; he confides to Bertha that he has been unfaithful to her—making her thus participate in his degeneracy as witness, accomplice, and sharer in responsibility unless she revolts against him. But he commits one primary mistake, as always, and his creatures escape from him; he discovers that they are double-natured, or complete, that Beatrice lays claim to a body and Bertha to a soul. He also makes another, much more serious, mistake with regard to the nature of the soul.

Richard-Joyce acts as though the soul were a body, or as though carnal awareness were only important when it involved the soul; many details emphasise this point of view, which shows how deeply disturbing it was for Joyce. When Robert, carried away by Richard's masochism, proposes "a battle of both our souls against all that is false in them and in the world. A battle of your soul against the spectre of fidelity, of mine against the spectre of friendship," the artist in Richard reacts against a direct confrontation. This is not the way to risk one's soul, one's individual self.

Joyce writes in his notes (p. 164) "It is the soul of woman left naked and alone that it may come to an understanding," for the soul has a nakedness of its own which is hidden by prejudices, lies, and social conventions in the same way that the body is hidden by its garments. The soul is also symbolised by Shelley, the immaterial lover whom the earth bears; "Shelley whom she (the earth) has held in her womb or grave rises". The man's soul is born from the cavernous body of woman as mother earth, and the woman is both a womb and a tomb to the soul, signifying yet again that the fleshly union which is so necessary is also tragic. This confusion leads Richard deep into error. When Joyce makes him "spiritual," he is allowing Richard in fact to lead a double life, for the history of Bertha and Richard is reproduced on a "spiritual" plane by the union of Richard and Beatrice. Richard wishes to keep these two existences completely separate from each other—and one can perceive here an echo of the attraction and repulsion which Joyce felt for Swift.

This explains his ridiculous lack of comprehension and its traumatic effect when Beatrice says to him, "Otherwise I could not see you". She looks at him for a moment and then turns aside quickly, whereupon he repeats, "uncertainly", "Otherwise you could not see me?" Why should she not *see* him, after all? Because his union with Beatrice, it is implicitly understood, is not to be in any sense of the word *carnal:* Richard and Beatrice have lived like the sculptor and the model in Ibsen's play, *When We Dead Awake*, they have loved each other and they have produced a child, "spiritually," which is the work of art, the statue. The child produced by Richard and Beatrice is the book which has been making for nine years in Richard's mind in the image of Beatrice, while Bertha, the bride of the flesh, has been bringing up the material child, the boy Archie.

And now Richard discovers that Beatrice does not love only his mind, as he wishes her to do; he questions her, "Then it is my mind that attracts you?" but it is evident that Beatrice loves him also with her senses. This is of course unpardonable, and she quickly realises it, and tries to escape. But it too late, and Richard holds her back, because he needs her. Long and painful scenes of unbridled sadism and masochism follow. Only the *voyeur* cannot attain reality, cannot imagine or enjoy real pleasure; he must always use someone as an intermediary, and this someone (whom he necessarily considers as merely an object) is in this case a woman. It is Richard and not Robert Hand, despite the latter's name, who really manipulates the others; he has put Beatrice into his work, he has made use of her, but as Robert says, he has refused her a "natural" existence. He has no wish for her body; he wishes that it did not exist, that it might be absent or even dead. All that they have shared, that couple bound together by sadism and masochism, is "pride and loneliness". Their relationship is composed of evils; each must witness the sufferings of the other. "You have watched me in my struggle," says Richard, without remembering how Bertha had not merely watched, but had also shared; he tells Beatrice of his sufferings, thus: "I expressed . . . in my character and life . . . something in your soul which you could not—pride or scorn?" Beatrice comes into Bertha's house to give piano lessons to her rival's son, and masochism is again in evidence.

Richard, who later accuses himself of having violated Bertha's soul, makes a manifest demonstration of cruelty now. The inquisitions of Act I are a kind of rape of the soul, pitilessly probing into Beatrice's soul, seeking in her the echoes of his own suffering, asking "Have you suffered?" and "Did my going make you suffer?" He bends over her to ask, "And so a coldness began between you, little by little. . . . Does nothing in life give you peace? O, if you knew how I am suffering at this moment! For your case, too. But suffering most of all for my own" (*Exiles*, p. 25).

He experiments on her with the tortures which he is later to inflict upon himself, and Beatrice docilely plays out the drama which he later makes Bertha and himself play. He has violated the virgin Beatrice and now she is different, she is a woman. "I was changed," she says, and adds, "I am given life and health again—when I cannot use them. I am convalescent" (*Exiles*, p. 26). Richard knows in advance the outcome of the drama which he directs, that the loss of peace ("nothing in life gives you peace") and the necessary wounding are inevitable; knowing this, he does not seek to avoid being wounded, but to offer himself to every opportunity of receiving a wound. Joyce tells us in his notes that this is "automysticism". The first page of notes is clear enough, defining Richard's "mysticism":

> His defence of her soul and body is an invisible and imponderable sword . . . The action of the piece should convince Robert of the existence and reality of Richard's mystical defence of his wife.
> Richard's jealousy . . . separated from hatred and having its baffled lust converted into an erotic stimulus and moreover holding in its own power the hindrance, the difficulty which has excited it, it must reveal itself as the very immolation of the pleasure of possession on the altar of love. He is jealous, wills and knows his own dishonour. (Notes to *Exiles*, p. 163)

Richard seeks for a union "in the region of the difficult, the void and the impossible". The invisible sword that constitutes the mystical defence of love is nothing but absolute freedom, the separation of the couple into two individuals possessing each full freedom, and as such must inevitably lead to the wounding of one or both; the magic sword harms even the person whom it defends. In effect, the tragic paradox of love is that it can only be great if it is "total and free," and that the supreme manifestation of love is the granting of freedom to the other person; yet since love cannot exist without a denial of that freedom, it is constantly necessary to bear in mind the possibility of a choice which would set all in jeopardy again. In order that the other person may feel free and may in fact be so, it is necessary for him to able to give himself to someone other than the beloved. Thus freedom is only to be experienced in causing or in feeling pain. By exercising it against onself, it is possible to manifest oneself as an individual and to declare one's difference, to show that one has been changed. "I" must not coincide with "you," and Bertha must not be identical with Richard, even when she most longs for so complete a union; Richard must still maintain his jealousy to the extent of poisoning their relationship thereby if necessary. Thus, when they were in Rome, with no obstacles to separate them, Richard had to create obstacles, to set the bodies of other women between them, to offer his own guilt as a sacrifice to Bertha's purity. In the midst of temptation Bertha must give herself to him, "She must appear also to be carried forward to the last point consistent with her immunity by the current of the action and must show even a point of resentment against the man who will not hold out a hand to save her" (Notes to *Exiles*, p. 164).

It is necessary to go to the very limits of suffering. But men are not gods, and Richard demands too much—deliberately. He reasons as illogically as Eve in *Paradise Lost*, book IX, 335–6, who says,

> And what is faith, love, virtue, unassayed
> Alone, without exterior help sustained?

in tones recalling Milton's *Areopagitica*.

Adam replies that man can control his frailty:

> within himself
> The danger lies, yet lies within his power (1.350),

yet that one must not trust too much to reason, for it can be suborned: "Seek not temptation then . . . trial will come unsought".

According to Joyce, it must be Robert who is the loser and his failure should be a lesson to him, yet this is not completely accurate: Bertha finally returns to Richard after having been possessed (perhaps) by Robert—for one cannot keep the body without holding the soul, and the soul of course belongs to the one who took its virginity, to its first love:

> The soul like the body may have a virginity. For the woman to yield it or for the man to take it is the act of love. Love . . . is in fact so unnatural a phenomenon that it can scarcely repeat itself, the soul being unable to become virgin again and not having energy enough to cast itself out again into the ocean of another's soul. (Notes to *Exiles*, p. 163)

If Richard knows that he has received the virginity of Bertha's soul, then he should not doubt or fear any more. But he seems to be unaware of Joyce's note in his attempt to recommence the game with a soul which is no longer virgin, which is what he claims that he is doing for love of Bertha. He feels that he is running a dangerous risk, and acts as he does out of masochism. The last lines of Act III sum up all the ambiguities of the play, revealing his reasons, "I will never know. Never in this world". "I do not wish to know." "I have a deep wound in my soul."

This fault in the structure of being is the form of exile which serves to define "living". He who has nowhere to live, who doubts even himself, who exercises all his ingenuity in the entanglement of the motives for his own actions, who thereby becomes divided against and estranged from himself, who makes his soul into his place of exile and his life a process of disengagement, who only desires a beloved object in order to feel vividly afraid of losing it, has passed far beyond the high Miltonic virtues, has passed by way of practising doubt and cultivating uncertainty to a region where faith, religion, and fidelity are rejected, and replaced by the mysteries of otherness and of distrust, by what, for him, makes an object precious.

> I have wounded my soul for you—a deep wound of doubt which can never be healed. I can never know, never in this world. I do not wish to know or to believe. I do not care. It is not in the darkness of belief that I desire you. But in restless living wounding doubt. To hold you by no bonds, even of love, to be united with you in body and soul in utter nakedness— for this I longed. And now I am tired for a while, Bertha.

In this speech Richard reveals the destructive fatal contradiction which is fundamental to him. His doubt is the very negation of that ideal love for which he longs; it is a double doubt, the doubt of knowledge ("I can never know") which is a lack of knowledge, and the doubt of belief ("I do not wish to know or to believe") which is a lack of faith. He wishes not to know, not to believe, yet he aspires "to be united in body and soul in utter nakedness" with Bertha, and how could such a nakedness of souls be attained except by knowledge or by an act of faith? The wish not to believe is in itself an assurance that the exile is a perpetual one; Joyce does not wish to believe in friendship or in love because they would threaten him with alienation. The stage-direction makes this clear: "gazing at her and speaking as if to an absent person". Faith is radically re-examined and seriously questioned, belief is refused and denied by one who could possess both knowledge and belief, and a supreme challenge is issued to the divinity that demands blind faith without knowledge. "All believe that Bertha is Robert's mistress. The *belief* rubs against his own *knowledge* of what has been, but he accepts the belief as a bitter food" (Notes to *Exiles*, p. 172). Thus, Richard knows that Bertha has remained faithful to him, but refuses to let himself move from knowing to believing.

To Bertha, Richard's attitude seems nothing more than irresponsible and cruel at the most; she feels that he is openly acting in bad faith, since it is clear that he confessed his infidelities to her in Rome because they were of no real consequence, while he refused to admit the much more serious, intellectual deception he was practising by spending nights away from her shut up in his study: "Did you not know? He passes the greater part of the night in there writing. Night after night . . . study or bedroom . . . He sleeps there, too, on a sofa" (*Exiles*, p. 138).

In fact, Richard's love for Bertha finds its expression in what she takes to be another infidelity, for Richard-Joyce can only really love the "absent person," the woman who is *not* there. Joyce loves and loathes Ireland, and makes it his own most fully when he is in exile; Stephen adores the ghostly, romantic figure of Mercedes; Richard used to write to Beatrice when he was with Bertha, because then Beatrice was the absent one: "You call that friendship? . . . My God, I feel it! I know it! What else is between you but love?" (*Exiles*, pp. 74–5). As Richard apparently comes nearer to Beatrice, as he returns to Dublin, he is moving away from the frigid, hostile woman, from the death she represents, and this apparent spiritual moving *away* which so grieves Bertha is a moving nearer to her—an indication of his real longing for her. Separation is inseparable from real love; it is Joyce's illusory means of protecting himself from being hurt. For this reason, when Bertha physically belongs to him, when it seems that no rival could threaten his possession of her, he has to create for himself (in the absence of a practical rival, a Robert Hand or Prezioso) a situation involving separation, deceiving Bertha in order to deserve her less.

Richard prompts Bertha to rebel, although such a rebellion is precisely what he fears. He arms others against himself in order that he may experience fear; Robert Hand is not another person, he is merely Richard's "hand," the hand which God raises against his creature and against himself. He is moved by impulses which are conveyed to him from and by Richard. He is destined to perish as a victim of this so-called freedom. "Have you the courage to allow me to act freely?" he asks Richard, naïvely proposing that they should engage in a kind of single combat. "Richard," he says, "you have driven me up to this point. She and I have only obeyed your will." A Satanic will, says Robert—you put these words, your own words, into my mind, you were the tempter. But Richard refuses any confrontation; freedom for him excludes other people, being simply a realisation and appreciation of one's own loneliness. "Fight your part alone," he says. "I will not free you. Leave me to fight mine". And again, "Free yourself," he mockingly orders, but what can the hand do without guidance from the mind?

Richard knows that one can only be free at the expense of someone's freedom, that a world completely populated by free beings would be a world of total anarchy, and that by imposing freedom on Bertha,

Beatrice, and Robert he in turn will bring them under constraint and free himself. But they are not deceived; Robert says to Bertha, "He has left us alone here at night, at this hour, because he longs to know it— he longs to be delivered". Also, "All his life he has sought to deliver himself. Every chain but one he has broken and that one we are to break, Bertha—you and I." Thus Robert enters into Richard's game of sado-masochism; similarly, Bertha accuses Richard of having let her off the leash so that he visit "her ladyship" Beatrice. Richard reasons in this way: if my creatures are not free, then I am not God, since I depend on their dependence. Thus, Richard wished to liberate Bertha in order that he might himself be free. *But,* if my creatures are free, then I cannot be free either. Richard discovers that it is impossible for him to be "God," or rather that to be God means to go before the others into exile, to be for them a model and example of divine impotence, of inability to live.

If Richard's behaviour seems equivocal, Robert's is apparently frank and open, and it is hardly surprising that Bertha should feel that she is despised by the one and respected by the other. Instinctively, she rejects the arranged trickery of time present; she wants nothing to do with her "freedom of decision". "Bertha is fatigued and repelled by the restless curious energy of Richard's mind and her fatigue is soothed by Robert's placid politeness" (Notes to *Exiles*, p. 173). Richard the sadist, masochist, and selfish coward, seems a very pitiful God the Father, abandoning those whom he has made; is he perhaps more satisfactory as an embodiment of Christ as love?

Exiles is the scene of a great debate, as master and disciple, throughout the play, try to define love in the parody-forms of a Socratic dialogue. Joyce's position expressed in his notes is, for once, quite clear: "love, the desire of good for another" (p. 163), and reminiscent of what Bloom was later to declare, "Love, I mean, the opposite of hatred". Joyce's definition is a Christian one. Richard and Robert stand for two concepts of the good to be sought in or derived from love, which Joyce labels "Nature" and "Spirit". Do these men really desire Bertha's good, we ask? Are the means they have chosen the right ones? In Act III Richard comes to see Robert (someone else to interrogate and torture) to discuss and compare the quality of their love; he is prepared to withdraw if the disciple can convince him that his is superior. Almost at once the radical opposition between the two becomes clear: they love, the one impulsively, the other hesitantly. Richard says, "I am afraid that that longing to possess a woman is not love" (*Exiles*, p. 88), and Robert replies, "No man ever yet lived on this earth who did not long to possess—I mean to possess in the flesh—the woman whom he loves. It is nature's law."

This is precisely what Richard refuses, for to him the human condition is "anti-natural" and consists of the refusal of one's desires to take and the refusal to let oneself be taken by others. Love is mingled with terror, and the voice that speaks is the voice of Stephen mocking the laws of history and of all arbitrarily decided legitimacy. Stephen, Richard, and Joyce are outlaws by vocation:

> *Richard:* What is that to me? Did I vote it?
> *Robert:* But if you love . . . What else is it?
> *Richard:* To wish her well.

To Robert love is a matter of taking; to Richard it is a matter of self-protection. The law of nature, says Robert, is simple, bestial, intending nothing more than "bodily union," and that by force if necessary. What Robert calls satisfied passion, Richard calls, in the phrase of Duns Scotus, "a death of the spirit". The body is the spirit's tomb. And Robert replies, echoing him, that only the impulse towards youth and beauty is immortal. " ' I give her freedom,' says Richard. . . . 'That is my fear. That I stand between her and any moments of life that should be hers, between her and you, between her and anyone' " (*Exiles*, p. 96). He fears, but he also desires to stand between her and another. Robert replies derisively, "And it makes you happy? And has it made you happy? Always? This gift of freedom which he gave you—nine years ago? . . . Because I had another gift to offer you then—a common simple gift—like myself. . . . The simple common gift that men offer to women. Not the best perhaps" (*Exiles*, p. 119).

While Richard wishes to give Bertha free control over her own soul —to dispose of it as she will—the gift that Robert would offer is the fusion and confusion of passion, his own body. He says, "You were like the moon. . . . In that dress, with your slim body, walking with little even steps. . . . Your face is a flower too," and talks of "the darkness and warmth and flood of passion". "Tonight the earth is loved—loved and possessed. Her lover's arms around her; and she is silent . . ." (*Exiles*, p. 125). Love is compared to falling "from a great high cliff, down, right down into the sea" (p. 46). To him Bertha is the round earth, material and maternal, the fruitful goddess, while to Richard, although still the mother-figure, she is identifiable with the Virgin Mother, the immaterial goddess of utter purity.

In Act I, a scene of exposition and explanation had already sketched out the pattern of this radical antagonism between flesh and spirit; it concerned the smooth stone which Bertha had brought home from the sea-shore, symbol of the body. Richard kisses the stone, just as he would kiss a woman, because it is beautiful and pleasing; "For me it is quite natural to kiss a woman whom I like. . . . She is beautiful for me. . . . Woman is a work of nature like a stone or a flower or a bird. A kiss is an act of homage" (*Exiles*, p. 55).

Robert goes even further; he claims that one loves a woman, not because she is different, but because she belongs to the "feminine kingdom" as to the "animal kingdom," and shares in a particular biological and physiological nature. The woman is the same as the smooth, voiceless stone, the beautiful object that lets itself be taken up and handled. Love, to Robert, is thus associated with an aesthetic judgement; man desires what is naturally beautiful. Hence every beautiful woman is lovable, and the dispersion must be good because it is natural. Robert says that God will tell him, "You were made to give yourself to many freely," and in this way he can envisage loving several people at once; this is why, at the end of Act II, he is able to ask Bertha whether she loves both Richard and himself.

If he has learnt anything, as Joyce in his notes states that he has, it must be the lesson that there is not room for two, that he must withdraw. Richard has difficulty in convincing him that love can only be precarious if it is based on a feeling for beauty, that it must suffer the same fate of degradation or obsolescence as all temporal objects; he opposes to this idea his own high, idealistic concept of giving oneself, freely and totally, to one single person. Yet in reality Richard confines Bertha to herself; love, far from being a participation in the material world, is a way of specially honouring and abstracting one particular individual, of making him free rather than of loading him with chains and obligations. The proof that I love you, he wants to say (and he wants Bertha to admit the truth of this too) is that I am giving you to yourself, that I feel neither desire nor jealousy towards you. When Bertha says, "you came back to see what I was doing, just like any other man," he is revolted by her lack of "understanding," for she is expressing in terms of middle-class comedy or farce what for him is a work of refined and aristocratic sadism; he came out of erotic curiosity, not out of jealousy. He did not even ask Bertha to follow him into exile, as he says, but simply accepted that she should do so on her own initiative.

It seems as though Richard should be the victor in the battle of souls. Bertha does not wish to be a stone, but does she wish to be a soul? Would she find happiness thus?[7] Certainly that she would not. The play may demonstrate that Robert is in the wrong, but Richard gains only a Pyrrhic victory. Richard and Bertha are overcome by a great weariness, and it seems clear that the gap between them has widened. Bertha calls desperately to her "strange wild lover" who for love's sake is torturing them both, but neither Richard nor Bertha is Christ, and their despair does not open out into a greater hope. The curtain falls on Bertha's hopeless gesture as she closes her eyes and stretches out her hands to Richard, who stands there alone. It seems that there can be no peace (as Beatrice had already answered), no possible happiness; yet there can be moments of reconciliation, when the woman's body may perhaps be the place where a union of souls takes place. Perhaps in this context the symbol of the Church might at last become meaningful. It grows clearer now that Bertha, however close she may be to Nora, is still for Richard-Joyce only a figure of Our Lady, essential to the usual blackmail-situation. "Bertha wishes for the spiritual union of Richard and Robert and *believes* (?) that union will be affected only through her body, and perpetuated thereby" (Notes to *Exiles*, p. 172).

But Joyce is sceptical: woman grants the "hospitality of her womb to the seed" of many, becoming both mother and prostitute, and again one finds the Other in the soul and body of the woman one had hoped not to have to share with anyone. Richard and Robert could perhaps be Bertha's brothers?

The theme of homosexual motivation is important to *Exiles*, and should be discussed here. Robert alludes frequently to love for Richard, for his strength or some other quality. What he loves in Bertha is what Richard has made of her; he wishes to be the reflection of Richard which in Beatrice's eyes he is. He wants more than this, wants to be Richard himself with Bertha, and he is often a feminine projection of Bertha to Richard, for he and she have been formed by the same master. At the same time he wants to be a woman for Richard, as two of Joyce's notes explain:—"To be united carnally through the person and body of Bertha . . . man to man as man to woman" (p. 173) and "Towards men he [Robert] is meek and humble"—like Bloom. And we have seen how Richard delegates his power to Robert. By a kind of cathartic projection

---

[7]Jean Jacquot, in *Etudes Anglaises*, 1956, no. IX, "Réflexions sur les *Exilés* de J. Joyce," p. 341, says, "When the curtain falls, the man and the woman are standing near each other, trying to find again the peaceful love they have known, as though nothing had happened"; but, in fact, neither Bertha nor Richard believes love in peace to be possible, and Richard at any rate does not desire it to be so.

Richard finds in Robert all the characteristics which he himself refuses to own, and thus he can pretend to be free of them. Robert and Richard live out their homosexual impulses by inverting their application. This process of identification and projection seems assured by the fact that Richard would like to love in the manly fashion of Robert, and that he identifies with him by attributing to Robert what he feels himself and by desiring to attribute to himself what Robert actually does feel. In one sense, Richard's wish that Bertha should have her freedom is a wish to be desired and possessed; freedom becomes symbolic of virility. But at the same time, he cannot wish this without admitting the feminine side of his nature.

They are mirrors for one another: as Robert seeks Richard in Bertha, so Richard seeks Robert in Beatrice—but he meets only Beatrice's cold gaze, and the mirror clouds over. The time is past when Richard and Robert lived in the same house and could read each other's thoughts and expressions. Richard no longer recognises the "language of youth" that Robert speaks to him. Robert is the only person to undergo any evolution during the course of the play: he is a good disciple and pupil, he learns a lesson; before his night with Bertha he is a disciple ready to betray, but afterwards he attains a new, ambiguous generosity; he returns Bertha to Richard, and becoming a new Richard himself, goes into exile. But already the game of inversion is in progress. We know that one exile calls for another, and at the same time constitutes an admission of defeat.

What are, after all, the connections between these three characters? Bertha's body is the scene of their encounters and of their loss. They have to pass through her in imagination just as Stephen and Bloom have to pass through the image of Molly, coming together by means of and by way of her, through the gaze that they both fix on the photograph of her which Bloom offers to Stephen. In this way there constitutes itself a trinity, which has in place of the Holy Ghost the woman's body. Richard's state of mind at the last moment is extremely complex: he has at last entrusted himself to Bertha's arms, as a child yields to its mother, as Joyce in his letters from Dublin after the storm seeks refuge in Nora's bosom and comforts himself with metaphors of the embryonic state which are later applied to Bloom.[8]

For a fleeting moment he abandons his body to pleasure without

---

[8]For instance, "O take me into your soul of souls and then I will become indeed the poet of my race. I feel this, Nora, as I write it. My body soon will penetrate into yours. O that my soul could too!" (Letter of 5 Sept. 1909.)

risking any real self-loss. God rested satisfied when he had finished his creation, and Richard is a creator, but he is also a destroyer and, as Satan, undoes God's handiwork; what he feels when he has finished is not satisfaction but disgust and weariness. But his renunciation is not complete: "I will remain. It is too soon yet to despair" (*Exiles*, p. 161). Like an alchemist, he has made his love undergo a series of mutations, with the purpose of determining the place and the limits of his exile. He cannot manage to coincide with others nor with himself; the abyss in his being is impassible, and he is satisfied. Joyce wishes us to hear the lament of Jesus left alone (I am hurt, lonely, listened to by no-one) and its echo, the cry of Satan (I am alone, naked, and beautiful in my suffering).

Richard and Bertha separate at the end of *Exiles*, although they are still within their blind and narrow together-ness, each seeking the other with no hope of ever coming near to him. They remain faithful to Stephen's heresy, knowing the ultimate inanity of trying to "approach" another.

Bertha could give Richard no further proof of her love except by accepting to follow him into exile once more. This time, he has condemned her to an exile of the soul, an exile of incomprehension and of the divided self; "Forget me, Dick, forget me and love me again as you did the first time," she implores, but love can only be felt towards the being who is one's equal, one's mirror and echo. Everyone loves the other person's mystery more than his reality. Everyone is alone, knowing the other to be inaccessible, side by side with him and sharing nothing but this knowledge.

The Lesson of Exile

After this cathartic play, the wounding of the spirit became a major literary theme in Joyce's work; to begin with, it had been an inevitable one because of its closeness to his life and its intimate connotations. Just as the accusation of heresy had been turned into the will to *be* heretical, so now exile by doubt was transformed and reinstated as a proud and voluntary choice. Joyce introduced here the theme of the executioner-God, the supreme and final form of self-duplication, the theme which was to make it possible for him to compose *Ulysses* as a parody. Since inspiration springs from the uneasiness caused by feeling that one has been, objectively, sent into exile, it becomes necessary to create artificially an exile-situation as essential for the production of the work of art. The Satanic artist chooses his friend in his own image, his other self, as it were, sends him to take the artist's place in real life, and catches him in his own trap. Then the next step is to dispose of the friend by whose agency one works against oneself, and to divide oneself into two antagonistic selves, artist and man, like God, who creates a world into which his son comes, to take upon him human form and to suffer.

It is obvious that the theme of the redemption is here being sacrilegiously used, for while Christ comes down to earth to die in order to save fallen mankind, man in Joyce's scheme experiences the world in order that the artist-God may recreate an universe in imitation of what he sees; Christ precedes Creation in the black theology of this aesthetic. God, divided into father and son, is also divided into sadist (or "executioner," as Stephen would say) and masochist; he is both creator and destroyer, manifested in carnage throughout history. God watches man live, and Joyce watches himself live, watches himself, according to Daedalus' definition, progressing sin by sin further into knowledge of himself. The sin is not a *felix culpa* because of any promise of redemption it offers; on the contrary, a true redemption would bring the work in progress to an end. Art is produced by the complicity of man the human being as voluntary victim offered to the artist. Robert and Richard are "doubles," which explains their resemblance to Joyce, a resemblance which would be most disturbing without the excuse that the author Joyce is two-natured; Robert has the creative sensual nature of Jim, and its ridiculous aspect too, while Richard has the power and the superstitious nature of Joyce. He says, "It is not in the darkness of belief that I desire you. But in restless living wounding doubt"; he speaks to Bertha "as if to an absent person," he declaring, "To hold you by no bonds, even of love, to be united with you body and soul in utter nakedness—for this I longed".

Exiles is not only the dramatic summary of a personal experience; it is the book of all the fundamental ambiguities that furnish Joyce's themes, the book of the Double, of Doubt, of the Divided Self. The theatrical space formed by this play, despite its outmoded appearance and its dependence on Ibsen, is in fact a kind of mystery play, an allegory of Joyce's ethic and aesthetic systems and of their foundation on the voluntary splitting of the self. The relationships between the characters symbolise the contradictory aspects of Joyce's own relations with the world, creation, and himself.

Robert and Richard are the projections of two opposing sides of

Joyce's soul. When he reaches the metaphysical maturity of his relationship with his art, in *Ulysses*, he no longer needs to create two characters
for the expression of his double self. Yet the existence of two distinct
persons does illustrate in a fashion readily comprehensible to the public
the two kinds of love and faith that are inevitably and constantly at war
within him. To connect this duplicity with reality, one might almost say
that Joyce's letters to Nora show how well he was able to assume two
different personalities, taking pleasure in the one—the "swine"—speaking, and then letting the other—the "poet"—condemn him. Robert's
speeches, and the whole emblematic substructure of sensual love, are
entirely Joyce's own; the metaphors, the exultation in confusing elemental nature and woman, are the same: "The rain falling. Summer
rain on the earth. Night rain. The darkness and warmth and flood of
passion. Tonight the earth is loved—loved and possessed. Her lover's
arms around her; and she is silent" (*Exiles*, p. 125).

These are the words that Joyce or Stephen would use. The dialogue
on beauty and love in Act I is in fact the classic dispute of the good and
the beautiful, the application of Thomism to the purposes of a tormented sensualist:

> *Richard:* Do you kiss everything that is beautiful for you?
> *Robert:* Everything—if it can be kissed. (He takes a flat stone which lies
> on the table.) This stone, for instance. It is so cool, so polished, so delicate,
> like a woman's temple. It is silent, it suffers our passion; and it is beautiful.
> (He places it against his lips.) And so I kiss it because it is beautiful. And
> what is a woman? A work of nature, too, like a stone or a flower or a bird.
> A kiss is an act of homage. (*Exiles*, p. 54)

And the sophist concludes that the beautiful is the good. Richard, of
whom it is rightly said that "The Church lost a theologian in you,"
replies, "It (a kiss) is an act of union between man and woman. Even
if we are often led to desire through the sense of beauty, can you say
that the beautiful is what we desire?"

The "theological" argument is just as specious as Robert's, and more
so because Richard is playing with a concept which he has emptied of
all meaning; what he has desired is not the beautiful but the sharing of
pain, not physical union but an impossible union. The ways of his desire
are tortuous: he cannot desire a natural object but only an object which
has been created by him. Bertha is that object, his work. And at the
same time he can only love an object that is free. Robert is not wrong
to point out that Richard has been seeking all his life through to free

himself from all moral obedience, and that Bertha and Robert have been made into the ultimate instruments of his liberation. The methods he uses are in direct opposition to the desired end, and yet they are the only ones available; setting Bertha free in fact constitutes the imposition of intolerable constraint, Richard is well aware of this, and is actually trying to bind himself. The action tends not towards the providing of answers, but to the immortalisation of the questions and to the re-creation of constraint and prohibition. What Richard finally achieves is a morality of loneliness and doubt which is the same as the condition of the first man, after his disobedience and before any redemption.

XX. The Artist and his Double

What happens to the artist after Stephen has left and Richard Rowan has returned? We meet him again in *Ulysses*—mortified but still as proud as ever—full of his experiences of travel, of his difficult time in Paris, where he read Aristotle in the Bibliothèque Sainte-Geneviève, and of the recent death of his mother. He is no longer living in his father's house, but is sharing a Martello tower with two companions whom he detests, his false friend Buck Mulligan and the Oxford under-graduate Haynes, lover of Irish paradox and amateur student of the Gaelic and its literary renaissance. This is Stephen's material situation as the 16 June 1904 dawns. In the first episode of *Ulysses*, 'Telemachus,' he gives up the key of the tower to Mulligan and begins his new book with a new departure; he never returns to this parody castle of Elsinore.

Repetition of significant action is a procedure frequently employed by Joyce, to whom everything takes on its meaning as it recurs and begins again in different contexts. The movement of the work consists of these repetitions, and the treatment of time is not merely a gratuitous game; it brings us to an awareness of the situation, and we recognise it as a repetition. Thus, Stephen's first act renews his exile and sets the form that this theme is to take in the book. Exile as a condition of art is elaborated by Stephen in connection with the theme of the ghost, and publicly expounded in the guise of a biography of Shakespeare, which in its different aspects takes up the 'Scylla and Charybdis' episode. Joyce here brings to a close his history of the artist's development, the living part of his aesthetic in its relation to the abstract ideology founded on Aristotle and Saint Thomas. The theory Stephen expounded in *Portrait* concerned itself with the work of art and the concept of the beautiful and culminated in the epiphany, while the theory expounded in *Ulysses* has as its objective the definition of the creative artist and the establishment of his power between his life and his creation.

To sum up this history of the artist, it can be said that in a sense this inner evolution is the movement that animates the whole of Joyce's work, although it may not appear to have a dynamic motion, since his problems are bound up not with some existential philosophy but with the nurturing to maturity of linguistic technique. It is possible to distinguish two rhythms of formation which are present throughout the work at all its levels. There is first a movement of acquiring knowledge of oneself and of the world, a kind of reciprocal setting in place of Joyce and his work, which lasts until *Exiles*. The moment of personal maturity when he is able to grasp his true self through all its ambiguities marks the end of the time of transformations, and from that moment onwards everything in the work and in his life begins again; all elements come back into play, not this time in a process of simultaneous cognition and creation, but with the added distance irony confers. By taking himself as his living experimental material, Joyce was able to eliminate the remaining traces of naiveté which had made the *Portrait* occasionally romantic in spite of the author.

In *Ulysses* Stephen's irony is constantly present; his existence in the world and the role he plays are accompanied by an inner commentary which reveals the nature of his duplicity as both strategic and defensive, and this intentional self-duplication finds its most complex expression when Stephen is offering his theories on Shakespeare to a hostile audience: he renews the tactics he had begun to use in Chapter V of *Portrait*, in order to pursue the game to the bitter end and in order to put into practice the notion of the necessary wounding which has already been given dramatic expression in *Exiles*, despite the risk he runs of being really hurt.

The Dissimulating Style

Since Joyce intended that every adventure—every hour, every organ, and every art that was intimately connected with the structural pattern of the whole—should "create its own technique," the 'Scylla and Charybdis' episode expresses its content by its form, and the matter of the experience is communicated in a language which is itself the illustration and the explicit judgement of that experience. Joyce's message, which centres on the necessity to the Artist of duplicity, is such that the form of the chapter is a mass of contradictions, of revelations followed by withdrawals; it comports presence and absence and a refined technical structure which is constantly being challenged and questioned. 'Scylla and Charybdis' seems to mislead the reader and to demand that he seek out the order hidden in its chaos.

According to the list of correspondences which Joyce made,[1] the scene takes place in the National Library of Ireland at two P.M. The organ is the brain, the art literature, the symbol Stratford and London, and the technique is that of dialectic. In other words, the scene of the action is twofold, being both the public space of the outside world and the private space that is the world of Stephen's thoughts. The symbol of Stratford and London indicates Shakespeare's own exile and is analogous to Stephen's journey from Dublin to Paris. Dialectic and literature are connected, and the points Joyce demonstrates are as follows:

Basically, Joyce demonstrates by means of Stephen what has become of the artist: he is now a god who makes use of God, or a demiurge, a creator, and this is possible because of his division into two, a process which is carried out in imitation of God the Father and God the Son. The Artist divides himself into a being, Christ, who lives through and who suffers from the assaults and the wounding pains of life, and a being, God the Father, who writes, making use of the experience and sufferings of the other.

God sends his Son out to suffer, not in order to save mankind, but in order that he may watch his own incarnated spirit undergoing the experience of life. God or the Artist writes his book from the outside, creating a world which is in fact the book. The Son or the Man aspect of the Artist is hidden within the work that tells his story and which reveals him through his person.

Stephen takes Shakespeare as his example, and Joyce makes it a game to demonstrate from real life the thesis that Stephen expounds by way of several disguises: Joyce is hidden by Stephen who is hidden by Shakespeare who is hidden by Hamlet.

Stephen chooses Shakespeare because it suits his purpose to do so. He

[1] He gave the plan of these to Stuart Gilbert, who published it in his book *James Joyce's Ulysses* (New York, 1930).

is asked whether he believes in his paradoxes, and he replies that he does not.[2] He takes pleasure in disturbing his audience, as Joyce does, and he is in fact Joyce's instrument, with the intention of founding an abstract aesthetic upon a living system of poetics.

Stephen contends that Shakespeare's work is not autobiographical and that Shakespeare is not Hamlet. There was one unique moment, however, in which the distance between the author and his creation was abolished, and this could be called "the *Hamlet* moment," just as for Joyce there must have occurred "the *Exiles* moment". *Hamlet* is a play of confession, and perhaps as much a self-inflicted punishment as *Exiles* is. *Hamlet*, as a continued creation, is a play in which Shakespeare puts his own soul on stage in an attempt to understand it. Hamlet is less a character than a series of comportments whose ambiguities reflect those of Shakespeare's soul, which he could not admit to himself. "Hamlet walks about reading the book of himself," it is said, and the quotation is from Mallarmé; and Shakespeare through him writes the book of himself. The play is "biopoetic"—it creates the author who creates it and who watches himself playing in it, suffering and playing at suffering. To write *Hamlet*, and in creating it to make oneself, is a way of being one's own progenitor, and here is sketched out one of the aspects of the theme of fatherhood, to which we shall return later on. Why does Stephen choose Hamlet, rather than, for instance, Othello, who serves as a mask for him in the house of Circe, or Lear, a ghost by absence who is also mentioned in the chapter? He does so because only in *Hamlet* can the mystery of the consubstantiality of father and son be revealed, and because the story of the creation of *Hamlet* contains several facts of which he can make use.

He proceeds to the following demonstration: that Shakespeare is an unhappy man, an exile by his own will and by his own fault. He has committed such wrong that he has had to leave Stratford. But in fact, as Stephen declared at the end of *Portrait*, he did not "fear to be alone or to be spurned for another or to leave whatever I have to leave," nor "to make a mistake, even a great mistake, a lifelong mistake, and perhaps as long as eternity too" (*Portrait*, p. 247). Art is born from experience, and experience is experience of misfortune. For Shakespeare, Stephen declares, "a man of genius makes no mistakes. His errors are

[2]"—You are a delusion, said roundly John Eglinton to Stephen. You have brought us all this way to show us a French triangle. Do you believe your own theory?
—No, Stephen said promptly." (*Ulysses*, p. 209.) And: "I believe, O Lord, help my unbelief. That is, help me to believe or help me to unbelieve? Who helps to believe? *Egomen*. Who to unbelieve? Other chap." (*Ulysses*, p. 210.)

volitional and are the portals of discovery" (*Ulysses,* p. 187). Thus it follows that the perfect Artist is he who has gone to the logical conclusion of his mistake, to the very ends of suffering and of himself. "The risk" is not a matter of life and death because the artist has a double nature; while he is passing through the portals of discovery, there remains within him someone who observes and takes notes. Furthermore, however grievous the wound from which the living man suffers, his recompense is his art; Shakespeare's work, says Stephen, was his rampart, behind which he hid, wounded but secretive, and his books were his defence.

Shakespeare's life is described like a progress, punctuated by psychological discoveries, between Stratford and London, *and the return journey* back. In the course of this double journey Shakespeare has time to encounter all experiences, and to repeat them in such a way that the repetition brings out the essential characteristics of one existence. 'Scylla and Charybdis' is not a textbook of psychology or sociology, but a chapter of life in search of its own meanings.

Joyce Behind Shakespeare

Joyce wrote the 'Scylla and Charybdis' episode between October 1918 and February 1919 approximately, with great rapidity, it would seem —for one must remember that this ninth "canto" is, apart from 'Circe,' the most complicated and the richest in themes and motifs of the eighteen episodes that comprise the book. Its place in the overall structure is of capital importance, for its long discussion takes place at what Joyce imagined as the juncture of two parts, under difficult conditions designed to stimulate Stephen's mental activity.[3] Stephen is encountering his literary enemies on their own ground, George Russell, the writer who signs A. E. (adopting the first letters of the word "aeon"), and the three librarians, Lyster, "a Quaker," Best, the youth, and Magee, who writes under the pseudonym of John Eglinton. Mulligan appears at the end, and Bloom furtively sneaks past at the end of the dialogue; Stephen sees only his timid back. A. E., the convinced partisan of Plato and theosophy, is politely indifferent to Stephen, while the three librarians

[3]The Ms. sent to John Quinn is labelled, "End of the first part of *Ulysses.* New Year 1918."

are sceptical or frankly aggressive. Stephen allies himself with Aquinas and in particular Aristotle, and by a skilful use of syllogisms, with dogmatic assurance (and occasional weakness), he builds up an ideal biography of Shakespeare and makes of it the key to elucidation of all his works, including in it every known detail. With the Thomist passion for order and completeness, he contrives to present a coherent whole, based on a multitude of quotations from Shakespeare's plays and poems.

It may well be asked why Joyce chose Shakespeare as the type of the artist, when he always used to affirm that Ibsen was the greatest dramatist ever, and why it is Hamlet who acts as his mask. Yet Joyce was fascinated by Shakespeare, despite his own denials; he had read all the recent studies and biographies of him in Trieste;[4] and it is likely that when far from Dublin he could more easily forgive the English for having produced such a genius. In 1913 he gave several lectures on Hamlet at the Università del Popolo. And finally, Hamlet is to him an archetypal figure, as Ulysses had always been.

While Ulysses, like Bloom, is what Joyce calls "an all-round man," Hamlet, like Christ, is incomplete; he explained to Budgen[5] that Christ is only a son, being neither father nor husband, and similarly Hamlet is only a son, a fatherless son, isolated on the very brink of non-existence.

On the other hand, *Hamlet* is a story of ghosts, treason, and fatherhood, three axial motifs essential to *Ulysses* and to Joyce's thought in general. The Shakespearean idea must have come to the forefront while Joyce was preparing his chapter, since at the end he identifies himself with Shakespeare at the moment of writing. At the age of eighteen he proclaimed himself the successor of Ibsen, and at thirty-seven he saw himself as Shakespeare or Dante—or rather both of them at once, with Dante providing him with the passionate and ecstatic images which Shakespeare lacks. As Ellmann points out (p. 467), in real life Joyce was caught between two dangers analogous to those of Scylla and Charybdis, on a comical level: he was in the middle of conducting a lawsuit against Carr, the clerk in the English Consulate at Zurich, and he was pursuing Marthe Fleischmann, writing passionately to her in French (with some inaccuracy on the subject of his age), "As for me, I am old —and feel even older than I am. Perhaps I have lived too long. I am 35. It is the age at which Shakespeare conceived his dolorous passion for the Dark Lady".[6] In this climate of comedy he wrote the serious chapter

---

[4]He had read, among others, Georg Brandes, Sidney Lee, Wilde, and Vining.
[5]See Ellmann, *James Joyce*, p. 449.
[6]*Letters*, vol. II, p. 432, translated by Christopher Middleton. December, 1968.

in which Stephen undertakes to "prove by algebra that Hamlet's grand-son is Shakespeare's grandfather and that he himself is the ghost of his own father". If Stephen succeeds in proving such a proposition by algebra, it is because everything is possible; the grotesque formula, made up by Mulligan as a joke, has still some meaning, for Stephen does found his ethical notions of the artist as ghost upon an Aristotelian argument from the "algebra" of possibles, that is, from the passage from potentiality to act, which thereby excludes all possibilities but one. The artist has free access to the world of all the possibles.

The Ghosts

Hamlet is a ghost story, and the expression recalls, apart from the spectre, the Holy Ghost; Stephen explains that there are three types of ghost, the ghost-by-disappearance (or death), the ghost-by-absence, and the ghost-by-exile. The Holy Ghost is a ghost-by-absence. Shakespeare when exiled from Stratford is a ghost-by-absence. In his play he takes the unexpected role of the king who returns from the grave, rather than that of Hamlet the prince, who, according to Stephen, is an imaginary projection of Hamnet, Shakespeare's son, who is a ghost by reason of his death. Stephen in his inner monologue oscillates between the king and the prince. An exile at the Court (represented by Dublin and the Library), he unsheathes his "dagger-definitions" as Hamlet unsheathes his words. But he is also Claudius, when "in the porches of their ears he pours" the poison of his brain.

Invisible, behind the ghost played by the actor, hides his ghostly double Stephen dressed as a romantic, Bohemian Hamlet, in the cas-toff mail of the court buck Mulligan. "—What is a ghost? Stephen said with tingling energy. One who has faded into impalpability through death, through absence, through change of manners" (*Ulysses*, p. 184).

Thus Stephen asks the first false question in his story. He must "catch" his audience, they must understand without seeing the speaker. Stephen goes about the seduction of their judgements like a good arranger, setting the scene with a wealth of circumstantial detail for "local col-our". "Ignatius Loyola, make haste to help me!" he thinks, asking the aid of the Jesuit in effacing himself for the time he needs to present all his revelations about the Swan of Avon. "It is this hour of a day in mid

June," he says, but it is not Dublin in 1904, we are in London of 1593, and "the flag is up on the playhouse by the bankside".

"The play begins," says Stephen, and in reality there are two plays and two theatres. There, William is playing out his life between Ann and his work, and here, Stephen is acting out his own disappearance, preparing his escape out of exile towards himself. Shakespeare and Stephen pass together through "the portals of discovery," but the audience sees only the image of the dead genius, and not the presence of the living.

In his role of author and actor of his own life, Stephen is Shakespeare, and as the latter is "made up in the castoff mail of a court buck," so the former at the beginning of the book is suffering because he wears the shoes given to him by "Buck" Mulligan. The play of doubles is given fuller meaning by this theme of humiliating alienation caused by deprivation and material dependence; the concrete sign of the dispossessed is this wearing of another's garment. When Stephen begins his story with the words "The play begins," he knows that it has already begun, that it began long ago when he was born, and that it began again that morning when Mulligan parodied the Mass in the open air on the gunrest of the Martello tower, brandishing his razor like a dangerous incense-boat. As victim and author of his own misfortune, Stephen is Shakespeare, and as Irishman, he is not; there is an essential difference between them here, emphasised by Joyce's subtle humour. Stephen the Irishman, a true son of his father Simon in this, has no conscience about debts. There are debtors of his in his audience, but this does not trouble him at all. Shakespeare, like all the English, has strong ideas on money, on material and spiritual economy, and does not like to spend or lose or owe anything. Furthermore, he is the son of a butcher who longs to be a gentleman.

Snobbish and bloodthirsty, he has about him that divine quality that terrifies Stephen, the godlike attribute of slaughterer. In Joyce's world, God is a bloodthirsty Jehovah who loves and favours the "slaughterhouses" of history. This is one of the reasons why Joyce chooses the moment when he needs Shakespeare as a mask to give him the role of the slain king rather than that of the son, who at the end acts like a butcher; the Artist is he who suffers, not he who inflicts, violence.

—A deathsman of the soul Robert Greene called him, Stephen said. Not for nothing was he a butcher's son wielding the sledded poleaxe and spitting in his palm. Nine lives are taken off for his father's one. Our Father who art in purgatory. Khaki Hamlets don't hesitate to shoot. The blood-boltered shambles in act five is a forecast of the concentration camp sung by Mr. Swinburne. (*Ulysses*, p. 184)

Stephen is neither a butcher's son nor a husband, but he has studied his own part as Shakespeare

> has studied *Hamlet* all the years of his life which were not vanity in order to play the part of the spectre. He speaks the words to Burbage, the young player who stands before him beyond the rack of cerecloth, calling him by a name:
>   Hamlet, I am thy father's spirit bidding him list. To a son he speaks, the son of his soul, the prince, young Hamlet and to the son of his body, Hamnet Shakespeare, who has died in Stratford that his namesake may live for ever. (*Ulysses*, p. 185)

Throughout his life Shakespeare has been waiting for the moment when, using no other weapon but craft, he could speak out and tell what had brought him to this disappearance and self-loss that are represented by his choice to play the part of the ghost. At once two inseparable themes enter the circle of operative revelation, that of awareness of self as an "I am," and that of fatherhood. Shakespeare in his role as Hamlet takes pleasure in rendering meaningless the prince's question on the choice between presence and absence; the problem is not that of choosing between being and not-being, for Shakespeare, like any other author, belongs to two essentially different worlds in which he is and yet is not present, the worlds of reality and imagination. But his message to the son is more tragic and immediate: if he wanders between two worlds, it is because he has been condemned by life to be something other than he seems. In his role as ghost, Shakespeare is a king who is no king, a father who is no father, a man who is no man. From beneath the ghost's helm come the words which Shakespeare could no longer speak to "the son of his body, Hamnet Shakespeare, who has died in Stratford that his namesake may live for ever". In other words, Stephen touches in passing on the idea that the loss by death of a son, a real grief, is a contribution to the flowering of the artist's genius.

The actor Shakespeare—a ghost-by-absence, speaking in the guise of the Dane who is a ghost-by-death to Hamlet who is only the son of his soul—says in effect, "You are the dispossessed son: I am the murdered father: your mother is the guilty queen, Ann Shakespeare, born Hathaway."

The audience protests against "this prying into the family life of a great man," as Stephen is in the process of demonstrating that it is the great man who makes his private life an open door upon his work. Ann is part of Shakespeare's creation. But, since there can be no negative mistakes for a man of genius, and just as Socrates derives dialectic from the shrew Xanthippe and intellectual midwifery from his mother, so Shakespeare owes to Ann, whose sixty-seven years of life enclose his own shorter life, a memory that was destined to become the origin of his imaginative power: "she saw him into and out of the world. She took his first embraces. She bore his children and she laid pennies on his eyes to keep his eyelids closed when he lay on his deathbed." Stephen explains, as he realistically sketches out his hero's life, that this memory made *Venus and Adonis.* Shakespeare had "a good groatsworth of wit and no truant memory," and the story of his affair with Ann can only be understood in one way, which is secretly related to us by *Venus and Adonis.* He who sang the beauty of Cleopatra and made Katherine the shrew a lovely girl would scarcely have been so blind as to choose "the ugliest doxy in all Warwickshire to lie withal". "Good: he left her and gained the world of men." But if he did leave her for the world in which feminine parts were played by young boys and where man gave words and thought and life to woman, it was because Ann had for him played the part of Venus. It all began in a cornfield with a grotesque action, with "a boldfaced Stratford wench who tumbles a lover younger than herself ".

In the game of Venus and Adonis the reluctant lover is doubly the victim. Violated by the insatiable sensuality of "the grey-eyed goddess," he only escapes from her embraces, in Shakespeare's poem, to die while hunting the boar, pierced in the groin by its tusk, "where love lies bleeding". The legend is symbolic; Venus has deprived him of his manly right to initiative and independent action, and by his submission he loses the virile strength necessary to the hunter and dies castrated. The reality of this death renews the castration mimed by the act of love. This wound, described by Shakespeare as castration, excludes the hunter from normal society and turns him into a creature of prey; yet again the image of Parnell comes to haunt Stephen's memory in the figure of an animal surrounded by the yelling pack.[7] Stephen's imagination links up with historical and personal memory and with his sensibility, hurt by

[7] The ambiguity of this metaphor of the hunt takes its full and ridiculous force in the article Joyce wrote in 1912, describing Parnell in terms which leave no doubt of the double meaning: "He went from county to county, from city to city, 'like a hunted deer,' a spectral figure with the signs of death on his forehead." (*Critical Writings,* p. 227.)

the howling mob and indifferent to those around him, to such an extent
that he sees himself as a child repudiated by the father of the Irish poets,
Russell, disguised as the god of the sea, Manannann mac Lir. "Cordelia.
Cordoglio. Lir's loneliest daughter."

He is interrupted: mac Lir is planning to bring out a collection of
young poets' verses, the white hopes of the Irish Renaissance, and
Stephen is not invited to contribute. At once the multiple image of
Shakespeare-Parnell-Stephen crystallises into the figures of the messiah
and the fox; the latter is suggested by the pseudonym adopted by
Parnell at the time of his secret activities, Mr. Fox, and the former is
the archetypal victim-figure in which all victims are combined:

> Christfox in leather trews, hiding, a runaway in blighted treeforks from
> hue and cry. Knowing no vixen, walking lonely in the chase. Women he
> won to him, tender people, a whore of Babylon, ladies of justices, bully
> tapsters' wives. Fox and geese. And in New Place a slack dishonoured body
> that once was comely, once as sweet, as fresh as cinnamon, now her leaves
> falling, all, bare, frighted of the narrow grave and unforgiven. (*Ulysses*,
> p. 190)

The Inevitable Self

Why did Shakespeare accept the role of victim, of the hunted man?
Could he not have avoided the torture? Again Stephen delves into the
imaginary library of his mind, where he can leaf through Aristotle
under the guardian aegis of Thoth, the writer god who looks after dead
thoughts and fossilized words. The room reserved for possibilities that
were never actualised is like the painted chambers whose walls are
made of brown, aromatic books piled high. He might have done . . . it
might have been . . . "he ponders . . . what Caesar would have lived to
do had he believed the soothsayer: what might have been: possibilities
of the possible as possible: things now known". *(Ibid.)*

Only what was possible is known, says Stephen, and then extending
the syllogism: for the man of genius the possible is also the sign of
destiny. Shakespeare "might have done" other things in a past unreal
time, but in the reality of his life as an artist aware of his nature,
everything that did happen had to happen—was good, right, and desirable—because it went to make up his own unique form. Stephen here
introduces a new essential theme, which is to be joined ultimately to the

various other principles of his theory, guaranteeing its permanence and universality: it is the law of the ineluctable self, in its earliest form as the law of the identity of man throughout the various changes caused by time, and for the artist it constitutes an identification and even a creation of the self for the self:

> As we, or mother Dana, weave and unweave our bodies, Stephen said, from day to day, their molecules shuttled to and fro, so does the artist weave and unweave his image. And as the mole on my right breast is where it was when I was born, though all my body has been woven of new stuff time after time, so through the ghost of the unquiet father the image of the unliving son looks forth. In the intense instant of imagination, when the mind, Shelley says, is a fading coal, that which I was is that which I am and that which in possibility I may come to be. So in the future, the sister of the past, I may see myself as I sit here now but by reflection from that which then I shall be. (*Ulysses*, p. 191)

From this lyrical discourse in which Stephen's favourite images recur (and in which he does not hesitate to repeat what he was saying to Lynch some months earlier) two propositions emerge: first of all, if the biological metaphor is correct and all the substance of the person is renewed, the original mark still remains that is the wrong or mistake the individual made, that by which he is recognisable. This mark is for Shakespeare the feelings aroused by the loss of his son; the dispossession which makes him into a father who is no father is the symbol of all losses and deprivations. Next, this cruel "presence in absence" determines the motion of the creative impulse, in its compensatory aspect. In the "instant of imagination" all differences between past, present, and future are annihilated, and there is but one constant landmark; the future is sister of the past, just as the present contains the future, and this circular time initiates the nightmare of history as cyclic, in which one only awakes in order to experience the same nightmare in the waking state. It is also at the origins of the creative act, causing pain yet fundamentally good, and the proof of this is contained in *Ulysses*, the book in which the future is indeed sister of the past.

The episode of 'Scylla and Charybdis' was already contained in 'Proteus,' and is repeated and reflected in 'Circe'. This is why the errors are volitional, why Shakespeare wanted a son in order to be truly a father, but also in order that he might lose that son, so that he might cease being father to the son of his body and become the father of a ghost. In fact, continues Stephen, as soon as Shakespeare is assured of the

consequences of "the swelling act"—as soon as Ann has borne him a son
—he leaves her: he no longer wants a wife. He had wanted a son, but
a son who should be an exile-by-absence, and life and death unite to
make this wish come tragically true with the real death of Hamnet.

Shakespeare leaves Stratford and goes into his first exile; now this
pattern is to repeat itself throughout his life, defined by Stephen as a
succession of betrayals undergone, accepted, and made use of:

> The note of banishment, banishment from the heart, banishment from
> home, sounds uninterruptedly from *The Two Gentlemen of Verona* on-
> ward till Prospero breaks his staff, buries it certain fathoms in the earth and
> drowns his book. It doubles itself in the middle of his life, reflects itself in
> another, repeats itself, protasis, epitasis, catastasis, catastrophe. (*Ulysses*,
> p. 208)

From the first act in the cornfield (or ryefield), the wound goes on
bleeding, inflicted by Venus, and he fosters it with care. He has the
escape-routes of homosexuality or of an affected Don Juan act and tries
out both, but without wishing to obtain his desire. He desires to desire;
possession can never give him back his self-confidence, and "he will
never be a victor in his own eyes after". Nor does he wish to be victorious; he sends young Pembroke to act as his replacement and to woo his
easily won lady for him. In his heart of hearts, like Richard Rowan, he
waits for the friend to carry off the dark lady, to rob him. He wants and
yet does not want her. His flesh is moved, but his soul has been poisoned
by the image of "the beast with two backs".

The woman's image is dark and troubled, driving him to a type of
homosexuality which is really a very complex voyeurism, for "There is,
I feel in the words, some goad of the flesh driving him into a new
passion, a darker shadow of the first, darkening even his own understanding of himself. A like fate awaits him and the two rages commingle
in a whirlpool" (*Ulysses*, p. 193). The flesh is forbidden, but only because
he forbids it to himself; the fox *could* catch the geese. But he no longer
wants this "tender people". "Ravisher and ravished, what he would but
would not, go with him from Lucrece's bluecircled ivory globes to
Imogen's breast, bare, with its mole cinquespotted." *(Ibid.)*

The commentary abruptly turns to deal with the incestuous desire of
the man as child for the woman as mother, and the obsession with the
mother's breast which exists in Shakespeare's work recalls obliquely by
way of Stephen the presence of Joyce, who used to long to be Nora's
child, casting her in the role of the Virgin, or her naughty little boy,
when envisageing her as awarder of punishment. Stephen feels that

Shakespeare dreams of being Adonis to Venus, and then, wishing to dominate in his turn, of being Tarquin to Lucrece, or, even better, of being Iachimo to Imogen, of feigning to have possessed a woman whom he has not touched, thus gaining the benefit of power without having had to pay the price of the flesh. In this circle of desired perversions, again we find Hamlet using all his power to destroy the pure Ophelia in order to take revenge on Gertrude the impure. The flesh, the world, and disgust haunt Shakespeare's and Joyce's worlds alike. Yet this disgust, which is experienced as a separation of soul and body, and this spiritual wound, like the physical wound, are intentionally acquired and are carefully fostered, because they contain the secret of the artist's whole relationship with his work.

Shakespeare has committed Adam's sin; yet even his sin does not belong to him. "He acts and is acted on." Like Adam, he has abdicated his manhood by yielding to Eve. He has acted "against nature" by reversing the relationship between man and woman, and cannot even lay claim to the pride in guilt of the first man. For this reason he is unable to love directly, but can only make the first gestures; he needs one or more intermediaries. "In *Cymbeline,* in *Othello* he is bawd and cuckold . . . His unremitting intellect is the hornmad Iago ceaselessly willing that the moor in him shall suffer".

How can one be both bawd and cuckold, the architect of one's own misfortune? Imperceptibly Stephen deviates towards what later becomes a fruitful type of heresy. Yet its premises were orthodox; he several times denounces the human "inclination to evil," Shakespeare's "sin". His original sin darkened his understanding and began his work, by means of a strong inclination to evil, to inflict it but above all to undergo it. "The words are those of my lords bishops of Maynooth: an original sin and, like original sin, committed by another in whose sin he too has sinned" (*Ulysses,* p. 208).

What the catechism of Maynooth says can be applied to Shakespeare as well as to Joyce: it says that because of Adam's sin we are all born without sanctifying grace. That our understanding is darkened, our will weakened; that our passions impel us to commit evil; and that we are subject to suffering and death. But what is said here in tones of regret and repentence is turned by Joyce to his own purposes and used with a completely different intention: that which is passion is now the form of action, and becomes thus intentional. To act is to be acted upon; to suffer is to discover.

This is why Shakespeare's life now takes place in a setting of agonising contradictions. In London he pretends to act, but his soul is not involved in the action, while in Stratford his voluntary absence encourages the recommencement of a situation which he both fears and desires—just as Bloom, another type of Shakespeare, favours the growth of Molly's adulterous affairs although he fears them. He acts as though he wished to exorcise the memory of his first defeat yet at the same time to keep it alive. Thus he plunges into a twenty-year sordid extra-conjugal debauch, passing from the "punks of the bankside" to the "quality woman," obsessed by the action that consisted of using his body—or of using the bodies of others—as his replacement when it came to dealing with "reluctant maidenheads". Shakespeare's loathing for this monstrous banquet of flesh is equalled by Hamlet's disgust at his mother's marriage feast, and by that of Bloom in the restaurant. There is "the holy office an ostler does for the stallion," says Joyce, the author of *The Holy Office*, with a smile at his own private joke. He has to find a replacement for himself—once mocked is twice mocked.

Stephen, as the audience harries or mocks him, becomes absorbed in his own game; his identity becomes porous, and we cannot tell whether it is Stephen or Will who is urged to action by the long inner monologue that keeps pace with the spoken exposition. "Act, be acted on" we hear; but who should act? Stephen's action becomes the same as Shakespeare's, and they defend each other by means of language. Stephen exhorts himself "Speech, speech. But act. Act speech. They mock to try you. Act. Be acted on," yet for Shakespeare the necessity for action is complicated by the knowledge that Ann in Stratford is making him into a ghost-by-dispossession. "Do and do. Thing done. In a rosery of Fetter Lane of Gerard, herbalist, he walks, greyedauburn. An azured harebell like her veins. Lids of Juno's eyes, violets. He walks. One life is all. One body. Do. But do. Afar, in a reek of lust and squalor, hands are laid on whiteness" (*Ulysses*, p. 198).

This "Penelope," as Stephen calls her, bringing to mind the image of Molly, a lusty Elizabethan Penelope, is only happy when yielding to the suitors; "she is hot in the blood," and the law of recommencement works for all alike. "Once a wooer twice a wooer." Shakespeare had chosen his betrayer as Stephen had chosen his Judas-figures, and it was his own favourite who took his place with the lady of the sonnets. In the same way he chooses suitors for Ann, and they are his own brothers. The evidence is in his work; "he had three brothers," and this time the choice falls on a rustic dullard. King Hamlet had *one brother* (Claudius) and Prince Hamlet compares the portraits of the two with amazement and fear: his father was noble, graceful, bold, and fair as Hyperion (it is obvious that Hamlet is in love with his father and not with his mother), but to this paragon Gertrude had preferred the ugly Claudius. Love, as Iago says, is a desire of the blood and a perversion of the will.

Shakespeare had *three brothers:* Gilbert, Edmund, and Richard. Gilbert was no doubt harmless; there is no trace of a Gilbert in the work. But there is a Richard, a sinister hunchback who woos a widowed Ann, persuades her and wins her. Joyce too had a brother and friends, and in *Exiles* his double, the writer Richard Rowan, is rivalled by his lifelong friend Robert Hand. "The theme of the false or the usurping or the adulterous brother or all three in one is . . . always with him."

The theme of exile with its corollaries of betrayal and banishment, associated motifs of Venus and Adonis and of replacement by another, is shared out between the two central characters in *Ulysses*: the figure of the father in all his real and symbolic functions as creator and protector, and the man deceived by his wife, by his brothers, but in reality by himself.

The relationships of dependence which constitute the work are centred around the father.[8] The father depends upon his son as the creator depends on his creation, and the engendered one assures his progenitor that he still exists. This simple dialectic has consequences which are often paradoxical or comic in Joyce's life as in his work; it is first to be noted that the son is only son *of a father* and not of a couple, because for Joyce the relationship is seen in the theological fashion. The reason for this insistence on fatherhood is not that Joyce is imitating Catholic dogma or wistfully looking back to its tenets, but that it originates in a fear of woman and of what she represents socially in Ireland. This explains the parallel importance of the theme of the deceived husband. Joyce finds an analogy with the Trinity in the triangular arrangement of adultery rather than in the idea of fatherhood. This does not mean that he particularly enjoyed the flavour of sacrilege involved, for his judgements are never value-judgements; to live and to create are for Joyce equally noble things, and equally small. All motifs are connected in the end.

To Stephen the analogy between the artist and God the Father is a proof supplied by bad faith, by faith of an heretical origin, as he well knows—Arian and Sabellian. He is explaining this aloud for the benefit of his audience by way of his Shakespearean mythology, when Mulligan, the enemy and the clown, appears, provoking in Stephen the bitterness

[8]See Edward Duncan, *Unsubstantial Father, A Study of the Hamlet Symbolism in Joyce's Ulysses* (University of Toronto Quarterly, Jan. 1950, pp. 126–40).

he feels at being a writer, a pariah who is esteemed less than the dilettante, the mocker. What he thinks but does not have the chance to say is a formulation of creation which is theological but not orthodox, in which the themes of wounding, fatherhood, and banishment are united in an unholy trinity:

> He Who Himself begot, middler the Holy Ghost, and Himself sent himself, Agenbuyer, between Himself and others, Who, put upon by His fiends, was nailed like bat to barndoor, starved on crosstree, Who let Him bury, stood up, harrowed hell, fared into heaven and there these nineteen hundred years sitteth on the right hand of His Own Self. . . . (*Ulysses*, p. 194)

The theory of vicarious replacement derives from Sabellius the African.[9] The first recital of spiritual identity recalls in some degree the Sabellian or Patripassian heresy, which considers that the three Persons of the Trinity are only modes of God, and that it was thus God Himself who died on the cross.

In fact, Stephen goes beyond pure Sabellianism by the touches of sadism he adds in his own theory. A man who has been wounded in body or soul leaves Stratford and goes off to Romeville or London or Paris, but he is also Shakespeare, bearing with him all his works *in potentia*, believing that in this way he will become creator of himself as artist. This is the real path of Shakespeare—self-exile and separation of self into man and artist—the man being "middler" of the word, who suffers so that the artist in him may create.

Stephen declares that Shakespeare is not solely a Christ-figure (the Son sent by the Father for the purpose of suffering) but that the heresy is yet more subtle. The artist-God has himself nailed to a "barndoor," watches himself suffer, takes notes on his sufferings, and makes a work of art therefrom. The Father detaches himself from his substance in order to watch it suffer. Can such a voyeurism really be called divine? Let us not forget, says Stephen, that "the most Roman of catholics call . . . the lord of things as they are *dio boia*, hangman god". The mystery of this God who calls forth and then uses his own suffering is accompanied by the mystery of fatherhood, that is, of creation. Stephen is only impelled to elaborate these complementary themes by his adversary Eglinton, who eggs him on to further paradox in the hope of catching him out in a misstatement. First, he is asked to prove that Shakespeare was a Jew, then, since he claims that a man's life is the material of his

---

[9]See William Noon, S.J., *Joyce and Aquinas* (Yale U.P., 1957).

work and that Shakespeare's wife, brothers, and children are as much grist to his mill as contemporary events were, he is challenged to find some traces of the father in this collection of autobiographical plays.

Stephen extracts himself from the first difficulty by a neat scholastic quibble; he reminds his audience that the man who created Shylock was a businessman and "a capitalist shareholder". This intellectual conjuring trick displeases Stephen, who mentally encourages himself by a stylistic grimace that heralds the melting pot of language in 'Circe': "I think you're getting on very nicely. Just mix up a mixture of theolologicophilolological. *Mingo, minxi, mictum, mingere*" (*Ulysses*, p. 201). But Joyce takes care that all elements are present in all, and if Shakespeare is a plausible Jew, then Bloom will have to be a plausible Shakespeare. As ever at moments of trouble Saint Thomas comes to the rescue explaining incest in terms of avarice and not from the standpoint of the Oedipus complex:

> Writing of incest from a standpoint different from that of the new Viennese school Mr. Magee spoke of, [he] likens it in his wise and curious way to an avarice of the emotions. He means that the love so given to one near in blood is covetously withheld from some stranger who, it may be, hungers for it. (*Ulysses*, p. 202)

Shakespeare, who loaned his wife to his brothers, held "tightly to what he called his rights," and the wife remained in the family like an inheritable object.

The father is a ghost who determines another set of grievous but necessary relationships that are made the subject of a brilliant exposition by Stephen, who is trying to reach a declaration, by the interweaving of the generations, that the artist is his own father and the father of his creatures; this is the artist's response to God the Father, the only being who does proceed from himself, and his attempt to imitate that independence.

John Shakespeare died when William was thirty-five years old, the same age as Joyce when he was writing 'Scylla and Charybdis,' the age of Dante when he began his great work, *"nel mezzo del cammin di nostra vita,"* as Stephen reminds us, and John Shakespeare is not a ghost. "From hour to hour it rots and rots. He rests, disarmed of fatherhood, having devised that mystical estate upon his son" (*Ulysses*, p. 203).

To Joyce this mystical estate is the only fatherhood that has any meaning; if motherhood has a meaning (for the child whom the mother has borne knows that he is the fruit of her womb), "paternity is a legal fiction,"[10] as Joyce wrote to Stannie after the birth of his son Giorgio. No man can be sure that he is the father of his son, and even the moment of conception is a mystery to him. "What links them in nature? An instant of blind rut." The slow gestation of the embryo links the child to his mother as the developing work is linked to the artist's imagination.

> Fatherhood, in the sense of conscious begetting, is unknown to man. It is a mystical estate, an apostolic succession, from only begetter to only begotten. On that mystery and not on the madonna which the cunning Italian intellect flung to the mob of Europe the church is founded and founded irremovably because founded, like the world, macro- and microcosm, upon the void. Upon incertitude, upon unlikelihood. *Amor matris*, subjective and objective genitive, may be the only true thing in life. (*Ulysses*, p. 204)

Stephen here is adopting for his own use views which he would not accept when they came to him from Cranly's lips. Mother-love, then, has nothing miraculous about it; but on the contrary, fatherhood—a mystical state founded on the void and on doubt—is a true mystery, and thus one can found one's work on the basis of this lack, as Joyce does, using doubt and absence as his starting-point.

The artist has nothing more to do but to become truly his own father. Sabellius maintains that the Father is Himself His Own Son; now how can Shakespeare be his own son? By the following syllogism that plays on the notions of possible and impossible, founded solely on the exploitation of the possibilities of meaning in the language because it is dealing with an abstract proposition. Saint Thomas falls a victim to this heresy, maintaining that the impossible does not exist. How, then, can a sonless father be truly a father, or a fatherless son truly a son? In Thomist logic, literally interpreted, he cannot possibly be. When John Shakespeare died, William, now fatherless, could thus no longer be called a son. On the contrary, he had two daughters, and thus counted as a father. "He was not the father of his own son merely but, being no more a son, he was and felt himself the father of all his race, the father of his own grandfather, the father of his unborn grandson. . . ." *(Ibid.)* As father of his race, sole progenitor, and hence father of himself, the artist is consubstantial with the work that he has engendered: he is father, son, and inspiration.

[10]Letter of 18 August 1905.

If Joyce's method of reaching his conclusion is original because it is basically Thomism turned awry, the conclusion in itself is not new, but is the nature of the artist, from Flaubert to Poe and from the German Romantics to Antonin Artaud, to call himself his own father. But Joyce was alone in transferring his creative paradox into ordinary, everyday life, in taking Bloom as its unfortunate illustration: Bloom who has neither son nor father cannot be truly father or son, he is nobody and is well aware of it. He is a ghost because he has been ejected from his racial background, by his own fault and not against his will, but he lacks the genius that makes the mistake an instrument of redemption; he is deserted, non-existant, often quite forgotten. Like Lear after the loss of all his titles except that of fool, he is a mere shadow of himself. Nor is he the God who tortures himself in order to become creative; his masochism is sterile. He is looking for his son, without much conviction, and his state of guilt is the place of his exile. It is generally said that Bloom finds a son in Stephen, and in fact he knows that Stephen is a son, but does not take any advantage of this. On the contrary, he tries to make Stephen take his place—to carry out the Holy Office for Molly. Bloom's passivity is not a form of action at all. When he repeats to himself, "All is lost," he does not consider this loss as a potential bringer of gain; he is only the man who sneaks furtively between Stephen and Mulligan, and who passes through the rest of the day meeting Molly at every turn, until at last, "childman weary," he falls asleep in the bed of exile, the bed of the living-dead.

Stephen finds his path, takes the way of the artist as he had described it in clear words in the Library; he knows now that he must depart; "Part. The moment is now. Where then? If Socrates leave his house today, if Judas go forth tonight. Why? That lies in space which I in time must come to, ineluctably" (*Ulysses*, p. 213). The destination matters not, since in space his own self is awaiting him; at the ultimate moment of the encounter with the self, "when the mind is a fading coal, that which I was is that which I am and that which in possibility I may come to be. So in the future, sister of the past, I may see myself as I sit here now but by reflection from that which then I shall be" (*Ulysses*, p. 191).

If matter is constantly being renewed, essence remains the same; thus, the artist always says the same thing, but the form changes. The creation is as it was on the first day God made it, but the pawns have shifted their positions. Only God is a circle that always returns to himself; my self is always myself; I am what I have been and what I shall be. Only the present instant, as seized by the artist's imagination in an epiphany, may seem different, because it contains in itself all possibles, and may give the illusory impression that there is a multiplicity of choice. The instant that contains *all possibles* contains eternity and an infinity of choices, just as in Hamlet's mind infinite space can be contained in a nutshell; it is defined by its very brevity. It is the inspiration, the breath that comes before the word, the trajectory of the living word before the written sign.

Joyce rightly says that the present only *reflects* the future by a projection of the self which is already there. The bets are laid and the game inevitably begins as soon as each individual commits the original sin proper to him. There seems no point in beginning to travel, if one only returns to the point from which one set out. Man, as Stephen says at the end of his experiences, is "what went forth to the ends of the world to traverse not itself. God, the sun, Shakespeare, a commercial traveller, having itself traversed in reality itself, becomes that self. . . . Self which it itself was ineluctably preconditioned to become".

Joyce avoids the difficulties inherent in this theory by means of his disguise, the mask of Hamlet, and by the game of self-duplication that he plays, turning himself by means of alienation into self and other. He may be a prisoner, but he is free because "I is another," I is two, I is God the Father and God the Son, Magician of the Word. It is now possible to come forth out of the self. Hamlet, a mature man, hard and authoritative, finds himself at the beginning of the play in a situation which he cannot control; he is allotted the role of a child, of a docile, obedient son. He must escape from the world in which he is a prisoner because he is the son of his father, of a ghost. He wishes to be the author of a play which has, in fact, begun without him, and to legislate for himself like Stephen. In order to do this, he has to reverse the mechanics of alienation: he plays at being mad, he simulates insanity, making himself into two people, thus obliging the rest of the world to play its part in his comedy. He transforms those who had thought they controlled the progress of the play into actors, making his uncle and Polonius, for example, into characters in his own play; his madness deprives them of reason and he robs of initiative and freedom of action those who thought themselves free. But the madness which removes him from the world soon brings him to a more radical exile: he is henceforth above the others as he had willed himself to be—but by that very intention he puts himself *outside* their circle.

Hamlet's solution is to be Hamlet the son—the madman, the dissimulator, driving the world round on a murderous course—Hamlet the father—the sane man, the one who knows—and the spirit, the Holy Ghost, the one who sees clearly through all things; this solution corresponds to Stephen's division of himself into three, "I, I and I. I" (*Ulysses*, p. 186). Because Hamlet's game involves risking one's life Hamlet can act, while pretending to be acted upon. Each character is put back in his original place and Hamlet could, in fact, become king by the death of Claudius; what Stephen calls a "reconciliation" could take place. But the game is dangerous, for there is a Hamlet who must be suppressed, the Hamlet who has served to restore order and right, the Hamlet who had been sacrificed beforehand. Hamlet the prince can only become King Hamlet by suffering death himself and by receiving the mortal wound that would restore his identity. Another *felix culpa* is involved.

The artist, the king, God, Stephen, Shakespeare, and Hamlet all have the right to be their own master, to legislate for themselves alone; they will their autonomy and break all the obstacles that prevent them from achieving independence. Authority, tradition, culture, society, the flesh, everything that hinders and tries to suppress the individual, is symbolically represented in the works of Shakespeare as in the works of Joyce by the figures of the father and the mother. Stephen, Hamlet, and Shakespeare share the same horror for the flesh which means also the desire to break away.

Stephen and Hamlet pass through three analogous phases; first, they abandon themselves to temptation. In *Portrait*, Stephen was afraid to give himself up to the arms reaching out to him, and Hamlet is afraid to let Ophelia love him. To know a woman means to accord her some importance, to let oneself be known, and through being known to lose oneself. For Stephen, the temptation is to enter the Church, for Hamlet, to accept Claudius' game and play the appropriate part in it; they both withdraw. *Non serviam*, I shall not accept mother or wife, I shall be alone and belong to myself. Furthermore, because he can never know who his father is, his distrust of the father is in fact a disguised form of disgust for the mother; not only does she share in the animal act of generation, but also she is the instrument of evil, Venus greedy for her prey, thieving man's substance from him. She is Eve the usurper, she is Gertrude, she wishes him dead. The son seeks to suppress the mother. Naturally, he succeeds to his father's place, but the mother is still there. John Shakespeare rots in the earth, the ghost of King Hamlet falls silent,

Simon Dedalus has faded away into the streets of Dublin, Ann Hathaway at sixty is still deceiving her husband with a preacher, Gertrude
returns to Claudius, and the fetid ghost of May Dedalus haunts Stephen
as far as the bordello, the house of Circe. If the painful sensations caused
by feeling "different" were to stop, if reconciliation followed separation, art would wither and die. The wound must be nurtured. Shakespeare wills his exile. The creation of Shakespeare as a type is both an
act of catharsis and an alienation. The belief that one must subject the
human being within oneself to the demands of art is not the first step
in a dialectic which finally brings man more suffering than he wants. In
effect, the artist only exists now in his artisanal activity; yet if he ceases
to write, he is condemning himself to death. He is obliged to write in
order to exist. He believed that he was his own master, and has succeeded in making himself his own slave; in terms of parenthood, this is
as much as to say, as Stephen has demonstrated, that the father is
dependent on the son—just as the ghost of King Hamlet has to be heard
by his son.

The ghost who falls silent simply disappears without trace unless he
has been heard and understood by the son whose father (in his second
proposition) he claims to be. This claim can only have any meaning if
the relationship is recognised by the one to whom the non-king *belongs*
now; the son is master of his father's existence and has the power to give
a body to this disembodied voice, and this explains the paradoxical
appearance of the theme of the father who is a father no more, and of
the father who is the son of his son. In the paradox, it is the work that
writes the author, the creation that guarantees the existence of the
creator, and the son that makes the father. Creation thus becomes
obligatory, which is an unbearable situation; the real prison has been
replaced by the imaginary prison, the state of Denmark by a simulated
madness, and exile in the world by exile inside Hamlet's nutshell. Stephen condemns this illusion: "He goes back, weary of the creation he
has piled up to hide him from himself . . . he passes on towards eternity
. . . untaught by the wisdom he has written".

Shakespeare as the victim of a fall early in his life—a fall in which he
had been a consenting party but which was still shameful—had built up
his work as a camouflage to hide his real insecurity; in the world he
played at being William the Conqueror in order to dissimulate the fact
of his first defeat, and to himself he acted out the comedy of his fatherhood in order to prove his manhood in spite of everything. By the flesh

he was the father of Susan, and by the apostolic fatherhood of the soul he was Hamlet's father.[11]

He was the author and legislator of a macrocosm in which politics and human beings were governed by laws which were not obeyed by the microcosm of his own being. In a tragically Machiavellian situation, the artist who is the apparent master of his creation is the first person to be excluded from it. While in the work conflicts are resolved and knotty problems loosed, in life nothing is solved. Nothing is lost or created, and Shakespeare does not change. He remains unfortunate, unable to surpass himself or to escape the ills in which he stagnates. What Stephen has proved is indeed that *a ghost exists;* the artist's vocation is but mortal. Either he wills his suffering because he sees it as a positive factor in a quasi-theological world where paradise lost promises paradise regained, or else his behaviour constitutes a flight from himself; he fears the man within him upon whom he inflicts pain, and in order to take his revenge for being made to fear, he causes the man within him further suffering. But at the same time he feels that he needs this man's humility; he scorns and yet respects this weakness in himself which, if seen clearly, would prevent him from acting at all. He has no other resource than to dissimulate to himself.

Joyce has already stated in *Exiles* that the artist can only create when wounded and doubting, but even if he knows that he is blind, is he really? To know that one creates for the purpose of self-dissimulation would seem to necessitate a denunciation of the imposture. This analysis of Shakespeare is the most subtle of Joyce's contrivances for hiding himself, for he never authorises any confusion between himself and the subject. He has refined himself out of existence, he claims; he is the great ungraspable Absence whose presence is felt on every page. The solution is expressed in terms of a game, and like Shakespeare he is everywhere in his work. But whereas Shakespeare, as he explains, has

[11]It is necessary to distinguish the connections of male lineage from those of feminine descent; to Stephen, death-by-absence or by change is reserved for the son. This is expressed in the opposition of two words which govern the structures of parenthood, "shadow" (the son), signifying the repudiation of son by father, and "image" (the daughter), meaning the imitation of the father's appearance. "If you want to know what are the events which cast their shadow over the hell of time of *King Lear, Othello, Hamlet, Troilus and Cressida,* look to see when and how the shadow lifts. What softens the heart of a man, Shipwrecked in storms dire, Tried, like another Ulysses, Pericles, Prince of Tyre?

Head, redconecapped, buffeted, brineblinded.

—A child, a girl placed in his arms, Marina." (*Ulysses,* p. 191.)

left his name everywhere in his creation (in the way that God has), he, Joyce, has left a succession of false names. Stephen, Shakespeare, Richard Rowan—all the artist's masks that Joyce adopts are as misleading as they are revealing, and Joyce furthermore treats them merely as cast-off clothes that he abandons by the roadside, for none of them appears in *Finnegans Wake.* They have simply acted as stages in the definition of his aesthetic. If Joyce proclaimed the necessity of the wound, he did so because at the time he wished to believe in it, and wished also that his readers should believe; but *Finnegans Wake* shows how he progressed beyond this idea.

It is he, rather than Shakespeare, who is afraid to open his eyes and see himself. For none may look upon the face of God—one would discover at once that he is not God. He requires us to bend over his mirror with our eyes closed; and, as an extra precaution, no mirror is ever to reflect Joyce himself. Narcissus looks at himself through the eyes of his replacements, Stephen and Bloom, and as one might expect, what they see is still the face of someone else, the face of a beardless, horned Shakespeare, paralysed and stuttering, the symbol of all that Joyce feels he is not, the artist who is banished from art for not having played the game to the bitter end, who yielded to the temptation to be simply himself and nothing more, a man amongst men.

Shakespeare had perpetuated the first sin and the first exile, knowing himself to be both victim and executioner of himself. At the end "he returns after a life of absence to that spot of earth where he was born, where he has always been, man and boy, a silent witness and there, his journey of life ended, he plants his mulberrytree in the earth. Then dies" (*Ulysses*, pp. 208–9). He has ended his journey as observer, actor, and creator, and this world outside has only ever been the actuality of what in his inner world was potentiality. The inner and outer worlds are identical because there is no objective reality, but rather a subjective relationship with what is outside.

This old dog who comes home to die has already passed through Stephen's consciousness when the latter was meditating on the mystery of the one and the many and the quest for the self, but then it was a real dog, called "Tatters," and its metamorphosis took place on the Protean beach; then he was a living symbol of the possibilities which are perceived by the artist but not realised. This lively, droll scene contains, in spite of its apparently insignificant subject, a moving epiphany of the progress of man through all the times of his life, under all his borrowed rags and tatters.

Sniffing on all sides, the dog looks "for something lost in a past life," following back the history of his "avatars" in search of primary self. Successively, as he moves back up the stream of time, the dog is, was, and will be hare, buck, bear, and wolf, until

> his speckled body ambled ahead of them and then loped off at a calf's gallop. The carcass lay on his path. He stopped, sniffed, stalked round it, brother, nosing closer, went round it, sniffing rapidly like a dog all over the dead dog's bedraggled fell. Dogskull, dogsniff, eyes on the ground, moves to one great goal. Ah, poor dogsbody. Here lies poor dogsbody's body. (*Ulysses*, p. 48)

The dog is often Stephen's emblem in *Ulysses*, and Stephen's quest for himself may have a double orientation; either the "dog" of memory is going back into time, searching for something *lost* in the past, or he is taking the route described by Stephen in 'Scylla and Charybdis' with reference to Shakespeare. "Every life is many days, day after day. We walk through ourselves, meeting robbers, ghosts, giants, old men, young men, wives, widows, brothers-in-love. But always meeting ourselves" (*Ulysses*, p. 209). All these "others" we meet are also objective versions of ourselves.

Stephen sums up the progress of the artist (Shakespeare, Stephen or Joyce) as it is made *in opposition to history*—or at least, in opposition to history as defined by Mr. Deasy in the 'Nestor' chapter:

> From the playfield the boys raised a shout. A whirring whistle: goal. What if that nightmare gave you a back kick?
> —The ways of the Creator are not our ways, Mr, Deasy said. All history moves towards one great goal, the manifestation of God. (*Ulysses*, p. 37)

As one moves back by various ways from animality to what should be "God," to what was manifest at the beginning as the First Cause, the Primum Mobile, the One that Aristotle does not name, that Saint Thomas and Mr. Deasy call God, what one finds is—a corpse—"Dogskull, dogsniff, eyes on the ground, moves to one great goal. Ah, poor dogsbody. Here lies poor dogsbody's body". The living dog and the dead dog are the two animal forms of Stephen as seen by himself and by Mulligan in 'Telemachus,' the first episode, the episode that gives his marching orders to one whose "great goal" is the manifestation, not of a God but of himself as artist, made into an artist after undergoing a series of ordeals. And at the end he goes back, like Shakespeare, to stretch out and rest, "an old dog licking an old sore".

The round stage on which the first act of *Ulysses* is played takes on the shape of the white china bowl into which Stephen's dying mother vomited up the bitterness of her life; "the ring of bay and skyline held a dull green mass of liquid". At the top of the Martello tower preparations seem to be in progress for a ritual sacrifice: "Buck Mulligan wiped again his razorblade.—Ah, poor dogsbody, he said in a kind voice" (*Ulysses*, p. 10). Mulligan's razor, the sledded poleaxe of the Stratford butcher's son, the concentration camps, are all the murderous instruments used by the Great Bad God to manifest his presence. Stephen is preparing to issue his challenge as artist to "the playwright who wrote the folio of this world and wrote it badly (He gave us light first and the sun two days later), the lord of things as they are" (*Ulysses*, p. 209).

Stephen comes out of the library; beneath the portico he is inescapably awaited by the Stephen he was a few months ago, he who dreamed of Thoth and watched the birds. "Here I watched the birds for augury. Aengus of the birds. They go, they come. Last night I flew. Easily flew. Men wondered" (*Ulysses*, p. 213). In the dream he was Daedalus, but today, 16 June, "no birds". Stephen's horror of the nightmare that is history is inspired by his feeling that the present is being stolen from him by the past, and that always the same story is being begun over and over again. Just as Bloom is always obsessed by the same woman, the whole of Dublin hums the nightmare refrain of this 16 June, "all is lost," and everything creaks and groans like the springs of that bed where Bloom is a stranger now. For Bloom, the misfortune is that he can never move beyond his feelings of loss, but simply repeats them. The present shares painfully in the past, and the past is the same as passivity in the grammar of mental suffering. "All is lost" expresses passively a loss which was inflicted on him by someone else, and which is thus irreversible.

All has been lost by someone, *actively* and in a manner that is hostile to Bloom; his feeling of helplessness is manifested by his physical impotence, and even the representation of his drama in the outside world is an action beyond his control. He is unable even to permit things to happen: in the 'Circe' episode, he is at the end uttering his most private and personal secrets, unable to stop himself. Eventually his impotence transforms itself into the *will* to be passive; he renounces any claims to the exercise of his own will, and consents to being managed and manipulated by others, abandoning his rights to the statement of a *cogito ergo sum* which in reality is very appropriate for him. And he falls into a passivity in which he is deprived by the world around him of any existence in the first person.

Stephen feels that the elimination of the past in order to be free to identify himself with a present self is a particularly difficult undertaking: "Behind. Perhaps there is someone". The bay of Dublin "lay behind him, a bowl of bitter waters" (*Ulysses*, p. 13), and there had been someone before, his mother, who washed his neck and scolded him, as he leaned over the white basin (*Portrait*, chapter IV).

And behind him too is death in the past; his memory crosses old battlefields, recalls past miseries, and personal or national failures every time he turns round. Life is like death by drowning, and any pity for a person other than oneself is a weakness that may be fatal.

> I am not a strong swimmer. Water cold soft. When I put my face into it in the basin at Clongowes. Can't see! Who's behind me? Out quickly, quickly! Do you see the tide flowing quickly in on all sides, sheeting the lows of sands quickly, shellcocoacoloured? If I had land under my feet. I want his life still to be his, mine to be mine. A drowning man. His human eyes scream to me out of horror of his death. I. . . . With him together down. . . . (*Ulysses*, p. 48)

This is not what Stephen wants; let each live his own life and die his own death, let each one have and accept his mother, his wrongdoings. The "I" is the one who begins the world with I, and who is travelling towards his "I". Exile and the promised land, fatherhood and creation, the same and the other, the purity of writing and the impurity of the flesh, presence and absence, life and eternity, God and the artist: all are expressed in their complex relations between Scylla and Charybdis by the plural voice of Stephen, the one who says, "I, I and I. I". This trinity stands, one and indivisible, in the space that extends between spoken language and wordless soliloquy. Stephen is telling the story of another man in order to tell his own, in which he is the narrator and the one who pours the poison of the Word into the porches of his listeners' ears; when he tells the tale of Shakespeare, he seems to have suspended his own existence for the time being, but in fact only his own drama is related here and only his own quest pursued.

This false biography is told under a triply negative sign, that of banishment, mistake, and treachery, which is represented by departure (or beginning), wrongdoing, and effacement. Shakespeare is exiled, wounded, disappointed, and rejected, and he creates the reverse of life as he lives it in a ghostly world over which he can reign supreme. If at the end of his life he returns to the point from which he set out, that of his original death and beginning, he does so because to the genius life and death are part of the same cyclic pattern—are acted out on the same stage—where all beings simply pretend to exist, where subjectivity can change with other people's attitude, where the only man to survive will be he who can establish a redeeming situation within himself by means of his spoken word, the word which listens to itself speaking. Finally, the story of Shakespeare is to be read as the account of a time, of a fertile, creative presence; misfortune teaches the genius the nature of its opposite, mistakes turn him in the direction of truth, shame inspires him with courage, and in his impotence as a man lies the secret of his omnipotence as creator.

In the library Stephen repeats the ontological Protean experience, the closing of his eyes in order to go into darkness, although knowing that even in the absence of his look the outside world was still there. The space in which his creative imagination moves extends around a twofold certainty: (1) that the form of all experience and thus of all life has always been and will always be the time present; and (2) that the soul is in some way everything that is. His attitude towards his own death is revealed in this definition of being as presence and as absolute possibility of repetition. Before, after, or without Stephen, the world is still there, is always there.

To repeat oneself, by reproducing oneself by one's writings, is a way of stating oneself to be, if not subjectively *in* the present, at least objectively present. When Stephen declares, "I, I and I," and then "I," he is at once placing himself somehow *beyond* the present in an absolute immortality which is not subject to the test which the possibility of his disappearance would constitute, and this brilliant move takes on its full meaning when compared with the actual experience of the disappearance of Bloom. Bloom on the beach says, "I am a . . ." and the sentence remains unfinished because Bloom is not a real person, but a being in suspended animation, "a . . .", with no real existence. Now, since "I am" is only experienced in life with the meaning "I am present," it supposes in itself a connection with presence in general, with being as presence. The appearance of the "I" to himself in the statement "I am" is in its origins related to the possibility of its *disappearance*, and to begin with, "I am" means "I am mortal". "I am immortal" is an impossible proposition. But "I,I and I. I" represents the only immortality possible for man, the immortality of the subject who repeats himself without taking on a temporal existence, without offering himself to the world of possibles, who enters into the present "non-existence" of the creator. Outside existence, "I" can exist, being represented by one or more "I am" statements in the world of presence as God is represented by His Son.

Stephen is making three speeches at once; he is addressing himself to the public audience with all the resources a pupil of the Jesuits might be expected to command, and under the protection of Loyola, the soldier of rhetoric, he is conducting a brilliant campaign with the intention of convincing others, skilfully making use of the grammar of irony, which informs his words subtly and invisibly; thus he brings to life a personality that has as much affinity with Iago as with Othello, with the Moor as with the Dubliner, whose history, or rather whose exemplary tale, has doubt as its main theme.

With his second voice Stephen is acting as confidant to himself, as Horatio and Hamlet, as the measured grave wise man and the man who pretends to be mad, as actor and as character in a play; within the self establishes itself an "intersubjectivity" which reproduces that without the self. The second person is an accomplice in the first person's lies, and at the same time his troubled vigilance is a form of the policing of self by self that Stephen practises, and of his presence to himself in his own mind. By an incessant interchange between the inside and the outside he makes sure of his mastery over his presence and over his "difference". He never for a moment confuses himself with Shakespeare, but on the contrary Shakespeare acts as a mask for him, as a proper name which he has himself chosen as evocative of himself (because his own name does not yet mean what he would have it mean). Stephen's second voice mocks his hearers Russell and Magee for being masked by anonymous names, A. E. and Eglinton. If Stephen borrows, he borrows from Hamlet or from Shakespeare. It can be seen how *duplicity gives an answer to doubt.*

Stephen's self-awareness appears thus in connection with the character he is playing, and thus the language of the first person is appropriate; his awareness is the voice that makes manifest, the spiritual body that continues to speak and to be present to itself, making heard in exile or in the absence of the world the inspiring breath of its own solitary self. Throughout the dialogue Stephen undergoes suspension of existence from time to time as a consequence of lack of attention, which brutally removes him from the scene in the outer world. At this point the second voice takes up the tale, for it is important that the inner speech should be a complete one, and not a silence by which Stephen would be consenting to his own elimination. The second voice is thus sometimes an ally of the public voice, its understudy, and sometimes the replacement of the first. In this case, it is necessary for the inner speech to be heard, and for some relationship to be established with the *object*, whatever it may, a relationship whose purpose is to take and comment upon what Stephen would call the "quiddity" of the world. This is hard, for the intention to speak, to mean something, is often threatened with suspension or interruption. The banished Stephen becomes a living awareness of banishment, felt as present to itself in relation to the outside world where it is not.

The only true life lies in this constantly renewed proximity to oneself, maintained by repetition of the act which ensures exclusion from the outer world; it follows then that banishment from the outside world guarantees presence in the world within. And within is he who speaks to Hamlet, he who is to become the artist. The spirit with its knowledge of death, the ghost of the King, is the double of that spirit in Stephen who knows day after day the death of one buried alive, that spirit who *sees himself killed* and, in disappearing from the sight of others, is deprived of the dull existence of the outside world. The second voice is the breath of the ghost. The ghost is not dead, but a live man suddenly hurled into the beyond unprepared. This is why he comes back, to protest, and he truthfully expresses his existence when he says, "*I am* the ghost" of the king who is no king, of your father. This statement "I am," which is in fact an awareness of *not being*, is made by someone who only exists by his absence from other people, by his disappearance; yet his disappearance is contradicted by his use of the pronoun "I," justified by his presence to himself. He is an invisible voice that calls up the non-king in the mind of the other person. And since all that he has left to him consists of that deadly knowledge, all his "*ergo sum*" is used up in his appeal, "hear! O hear!" He calls to Burbage the actor "who stands before him beyond the rack of cerecloth," who is only his son if he will accept the ghost's words, "I am thy father's spirit". The only thing of which the ghost can be certain is the intuition of the subject of that first affirmation, which does not depend on any other person's look, on any other synthesis, social or empirical.

When Stephen says that *Hamlet* is "a ghost story," this means not only that it is a story involving superstition, but also that it is a story of voices speaking; the ghost is in fact one who is represented in this world by the power of the speaking voice, and he who is nothing outside this world may be reconstituted and repeated in this medium which preserves presence-to-self and the absolute proximity of actions to themselves. The voice, and what Saussure calls the "acoustic images," are heard and understood by the ghost-self who utters them in absolute proximity, in their time present; the ghost-self does not have to move out of the domain of himself to be immediately affected by his own words.

The spirit and the inspiration are inseparable in what is still only an "inner monologue," a transparency. The ghost who says "I am," be he Stephen, Shakespeare, or the king, listens to himself in the time of his speech. This presence to the self of the act that animates, in the transparent spirituality of that which is animated—this living word that is only heard in time present—is a kind of direct affecting of the self; it differs from the operation of the eyes, from watching or looking at something, in that the latter has to pass through something accessory, something foreign to the self. In order to see himself, Bloom has to be seen, by a mirror or by another person, and in order to be touched Stephen needs a woman; in both cases the body is exposed to the world, which for Bloom brings pain and for Stephen a feeling of nakedness.

But in *listening to oneself speaking* one can abolish the outer world, and may even reduce the inner space to nothing; in the speaking of the inner world space is annihilated, and with it the very place of possible exile—there can be no separation or distance between "I" and "I".

Part Five: Joyce's Poetics

XXI. Approaching Reality

Language as the Meeting-Place of Subject and Object

The primary work of the young Joyce was to meditate upon and to evolve the principles of an aesthetic based on Aristotle and Saint Thomas, and to note down in exercise-books or on scraps of paper instants of reality as they were seized by hearing, sight, or taste, or caught in a word, a phrase, or several phrases. These momentary snapshots, collected and preserved because they had resuscitated some thought or emotion in the observer, in spite of their brief or banal nature, he called "epiphanies," and on these selected scraps of reality he founded books whose meaning is not provided by plot, analysis, or social event, but by the revelation they give of a certain universe in a certain order.[1] The nature of the epiphany is by definition twofold: as manifestation (the real meaning of "epiphany") it is an object that offers itself to the watcher, a free image. But not everything is epiphanised, for some conjunction must be operative between subject and object; an object may exist for centuries before its "soul" is manifested in this way.

[1] *My Brother's Keeper* (p. 134) shows us Joyce "noting what he called 'epiphanies'—manifestations or revelations. Jim always had a contempt for secrecy, and these notes were in the beginning ironical observations of slips, and little errors and gestures—mere straws in the wind—by which people betrayed the very thing they were most careful to conceal. 'Epiphanies' were always brief sketches, hardly ever more than some dozen lines in length, but always very accurately observed and noted, the matter being so slight. This collection served him as a sketch-book serves an artist, or as Stevenson's note-book served him in the formation of his style."

There is some sort of appeal made by the subject, to which the object responds; and from being merely a surface perceived by the senses and objectively delimited, the epiphany becomes a unique instant in the series of succeeding instants, the moment in time when it is suddenly perceived by a subject in its unity. In this movement and at this instant, what had been just an object among objects becomes suddenly a "vision" apparent in its wholeness, detached by the watcher's gaze from the whole of which it forms a part—it becomes a particular thing by itself that radiates in the subject's mind.

This vision may be treasured and preserved in the memory with no thought for communication, but for Joyce the epiphany should be communicable, and the unique instant as perceived in one unique motion must be reproduceable by art, in this case by language. The difficulty arises from the fact that the epiphany does not bring some miraculous vision to light, but rather the banal in its full banality. In sum, this means that the artist, with some reader as companion, follows a passer-by until the latter's very soul becomes clear to them—without having had any need of interrogation or explanation, and without any extraordinary occurrence having taken place—in the manner of a detective novel. Joyce then assails the epiphanised object (and by object, we may mean generally anything that constitutes the reality which is transposed into the book, be it a thing, a person, a dialogue, a situation) by all the means that cause language to be both matter and the instrument of that matter's transformation. Everyday language has to be seen as artistic substance. Joyce attempts to renew the power of everyday words, in order that the ordinary may be both its banal self *and* revelatory of something other than its outward appearance; the outer surface has in fact become so worn that it is virtually invisible. This renewal can only be achieved by means of comparison and modification, by the introduction of an element or form that catches the attention.

Thus, the banal when placed in a literary context takes on the full force of its vulgarity and plainness. In the same way, Joyce makes use of repetition, of fragmentation of phrases overheard, and of scenes succeeding each other in an order which is only apparently haphazard —their meaning becomes clear at the end of the sequence, as does that of the actionless scenes that make up Chapter V of *Portrait*. One of Joyce's favourite methods of composition in *Portrait* is a kind of montage, as original as it is unique in the book; he inserts into the body of the work a number of quotations, scraps from poems that are part of the English nation's cultural heritage, obsessive childish phrases, short foolish rhymes that occur to the adolescent mind in moments of depression.

They are perfectly integrated in the contexts where they occur, and together make up a strange baroque picture quite in harmony with the book's subject; their total effect is a living metaphor of what is happening in the Artist's soul, and they all have their origins in the need Stephen feels to give his life some musical quality or form. The message varies with the time at which it is given, sometimes depending also on the climate. The reader is struck in both his auditory and his visual sensibilities: as he leafs through *Portrait*, he gets the impression of a prose background sown with lyrical exclamation. The musical quotations of the first chapter, if collected and examined, reveal what haunted the mind of Stephen as a child, and from their alternating order springs the Portrait of a soul. To begin, we find

1) O, the wild rose blossoms
   On the little green place.

2) O, the green wothe botheth.

3) Tralala lala,
   Tralala tradaladdy,
   Tralala lala,
   Tralala lala.

4) Pull out his eyes,
   Apologise,
   Apologise,
   Pull out his eyes.
   Apologise,
   Pull out his eyes,
   Pull out his eyes,
   Apologise.

5) Wolsey died in Leicester Abbey
   Where the abbots buried him.
   Canker is a disease of plants,
   Cancer one of animals.

6) Stephen Dedalus
   Class of Elements
   Clongowes Wood College
   Sallins
   County Kildare
   Ireland
   Europe
   The World
   The Universe.

7) Stephen Dedalus is my name,
   Ireland is my nation.
   Clongowes is my dwellingplace
   And heaven my expectation.

8) O Lord, open our lips
   And our mouths shall announce Thy praise.
   Incline unto our aid, O God!
   O Lord, make haste to help us!

9) Visit, we beseech Thee, O Lord, this habitation and drive away from it all the snares of the enemy. May Thy holy angels dwell herein to preserve us in peace, and may Thy blessings be always upon us through Christ our Lord. Amen.

10) Dingdong! The castle bell!
    Farewell, my mother!
    Bury me in the old churchyard
    Beside my eldest brother.
    My coffin shall be black,
    Six angels at my back,
    Two to sing and two to pray
    And two to carry my soul away.

This is the song of rhythm, dance, and terror that fills the small child's awareness; then comes the age of obscenity and the time of disgust:

11) Balbus was building a wall.
    Julius Caesar wrote the Calico Belly.

12) It can't be helped;
    It must be done.
    So down with your breeches
    And out with your bum.

Chapter II has virtually no such quotations; it shows Stephen enclosed in a world of images dominated by the figure of "she" and absorbed in silent contemplation. Chapter III is of course concerned with his fall into hell, and the subject is alienated to such an extent here that he is nothing but a sounding-board for the sermons he hears.

Music and incantation appear again in Chapter V. This time the culture for which he longs and the now-empty charms of Latin are in rivalry with the first invented phrases, some beautiful and others non-sensical:

13) I was not wearier where I lay . . .

14) The ivy whines upon the wall,

> And whines and twines upon the wall,
> The yellow ivy upon the wall,
> Ivy, ivy up the wall.

15) Contrahit orator, variant in carmine vates.
> Impleta sunt quae concinit
> David fideli carmine
> Dicendo nationibus
> Regnavit a ligno Deus.

16) Are you not weary of ardent ways,
> Lure of the fallen seraphim?
> Tell no more of enchanted days.
> Your eyes have set man's heart ablaze
> And you have had your will of him.
> Are you not weary of ardent ways?
> Above the flame the smoke of praise
> Goes up from ocean rim to rim.
> Tell no more of enchanted days.

17) Bend down your faces. Oona and Aleel.
> I gaze upon them as the swallow gazes
> Upon the nest under the eave before
> He wander the loud waters.

18) And when we are married,
> O, how happy we'll be
> For I love sweet Rosie O'Grady
> And Rosie O'Grady loves me.

This is the musical history of Stephen's state of separation, as expressed by the devices of typography, which can act as a kind of mechanical epiphany; Joyce uses it as such, in a spirit of parody, by presenting the whole of the chapter 'Eolus' in *Ulysses* as a newspaper layout.

In Joyce's work, the art of language is essentially connected with his theory of the epiphany, and inversely, the epiphany is itself a contributor to his linguistic experiments. Often a word is the key to the house of memory, or may precipitate the subject into a labyrinth of perception, as do the words "kiss" and "suck," or may take him further—into rebellion and its long-lasting consequences. Stephen's interview with the dean in Chapter V of *Portrait* takes place to the accompaniment of Stephen's own reflections, interacting with an almost allegorical epiphanisation of what is happening before him (with the sudden modification of his thought) and with flashes of imagination about his destiny, caused by the shock of particular words. The symbolic scene in which

Stephen and the dean discuss aesthetics in Thomist terms is composed
of two concurrent and parallel monologues, each of the speakers pursuing his own idea until some turn of phrase orients him suddenly towards
one or other of the superimposed themes of vocation, of the purpose
of art, and of the value of words. Stephen watches the shadowy figure
of the priest:

> Kneeling thus on the flagstone to kindle the fire and busied with the
> disposition of his wisps of paper and candle-butts he seemed more than
> ever a humble server making ready the place of sacrifice in an empty
> temple, a levite of the Lord. . . . His very body had waxed old in lowly
> service of the Lord—in tending fire upon the altar, in bearing tidings
> secretly, in waiting upon worldlings, in striking swiftly when bidden—and
> yet had remained ungraced by aught of saintly or prelatic beauty. (*Portrait*,
> pp. 184–5)

He thinks of the absence of fire and strength in this soul which should
be illuminated by its service of God: "a mortified will no more respon-
sive to the thrill of its obedience than was to the thrill of love or combat
his ageing body, spare and sinewy, greyed with a silver-pointed down."
(*Ibid.*)
        Yet the dean's practical activity, which is obviously quite fascinating
to him, forms an ironical counterpoint to Stephen's observation that "in
his eyes burned no spark of . . . enthusiasm". But he knows how to light
a fire, and "there is an art in lighting a fire. We have the liberal arts and
we have the useful arts. This is one of the useful arts".
        Stephen wishes to practise the liberal and disinterested art of writing.
As though to challenge the Jesuit on his own territory, he quotes Saint
Thomas to such effect that he at once confounds his adversary. But the
other wriggles out of his difficulty by provoking Stephen with his metaphorical and conventional description of the dangers of the artistic
vocation. As the exchange continues, Stephen adapts Aristotle in a
cavalier way, as well as Aquinas, and the dean, as though obsessed by
the real flames which the technician of the useful art has brought forth,
alludes to Epictetus and his lamp. From all this imagery of sparks and
hearth and ash and coals comes up a smell of molten tallow, which fuses
itself in Stephen's consciousness with the jingle of the dean's words,
"lamp and bucket, bucket and lamp".[2] The names of these utensils and
their sound hypnotise him, and bring him into that stasis where he is
ready to receive an epiphany. "The priest's voice, too, had a hard

---

[2]This may perhaps be a recollection of the ridiculous word-play, "soup and salad, salad
and soup," in *Tristram Shandy*.

jingling tone. Stephen's mind halted by instinct, checked by the strange tone and the imagery and by the priest's face which seemed like an unlit lamp or a reflector hung in a false focus" (*Portrait*, p. 187).

There is misunderstanding too; Stephen speaks of working "by the light of one or two ideas," and then extends the metaphor. "I need them only for my own use and guidance until I have done something for myself by their light. If the lamp smokes or smells I shall try to trim it. If it does not give light enough I shall sell it and buy another." *(Ibid.)*

Whereupon the Jesuit speaks of Epictetus' actual lamp. The real lamp and its metaphorical use in a rhetorical sense bring Stephen a momentary triumph, of which he proudly makes full use; he decides to explain to the dean the difference between a metaphor and a word used literally: "One difficulty, said Stephen, in aesthetic discussion is to know whether words are being used according to the literary tradition or according to the tradition of the marketplace." *(Ibid.)*

He gains some ground, he quotes Newman, causes a further confusion, and smiles . . . he is the legitimate owner of language, and the priest is but a powerless servant of the divine word.

Then, suddenly, the tables are turned in a way that has a profound effect on Stephen; the Jesuit returns to the lamp and to the oil-funnel:

—What funnel? asked Stephen.
—The funnel through which you pour the oil into your lamp.
—That? said Stephen. Is that called a funnel? Is it not a tundish?
—What is a tundish?
—That. The . . . funnel.
—Is that called a tundish in Ireland? asked the dean. I never heard the word in my life. (*Portrait*, p. 188)

Stephen is so humiliated that he feels the simple word has dispossessed him of all the culture whose treasures he was displaying for the priest's bedazzlement. Can this ageing, foolish, lightless Philistine have more right to their common language than he, Stephen Dedalus? He has to admit that this foreign language, which he loves, rejects him and fills him with unhappiness.

The epiphany dies down in shame. Yet, at the other end of the book, when Stephen is going out into artistic exile, he notes down in his journal for April 13 that he has regained the mastery of words, thus, "That tundish has been on my mind for a long time. I looked it up and find it English and good old blunt English too. Damn the dean of studies

and his funnel! What did he come here for to teach us his own language
or to learn it from us" (*Portrait*, p. 251).

In a sense, while *Stephen Hero* deals with aesthetic gestation, *Portrait*
is the gestation of a soul venturing among words, while in *Ulysses* and
after the sentence itself becomes the scene of experience. Finally, in
Finnegans Wake, the words themselves contain the meaning carried by
an ordinary sentence, while the linear construction of the latter is burst
asunder and replaced by a kind of verbal galaxy. At a certain level of
prose and of the artist's sensibility, the word and the perceptible appearance of the thing resuscitate similar visions, as though the word
itself were an object which one encountered and turned into epiphany.
The most brutal example of a word as object is found in the incident
where Stephen sees the word "foetus" engraved on a desk, and receives
a severe shock. Often a chain-reaction is set up, and a word calls up a
vision which, as it fades, calls up further words to mark its passage. Joyce
or the artist, because he is aware of this process, requires language more
and more to serve as his meeting-place with reality; he is constantly on
the watch for the word or fact which he feels he needs. The chaotic,
grey, ugly reality is repellent to him, and nothing would retain his
attention here or bind him at all to the present, were it not for the
epiphanies, which function as landmarks fixed by writing; in them the
difference between the self and the world is momentarily effaced, and
the image or fact or word enters into the artist, and he into the world,
in a brief mutual comprehension. To "comprehend" even the ugly is
the first step in art; it is the open door to beauty, which is the same as
the definition Stephen gives Lynch of the reconstitution of the epiphany by means of art:

> To speak of these things and to try to understand their nature and,
> having understood it, to try slowly and humbly and constantly to express,
> to press out again, from the gross earth or what it brings forth, from sound
> and shape and colour which are the prison gates of our soul, an image of
> the beauty we have come to understand—that is art. (*Portrait*, p. 206)

This technique the young Stephen had already tried out on language
itself; in *Stephen Hero* he tries to transform ordinary words into wonderful words, by eliminating what he calls "the hell of hells, the region
wherein everything is found to be obvious". He follows the opposite
path from that of the romantic visionary—but in the same romantic
spirit—seeking wonders not by way of banality but in the banal material
itself. "It was not only in Skeat that he found words for his treasure-

house, he found them also at haphazard in the shops, on advertisements, in the mouths of the plodding public. He kept repeating them
to himself, till they lost all instantaneous meaning for him and became
wonderful vocables" (*Stephen Hero*, p. 36).

The people of Dublin whom Stephen observes and follows in *Dubliners*, *Portrait*, and *Ulysses* can no longer see Ireland as it is. Objects are
divided into two categories: if they belong to the group which is sacred,
they are closed, full of their mystery and power, more respectable and
respected than the ordinary human being; if they are merely useful
objects, they stand without mystery, flat surfaces, invisible by dint of
their figurative nature.

Stephen wishes to invert the relationship between interior and surface, and to recover from holy objects their privileged profundity; the
epiphany is to be a revitalising devotion to the ordinary real. The clock
of the Ballast Office, which is the object chosen for the first demonstration of rehabilitating reality, is no longer just a machine that tells the
time, and in truth the time is no longer the time of Masses and Confessions, dividing life into daily ceremonies. The clock has a form, and
qualities which belong to it apart from its functional existence. It can
be looked at without the a priori establishment of a relationship which
makes it disappear, subordinate to its function.

The Doctrine of the Epiphany and its Context

When Joyce left the Church at the end of the nineteenth century, he
found himself caught up in cultural waves into which he enthusiastically
dived. His mind, formed by the discipline of scholasticism but inclined
to the euphoria of mysticism, hesitated between two literary currents:
one English, one European. He was sensible of the charms of decadent
prose—of Walter Pater, Oscar Wilde, and the French symbolists by way
of Arthur Symons—for it appealed to his taste for formal beauty which
had been temporarily eclipsed by his desertion of the Catholic religion.
Their Irish equivalents, the supporters of the "Celtic Revival," who
advocated what to him was a return to the childish babblings of early
art, turned him against this taste. From Europe came the realism of
Flaubert and Ibsen.

In his earliest essays[3] Joyce shows a preoccupation with realism,

[3]See above, our analyses of 'Drama and Life' (1900), 'Ibsen's New Drama' (1900), 'Day
of the Rabblement' (1901), and 'James Clarence Mangan' (1902).

which he defined as an approximation, as exact as possible, to psychological and historical truth. What he says in 1900, "life we must accept as we see it before our eyes, men and women as we meet them," he said thirty years later too in a conversation with Arthur Power: "Literature . . . should be life, and I remember that one of the things I could never get accustomed to in my youth was the difference I found that existed between life and literature."[4]

He confuses beauty at that time with the notion of it, propagated by Wilde and his circle, as something weakening, the search for which touches only the forms of things, producing a sickly, unhealthy art.

The truth has to be defined; it is not the scientific veracity of naturalism, nor a concession made to the general public by the artist, for the true artist, lover of truth or good, cannot but abhor the vile crowd. Truth is reserved for a select few, whose patrons are a philosopher, Giordano Bruno, and a poet, James Clarence Mangan. It seems that we are deserting the realism of Ibsen and drawing nearer to the symbolists, but Joyce points out the difference: Mangan carries imagination to the limits of the visionary. This might, indeed, be a mere repetition of Carlyle's ideas, and in the exaltation of artificial means of inspiration (such as the opium Mangan used to bring forth his world of magnificent and terrible images) we surely have a romantic commonplace, but Joyce builds it to a degree of intensity where what the poet-visionary perceives is not the bright hallucination but a luminous penetration of reality. The vision may be magnificent and exalting, but its object can be two Dublin old maids on a day's outing, or a butcher-boy's basket. When Joyce declares in his Italian lecture on Mangan in 1907 that "there are certain poets who, in addition to the virtue of revealing to us some phase of the human conscience . . . also have the more doubtful virtue of summing up in themselves the thousand contrasting tendencies of their era, of being, so to speak, the storage batteries of new forces," he is speaking of the poet as seer, but at the same time he is establishing the bond between truth and beauty. From this point of view, truth is only revealed through beauty; the good and the true remain separate, and beauty born of imagination is the only valid truth.

These floating, contradictory elements are soon to be fixed in a system which sets beauty in a definitive place, allotted by its real presence in life; in fact, Joyce was so impressed by Ibsen's absolute indifference to watchwords and to the established laws of art that he felt the necessity to construct a work which should define its own norms without paying

[4] *James Joyce Quarterly* III. 1, Autumn 1965, p. 43.

attention to the fixed laws, without being founded on some abstract cult of beauty. In his notebooks in Paris and in Pola, and in *Stephen Hero*, he worked out an aesthetic in which realism took on a Joycean aspect and the gleams of the decadent style remained only as influences on his prose. But at the heart of this theory with its scaffolding of scholastic forms there glows, like the roses that illumine every critical moment in *Portrait*, the notion of the epiphany, whose petals had already opened for Marius the Epicurean.

Walter Pater declares,[5] at the end of his essays on the Renaissance, that modern thought has come to regard "all things and principles of things as inconstant modes". Physical life is a perpetual motion of instincts and perceptions, and knowledge of the objective world is made up of ephemeral impressions that pass vaguely through our consciousness.[6] The vision of this fluid world is introduced by a quotation from Heraclitus. In this dissolving time, the purpose of life must be to retain for an instant as intense an impression as possible; the purpose of art must be to seize that instant and to represent it as it is. "Every moment some form grows perfect in hand or face; some tone on the hills or the sea is choicer than the rest; some mood of passion or insight or intellectual excitement is irresistibly real and attractive to us—for that moment only."

It is this instant in its uniqueness, says Pater, that gives life its value, that is "success in life". The instant is described as an "ecstasy," a "hard gemlike flame," using a vocabulary like that of Mallarmé, who also tried to grasp the ungraspable. And Pater adds, "Not the fruit of experience, but the experience itself, is the end". He defines this mode of living, this state of becoming, because he feels that the present-day consciousness is sinking amid a welter of "conflicting claims and entangled interests," and that the mind needs to understand itself and to find some unity again. His analysis of Leonardo de Vinci was particularly famous because he discovered Leonardo to be a modern insofar as he renders time personal and subjective. "He trifles with his genius, and crowds all his chief work into a few tormented years of later life": his work is based on his impressions and personal experiences, and his "realism" is founded on life. The Mona Lisa[7] expresses all passions of mankind in her mystery, and appears as "the symbol of the modern idea," since "mod-

[5]He is indirectly alluded to, though not named, in the early part of *Stephen Hero*.
[6]See Jerome Hamilton Buckley, *The Triumph of Time* (Harvard U.P., 1967), on the concepts of time, history, and progress in formation towards the end of the Victorian age.
[7]Pater's view of her may well have contributed to the blue-gold-ivory unreal image that inspires Stephen.

ern philosophy has conceived the idea of humanity as wrought upon by, and summing up in itself, all modes of thought and life". This instant, fixed for ever on canvas or in a phrase, is both unique and universal, being a visual or verbal *résumé* of the history of the human soul; it is a relative absolute, a miracle of contradiction, and as such illuminates Stephen's aesthetic concepts. It is obvious that this romantic idea makes art into the property of a privileged few souls, and that from this point of view the poet is indeed the intense centre of his age, the explorer to whom it is granted to contemplate the being of the visible world. But he is also the one who can seize this world, the one who guards its beauties and protects its values—who transmits reality through language.

So far Dedalus is a good disciple of Marius; but as soon as he has outstripped reality, he takes a different path. What he takes and fixes forever as art is not the beauty of a smile, the perfection of a colour, but *any* characteristic that sums up the world as it is in the raw state. The effect produced upon him by the epiphanies is still described in the style of Pater—"He received an impression keen enough to afflict his sensitiveness very severely"—but the cause is not a choice tone on the hills or the sea; it is the following dialogue:

> The Young Lady—(drawling discreetly) . . . O, yes . . . I was . . . at the . . . cha . . . pel . . .
> The Young Gentleman—(inaudibly) . . . I . . . (again inaudibly) . . . I . . .
> The Young Landy—(softly) . . . O . . . but you're . . . ve . . . ry . . . wick . . . ed . . . (*Stephen Hero*, p. 216)

The first epiphanies Joyce collected were slow dismembered dialogues, trivial phrases, verbal tics, and dreams, and they are signs of the world as he perceives it: "This triviality made him think of collecting many such moments together in a book of epiphanies. By an epiphany he meant a sudden spiritual manifestation, whether in the vulgarity of speech or of gesture or in a memorable phase of the mind itself". *(Ibid.)*

The world thus revealed is neither beautiful nor exalting nor unduly promising; it is weak and invalid, stricken by aphasia. The situation of the poet is indeed at the centre of life, but the mission of the poet to "fling abroad amid planetary music" his discoveries meets inevitably, and clashes with, the ugliness of the object discovered. Even if in its origins the epiphany is still noble, even if it retains its quality of spiritual revelation, the realistic intention which the young artist has learned from Flaubert and Ibsen causes him, as he emerges from the world of ecstasies and inward joys, to take cognisance of the difference in quality between aesthetic experience and practical experience. In fact, if in *Stephen Hero* the discrepancy is not emphasised because the heart of the book consists rather of a pursuit of aesthetic principles, in *Portrait* there are epiphanies whose power is completely that of irony, showing how the process of epiphany can be painful, as well as the exalting happiness that Pater portrays.

Stephen is able to absorb himself in making an inner inventory of all his treasures of knowledge, philosophy and poetry, until the outer world disappears: "His thinking was a dusk of doubt and self-mistrust, lit up at moments by the lightnings of intuition, but lightnings of so clear a splendour that in those moments the world perished about his feet as if it had been fire-consumed" (*Portrait*, p. 176).

This happens because he feels "that the spirit of beauty had folded him round like a mantle"; this metaphor conceals really a flight far from reality, which he has rejected as he has rejected the possibilities of ecstasy, "by an angry toss of his head . . . stumbling through the mouldering offal, his heart already bitten by an ache of loathing and bitterness". The epiphany here has all the intensity of the aesthete's flight, of the feeling the soul has of being "loosed of her miseries". There is no question of flinging abroad amid planetary music the discord of Dublin, but simply of taking refuge in the unreal world of art.

At once, then, a second paradox becomes clear; the first was that of the sudden conjunction in a flash of realism and of its spiritual transposition by means of writing, and the second is that the epiphany as a way of confronting reality may also constitute a flight or escape from the real. Reality has a maleficent power conferred by its very trivial and inane nature, and the revelation of the void eventually wears out the soul who undergoes it. Stephen Hero can make notes on Dublin as though he were a mere observer or a stranger, but Dedalus is caught in the city's net; he turns this feeling of belonging into an epiphany of objective and ironical character, realising that what appears before him can only with difficulty be considered a vision of beauty in itself. "He found himself glancing from one casual word to another on his right or left in stolid wonder that they had been so silently emptied of instantaneous sense until every mean shop legend bound his mind like the words of a spell and his soul shrivelled up sighing with age" (*Portrait*, p. 178).

The relationship between reality and art has changed since the time of *Stephen Hero*; the epiphany which was directed from object to subject seems in *Portrait* to have acquired some autonomy of movement, so that on occasions it is the subject who is revealed by the method in which the revelation of reality is made. The distance between subject and reality has also grown less.

The "objective" epiphany also provides the dull gleams perceptible in *Dubliners*; the origin of many of the novellas, as is well known, was a real fact or happening such as the death of a slightly crazy old priest, a domestic scene, the meeting of two friends, and that reality is set into a narrative and descriptive context composed of accumulated details whose very insignificance eventually takes on meaning. The accumulation of the banal often means nothing more than itself, as in the French novel of the present day boredom is communicated by a form which is productive of boredom, or mystery by a form which misleads. But in this insignificance of Dublin life there is something uncanny, and the repetition of colours, vague emotions, and key words eventually brings us to a moment when reality seems to break under the strain of misfortune, just long enough for us to perceive the abyss below. The epiphany in *Dubliners* springs from the artist's work on the material of time; the emotional curves of the stories imitate the gestation of an awareness that is awakening gradually to the knowledge of its own misery. Thus, in 'The Sisters,' the epiphany extends throughout the story, from the first words with their evocation of futile waiting and fascination to the last slow and funereal scene which also tells, in a low voice, of void and futility. The reader is hypnotised by the evenness of the surface, by the nervous intensity and by the unanswered riddles, until he too comes to share in the lethargy of the world depicted. On the contrary, the passage of time in 'Eveline' has the quick, staccato quality of a frightened animal's breathing, as memories and plans clash, and the scenes of the past eventually cover the present with dust; the attempt to escape towards freedom, life, and "perhaps love, too" ends in shipwreck of the heart, with Eveline's lifeless body gripping the barrier that separates her from the ship. The epiphany gains in irony by its imagery of fear; the real waters that were to carry her to freedom bring imaginary waves "about her heart" to drown her, and the prose narrative forms its unbroken surface again over the girl and her anguish. Rhythms, broken by moments of horror (Chandler's tears, Corley's smile, Polly's sighs, or Farrington's cries of anger), find their final expression in 'The Dead,' which Joyce was writing at the same time as he was rewriting *Portrait*. In 'The Dead,' there is no one climactic instant, but a series and accumulation of revelatory moments. The artist does not only have to "disentangle the subtle soul of the image from its mesh of defining circumstances most exactly and re-embody it in artistic circumstances chosen as the most exact for it in its new office" (*Stephen Hero*, p. 82).

The whole long novella is a single epiphany of multiple meaning (death in life, life in death, the presence of death, evocation of the dead, all the forms a mind could invent for the imagining of death, or as means of avoiding the notion), and it is furthermore composed of a host of epiphanies which are all the more refined in that they have both a "soul disentangled from the mesh" of circumstances and a constructive part to play within the whole. The longest and most subtle of these images that form, as it were, a microcosm within the larger setting, is that which Gabriel imagines and conceives as a painting; first there is a zone of silence in a babble of voices, and it isolates a strange image, disturbing by the simplicity of its mystery:

> He was in a dark part of the hall gazing up the staircase. A woman was standing near the top of the first flight, in the shadow also. He could not see her face but he could see the terra-cotta and salmon-pink panels of her skirt which the shadow made appear black and white. It was his wife. She was leaning on the banisters, listening to something.

Gabriel is surprised as he spies on this woman and he is himself two men at once: both the husband and the sensitive intellectual who is able to detach a beautiful or a moving image from its context in order to give it its unique value. The recognition of the woman as his wife, given that he cannot see her face, and that he is looking up from below, may simply be an example of slowness to interpret sense-data, but it is also the second stage of the epiphany; when he sees "a woman," he passes through the phase that Stephen calls *integritas*. The aesthetic image is perceived as a whole, clearly delimited upon a spatial area. Then Gabriel apprehends it in its complexity, multiple, divisible, separable, harmonious, and finally he sees that the woman is "his wife," an object that abruptly reveals its inner self while absorbed in mysterious contemplation. Fascinated by the epiphany, he stands motionless. "The luminous silent stasis of aesthetic pleasure, a spiritual state very like to that cardiac condition which the Italian physiologist Luigi Galvani, using a phrase almost as beautiful as Shelley's, called the enchantment of the heart" (*Portrait*, p. 213).

The epiphany continues as Gabriel himself, standing there motionless and fascinated, becomes an object of it, his thoughts forming yet another kind of revelation:

He stood still in the gloom of the hall. . . . gazing up at his wife. There was grace and mystery in her attitude as if she were a symbol of something. He asked himself what is a woman standing on the stairs in the shadow, listening to distant music, a symbol of. If he were a painter he would paint her in that attitude. Her blue felt hat would show off the bronze of her hair against the darkness and the dark panels of her skirt would show off the light ones. *Distant Music* he would call the picture if he were a painter.

The picture *Distant Music* is a reproduction in miniature of the situation as experienced in real life. Through it "the enchantment of the heart" is propagated from echo to image.

Henceforth the image is no longer isolated, but is caught in a network of other images which are not luminous appearances manifesting the meaning of reality, but rather the appearance which the artist confers upon reality as he has perceived it. Gabriel stops to reflect for a moment on the stairs, and the reader sees not only what Gabriel sees, but also what lies beyond; the scene is not detached and isolated as it is for Gabriel, but has meaning in a wider, carefully constructed whole. Gabriel is still in the present and the world of reality, suspended a moment in contemplation of revealed beauty, but the artist can take us, "by the syllogism of art," as Dedalus would say, from one world to another. Gabriel expresses a certain quantity of meanings, but what we grasp from present objects is always their unexpressed meaning.

The moment of "distant music," whose meanings become clearer and more profound because of the proximity of various details (such as the picture of Romeo and Juliet hanging on the drawing-room wall, in front of which pass the dancing couples without glancing at it), has an almost tragic counterpart at the end of the novella; epiphany through music takes on an unexpected fullness of meaning when the emotional processes that have brought it to its *claritas* and maturity are repeated inversely as Gabriel passes from fascination and hope to loneliness and separation. He is with Gretta in their hotel room; in the dark, feverish with desire for "the touch of her body, musical and strange and perfumed". He could have thrown his arms round her hips and held her as she walked up the stairs, but the porter was there; he had to drive his nails into the palms of his hands. This woman is a woman, and his wife. And yet when she turns to him, musical, strange, and perfumed, she is listening to other voices and not his; she is still listening in the dark alone, strange and distant as she was on the stairs in the darkness. "Why did she seem so abstracted? He did not know how he could begin. Was she annoyed, too, about something? If she would only turn to him or come to him of her own accord! To take her as she was would be brutal.

No, he must see some ardour in her eyes first. He longed to be master of her strange mood."

But now comes the moment of reversed epiphany. She breaks loose from him, and, running to the bed, hides her face. Gabriel stands petrified with astonishment for a moment and then follows her. As he moves towards her, this weeping woman, he notices himself in the mirror, and the image catches his attention; "his broad, well-filled shirt-front, the face whose expression always puzzled him when he saw it in a mirror, and his glimmering gilt-rimmed eye-glasses" fling him back into the ordinary world in which he is not the consumptive young lover but "a nervous, well-meaning sentimentalist, orating to vulgarians and idealising his own clownish lusts". A series of key-moments follows this first feeling of horror inspired by oneself; successive paragraphs widen the moment of awareness from shameful egoism to pity, equanimity, solidarity in grief, communion with others far and near, dead or alive, until to the accompaniment of a verbal music the soul that had perceived its outward appearance in the mirror is dissolved in that one and only phase of time when the boundaries between life and death are buried under the snow, swooning into sleep. The separation of Gabriel and Gretta is described in serious tones, but with the same universalising of the particular that we find also in the more vulgar separation between Molly and Poldy Bloom.

> He watched her while she slept, as though he and she had never lived .together as man and wife. His curious eyes rested long upon her face and on her hair: and, as he thought of what she must have been then, in that time of her first girlish beauty, a strange, friendly pity for her entered his soul. He did not like to say even to himself that her face was no longer beautiful, but he knew that it was no longer the face for which Michael Furey had braved death.

In that moment of pity and knowledge, Gabriel again reaches the luminous stasis, the enchantment of the heart that suspends death for an instant. He is ridiculous and unattractive; she is no longer what she was; Michael is forever the seventeen-year-old boy in the snow; and they are all dead. Joyce has here contrived not only to detach the images from their spatial context, but also to develop two parallel movements of images against a temporal background, and it perhaps is the height of this revelatory art to have transformed 'The Dead' into "the radiant body of everliving life". Art no longer consists simply of reproducing vision or dialogue, but itself generates visions—even a certain vision of reality transmuted to epiphany. Joyce has passed from the isolated note collected and preserved in a notebook to the creation by the artist of an organic form, and the epiphany is no longer the apparition of the "quidditas" of an object, supposing an objective structure and available to all, but the final term in a verbal strategy arranged by the artist, giving the object a designated place of its own in a composite pattern of events and emotions.

The structure of *Dubliners*, whose meanings are made clearer by the introductory or final epiphanies, shows that Joyce's intention was to experiment with the help of this notion, the aesthetic import of which he had already determined for himself; the result is a suggestive realism, apparently objective, which suits his purposes very well. He had wished to write a chapter in the moral history of the Dubliners, and to show them their collective portrait in the mirror of a prose style that imitated them. But once the purpose in hand is to paint a Portrait of the Artist, objective revelation of reality has no more importance; modifications in the vision of reality exemplify the character's own growth and development. The epiphany, insofar as it still exists in *Portrait*, changes its nature, or rather is divided into two: Stephen the artist adopts it for his own use, and quotes some specimen epiphanies, either as illustrations of his own theory or else because certain objective phenomena do really take place before his eyes—to this class belong the stained table that we see at the beginning of Chapter V and the cries of the mad nun in the convent garden. But to Joyce the epiphany of an object is no longer a special, privileged moment, since the material being placed under observation is less reality than the language itself. To begin with, these sudden illuminations, supposed to proceed from the inner self of the object, were contrasted with the conjunction of words and objects in the outside world. Later on the real world disintegrates, and the artist's experiences become more and more subjective, and even almost incommunicable. The epiphanies in *Portrait* tend towards inversion, many of them being dreams or hallucinations, and as such closer to symbolism than to suggestive realism. They form part of the artist's different states of mind, and sometimes he does not attempt to integrate them into a whole or to draw out their meaning; they remain unexplainable and obscure like the dream noted down in the journal at the end of *Portrait*:

> *March 25, morning.* A troubled night of dreams. Want to get them off my chest.
> A long curving gallery. From the floor ascend pillars of dark vapours. It

is peopled by the images of fabulous kings, set in stone. Their hands are folded upon their knees in token of weariness and their eyes are darkened for the errors of men go up before them for ever as dark vapours.

Strange figures advance as from a cave. They are not as tall as men. One does not seem to stand quite apart from another. Their faces are phosphorescent, with darker streaks. They peer at me and their eyes seem to ask me something. They do not speak. (*Portrait*, pp. 249–50)

This dream, transcribed without comment, is in fact one of Joyce's own.[8] The unconscious is allowed to speak, or rather the unconscious produces wordless images; this is a recognition by Joyce of the existence of non-verbal zones, but also an absolute negation of the original definition of "epiphany" as the *claritas* of an object or emotion. One may, reading *Ulysses*, retrospectively shed light on this gallery of idols and see them as the dead generations of petty Celtic kinglets and the dream as the image of History as Nightmare; but there is no proof of this, and no contextual justification for thus limiting and "reincarnating" the vision. In fact, by the end of *Portrait*, Joyce has ceased to believe in the epiphany, its spiritual connotations being opposed to the practice, in his life and in his work, of a progressive detachment. It becomes impossible for him to believe in a kind of autonomy of reality as it may be objectively manifested.

In *Portrait* he is operating a synthesis between two notions which until then had been separate in his mind, and which he had been elaborating along Aristotelian lines in his Paris and Pola notebooks: the ideas of aesthetic pleasure and of the suspension of the passions. In his Paris notebook, on the pretext of defining the superiority of comedy to tragedy (comedy causes joy, hence satisfaction),[9] he emphasises the necessity for a "stasis" of the emotions if artistic creation is to take place.

In his Pola notebook, beginning with a phrase from Saint Thomas, *"Bonum est in quod tendit appetitus,"* Joyce declares that if only the good is desirable, then, since the true and the beautiful are the most persistent orders of the desirable, the true and the beautiful are good. Then, beginning from the famous phrase, *"Pulchra sunt quae visa pla-*

[8]See *My Brother's Keeper*, p. 135: "My brother's purpose was different and his angle of vision new. The revelation and importance of the subconscious had caught his interest. The epiphanies became more frequently subjective and included dreams which he considered in some way revelatory. Some of these 'epiphanies' he introduced here and there into *A Portrait of the Artist* where the occasion offered and some into the imaginary diary at the end."

[9]He also defines pity and terror, but without referring to Aristotle's *Poetics*, as though he had not yet read the work.

cent," and modifying it slightly, he says that every thing the apprehension of which pleases is beautiful; since the "pleasure" involved is purely an intellectual satisfaction, a judgement is made upon the object perceived, whether it is "beautiful" or "ugly," and as a result of this judgement the object satisfies, if it possesses a form realised in matter and if it has attained formal perfection in its category. "Even the most hideous object may be said to be beautiful for this reason as it is *a priori* said to be beautiful in so far as it encounters the activity of simple perception" (*Workshop*, p. 82).

The difference between the beautiful and the ugly may be measured by the nature, duration, and degree of the satisfaction resultant from the apprehension of any sensible object. Aesthetic apprehension has three types of activity: that of cognition of simple perception, that of recognition (which is the act of judgement), and that of satisfaction. The notion of "satisfaction" goes beyond Aquinas' notion of "pleasing," for Joyce is trying to bring this theory of the necessary "stasis" (expounded as a result of analysing dramatic forms) into conjunction with his theory of *claritas* or radiance, both being the supreme goal of art. The "satisfaction" involved is the feeling of plenitude or perfection produced by the appeasement of desire or emotion, as joy is the ecstasy in which pity and terror disappear. Aristotle is interpreted in a rather unorthodox manner, since a stasis takes the place of his dynamic catharsis in which the soul purifies itself of its passions by an intermediary.

In *Portrait*, under the protection of Aristotle in disguise and "applied Aquinas," Stephen invents a formula in which satisfaction and stasis are united in the "luminous silent stasis of aesthetic pleasure". The suspension of emotions, light, and silence distil into those mysterious moments of time when nothing has yet been said, when the word, heard but unexpressed, still fears the destructive contact that being actualised would involve—the moments Shelley speaks of in his *Defence of Poesy*. Joyce does not hesitate to move from the almost therapeutic rationalism of Aristotle to the mystic experience of the romantic poet; he finds himself at the other limit of language, on the boundaries of the ineffable, close to that absent but guessed-at word that so charmed the symbolists, and the epiphany comes forth from an ordered mediaeval universe in which everything has its place, meaning, and function, whose imaginary representation could be made into a three-dimensional model. From now on it is the subjective transposition of one moment of spiritual espousal: the artist "sees" the object in such a way that his action is one of possession rather than of recognition, and this is at once followed by the extinction of the static light and by a feeling of despair and dispossession. This is described by Joyce in his account of the composition of the villanelle in Chapter V of *Portrait;* the artist, in order to retain a minute part of his vision of that reality, makes haste to write, while he still feels beating within him the tides of emotion aroused by the verses. The epiphany has become—not a discovery of the world any more—but the moment of gathering and peace prior to the creative act.

In this way, the notion analysed by Stephen in *Portrait* becomes entirely subjective. We seem far from *Dubliners* here, and yet it is of a book of this kind that the young man seems to be thinking when he goes "to encounter for the millionth time the reality of experience and to forge in the smithy of [his] soul the uncreated conscience of [his] race". How can he forge the collective conscience if he starts from a subjective experience which is practically incommunicable—unless he believes what Stephen never says he believes, namely, that "life" and "art" are nothing but purely artistic creations? The *Portrait* shows us the gestation of a sensibility rather than of an aesthetic. Joyce no longer believes what Stephen professes, even if he loans him his own old notebooks.

When Joyce finished *Portrait,* he had already been thinking for a number of years about *Ulysses.* The fictitious date of the latter, 16 June 1904, sets it a few months after the end of *Portrait,* and it is possible to estimate how much the artist has matured in those months by considering the mocking phrases in the scene on the beach which form his commentary on existence: the style is new and Protean, and seems to belong to a different world and a different generation from those inhabited by the disciple of Pater. "Remember your epiphanies on green oval leaves, deeply deep, copies to be sent if you died to all the great libraries of the world?" (*Ulysses*, p. 42–3).

This is not Lynch's teacher speaking now; but perhaps Stephen was already mocking, if not his researches, at least the outdated forms of his theory, which made it unusable for *Ulysses*—in which reality in all its diversity appears against a background of myth and culture rather than of space and time.

The Evolution of the Notion of Epiphany

It may well be asked whether from the outset it was not obvious that the epiphany would evolve towards the rendering of subjective reality

which it became. An early epiphany, preserved by Stanislaus, already
has this mixed nature:

> Dull clouds have covered the sky. Where three roads meet and before
> a swampy beach a big dog is recumbent. From time to time he lifts his
> muzzle and utters a prolonged sorrowful howl. People stop to look at him
> and pass on; some remain, arrested, it may be, by that lamentation in
> which they seem to hear the utterance of their own sorrow, that had once
> its voice but is now voiceless, a servant of laborious days. Rain begins to
> fall. (*My Brother's Keeper*, p. 136)

The first striking characteristic of this piece is the lack of logical or
necessary connection between the scene-setting, the scene, and the
occurrence. But this may have no meaning. A dog is howling—only a
dog; but people stop to look, and some of them even recognise themselves in the dog. And now a passage is opened up between object and
subject, or rather, the difference between them is abolished. There is
no more distance between object and subject, and the dog's howling
becomes a wordless voice of human grief. The epiphany makes its
revelation in a language without words; any words that are heard are
those the subject attributes to the object. Curiously enough, people
stop, as though concretely to carry out that stasis which emotionally
corresponds to their recognition of the phenomenon. And the artist's
work is to comprehend the extent and the significance of the scene, to
reproduce the sad eloquence of silences and howls. It is as though the
dog or the object were expressing the very souls of the passers-by; in
their act of recognition there is tacitly a surprised admission of the fact
that it is the world that expresses man, and not man who makes the
world by his word. When King Claudius in *Hamlet* sees the actors
playing out the secrets of his inner life, this is "normal," but when a dog
howls thus for the sake of humanity, it becomes more sad and frightening. From the beginning the epiphany has a potential capability for
personalisation which develops until it can reverse the relationship that
previously existed: that of the subject receiving some manifestation
from the object.[10]

Portrait offers several instances of this reduction of the distance between the self and the world; in some cases the distance is completely
annihilated, as it is at the time of that spiritual crisis that so strongly
affects the young man's awareness and separates him from reality by

[10]This fable of the dog recalls Kafka and the objectivity of the subject in *Metamorphosis*.

means of the concept of sin. The world loses its concrete, real, and limited characteristics because Stephen feels that he has been shut out from the world; his guilt, projected on to reality, destroys it. His feelings of alienation, his inability to join in the group activities of his contemporaries, are expressed physically in fits of dizziness; his legs feel weak, and he staggers—the world on which he treads is unsteady. His fear of Hell transforms the whole outside world into a hell, and the sickness that afflicts reality at once infects language; words seem to get out of control, and he hears:

> We knew perfectly well of course that though it was bound to come to the light he would find considerable difficulty in endeavouring to try to induce himself to try to endeavour to ascertain the spiritual plenipotentiary and so we knew of course perfectly well. . . . (*Portrait*, p. 136)

> Soft language issued from their spittleless lips as they swished in slow circles round and round the field, winding hither and thither through the weeds, dragging their long tails amid the rattling canisters. They moved in slow circles, circling closer and closer to enclose, to enclose, soft language issuing from their lips, their long swishing tails besmeared with stale shite, thrusting upwards their terrific faces. . . . Help! (*Portrait*, p. 138)

He sees an apocalyptic vision when the time comes for him to "say in words" all that he has done. "His blood began to murmur in his veins, murmuring like a sinful city summoned from its sleep to hear its doom. Little flakes of fire fell and powdery ashes fell softly, alighting on the houses of men. They stirred, waking from sleep, troubled by the heated air. The slide was shot back. The penitent emerged from the side of the box" (*Portrait*, p. 142).

In these incoherent moments, the epiphany becomes merely subjective, being perceived by the neurotic mind and disturbed senses of the actor or victim, rather than by the reader; the transition to the world of delirium from the ordinary world is made without warning. There is an anguished continuity between the two "realities," which is probably maintained by the power that language has for Stephen, for the form of his mind is such that he has adopted the habit of turning his active or outward life into inner life by means of verbal commentary or meditation which he makes to himself; since he was a child, his secret existence has proceeded in this way—in the parallelism between his words and reality which marks him out as a potential writer. This same disposition, which causes him always to hold back a little from what is happening and to relate events to himself by means of words, also permits a dislocation of the awareness in moments of crisis; he continues to speak and to tell his own tale, but he has difficulty in resuming contact with reality. Everything, including his own room, becomes alien to him, and objects no longer make epiphany in communion with him, but manifest their own different and unrecognisable "soul," "A doorway, a room, the same room, same window. He told himself calmly that those words had absolutely no sense which had seemed to rise murmurously from the dark. He told himself that it was simply his room with the door open" (*Portrait*, p. 136).

The boundaries are abolished; concrete and abstract become interchangeable: "His sins trickled from his lips, one by one, trickled in shameful drops from his soul, festering and oozing like a sore, a squalid stream of vice. The last sins oozed forth, sluggish, filthy" (*Portrait*, p. 144).

Words turn into objects, as objects are made slaves to words, and shameful thoughts cover his soul with a fine layer of ashes. At last, God Himself addresses Stephen in an hallucinatory experience so close to reality that it seems almost comical: "Yes? What? Yes? . . . A wave of fire swept through his body: the first. Again a wave. His brain began to glow. Another. His brain was simmering and bubbling within the cracking tenement of the skull. Flames burst forth from his skull like a corolla, shrieking like voices: Hell!" (*Portrait*, p. 125).

This supreme epiphany takes on a new ironical aspect when Stephen later hears a nebulous music floating from the clouds that pass over Ireland in "one long-drawn calling note, piercing like a star the dusk of silence. Again! Again! Again! A voice from beyond the world was calling" (*Portrait*, p. 168).

The two separate epiphanies, the one hellish and the other angelic, come together in symmetry, in *consonantia*, or even in discord.

In *Portrait* the epiphanies often assume a visionary aspect which still recalls their spiritual origins; but the close connection of apparition and language is already indicative of the direction *Ulysses* and *Finnegans Wake* are to take.

The seeds of the delirious pantomime and language of 'Circe'—the chapter in which Joyce makes a game of destroying and disfiguring all the psychological, moral, and aesthetic meanings and connotations hitherto assembled in his work—are to be found in *Portrait*. He turns madness and mockery loose in order to make a clean sweep, in order to invent a space in language in which to write *Finnegans Wake*. As early as *Portrait*, his style reflects the disturbances from which the self suffers, and the confusion between exterior and interior, between thought and action, and the pathological phenomena of 'Circe' are basically only extreme forms of the epiphany. The doorhandle that says "Theeee" accusingly to the guilty Bloom in 'Circe' belongs to a world in which objects abruptly begin to speak and to manifest themselves in mad epiphanies, giving forth meanings which have nothing to do with the *integritas* of the object, but rather with the disfigurements the subject attributes to the object. "The grey block of Trinity on his left, set heavily in the city's ignorance like a dull stone set in a cumbrous ring, pulled his mind downward . . . he was striving this way and that to free his feet from the fetters of the reformed conscience" (*Portrait*, p. 179).

Even the disembodied voices, heard in the absence of any speaker and coming from one knows not where, are reminiscent of the auditory hallucinations suffered by Bloom in the house of Circe; and the procession of ghosts that passes through a history lesson ("Royal persons, favourites, intriguers, bishops, passed like mute phantoms behind their veil of names. All had died: all had been judged") reappears in a grotesque form as the vision of King Edward and the crowd of citizens around Bloom or Stephen in 'Circe'.

In fact, the history of Stephen's resistance to the outside world makes it clear that the artist lets himself become more and more deeply affected by dreams and fantasies, whose clash with reality becomes in its turn productive of epiphanies; thus, every vision is roughly interrupted by a relapse into the sordid or vulgar, as though reality were manifesting itself more powerfully than the romantic imagination can. Stephen can abandon himself willingly to the unreal world, since he is assured of a brief stay there and of a necessary return to this world.

'Applied Aquinas' and Irony

"I will tell you what I will do and what I will not do. I will not serve that in which I no longer believe, whether it call itself my home, my fatherland, or my church; and I will try to express myself in some mode of life or art as freely as I can and as wholly as I can, using for my defence the only arms I allow myself to use—silence, exile, and cunning" (*Portrait*, p. 247).

The young man states his intention of no longer serving the established order, no matter what disguise it assumes, and of expressing himself completely and freely, using spiritual weapons only. Stephen, like Joyce, always admits that he is the product of his race, of his country, and of his formation in the "school of old Aquinas". If he wishes to express himself "wholly," he must express himself as he has been made by that in which he no longer believes. This might anger him, but in fact does not. He is determined not to serve home, fatherland, or Church, but to make use of them for the expression of himself in his life and art.[11]

From Saint Thomas, Joyce borrows the foundations of a large part of his aesthetic theory. His need for order and his need for freedom are reconciled in the pleasure he derives from obtaining for his art the benefits offered by an ethical vision of the world. His use of the Thomist order and rejection of the faith that inspired it guarantee sufficienctly his freedom to form "a theory of art which was at once severe and liberal. His Aesthetic was in the main applied Aquinas, and he set it forth plainly with a naif air of discovering novelties. This he did partly to satisfy his own taste for enigmatic roles and partly from a genuine predisposition in favour of all but the premises of scholasticism" (*Stephen Hero*, p. 81).

Stephen does not, however, make direct and exclusive use of Saint Thomas; his aesthetic is neither Thomist nor orthodox, but a combination of characteristics borrowed from theories of his own times and skilfully annotated quotations from Aquinas. It may be asked to what extent had Joyce already determined the form of his conclusions, justifying them afterwards by an apparently honest chain of deductive reasoning. In the reasonably extensive field covered by his reflections, what seems to concern him most is a certain definition of the artist's function and of his mediating situation between art and the world, followed by the elaboration—by way of his definition of beauty—of a new form of art whose essence is the theory of the epiphany (which was originally a rather artificial addition to the rest of his theories).

One whole section of the meditations of Stephen has no interest for the reader apart from the eventual justification it provides for the theme of the artist as absent from his work. It is rigorously worked out in *Portrait*, along the lines of the more hesitant version introduced in *Stephen Hero*, and is based on the idea that art can be divided into three

[11]In *Stephen Hero* he is even more explicit: he says to Cranly in the course of their conversation about religion, "I am a product of Catholicism. I was sold to Rome before my birth. Now I have broken my slavery but I cannot in a moment destroy every feeling in my nature."

main types—lyric, epic, dramatic—according to the relationship between the artist and the image he is presenting. The interest of this theory lies less in its content (which presents a classical tripartite division derived from Aristotle's *Poetics*, 1447 a, b, 1456–62 a and b), than in its formulation, which is very close to Joyce's first essay on Mangan, for example (which in its style is still under the influences of Pater, as were Stephen's first artistic outpourings too).

In *Stephen Hero*, Stephen declares that art is the disposition of intelligible or sensible matter for an aesthetic end, the disposition falling into one of "three distinct natural kinds, lyrical, epical and dramatic. Lyrical art, he said, is the art whereby the artist sets forth his image in immediate relation to himself; epical art is the art whereby the artist sets forth his image in immediate relation to himself and to others; and dramatic art is the art whereby the artist sets forth his image in immediate relation to others." *(Ibid.)*

What interests the young man more than anything else at this moment is the attainment of his own definition of "the relations which must subsist between the literary image, the work of art itself, and that energy which had imagined and fashioned it, that centre of conscious, re-acting, particular life, the artist" (*Stephen Hero*, p. 82).

It is clear that the hero is fascinated by this centre of energy; and it may be that the artist is seen as the hero of modern times, as Carlyle sees him. But Stephen sees him as mediator between the world of his experience and the world of his dreams. Yet, aware of the dangers of "spiritual anarchy," he still takes great pains to acknowledge the importance of the classical style, by means of which one can pass from one world to another. The temper of classical art is here defined as "security and satisfaction and patience," and its way leads to the concept of the epiphany as luminous stasis.

The bare, brief definitions of the earlier book are replaced in *Portrait* by a long, flamboyant speech from Stephen, which *follows* the theory of the epiphany and adds nothing to it; the order of its development is probably dictated by Joyce's wish to end his series of manifestoes on the famous comparison of the artist to an indifferent God.

> The lyrical form is in fact the simplest verbal vesture of an instant of emotion, a rhythmical cry such as ages ago cheered on the man who pulled at the oar or dragged stones up a slope. He who utters it is more conscious of the instant of emotion than of himself as feeling emotion. The simplest epical form is seen emerging out of lyrical literature when the artist prolongs and broods upon himself as the centre of an epical event and this form progresses till the centre of emotional gravity is equidistant from the

artist himself and from others. The narrative is no longer purely personal.
. . . The personality of the artist, at first a cry or a cadence or a mood and
then a fluid and lambent narrative, finally refines itself out of existence, so
to speak. The aesthetic image in the dramatic form is life purified in and
re-projected from the human imagination. The mystery of aesthetic, like
that of material creation, is accomplished. The artist, like the God of creation, remains within or behind or beyond or above his handiwork, invisible,
refined out of existence, indifferent, paring his fingernails. (*Portrait*, pp.
214–5)

It will be observed that the *fin-de-siècle* terminology that was absent
from *Stephen Hero* here harmonizes with the next episode, which concerns inspiration, and is in direct contrast with what immediately follows this speech, which Lynch calls "prating about beauty and the
imagination". The reality of the rain and of the undergraduates' banal
conversation puts beauty in its place, he feels; and Stephen remains in
a state of non-divine absence, "emptied of theory and courage, lapsed
back into a listless peace".

The theme of the impersonal artist is taken from a tradition which
was represented at the end of the nineteenth century by a number of
people, including Flaubert and Yeats; but it also corresponded to an
almost instinctive personal attitude peculiar to Joyce, who protected his
sensibility by an affected indifference and admired the aloof haughtiness of his heroes Parnell and Ibsen. In *Stephen Hero* he expresses in
terms of epiphany the delight he felt on encountering "the spirit of
Ibsen". "The minds of the old Norse poet and of the perturbed young
Celt met in a moment of radiant simultaneity" (*Stephen Hero*, p. 45).
All past drama, including Hindu, Greek, and Chinese plays in translation, seems to him merely an anticipation of Ibsen's genius. The dramatic form is the most perfect form of art, insofar as the artist's vitality
confers an autonomous existence on the men and women of his invention. Once this mystery has been accomplished the artist simply has to
withdraw. Joyce felt that Ibsen had attained excellence in this form.

And yet it was not this excellence alone that captivated him: "It was
not only the excellence . . . which he greeted gladly with an entire joyful
spiritual salutation. It was the very spirit of Ibsen himself that was
discerned moving behind that impersonal manner of the artist." *(Ibid.)*

The artist's "impersonality" means for Joyce his "invisibility," his
absence as commentator, but this does not imply that art should be
"objective". On the contrary, even in the most impersonal form, the
drama, there is the expression of a spirit which is sensed through its

creation. The artist creates the world, starting out from a personal and critical vision of reality, and this is what resolves the passage, or (as Stephen would say) the "mediation," from one world to another, and the definition of a realism that is marked by the god hidden within. Joyce had first conceived the problem of the two worlds in romantic terms: there was the real world which his intelligence showed him in all its sordid and deceptive details and there was the world of the artist's dreams—the monster in him and the hero in him. He felt overwhelmed by the impossibility of reconciling the two, and wondered how to live in two worlds that were foreign to each other, when he found his saving revelation in Ibsen: the second world must not be the world of dreams, but the dramatic and "dis-illusioned" form of reality. The artist may be "personal" and give his creation his own vital energy, and still stay *outside* this recreated existence. He has here a way of expressing himself without being caught in the form of expression; the work is to be an imitation of life that replaces life, closing in upon itself and forming a world that has its own system of references within itself, not aspiring to a more lovely life but finding its perfection in its own complete comprehensiveness.

Saint Thomas does not contradict or weaken this theory, and so Joyce deduces that he confirms it—a view neither true nor false. It is true that the "artist" has no privileged status in the world of Thomism, and the problem of his personality or "impersonality" simply does not arise, since the value of an object is defined solely by its way of fitting into its determined place in the order that God has willed and protects. The artist is the man who can create an object that will find its place and function in this universal harmony. Its "beauty" is not an absolute quality, and there is no such thing as purely imaginary work of art; beauty is measured according to the laws appropriate to the object. The "aesthetic end" of which Stephen speaks, the intent of the artist, does not exist in the Thomist schema.

Joyce knows this. But it is understood that he is going to make use of "applied Aquinas" for his own purposes until he finds it necessary to adopt "a new terminology" for explaining "the phenomena of artistic conception". From the moment when the subject under discussion ceases to be "Criteria of Beauty" and becomes "Art for Art's Sake," the Thomist has no further contribution to make. When Joyce omits discussion of the relationship between the beautiful and the good or true, he does so because he does not consider art as a "technè"; that is, the object which attains perfection in formal harmony, the *perfectio prima*, has no need of the *perfectio secunda* which consists in being adapted to its function. When Saint Thomas says *"Pulchra sunt quae visa placent,"* the satisfaction derived from the beautiful objects is a double one: there is the pleasure given by the objects' form, and the pleasure derived from certainty that this form means suitability to the objects' eventual functions. This omission of finality permits Joyce to move on to the purely formal concept of "aesthetic emotion".

In *Stephen Hero* we find the first expression of "applied Aquinas," in the procedure so dear to Joyce of removing a quotation from its context and fitting it into his own system for his own purposes. He takes pleasure, however, in condemning Stephen's skilful evasive tactics in the short scene of his conversation with the Very Reverend Dr. Dillon, censor at University College. The latter reproaches Stephen with intending to "emancipate the poet from all moral laws," and says, "I suppose you mean Art for Art's sake" (*Stephen Hero*, p. 100). Stephen, having gauged his adversary's incompetence in the course of the preceding conversation, replies daringly,

> —I have only pushed to its logical conclusion the definition Aquinas has given of the beautiful.
> —Aquinas?
> —*Pulchra sunt quae visa placent.* He seems to regard the beautiful as that which satisfies the aesthetic appetite and nothing more—that the mere apprehension of which pleases. . . .
> —But he means the sublime—that which leads man upwards. *(Ibid.)*

Stephen is then able to drive the Jesuit into supporting a moral code which obliges him to deny Saint Thomas, and at once to seize the opportunity this offers him:

> There are parts of Aquinas which no priest would think of announcing in the pulpit.
> —But what if I, as an artist, refuse to accept the cautions which are considered necessary for those who are still in a state of original stupidity?
> —I believe you are sincere but I will tell you this as an older human being than you are and as a man of some experience: the cult of beauty is difficult. Aestheticism often begins well only to end in the vilest abominations of which. . . .
> —*Ad pulchritudinem tria requiruntur.* . . .
> —It is insidious, it creeps into the soul, little by little. . . .
> —*Integritas, consonantia, claritas.* There seems to me . . . to be effulgence in that theory instead of danger. The intelligent nature apprehends it at once.

—St. Thomas of course. . . .

—Aquinas is certainly on the side of the capable artist. (*Stephen Hero*, p. 101)

No further progress is made that day. Father Dillon is unable to counter this last usurpation, and stands paralysed before the sacrosanct words of Saint Thomas without realising that Stephen is justifying his aesthetic by the simple procedure of suppressing Aquinas' ontology.

Much later, having satisfactorily acquired the precious formula by means of formalist logic-chopping, that is, by a trick, Stephen explains these three points to Cranly, together with the epiphany which has just been revealed to him in the trivial dialogue overheard in Eccles Street between the Young Lady and the Young Gentleman. This epiphany has inspired him to write ironical verses which are the first draft of the Villanelle.[12] The text of Saint Thomas, in the *Summa Theologica*, Prima Pars, q. 39, a 8, runs as follows: *"Ad pulchritudinem tria requiruntur. Primo quidem integritas, sive perfectio: quae enim diminuta sunt hoc ipso turpia sunt. Et debita proportio sive consonantia. Et iterum claritas, unde quae habent colorem nitidum, pulchra esse dicuntur."* From this paragraph Stephen has only selected the three nouns which he quotes, and given them his personal interpretation. In *Stephen Hero*, *integritas* is first defined as a way of detaching and isolating the object from all that is not the object and of perceiving it as an integral thing of itself. Here Stephen is distorting Aquinas' thought, for what the saint says is that *integritas* or *perfectio*, completeness and fulfilment in all formal qualities of the object in relation to what it must be in God's eternal design, is the first condition—not of the object's isolation but of its participation in this universal pattern conceived by God. Next Stephen defines the "analysis" performed by the mind upon the object. It has to be examined as a whole and as the sum of its parts, in relation to other objects and to itself, and one must verify the equilibrium existing between those parts in order to be fully assured of its symmetry and to recognise it as an independent composite entity. This is the Thomist *"proportio,"* which connects with what Joyce calls "the rhythm of beauty". In *Portrait* he says, "Beauty awakens in us, or ought to awaken, or induces, or ought to induce, an aesthetic stasis, an ideal pity or an ideal terror, a stasis called forth, prolonged, and at last dissolved by what I call the rhythm of beauty" (*Portrait*, p. 206).

[12]There is an example of the ironical presentation of Stephen as melancholic poet in *Portrait*, as contrasted with the fine satirical sensibility of Daedalus; in *Stephen Hero*, the villanelle is inspired by the ugliness and paralysis of Dublin.

Rhythm is *proportio,* and the idea of formal harmony leads to *claritas,* a quality which does not seem to serve Stephen's purposes and which he eventually replaces by the term *quidditas,* meaning the essence of the object, or its "soul," the clear radiance of the image that manifests itself in the epiphany, when the object puts off the vesture of its mere appearance.

The concepts of "soul" and "epiphany" are clearly spiritual ones, and in *Portrait* Stephen suppresses both of then; in their place he introduces the artist's "imagination". In *Stephen Hero* aesthetic apprehension was not reserved for the artist alone, and in order to bring in the notion that it is so reserved, Stephen has to twist Aquinas' thought and misrepresent his intentions. He says, "I thought that he might mean that *claritas* is the artistic discovery and representation of the divine purpose in anything or a force of generalisation which would make the aesthetic image a universal one, make it outshine its proper conditions. But that is literary talk".

This "literary talk" is in fact close to the Thomist conception; but Stephen wishes to separate aesthetic apprehension from its metaphysical implications, to keep the vision but to connect it with an activity of the imagination, to formulate it in romantic terms rather than theological language. The concept of imagination enables him to free himself from this divine interference: "Beauty is beheld by the imagination which is appeased by the most satisfying relations of the sensible," he tells Lynch. Thus he establishes a relationship of mutual determination between imagination and beauty; the liberation here accomplished is expressed, when the stages of aesthetic apprehension have been analysed, in these words: "This supreme quality *(claritas)* is felt by the artist when the aesthetic image is first conceived in his imagination. The mind in that mysterious instant Shelley likened beautifully to a fading coal" *(Portrait,* p. 213).

Claritas, the object's manifestation of itself, coincides with its creative conception; perception and conception unite to form "discovery by art," the artist's appropriation of reality. "The symbol has no previous existence; it is created by the artist, invented in the moment of illumination" (J.-J. Mayoux, *James Joyce,* p. 70).

XXII. Going Beyond Reality

The Irish symbolism which had so much influence on literary circles at the beginning of this century was deeply dyed in occultism and esoteric doctrines. Far from being a romantic form of communion between the individual and the world, or a recovery of the harmonious order of the mediaeval or Renaissance world, the symbolist exercises of a Russell or a Yeats were attempts to transcend reality and to ignore the ugliness of social or political conditions around them in order to attain knowledge of the Neo-Platonic eternal essences. Joyce, with Gogarty, mocked at the "Yogibogeybox in Dawson chambers. *Isis Unveiled.* Their Pali book we tried to pawn. Crosslegged under an umbrel umbershoot he thrones an Aztec logos, functioning on astral levels, their oversoul, mahamahatma. The faithful hermetists await the light, ripe for chelaship, ringroundabout him" (*Ulysses*, p. 188).

His disgust for such spiritualistic activities no doubt brought him closer again to that scholasticism whose faith and whose masters he repudiated, while keeping its clarity and its care in rationalising. Yet in his work there also exists an occult parallel world, whose symbol is Thoth, and which would seem to bring him necessarily into contact again with the hermetists of Dublin. But what interests Joyce is not the "oversoul"; just as Thomism expresses his atheistic philosophy of aesthetics, so symbolism is only one way among many to multiply meanings, or at times to modify them by reference to a purely formal and transcendent world. In fact, apart from the sign of Thoth, the little Egyptian god who appealed to Joyce so much, the vast majority of symbolic systems or of isolated symbols in his work undergo the fate reserved by Joyce for all idealisms; one might almost say, parodying the initiatory formula of the hermetists, that "what is above is as what is below," that to Joyce "that which is below"—the mean, small, and trivial—is the model of "that which is above," and that the symbolism is inseparable from the irony upon which it rests. It is also inseparable from the technique of repetition which permits Joyce to draw a twofold effect from his use of symbols: that of the signified in itself and that of the signified in its relation to a wider structure in which it is set. According to the context, an apparently serious motif can become ridiculous; time transforms one's vision of the world, and repetition may be productive of comic effect. Everything depends on the reference which guides the direction and manner of our interpretation. The classical system of references supposes the existence of a macrocosm and of a *Weltanschauung* known to all, with relation to which the symbol has an immediately perceptible value and meaning, but Joyce may well resort to another system, little-known or completely invented by himself, so that the reader can only identify the meaning retrospectively when he has recognised the structure in "the now, the here, through which all future plunges to the past".

The time of creation is not the same as the time of living and of the process of becoming, but it is the time of the book itself; Joyce's art begins a new era for readers, the age of *double reading*. Just as Shakespeare's progress is a journey and return, so the discovery of the Joycean experience requires the reader to make a double journey. "This vision is presided over not by the time-scheme of the builder but by that of the poet, that of the imagination its master, for which time and the vision are reversible".[1] Recurrence is opposed to reversibility and connected with contiguity. Roman Jakobson[2] has demonstrated that the spoken word makes its appeal to two essential and complementary functions, to the selection of similar units and to the combination of contiguous units. The first operation takes place at that pole of language which rhetoric calls metaphor (the transfer of meaning by analogy) and the second at the pole represented by metonymy (the transference of meaning by contiguity). Poetry is founded on metaphor and its corre-

---

[1] J.-J. Mayoux, *op.cit.*, p. 79.
[2] *Deux aspects du langage et deux types d'aphasie. Essais de linguistique générale* (Paris, 1963).

spondences, and the novel on narrative that follows the order of spatial and temporal contiguities. Joyce makes use of metaphor in contiguity in order to bring out its meaning; the succession of scenes which are alike without being absolutely the same tends to produce an impression of recognition at first, and eventually of cognition. He also makes use of *repetition*, scenes or phrases being identically reproduced at intervals of such length that the reader's memory does not superimpose the two but rather awakes suddenly to the direction of meaning thus pointed out.

Joyce is always telling the same story, but in a relationship with language which is always changing, from *Stephen Hero* to *Finnegans Wake*. It can be said that in a sense *Dubliners* is a mockery directed at the soul that is so afraid of recognising its body's existence that it makes itself as vague and transparent as a ghost at daybreak; and from ghost to ghost, from alienation to return from the dead, the Spirit moves, avoiding bodies of real flesh and all that tastes of life. The loathed and rejected bodies wither and stiffen in paralysis, not daring to manifest their presence except in outbursts of paroxysm that cause the soul deep shame. And the pilgrimage ends in the snow of 'The Dead,' where it is said that the body must abandon all hope.

On the contrary, *Ulysses* is shaped like a monstrous dismembered body, functioning at the lowest organic level, demonstrating Joyce's view that the City of God, if it practises a mortifying spirtuality, destroys not its flesh but its spirit, and condemns itself to the prison from which it was trying to escape. If there is any connection established with God in *Ulysses*, it is established by the flesh. *"Corpus Meum"* is more important than the Holy Ghost, and "transubstantiation" is a form of cannibalism. The Dubliners and God live in a strange relationship: they eat Him and He contains them. Men are fed by a God in whom they exist. "Ireland is an old sow that devours her farrow," says Stephen.

The most richly meaningful symbolism is that which Joyce has most deeply buried in the work, and that whose presence he has most clearly pointed out. There is an irony which must have pleased him in the official divulgation of his technical secrets of construction and composition, a way of ensuring the critics' allegiance by giving them advance knowledge of all the gates along with the keys that would open them. The network of Homeric correspondences was to be a mystery to the public, if not to his close friends. The building of *Ulysses* appears as a kind of game played by Joyce, the construction of a motion which would constantly confront him with new technical problems as it proceeded;

he would ask all his friends for help in answering these, or for inspiration, as we can see from this letter to Budgen:

> Dear Budgen: Have met Sargent several times and dined. He is held up
> here for a week. The stories he tells me of mob manners in London are
> almost incredible. Have worked some of it into *Circe* which by the way is
> a dreadful performance. It gets wilder and worse and more involved but
> I suppose it will all work out. . . . I am sorry you do not think your ideas
> on Circe worth sending. As I told you a catchword is enough to set me off.
> *Moly* is a nut to crack. My latest is this. Moly is the gift of Hermes, god of
> public ways, and is the invisible influence (prayer, chance, agility, *presence
> of mind*, power of recuperation) which saves in case of accident. This
> would cover immunity from syphilis (σύ φιλις-swine-love?) Hermes is the
> god of signposts: i.e. he is, specially for a traveller like Ulysses, the point
> at which roads parallel merge and roads contrary also. He is an accident
> of providence.[3]

He gave a very superficial outline of the plan to John Quinn[4] and to
Carlo Linati some very valuable indications, in strict confidence:

> I think that in view of the enormous bulk and the more than enormous
> complexity of my three times blasted novel it would be better to send you
> a sort of summary-key-skeleton-scheme for your personal use only. . . . I
> have given only catchwords in my scheme but I think you will understand
> it all the same. It is an epic of two races (Israelite-Irish) and at the same
> time the cycle of the human body as well as a little story of a day (life).
> . . . For seven years I have been working at this book—blast it! It is also
> a sort of encyclopaedia. My intention is to transpose the myth *sub specie
> temporis nostri*. Each adventure (that is, every hour, every organ, every
> art being interconnected and interrelated in the structural scheme of the
> whole) should not only condition but even create its own technique. Each
> adventure is so to say one person although it is composed of persons—as
> Aquinas relates of the angelic hosts.[5]

He refused to give a copy of the scheme to Edmund Wilson in 1928, but
gave it to Valéry Larbaud and Stuart Gilbert, whose study of *Ulysses*
came out in 1930.[6]

[3] *Letters*, vol. I, pp. 147–8.
[4] *Ibid.*, p. 145: "*Ulysses* is in 3 parts (Telemachia, Odyssey, Nostos). This is the scheme:
I. Telemachia. 1. Telemachus. 2. Nestor. 3. Proteus. II. Odyssey. 1. Calypso. 2. Lotus
eaters. 3. Hades. 4. Aeolus. 5. Lestrygonians. 6. Scylla and Charybdis. 7. Wandering Rocks.
8. Sirens. 9. Cyclops. 10. Nausikaa. 11. Oxen of the Sun. 12. Circe. III. Nostos. 1. Eumeus.
2. Ithaca. 3. Penelope."
[5] *Ibid.*, pp. 146–7.
[6] For the diffusion of this scheme, see *A James Joyce Miscellany*, Second Series, ed.
Magalaner, pp. 9 ff.

But to the general public *Ulysses* was to appear in the form of a perfection whose secrets belonged only to its creator; Joyce's intention was not to publicize abroad his technical discoveries, nor that he should be mistaken for an artisan, nor his work for a book. Rather was it a world, in which the presence of the arranger should be hinted at rather than demonstrated. In short, the work had to be given that mystery and opacity that daily reality offers to mankind. *Ulysses* was to be a moving surface, even if that surface was founded on permanence. To this end, all the symbolism that acts as bearer of echoes and correspondences, and the scrupulously detailed plan, all succeed in luring the reader away to follow different tracks—but in vain, because no ultimate meaning will be forthcoming, for the equation was solved at the beginning. The real point of this procedure lies in the fact that this symbolism, first suggested and then effaced, is not the signified but the signifier; reality takes on its meaning in the here and now by its relation to the permanent "objective" world.

The hidden image is the most clear, for Joyce designed the plan of his works as a challenge to the enemy, reproducing in a structure composed of one single gigantic metaphor the unbearable situation which his writing was intended to destroy: the separation of soul and body caused by the national guilt-complex of Catholic Ireland.

The use of conventional symbols is opposed to the epiphany, which is individually perceived by one person and of significance to only this one to begin with.

Why should Joyce make use of magical correspondences of the kind found in the hermetists' books? What is the real connection between Stephen and the birds he sees? And what is the real relationship between Joyce and the known codes of symbolism, and the French symbolist writers? There are in fact two codes: at first, the symbols used in *Dubliners* refer clearly to the culture of Ireland, and the objects that bear the symbolic meanings are borrowed from the Catholic religion. Emblematic colours are also ceremonial. The native reader can easily recognise these objects: the ivy standing for Parnell, the piano, beer, the fog, and so on. Everything refers back to the Mass or to the City. And Dublin is the place of pitiful reality between the Biblical imagery of Paradise or Promised Land and the pagan Land of Joy. Even the dreams are not original: the scenery of 'Araby' which is the theme of the novella bearing this title, and the disappointing bazaar with the exotic name ("an Eastern enchantement") are not invented. A bazaar named Araby did take place in Dublin, in May 1894, and Ellmann thinks (*op. cit.*, p.

40) that the tale of the nephew deceived by the wicked uncle may well be autobiographical.

With *Portrait*, the use and application of symbols become wider; basing itself on the network established already in *Dubliners*, the process now becomes twofold. There are two codes, which gradually become autonomous and doubly meaningful, both in connection with reality and in the opposition of their values. The one has the value of a traditional symbolism and the other that of a personal symbolism; the first has as its scheme of reference that assemblage of Western culture to which Stephen feels he has been invited as a poor relation, and the second is a closed circuit of references to Joyce himself and to his books. The second reveals his vision of the world while the first, the borrowed symbolism, is a sign of irony and bitterness, corresponding on the historical level with the theory of man's identity throughout time, despite change and degeneracy. This symbolism maintains a parody-view of the world, while the personal symbolism is in fact a discrete form of reality itself.

But paradoxically the two types of symbolism are both responses to the same experience: the approach of reality, as described in the preceding pages, brings an awareness of disorder, destruction, and separation such that the very self is threatened with dissolution. If Joyce were intending an intensive conversion of reality into epiphany on a large scale, one would never move beyond Stephen's disturbed consciousness; the book would be completely chaotic and confused, Protean or Circean, imitating the monologue of a solitary schizophrenic or the conversation of a paranoiac with his fantasies. But *Portrait* and *Ulysses* are works constructed, foreseen, and organised within structures that arrange the disorder—arrange it in such a way that the reasons for the world's madness are shown along with the signs and representations of that madness.

Joyce attains this formal order by making division the instrument of reconstruction instead of merely another symptom of fragmentation. Disorder, exile, and alienation are still constantly present, but present within the limits of an instant, which, if isolated, would be a moment of folly or absurdity, but which in this cyclic time and this system of echoes becomes epiphany gradually; it takes its place then in a story, the story of a hero like that of the traditional novel, but with the difference that this story has been accidentally shattered and is being reconstituted from memory. The modern world and man have changed and become decomposed, but they have not lost all trace of the old images that were powerful when the culture of the Western world was homogenous, when everyone spoke the same moral and metaphysical language and understood immediately the vertical connections between the degrees on the ladder of being and the horizontal connections between the different orders of reality, when to signify a king, for example, one could use the bestiary image of the lion. Some systems or mythologies are still present to the modern memory. Homer, the Catholic liturgy, and theology are still fairly close, although they are but traces of greater worlds that have disappeared, so that Homeric or Christian imagery may serve as points of reference in chaos or as the landmarks which they are for Joyce. He imposes upon the experience of the disintegration of reality a network of traditional symbols, and to the actuality of separation and non-communication he attaches patterns of correspondences, borrowed in *Portrait* from the theological world he is striving to destroy and in *Ulysses* from the cosmos that his work is attempting to devalue and replace.

The Use of Catholic Symbolism in *Portrait*

The use of Catholic symbolism is naturally suggested by the axial theme of the rivalry between priest of religion and priest of the imagination. There are two main groups of emblems to be distinguished, presented in such a way that their original meanings are provided with a bizarre twist. The first consists of the sensual and perfumed presence of the Virgin and of all the figures who are types of her. Colours, scents, mystery, and fascination are arranged about her through the beauty of the language and of the metaphors that are her praise; and the young man's spiritual evolution can be followed through the movement of emotions aroused in him by the idea of Our Lady, "spikenard and myrrh and frankincense, symbolising her royal lineage, her emblems, the late-flowering plant and late-blossoming tree, symbolising the age-long gradual growth of her cultus among men" (*Portrait*, p. 104). By the blue, gold, and ivory that fade as the book progresses and flare up again in the vision on the beach of the girl's "thighs, soft-hued as ivory, slate-blue skirts and long fair hair"—and at the end all that remains of the cult of beauty is a language freed from all beliefs but still apt for the fashioning of fair profane images.

"Quasi cedrus exaltata sum in Libanon et quasi cupressus in monte Sion. Quasi palma exaltata sum in Cades et quasi plantatio rosae in Jericho. Quasi uliva speciosa in campis et quasi platanus exaltata sum juxta aquam in plateis. Sicut cinnamomum et balsamum aromatizans odorem dedi et quasi myrrha electa dedi suavitatem odoris" (*Portrait*, p. 105).

The other symbol borrowed from the Christian mythology is that of the Rose.[7] If in the *Portrait* there is a whole procession of roses possible and impossible, it is openly a matter of parody. Joyce's rose is to some extent that which he stole from Dante, whom he genuinely admired. It was a favourite image of Joyce's, used on many blasphemous occasions, such as when he was acting as Dante-Shakespeare for Marthe Fleischmann, and in *Finnegans Wake* they are the compass of the circle that means closing, introversion, and new beginning.

The importance of the theme is shown by the fact that *Portrait* begins with the song of the rose; it is at first simply a flower and a mystery, and then by its disfigurement into a green rose it takes its place at once in a double mythology—that in which all the traditional allegorical roses grow and that, Joyce's, where a spiritual rose grows, as mistreated as the white roses in the Queen's garden that are repainted red in *Alice in Wonderland*.

At the beginning of the *Divina Commedia*, Dante finds himself in the middle of life's way, lost in a dark wood. By rereading Joyce from *Finnegans Wake* downwards (since the *Wake* contains all its own system of reference within itself), one could see in the very first episode of *Portrait* an analogy between the situation of Dante setting out on his allegorical pilgrimage and meeting the three beasts that frighten him—leopard, lion, and she-wolf—and that of the worried little boy setting out and meeting a cow, and then being threatened by the eagles. Dante's leopard, lion, and she-wolf represent the moral, political, and theological distress of which he suddenly becomes aware in the chaos of Florentine life at the time. One could go on and on finding meanings other than the literal one provided by the three allegorical levels on which Dante conceived his "polysemous" work, as he explains them to Can Grande in the

---

[7]For the function of symbol and allegory in the Middle Ages and the Renaissance, and the use Joyce makes of them, see Rosemond Tuve, *Elizabethan and Metaphysical Imagery* (Chicago U.P., 1947); W.Y.Tindall, *The Literary Symbol* (Colombia U.P., 1955); Christine Brooke-Rose, *A Grammar of Metaphor* (London, 1965).

prefatory epistle to the *Paradiso*.[8] If it is not sure that a metaphorical analogy does exist between the *Commedia* and *Portrait*, the situations are at least similar: morality, politics, and theology unleash their ferocious animals upon the child, and like Dante he flees towards the rose.[9] But Dante has Virgil to guide him towards a rose that is visible and real, although it is allegorical to Dante. The sun is God because of its warmth, its spherical shape and its light; but for Joyce there can be no God in the fog and rain of Dublin, and Paradise cannot be there. But there *are* roses, real roses on the hedges and roses of the imagination. At the end Dante contemplates a huge glowing rose, white with a yellow heart, around which the angels flit like bees, which resembles a garden of concentric petals in whose centre sit Beatrice, Our Lady, and the blessed. Dante's rose is white and pure and angelic. When Stephen reaches Paradise by the ways of the imagination, with no other Virgil or Saint Bernard but himself, he sees "glimmering and trembling, trembling and unfolding, a breaking light, an opening flower, it spread in endless succession to itself, breaking in full crimson and unfolding and fading to palest rose, leaf by leaf and wave of light by wave of light, flooding all the heavens with its soft flushes, every flush deeper than the other" (*Portrait*, p. 173).

The gestation of Stephen's soul is like a version of Dante's progress; the latter changes as he crosses the different circles of Hell, acquires experience of evil and sin by hearing the confessions of the damned, and then passes from the role of observer to that of actor as his purification is accomplished. This purification corresponds to Stephen's detachment, as he crosses a hell and a purgatory before taking flight. And Dante has two guides, the poet Virgil and the beloved Beatrice, who

[8]"For the elucidation, therefore, of what we have to say, it must be understood that the meaning of this work is not of one kind only; rather the work may be described as 'polysemous,' that is, having several meanings; for the first meaning is that which is conveyed by the letter, and the next is that which is conveyed by what the letter signifies; the former of which is called literal, while the latter is called allegorical. And for the better illustration of this method of exposition we may apply it to the following verses: 'When Israel went out of Egypt, the house of Jacob from a people of strange language; Judah was his sanctuary, and Israel his dominion'. For if we consider the letter alone, the thing signified to us is the going out of the children of Israel from Egypt in the time of Moses, if the allegory, our redemption through Christ is signified; if the moral sense, the conversion of the soul from the sorrow and misery of sin to a state of grace is signified; if the anagogical, the passing of the sanctified soul from the bondage of the corruption of this world to the liberty of everlasting glory is signified."

[9]Joyce was reading Dante a good deal when writing *Stephen Hero*, and we have shown that 'Grace' is a parody of Dante's ascent.

comment on visions which the traveller cannot understand; Dante always takes great care to explain exactly anything that goes beyond the literal understanding. The meaning and intention of the allegory are rigorously controlled.[10] In *Portrait*, the trinity of Dante, Virgil, and Beatrice is represented by the young man, the artist, who is sometimes shown as Thoth and sometimes as Daedalus, and by the beloved, whose different vague faces are all the images of Stephen's desire. This is in effect as much as to say that Stephen is in himself Dante, Virgil, and Beatrice. The reduction of the trinity-pattern into the sole figure of the Artist is found in this form in *Portrait* and *Ulysses*. Joyce carries out by this means various processes of deconsecration, which take on the form of parodies, but whose intentions betray a certain longing for the devalued past; he is aware of belonging to an age which is disagreeable to him, but which must be experienced because the here and now have all the force of reality for him.

Dante's vision was a blessing and a promise of redemption; Stephen's roses also promise salvation, but a salvation that will be accomplished by the liberation of the soul from the body politic and catholic. At the heart of this rose is the offer of exile. And the concentric petals open out sin by sin until the self comes to knowledge by the experience of a voluntary fall. The rose has become the flower of sin, and as such is stained scarlet; incense is no longer burned to the rose of Jericho but to the "lure of the fallen seraphim," the temptress of the villanelle:

> He turned towards the wall, making a cowl of the blanket and staring at the great overblown scarlet flowers of the tattered wallpaper. He tried to warm his perishing joy in their scarlet glow, imagining a roseway from where he lay upwards to heaven all strewn with scarlet flowers. Weary! Weary! (*Portrait*, p. 221)

The metaphor, once a sign of identity, and then reduced at the Renaissance to the status of mere allegory supported by the comparison, is thus brought to disintegration by Joyce, who reconstitutes a new metaphor, no longer harmonious but discordant. Stephen is indeed transported in ecstasies like those of a saint, but the essential equation is lacking to make both terms of the metaphysical metaphor into epiphany and to unite reality with the Christian supernatural. Stephen's roses are vulgarly realistic, printed on the wallpaper of his room, or else

[10]For Dante's allegory, see Angus Fletcher, *Allegory, Theory of a Symbolic Mode* (Cornell U.P., 1964), pp. 318–9.

completely detached from reality, they are seen in a dream and serve to emphasise the ridiculous discrepancy between the poet's aspirations and what life actually offers him. At this time he is experiencing a non-courtly (or non-feudal, as he would say) but romantic kind of love, modelled on that of the Roman de la Rose; he is acting the part of Guillaume de Lorris for the lady who is enclosed in the garden, the unattainable rose, or Mercedes, or "she". Here Joyce can be seen as the learned but disbelieving heir to the mediaeval *Imago Mundi*.

Marjorie Nicolson has demonstrated that when the mediaeval world died the system of analogies which sustained the structures of its imagination was broken, so that the metaphor, freed from its connection with the nature of things, became detachable and took on the function of a mere decorative comparison.[11] The chain of being was broken in the middle, and the upper portion—that of the angels, the seraphim, and above them, of God—was no longer the summit of creation, but moved further away and became the "supernatural" or the improbable. The lower portion then appeared as reality alone, but the cosmic pattern of correspondences was no longer operative; the two realms were now separate and not symmetrical. Romanticism in art is characterised by the rehabilitation of significant imagery after two hundred years of reason, and by its association with the discovery of history. The French Revolution played the same part for the poets of the time as did the Gaelic rebellions and attempted revolts at the beginning of this century, with this difference: that the Romantics were disappointed in their hopes for a social apocalypse and the emergence of a new world, while the Irish theosophists, symbolists, and folklore revivers were in fact basically middle-class and reactionary, deeply attached to class distinctions and values.

The reaction to a political chaos has, at any rate, the same effect on the political spirit: the Romantics, and a century later the symbolists, transposed their thirst for revolution or their longing for a mythical world from the outer to the inner world, and their impulses towards a new order were turned inward to the soul. If there was revolution it was in the individual mind, and Paradise was no longer celestial or terrestrial, but within. The quest was no longer a matter of ascent, but of descent into the depths of the consciousness, for at the very boundary of the unconscious is made the essential fusion between the self and the images. This is the attainment of self-knowledge through spiritual ordeals as described by Shelley in his *Prometheus Unbound*, that allegory

[11]Marjorie Nicolson, *The Breaking of the Circle* (New York, 1960).

of the artist's soul in search of the inner place where all the forms of his
being may be reconciled. Asia and Prometheus, the masculine and
feminine principles, vegetate gently in the depths of their mossy cave,
discussing things unknown, and are the prototypes of the androgynous
imagination attributed to Stephen, which receives the echoes of the
world outside and makes them into poems.

Insofar as *Portrait* is the image of a soul in gestation, Joyce has indeed
inherited Shelley's ecstasies; but always between ecstasy and art lies an
ironical reality that must be crossed. Metaphors detached from the
vanished cosmos are revived by Joyce for purposes no longer decorative
but depreciatory. Symmetry no longer manifests harmony, but lack of
resemblance. Yet the derisive intention is not only an expression of that
blasphemous disbelief which always appealed to Joyce; it can also be
seen in its contemporary Irish context, that of the young Joyce beginning to write and seeing Yeats as a possible rival. One cannot estimate
exactly the presence of Yeats in Joyce's work, because the latter has
hidden his tracks as he often did, assimilating or dissimulating his
sources. But he owes a great deal to Yeats; many passages of *Portrait* are
written both for and against him, and it may have been Yeats's genius
that helped to estrange Joyce from the Gaelic heritage which he did not
want or need, as he claimed, for reasons of literary policy.[12] Irish mythology, Cuchulainn, Conchubar, Diarmuid, and Grainne seemed to belong to Yeats by right, and he had made them his own to such an extent
that Joyce would not go near them. Yet naturally he would have been
tempted to make use of the system of references they offered as he had
made use of the liturgy, of Homer, or of theosophy.

It seems that Yeats's presence kept him away from this fertile field
until he felt sufficiently assured to annex Gaelic culture as his own and
to give it a place of importance equal to that allotted Homer in *Finnegans Wake*. But at the time of *Portrait*, Yeats was still the guardian of
these mysteries and their despised values. Like Wilde and like Joyce,
Yeats practised substitution by identity or by equivalent rather than by
analogy, substitution of poetry for religion, and deification of the poet.
The introduction into *Portrait* of a fragment of his play, *The Countess
Cathleen*, the speech of the dying countess to her bard Aleel, is an act
of homage to the author from Joyce, who had translated the play into
Italian in 1911:[13]

---

[12]On Yeats and Joyce, see Ellmann's *James Joyce*, and his *Eminent Domain* (Oxford,
1967), chapter 'The Hawklike Man'.
[13]Yeats claimed that he had used an inaccurate version of the play to translate.

What birds were they? He thought that they must be swallows who had come back from the south. Then he was to go away for they were birds ever going and coming, building ever an unlasting home under the eaves of men's houses and ever leaving the homes they had built to wander.

Bend down your faces, Oona and Aleel.
I gaze upon them as the swallow gazes
Upon the nest under the eave before
He wander the loud waters. (*Portrait*, p. 225)

Joyce allusively associates Stephen with the countess, for both are victims of the unhappy race for whom they have given their souls; the imagery of water and flight is a foreboding and an echo of Stephen's prophetic vision.

Joyce admired Yeats, who was seventeen years his senior, and despite Joyce's insolence Yeats made an effort to admire the younger man's unquestionable talent; but their famous first meeting in 1902, in which Joyce is supposed to have said to Yeats, "You are too old for me to be able to help you," although inaccurately reported, does suggest that Joyce felt some need to outdo Yeats, and that behind the rude remark there might lie some regret that Yeats had come before him into a field rich in literary resources, but that he could do nothing against a writer of such genuine worth. Yeats is the adversary who is always there at the other side of Stephen's words, the man the artist wants to imitate and whom he eventually exorcises by mimicking his very symbols and rhythms. This is why the rose of Dante corresponds to the rose of Yeats, and from this correspondence over dead time and broken worlds there spring new kinds of metaphor, whose inferior terms are meant in mockery of their superior terms. After all, the "green rose" that does not exist could be a bud from Yeats' own *Secret Rose*.

In fact Yeats had preceded Joyce in the employment of Christian imagery in poetry that made no concessions to the Christian faith. The stories in *The Secret Rose* worried the editors Lawrence and Bullen so much that the book nearly suffered the same fate as *Dubliners*, but for very different reasons: Yeats's impure pagan mythology celebrating the glory of the Druids and the disloyalty of the priesthood was more impious than Joyce's realism. Yeats even went so far as to predict the advent of a new God, which he did in a book Joyce admired, *The Tables of the Law* (1897). His poems to the Rose have several meanings, being associated with politics (the Dark Rose is Ireland), Rosicrucianism, with its theme of the spirit nailed by time to the cross of material being, alchemy (where the rose signifies the transmutation of matter), and love; but unlike Joyce, who always planned and organised the associations his symbols should evoke, Yeats used to say that his symbolic poems had always had many meanings, but that these were constantly changing.[14] For him, the symbol depended on the author's and the reader's individual caprice or state of mind.

Joyce has no free symbolism; when he quotes a verse from *The Countess Cathleen*, he does so not only because it evokes the poetic charm and cadence of 'Who goes with Fergus,' but also because the motif-complex of death, deity, and motherhood springs from the one allusion. In the same way, the secret of the Rose has not merely the simple value of beauty; what attracts Joyce is the *secret*, the feelings of the poet waiting for the Rose that men have sought in the artificial paradises of wine, beauty, or dream to come to him of its own accord and to reveal its secret essence. Yeats ends by admitting that he does not know the meaning of the secret except insofar as it is an unknowable mystery.

For Joyce, every secret must have at the end its moment of epiphany, and so he plants his enigmatic roses throughout his work with the purpose of showing what symbolism should be, an image of reality, "a disposition of sensible matter . . . for an aesthetic end". The roseway which began in mystic radiance ends on the railway lines in Lenehan's pun in *Ulysses*; Lenehan is Boylan's clownish companion, the parasite and jester who misuses the language, and in the 'Sirens' episode, the motif is introduced, first in the musical overture, thus: "Gold pinnacled hair. A jumping rose on satiny breasts of satin, rose of Castille". "Last rose Castille of summer left bloom I feel so sad alone." Variations are elaborated on Bloom's sad loneliness, and we recall that he signs his letters to Martha "Flower". Visual variations such as the image of the rose on the barmaid's satin bosom echo one of the paragraphs of 'Eolus,' which was entitled '???' "Lenehan said to all:—Silence! What opera resembles a railway line?" The answer, in caricature of the Secret of the Rose, is gladly announced by Lenehan: "The Rose of Castille. See the wheeze? Rows of cast steel". This phonetic word-play in the setting of Eolus' cave is a figure of rhetoric, paranomasis—but it is more particularly one of the verbal epiphanies that occur throughout Bloom's journey. Molly is associated with the rose and with Spain by her origins, and with opera by her singing engagements, and this rose of Castille haunts Bloom all day, to his distress and confusion. In the house of Circe,

[14]Tindall, *The Literary Symbol*, p. 40.

Molly's image pursues him, and he just manages to avoid a railway line. The secret of the rose has undergone the vulgar metamorphosis which the world in which Bloom is a hero imposes upon all values.

Pagan myths and the Hermetic tradition are treated in much the same way. Joyce had been attracted by curiosity into the magic universe where Kabbala, Hermeticism, and alchemy unite in the search for the secrets of man's omnipotence; but while his Aristotelian-Thomist philosophy served as basis and infrastructure to his thought, his readings from the masterworks of Hermeticism contributed only elements of decoration which were soon discarded.

Establishment of a Personal Symbolism

Portrait is illustrated by two types of iconology, the one of good omen and the other sinister: the one is a kind of symbolic ornithology fabricated by Joyce from the development of various theories, myths, and metaphors, and the other an original reconstitution of the mediaeval bestiary. The German theologians of the Renaissance, Swedenborg, Daedalus, and Thoth preside over Stephen's destiny and his creative exile, and his mind becomes a meeting-place for the mythologies and philosophies of the Greek world and the mysticism of the East as interpreted by Germanic and Lutheran philosophy. It seems as though Joyce is trying to fuse together in one single form the cultures of East and West, and to make the artist the master of all possible ways of translating the world into words. This multiplicity can be sensed with the first revelation of the two worlds' correspondence and of the role Stephen is destined to play in the confused mystic experience he undergoes:

> Now, at the name of the fabulous artificer, he seemed to hear the noise of dim waves and to see a winged form flying above the waves and slowly climbing the air. What did it mean? Was it a quaint device opening a page of some mediaeval book of prophecies and symbols, a hawk-like man flying sunward above the sea, a prophecy of the end he had been born to serve and had been following through the mists of childhood and boyhood? (*Portrait*, p. 169)

Stephen hesitates to decipher the message; his only certain knowledge is the name which resuscitated the vision, the name of Daedalus. But the winged figure might have come from a mediaeval prophecy or a grimoire, and the atmosphere that surrounds him has nothing of Ovid's almost realistic simplicity about it; rather do these hazy visions, with their music and with Stephen's spiritual ascent, recall the ecstasies of Swedenborg or Blake. The description is couched in passionate terms which are nevertheless disciplined by art, for Joyce takes care to set this fantastic scene between two resolutely banal incidents, reproducing, as it were, the visionary world of Blake, who, visited by elemental beings and spirits, "would leap out of bed, and, seizing his pencil, remain long hours in the cold London night drawing the limbs and lineaments of the visions" (*Critical Writings*, p. 218).

The second appearance of a messenger from the world of art takes place, on the contrary, in a state of stasis in which, however, Stephen does not lose his consciousness of space and time; a phrase from Cornelius Agrippa and some scraps from Swedenborg set the poetic imagination working, and it is a reverie rather than a vision, centred on the figure of Thoth, that Stephen follows. He *thinks* (and this word is repeated) about the signs of departure, without experiencing the ecstasy of flight. What had appeared to him on the beach as a mysterious omen full of promise is here subjected to the tests of doubt: instead of crying "On! On!", he thinks that all visions, prophecies, and calls of this kind are "folly".

This hesitation between poetic folly and craftsmanlike reason, representing Stephen's doubts, shows that Joyce himself does not believe in any of these revelations, and that he is using the "insane" or "pathological" aspects of the visions for purely artistic ends, reorganising into an ironic whole the experiences of others. All of these owe their allegiance to Hermes and to the theory of correspondences, and each contributes in his own fashion to the elaboration of Joyce's correspondences. The traditional connections which link books and ideas together are no longer following their original courses, but are now linking together a great variety of world-visions which are themselves unified by their own system of correspondences. *Ulysses* is really an encyclopaedia of these worlds of correspondences, linked together by the chains of irony which Joyce had fabricated and put in place in *Portrait*.

The name Thoth is the Greek transcription of the Egyptian moongod's name; Thoth or Djhoutey was worshipped in Upper Egypt at Khmun, Hermopolis Magna, and as god of the moon and its lunations he became the patron also of the passing of time. He then became the god of arithmetic and, by extension, of knowledge, the inventor of writing and founder of the social order, and a kind of Prometheus figure, unpopular with the other gods, whose secretary, interpreter, and adviser he was. On earth he was the representative of the great sun-god Ra. His presence is introduced in *Portrait* by the recurrence of his name as *leitmotiv* associated with Stephen's frequent moon-melancholies. As scribe and mathematician, he was charged with the task of weighing dead men's hearts and souls for Osiris and the judges of the dead. Such a god—master of arts, language, and criticism—was a perfect idol for Stephen to choose. The animals sacred to him were the ibis and the baboon, and he was represented in the form in which Stephen sees him in Chapter V, an ibis-headed man. The Greeks identified Thoth with their Hermes, and attributed to him the authorship of books of magic under the name of "Thrice-great Thoth" or Hermes Trismegistus, by reason of his triple function. Hermes' magic works deal with the nature and power of the Logos, and are collected under the title of *Corpus Hermeticum* or *Poimandres*; they enjoyed great popularity from the second century A.D. onwards. To Hermes the cosmos was a whole constituted of independent parts, all connected together by sympathies and antipathies, analogical bonds, or, as Hermes says, by a relation of reciprocity which unites all things into a chain that reaches from highest to lowest by means of mutual correspondences.

Hermeticism went underground in the Middle Ages, to reappear in the fifteenth century with Ficino's translation of the *Corpus* in 1463. But with the Renaissance alchemists such as Cornelius Agrippa and Jacob Boehme, who were more theologians than magi, the new Hermeticism gained ground—to some extent because the *Imago Mundi* it inherited from Thomism was completely in harmony with the order of nature and the corresponding likenesses between microcosm and macrocosm. For Sir Thomas Browne, whose thought is a synthesis of the two "philosophies," the visible world is an image of the invisible. Hermeticism produced many variants, particularly after the disappearance of the belief in effective communication between the two worlds.

In fact, the Hermeticism which was known to Joyce had undergone many changes and been bastardised by the addition of much alchemical material, theology derived from Meister Eckhart, and simple magic during the nineteenth century. It had been much affected by poets, especially after the publication of Eliphas Lévi's *Dogme de la Haute Magie* in 1855. Baudelaire,[15] Rimbaud, Villiers de l'Isle-Adam, and Mallarmé read it because it was a book on the power of language rather than for the world-vision it offered. Lévi's work is astonishingly modern

[15]He writes, in *Salon de 1859*, ch. IV, "The whole visible universe is but a storehouse of images to which the imagination must give their places and relative values".

in its expression, although he claims he is lighted only by the lamp of Trismegistus; in order to dicover the secrets of reality (which was, of course, Joyce's ambition), the magus (Rimbaud's *voyant* or Baudelaire's *savant chimiste*) has to move through the whole vertical scale of being and decipher "the analogical correspondence between the sign and the thing signified". It is clear that here is no Boehme-like theology nor mediaeval world-pattern, but a linguistic formulation of the relationship between intellect and reality. Lévi connects the sign and the thing signified with the evocative powers of the symbol, which he considers a legacy from Adam, who was given the task of naming the creatures. "To pronounce a name," he says, "is to create or to call up a being or a thought". This is often what happens to Stephen; for instance, the name Dedalus which he hears called out evokes and calls forth the winged figure of the hawk-like man.

The bond between the word and the being was a natural one for the artist who had since his childhood been unconsciously building up the complicated system of correspondences which is presented in *Portrait* in its guise of associative memory. The present constantly calls to the past by means of language, and in Stephen's own life exist several levels of time analogous to the Hermeticists' worlds of above and below, connected by analogy and similarity. The time spent at Clongowes and the incidents occurring there correspond to the time spent at the University, as the material world to the spiritual. By way of the present, the world above is connected with the world below.

The theme of flight, escape, and exile in Joyce's life could scarcely avoid being connected with groups of traditional images illustrative of the misfortunes of Ireland; such are the flight of the "wild geese" towards America, which Joyce mentions in his lectures in Trieste, and the passive condition of the "tame geese" who remain enslaved by Church and Empire. "Bard," *vates*, priest, poet, and prophet, the idea Stephen has of himself in *Portrait* and the image that he projects—these concepts are not those of a revolutionary or moralising artist, but those of an inspired poet who reveals mysteries, who is threatened, and who is grieved by his feeling of being different from other men. Ever since he was a child, he has been awaiting the revelation of his true nature. In Chapter V, he stands on the steps of the library on two occasions, a troubled augur taking the auspices under a temple colonnade; the first time, the only birds to appear are the young ladies of Dublin, who stand on the steps with the wings of their umbrellas unfurled, watching the clouds like frightened swallows. The life that is promised to him may be symbolised by the girl with "her life simple and strange as a bird's life, gay in the morning, restless all day, tired at sundown".

But that night, Stephen is warned by prophetic dreams that his nest is not to be on this earth, and again he returns to the temple: "Why was he gazing upwards from the steps of the porch, hearing their shrill twofold cry, watching their flight? . . . What birds were they? He stood on the steps of the library to look at them, leaning wearily on his ashplant" (*Portrait*, p. 224).

To begin with, Stephen was called "baby tuckoo," the cuckoo that is born in another bird's nest, and perhaps Joyce took this opportunity of beginning a chain of symbols with the artist's birth; this view would be confirmed by the virulent assertion of Stephen Hero that the Irishman's soul is sold to the Church before he is born. Thompson tells us that in legend, mythology, and the fables of Aesop the cuckoo *(cuculus)* is confused with the hoopoe *(cucupha)*, and that the latter is metamorphosed into hawk and magician as its last incarnation.[16] Cornelius Agrippa gives the bird *cucupha* a meaning which seems surprising in the context of *Portrait: "Cucupha gratitudinem indicat: sola enim haec parentibus senio confessis gratia refert"*. It can only surprise us that the cuckoo should symbolise filial piety; but on the other hand, the hoopoe is often confused with the lapwing, and thus the circle cuckoo-hoopoe-lapwing brings the unwanted character from the road at the beginning of *Portrait* to the bay at the beginning of *Ulysses*. The hoopoe, sacred in Egypt (the land of exile), is impure to the Jews (Leviticus, 11, 19) under the name of lapwing; in other words, what is sacred on the banks of the Nile is impure beyond, and the same bird is a good omen in the land of hieroglyphics (that is, of art) and evil in the land of God. According to Leviticus, the heron, stork, bat, and lapwing are impure, and what makes the lapwing *(upupa)* so undesirable is its filthy reputation as a haunter of dunghills. Pliny calls it *"avis obscoena pastu,"* and Saint Jerome, *"avem spurcissimam, semper in sepulchris, semper in humano stercore commorantem"*. The boy Stephen undergoes the same humiliating fate as the bird that is condemned to seek its nourishment in the dunghill. In fact, the failed attempts at flight and the metamorphoses into birds of the same species but different names correspond to the artist's necessary exile, which is real because it consists of a migration yet false because Stephen only moves away in order to be more completely *in Dublin*.

[16]D. W. Thompson, *A Glossary of Greek Birds* (London, 1936), quoted in Ronald Bates, *James Joyce Quarterly*, vol II, no. 4, Summer 1965, pp. 281–9.

What birds were they? He thought that they must be swallows who had
come back from the south. Then he was to go away for they were birds
ever going and coming, building ever an unlasting home under the eaves
of men's houses and ever leaving the homes they had built to wander.
Bend down your faces, Oona and Aleel.
I gaze upon them as the swallow gazes
Upon the nest under the eave before
He wander the loud waters.

A soft liquid joy like the noise of many waters flowed over his memory
and he felt in his heart the soft peace of silent spaces of fading tenuous sky
above the waters, of oceanic silence, of swallows flying through the sea-
dusk, over the flowing waters. (*Portrait*, p. 225)

The flight of swallows that Stephen watches associates the visible sign
both with his personal mythical images (himself as Daedalus the hawk-
man, and himself as Thoth the Scribe) and with a literary and historical
reminiscence. The verses quoted are from Yeats's play *The Countess
Cathleen*, which had been hooted down by the reactionary and stagnant element in Irish culture. The poet must leave, because the birds
tell him to do so and his public demands it.

Yeats's words do not receive Stephen's full approval; he will not bend
down his face. Once he had dreamed vaguely of a pure brother-and-
sister love between himself and Emma that would be blessed by the
Holy Virgin, but now he does not believe in it any more. He gazes on
the nests of others and then takes his flight. Yeats had said, "as the
swallow gazes . . . before/She wander the loud waters," but Stephen
modifies the quotation to suit himself, and becomes metaphorically the
swallow: "before/He wander the loud waters". This change is all the
more important because the countess compares herself to the swallow
as she lies dying, expiating her over-great devotion to her people; in the
same way, Stephen is leaving in order to forge the conscience of his
race, but also in order to save himself. The style of this passage mimics
the movement of the birds that fly past and return, as Stephen watches
them enquiringly. Thoughts also fly back and forth between the past
moment and the present, moving through space without ever stopping
to perch:

A phrase of Cornelius Agrippa flew through his mind and then there flew
hither and thither shapeless thoughts from Swedenborg on the correspondence of birds to things of the intellect and of how the creatures of the air
have their knowledge and know their times and seasons because they,

unlike man, are in the order of their life and have not perverted that order by reason. *(Ibid.)*

Joyce was probably acquainted with Agrippa through the re-edition of his major work, *De Occulta Philosophia,* which appeared in 1898 under the title *Three Books of Occult Philosophy.* It is composed of a mixture of Neo-Platonism and Christianity, centred around Kabbalistic philosophy; Agrippa states that magic is a perfect science which leads to knowledge of nature and of God. His doctrine of the three worlds also fits into the vast Hermetic pattern, with the elements, stars, and spirits corresponding to the physical, celestial, and intellectual worlds. As he thinks of these correspondences, Stephen also recalls those of Sweden-borg, as expounded in *Arcana Coelestia*: "Birds signify things spiritual, rational, and also intellectual . . . a domestic bird or birds will stand for spiritual truth, a wild bird for natural truth, and a winged object for sensual truth". Ronald Bates has shown what use Joyce made of Agrip-pa's treatise, and how in his usual fashion he selected details which could be inserted into the system of correspondences that he had estab-lished at the beginning of *Portrait*; bats, eagles, herons, and domestic fowl have their symbolic meaning by reference to a much larger and more complete aviary. Agrippa sees birds as having meaning as omens: the bat, for instance, signifies escape: *Vespertilio fugienti occurrens, evasionem significat; nam ipsa licet pennas non habeat, tamen evolat.* The heron stands for an obstacle, and the stork for reconciliation. The reader will remember Vincent Heron and the battle over Byron.

"Ardea rerum arduarum auspicium est. Cyconia, concordiae avis, concordiam facit. Grues a gruere antiquo verbo, quasi congruere dicti, semper adferunt quod expedit, atque inimicorum cavere faciunt."

Thus the crane is seen as the opposite of the heron; it points out the traps the enemy has laid. When the bird-girl appears, the emblems and the metaphors of the one feminine image suggest both Thoth and Our Lady. She is compared to the crane, the *Grues* who is a beneficial messenger.

The introduction to Latin *Gradus ad Parnassum* gives two epithets for *grues:vigil* and *praesaga,* vigilant and prophetic; it is clear that the attributes of the bird-girl may be related to a form of Messianism which links Christian iconology to Hermeticism, as the description of her contains characteristics from both iconographies. The switch to imagin-ing her as a being magically transformed into a sea-bird makes her participate in the Ovidian *Metamorphoses* that had suggested to Stephen his own transmutation:

> A girl stood before him in midstream, gazing out to sea. She seemed like one whom magic had changed into the likeness of a strange and beautiful seabird. . . . Her thighs, fuller and soft-hued as ivory, were bared almost to the hips where the white fringes of her drawers were like feathering of soft white down. Her slate-blue skirts were kilted boldly about her waist and dovetailed behind her. Her bosom was as a bird's, soft and slight, slight and soft as the breast of some dark-plumaged dove. (*Portrait*, p. 171)

Agrippa recalls that *grues* corresponds to *geranos*, the bird sacred to Thoth; thus, the girl is both the sweet inaccesible figure with the dove's breast that arouses in Stephen the same emotions of adoration as does Our Lady, and a messenger from the god of writing, whose emerald-green colours she wears. The ambivalence of masculine and feminine, Catholic and Hermetic, is underlined by a meaningful detail:

> "Her long slender legs were delicate as a crane's and pure save where an emerald trail of seaweed had fashioned itself as a sign upon the flesh."
> *(Ibid.)*

She is both virginal dove and Hermetic crane, beauty revealed and significant as the first living epiphany; she signals to Stephen the message that he must migrate, that he must write. She is the angel of his annunciation, just as Gabriel was in the dream which produced the villanelle; Gabriel was a messenger of God, and she is a messenger of Life. It would seem, from the opposition suggested by the phrase, "pure, except where marked by a sign," that writing is considered as a kind of impurity, and as we have already seen, Thoth was accused of theft and impiety for having invented the art of writing; thus there recurs here, discreetly but inevitably, the correspondence between writing and guilt which makes the artist desire his exile; he sees himself as following the example of the hawk-like man.

Eugene Waith states that Stephen's emotions at this moment are free from all sensuality,[17] but Harry Levin defines his ecstasy as "a metaphor of sexual fulfilment and artistic creation."[18] His encounter with the vision may be interpreted as flight or escape, as a fall or as attraction upwards. In the first version of *Portrait*, written in 1904, Joyce had

---

[17]'The calling of Stephen Dedalus,' *College English*, XVIII, Feb. 1957, pp. 256–61; see also p. 241.
[18]Levin, *James Joyce, A Critical Introduction*, p. 59.

already made the artist go to the sea to hear the voice of life. He met with a similar impassioned ecstasy, but there was no girl there. Instead of the girl there was a quotation from Saint Augustine, "reconciling" life with sin, "those things only are good which are susceptible of corruption". "A philosophy of reconcilement" was what the young man found on that beach, a possibility of accepting the dreadful duality of body and soul, or, as he called it, "mortal beauty". This reconciliation between body and soul was what Joyce in 1904 called "espousal": "He had gone out, out among the shallow waters, the holy joys of solitude uplifting him, singing passionately to the tide. Sceptically, cynically, mystically, he had sought for an absolute satisfaction. . . . A philosophy of reconcilement . . . possible . . . but the lights in the chambers of the heart were unextinguished, nay, burning as for espousal".

Such an espousal is celebrated in *Portrait*, a strange union whose essence and whose magic we must try to define. After the bird-girl has appeared and disappeared, Stephen imagines her to have been a messenger—an angel from the courts of life—sent to warn him of the birth of the artist and of the deposition of his material humanity.

> Her image had passed into his soul for ever and no word had broken the holy silence of his ecstasy. Her eyes had called him and his soul had leaped at the call. To live, to err, to fall, to triumph, to recreate life out of life! A wild angel had appeared to him, the angel of mortal youth and beauty, an envoy from the fair courts of life, to throw open before him in an instant of ecstasy the gates of all the ways of error and glory. On and on and on and on! (*Portrait*, p. 172)

Stephen was aware of life and will within himself before he met the symbolic bird, but in this solitude he truly gives himself to himself, in "a waste of wild air and brackish waters and the sea-harvest of shells and tangle". The bird, once her message is delivered, once the image has been sown in the imagination where it will germinate, disappears and leaves the artist alone with his visions. The only union which is vital rather than sinister is that of the artist with mortal beauty, the only marriage in which neither is destroyed but each weds the other by contemplating it; the promise does not deprive its maker of anything, but gives him fullness. The woman's image is there, of necessity, but it is fortunately motionless, harmless, and innocent.

The artistic gestation that takes place in this ecstasy of the soul is an exactly opposite reproduction of the physical gestation that takes place in the mother's womb. Stephen in celebrating his espousal with himself does so with no witnesses except "life" or "the angel of mortal youth and beauty," and in so doing discovers at last the secret of art and the voice of his freedom. The living work issues forth from two successive births, separated from each other by a fall. From the first birth, human and physical only, which makes him a prisoner of the life he leads as son and as guilty one under the accusing eyes of the motherly powers, he must pass to his second birth, after having avoided the offers of the Temptress; he has to accept his fall and his life of solitude until the moment comes when he feels master of his isolation, when he is able to fly; he has to render himself innocent again, even in transgression, for what was a barrier before is now an open gate to life. The second life is born from the first. Life recreated with life belongs totally to Stephen, and in this second life the woman is no longer the mother; she is only an image that arouses creative emotion in the man's imagination. The emotional flight is a holy masturbation, after which the artist brings forth into silence his own power made fruitful by the image. "On and on!" Stephen stops, and the only sound to break the holy silence of ecstasy is that of his own heart.

Ovid does not mention a hawk in the account of Daedalus, but simply says "a bird" *(avis)*. Stephen sees "a hawk-like man flying sunward" and identifies him with Daedalus. The vision is inspired by Swedenborg, for it is no longer a metamorphosis, but rather a spiritual experience. To Swedenborg, the hawk represents natural man separated from spiritual man, and the swallow stands for natural truth. In the hierarchy of the celestial arcana, it seems, natural truth is the highest kind, and thus the swallow is the forerunner of the hawk. Swedenborg's place in the hierarchy of the young artist's masters in thought is a provisional one, for Joyce does not believe in mysticism and revelations. But Swedenborg is associated with Blake, who succeeds him as doorkeeper of eternity in *Ulysses,* and whom Joyce did admire greatly. All the same, the heretical aspect of Swedenborg's theology could not fail to please him. The winged vision recurs in several pieces he wrote on both Swedenborg and Blake:

> The influence of Swedenborg, who died in exile in London when Blake was beginning to write and draw, is seen in the glorified humanity with which all of Blake's work is stamped. Swedenborg, who frequented all the invisible worlds for several years, sees in the image of man heaven itself and Michael, Raphael, and Gabriel, who, according to him, are not three angels, but three angelic choirs. Eternity, which had appeared to the beloved disciple and to St. Augustine as a heavenly city, and to Alighieri as a heavenly rose, appeared to the Swedish mystic in the likeness of a

heavenly man, animated in all his limbs by a fluid angelic life that forever leaves and re-enters, systole and diastole of love and wisdom. From this vision he developed that immense system of what he called correspondences which runs through his masterpiece *Arcana Coelestia*, the new Gospel which, according to him, will be the apparition in the heavens of the Son of Man foretold by St. Matthew. (*Critical Writings*, pp. 221-2)

Eternity in its three aspects of heavenly city, heavenly rose, and heavenly man is a sublime transposition of art as epiphanised in *Portrait* by way of the city, the rose, and the young man, but within the sordid reality of Dublin; the cosmic visions of Swedenborg and Blake correspond inversely to those of Joyce, especially in *Ulysses*. The flight experienced by Blake, "flying from the infinitely small to the infinitely large, from a drop of blood to the universe of stars, his soul is consumed by the rapidity of flight, and finds itself renewed and winged and immortal on the edge of the dark ocean of God" (*Ibid.*), is analogous, on the level of eternity, to Stephen's flight on the beach.

Swedenborg's researches into science and philosophy are less known than his theological works, because of the visions which led him from an intuition of nuclear physics to the spiritual world at the express command of God.[19] He was a mystic in the style of Blake, but particularly unorthodox, being persuaded that his visions were in fact signs heralding a new Messianism; especially he rejected the doctrine of the Trinity, finding three persons in one inconceivable, but accepted God as Divine Man in whom exists a trinity of love, wisdom, and action; it was God who came to earth as Jesus, whose soul was the Divine Nature. Our Lady mediates between the Divine and human nature. Jesus by living in the fullness of humanity eliminates all of the merely human and refines himself into the perfection of the Incarnate Word, and thus human nature, inhabited by a divine spirit, becomes the divine incarnation that is the Holy Ghost, the active and living overflow of the human-divine. This heresy, distantly reminiscent of Sabellianism, eliminates any threat of hell, because Jesus as the human-divine interposes himself between man and temptation.

The orign of Swedenborg's "correspondences" is expounded in his *Arcana Coelestia* (London, 1749-56, 8 vols.), which provided Joyce with

[19]Emmanuel Swedenborg (1688-1772), was born in Stockholm, was a great admirer of Newton, and between 1716 and 1718 brought out a scientific magazine called *Daedalus Hyperboreus*.

material for his own symbolic structure, and in *Apocalypsis Explicata* (London, 1785–9, 4 vols.). In the one Genesis and Exodus, and in the other Revelations, are analysed according to a system whose basic principle is as follows: that all created things are necessarily forms and effects of aspects of the divine love and wisdom, and correspond on the material plane to spiritual realities.

No thinker has been so close to Swedenborg's ideas as William Blake was, and it is by the intermediary of Blake that Joyce shares in this world which he refuses to call "mystic" but instead labels "idealist". There exists a very fine text, unfortunately incomplete, of a lecture given by Joyce in March 1912 (at the time when he was writing *Portrait*) at the University of Trieste, entitled *Verismo ed idealismo nella letteratura inglese: Daniele De Foe, William Blake.*[20] Blake's Albion, universal man and symbol of eternity, is one of the types of H. C. E. in *Finnegans Wake.*[21]

It is interesting to see that Joyce, who identifies himself with Blake quite literally at some points (in particular in his personal life with Catherine Blake), should insist upon the fact that in Blake "the visionary faculty is directly connected with the artistic faculty". He is taking Blake out of the ranks of the mystics in order to give him "a unique position in the category of artists". He seems to be discussing himself when he says, referring to Michelangelo's influence on Blake, "the importance of the pure, clean line that evokes and creates the figure on the background of the uncreated void" (*Critical Writings*, p. 221). This sounds like a description of Joyce's own procedure, his utilisation of almost vanished correspondences in which he no longer believes, for the creation of a space in which images and signs may be evoked.

Joyce makes use of another network of personal symbols which seems to recall the mediaeval bestiary, but which is in fact a consequence of the distortion exercised by Stephen's disgust on the world he sees around him. It is very close to the vision of Joyce as a young man, as he expresses it in his essay *Day of the Rabblement*, in which his indignation was inspired by Giordano Bruno's scorn for the *Spaccio de la Bestia Trionfante*. From one point of view *Portrait* is an expanse of animality: life begins for baby tuckoo with an imaginary meeting with a cow; two monsters, cow and eagle, awake his first fear and distrust; when he grows to the stature of a Theseus or a Daedalus, he will dare to fight

[20]The first ten pages are missing; the Italian ms. is in the library of Yale University, and a translation appears in *Critical Writings*, pp. 214–22.

[21]See Northrop Frye, 'Blake and Joyce,' in *James Joyce Quarterly*, Feb. 1957, pp. 39–47.

cattle and eagles at last, and will be a hero, ready to save his island-home
—if it wishes to be saved. If not, he will deliver his soul-spouse. Dangerous animals are everywhere in his path; he has to suffer from all kinds
of vermin, from rats to lice. The appearance of beasts is associated
always with corresponding forms that suggest imprisonment; the world
is often like a cage or hen-house, while he is not yet ready to fly. Traps
and nets take on precise geometrical forms, depending on whether
they are designed to catch the young man's body or soul. From *Dubliners* onwards, circles and spirals are designed to arouse or suggest beastli-
ness, and every curving motion is a sign of animal lust: "He would follow
a devious course up and down the streets, circling always nearer and
nearer in a tremor of fear and joy, until his feet led him suddenly round
a dark corner" (*Portrait*, p. 102).

The course he follows finds its end in hell, as

> Goatish creatures with human faces, hornybrowed, lightly bearded and
> grey as india-rubber. The malice of evil glittered in their hard eyes, as they
> moved hither and thither, trailing their long tails behind them . . . they
> swished in slow circles round and round the field, winding hither and
> thither through the weeds, dragging their long tails amid the rattling
> canisters. They moved in slow circles, circling closer and closer to enclose,
> to enclose, soft language issuing from their lips, their long swishing tails
> besmeared with stale shite, thrusting upwards their terrific faces. . . ."
> (*Portrait*, p. 138)

Transposed down into the depths and darkness of sin, Stephen is
allowed by God to glimpse the hell reserved for him, "stinking, bestial,
malignant".

As Stephen undergoes the crisis of puberty, he is like a wild beast
prowling about Dublin. But the favourite place of assembly for the
allegorical bestiary is in fact the University; in the house of the spirit
where there should be such abundance of magicians, poets, and learned
men, there is in fact the greatest variety of animals. It is like a jungle
or a farm-yard, but the metamorphoses are so discreetly and "naturally"
made that at first one does not notice this. Joyce does not adopt the
elementary procedure of turning men into Yahoos; the change from
man to animal or unnatural man is made indirectly, there is no sorcerer,
and the process of denaturing is more serious than a simple metaphorical identification would be. Each one is distorted and changed into an
animal in the eyes of others, partly because everyone is quick to seize
on the weakness of another and partly because each person projects
upon the other a disgust and animosity which are really the image of

himself; thus Cranly treats everyone as a pig, because there is something of the pig in everyone's nature, but also because Cranly is afraid of the pig in his own nature. The variety of species corresponds to the existence of differences among the students, but they all have one characteristic in common: they are animals that remain near to the earth, domestic fowl, rodents, or serpents. The irony that springs from the obligatory aspirations each one cherishes towards a virtue which should be the dispenser of holiness is underlined by another series of symbols. Their own weight pins them down to the mud and the rotting smells of Dublin; it is not by chance that Joyce describes Lynch's ponderous gait, and that other undergraduates wear heavy shoes. The sporting Davin possesses an impressive collection of boots, and this inspires an amusing sketch of the down-at-heel poet parading before the shoes of the rude Gael:

> Often, as he sat in Davin's rooms . . . wondering at his friend's well-made boots that flanked the wall pair by pair and repeating for his friend's simple ear the verses and cadences of others which were the veils of his own longing and dejection, the rude Firbolg mind of his listener had drawn his mind towards it and flung it back again. (*Portrait*, p. 180)

Stephen's friends or acquaintances often have disturbing faces, less "realistic" than repellent. Temple, the double of Stephen and Cranly's surrogate, is a chameleon, "A lean student with olive skin and lank black hair thrust his face between the two, glancing from one to the other at each phrase and seeming to try to catch each flying phrase in his open moist mouth" (*Portrait*, p. 195).

Pursued, he naturally turns into a bleating goat, and then a light-footed beast of uncertain nature. Lynch has a snake's head and the walk of an elephant.

But the bestiary draws its lowest and most comical symbol from Stephen and his lice. Joyce was always obsessed by "vermin," originally using the word to denote the intellectual parasites that he considered the Irish to be. In his Pola notebook, the first group of words refers cruelly and succinctly to Ireland: "Catacombs and vermin" is followed by "Ireland—an afterthought of Europe". In *Stephen Hero* he developed his repulsion, emphasising it by a choice of words which he was later to use as reference-points:

> The deadly chill of the atmosphere of the college paralysed Stephen's heart. In a stupor of powerlessness he reviewed the plague of Catholicism.

He seemed to see the vermin begotten in the catacombs in an age of sickness and cruelty issuing forth upon the plains and mountains of Europe. . . . They obscured the sun. Contempt of human nature, weakness, nervous tremblings, fear of day and joy, distrust of man and life, hemiplegia of the will, beset the body burdened and disaffected in its members by its black tyrannous lice. Exultation of the mind before joyful beauty, exultation of the body in free confederate labours, every natural impulse towards health and wisdom and happiness had been corroded by the pest of these vermin. *(Stephen Hero,* pp. 197–8)

What is expressed with fierce hatred but figuratively in *Stephen Hero* becomes in the focus of *Portrait* a double symbol: the vermin crawling over Ireland are more than metaphorical. Stephen is still in Dublin; to be there is to participate, even if only a little, in the general state of paralysis.

While he was striving this way and that to free his feet from the fetters of the reformed conscience he came upon the droll statue of the national poet of Ireland.

He looked at it without anger; for, though sloth of the body and of the soul crept over it like unseen vermin, over the shuffling feet and up the folds of the cloak and around the servile head, it seemed humbly conscious of its indignity. *(Portrait,* p. 179)

The bird-man is still covered in vermin; he is free but dirty and afflicted by parasites.

A louse crawled over the nape and, putting his thumb and forefinger deftly beneath his loose collar, he caught it. He rolled its body, tender yet brittle as a grain of rice, between thumb and finger for an instant. . . . But the tickling of the skin of his neck made his mind raw and red. The life of his body, ill clad, ill fed, louse-eaten, made him close his eyelids in a sudden spasm of despair and in the darkness he saw the brittle bright bodies of lice falling from the air and turning often as they fell. *(Portrait,* pp. 233–4)

This vision in the dark behind closed eyelids is not an isolated one; it fits into a vast network of correspondences which spreads its ramifications out to *Finnegans Wake,* forming a meaningful whole of baroque richness of detail. As ever, the interlacing themes alternate with beautiful phrases; here the vermin's presence is accompanied by the echo of a verse from Nash, around which cluster the themes of opposition between light and dark, departure and stagnation, poetry and reality.

Just as Yeats's lines were quoted with an important modification, so is the line from Nash wrongly quoted, but this time the mistake is quickly picked up and corrected because it contains the key to all these correspondences. Stephen repeats the poem in an atmosphere of loneliness and treachery, having just seen the beloved come out of the library and greet Cranly, ignoring him.

> The swallows whose flight he had followed with idle eyes were sleeping. She had passed through the dusk. And therefore the air was silent save for one soft his that fell. And therefore the tongues about him had ceased their babble. Darkness was falling (*Portrait*, p. 232).

At once he takes refuge in words: "Darkness falls from the air," and he is carried back to the age of Dowland, Byrd, and Nash. The chosen line, distorted by his awareness of Dublin's darkness, comes from a poem which Joyce had removed from the book—yet which remains disturbingly in Stephen's mind—from a song of premature death, unjust loss, and abdication, *Summer's Last Will and Testament*. The exact text will intensify the allusion:

> Beauty is but a flower
> Which wrinkles will devour;
> Brightness falls from the air,
> Queens have died young and fair.

Beneath the traditional themes we recognise the involved anguish of Joyce, which he attributes to Stephen.

Isolated and incorrect, the line has no meaning in the text as it stands; it is merely a sensual compensation to Stephen for his frustration:

> A trembling joy, lambent as a faint light, played like a fairy host about him. But why? Her passage through the darkening air or the verse with its black vowels and its opening sound, rich and lutelike? (*Portrait*, p. 232).

It was not to be hoped that grace could descend among the rotting rubbish that encumbered the streets and souls of Dublin, or emerge from the box on the kitchen table, "speckled with louse marks," in which pawn tickets are kept, white and blue like the robes of Our Lady. Lice destroy the illusion and bring the dreamer back to reality.

> Yes, and it was not darkness that fell from the air. It was brightness. 'Brightness falls from the air'. He had not even remembered rightly Nash's line. All the images it had awakened were false. His mind bred vermin (*Portrait*, p. 234).

As Fritz Senn has demonstrated,[22] the fable of the Ondt and the Gracehoper (*Finnegans Wake*, p. 414) is part of the abundant metaphorical burgeoning for which Joyce employed all his talents as amateur "entymologist," a half-serious and half-comical view of the chaos of sexuality compared with the blind fertility of the insect world. Insect and incest go together in *Finnegans Wake*, as the bat and the libido in *Portrait*. In 'Scylla and Charybdis' in *Ulysses*, Stephen compares incest to "an avarice of the emotions". The *ondt* is the "ant" who stands for shame, and the prohibition, "don't," and is as avaricious as the ant in the fable; the emotional avarice that leads to incest is rather a typically Irish form of inhibition than an Oedipus complex too Greek in its blind directness. It is the prohibition that agitates the conscience. But the Irish "superego" is less God the Father than Mother Church. Stephen leaves the Church, we know, but keeps a friendly respect for Jesus, who has nothing to do with its abuse of the maternal authority. The emotional avarice is absorbed by the child from the very beginning, along with its mother's milk, that magical milk for which Stephen feels such disgust. The circle of emotions is a closed one, and the child, then the man, must pass from mother to mother until he dies; the Church claims all emotions as its due. Joyce was most amused by the fanatical feminism professed by his friend Francis Skeffington, or Sheehy-Skeffington as he became after his marriage with Mary Sheehy; Irish women were either bats or "ondts," and in no way could be considered as having any sense of life or notion of politics, or indeed anything but the blind instinct of continuous fertility. "Votes for women" means "foods for vermin" (*Finnegans Wake*, p. 239).

In *Portrait* the mother is constantly reminding Stephen of "shame," from the beginning of Chapter I to that of Chapter V: "Ah, it's a scandalous shame for you, Stephen," she says. She cleans his dirty face and ears, and his father offends the artist's delicate ears by his vulgar insults.

Stephen as Gracehoper in *Portrait* is eaten up by vermin; Stephen Hero laments the corruption of all natural instincts by vermin. In order to appreciate the scene in which Stephen's mother washes him in the presence of all his brothers and sisters, the passage from Freud should be borne in mind which says that "small animals and vermin are substitutes for small children, for unwanted siblings".[23] In 'Circe,' Stephen-

---

[22]Senn, 'Insects Apalling,' in *Twelve and a Tilly*, edd. J. P. Dalton and Clive Hart (London, 1966), pp. 36–9.
[23]Senn, *op. cit.*, p. 38.

Simon Dedalus, metamorphosed into a cardinal, is suddenly covered by thousands of crawling insects.

The Illusion of Surpassing Reality by Language

In spite of the establishment of a symbolism which implies the existence of a double reality, language remains an intermediary between subject and object in *Portrait,* and "the other side" is only projected through the subject and then at once given fixed form in prose; the reader's comprehension of the material is not interrupted by any alien elements. The sensile world is commented upon rather than experienced, but commented upon in realistic fashion, so much so that once the notion of "the subject's own style" has been grasped and accepted, one can easily follow Stephen's mental development as it is mimicked by the language; as the world gradually moves inwards, realism moves also, towards consciousness of the self. Time, which is the present rooted in memory, does not escape from the control of either author or reader; the associations which bring the past into the present are always perceptible. Joyce has not yet adopted the technique of fragmentation and dispersion of moments that makes *Ulysses* more difficult to read. The only innovation, though an important one, lies in the increased power and the place allotted to language in the work as a whole. Gradually it becomes, not only the vehicle of reality, but also something which has a role to play in the book similar to that of the typical characters or situations or the great figures of authority: Family, Country, and Church. Language tends, indeed, to become Stephen's replacement-universe. His word becomes twofold, and the inner monologue, as reduplication of the self shown as conversation in a space it has itself created, starts to appear, although still in an indirect style, in Chapter V. At certain moments words become actual objects which his consciousness encounters.

As the world moves on to the inner stage, a new world emerges which is not autonomous, but which is not entirely dependent on its creator either; there is reciprocal influence of the word and the self on each other, because of two phenomena—the one subjective and the other objective. Language seems at times stricken by disease, so much so that words become completely meaningless for Stephen; this happens because of the neurosis of the self, which feels that it has lost the meaning of its own presence in the world. Or it may happen, on the other hand, that the subject feels robbed of his rights over language because he is simply an uninvited guest at the banquet of a foreign culture. In this case he reacts energetically by reappropriating for himself the language of his own alienation, opposing to the English which pains his Irish nature the Latin which is universal, and which belongs in particular to him as Catholic. If Ben Jonson or Nash please or distress him, he can claim the right to handle Horace and Aquinas.

As soon as he begins to disengage himself from Ireland and to prepare for exile, the reality which had been distressing becomes intolerable, and this is manifested not objectively but subjectively by his retreat into a time-scale close to that of dream, which is sometimes so far removed from real time as to border on hallucination. The destruction of real time is shown in a fashion both comical and symbolic at the beginning of Chapter V by a great deal of play with clocks that will not tell the right time and which contradict each other; they draw the reader's attention to modifications which are transforming the world from which Stephen has already fled in imagination, from the clock in the dairy that says five to five when it is eleven in the morning to the alarm clock lying on its side at home, which is an hour and twenty-five minutes fast for some unknown reason. From that day on, duration becomes a purely inner matter; the Thursday which it is in reality has no date and seems to extend throughout the whole of the vast chapter, which takes up a third of the book.

Apart from the month which is represented by the journal, it lasts for approximately twenty-four hours, and ends with Stephen, ready at last, taking up contact again with chronology, with the days and months that mark out a reality now open to the future. He has lived between reality and delirium in a ghostly city, and the first ghost was a sinister double of himself, a consumptive man who walked with little steps, holding a furled umbrella "like a divining rod" that is a sterile caricature of Stephen's own ashplant. His spirit moves about the streets of Dublin dreaming of reality and distilling its dreams. Space and time open and close like the artist's eyes, and his thoughts wander. Here can be there and yesterday can be now. In his mind, fearlessly open like a stage, the Dubliners play out their daily life and death. The city speaks a concrete language intended for the senses, and Stephen replies with an inner word of his own, so free that it surprises the self who is listening. The paths of memory cross the ways of imagination, and every picture resembles some other image, real or dreamed. A permanent exchange is taking place between the phenomenal world and the young man's mind. The world is the sensile space in which Stephen's vision is imprinted, and he is sorcerer as well as artist. The passage from the mental universe to the sensile world is made by means of language as intermediary. Everything that is perceived is at once commented upon by Stephen and fitted into its place. Everything that is imagined is at once established in a "representational space" that is as real to Stephen as the street in which his legs are carrying him along.

Language establishes the continuity between the two worlds until Stephen feels himself exiled from the one by excess ugliness and from the other by excess of loneliness. At this point *he passes into the third world, that of words,* where the streets are sentences and the palaces are poems, and the poor quarters are disconnected speeches. This is where what Stephen calls his "soul" resides.

At eleven o'clock, he stands in the street, consulting the placard in a newsagent's shop to find out what day it is:

> Eleven! Then he was late for that lecture too. . . . He fancied to himself the English lecture and felt, even at that distance, restless and helpless. He saw the heads of his classmates meekly bent as they wrote in their notebooks the points they were bidden to note, nominal definitions, essential definitions and examples or dates of birth or death, chief works, a favourable and an unfavourable criticism side by side. . . . His thoughts wandered abroad and whether he looked around the little class of students or out of the window across the desolate gardens of the green an odour assailed him of cheerless cellar-damp and decay. (*Portrait*, p. 177)

At eleven o'clock, then, he is in the street, and the date and time of day are given to him by the outside world; but within himself he is sitting among his fellow-students, sadly undergoing his passion. Bending over the notebooks, the symbol of intellectual alienation, his classmates docilely permit themselves to be led through a dead past, which, unlike Stephen's, cannot be evoked into any life in time present. Stephen's thoughts sail freely out through the window, while the minds of the group remain bent down towards the notebooks. In appearance we are attending a lecture, but in reality as lived by Stephen we are down in the catacombs—in the graveyard of Dublin's minds. He is repelled by the reality of the street and by the magic formulae which are in fact trivial shop signs, emptied of all meaning. This world is typically that of the alienated individual, for whom the inanity of the world becomes suddenly mysterious and threatening, as though personified: "He found himself glancing from one casual word to another on his right or left in stolid wonder that they had been so silently emptied of instantaneous sense until every mean shop legend bound his mind like the words of a spell and his soul shrivelled up sighing with age as he walked on in a lane among heaps of dead language" (*Portrait*, p. 178).

Language decomposes when it comes into contact with this corpse-silence; thought is not safe from mutability, because it is a living, organic thing; and Stephen's language which is the product of his mind, his history, and his will aspires to freedom, order, and luxury. The language of Dublin carries along with it the refuse and filth of its moral wretchedness. Language resembles the man, and the words of Dublin can signify nothing but the foulness of Dublin. Like the flow of sins oozing forth, the flux of that language whose master Stephen is drips away in a nonsensical arrangement of words, set to a rhythm by a last glimmer of poetic awareness:

> The ivy whines upon the wall,
> And whines and twines upon the wall,
> The yellow ivy upon the wall,
> Ivy, ivy up the wall.

Stephen, who has just been deriving solace from a precious Elizabethan poem, can no longer recognise such foolishness, and so the lines cannot have come from his store of poetry and phrases; the intruding lines may imitate the cadence of a small poem, but it cannot make itself pass for art.

Joyce's taste for comic songs was inversely paralleled by his love for the charms of lyric; short poems and limericks illustrate two intuitive and mutually contradictory visions of the world of emotion, because their formal qualities, and perhaps other qualities too, are similar; their brevity and their rhyme are particularly apt for the transmission of intensely dramatic or intensely comical messages. This is why Stephen in *Portrait* is constantly toying with rhymes, amateurish rondeaux of nostalgia, or nonsense verses. In fact, the content of poems and sung verses provides for a two-way current of parody; the day which Stephen begins on a note of weariness with Ben Jonson's line, "I was not wearier where I lay," continues its course through limping rhymes and doggerel to the walls where the ivy whines and to Stephen's Green; here the image of the billiard table occurs, called up by the unconsciously obscene rhyme used by the professor of physics in his lecture on the elliptic:

> On a cloth untrue
> With a twisted cue
> And elliptical billiard balls.

The words "yellow," "Ivy," "whine," and "wall" are not merely capricious visitors to Stephen's mind; melancholy words that roll softly off the tongue, they wind sinuously like snakes or like the ivy on the wall as hieroglyphs of Ireland's cultural alienation, the result of its political and economical alienation. The ivy climbs hopelessly up the wall of a prison, for even the illusion of freedom died with Parnell. "Who ever heard of ivy whining on a wall?" And the ivy is yellow, because in Stephen's over-sensitive imagination the sounds of "ivy" and "ivory" are confused; the two words are brothers, yet enemies to one another, for the ivy dies through the ingratitude of Ireland while the ivory is one of the fundamental words of Stephen's poetic imagination. Yet from now on he is far from the mystery of the tower of ivory and much more sensitive to the interplay of sounds. Ivory no longer suggests Our Lady, but "The word now shone in his brain, clearer and brighter than any ivory sawn from the mottled tusks of elephants. *Ivory, ivoire, avorio, ebur.* One of the first examples that he had learnt in Latin had run: *India mittit ebur.*" *(Ibid.)*

From one word to another in this reverie of the senses is sketched out the drama of the dispossessed artist and his wish to recover the beauty of words—a substitute, as the context shows, for the worship of Our Lady. The book from which he learned Latin versification was indeed written by a Portuguese priest, and he recalls "the shrewd northern face" of the rector who taught him to construe Ovid's *Metamorphoses,* but beyond the voice of the rector, the Latin words *implere ollam denariorum* really do "fill a pot with denaries". The evocative power of the word is the only reality, even if the word is spoken by a stranger or foreigner. In the same way, he finds life in an ancient, yellowed book. And why should he not take his place in the pre-Christian culture of antiquity? Horace stands near to him:

> The pages of his time-worn Horace never felt cold to the touch even when his own fingers were cold; they were human pages and fifty years before they had been turned by the human fingers of John Duncan Inverarity and by his brother, William Malcolm Inverarity. Yes, those were noble names on the dusky flyleaf and, even for so poor a Latinist as he, the dusky verses were as fragrant as though they had lain all those years in myrtle and lavender and vervain. (*Portrait*, p. 179)

The myrtle, lavender, and vervain are more emotionally moving and less rare than the spikenard and myrrh and frankincense of Our Lady.

The language of poetry is unalterable, and faded verses survive poets and survive the lips that first spoke them in a scented slumber; not only life is there, which only belongs to the present, but also the delightful eternity of memory. This is the language that is heard across seas and centuries. Stephen's words are not understood by the Dean, and not listened to by his friends. The Dean uses words which Stephen does not know, and this is simply a sign that the mediocre or servile word is incapable of changing places with the intransigeant and troubled word of Stephen. He does not know whom he should address: Horace is dead, Newman is dead, Ibsen is too far away, Davin who attracts his attention "by a quaint turn of old English speech" also repels "swiftly and suddenly by a grossness of intelligence". Yet between the Roman empire in all its glory and the Gaelic myth in its intermittent gleaming, Stephen is wounded "to think that he would never be but a shy guest at the feast of the world's culture and that the monkish learning, in terms of which he was striving to forge out an aesthetic philosophy, was held no higher by the age he lived in than the subtle and curious jargons of heraldry and falconry." *(Ibid.)*

Suffering provokes the defensive attitude. Joyce is to impose upon the world lost erudition and disciplines. With the myrtle, vervain, lavender, crises, struggles, and victories in these pages, near the grey block of Trinity College "set heavily in the city's ignorance," he introduces one of the most attractive leitmotifs in his work, a motif that begins with three flowers and an ancient book to lead on eventually to Edgar Quinet's sentence which he reproduces in its entirety in *Finnegans Wake:*

Aujourd'hui comme au temps de Pline et Columelle, la jacinthe se plaît dans les Gaules, la pervenche en Illyrie, la marguerite sur les ruines de Numance et pendant qu'autour d'elles les villes ont changé de maîtres et de noms, que plusieurs sont entrées dans le néant, que les civilisations se sont choquées et brisées, leurs paisibles générations ont traversé les âges et sont arrivées jusqu'à nous, fraîches et riantes comme aux jours des batailles. (Finnegans Wake, p. 281)[24]

Today as in the days of Pliny, today in the days of Joyce, civilisations become degenerate and slaves change masters or replace them with others. As in Saint Patrick's day, the Irish continue to go to confession, and history repeats itself; it is always the same story, the disappearance of man and the appearance of ghosts, while the flowers can laugh at

[24]See the analysis of this motif in Clive Hart, *Structure and Motif in Finnegans Wake* (London, 1962), pp. 182ff.

death. Joyce detested flowers, and Stephen likes only the symbolic rose. The artist is not to be consoled by a vegetable continuity; the flowers that are reborn are only the scent of his phrases, the breath of the poet that is transmitted to every reader. Joyce-Stephen is obviously not interested in the Golden Age type of poet, but in the lover of fine language.

The good old times of Horace or of Simon Dedalus are times that will not come again, but their songs live on. Stephen dreams of escaping into the time of scent and sound, although the world, and the work, are still to come. When Stephen declares war on death, he is proclaiming his faith in the future, and his loyalty to the past; he always bears the past in mind, because he knows that it has produced him as he is, but the Dublin consciousness is a dark and confused one that leaves no trace of itself behind. It is certain that Heron is not aware of repeating an act of cruelty, and that, no matter what Lynch says, E. C. does not wish to remember past feelings. Stephen's last declaration is of capital importance: "the present is living only because it brings forth the future". The young man only lives because he is to bring forth the artist. The formula is an open one, open to the possibilities of life and the time of creation. In the 'Proteus' episode of *Ulysses* he adopts it and reverses it, thus: "Hold fast to the here and now, through which all future plunges into the past".

The meaning of this second formula is revealing: the leap towards the unknown is replaced by a dive into the known. Between these two temporal experiences one is to look for the secret of the craftsman. The lesson which Stephen has learned in the time between *Portrait* and *Ulysses* boils down to the discovery that the Universe awaiting him beyond the known, beyond the limits of the city and of time present, beyond the nets and traps, is *the same* universe still; the same, but recognised, caught in the bounds of the artist's imagination and in the nets of his awareness, it is "reflected" and experienced *within*. The belief in a completely different unknown, in a transcendence, in the possibility of being the first to gaze upon a beauty that had not yet come into the world, in the existence of some virgin territory not yet named by anyone else—this vague but exhilarating belief that bore up Stephen's soul throughout *Portrait*, from liberation through detachment to ecstasy, has now disappeared. This result was never entirely an unforeseen one; the voice of Daedalus in Stephen had never ceased to remind Icarus of the dangers of flying too near the sun.

As he is making his last preparations, having already had his Annunciation and his vision of the hawk-like man, he still feels some fear of the unknown, of symbols and omens, and of the bird-man whose name he bears, flying away from his prison on wings that he has made. An intuition of the truth appears: *Portrait* had been the book of signs and symbols. To Stephen every detail is full of meaning and importance. The world speaks a secret language to him now, and he understands all its meanings. No scene, thought, or moment has been without its significance, and everything, down to the most common object, has had its message to deliver. Stephen has lived through the world as though the world were a book; at first he was not able to decipher it all, but as he continued to observe its words, he understood more and more. Beings, animals, objects, colours, sounds, expressions, and dreams were all signs in an elaborate and complicated code, and he soon believed that he had discovered their values. The book related a story that was already imprinted in time, but, like every book, it was the written expression of some reality.

This, at any rate, was what Stephen believed. He watched the outside world as though it were capable of epiphany: "Imagine my glimpses at that clock," he says in *Stephen Hero*, "as the gropings of a spiritual eye which seeks to adjust its vision to an exact focus".

When the focus is exact, the spiritual eye sees the real "clock"; and what has happened between *Portrait* and *Ulysses* is precisely that: the clock has become epiphanised. And the artist recognises that the clock is *a* clock, but also that *this* clock is a *clock*. And the world towards which the not-yet-epiphanised world was directing him is *the* world and the *world*. Reality places itself between these two visions—that of the object-world which belongs to anyone and everyone, and that of *the* world which is Stephen's, seen by his young, myopic, smarting eyes, attentive, open, and distorting. As he draws away from reality because of his desire for exile, he becomes more and more sensitive to reality, until he is almost completely permeable to it, as he will be in *Ulysses*. Dublin penetrates into him by all his senses, saturating his thoughts, "An odour assailed him of cheerless cellar-damp and decay. . . . But the trees in Stephen's Green were fragrant of rain and the rain-sodden earth gave forth its mortal odour, a faint incense rising upward through the mould from many hearts".

The odour is that of Irish history, of corruption and venality, he feels. The material world has become nothing more than a vague fluid atmosphere seeping from his brain to impregnate space through the fluid and melancholy language of doubt; the grey monochrome of the present is the very colour of alienation. The world of Dublin is a stagnant socio-historical setting whose "veil" of fog and grey mist prevents the eye from conjuring up any vision of a future. When Stephen revolts against this lack of any change, this automation of behaviour and the hereditary transmission of prejudice and blindness, he is claiming his right to have a destiny of his own, and space after that takes on the form of his thought; the climate becomes that of his mind. The fog of doubt is illuminated by brief flashes. Fear of staying and fear of going are at once given verbal expression, and there is coalescence rather than correspondence between the self and the world. "His thinking was a dusk of doubt and self-mistrust, lit up at moments by the lightnings of intuition" (*Portrait*, p. 176).

Doubt as intellectual irony clearly constitutes the transition-place from reality to dream and from symbolism to personal symbolism. It is a recognition of the instability of the awareness and of the absence of the world—or rather, of one's own absence *from* the world. The exchange of characters, mutations, and absorbing encounters with people or words are already a preparation for *Finnegans Wake*. Stephen is he who possesses his own name, yet feels constantly that *in potentia* he is someone else, and he sees himself as monk, bard, or bird, as the world around him grows disfigured more and more. As an open awareness, he receives into him this world which drowns him, and he fills it with a mad language which is already that of *Ulysses*, although lacking the irony of the latter.

The *Portrait of the Artist* preparing for his life-work was a workshop in which the instruments for that work were being forged; *Dubliners* was a lexicon of primary symbols, from which developed Joyce's personal symbolism that could then inform any of the future books; *Ulysses* consists of the restoration to freedom of a reality that had previously enjoyed only a relative autonomy, controlled by the nets woven in *Portrait*. Joyce can permit the larger book to develop so because *Portrait* and *Dubliners* are veritable treatises of symbolism, yet also because the dreams in *Portrait* open out not into mystery but into the eternal world that we all share. In *Portrait* everything converged into one impulse towards the heights, and gradually became sublimed into revelation. The mystery of the awareness, of the imagination as womb, oriented the whole book towards an escape and an emergence. But now the mystery is revealed as being the faculty of detachment proper to creation, which must be applied to reality. And for Joyce, as for Stephen, reality is Ireland. It could be history, or the social revolutions of the twentieth century, or scientific evolution, or a concrete universal reality; but it is Ireland. Joyce was far too indelibly marked by Ireland and Catholicism ever to be able to expatriate his mind and his intelligence. His problems are still the same problems which made him contradict his fellow-creatures, and his phantasms are but the creations of his ghost-surrounded imagination. But in *Portrait* the artist simulates the sensibility of an uneasy conscience tormented by hallucinations, while in *Ulysses* the visions amuse the visionary. A lament such as this —"O the grey dull day! It seemed a limbo of painless patient consciousness through which souls of mathematicians might wander, projecting long slender fabrics from plane to plane of ever rarer and paler twilight, radiating swift eddies to the last verges of a universe ever vaster, farther and more impalpable" (*Portrait*, p. 191)—is echoed in *Ulysses* by a crazy dance of words: "Across the page the symbols moved in grave morrice, in the mummery of their letters, wearing quaint caps of squares and cubes" (*Ulysses*, p. 30).

Stephen, having returned to Dublin at his parents' behest, is in search not of a father, but of a means of rejoining the Dream without having to go by way of words. *Ulysses* is written in a language which is attempting to live by its own phonetic substance and at the same time is written partly in the sickly language of classical literature, which strives to repeat and transmit the same ancient messages of the human mind. Bloom's abundant speech is a recognition or statement of the spiritual weariness of his world. He fails to resuscitate one or two dead words such as "love" and "nation," because it is not merely the words that should be cured, but the whole language—which is alienated and should be replaced. As a challenge to the Word, Joyce writes the chapter 'Oxen of the Sun,' in which Mrs. Purefoy gives birth to a son, in parody of gestation and parturition, using a parallel "embryology of language," demonstrating its inanity and instability by way of various grotesque mutations. Then he moves from the hospital where the Logos was in the ante-chamber of birth to the bordello of Crice, where the mother's breast is replaced by the imaginary breast, obstetrics by magic, God by the butcher, and His logic by hallucination.

After the diagnosis of *Ulysses*, the only thing to do is to set out again. And Joyce moves on to the world of dream and of the infinity of possibles, playing with an unlimited language which is the only space where one is not required to leave: the only "place" which is truly his own. Here the artist is an outlaw beyond every law, including those of grammar, and he can move around freely, indefinitely, without needing to fear that at the mouth of the labyrinth reality may be lying in wait for him. *Finnegans Wake* is, in short, the final statement of the artist as heretic, and the admission that if one wishes not to be subject to the control of theology, there is only one solution—not to come out, not to be born, to refuse to answer "present," to refuse to represent the world in the traditional terms which are already dictated by the Divine Tyrant (as Artaud would say). "Realism," from this point of view, is nothing but art obeying the orders of Creation, reciting or quoting from the work of an Other who holds all the copyrights.

XXIII. The Language of Reality

After the moral history of *Dubliners*, after the spiritual gestation of the archetypal artist and the discovery of the subject's own style, after the skilfully demonstrated statement that the Artist creates, starting from his inner exile, a work outside which (or far from which) he stands, Joyce wrote *Ulysses*, the work which reconciles unity and multiplicity to an end which is both realistic, moral, and universal. The Artist is both within and without, and the style of the object responds to that of the subject. The relationships of symbolism and realism are modified, sometimes to such an extent that the code and the message, the surface and the depths, are confused with one another. The object of realism is not "reality," for the reality of Ireland is only a part of an infinitely larger whole. *Ulysses* is not the modern *Odyssey*; the Odysseyan symbolism with its network of correspondences leads scarcely further than an ethical statement, and in fact the *Odyssey* is also part of an infinitely larger whole, taking on its meaning from that whole (all Western culture, its historical duration, and its myths) and from its relationship with the concrete reality of the here and now. The best definition of Joyce's intentions is to be found in a letter he wrote to Carlo Linati:

> I think that in view of the enormous bulk and the more than enormous complexity of my three times blasted novel it would be better to send you a sort of summary-key-skeleton-scheme, for your personal use only. . . . I have given only catchwords in my scheme but I think you will understand

it all the same. It is an epic of two races (Israelite-Irish) and at the same time the cycle of the human body as well as a little story of a day (life). . . . For seven years I have been working at this book—blast it! It is also a sort of encyclopaedia. My intention is to transpose the myth *sub specie temporis nostri.* Each adventure (that is, every hour, every organ, every art being interconnected and interrelated in the structural scheme of the whole) should not only condition but even create its own technique. Each adventure is so to say one person although it is composed of persons—as Aquinas relates of the angelic hosts.[1]

Joyce's programme, in its methodical formulation and with its encyclopaedic intention, is in its universality nothing less than a project to write the book of books, to find a form or "structural scheme" in which everything may be said in relation to everything, in which each component part (art, organ, hour, etc.) should create its own language. This monstrous epiphany is to be the total manifestation of reality through language.

The first point to notice is the idea of a "summa," a mediaeval idea from which Joyce takes the concept of totality, while abandoning its content, that order and hierarchy which made the correspondence-system possible; the form of the summa is dictated by the demands of language. Joyce rejects the idea of one unique style, one author's commentary, and replaces it by a multiplicity of styles. At the very most, he admits that the word "style" may have a meaning. He explains to Miss Weaver that it is the mode of language of any one generation, thereby reducing it to the garment of writing, not even the garment of thought; by this he means that the men of any given generation will command the same resources of language, drawn from their vocabulary, and that in this sense one can speak of the purple style of the symbolist decadents, or of the style of the generation of Pope. But when "style" is meant as a purely formal and objective term, it is simply the historical aspect of the language, that which permits the reader to date the work. Apart from this meaning (in which style appears as that which is not the man, but that which is the age in which he lives, the very reverse of the original expression), he always insisted, in the explanations given to friends while the work was in progress, on the primordial function of the "multilanguage" of *Ulysses*: "The task I set myself technically in writing a book from eighteen different points of view and in as many styles. . . ."[2]

[1] *Letters*, vol. I, pp. 146–7, 21 Sept. 1920.
[2] *Ibid.*, p. 167.

There might seem to be some contradiction here, in that the idea of totality is limited by the order Joyce has chosen, in that there are to be eighteen styles and no more. The traditional idea of style is indeed destroyed, but it is replaced, given the artifice of the choosing of the eighteen styles, by an experimental style which is a kind of summa of all styles, including the philological parody of the English language from its origins to the present day. He does this in one chapter alone, 'Oxen of the Sun,' whose corresponding co-ordinates are in themselves a comic metaphor of what Joyce considers literature to be; the organ of this chapter in which literary style develops like a technical embryo is the womb.[3]

Yet *Ulysses* may further be a summa of all possibilities of literary representation, a kind of critical anatomy of genres, myths, and modes; in this way the work becomes a part of culture, if only with purpose of destroying it from within, for "each successive episode, dealing with some province of artistic culture, (rhetoric or music or dialectic) leaves behind it a burnt up field."[4]

The context of experiences is always the same, that of culture as expressed through language and, through culture only, a very definite vision of the universe in its spatio-temporal categories. This limitation is expressed in the choice itself of a unity of time and space: "everything" happens in one single day, in one place, and Joyce remains in the main stream of Western thought, with its vision of the world always directed towards the One or the Absolute.

This multiplicity caught in unity permits the author-as-demiurge to withdraw, leaving reality to speak its own language. There is sometimes a perfect equation established between the code and the message it conveys, between the world and the way in which it is expressed, which may go so far as to include phonetic mimicry like that of the four words spoken by the tide: "seesoo, hrss, rsseeiss, ooos. Vehement breath of waters amid seasnakes, rearing horses, rocks. In cups of rocks it slops: flop, slop, slap: bounded in barrels. And, spent, its speech ceases" (*Ulysses*, p. 52). But there is still, of necessity, a permanent presence, a witness of reality, one who hears this language. In the 'Proteus' chap-

---

[3]Bloom, Stephen, and the medical students meet at the maternity hospital at ten in the evening. Stephen as artist is in a sense the apostle of fecundity, but as prodigal son is the enemy of Ireland and of every mother-figure; he conducts a discussion about life and death and man's last end. Parodying Aristotle again, he remarks, "What of those Godpossibled souls that we nightly impossibilise, which is the sin against the Holy Ghost, Very God, Lord and Giver of Life?" (*Ulysses*, p. 383.)

[4]*Letters*, vol. I, p. 129, 20 July 1919.

ter, everything passes through Stephen's consciousness; but Stephen is not the author of the chapter, he exists in the flux of reality as do the objects which he perceives. In fact, the author and the character are replaced in *Ulysses* by a new sort of subject, who participates in both the action and the creation; the epiphany is still there, but an enlarged, totalitarian epiphany that includes space and all moments. It ensures the harmony of this chaotic universe by wrapping it in a "verbal clothing". The epiphany-as-cosmos allows for the depersonification of art in *Ulysses*.

A work such as *Ulysses* was only possible in a prolongation of *Portrait*, and by means of greater flexibility in the technique of the epiphany, which becomes a focus of metamorphoses, the meeting-point of *stasis* and *movens* where they unite for an instant, the brilliant reconciliation of contraries; *Ulysses*, freed from the limitations imposed by the single gaze of the artist, can include the sounds of the everyday world and of the elements, individual images and images from myth, banal moments and moments from Biblical legend. Objects are given speech: the cat, the church bell, the beach strewn with shells, the mirror and its glancing reflections, can all speak. The art of *Ulysses* is not only impersonal, but also often depersonified. The depersonified passages by finding verbal expression take their places in the general established order, and at the same time ensure its mobility and freedom. The ultimate function of the epiphany is to express the mobility that exists within the order Joyce has fixed, and this function of mediation between subject and object is precisely that which Joyce in his earliest aesthetic allotted to the artist himself. The language of epiphany has become the vital centre of art; through it, what was hallucination in *Portrait* becomes a liberation of subjective and objective reality in *Ulysses*. When Stephen at the beginning of the 'Proteus' chapter says that "the soul is in a manner all that is," we can see from this wider conception of the "soul" how far he has progressed, and how much the idealistic definition of existence has been expanded. The "soul" is here understood in the sense of the Aristotelian "form".

Everything that is is also caught in the "form of forms," which is the summa, *Ulysses*. The "hero" of *Ulysses* is the "form of forms," just as the "hero" of *Finnegans Wake* is not the dreamer but the dream in which he is dreaming (just, indeed, as Alice is "dreamed" by the King, according to Lewis Carroll's formal logic). When the human mind is embodied as part of the world, persons and objects may be of equivalent status; Stephen's mind, on the beach, eventually scatters his thoughts about like sand. Bloom, who is more closely sympathetic to the animal kingdom, is so near to the seagulls or to the cat that he reaches a kind of communion with them, foreshadowing the abolition of the function of difference between the world and the self which occurs in the 'Circe' episode. In 'Calypso,' Bloom is in a state of osmosis with the cat:

> —Mkgnao!
> —O, there you are, Mr. Bloom said, turning from the fire.
> The cat mewed in answer and stalked again stiffly round a leg of the table, mewing. Just how she stalks over my writingtable. Prr. Scratch my head. Prr. (*Ulysses*, p. 54)

"My table and "my" head do not refer to the same subject; the cat-as-object enters the porous consciousness of the subject in such a way that the first person may indifferently be Bloom or the cat, in the same speech. Bloom-as-cat links up with Molly-as-cat, her mewings and sighs echoing this first scene, and "she" may mean either Molly or the cat in this monologue of Bloom, as he goes about the feeding of his pets:

> She didn't like her plate full. Right. . . .
> —Milk for the pussens, he said.
> —Mrkgnao! the cat cried. . . .
> She understands all she wants to. Vindictive too. Wonder what I look like to her. Height of a tower? No, she can jump me.
> . . . She might like something tasty. Thin bread and butter she likes in the morning. Still perhaps: once in a way.
> He said softly in the bare hall:
> —I am going round the corner. Be back in a minute.
> And when he had heard his voice say it he added:
> —You don't want anything for breakfast?
> A sleepy soft grunt answered:
> —Mn.
> No. She did not want anything. (*Ulysses*, pp. 54–5).

Gradually, objects are drawn into the epiphany, which becomes full of memories, associating the present with the past, memory with hope, and Dublin with Gibraltar. There are certain focal points which direct and hold the reader's attention, as though to continue the first form of the epiphany, that of the image isolated from reality and set in a context which it illumined and which caused its soul to show forth clearly; they may be words, such as "parallax" or "metempsychosis," which (as in *Portrait*) are planted in reality and then germinate and branch out to form recurring psychological themes. Or they may be snatches of song which play the role taken in *Portrait* by such phrases as "Tower of Ivory" and "House of Gold". Examples of these latter are the song "All is lost now" and the aria *Vorrei e non vorrei* from *Don Juan*, which is quoted with a mistake in it that reveals the whole of Molly's intrigue with Boylan. Other focal points may be mistakes such as that made by Bloom's secret correspondent Martha Clifford, who writes "world" instead of "word"; the sentence "I do not like this other world" becomes allegorical, and allows a transition to take place from "word" to "world". It acts, in fine, as a disguised epiphany, a signal from Joyce to the attentive reader. More and more, objects are becoming signs, though these were still rare in *Portrait*. They are often mysterious: for instance, Bloom carries a potato around with him all day in his pocket, and when he gives it to a young prostitute in the house of Bella Cohen or Circe he explains that it is a talisman, for good luck. The contents of his pockets, indeed, would deserve an inventory to themselves—not a realistic one like that made of Gulliver's pockets by the Lilliputians, but a symbolic, and epiphanic, list. The soap he buys for Molly eventually turns into the moon, Molly's bed creaks all day long, and the newspapers sum up the immediate present. Some insignificant details seem to secrete a kind of mystery, and an abundance of small unexplained elements makes up the substance of everyday life, in which, as in the substance of culture, Joyce carves strange, unexpected shapes.

There is an intellectual order hidden within and beyond the apparent chaos of details. Just as Saint Thomas trained Stephen's mind for its conflicts in *Portrait*, here in *Ulysses* we find Aristotle, or rather Aristotle as revived, contradicted, or, on occasions, supported by his Semitic disciples Averroes and Maimonides. The philosophical key to *Ulysses* is certainly borrowed from the Stagirite, and it opens the two worlds, that of the possibles and that of the actual, the gap between which Stephen is trying to bridge. Furthermore, and as always in this work where everything follows two paths, that of Stephen and that of Bloom, if Stephen is thinking in fashions which agree or disagree with Aristotle, Bloom is to be seen, in a way both comical and unexpected, as the living object of a demonstration of a particular Aristotelian mode of being. Aristotle is no more important to the pattern of *Ulysses* than Saint Thomas was to that of *Portrait*, but he is present in *Ulysses* as master of the stability of the world, in relation to whom the apparent instability of *Ulysses* takes on its full meaning.

If one could speak of a philosophy of Joyce that informs his poetics, one would have to define it as "anti-history," with its basis in the permanent nature of art. Aristotle's causality serves Joyce's aesthetic purposes, but, although he was able to be a Thomist without involving himself in any profession of faith, he had to oppose Aristotle insofar as the latter's theory of the actualisation of possibles produced in him a movement of metaphysical rebellion. Joyce's reply is an ambiguous one: he knows himself to be the product of the Aristotelian world-vision, but he feels much closer, by a spiritual affinity, to Aristotle's Semitic commentators Averroes and Maimonides.

These two are spiritual brothers of Stephen. Joyce was probably acquainted with them through the intermediary of another of his allies, the rebellious thinker Ernest Renan, whose works he still read with excitement when he was living in Italy.[5] The dark-eyed philosophers, contemporaries and enemies, played the same chess-games with the truth as did Stephen and Joyce; both, as readers and commentators of Aristotle, sought to establish an enlightened humanism at the crossroads between history and theology, between Faith and Reason.

Averroes (1126–98), astronomer, doctor, and favourite jurist of the Almohad princes, wrote a commentary that was both a defence and an apology for Neo-Platonism and Aristotle's philosophy, entitled "The Incoherence of Incoherence," *Tahafut al-Tahafut*, which takes its first principles from Plato's *Republic*.[6] In Aquinas' treatise *De Unitate Intellectus*, written in 1270, there first occurs the word "Averroistae," used to designate the adherents of heterodox Christianity who were remarkable for their support of the doctrine of "monopsychism," that is, of Averroes' version of Aristotle's *De Anima*. Averroes was a rationalist and a man of science before anything else, and he would not hesitate to question the apparent irrationalities of his religion.

Until recently, all studies of Averroism stated, incorrectly, that Averroes adopts the theory of the Two Truths, that of religion and that of reason, and accepts that they may contradict each other. It can be seen what affinities Joyce would feel for this philosopher of destruction, this man who redeems reason by cunning. His compatriot and companion Maimonides had a fate of such ironical import that Joyce could not have failed to be struck by it: he was born at Cordova, an Arabic scholar and doctor like Averroes, but was expelled because he was a Jew. His

---

[5]There was virtually no available translation of the two philosophers, except one into French, but Joyce was able to make use of Saint Thomas' commentaries on them and of other works of scholastic philosophy.

[6]Renan claims, although this is contestable, that there is an Averroistic influence discernible in scholastic philosophy from the thirteenth century onwards. The works of Aristotle, translated into Latin by Michael Scot, in the years 1217–30, were being read shortly after in Paris and Oxford.

travels took him in a direction opposite to that of his namesake Moses, not *de Egypto* but into Egypt, where he became physician to Saladin in Cairo. His *Mishned Thorah* in fourteen volumes is a *Summa Theologiae* of Judaism, inspired by the philosophy of Aristotle as he had found it, and as Averroes had found it, with its commentary by Avicenna. His famous *Guide for the Undecided* is a treatise in Arabic interpreting Biblical and Rabbinic theology by means of an Aristotelian Neo-Platonism. In the episodes 'Proteus' and 'Nestor,' Stephen thinks of these two men, associating them with stars and with exile beyond the bounds of the actual: "Gone too from the world, Averroes and Moses Maimonides, dark men in mien and movement, flashing in their mocking mirrors the obscure soul of the world, a darkness shining in brightness which brightness could not comprehend" (*Ulysses*, p. 31).

Averroes and Maimonides, the Arab philosopher and the Jewish philosopher, both born in Cordova in the twelfth century, both Hebrew scholars writing in Arabic, both writing out the truth from right to left in order that its reflection might be deciphered by some infidel, dark men like Stephen, all disciples of Aristotle, are scholars who penetrate the night of the soul and whom the light of the Catholic revelation cannot comprehend; dark, Odysseus-like Semites, they participate in the young Dubliner's imagination in the infinite adventure of the book, in the dark and infinite freedom of writing and the Word.

The Policy of Recovery of the Possibles

The problem which occupies Stephen's mind in his Aristotelian meditations is connected with the concept of History as actualisation of the possible: the problem of the imaginary is introduced during the history lesson he gives to the pupils of Mr. Deasy, in the 'Nestor' episode. Is the history of Ireland, he wonders, the sum of a number of absurd accidents like the assassinations of Pyrrhus or Caesar, for example, or "was that only possible which came to pass?"

> For them too history was a tale like any other too often heard, their land a pawnshop.
> Had Pyrrhus not fallen by a beldam's hand in Argos or Julius Caesar not been knifed to death? They are not to be thought away. Time has branded them and fettered they are lodged in the room of the infinite possibilities they have ousted. But can those have been possible seeing that they never

were? Or was that only possible which came to pass? Weave, weaver of the wind. (*Ulysses*, p. 28)

In other words is it chance, or destiny, or God who makes history into a bloodstained, inevitable nightmare? Where are the infinite possibilities which reality, or what Aristotle calls "the act," has ousted? For the artist, who can create a world which is not actualised, all possibilities are good; in spite of the given order and the constraint of the already-established unity, the artist wishes to try to keep the richness of multiplicity. What Stephen retains of Aristotle's metaphysics and brings forth in fragments illustrated by Blake-like visions in *Ulysses* can be summed up as follows.

The One and the Many: The basic principle of all Western metaphysics is the absolute affirmation of being, the absolute truth of the first principle, that of identity, in its application to everything that can exist in the consciousness. This absolute truth of the first principle is posited as necessary and undemonstrable. It is the point of departure for the science of metaphysics, and its omission would involve the relativity of being and the instability of all appearances. Secondly, the unity of being appears to us by way of a diversity which splits it up into fragments; the many modes of belonging to the One have to be collected into a system. The monism of being, when confronted with this multiplicity, seems to give rise to a number of inescapable antinomies. Thirdly, they can be reconciled in a general synthesis of being and not-being, as Aristotle observes it in the process of movement, kinesis, and metabolism.

Everything that exists in our minds as thought is first given to us in the form of kinesis, because it is the data derived from the senses that provide us with our mental concepts; the sensile object is mobile, according to the four modes of change—*quid, quale, quantum, ubi*. From the notion of movement Aristotle draws the elements of his general theory of the four causes: essence or form, matter or subject, principle, and intended end.[7] He then discovers at the root of the duality between form and matter the two great metaphysical principles of Act (*energeia*) and of what one might call Non-act, Potentiality (*dynamis*). The non-act, the potentiality—or what Stephen would call the possible—is a positive possibility, a disposition to *be* more fully; in the last analysis, it is the result of a prior act upon which it is supported, for passive potentiality is simply the "objective" expression of the "active potentiality"

[7] *Metaphysica*, A, 983.

of a previous positive dynamism, and so on. Thus the keys of existence are given to him who wishes to find the ultimate end, unity, and identity. At the level of *Ulysses*, Stephen is no longer sure that he does wish to be one; since the real world is subject to constant change, being appears to the subject's intelligence as a *process of becoming*, divided between the act and the possibles. "It must be a movement then," he thinks, "an actuality of the possible as possible" (*Ulysses*, p. 28).

By way of this process of becoming, thought of as act *plus* potentiality, the totality of the being must be revealed, since every process of being proceeds from an act which is its motive principle *(kinoyn)* and tends towards an act in which it finds its accomplishment *(telos)*.

Throughout his mental and physical itinerary of 16 June, Bloom lives over his own history again, and its form is a tragical-ironic illustration of "applied Aristotle".

"Kino" is one of the bizarre motifs of Bloom's preoccupation, and it contains an unexpected amount of meaning:

> But then why is it that saltwater fish are not salty? How is that?
> His eyes sought answer from the river and saw a rowboat rock at anchor on the treacly swells lazily its plastered board.
> Kino's
> 11/-
> Trousers.
> Good idea that. Wonder if he pays rent to the corporation. How can you own water really? It's always flowing in a stream, never the same, which in the stream of life we trace. Because life is a stream. All kind of places are good for ads. That quack doctor for the clap used to be stuck up in all the greenhouses. Never see it now. Strictly confidential. (*Ulysses*, pp. 149–50)

If Stephen *is* a reincarnation, however brief, of the philosopher, Bloom is a living example of an object (not a subject) which is liable to change, presented to the reader in process of becoming by a sarcastic subterfuge of the author. Bloom's process of becoming proceeds from the motive principle *Kino*, an obsessive word which he connects with trousers, one of his chief preoccupations (as the reader will not have failed to notice, the object of an apparently ridiculous amount of attention from the end of the 'Calypso' episode onwards). The motif of "Kino" gives away the secret of Bloom's inertia right at the beginning of this Odyssey; the 'Laestrygones' episode corresponds, in the elucidation of the motives behind both Stephen's and Bloom's movements, to the 'Proteus' episode. These two episodes, which Joyce presents to us inside the minds of the two characters, develop two lines of metaphysi-

cal thought, starting from a set of problems which resemble each other
in their first questions; they are both concerned with the eternal trouble
of man in Western civilisation, asking what is the meaning of life in its
relation to death and to reality, what is the meaning of individual
duration in its relation to the chaos of history, and how can one preserve
any permanent identity of the self throughout multiplicity and
changes? From this point of view, sarcasms and subtleties of structure
take on such meaning that the history of Bloom and Stephen, through
Joyce's desperate irony, becomes exemplary of the entire crisis of culture and humanism at the turn of the century.

'Laestrygones' is by definition an episode of absorption and transformation of matter, and of a parallel reflection on the origin and the ends
of all things. Bloom is given up to himself in this episode, and the
meditation which began in 'Hades' with the idea of death is here complicated by a rumination on the modalities of existence as physiological
survival and emotional destruction. Appropriately, the list of correspondences indicates for this chapter the peristaltic organs; we follow
Bloom's thought on its journey like a pill travelling through the system,
whose foreseeable destination can but determine the conclusion of his
intellectual rumination. Inevitably, he concludes that from our entry
into life until our death, we change ineluctably, by decomposition.

The word "Kino" is carried along by this typically Bloomesque stream
of consciousness; it follows the lines of reality very closely, while Stephen's stream of consciousness moves away from the reality where it
begins. Bloom goes south towards the Liffey, where, without his knowledge, he assumes the mask of the Presocratic philosopher Heraclitus, to
whose theories Aristotle's theory of becoming was designed as an answer. The most celebrated phrase surviving from the cosmogony of this
ancient philosopher of Ephesus (fl. 544 B.C.) is "One cannot step twice
into the same river, for it is constantly bringing fresh waters past". This
notion of becoming states the variability and inner contradiction of
moving objects, which flow past in time. Heraclitus recovers metaphysical thought on the very brink of dissolution by a kind of instinctive
self-preservation which impels him to find some sort of unity within the
very form of becoming: realism remains, but objects and thoughts are
carried along at the same pace always by an "active principle" which
is "fire". Thus the unity in multiplicity of existence is merely a formal
unity.

This is the river whose course Bloom sceptically follows in the 'Laes-
trygonians' chapter. What, he wonders to himself, is the use of religion
if it only protects the insane process of becoming by preaching the

perpetuation of the species? At the most, it stains the waters blood-red: "Are you saved? All are washed in the blood of the lamb. God wants blood victim. Birth, hymen, martyr, war, foundation of a building, sacrifice, kidney burnt-offering, druid's altars. Elijah is coming. Dr. John Alexander Dowie, restorer of the church in Zion, is coming" (*Ulysses*, p. 147).

And the prophets—what of them? There are always new ones appearing, to prophesy the end, but what never comes to an end is hunger; the prophets, like the seagulls and all sorts of animals, must be fed in this world until they die:

> His eyes sought answer from the river and saw a rowboat rock at anchor on the treacly swells lazily its plastered board.
> Kino's
> ll/-
> Trousers.

Kino sells clothes; Kll, as he becomes in 'Circe,' has chosen to sell them cheaply. K is the eleventh letter of the alphabet, that of new beginnings, whose number is ll in the Kabbala. Bloom is struck by the advertisement for more than one reason: first, as a man concerned with publicity, he thinks it is a "Good idea that. Wonder if he pays rent to the corporation. How can you own water really? It's always flowing in a stream, never the same, which in the stream of life we trace. Because life is a stream."

All drawers remind him of Molly and all trousers of his rival Boylan. The interplay of association of ideas reminds him of the flow of other liquids, urine, "the greenhouses," "the clap," which he almost wishes on Boylan. Kino sells trousers for only eleven shillings, and Bloom has had to pay more than that to have his old ones repaired. Faced with the rapidity of the stream of life that seems to be escaping from him, he turns from the peaceful current to the image of the strongly flowing stream. At the hour of the Sirens, his meditation passes out to sea, with its philosophical conclusion, on the subject of Molly, "As easy stop the sea."

In Bloom's universe, the state of becoming proceeds from an act whose motive principle (hunger or lust) causes it to move towards an act in which it finds its accomplishment (defecation, decomposition). If the principle and the end of any particular process of becoming contain potentiality as well as act, then they are themselves processes of becoming and in their turn require an act to be their principle and another act to be their end. Thus, Bloom does not satisfy his hunger (he flees from the restaurant and "men, men, men" to the pub for a cheese sandwich) nor his sexual frustration; Boylan is ubiquitous, and all the more so because Bloom *believes* he can see him at every turn. Only in 'Nausikaa' does "potentiality" find an ironical and very relative actualisation. At the end, the totality of becoming, or the process of becoming as such, will develop from a universal principle, a "first mover," which is a pure act, and an absolutely final intention and ending which is equally a pure act. Bloom's process of becoming is characterised by the minimal quantity of *energeia* exercising within it any positive dynamism, and inversely by an excessive "potentiality," a negative dynamism which is that of emptiness and lack; it calls to the "act" which Bloom is gradually suppressing and depriving of opportunities to achieve its end.

The fact that *Ulysses* is begun by an appearance of Stephen shows the author's intention to challenge and defy. Stephen has come back after six months in Paris studying Aristotle. His theory of aesthetics is ready at the end of *Portrait*. His return to Dublin, which could have been so humiliating for him, brings him into a situation where he is able to measure his theories against reality. He is in a transition-stage; he is no longer the Artist as a young man, and he is not yet an Artist; he is seeking, on the borders of the concrete world and of society, for the abstract space in which his book is to be written. The first three chapters of *Ulysses* are the mere repetition of the breakaway he had already made, but which was presented to him in a new and doubtful light by his involuntary return. Indeed, his personal situation has changed, with the death of his mother, his spiritual enemy, and he now has to redefine the form of his exile within Dublin. Successively, and in a style very different from that of *Portrait*, he rejects over again his Catholic education, the adult defenders of reactionary and middle-class values, and finally the image and hierarchies inherited by the Christian world from Aristotle. His attack is presented in a fashion that is both grandiose and theatrical, and more absolute too, for his thought is cosmic, in harmony with the dimensions of the book itself. It is no longer Ireland that is accused and identified with the old sow who devours her farrow, but by way of Ireland it is the theological world, and beyond Catholicism, it is God he attacks, God masked as the hangman-god who delights in the slaughter-houses of history.

In the first chapter, he leaves the Church's stage, leaving its actions in the hands of those who have to mock their Church in order to remain subject to it; in reality Buck Mulligan's liturgical parody is a form of shameful submission. In the second chapter, he abandons history to its

Chief Butcher, and leaves by the porch that is flanked by two toothless, and possibly Mycenian, lions, facing Vico Road. In the third chapter, he passes on to the edge of the world, to the sea-shore where the universe ends and is bounded neatly by a line; passing beyond that line, the "spiritual eye" of the artist can turn time and space into epiphany. In 'Proteus' he replies to the first metaphysical question which had occurred at the beginning of *Portrait*, the question which had started him wondering and which had impelled him to climb up the ladder of being, from "Stephen Dedalus" at Clongowes Wood to "Ireland, Europe," to "World, Universe".

At the age of six he wondered "what was after the universe? Nothing." "But was there anything round the universe to show where it stopped before the nothing place began? It could not be a wall; but there could be a thin thin line there all round everything" (*Portrait*, p. 16).

In 'Proteus,' Stephen is walking along this line between concrete reality and the "nothing place," having "thought about things" and listened to words for a long time. The chapter begins with the famous quotation from Aristotle's *De Anima* (VII, 30 a), "Ineluctable modality of the visible: at least that if no more, thought through my eyes".

Stephen has no audience but himself on the beach at Sandymount, but he who walks there is already the Artist, applying art to reality, as he defined it to Lynch in *Portrait*: "To speak of these things and to try to understand their nature and, having understood it, to try slowly and humbly and constantly to express, to press out again, from the gross earth or what it brings forth, from sound and shape and colour which are the prison gates of our soul, an image of the beauty" (*Portrait*, p. 206).

'Proteus' is the chapter of transience and transition. Essentially, it is represented on the level of the genesis of writing itself, as an example of the triple movement of art—that is, the perception of material things, followed by the expression of that image of beauty which Stephen has succeeded in extracting, an expression not only conditioned but indeed created by the episode, in a way which Joyce sets forth in his letter to Carlo Linati (21 Sept. 1920). The artist has to step over the line that surrounds the created universe, and thus necessarily to exile himself from the created sphere; this alone can allow him to survey the universe from outside, and to escape from time, space, and immediacy in order to move into the place of creation between World and Words. Having destroyed his objective connections with reality, Stephen re-establishes a world which is similar to the world he has left, but which begins at his word. This recovery is made by meaning, by language, and by writing, and the result is not a dissolution of objective reality, but clearly a disappearance of the difference between reality and the self; the self can thus enter into a very direct contact with the world, yet with the benefits of reflection and decision. This process is a clear and distinct one, and the voluntary suppression of barriers between the self and reality must not be confused with the "lowering of the mental level" that Jung called it (to Joyce's great annoyance).[8]

This breakaway by exile, followed by the recovery of the world, should be seen as a "phenŏmenological reduction"; Joyce acted thus without having read Husserl, and rather because he had only succeeded in defining his art with relation to the human word that gives objects their names, to the sound of the voice that creates space, and to the subject that grasps time in its relationship to its self. The barrier is replaced by the written line. Joyce does not imagine himself to be or to contain the world; what he is doing is refusing to pass to reality by way of an outworn culture. Reality tells itself to whoever will sincerely call upon it. This is why "style" ceases to have any meaning for Joyce; he writes the world, but refuses to "explain" it. The reader must *read* it. Reading and writing are the two inseparable phases of creation. Stephen undertakes to decipher it. "Ineluctable modality of the visible: at least that if no more, thought through my eyes. Signatures of all things I am here to read" (*Ulysses*, p. 39).

Aristotle walks along the Protean beach with Jacob Boehme[9]. Greek rationalism meets German mysticism, and within Stephen's mind is accomplished as epiphany the *Mysterium Magnum*.

Form as Immediate Message

The manner of writing, what Joyce calls the "technique," depends not on the moment of creation but on the object of the work; writing is intended to be a comprehension of reality, and the form of what is written is a language which resembles the reality, not the writer. The

[8]See Jung's article "Ulysses" in *Europäische Revue*, 1932.

[9]Boehme, the visionary cobbler (1575–1624) joins Blake and Nicolas Cusanus in suggesting to Joyce his theory of contraries and of progression by their reconciliation, uniting Shem and Shaun in H. C. E. Boehme's formula is, "All things consist in Yes and No". In his main work, *Mysterium Magnum* (1623), he says that the world is a book in which man can everywhere decipher God's signature. He had some considerable influence on the Romantics and on Berkleyan idealism.

form mimics reality, without commenting upon it or passing any judgement. The technique is not simply that of identical reproduction; Joyce makes use of language and of all its almost infinite possibilities of expression as *equivalent matter*. The juxtaposition of the work and the world with no intermediary should, if the artist is very good, bring out all the hidden meanings in the concrete objective. Commentaries are made only at the moment of reading, by a simple confrontation of the work and the world; all the meanings are already contained in the discrepancy or difference between absolute reality, reality as read, and reality as written.

Thus, instead of relating that Stephen was thinking that day of Aristotle and his *ubi, quantum, quale, quomodo,* Joyce offers us directly Stephen's changing thoughts, in which he is at one moment Aristotle himself, at another Stephen, or a dog, or a drowned man. Carried along by the stream of his thought, he works out syllogisms which become mixed up with snatches of song: "Limits of the diaphane. But he adds: in bodies. Then he was aware of them bodies before of them coloured. How? By knocking his sconce against them, sure" (*Ulysses*, p. 39).

He moves gently from reason accompanied by experience ("Shut your eyes and see") towards the fantasies of personal misery; the waters dilute the world of actuality, and the imagination gains ground from the firm Aristotelian logic as the rising tide overwhelms the beach. Imagination cannot be confined by the claims of the present to have been the only possibility which could have passed on to actuality; it recalls the other possibilities which remained such, and which wallow in the waters of regret and oblivion like still-born children in Limbo, and confers on them a profane baptism by refusing to eliminate them under the pretext that a unity exists which excludes alternatives. Thus it can recover a certain freedom of choice, and may infinitely extend the domain of the possible. All Stephen's defiance and challenges to the logic of causality are to be understood in this way, and Aristotle can be seen to some degree as the *dio boia* who threatens the omnipotence of the imagination with his statements that what has been actualised is, that what is not possible is impossible, and that A is A and not B. Neither Joyce nor Stephen have any use for such a system. Thus, while Stephen is writing a poem on death, his shadow falls on the rocks and he wonders why it should not be "endless," why physics should be more "true" than metaphysics, and why the world should be limited, when the universe of stars offers no limits to the gaze but the invisible ones of scientific laws.

Why not endless till the farthest star? Darkly they are there behind this light, darkness shining in the brightness, delta of Cassiopeia, worlds. Me sits there with his augur's rod of ash, in borrowed sandals, by day beside a livid sea, unbeheld, in violet night walking beneath a reign of uncouth stars. I throw this ended shadow from me, manshape ineluctable, call it back. Endless, would it be mine, form of my form? Who ever anywhere will read these written words? Signs on a white field. (*Ulysses*, p. 50)

There is no difference between the space of the dark worlds that shine in the brightness of the sun and the creative imagination that shines in the darkness of Stephen's body. The sky is a book signed with the delta of Cassiopeia, and we are told in 'Charybdis and Scylla' that this constellation was that of Shakespeare's birth. If Stephen had no limited form, if he was not trapped in the nets of his body, his family, his country, he would be pure form. When he writes, he *is* "form of my form"; then he can recover the possibles assassinated by the Act, the possibles which are now called impossibles (and, as Blake says, "Everything possible to be believed is an image of truth"), and can prepare the way for the operations of chance, the champion of all possibilities. Stephen shuts his eyes, which may mean his falling over a cliff; he lets his legs carry him along, and they may take him to see Aunt Sara and Uncle Richie Goulding. At least, he visits them in imagination: "I pull the wheezy bell . . . they take me for a dun . . . a bolt drawn back . . . in the broad bed nuncle Richie . . . Walter squints vainly for a chair. . . . His tuneful whistle [Richie's] sounds again . . . his fists bigdrumming on his padded knees". The wind becomes sweeter.

As it does so, we realise that the time is the same and that Stephen is the same, but that we are in the present-possible; the reader has been taken to visit Uncle Richie, has drunk his whiskey and listened to Ferrando's aria, and yet he is there in the wind blowing over Sandymount. It is difficult to tell where we are, or where Stephen is, or what the difference is between here and there, since they both have the same form and the same time-context. He moves on to the supreme hater of his kind, the horsenostrilled man with eyes like stars, the dean of Saint Patrick "Abbas father": "A garland of grey hair on his comminated head see him me clambering down to the footpace *(descende)*, clutching a monstrance, basiliskeyed. Get down, bald poll!" (*Ulysses*, p. 42).

In this way Stephen moves from thought to image, bearing the provoking present through time and space by means of association. From uncle to father, from Swift to Berkeley, he lets himself be carried along by a tidal rhythm of memories and ideas which sweeps him far away from Aristotle's rigorous rhythms. For the space of an allusion to a minor detail in literary history, Stephen becomes Swift, without truly being he: "Cousin Stephen, you will never be a saint". Then Swift joins the troop of anti-selves, "equine faces, Temple, Buck Mulligan, Foxy Campbell," while Stephen follows in mimicry the service that takes place in the great empty cathedral; while Swift fumes, we are on the beach, and listening to Uncle Richie, while "at the same instant perhaps a priest round the corner is elevating it. Dringdring! And two streets off another locking it into a pyx. Dringadring! And in a ladychapel another taking housel all to his own cheek" *(Ibid.).*

"Down, up, forward, back," tomorrow, today, yesterday, still everything may be possible, for it is enough for Stephen to write in the present. During this time his feet are walking, marking out a rhythm, and his shoes are crushing what remains of history, for history cannot exist if there is no more time: "His boots trod again a damp crackling mast, razor-shells, squeaking pebbles, that on the unnumbered pebbles beats, wood sieved by the shipworm, lost Armada" (*Ulysses*, p. 43).

Action mingles with fiction and objects that are perceived enter the inner monologue; shortly, a dog will take up the whole of the inner space, while in the distance a man and a woman gather shellfish. Clongowes, Paris, the dream he had last night, Dublin as Zion seen from afar, the isle of thirst, the beach strewn with hoops from barrels, the history of Ireland from the Vikings to the Fenian Movement—all this floats in time, as fluid as the waves. A drowned man appears, and joins the company of Dan Occam, Berkeley "the good bishop of Cloyne," and God himself in the darkness of Stephen's soul, which has become the Protean form of thoughts on the origin and end of all things. *"Et vidit Deus. Et erant valde bona."* Everything is possible in such a cosmos, as amorphous as the sea. Stephen himself is subject to as many metamorphoses every instant as is the dog-buck-bear-wolf, according to the angle from which he is seen; in the same sentence he can be first or third person: "He halted. I have passed the way to aunt Sara's."

He can also be the second person, and address himself as, "Reading two pages apiece of seven books every night, eh? I was young".

In the end, this formal Proteism, at least in Stephen's case, could be confused with Berkeley's idealism; when he wonders "Who ever anywhere will read these written words? Signs on a white field," he is using the same formula as the Irish bishop, who considered reality to be a divine writing addressed to man, whose task is to decipher it. Rather than an acceptance of Berkeley's views, we should see here a half-serious reference to them, since the signs in question are inscribed by

Stephen and not by God. This is an impertinent form of challenge to the old theories of knowledge, one typical of Stephen; for the Joycean artist the world is no longer the well-ordered creation of God, but the totality of all relationships established between the world of reality and the self.

The form of this episode reproduces the moving perception of reality as taken in by the consciousness of an individual self which is also in motion; the relationships between the subject and the world are all the more subject to change because the display of reality and its accidentals are constantly making modifications in the consciousness that perceives them. 'Proteus' is thus the most typical example of a poetic that is in motion expressed by the form itself of the chapter. It is what Umberto Eco has called "the poetic of expression form."[10]

The episode 'Eolus' takes place in the offices of the *Freeman's Journal*, where several of its contributors, lovers of this chapter's art, rhetoric, are assembled. The symbol indicated by the list of correspondences is "the editor," and the organ "the lungs". The winds of Eolus scatter the words abroad in small paragraphs, which bring out clearly the foolish incoherence of a newspaper, with its mosaic of disparate chapters whose only connecting unity is that of the date. The headings symbolise the nature of the newspaper, in their rough, enigmatic succession: "In the Heart of the Hibernian Metropolis—The Wearer of the Crown— Gentlemen of the Press—With Unfeigned Regret it is we announce the Dissolution of a most respected Dublin Burgess." Then the tone changes, and grows quicker:—"Short but to the Point—Sad—His Native Doric—Spot the Winner—Clever, Very". As Stuart Gilbert has pointed out,[11] the style of the headlines passes from that of the Victorian tone and the discreet allusion to the vulgar expression of modern slang, fast losing all meaning it might have; we watch the devaluation of language.

From the lungs of Dublin blows a wind both real and metaphorical; people appear as though borne along by it:

> Mr. Bloom, breathless, caught in a whirl of wild newsboys near the offices of the *Irish Catholic* and *Dublin Penny Journal*, called:—Mr. Crawford! A moment!
> —*Telegraph!* Racing special!
> —What is it? Myles Crawford said, falling back a pace. A newsboy cried in Mr. Bloom's face:

[10]Eco, *L'Oeuvre Ouverte* (Paris, 1965), pp. 218ff.
[11]Gilbert, *James Joyce's Ulysses* (New York, 1930), p. 178.

—Terrible tragedy in Rathmines! A child bit by a bellows! (*Ulysses*, p. 143)

This fragmented, breathless, inane prose has its own hero in the person of the pompous MacHugh, and its jester in Lenehan, the punster. In this chapter is heaped up, to illustrate its vanity and lack of continuity, every rhetorical figure known to man; they demonstrate how useless it is to know the techniques of a language if one only considers the form and not the content. The list of these figures, of which Stuart Gilbert has counted seventy, is enough to make the reader dizzy: metathesis, chiasmus, metonymy, asyndeton, anacoluthon, synechdoche, hyperbaton, apostrophe, and many more. Joyce does not label them, but they form each paragraph in its own characteristic fashion. If the form of the chapter is expressive, it can be read as Joyce's judgement of the rhetoric practised by his contemporaries, of this language that is lost in the air around him, of its abundance, inanity, and fragmentation. If one feels that language is in principle a mediator between individuals as much as between one individual and reality, one cannot fail to sense the emptiness of these words.

This summa of mockery is not solely designed "to stigmatise the paralysed life of Ireland, and, by way of this, the paralysis and fragmentation of the whole world" (Eco, *op. cit.*, p. 219), by satirising the empty speech of the journalists, but, more precisely, to devalue the language. Not only the language of Dublin or of the newspapers, but the language that claims it can reduce the whole world to words, including the artist's own word, is subjected to destructive criticism; the accumulation of rhetorical figures shows a manifest disgust for language, for its laws and for its lies, which is emphasised by the remarkable epiphany of the printing machines. Bloom the outsider is watching the Italian foreman who is "more Irish than the Irish," and continuing his meditation on death, when he suddenly imagines an apocalyptic doom: "The machines clanked in three four time. Thump, thump, thump. Now if he got paralysed there and no one knew how to stop them they'd clank on and on the same, print it over and over and up and back. Monkeydoodle the whole thing" (*Ulysses*, p. 117).

Machines "rule the world today". The printed pages meet with various fates which only emphasise the superficiality of the information they bring to the world: "Miles of it unreeled. What becomes of it after? O, wrap up meat, parcels: various uses, thousand and one things" (*Ulysses*, p. 118).

In this chapter where human vanity is emphasised by the headlines and their language, Joyce defines the language of inanimate objects:"Sllt The nethermost deck of the first machine jogged forward its flyboard with sllt the first batch of quirefolded papers. Sllt. Almost human the way it sllt to call attention. Doing its level best to speak. That door too sllt creaking, asking to be shut. Everything speaks in its own way. Sllt" (*Ulysses*, p. 120).

The speech of objects, as phonetically grasped by Bloom, takes its place in a network of problems which is much wider than that of the (comic) history of language as spoken, since it draws attention to the value of the message in its relationship with the code used, and leads to a comparison, in this chapter full of winds and spirit, between the spoken word which the wind scatters and the written word which remains. Again, this battle of words takes place in Stephen's mind: its boundaries are history (the space in which events occur) and prophecy (the revelation of God's plan). Between the two stands the artist, jealousy watching over every speech in his constant search for spoken beauty and the virtue of writing.

If Bloom and Stephen are both to some extent Moses-figures, Bloom is a Moses of parody, while Stephen lives through the prophet's misfortunes in a way which is almost tragic, since his exile is an exile of the word. The vociferations of the politician, the art of oratory, the declamatory rhetoric of the newspaper, the daily news which is forgotten by evening, these are the voices that move the crowds and make history; the words of the political or religious preacher are a poison, and they persuade the audience to carry out some meaningless action. All the foolish declaimers whom Stephen observes in this episode do nothing but turn the mills of Hell with the hot air and the unreal energy that is all they produce. Their heroes are Gallaher the journalist who can report sensational news with the speed of a telegraphist, Moses the prophet who is the idol of Professor MacHugh and patron of lawyers, and O'Molloy and Taylor of the Historical Society who listened to the voice of the Egyptian highpriest "raised in a tone of like haughtiness and like pride" (*Ulysses*, p. 139). While MacHugh echoes an echo by reporting word for word the speech of Taylor reporting the speech of the highpriest addressed to the youthful Moses, with a solemn eloquence hardly interrupted by an accidental belch, the audience listens, rapt and carried away by the incomparable charm of the echo's echo's voice: "It seemed to me that I had been transported into a country far away from this country, into an age remote from this age, that I stood in ancient Egypt and that I was listening to the speech of some highpriest of that land addressed to the youthful Moses". *(Ibid.)*

Stephen's wounded self-esteem arouses his pride in rivalry to that pride that expresses itself in "noble words":

> Could you try your hand at it yourself?
> —And it seemed to me that I heard the voice of that Egyptian highpriest raised in a tone of like haughtiness and like pride. I heard his words and their meaning was revealed to me. *(Ibid.)*

The audience, enchanted by the cadences, loses all powers of criticism, and no revelation is made; they forget the meaning completely, destroying the real but inaudible greatness of the youthful, silent Moses in their midst, hidden in the person of Stephen. The object of MacHugh's peroration is thus both attained and annihilated by the power of his rhetoric. What he wished to demonstrate was simply the persuasive effect a good speech may have, but what is clearly established at the end of the demonstration is simply the silence of his hearers. Silence as mute speech can lend itself to all equivocal interpretations possible, and MacHugh is answered by two silences: that of the journalists and teachers and that of Stephen. "He ceased and looked at them, enjoying silence."

The exact meaning of Stephen's silence is at once revealed by a parenthesis opened by Joyce upon his inner speech, with which we remain in constant communication. "It was revealed to me that those things are good which yet are corrupted which neither if they were supremely good nor unless they were good could be corrupted. Ah, curse you! That's saint Augustine."

The irony of this remark is triple: firstly, in spite of himself, Stephen echoes MacHugh's words, "their meaning was revealed to me," which introduce his automatic oration, although at the time Stephen is in revolt against the usurping power of eloquence; secondly, in spite of himself again, he replies in a long, proud, complicated sentence, because the silent Stephen cannot help being unconsciously jealous of all who present themselves as orators—his reaction takes the form of a defiant challenge, and his sentence is intended as a rival to the other in form and beauty; thirdly, he realises at once the reason for his annoyance, and in horror discovers the cheating trick his unconscious has played on him by presenting the rival sentence as his own, when in fact it is Saint Augustine's.

Everything happens at this level, as though Joyce were taking a sarcastic pleasure in demonstrating the irresistible attraction the *sound* of the human voice has for even the most recalcitrant mind. But however seductive the spoken word may be, it can have no power over thought. There still exists a defence mechanism which saves the pure values that are in jeopardy by reduplicating the apparent failure of the unconscious and restoring meaning to its rightful place. For, after all, the sentence from Saint Augustine is not merely an elegant extract that goes with its context; it is also a very severe criticism of the inanity of style when the latter is taken as an end in itself. What Saint Augustine says, when applied to rhetoric as abuse of the spoken language, means that good language is corruptible because it is *only good* (that is, oral), and that if it were *supremely good* it could not be corrupted. The supremely good, and hence incorruptible, language must be that which is written, for no-one could corrupt what is written or engraved without being accused of forgery and falsification. Oral speech, a mere inane breath, may be the cause of change, but once the speech is finished its words are dead and its work handed over to corruption. This is the lesson that Stephen learns in the cave of the wind-god, and as Lenehan the joker takes up and disfigures grotesquely the echoes of MacHugh's words, Stephen comes to the same conclusion on the death of words; he does so because he is the critic of the inevitable lie of history and of time that feeds on dead words and bloody battlefields. The hollow-sounding speech makes him think of "Hosts of Mullaghmast and Tara of the kings. Miles of ears of porches. The tribune's words howled and scattered to the four winds. A people sheltered within his voice. Dead noise. Akasic records of all that ever anywhere wherever was. Love and laud him: me no more" (*Ulysses*, p. 141).

Writing alone is incorruptible; by it alone can one give the lie to history and it alone is the truly living word. Stephen is to be the Moses of Sinai, not he who spoke "with the Eternal amid lightnings on Sinai's mountaintop" nor he who "came down with the light of inspiration shining in his countenance," but he who bears "the tables of the law, graven in the language of the outlaw."

The scene is recalled and extended later on in the National Library, where a group of orators discusses dialectic rather than eloquence. The smoke of their cigarettes ascends "in frail stalks that flowered with his speech" in the newspaper office, and the phrase "and let our crooked smokes" occurs in anticipatory parody of the hierophantic altar at the end of 'Scylla and Charybdis,' with the same allusion to *Cymbeline*:

Laud we the gods
And let our crooked smokes climb to their nostrils
From our bless'd altars.

Joyce is insinuating that the journalistic style is much the same as the style of classical culture.

If we admit that the author of *Ulysses*, following Stephen's ambitious plan, has created his characters and then refined himself out of existence and that his story is built up in a "natural" fashion, according to its own laws, with no point of view indicated for the reader's guidance, then if the book is to remain a book rather than a filmed documentary we must choose before we read some centre of reference, some character, plot, place, or time, which will give a relative meaning to the vast amount of material confronting us. If the hypothesis of the disappearance of the author is set aside, most readers would agree on a number of points—for instance, that *Ulysses* does not relate one story, and that it has no "unity". But it has a limited polycentricity, rather than an unlimited formless multiplicity. Bloom, Molly, Stephen, and Dublin are undeniably present, and the author's withdrawal is only such on the level of the traditional novel's categories; he is invisibly present on the level of the individuals in the book. We shall now discuss the different methods he uses to preserve their individuality.

The fluidity of form in *Ulysses* is caused by the displacement of reality, or rather by the modifications which the notion of reality here begins to undergo; reality is no longer a common universal objective experience, but a particular, subjective, often incommunicable experience. If *Ulysses* apparently takes place in Dublin—a Dublin laid out with the exactness of a cartographer or a guide for tourists—it is really only a framework and a setting. Dublin exists, but much more as an animate object, a giant body, a corporate character, than as a stage; the true place of action is the consciousness of the central characters. "The" consciousness is made up of all individual conscious minds, and the absence of anyone else as audience means the disappearance of all the traditional signposts used in prose writing to facilitate the transition from one person or place to another, such as "he said," "he replied," and so on.

The book begins *in medias res;* we are immediately in Dublin, with no map or guide, and with no visible set of correspondences, for even if the book is called *Ulysses*, with eighteen episodes corresponding (all except one, the 'Wandering Rocks,' which is Joyce's own addition) to books of Homer's *Odyssey*, the author has taken care to eliminate all explicit reference to the classical antique background, refusing even to leave the eighteen episodes the titles which he had at first given them. We find ourselves in a section of time which is obviously cut out of a larger and more extensive expanse of time; after Mulligan's satirical *"Introibo,"* the first chapter, a fairly classical opening chapter of exposition, indicates the presence of a whole stretch of time past which is to weigh heavily upon the whole book. The "plot," if so it can be called, has begun before the book opens, and the characters on stage are separated by a mysterious resentment when we first see them. Malachi Mulligan, with his sparkling eyes and wit and his gold-filled teeth, appears in treacherous and attractive ambiguity as the false friend—brutal yet flattering, moralising immoralist, as observed, examined, and seen through by Stephen. "Buck" (a nickname that suits him well) is acting a part; he is on a stage, kept at a distance by Stephen the Kinch (a nickname derived from the sound of a knife scraping), as Stephen begins his inner monologue. He is a puppet, and Stephen an abnormally sensitive consciousness divided into "he" (who may be *ipse* or *ille*, depending on the scornful or adulatory reactions of his interlocutor) and the secret self, "I". The latter lives on three time-levels: he is haunted by the past, and "she" has come to pursue him even in his dreams:

> Stephen, an elbow rested on the jagged granite, leaned his palm against his brow and gazed at the fraying edge of his shiny black coat-sleeve. Pain, that was not yet the pain of love, fretted his heart. Silently, in a dream she had come to him after her death, her wasted body within its loose brown graveclothes giving off an odour of wax and rosewood, her breath, that had bent upon him, mute, reproachful, a faint odour of wetted ashes. Across the threadbare cuffedge he saw the sea hailed as a great sweet mother by the wellfed voice beside him. The ring of bay and skyline held a dull green mass of liquid. A bowl of white china had stood beside her deathbed holding the green sluggish bile which she had torn up from her rotting liver by fits of loud groaning vomiting.
>
> Buck Mulligan wiped again his razorblade

And the present became overcast with bitterness and mourning. The present slashes woundingly and humiliatingly at Stephen, and he reacts by piercing his adversary with a number of brief jabs, lancet against razor. "Parried again. He fears the lancet of my art as I fear that of his. The cold steelpen" (*Ulysses*, p. 11).

> Buck Mulligan . . . said solemnly:
> —He who stealeth from the poor lendeth to the Lord. Thus spake Zarathustra.
> His plump body plunged.
> —We'll see you again, Haines said, turning as Stephen walked up the path and smiling at wild Irish.

Horn of a bull, hoof of a horse, smile of a Saxon.

• • •

I will not sleep here tonight. Home also I cannot go.
A voice, sweettoned and sustained, called to him from the sea. Turning
the curve he waved his hand. It called again. A sleek brown head, a seal's,
far out on the water, round.
Usurper. (*Ulysses*, p. 26)

He proceeds in particular by long speeches that are reflection, evocation, and vision together:

The proud potent titles clanged over Stephen's memory the triumph of
their brazen bells: *et unam sanctam catholicam et apostolicam ecclesiam:*
the slow growth and change of rite and dogma like his own rare thoughts,
a chemistry of stars. Symbol of the apostles in the mass for pope Marcellus,
the voices blended, singing alone loud in affirmation: and behind their
chant the vigilant angel of the church militant disarmed and menaced her
heresiarchs. A horde of heresies fleeing with mitres awry: Photius and the
brood of mockers of whom Mulligan was one, and Arius, warring his life
long upon consubstantiality of the Son with the Father, and Valentine,
spurning Christ's terrene body, and the subtle African heresiarch Sabellius
who held that the Father was Himself His own Son. (*Ulysses*, p. 24)

Stephen's inner world is populated by ghosts and dead thinkers;
the young man in black lives in a world of theology and culture that
exists now in the eternity of memory. His consciousness is metaphysical, egocentric, and ornamented with fine language; he thinks
across books and centuries, constantly reorganising the flow of his
thoughts and emotions, starting out from intelligible matter and following an aesthetic plan; the rhythmic formation and the modula-
tion of styles to include isolated thoughts, ideas, and relived instants
of the past all show to what extent art has become second nature to
Stephen.

To the reader unacquainted with *Portrait* and not sufficiently familiar
with literature, theology, and the history of philosophy, Stephen's inner
monologue will appear to be written in a "closed-circuit" language,
often incomprehensible, for if the flow of individual experience is unin-
terrupted, the system of reference which gives it meaning has been
shattered and the fragments strewn about; the reassuring known space
of the traditionally-built novel is not here given as objective, but is
reconstituted by an inner gaze which at once makes it subjective.

Woodshadows floated silently by through the morning peace from the stairhead seaward where he gazed. Inshore and farther out the mirror of water whitened, spurned by lightshod hurrying feet. White breast of the dim sea . . .

A cloud began to cover the sun slowly, shadowing the bay in deeper green. It lay behind him, a bowl of bitter waters. Fergus' song: I sang it alone in the house, holding down the long dark chords. Her door was open: she wanted to hear my music. Silent with awe and pity I went to her bedside. She was crying in her wretched bed. (*Ulysses*, p. 13)

The mother's presence is as dangerous and all-enveloping as that of the country. The flow of consciousness is composed of many disparate elements, memories, quotations, judgements, self-criticism, decision, dreams floating up to the surface again, sometimes conversation with the self, satire, apostrophe—a whole and entirely original rhetoric, in which the world and other people have their place, but a place which is quite the reverse of that they occupy in the order imposed by the omniscient Author. The macrocosm is the consciousness of the subject, and all objects outside this conciousness are brought into it as images or as words, in obedience to laws which are not given to the reader, at least to begin with. The author is still a "realist" in his intention to reproduce without explanation all elements of the inner discourse; but in fact he is limited by the necessity of selection, as is every realist. Flaubert does not follow Madame Bovary from the cradle to the grave, but selects details; the history of Frédéric Moreau begins and ends at dates decided upon by Flaubert; and if the inner monologue is realistic (that is, true in its form and in its refusal to rearrange the fragments logically into a comprehensible whole), it is none the less limited to whatever is said in a certain chapter within the book; reality is not the objective world, but the invisible structure of the work. If the soul is in a manner all that exists, as Stephen says, reality or life is in a sense everything, but is also only that which is said or suggested.

Once one has registered the fact that *Ulysses* is a book of consciousness, history ceases to exist. The reduction of chronological and objective time is expressed as an image by the compression of all time into one single day, 16 June 1904, all the hours of which are lived through as experience but at different depths and to different rhythms. The space of reality is, as we have said, that of one consciousness which is globally and cosmically inclusive, so that events in outer or inner worlds have the same spatio-temporal setting and attributes. Finally, because

the characters are not identified by an omniscient Author but represented by whatever they think or say, the reader eventually becomes
unable to distinguish where he is, in whose mind or at what time in that
mind. In effect, everyone has two languages; the one carries along with
it the specific signs of the individual's existence and thought as they are
in the present, but marked by the past, in a form that is absolutely
personal and recognisable, while the other is the common language of
the senses, of permeability to daily life—the colourless language of
indifference common to all of the inhabitants of the same city, who are
all informed to much the same extent of those facts and circumstances
which do not affect their personal lives.

In the outside world, which is embodied in the crowd of all Dubliners,
the mass of citizens who are seen in groups in a pub or hospital waiting-
room or cemetery is divided into individuals—but only their names
differentiate them, because they are all alike and all like Dublin. Their
language is superficial, their speeches interchangeable, and the reader
has to pay very close attention in order to see how the roles are distributed among these minor characters. Similarly, in the inner world in
which Bloom, Stephen, and Molly move (accompanied occasionally and
briefly by other individuals who suddenly impinge on their consciousness, such as the two Siren-barmaids, glimpsed for the time of a sigh and
no more), images, facts, or events may be encountered in exactly the
same way by Bloom's mind and by Stephen's mind, as though the
universal consciousness were really a continuous space permitting any
idea to be thought, without telepathy, by anyone. This notion indicates
that the author's vision of reality has nothing left in common with the
traditional arrangement usual in novels. And if a thought is no longer
the property of one particular ego, then the sum of all thoughts is
reality, and Bloom, Molly, and Stephen are nothing more than objects
of cognition floating in a *continuum*—a not inconceivable situation, and
one which is basically the same as that of Alice when she learns that she
is being "dreamed" by someone else; this is where the dream of *Finnegans Wake* begins.

Nevertheless, Joyce does not carry this technique of interpenetrabil-
ity to its limits: only in the 'Circe' episode are the boundaries of the self
shattered, as the experience of dissolution is dramatised in a kind of play
whose theme is guilt. The polycentricity of this play is apparently pola-
rised and made to focus on one of the two minds which act as the stage
for their hallucinations, but in fact the space in which they occur is not
separated from the surroundings in the way the normally perceived
world is separated from and arranged round the observer. There is no

"omphalos," as Mulligan would say, precisely because 'Circe' represents an attack upon the unity of the theological world with its single centre; Joyce is attempting to set up a vision of his own, ex-centric as far as the Creation is concerned, a world which can escape from the Absolute which rules the world God has created. Everything which usually constitutes or contributes to the traps and nets in which God holds the world and the mind captive, subjected to his Presence and Omnipotence, is endangered by Joyce's art—spatial orientation, currents in time, duration and evolution, dialogue which supposes a relationship between two people and hence a space established firmly between two fixed points, and grammar that imprisons words between the rails of reason, obedient to the laws of the divine Logos. All these suffer in Joyce's world.

Joyce also tries to replace the imagery common to Western thought, with its implications of a beginning and an end, a here and a there, a past and a present, a self and an other, by a world without history, a continuous world of osmosis. Space is then no longer defined by personal landmarks, and one's surroundings are not a line separating the known and visible from a beyond which is different and strange. The outlines of reality become blurred, the horizon clouds over, and people and things can appear to us without being subjected to our minds' usual process of examination and recognition; races, knowledge, cultures, personal histories, childhood memories, desires, all mingle, with no concern for the normal boundaries of mine and thine, *hic* and *ille, tunc* and *nunc.* This is not chaos, but the polycentricity that has replaced egocentricity or theocentricity. Even Bloom and Stephen only succeed in directing the disorder to a limited extent; their minds interpenetrate, and fantasies move from one to the other, without at once being noticed. Life and death communicate in the vertiginous movements of the *danse macabre.*

In *Ulysses* the devaluation of space and that of time are parallel processes; 'Circe' inverts the spatio-temporal manifestation of Stephen's reason that took place in 'Proteus'. As soon as doubt affects the *nacheinander* and the *nebeneinander,* everything may become reversible or simulated, even life and death, age and youth, male and female, here and there, yesterday and tomorrow. Logic leaps in any direction, and no-one is concerned with contradiction. The lack of continuity between the perceived reality and that which it impresses on the mind is replaced by continuity of such a kind that characters can move freely about on a continuous stage. Here, for instance, causality can do away with the temporal interval which generally separates cause from its consequence, and either manifest both simultaneously or invert the logical order and make the effect seem the cause.

It is thus possible to dismember history and time, conjugating past and future in the present tense, and even going so far as to attribute to the dead past an imaginary future which contradicts the real past, permitting, for example, the final apparition of Rudy, Bloom's son who died at the age of eleven days.

Co-Ordinates of the Personality

In fact, if the citizens of Dublin remain supernumerary characters, Bloom, Molly, and Stephen are different; they are perfect and defined, infinitely more complex than the traditional character in a novel. The latter is only ever seen in a partial, reduced aspect, and we never know him personally; we are simply given his history as at one specified moment, and this is defined by means of psychological factors or by the traditional concepts on which a novel rests, such as the part played in an intrigue or the function fulfilled in society by the character. He is judged according to a conventional moral code of good or bad, passion and will, sexuality and purity. But Bloom, Molly, and Stephen are not judged; they exist. They are not caught in a dramatic situation which requires them to manifest their freedom; they are simply living through an ordinary day.

In any ordinary day, every occurrence and every gesture is the sum and fruit of a whole life, and every thought is determined by the totality of experience rather than by some extraordinary event that distorts the consciousness. With no defence, no shame, and no limits, the consciousness of each one of these three people gradually yields up all its secrets, and eventually we can know Molly or Bloom in a way which is strictly impossible in either reality or fiction. They give themselves by means of a language which is individually theirs, or rather by means of a style which is determined by the inner personality—the style of the self which is never the same as the style of other men's words—behind which one normally hides.

This style of the consciousness is formed by personal obsessions and dreams, some more serious than others, some lasting longer than others, all determining or determined by factors of the past or the present. Each of these three egos has a complicated inner life which revolves around certain essential but personal questions and motive events; their movements, hopes, and silences are all identifiable, and out of the chaos of material or psychological experiences undergone by each there soon emerges a system, or rather several systems, of co-ordinates. These reveal below the trivial surface many pitiful, and indeed exceptional, dramas; *Ulysses* contains a portrait of Everyman, but beyond Everyman is the chronicle of Molly and Bloom—of their unique pettiness and their greatness.

It is not necessary to relate here the personal history of Bloom or of Molly, but it must be demonstrated that *Ulysses* is not the pattern of a man's life reduced to its elementary structure of birth, death, feeding, deception, and return. The organisation of a multiplicity of possibles (which we have previously seen Joyce achieving from without by the imposition of a network of traditional orders upon lived material) now assumes its full value with reference to the person whose identity is finally guaranteed by the organic constitution of the whole, for if there is an Odyssey here, it is present in order to confer upon the situation of Leopold Bloom, the simple man, its true tragic meaning of exile in a world both familiar and unknown. If the pattern of the Trinity is found everywhere, in its degenerate form of the "triangle," it is there to point out the tenuous, difficult, and even morbid relationships that exist between three people who can never satisfactorily achieve their communion. All order emphasises and informs the disorder that there is, and the harmony of the closely-woven form holds in its networks disintegrating individuals who are separated from one another. The ambivalence of *Ulysses* shows what Joyce's judgement is: the disintegration of the world of the consciousness shows how necessary some form of integration is, and (inversely) the formal order has most value when it is imposed upon the greatest disorder. Art has become Joyce's reply to man's mental disorder and confusion.

Dublin is not experienced by Stephen or by Bloom as an ordinary town: for each of them it is the scene of his exile, chosen by Stephen and inevitable for Bloom. While we believe that we are in Dublin, Bloom and Stephen are carried by their desires or fears into two types of place, the place where they dream of living and the place into which they are thrown by their daily trivial contacts with others—their personal hells and heavens, in fact. Thus, from dawn onwards, Bloom vacillates between a promised land and a judgement seat in a typically Jewish polarity. From morning to evening, both are dreaming of ways to escape. Their minds attempt the decentralisation necessary for any detachment. For Stephen, this means constantly renewing his alienation from the three powers that fascinate and bewitch his soul, the Church, the family (reduced in *Ulysses* to the ghost of the mother and nothing more), and Dublin (as an intellectual centre where there is no room for him). Bloom tries to exorcise the one power that fascinates him, Molly, by taking advantage of Stephen's night escapade, appointing himself the latter's guardian in the disreputable district (into which he, Bloom, would never have dared to venture by himself).

When Bloom and Stephen arrive at the house of Circe, they enter a space which is quite unlike any other, a theatre of the guilty conscience where each one seeks out and finds the wound that has disabled him; they have to pass through this place of wrongdoing and justification before they can reach Ithaca, before Bloom can reach Penelope and Stephen the brink of the universe that he must leave.

The second aspect of the inner personal space is its sacred nature, which clearly suggests to Joyce the notion of sacrilege; thus, a number of places become anti-temples, in the way that the National Library was like a temple in *Portrait*. The Martello tower that overlooks the bay, where Buck Mulligan celebrates a parody of the Mass, is compared to the navel of the earth, and Stephen starts from it, that is, from the centre of the world, at dawn, only to find himself when night falls in the house of Circe, the bordello kept by Bella Cohen, a vast, monstrous woman who can change herself into a man, and who can change men into whatever they are ashamed to be, or do not want to be, or darkly and ignobly desire to be. Stephen's day had begun with a double dream, the one being of his mother's terrifying ghost in its shroud, pursuing him with her corpse-like breath, and the other a dream of the exotic: "After he woke me up last night same dream or was it? Wait. Open hallway. Street of harlots. Remember. Haroun al Raschid. I am almosting it. That man led me, spoke. I was not afraid. The melon he had he held against my face. Smiled: creamfruit smell. That was the rule, said. In. Come. Red carpet spread. You will see who" (*Ulysses*, p. 49).

These two dreams were premonitory: the bordello and his mother await him unavoidably at the end of the day, and in the house of Circe his painful ambiguity is finally exposed; he plays his own contradictory roles of free-thinking, liberated son, blasphemer, and master of history, and he acts out all the images of remorse. He drives away the ghost of his mother, that cries for him to repent, and he assumes the grotesque disguise of a music-hall cardinal.

Bloom's day is regulated by Molly's timetable and arranged around the time of her meeting with Boylan; his entire progress is nothing but an attempt to run away, and he traces out as large a circle as possible around a centre which is always Molly's bed. In the house of Circe he becomes what he has always wished, and not wished, to be with Molly. For the *choice* of what creature the soul will be reincarnated as rests not with some sovereign judge but with the self-judge who presides at the trial of the guilty self in its delirium; this is why all the transformations and all the conversations between Bloom and his *alter ego* or his anti-Bloom, all the dialogues between Stephen and himself, or between Stephen drunk and Stephen sober, personify concretely all the shameful and hidden personalities the two men believe or know that they contain. Each is Ulysses in his own fashion, each is attracted and terrified by the power of woman, and each approaches her cautiously, armed with his medicinal "moly". Each is changed by Circe into what he does not want to be, what he fears to be; Bloom's masochism and Stephen-Joyce's superstition co-operate in the magic that punishes them. "The soul" is indeed the consciousness of these two types of Ulysses, as we can see from their relationships with their respective pasts. Each feels that he is being watched by a "Supergo" (a Freudian term which is used here simply as a matter of convenience) chosen from his personal history. Stephen's is determined by his first encounter with prohibitions and threats, and Bloom's by his feelings of duty towards his lineage. Stephen is defined as an outlaw with relation to the structures of Irish thought and society, while Bloom feels responsible in the eyes of his ancestors. The conflict that Stephen sustains sets him against his mother as incarnation of Ireland, and against his *dead* mother as representative of death; Bloom stands before his father and grandfather as the representative of a culture and a tradition which he has betrayed by not doing his duty. He is expected to perpetuate his race and his own lineage, but for eleven years now he has been running away from his wife. Thus, indirectly, Stephen and Bloom are conducting their struggles against two aspects of the same theological world.

While Bloom's inner space is reduced, while life leads him gradually round to the only safe place—the place of his surrender and abdication, the end of his woes where every dream and hope is excluded—Stephen's space opens out into infinity; his imagination enjoys the freedom of the outlaw who is no country's subject.

There is an intellectual correspondence with these personal inner spaces, a way of rivalling the sacred nature of things which are sacrosanct to others: Stephen tries to reduce the gap between the One and

the Many, and Bloom tries to achieve the squaring of the circle. Both
are in search of a humanly impossible absolute.

Place is normally oriented around some centre, home, church, country, for instance, just as psychology is organised around one central ego.
But Bloom and Stephen have really and spiritually lost their bearings.
The idea of the centre as pivot of the consciousness is clearly a notion
belonging to the theological world, and the centre of a being is either
a projection of God or some substitute for the Deity.

For Stephen, the centre which he has lost is the Catholic faith as
represented by his mother. Bloom has transferred his notions of divinity
to Molly. And both men are repelled and attracted by their fear and
desire for the unique being, be it God or Molly. Stephen has not yet
succeeded in completely replacing God within himself, because God is
ably assisted in defending himself by the ghost of Stephen's mother. But
if he succeeds, theocentricity will be replaced, as it was for Joyce, by
egocentricity.

> Stephen—Here's another for you. (He frowns). The reason is because the
> fundamental and the dominant are separated by the greatest possible
> interval which . . .
> The Cap—Which? Finish. You can't.
> Stephen—(With an effort) Interval which. Is the greatest possible ellipse.
> Consistent with. The ultimate return. The octave. Which.
> The Cap—Which?
> (Outside the gramophone begins to blare 'The Holy City').
> Stephen—(Abruptly) What went forth to the ends of the world to tra-
> verse not itself. God, the sun, Shakespeare, a commercial traveller, having
> itself traversed in reality itself, becomes that self. Wait a moment. Wait a
> second. Damn that fellow's noise in the street. Self which it itself was
> ineluctably preconditioned to become. *Ecco!* (*Ulysses*, p. 473)

To be oneself from all eternity because being *oneself*, to persevere
in being that which has its essence in such a perseverance, to perpetuate oneself and thus every moment to renew oneself, to be one's own
father and son, ghost and spouse, knowing life to be but the illusory
interval between one's person and one's self—this means eventually
that one will do away with *every* interval and remove the element of
mystery from all progress and travel. Thus, the difference between the
One and the self disappears at the moment when Stephen discovers
that he is Stephen and that he is one. His "I" is now the name of one
who knows that he is himself, an indivisible individual free of place and
time. He emerges from the finite and the temporal, to enter the com-

pany of God, Shakespeare, and every complete being.

Nicolas Cusanus says that human reason draws always nearer and nearer to the divine Reason, as a polygon draws nearer to the shape of a circle when the number of its sides is increased. Bloom, who does not seem to be so troubled by God as Stephen is, is in fact a maniac for the absolute. His ambition is to square the circle; he makes use of an applied Blakean philosophy when confronted with the immensity of the starry sky. He measures God and his creation by the vertiginous infinites of a never-ending calculation. His search for the impossible expresses his despairing relationship with reality.

In order to calculate the area of a circle, one needs to use the sign π, which is not fully defined, since it is in fact the figure 3.1416. It is an endless number, and thus cannot allow a totally exact calculation. In order to achieve exactitude, Bloom tries to inscribe a number of squares inside a circle to make the nearest possible approach to the truth, but the actual impossibility of a complete coincidence, although minimised, remains.[12] Bloom by seeking the squaring of the circle in such a world, seeking the periphery in a world of hallucination, contrives to turn space into mere surface. Reality loses its depth, and objects appear near at hand without having had to traverse any distance. Time past attains to simultaneity with time present. Places cannot be defined with any precision because of the lack of depth. Differences in all fields can thus be abolished, and if the relationships of differentiation no longer exist, anything can be anything else: a butterfly may be someone's grandfather, and Bloom may be a woman.

Bloom's time-scale is that of loss, and his personal space is characterised by return, which also stands for loss of the self, or, as Joyce puts it, "An unsatisfactory equation between an exodus and return in time through reversible space and an exodus and return in space through irreversible time" (*Ulysses*, p. 652).

Bloom's conflict takes place not on a political plane but on a much more weightily theological and ontological level; his problem is not "to serve or not to serve," but "to succeed or not to succeed". By his origins

---

[12]"Some years previously in 1886 when occupied with the problem of the quadrature of the circle he had learned of the existence of a number computed to a relative degree of accuracy to be of such magnitude and of so many places, e.g., the 9th power of the 9th power of 9, that, the result having been obtained, 33 closely printed volumes of 1000 pages each of innumerable quires and reams of India paper would have to be requisitioned in order to contain the complete tale of its printed integers of units, tens, hundreds, thousands, tens of thousands, hundreds of thousands, millions, tens of millions . . ." (*Ulysses*, p. 624).

he is subjected to a renewal of time and to reproduction of the species as a law; his mission should be to bring men into the world, just as Stephen's should be to set man, himself, in the context of Ireland, in prison. Bloom feels that he is the slave of a temporal succession which he is guilty of having interrupted (though not voluntarily) and so he reflects on that simultaneous time in which history disappears, the opposite of successive time; if the past, which for Bloom is simply a record of failures, could be effaced, or if from one's standpoint in time present one could act upon time past in the same way that one can influence time future by preparing for it, then Rudy would be alive and Bloom would be a father. His attempt to appropriate Stephen as a substitute son indicates his wish to break the inevitable order of successive time and its accidentals.

Thus Bloom in his madness seeks to suppress the progress of time, to counterbalance its irreversibility by a kind of indefinite suspension, and even, if possible, to confuse the active and passive paths between which existence normally proceeds, in favour of an "infinitive" path which has no subject nor agent.

For Bloom, the reciprocal relationship between the world and the self, an alternating relationship of autonomy and heteronomy, has come to an end; what happens in 'Circe' is that he is able to be powerless and omnipotent at one and the same time—he can be everything and nothing, not in a coincidence of opposites such as that discussed by Nicolas Cusanus, but in presence and counterpresence.[13] Thus for Bloom to be both man and woman does not indicate hermaphroditic nature, but an existence as masculine *against* feminine, not co-presence but counterpresence. Bloom is powerless against other people, who can manipulate him as they will; he has no more power over the organs of his own body, and yet he can also manipulate other people, and turn Bella into Bello. *But* he has no feeling that *he* is doing this; it seems to him that someone is affecting others, but that it is not his doing. His presence is neither personal nor active, but rather *infinitive;* the relation of active and passive is done away with, and replaced by the infinitive of counterpresence.

Bloom says that "Time is the time the movement takes," and such a concept of time, connected with the idea of action in the immediate sense of activity, reduces the power of time as the stage of history to a

---

[13]For example, a schizophrenic patient might say, I am the universe, my liver is Japan, and so on, but I am connected with it by a recurrent pain; yet even that pain does not belong to me personally.

minimum. Bloom cannot admit that there is any connection between time and history, since he himself stopped developing long ago; from henceforth he only eixsts in a fragmentation of temporal continuity, into which he may surreptitiously introduce some possibility of change. Time does not belong to him, and by his definition he is only the limited space in which an almost impersonal energy acts. Time is allotted to the body and to objects that move in space, but not to the mind, for which time should be the theatre of life. But life is not a temporal continuity for Bloom; it appears rather as a succession of ages closed by death and punctuated by changes of address. His own life is not a history, but rather a succession of accidental breakages, with which he has little or nothing to do; the death of his father, the death of Rudy, the loss of Molly, the departure of Milly—all these in their ironical repetition of death eventually impose upon him a kind of law of the reversibility of responsibility.

The statement that Bloom makes no plans is only superficially para-doxical: in fact, since he has lost his right to the past because he is no longer the same as he was, and since he has lost his rights over the future because he has ceased to exercise his individual self directly in the world, he has no time that belongs to him; he is as old as his increasing waistline and his thinning hair, and he can be said to own the fictitious and sometimes romantically-designed time of his own invention, filled with landscapes and houses that are familiar and unspoiled. But the real future belongs to others, and into this Bloom makes only occasional incursions. In fact, all his imaginations about the future are centred around people who would normally be considered for their promise and their potentialities, yet Milly is already lost to him and Rudy can only be thought of by his father in the past conditional. His numerous dreams of retirement, success, and peaceful old age are completely unreal and impossible figments of his imagination. Even the most sim-ple domestic plans, such as the intended visit to Milly, who is in Mullin-gar, quite near Dublin, are condemned to failure before they can be made operative, for this maker of plans and dreamer of dreams is a man of fantasies who will always be lazy and impractical. He only dreams of making something or of raising himself by his own ingenuity when he is thinking of some impossible plan or contingency. As soon as the future draws near, he hastens to shift the responsibility that might be his: he will go to see his daughter if *someone else* can provide him with a cheap railway ticket. This is not cowardice so much as a systematic, obscure negative will which denies all hope of ever achieving autonomy. Bloom is destined never to be his own master.

He who loses all is he who has willed the loss of all; gradually Bloom becomes a contributor to his own downfall, and, in tragic fashion, retraces the path of his life, as though demanding his punishment from the painful events of the past. He says, in 'Ithaca,' that one cannot foresee the future or recover the past. But one can recover the feeling of guilt and of wrongdoing. He goes on down the stream of time: diminishing constantly, reducing the powers of his self, renouncing enjoyments except those of dreams, and at the end of the day (having reduced himself to zero) he comes back to shelter under the all-embracing spherical power of Molly. If Molly represents the promised land (and Joyce does make several more or less obscene puns on the image of the promised moon, which appeared first at dawn in the form of a melon), then Bloom as Moses renews the myth of the loss of a desirable place—renews it, that is, on the level of a parody. An analysis of the Mosaic pattern mimicked in Bloom's movements reveals the familiar formula of voluntary exile, so dear to Joyce. Moses (or Bloom or Joyce) can never reach the promised land, but can only glimpse it from afar. It is lost from the beginning, and is all the more fair, and all the more desired, because it is inaccessible. Bloom does not mind that Molly no longer belongs to him, as long as he can still see her. *There* and *then* she was very beautiful and alluring, as seen from the here and now. Yet Bloom would not wish to return *there* in order to retrieve *then*, quite simply because what he in fact loves is the hope and despair, the knowledge of the loss which has already taken place, thus leaving him safe from disappointment or deception—love, itself, in fact. Molly furnishes him with a pretext for idolatry and for self-torture. Subjectively, the delights of jealousy, sharpened by renunciation, are more important than love; basically, the emotion that agitates and torments Bloom the whole day through is his entire life. He runs, flees, dodges, acts entirely as a function of the signs made by Molly and her brutal lover, and at the end of the day he is tired.

When Stephen disappears, followed by his echo as he had been followed by the sound of his ashplant when he left the Martello tower that morning, the world reverberates to his steps in symbol of its response to his presence.

> Alone, what did Bloom feel?
> The cold of interstellar space, thousands of degrees below freezing point or the absolute zero of Fahrenheit, Centigrade or Réaumur: the incipient intimations of proximate dawn. (*Ulysses*, p. 629)

Outside it is as cold as death, the absolute zero that Bloom fears: "wake no more". And life is just a period of waking between two zeros. "Did he remain?" The way in which Bloom comes home, fearing to spark off an argument with Molly, and the symbolic expedient to which he has to have recourse, determine his final decision: because he has forgotten the key, he has to climb in like a prisoner anxious to re-enter his cell, even at the risk of a fall.

Thus Bloom comes home alone, fleeing from cold loneliness in order to regain his warm loneliness. And he shuts the door after him. His morality is a morality of inertia, inspired by his fear of death. He knows that in order to escape degradation he should leave; but if he left, he might have to suffer cold and hunger. He follows the law of least effort and chooses the "fleshpot" with its rounded, smooth, reassuring walls; to enter here he must stifle all awareness and "put out the light". He is himself the sacrificial victim. The motif "Fleshpots of Egypt" recurs often in *Ulysses*, associated with "Plumtree's Potted Meat" and with Bloom's macabre ideas about corpse-flesh as potted meat; eventually the following meaning emerges. The Herbrews during their Exodus longed again for their slavery in Egypt, which stands for alienation or death, because it had involved the compensation of an assured daily ration of food, and similarly Bloom prefers Molly's warm bed, even with all the humiliations he suffers there (he finds scraps of potted meat in the bed, which she had shared with someone else earlier in the day), to the cold of loneliness.

He can forget and forgive, because this forgetfulness ensures him "the best death," the sudden quick death which he had envied Patrick Dignam that very morning. Probably the most famous of Bloom's inventions is this avoidance of truth as soon as it manifests itself, in a juxtaposition of the revelation and its annihilation, carried out by the frightened conscience. Joyce by his art can bring out the fundamental meaning of this "alio-relativity" of Bloom, leaving it intact, with no commentary to distort it; he puts off the moment of illumination which both reveals it and reduces it again to nothing, until Bloom himself "understands". What is important in the following quotation is to be found in what is not written down; as the three riddles are asked, he decides not to take the road of exodus and exile, which would make it "unreasonable" to come back:

(first riddle) What selfimposed enigma did Bloom about to rise in order to go so as to conclude lest he should not conclude involuntarily apprehend?

The cause of a brief sharp unforeseen heard loud lone crack emitted by
the insentient material of a strain-veined timber table. (*Ulysses*, p. 653)

There seems to be here some disproportion between the extreme
anguish of departure and the occurrence which seems to prevent it, a
cracking sound made by a wooden table; it must also be emphasised
that the apprehension of this noise is *involuntary* on Bloom's part:

(second riddle) What selfinvolved enigma did Bloom risen, going, gathering multicoloured multiform multitudinous garments, voluntarily ap-
prehending, not comprehend?
Who was M'Intosh? *(Ibid.)*

At the cemetary, the man in the mackintosh was the thirteenth, as
Jesus was the thirteenth guest at the Last Supper. Bloom wondered
then, "Now who is he I'd like to know?" His thoughts move slowly and
involuntarily about the figure of this stranger, whose inexplicable appearances punctuate the course of the day and seem to worry Bloom
a great deal. Macintosh is nobody to anyone, is quite unknown, and yet
seems to be everywhere as Bloom carries out his petty daily negotiations with life. All Bloom knows of him is the anonymous mackintosh
that envelops him. Why did he go to Paddy Dignam's funeral, and what
is he doing in the house of Bella Cohen? A man in a mackintosh keeps
his identity hidden completely, but he is still there, frightening Bloom.
At the funeral, Bloom counts the people present, and at first believes
that he is himself the thirteenth man, but then he sees the other, come
from no-one knows where, replacing him and taking the sinister position of the thirteenth. In the house of Circe, only the coat is present,
and for a moment Bloom thinks that it is the ever-absent Boylan. He
knows by the end of the day who M'Intosh was, although by then he
has no desire to ask the question. The garment has become transparent
to Bloom's "unconscious substance," and he has now to struggle against
the truth that is self-imposed.

Robert Adams has taken great pains to retrace the footsteps of all the
Dubliners who wander in and out of *Ulysses* during the day; he accepts
uncritically Stuart Gilbert's statement, reported by Ellmann (*op. cit.*, p.
530), that M'Intosh was a person named Wetherup, who is twice mentioned in the book and who was employed at the Central Tax Office at
the same time as John Joyce. The truth of this statement may be questioned, but it is of no consequence; what is important is that Bloom feels
as he does. We can see why M'Intosh concerns him more than anyone

else except his family (and Stephen, after nightfall), and why he makes his defence against the dull-coloured mackintosh by gathering multicoloured multiform garments. Tindall points out that "Mac" means "son of," and "Macintosh" may be seen as the son and representative of a faceless, nameless being; he is at first only recognised by that which hides him, but what does the garment conceal?

When Bloom has returned to Ithaca and to his faithless, slumbering Penelope, he mentally reckons up the day, and his life, noting gains and losses to himself:

> What imperfections in a perfect day did Bloom, walking, silently, successively, enumerate?
> A provisional failure to obtain renewal of an advertisement, to obtain a certain quantity of tea from Thomas Kernan (agent for Pulbrook, Robertson, and Co., 5 Dame street, Dublin, and 2 Mincing lane, London, E. C.), to certify the presence or absence of posterior rectal orifice in the case of Hellenic female divinities, to obtain admission (gratuitous or paid) to the performance of *Leah. . . . (Ibid.)*

His regressive desires for the motherly moon he has lost circle around the ideas of orifice and entry, and the image of the teapot. Between hope and calculation stands the anguish that constitutes an obstacle to any expenditure of energy—centred on an enigma, an insoluble mystery, the incomprehensible at the centre of all life, the unknown from which consciousness flees and towards which thought moves. He stands on the threshold, ready to depart, in *voluntary* apprehension. The next riddle leaves him in suspense, with a further question: "What selfevident enigma pondered with desultory constancy during 30 years did Bloom now, having effected natural obscurity by the extinction of artificial light, silently suddenly comprehend? Where was Moses when the candle went out?" *(Ibid.)*

The reply is given *at once, without a word*. It is now necessary to establish the connections between these three riddles, that occur in no apparent order, yet whose formulation brings about Bloom's consequent abdication and renunciation of the idea of leaving.

He removes his "*remaining* articles of clothing," takes a "folded long white nightshirt" (or shroud?) and enters the bed, "with circumspection . . . with solicitude, the snakespiral springs of the mattress being old," "prudently, as entering a lair or ambush of lust or adder," and "reverently, the bed of conception and of birth, of consummation of marriage and of breach of marriage, of sleep and of death". If he had smiled, records the clerk, implying that he did *not* do so, he would have smiled "to reflect that each one who enters imagines himself to be the first to enter whereas he is always the last term of a preceding series even if the first term of a succeeding one, each imagining himself to be first, last, only and alone, whereas he is neither first nor last nor only nor alone in a series originating in and repeated to infinity" (*Ulysses*, p. 655).

But he does not smile, because although he knows that he is neither the first nor the last to lie in this bed of death-in-life, it is nevertheless true that each one can but imagine himself to be the first, even if he is Bloom. Each one knows nothing, except his own death at the moment of its occurrence, and a dying man does not smile because he does not yet know the face his own death will take; death is the only time one always and truly is the first, for no-one, even God, can live another's death in his place. Yet at the same time, the paradox of death lies in the fact that it is the only act common to all creatures, that it is their common ground where the feeling of being "alone" is abolished, because one is with all.

Bloom understands that all the riddles of his life have one and the same answer: a fear of death and an even stronger attraction towards it. This day, 16 June, is not an ordinary day, not "the dailiest day possible," as Arnold Bennett called it, for even if one can go to a funeral, or visit bawdy-house or hospital any day, it is not every day that one will find one's own truth there.

Sixteen June is a day like any other in its temporal substance, but chance so wills it that on this day Bloom realises the presence of his death and Stephen discovers the direction of his escape. "Bloomsday," as Joyce Societies now tend to call this day, is the day on which Bloom disappears, learning suddenly that he has been dead for a long time, and that what he thought to be himself was in fact his remains (or, as Stephen would say, his ghost).

The first riddle finds its answer within the question, insofar as Bloom is not a schizophrenic: it must be assumed that signs are heavily charged with meaning, to a degree commensurate with their effects. Bloom's apprehension is all the stronger because after the session in the house of Circe his relationship with reality is still that of an accused man before his judges. The trial of Virag may begin. We have seen Bloom's subterfuges and attempts to make up for his own lack of existence by means of symbols and images. He is afraid of the table, as he is afraid of the high-society ladies and of Bella-Bello; one sharp warning noise from the unconscious is sufficient to set in motion all the mechanisms of memory and to make Virag-the-Superego fall down upon Bloom-the-guilty, now more guilty than ever. That one noise may wake Molly. For the first time, thanks to Stephen, Bloom has come to the very brink of action. Only in action, in actualising a possible, would he reach the certainty which until now he has rejected and tried to conceal—the truth about his relationship with Molly. What holds him back on the brink of truth is the fear of a noise. It is clear that he also hopes for that which he fears, for he is ready to leave "so as to conclude"; his distress is a premonition, a warning sign which alerts the defence system (inertia, self-destruction, lies) of a self which is dangerously close to seeing itself. This explains the very elaborate form of the riddle, which Bloom rearranges in order not to have to pay attention to the subject he secretly fears; the rearrangement gives him away, for the real question is not, "Why should the table make this noise?" but "Why is it so important that it should or should not do so?" The answer lies in the second riddle: because Bloom is afraid that he will recognise Macintosh, whose identity he has guessed and whom he has no wish to name.

If the table (which stands for both chance and the unconscious) should make a noise, he will be trapped, imprisoned, made to speak Macintosh's name; he will have to let him in. This is the same as Hamlet's "To be or not to be," but it is only indistinctly articulated, because if Bloom were to answer the second riddle honestly, he would have to take flight at once. Truth is stifled by silence and by the suppression of the movement towards departure. The second riddle is in its turn a question of life and death, and it holds the keys to both doors, while the first riddle prophesies and judges.

Bloom's silence and hesitation signify that it is certainty, which he has anticipated in the time he has been taking to understand who he is, that now determines his new anxiety to hasten the moment of conclusion; he fears that he may no longer have the strength to conclude. His own anxious haste appalls him like a movement which he could make but has not made for a long time (a feeling which had already occurred to him in the house of Circe), and once he has taken cognisance of it, it stops him in his tracks. He has not made a real move towards departure, but rather a gesture expressing his newly-gained knowledge of his being; this knowledge is now only bearable in the silence in which he at once buries it, in the necessary simulated blindness. Where is Bloom when the candle goes out? He must not say, because *he is not really there at all;* his pretence of existence is his own means of defence against "fading" away.

He stands between the "primal language" of his desire, the wordless language that must not attain to the level of speech, and the absolute silence of the vanished: vegetating, floating like a lotus-plant between the dark currents of dead knowledge and absence from the self. He *distracts* himself from the watch he is keeping, and the silence says more than unspoken or inner words; it is an anti-word, death of speech and knowledge. What Bloom does not say is precisely that which he knows and does not wish to know. When the light went out, Moses was in the dark. When Bloom's light goes out, he is in Molly's bed, which represents the starless black sky of death. We realise that he wishes to start again with a clean slate, ignoring everything of himself that he discovered by chance in the house of Circe; the voice of Virag, the voice of God speaking to the people gathered around Sinai, and the same voice speaking to Moses on Mount Pisgah, the voice of the Other who threatens death. These are all, as Stephen would say, "dead noise." Only the word registered and set down could survive; but the table is no table of the law. Nothing is written there, there is no Law; it can simply make a sound that might change the world. Moses himself did not wish to enter the promised land, but, being a *voyeur*, wished only to see it.

So Moses dies outside the promised land, yet having seen it first in fated contemplation, projecting his thought beyond his imminent death into the land flowing with milk and honey; and at that moment his soul left his body. Bloom perceives what separates him from life, and knows that he stands on a threshold he cannot cross. In 'Nausikaa,' the episode which demonstrated the distance between the image and object of desire and the lonely ego of Bloom, he had prefigured what would happen to him in the end. After he had acted out a long game, deceiving himself into the belief that he was omnipotent (to the point of exhaustion), seducing in imagination the distant lame girl, night came to fall on his conscience, bringing the bats and a dream of self-punishment:

> Curse seems to dog it. Dreamt last night? Wait. Something confused. She had red slippers on. Turkish. Wore the breeches. Suppose she does. Would I like her in pyjamas? Damned hard to answer. Nannetti's gone. Mailboat. Near Holyhead by now. Must nail that ad of Keyes's. Work Hynes and Crawford. Petticoats for Molly. She has something to put in them. (*Ulysses*, p. 375)

He was sure that Nausikaa would come back; in *Ulysses*, women do come back, as it were, but in the form of ghosts or phantasms. "What about men?" wonders Bloom, or rather, "What about me?"

Mr. Bloom with his stick gently vexed the thick sand at his foot. Write a message for her. Might remain. What?

I.

Some flatfoot tramp on it in the morning. Useless. Washed away. Tide comes here a pool near her foot. Bend, see my face there, dark mirror, breathe on it, stirs. All these rocks with lines and scars and letters. O, those transparent! Besides they don't know. What is the meaning of that other world. I called you naughty boy because I do not like.

AM.A.

No room. Let it go. *(Ibid.)*

Bloom's message on the sand is the first draft of a will; it is not by chance that he chooses the sand, on which no trace of his writing will remain. All his thoughts centre on the single obsession which is expressed a moment later in the words, "All fades."

"All fades" follows on "All is lost," and is the final expression of death and total disappearance. One dies without leaving male heirs; one disappears without trace. Bloom has lasted so long that, when he bends over the dark water, he can say, "I see myself," with no audience other than that *self.* But if Bloom as "I" cannot maintain Bloom the self in existence, then Bloom will fade away, having ceased to be object or "other person" for anyone. His ego itself is inconsistent, worn, and more dead than alive. His relationship with his self deteriorates and becomes eroded during 16 June. Increasing loneliness enlarges the distance between "I" and self. Gradually the Word of present existence is slipping away from Bloom; to say "I am" is an expression of a wish to live, but to say "me, myself" is a kind of abdication (in the proper sense of the word). When Bloom chooses the sand to receive his last declaration in the first person active (though not entirely in good faith), he is in fact demonstrating that he has already renounced present existence and the conviction of being qualified to say "I am." His "I" detaches itself from time present, alone and hieroglyphic, without the verb that could inform the world of its being; it stands derisively like a useless pole, the sign that "someone" has written it and at the same time symbolic of the absence of that "someone," and Bloom at once recognises its symbolic value. The sign "I" traced on the sand reproduces the shape of the object with which it was traced; this Bloom throws away because it is useless: "he flung his wooden pen away". In so doing he is abandoning the object (and part of the body) which Stephen has kept. He gives up the idea of finishing the sentence or of signing it, and forestalls the natural action of the sea which would wash it away, as though by erasing the ephemeral signs before their time he were choosing, by a final gesture as owner of his own self, to adjudge himself worthy of this inevitable death, deciding on its hour since its inevitability was already established.

A close examination of this episode will show that it is a rehearsal for Bloom's suicide as it does take place later, in 'Ithaca'; it happens in the interval between the writing of "I" and the writing of "AM.A". This brief interval constitutes an infinity, the sudden gap in Bloom's continuity which permits us to see his basic unhappiness taking shape within him, the moment by which death enters his being. It should be noted that he only writes "AM" as an automatic gesture, inspired by his reason, which is still trying to preserve its continuity. It is as though in the interval the "I" had been washed away by the tide of time, and as though the self were still putting up some resistance, causing the body to move about when the soul had already left it; the last spasmodic movements are appalling, because of the extreme fragility of the defences. Bloom has just said to himself that he cannot read what is inscribed on the rocks, and yet the signs are "letters"; in that case, how could anyone else read the lines and scars left by him when he had disappeared? There is no memory either, no possible "other world"—no last word and testament, no existence beyond.

"All fades." The conviction that this is true limits Bloom to the present, although he knows that he is absent from it. This explains the terrible unresolved sentence, AM.A. He is nothing, a zero, because there is "no room" for him. Yet how can there be "no room" in the world? This again is a metaphorical subterfuge intended to conceal the meaning of the silence that follows A. It is not that literal space is lacking, but that in *time* there is no more room for Bloom's ego; he is no longer what he used to be. Once he was "I," belonging to a couple, "we," whose other factor, "you," was Molly, but now, as he says with the harsh realism of suffering, "All quiet on Howth now. The distant hills seem. Where we. The rhododendrons. I am a fool perhaps. He gets the plums and I the plumstones. Where I come in. All that old hill has seen. Names change: that's all. Lovers: yum yum" (*Ulysses*, p. 370).

In a situation like that, why should Bloom go to pick the nightblue fruit that hangs on the heaventree of stars? Stephen does not pick fruits for another's enjoyment, we know. But every fruit Bloom picks goes straight to the Other, and he is quite aware of this; because he intends it to be so. He accuses the heaventree of being an unreal Utopia because the fox cannot reach the fruit it bears.

The self is a monolithic object, relic of an ego that was once young and lively; it is the word spoken by a subject isolated from the world by the knowledge of its end. And its end has already come; it is present in Bloom's mind every moment. It represents the past in a state of absolute reality, "the time left behind one" which is connected with the knowledge that is already making Bloom a thing of the past, the knowledge that after his physical death he will be totally abolished.

Joyce brings the days of "I" to an end with the sinister joke that closes the episode. The reader wonders what Bloom would have written if he had completed his sentence, I.AM.A., and something replies:

> Cuckoo.
> Cuckoo.
> Cuckoo.

The *sound* is in fact nothing more than the echo of Bloom's anguish, which he masochistically translates into words. But the word which he does not write cannot be written by this world; it is the black or white of the censured word, the lie which is held back and which acts as a substitute for truth. It could eventually be formulated, but one should bear in mind the fact that Joyce wrote the whole book to replace this word that was not written; the most important thing is to understand that the vast amount of energy expended by Joyce on Bloom's behalf and on his own for the filling of this gap is in itself indicative of that complex fear of truth which tells us, in order to mislead us, "I am a (man), a self with no ego, an awareness of not being what I am, I am what I am not."

Such an absence requires to be commented on, because it only assumes its full ghostly, negative reality when opposed to Stephen's repeated assertion, "I am, I am complete, I am that I am," and to Molly's affirmation that is complete in itself, her *yes* that makes up the nothingness of Bloom, meaning *Ich bin das Fleisch das stets bejaht.*

Each in his own way, both Bloom and Stephen show the same concern for unity and integration as Joyce felt. The problem faced by Stephen as artist is expressed by his analysis of the relationship of cruelty between father and son, and ends with the affirmation of the eternal division of the person. In his personal life, it is the ghost of the mother, not that of the father, which is trying to prevent him from living fully; it is generally said that he is weighed down by remorse for having refused to pray at her deathbed, and for having been to some degree his mother's murderer. But in fact it is the mother who is endeavouring to kill his desire to soar away into the limitless spaces of art. The ghost of the mother is inseparable from his soul, which is defined by her constant attacks, and his response to death is his writing. In

Portrait, poetry replaced the act of physical love, and in *Ulysses* he goes even further, establishing his exile beyond the real universe, in the world of the book. Yet again, a group of strange rhymes from a poem makes his secret clear; they are given to him in 'Proteus,' yet not until the end of 'Eolus' does their form yield up its meaning to him:

> Rhymes and Reasons
> Mouth, south. Is the mouth south someway? Or the south a mouth? Must be some. South, pout, out, shout, drouth. Rhymes: two men dressed the same, looking the same, two by two.
>
> .... *la tua pace*
> .... *che parlar ti piace*
> .... *mentrechè il vento, come fa, si tace.*
>
> He saw them three by three, approaching girls, in green, in rose, in russet, entwining, *per l'aer perso* in mauve, in purple, *quella pacifica oriafiamma*, in gold of oriflamme, *di rimirar fe più ardenti.* But I old men, penitent, leaden-footed, underdarkneath the night: mouth south: tomb womb.
> —Speak up for yourself. (*Ulysses*, p. 136).

The Stephen caught in the bag of Eolus wonders about the meaning of the poem written by Stephen on the beach in 'Proteus'.

> Bridebed, childbed, bed of death, ghostcandled. *Omnis caro ad te veniet.* He comes, pale vampire, through storm his eyes, his bat sails bloodying the sea, mouth to her mouth's kiss.
> Here. Put a pin in that chap, will you? My tablets. (*Ulysses*, p. 50)

The vampire who kisses and who turns the sea bloody is death, not named; 'Death' is masculine. And when Stephen says *Omnis caro ad te veniet*, "all flesh comes to thee," "thee" is Death, the husband of Stephen's dead mother. The tiny and immediately meaningful phrase, "put a pin in that chap" takes on tragic status and meaning in the continuation of a Donne-like array of imagery; it means "seize that ephemeral phrase, which is to begin the poem," but one can also read into it the gesture of Hamlet, "slay that man, slay Death the Devourer of all." Slay the Killer of men and his accomplice who clings to him in a kiss; the beast with two backs that terrifies Stephen—the secret animal of his nightmares—is composed of corpse and vampire, of this blood-thirsty God and his mother as hyena. How could Stephen ever embrace real flesh, when all flesh leads to the "allwombing tomb"? His lips will kiss nothing but air: "His lips lipped and mouthed fleshless lips of air."

His lips create by their breath insubstantial lips for the air; 'His mouth moulded issuing breath, unspeeched". This is the origin of written language, the separation of the Word from flesh. The definitive version of the poem is not given until 'Eolus,' under the triple sign, oracular by its nature, that heads the paragraph with the double riddle of death, '???'. When Lenehan asks, "What opera resembles a railway line?" Stephen recites to himself the answer to the riddle of his own existence:

> On swift sail flaming
> From storm and south
> He comes, pale vampire,
> Mouth to my mouth.

By a transference of image, the vampire of the poem comes to place his lips on Stephen's mouth. He must escape. Within is the Hell of confusion and self-loss. Dante's rhymes repeat themselves in Stephen's head as he listens to his own stifled voice: *"la tua pace. . . . . . . che parlar ti piace . . . . . . mentrechè il vento, come fa, si tace."*

As Tindall points out,[14] four of these fragmentary quotations come from the second circle of Hell where Paolo and Francesca suffer. But *quella pacifica oriafiamma* and *dirimirar fe più ardenti* recall the beatific crimson of the Mystic Rose in the *Paradiso.* The girls entwining replace feminine rhymes, and all real flesh. Yet their colour is the colour of death. Stephen has renounced life in order to escape death.

After his last combat, in the house of Circe, he seeks nothing more but to flee, to escape far away with the moving stars: "ooeeehah: roar of cataractic planets, globed, blazing, roaring wayawayawayawayawayaway."

The Paradoxes of Art

The fact that the mosaic can be reconstructed from the fragments which Joyce has scattered throughout the book is a proof of the intentional contradictions contained in his original plan; dispersion of details gives the impression that the author who might have organised them into a whole is absent, but selection and especially repetition of those details demonstrate his presence. The idea of a hierarchy is destroyed

[14]Tindall, *The Literary Symbol*, p. 197.

by the apparently equal status of all the fragments, just as the establishment of a generalised time present in which future and past are mingled destroys the ideas of development and becoming; and there is no
system of values because the pattern of correspondences does not proceed from "below" to "above," and because its terms are all reversible.

In fact, the organic character of *Ulysses* is apparent on all levels;
contradiction, disorder, and ambiguity have their own reasons for existence, so much so that if there were no chaos and division in the outside
world, Joyce would invent it. We shall see later on what his intention
was, but at present our task is to identify the arrangement and the
values which it creates.

Ulysses is, on the one hand, a summa of correspondences, on
the other a structural system, and altogether a globally inclusive
form.

The superstructure of the *Odyssey* gives the division into chapters
and the allegorical quest of Ulysses himself, while the mediaeval image
of the world supplies the idea of a set of horizontal correspondences
between chapter, hour, organ, art, technique, colour, and symbol.
Within this organic pattern, the three persons of the profane Trinity
dictate in turn divisions which correspond to the movements of their
respective minds and consciousness. The first three chapters, devoted
to Stephen, represent his triple revolt; the following twelve chapters
summarise in epiphany-form Bloom's entire life and destiny; then follow two chapters, 'Eumeus' and 'Ithaca,' in which the return of Ulysses
and the identification of the hero with Moses are mercilessly caricatured, and the themes of the son in search of a father and the father in
search of a son are explicitly denied. Finally, the last chapter is spoken
by Molly alone, and her words envelop the life and death of all three
in the fluidity of her final affirmation, which flows on until it joins with
the waters of Anna Livia Plurabelle.

Nothing remains of the heroic or Christian values, nothing, that is, of
their orthodox significance, for one can still say that Bloom is Christ or
Ulysses. From the conjugation of styles and structures emerge the
figures of truly living creatures in a series of epiphanies, and beyond
their personal destinies rises an harmonious global form which reminds
the reader of the young Joyce's Thomism and of his theory of the three
criteria of beauty. *Ulysses* has been compared to a sonata because of the
clear musical proportions of its rhythm; the polyphony of Bloom accompanies the symphony of Molly, the fugue and variations of Stephen, and
the *leitmotive* borrowed from opera or fashionable songs of the time,

while the concord of all these recalls that the mediaeval image of the world, with its hierarchies and its concordance of part with part, was associated also with the superior harmony of the music of the spheres. The Middle Ages identified *proportio*, which is mathematical proportion, rhythm, and relation of the parts to the whole, with *consonantia*.

From *Portrait* to *Ulysses*, the Thomist theory of the beautiful evolves from "that which pleases the eye" to "that which pleases the ear, or the mind"; proportion and rhythm replace epiphany and revelation, as symmetry replaces repetition. The eighteen organs of the body in *Ulysses* are echoed in the eighteen paragraphs of the 'Wandering Rocks' episode, and the eleventh chapter, the 'Sirens,' reproduces in miniature a popular operetta by its separate themes, and a treatise on musical composition by its form. 'Circe' is presented as an apocalyptic opera, too.

All the verbal or psychological themes, ideas, reminiscences, and personal data derived from the senses define by a system of echoes a musical space; at this level the problem of meanings determined by their context shows in what direction, phonetic and polysignificant, Joyce is progressing. Any word or incident has a double effect as soon as it appears at a given moment in *Ulysses*; it is connected by various associations to the point at which it first occurs, making its commentary and being commented upon by its specific context, but it is also prolonged like a musical echo, so that its meaning may be extended throughout several chapters.

The musical analogy confers form on this mobile, fluid order, the trinity-pattern associates three solitudes, and the odyssey permits references to be made allegorically to eternal man. But what is definitively their function, one may ask? For Joyce, the Homeric system of correspondences was a necessary stage in the construction of the work, as the metal skeleton is necessary to a sculpture, yet is later removed or covered over by the material that is built up on it.[15] Apart from the title, nothing remains on the surface of Joyce's precise references to details of the *Odyssey*; one has to have read the works of commentators, and of those in whom Joyce confided, in order to recognise these in their present disguises. For the first readers of *Ulysses*, of course, this was

---

[15]See A. Walton Litz, *The Art of James Joyce* (Oxford U.P., 1961); Frank Budgen, *James Joyce and the Making of 'Ulysses'* (London, 1934); Stuart Gilbert, *James Joyce's 'Ulysses'* (New York, 1930); M. Magalaner, *A James Joyce Miscellany* (Second Series), (Southern Illinois U.P., 1959); and, in the last, M. K. Croessmann's article, "Joyce, Gorman, and the schema of *Ulysses*", p. 9, with the reproduction of this schema, p. 48.

impossible. *Ulysses* appears enigmatic from the very beginning, for the title naturally suggests to the reader that he should look for Homer beyond Joyce, and the function of the correspondences is at once reversed: having been at the beginning a means by which the author arranged and imposed order upon his material, they become in their turn symbols which have to be deciphered. The hidden structure becomes one of the meanings of Joyce's message.

Here, in the fusion of code with message, in their functional reciprocal influence, the intention of parody insinuates itself; thus, Molly is Calypso before she is Nausikaa, she appears as Zoe, the young prostitute with Oriental looks, in 'Circe,' and then she is Penelope, that is, all women; she follows the rules pronounced once in a moment of hallucination by the picture of the nymph that hangs on the bedroom wall: "I have seen everything," and "you will recognise me again". But she is also an anti-Penelope, welcoming and accommodating to the wooers, whom she does not love. And finally, since transpositions are reversible, Penelope can be a Molly. Joyce, having destroyed the substance of culture by an accumulation of systems, has now to destroy the value of those myths that make man heroic; when he was thinking of writing *Ulysses* as a novella, at the time of transition from *Dubliners* to *Portrait* his hero Ulysses was a dark-skinned Dublin Jew named Hunter, who was, according to rumour, deceived by his wife. This was how Joyce presented the outline of the story to Stanislaus.

Joyce always considered man a ridiculous being, hiding his emotions with an affected irony, and no-one is more ridiculous than Bloom; all the accidents which happen to him make him appear more of a clown (the trouser button that falls off, the affair of the biscuit tin, the forgetting of the key, and sweepstake bet, and so forth), and yet his story as told without reference to *Ulysses* would be as tragic as it is ridiculous. One cannot imagine *Ulysses* written by Italo Svevo, or reduced to nothingness by Beckett. In 'Charybdis and Scylla,' Stephen provides the key to Joyce's irony. Having admitted to himself that after his mother's death, "I wept alone," he sees himself as Don Quixote: "Stephen looked down on a wide headless caubeen, hung on his ashplanthandle over his knee. My casque and sword" (*Ulysses*, p. 189). Then he plays the parts of Hamlet and Shakespeare, and suffers from his own pride and from the sceptical smiles of his audience. "Are you condemned to do this?" he asks himself, and he explains, still using Shakespeare as his mask, that he laughs in order to free his mind from the tyranny of his mind. This is the laugh that recognises that the masochist hidden within the work knows that if he leaned over Circe's mirror with Bloom and Stephen, he would see himself as well as them in the one image it shows: the image of a guilty, stammering Shakespeare, the cuckold, the lucid man who reminds his fellowmen that they are not invisible, the man who cries, "Iagogo," the word of Othello to the traitor he desired.

XXIV. Conclusion—Joyce's Dream

If Stephen recalls so insistently the magnificent "slaughter-houses" of history at the beginning of *Ulysses*, and if the Lamb is led to slaughter in virtually every chapter, this is not solely because of Joyce's very real and often-proclaimed pacifism; it is also because Joyce is as concerned with his nightmare as with real life. In fact, if history really were a process of becoming, if dialectic existed, and if the nightmare could come to an end, then Joyce the artist would have no more reason to write; it is necessary for blood to flow, so that Joyce may be a man of peace. It is also necessary for all to be in all, for Catholicism to affirm the eternal essence of man, and for symbolism, following the path of the Hermetic tradition, to establish a network of correspondences such that possession of the minor terms will ensure by analogy knowledge of how to find the major terms and meanings.

If all is in all, as in a dream all may replace all, and the hierarchy of values may be reversed as one pleases. Events are neither amusing nor sad, since they do not have a place in any progression; they are merely echoes of a permanent situation. God may be used as a symbol for the act of defecation, and excrement may have the same value as ink; a dog may bark in place of the Word, and God may enter a dog's body. In this world, where Joyce acknowledges no priorities, the artist is free within the nightmare. To Joyce, the fruitful paradox of history is this: by definition, a nightmare is an adventure in which one is involved, whose contradictions one is absolutely powerless to resolve. Yet it is in constraint that the imagination is free. The tension between contradictions is the energy of art and the origin of language; helplessness in the face of destiny justifies the artist's decision to exile himself.

Metaphor of a Crisis of Awareness

Ulysses appears to be a work balanced on the void, on chaos and the improbable, drawing its existence from the very incoherence of reality.

As an harmonious work, an historical metaphor, representing that moment of the modern mind when the critical spirit of the nineteenth century has successfully challenged the theological world, while the sensibility of the twentieth century is still seeking for its place and its form in a fragmented universe, *Ulysses* is a whole, yet a whole dissociated by its relativist point of view. It is above all the book of the self's reconciliation with the world by way of language, whose modern surface rests on ancient foundations.

It is necessary here to distinguish the two levels of the Joycean experience, the universal and the particular, and their relationships.

In principle, *Ulysses* may be considered as an epic story whose modern episodes constitute an indirect criticism of the heroic age, yet whose intention is identical to that of Dante or of Homer—the total representation of the problems of the typical man in a given civilisation. In this sense, it still belongs to a humanist tradition, even if its values have been degraded.

The image of man that emerges from these different points of view is modern insofar as his relationship with the world by which he is defined is no more that which had determined the character in a novel until Joyce's time, for he is no longer "man in society". He is no longer presented as a subject placed in the world to interpret or modify it. Since the end of *Portrait*, duality has disappeared. In *Ulysses*, there is no more separation between the inside and the outside, spirit and matter, reality and the self, no more guarantee of what Jaspers calls *Meinigkeit* or the feeling of the self to be distinct and not alienated. All that exists is a movement which animates simultaneously objects, one's body, society, and the self, in a general interference with nature and culture, the physiological and the spiritual planes. Eventually the *Mei-*

nigkeit, lost in a world of disorder, takes refuge in the body, the only place in which one can still be aware of one's own integrity; and this is the reason for Joyce's insistence on Bloom's various bodily functions. This is less a form of scatology than a type of defensive narcissism; it happens because Bloom is the most threatened and the most ghostly of the three main characters, because he therefore becomes more attached to his body as to a place from which he cannot be dispossessed. With him, everything is expressed in terms of appetites, because he is starved of affection.

> No more wandering about. Just loll there: quiet dusk: let everything rip. Forget, Tell about places you have been, strange customs. The other one, jar on her head, was getting the supper: fruit, olives, lovely cool water out of the well stonecold like the hole in the wall at Ashtown. Must carry a paper goblet next time I go to the trottingmatches. She listens with big dark soft eyes (*Ulysses,* pp. 77–8).

The peristaltic rhythm and meditation on art are naturally associated:

> Quietly he read, restraining himself, the first column and, yielding but resisting, began the second . . . he allowed his bowels to ease themselves as he read, reading still patiently, that slight constipation of yesterday quite gone. Hope it's not too big to bring on piles again. No, just right. So, Ah! Costive one tabloid of cascara sagrada. Life might be so. It did not move or touch him but it was something quick and neat. Print anything now (*Ulysses,* p. 68).

The world is no longer that space ruled by hierarchy in which the animal functions are inferior to the operations of reason, but rather an horizon made up of chains of insignificant factors; and would be nothing but the absurd and devalued world of chance, with no differentiations, if it were not for the other plan of Joyce to work against and simultaneously with the first one. The epic tale of the ordinary man, the allegory of the unmeaning, the correspondences and the summa of culture—all eventually give the impression that all is no matter what and that there is neither "above" nor "below".

Yet within this degenerate cosmos Joyce introduces his vision of man and of woman, by way of stories transposed from his own lived experience; his universe is still attached to the mediaeval forms, as well as to the new images of the world provided by Einstein's physics and the quantum theory. Molly, even if she is Gea-Tellus or Penelope, is above all a buxom Madame Bovary with a sense of humour, whose ignorance of all culture does not prevent her from being intelligent, humane, perspicacious, and basically charitable despite her idleness and egoism.

If she is compared with some mythical Cybele, it is easily forgotten that her monologue sums up a woman's life, with the suffering caused her by the inanity of an existence which she shares without being able to dominate; such a woman is very like Joyce's own imaginary woman, his typical female.

These individuals, shut inside their own life-stories, are, like modern open-minded man, caught up in a vast plan more extensive than humankind and its world, a plan which contains all this, Joyce's real dream: they belong to a written work which is to escape all the laws and metamorphoses which history imposes upon reality and to build itself up as a universe of its own, obeying its own linguistic laws. The work of substitution begins in *Ulysses* with Stephen's monologue, insofar as this inner speech constitutes a world separate from the outside world (as Molly's and Bloom's monologues do not).

Language Replaces Reality

In the presence of other people he is content to stroll through ironical galleries, pursuing aloud his monologues which are intended to deceive or amaze his thick-witted courtiers. Like Hamlet, he only speaks directly to death and to the ghost of himself, simulating a Bohemian and poetic excentricity in order to deceive those around him and to keep hidden his true grief. To speak would be to move away, because Stephen has built an impregnable language for himself. His exclusion from the outside world has established him in a non-place of his own, to which he will admit no visitors. His country is the space on the threshold of language where he first built his dwelling-place, surrounding himself in his loneliness with books and with a garden of magic phrases, where beautiful phrases were tasted with as much pleasure as the fruits of the worldly garden. In the centre stands the theoretical construction of his aesthetic, in the shelter of which and on the threshold of which he cultivated his self and created. At the end of *Ulysses* he undergoes a fit of delirium, which could be attributed to a physiological cause, but which is more properly the violent expression in the outer world of thoughts which assume the disguise of madness in order to be able to speak the truth. Stephen in the house of Circe is Hamlet *"le distrait"* before Polonius or Ophelia, never so wise as when he is believed mad and speaking strange familiar words. It will be further noticed that both

Stephen and Hamlet are travellers haphazardly embarked by someone else in a ship that is destined to founder, thrown up by chance on the first dry land after a mock death.

This voyage is the subterfuge adopted by Reason when threatened by the constraining hostility of the world, with the intention of returning in disguise after the drowning of all suspicions; Reason returns, dissimulating guilt under the pitiable mask of "innocence," of a superficial innocence which has nothing to do with ignorance. Stephen's "distraction" is the very opposite of the ingenuous innocence of Voltaire's characters who regard the world with fresh unsullied eyes. Stephen's eyes are forewarned and forewarning, and his gaze is the gaze of Joyce, the silent word that comments on reality without having to make use of speech, the gaze that pierces through the false to the true and brings the true forth as epiphany. It is not by chance that Joyce parodies the *Danse Macabre* in the 'Circe' episode; the imagery of death, the physical liberation, the ironical denunciation of false values, the stripping down to the bone and the mockery of woman's proud flesh—all find their most crazy and appropriate setting in this dark circus in which man wavers towards non-existence.

If Joyce has no wish for an apocalypse or absolute ending, this is because he is not interested in the end of time, but rather in the mockery of life and its meaninglessness. Death-in-life is more frightening than death. In 'Circe' the romantic veils that usually cloak feeling are torn away. It is necessary to expose the cheating of the sentiments and the blackmail passion exercises, to prostitute Beatrice and insult Dante; the immortal and immaculate women of poetry are so many icons to be destroyed, for their scented flesh already contains death. Myrrh and incense mingle with the smells of garlic and onion, as they do in life. And this is death. And life and death co-exist in a time present which must not deceive us; nothing is lost, because all is lost to begin with. All, that is, except language, for language is the replacement of every Absence.

Bloom retraces his steps to Ithaca, where he hopes to find Stephen; but this time the artist is ready for his definitive exodus towards the promised land of the Word made book. As he walks off into the night, Stephen intones Psalm 113:[1]

---

[1] This is a Pascal hymn, celebrating the Exodus and the crossing of the Jordan: "When Israel went out of Egypt, the house of Jacob from a people of strange language;/ Judah was his sanctuary, and Israel his dominion./ The sea saw it, and fled: Jordan was driven back./ The mountains skipped like rams, and the little hills like lambs."

In what order of precedence, with what attendant ceremony was the exodus from the house of bondage to the wilderness of inhabitation effected?
Lighted Candle in Stick borne by
BLOOM.
Diaconal Hat on Ashplant borne by
STEPHEN.
With what intonation *secreto* of what commemorative psalm?
The 113th, *modus peregrinus: In exitu Israel de Egypto: domus Jacob de populo barbaro.*" (*Ulysses*, p. 622)

The psalm is doubly meaningful: it stands for escape from the land of exile, and for Joyce it is in particular the sign of Stephen's entry into literature, because it is the psalm that Dante used as an example to illustrate his aesthetic in his epistle to Can Grande.

Form and Function of Language in 'Ithaca'

In Bloom's guilty conscience, his Hungarian grandfather Virag appears to avenge Bloom's offences against racial memory and genealogy; one may be unfaithful to oral tradition and make the excuse of having forgotten it, but no-one can be ignorant of the written law. Writing is a way of reducing the domain of death and of answering the anguish the thought of death causes. Bloom and Stephen both belong to races which history has threatened with extinction, surviving with great difficulty—expropriated, diminished, worn—possessing nothing but the memory of their shared sufferings; for Joyce Hebrew and the Gaelic are both dead languages, which cause memory to fail and whose speakers risk losing the past as well as being banished from the present.

Was the knowledge possessed by both of each of these languages, the extinct and the revived, theoretical or practical?
Theoretical, being confined to certain grammatical rules of accidence and syntax and practically excluding vocabulary. (*Ulysses*, p. 613)

They indulge in "a glyphic comparison of the phonic symbols of both languages".
The enumeration of the points of contact between the two languages

and the two peoples justifies the striking confidence which both Bloom and Stephen have in writing; both appeal to a tradition in which the written letter is powerful and the combination of letters is a part of magic. For Bloom the Kabbala and for Stephen the Book of Kells do in fact handle writing as a specific art; the letters of the Hebrew alphabet may be productive of ecstasy if assembled according to their numerical values. They open the secret paths of the world of beatitude and the illuminated letters in the old Irish manuscripts figure the invisible in hieroglyphic mysteries.

Joyce prompts the two apprentice sorcerers to their lesson in phonology; when Bloom writes, he chooses the characters *ghimel, aleph, daleth* and *goph,* indicating their arithmetical values, 3, 1, 4, 100. His choice is doubtless inspired by the recollection of his great project of squaring the circle, but he is also replying to Stephen, who began by writing down the Irish characters standing for *g, e, d,* and the *m* which Bloom had to replace by *goph.* In Joyce, isolated letters always suggest the presence of some latent code. By repeating these—*g, e, d* and *m*—he wishes to strike the reader's eye and ear, and to convey a message, the meaning of which, ironically enough, escapes the messengers' understanding; the identity of sound between the words that are written down with Stephen's pencil—*ged, gad, m,*—and the word *god* can only be interpreted (by the reader who joins them together as he reads) as "a sort of phonological allusion to their semantic proximity".[2] On the other hand, the *opposition* phonologically established between the dull tonality of the consonants and the lighter tonality of the vowels has its own direct meaning too, as though the living material were caught between the dull phonemes that stifled it, ending in an *m* which may stand for the mute presence of some being whose initial is *m, me, mother,* or *Moses,* for instance.

The critic may object that it is unnecessarily ingenious to seek out the meaning behind these letters; but there seems to be some justification for the procedure, both in the whole of *Finnegans Wake* (in which, as Mallarmé says in his essay *Crise de Vers,* Joyce "makes up the lack of languages" by using the autonomous icon-values of phonological oppositions) and in the reactions of Bloom and Stephen. One should not be surprised by the power of these neologisms to which they are inspired during the night that follows a day that has been lived through in defiance or opposition to God, and one should also take into account the

---

[2]Roman Jakobson gives the example of "gather," "mother," and "brother," in *"A la Recherche de l'Essence du Langage," Problèmes du Langage* (Paris, 1966), p. 32.

express intention of the author to make 'Ithaca' the episode in which everything is said "so that . . . the reader will know everything and know it in the baldest coldest way".[3] It was Joyce's favourite episode, for he liked what he called its "reassuring ghostliness."

If we recall that the art designated for this chapter in the list of correspondences is science, and the organ the skeleton, we shall understand how this voluntary stripping away of the flesh is designed to show up the elementary human form, the simple structures that are common to Bloom and Stephen, and to ask the primary questions, "where does death begin?" and "when does the "I" cease to pursue its illusion of life?" and finally, "when will our exile end and where is the promised land?" These questions have been given as a destiny to the Irish and the Jews by history and by the Will of God, as the representatives of both races realise: "The restoration in Chanan David of Zion and the possibility of Irish political autonomy or devolution" (*Ulysses*, pp. 612–3).

The answers are given in Old Irish and ancient Hebrew; Stephen first recites the formula for departure, "walk, walk, walk your way, walk in safety, walk with care," and then Bloom replies with a quotation from the Song of Songs, in which the voice of love and loss is heard, mingled with Joyce's own speech of enjoyment and of sadness for times past and with Bloom's own voice: "thy temple amid thy hair is as a slice of pomegranate". *(Ibid.)* The endless road is offered to the man who is leaving, and to the man who remains the fruit, pomegranate, or melon. But the endless road is infinite, measured only by the length of one's progress along it, and the fruit offers only a finite joy that is over when the fruit is gone. The one has the painful hopes and distresses of art, the unknown, and the future, while the other is left with memory, the known, and the past.

Stephen alone will leave any track behind him; this is why, at Bloom's request, he signs his name twice. Both have heard and seen: "What was Bloom's visual sensation? He saw in a quick young male familiar form the predestination of a future" (*Ulysses*, p. 614).

From the commentary of 'Ithaca,' we move back into zones which were still hidden in darkness in 'Circe,' now illuminated by the candle Bloom holds "to lighten the Gentiles" in the fashion of Saint Paul; and if we now reread the speech Bloom makes as emperor-Pope-renegade to the applauding populace in 'Circe,' we see the meaning which was hidden there, on the surface. Draped in the cloak of His Most Catholic Majesty, Bloom recites symbolically the life of a Jew, "Aleph Beth Ghi-

[3] *Letters*, vol. I, p. 159, late Feb. 1921.

mel Daleth Hagadah Thefilim Kosher Yom Kippur . . ." (learning letters, childhood, history of the flight into Egypt, Pascal rite, prayers, permitted food, fasting and contrition). By his appeal to *aleph, beth, ghimel,* Bloom is passing back through ancestral generations in the fashion of the being described and put on trial in *Finnegans Wake* (pp. 104–8); it is said that he has had many names in all ages, but that his story is always "semper as oxhouse humper"—that is, as simple and everlasting as the alphabet, *aleph* (ox), *beth* (house), *ghimel* (the camel, humper). The being himself is a "nonoun," like "husband," "husboat," or "hosebound."

> In fact, under the closed eyes of the inspectors the traits featuring the chiaroscuro coalesce in one stable somebody as by the providential warring of heartshaker with housebreaker and of dramdrinker against freethinker our social something bowls along bumpily, experiencing a jolting series of prearranged disappointments, down the long lane of (it's as semper as oxhouse humper) generations, more generations and still more generations. (*Finnegans Wake*, p. 107).

As Bloom and Stephen come out "by a passage from the rere of the house into the penumbra of the garden," they perceive the promised space in the form of "the heaventree of stars hung with humid nightblue fruit". The starry field that awaits Stephen is a greedy, fertile, mother-like space, but also an open space containing the infinity of all possible fruits, which Stephen can actualise by an eternal harvesting. The contradiction between the actualising of reality (which puts an end to the infinite richness of the possibles) and the desire to enjoy an unlimited freedom and creativity is resolved for the artist by means of the wondrous promise of language; if the tree, which is a finite material object excluding all other possibilities, can be the infinity of heaven, this is so because language does not acknowledge the limitations of the real world. The human imagination may enjoy the infinite possibilities of language and the heaventree may open to Stephen an inexhaustible treasure of words. As in the Word, there cannot exist the agonising separation that divides the human being against himself, since the word does not have to reconcile flesh and spirit within itself; since sound and meaning admit of continuity and words may communicate like vessels of liquid; since meaning may move through chains of sound as though through unlimited space. And because words belong to the man who pronounces them, Stephen's riches consist of the whole world's words, and the possible infinity of *Finnegans Wake* is already there, sleeping beneath the tree. Yet there is on the horizon of language, very far away of course, a line that acts as a boundary, for Joyce-Stephen cannot dislocate grammar without falling into a sea of phonemes and drowning there, eternally alone.

'The', Article of Death

Joyce is a learned man of language, a prey to despair and a rival of God, whose ambition is to create the ever-elusive—not Mallarmé's "The book," but the Book which, once read, would not contradict its creator even by its "impression," the Book that would remain alive, ever-changing, moving, ageing, never fixed on the page as a given, signed, complete universe. But every book must die when the pen stops writing, ink is the blood of sin (Stephen's history book is streaked with blood), and the writer who stops writing is the murderer of his own art as soon as he ceases to invent. Joyce well knew this successive death that catches up with the writer; every book of his, as soon as he had finished it, disgusted him, like a corpse, and sent him on eagerly to the next that was not yet written. The need to speak, to hear the spoken word with its assurance that he was alive—to say merely "I am he who writes"— was what drove Joyce to seek out and invent a kind of writing that would not stop its evolution and development once the writer had left it, which would continue developing because it contained an infinite supply of meanings.

This explains the pride behind the apparent raving of *Finnegans Wake*, which is not a finite *book* but an example of this writing that withholds the last word, that is intended to last forever, mouthing a breath that never ceases to be, like Stephen's lips when he walked on the beach at Sandymount. This was Joyce's ambition and we must examine his success. The final discovery that keeps the reader forever in suspense on the brink of the last page of *Finnegans Wake*, that *the* which opens on recommencement, is an admirable but unique contrivance; but it is not that infinity of Joyce's dream but rather the suppression of the ending, which is instead replaced by the beginning. In this, *Finnegans Wake* is indeed Joyce's last will and testament. And after all, the work is still limited, by the very fact of its having a beginning. "At the end," it succeeds itself, and since its beginning is its end, it is both mother and murderer of itself, giving both birth and death to itself; it is therefore not surprising that the word chosen to be the last and designated to be the first should be "the"—the definite article, the word which points out but which by itself means nothing, a dead word, a sign which depends upon what follows. it.

When Borgès speaks of Joyce, who was like himself caught in the labyrinth of mortality, he understands him, follows, holds and enfolds him—embraces him in their shared misfortune; he calls him "the entangled and almost infinite Irishman who could weave *Ulysses*".[4]

This is true; he *is* entangled, and he is *almost* infinite. This *almost* is an infinity that separates him from infinity just as Bloom is separated from a successful squaring of the circle. The thirst for the absolute cannot be quenched. This is what makes it absolute. And the entanglement is the multiplication of language and of possible meanings to the very limits of one's creative powers, carried out within the boundaries of a radical knowledge that admits its contradictory nature. To attempt the impossible with all the energy and eagerness one would employ in attempting the possible, knowing all the while that it is impossible, is the type of the heroic duel that is pursued to the last gasp—heroically, but to no purpose. In uselessness, madness, and terror, the hero writes, like Joyce, until he is himself nothing but the effort of writing.

In the last analysis, what Joyce says is what also overwhelms Stephen: the fact that freedom only exists outside the culture in which one is irremediably imprisoned; that one sleeps out one's life to the accompaniment of history as told by a God who speaks the same language as oneself; that only within this history does one have a place to occupy and a part to play. If God speaks the language of men, He does so because men have invented God speaking their language, and because they claim to justify themselves and to render themselves innocent by attributing to God the Word that gives the signal for the slaughter to begin.

[4]J. L. Borgès, *Discussion* (Paris, 1966), p. 130.

Appendix

I. Thoth and Egyptian Religion

Egyptian, Babylonian, and Assyrian mythologies make the god Thoth the centre of a network of ideas concerning the origin and value of writing. These ideas are founded on the fundamental and corresponding oppositions between life and death, father and son, written and spoken word, good and evil, day and night, sun and moon.

The god Thoth is the eldest son of the king-god or sun-god Amon Ra, who is the creator. Ra engenders by the mediation of the spoken word; he speaks, and all things are born. He hides himself under the name of Amon, which may be the same as the word *amon*, meaning "to hide oneself". The sun Ra is hidden behind Amon. He is often represented by the king. Amon is born from an egg, and the sun comes forth from a shell; thus the shell plays the part of the spoken word, hiding and protecting the light. Amon, because of his birth from an egg, is often called "the great falcon"; as a sun-bird, he reminds the reader of Joyce of the hawklike man wrongly called Thoth in *Portrait* and of Humpty Dumpty the egg.[1] Thoth and his companion Horus share the task of transmitting the word of Ra; Horus conceives it and makes it into

---

[1] H. C. E. reconstitutes himself piece by piece like Osiris after his fall: "Even if Humpty shell fall frumpty times . . . there'll be iggs for the brekkers come to mournhim" (*Finnegans Wake*, p. 12).

thought, while Thoth puts it into words. Thus Thoth the messenger is a secondary god, since he merely borrows the concept (or the matter signified) from Horus, in order to enunciate it in words. Here is the germ of the relationship of complementary subordination that exists between Shem and Shaun. Thoth is interpreter, messenger, go-between and substitute, like his Greek counterpart Hermes the god of cunning, of theft, and of communication (like Shaun the Postman); he may carry or steal; he is both necessary and dangerous.

Thoth is not the author of language; at the most, he is occasionally asked by Ra in half-serious, half-joking tones to replace him as the moon replaces the sun. He becomes the moon on one occasion by means of a play on words which Ra makes, thus: "Stand in my place in the heavens while I go to shine for the blessed in the lower regions. You are in my place . . . and you will be called Thoth the substitute for Ra". He says, "I shall cause you to embrace [*iohn*] both heavens with your radiance and beauty," and the moon *(ioh)* is born. Thoth's emblem, the ibis *(hib)* is also the result of an play on words, on the word *hob*, meaning "those greater than you". Shem and Shaun are similarly desig-nated and created as *different* by the constant game played with their ever-changing names: Shem can be "Sham" and "Shame," for instance.

It is a remarkable fact that Thoth's modifications and his subordinate position are caused and connected by plays on words. Thoth, like Shaun or Shem, is jealous of the person who has conferred such power on him by means of a subterfuge. The theme of usurpation rules all his family relationships, as it determines the brotherly hatred of Shem and Shaun; Thoth plots against Ra in the interests of the mother of his five siblings. He allies himself against his brother Osiris and the latter's sister-wife Isis, with the evil brother Set who slays and dismembers King Osiris. Then he allies himself with Horus (the son born to Isis and to the dead Osiris after the latter had been put together again) and fights against Set. During this violent struggle he shows his skill as physician and chemist, a skill also attribued to Hermes.[2] As secretary to the gods, he is the custodian of the written characters before becoming scribe and accountant to Osiris; he helps him, in the *Book of the Dead*, to make the necessary calculations of a soul's length of life, weight of sin, and so on.[3]

---

[2]Shem is also a physician; his address is "Null Null Medical Square," which is a pun on "null," meaning death, and on "nulla-nulla," the magical staff of the Australian witch-doctor.

[3]There are many allusions to the *Book of the Dead* in *Finnegans Wake*; see Atherton, *The Books at the Wake*, pp. 194ff.

II. Thoth as Shem or Shaun

Thoth is an ambivalent god, master of writing by which things are preserved and also god of death. Writing is associated with the death of the active memory *(mnemé)*, and replaces it by the passive memory which remains outside the consciousness, concerned only with the book in which the facts are to be found written down. Shem and Shaun similarly share death and life, speech and silence, between them. Thoth as the substitute moon opposed to the sun and the son substituted for the father is the night of day and the West of East; and in the same way Shem and Shaun move round the earth in orbits that incline towards each other, Shaun moving from east to west and Shem from north to south by way of the antipodes. Their spatial cycles correspond to the spiritual cycle of exile and return. Thoth is an ambiguous character because he is asked by his father to replace him, when he would much rather usurp than tamely replace.

He is the sun, the father, life and the word, yet not absolutely. He is the god of translation as of transition. He imitates out of obedience; he is the god of reproduction and repetition. This function of his, to act as a stage on which opposites coincide, recalls the play of shifting identities that goes on between Shem and Shaun, who are both the Same and the Other to each other. As Clive Hart has pointed out,[4] the Same and Th'Other (a pun on the name of Thoth) entered the Joycean cycle both together through the influence of Yeats, whose *A Vision* consists of a reading of Plato's *Timaeus*. The succession of meeting points between contraries in *Finnegans Wake*, if plotted like a graph, forms the shape of a cross.

Joyce took his inspiration from Plato by way of Yeats, exercising the same freedom of fancy and deep scepticism that had previously characterised his use of theosophy, Hindu mysticism, Vico and Freud; he takes his myths from wherever they are to be found appropriate to his system. Plato recounts the creation of the World-Soul in his *Timaeus*, explaining how the Whole, the sum of all things, was split lengthways into two pieces, which are laid over each other to form an equal-armed cross. Its two limbs are then curved round to form circles, which meet again at a point opposite the original point of contact. Then the two circles are set in motion, the outer movement being that of the Same and the inner that of the Other. This system of oppositions is also reproduced in the

---

[4]Clive Hart, *Structure and Motif in 'Finnegans Wake'*, p. 129.

polarity of Shem and Shaun, within, without, meeting (in book I, in the conversation between Mutt and Jeff, who are emanations of Shem and Shaun), separation again in book I and meeting in book III (Butt and Taff), further separation and new connection, between Muta and Juva. In the same way Thoth and Osiris are united, separated, meet again; sometimes one is dominant and sometimes the other, but the functioning of the one depends on that of the other as the moon on the sun, or as the written on the spoken word.

III. Joyce and Plato

Shem is dominant in the first part of the cycle; the letter, the written letter, is taken seriously. In book III Shaun overcomes and scorns Shem; in book II the supremacy of these "twinnt platonic yearlings," Shem and Other and Shaun the Same, is reversed. Th'Other moves, as he does in Plato, to the left, "with his sinister cyclopes". Plato had attributed the supremacy to the Same, whose motion is uniform and indivisible; the inner circle, that of the Other, is divided into seven unequal circles which move in different directions, three at the same speed and four at different speeds but in order. Shem and Shaun move also, driven by various causes whose comical form does not prevent them from echoing those of the *Timaeus*. Shaun's mission is to carry the letter that Shem has written. Thoth's task is also unequally divided. Shaun is the means of communication.

He has also a public role, which he plays successfully, but without intelligence: he is the speaker or actor of a text which he did not write. His journey towards the west predestines him to decline, as does that of the dead Egyptian; the latter is buried with a small idol representing himself, a *shwabti* of stone, alabaster, wood or terracotta, bearing the text of the sixth chapter of the *Book of the Dead*. The figurine is invoked by the dead man's name, which is carved or painted upon it, to carry out in his place the labours which he will have to accomplish in the next world. Joyce alludes to this sixth chapter in the following terms: "We seem to us (the real US) to be reading our Amenti in the sixth sealed chapter of the going forth by black" (*Finnegans Wake*, p. 62). The word *Amenti* means both the west and the land of the dead. The lively "postman" disappears in book III; Shaun has become Yawn, and is now merely the instrument of Shem's will.

"Further," says Plato in the *Timaeus*, "as concerns the motions, the best motion of a body is that caused by itself in itself; for this is most nearly akin to the motion of intelligence and the motion of the Universe. Motion due to the agency of another is less good; and the least good motion is that which is imparted to a body lying in a state of rest and which moves it piecemeal and by means of others"; this is the case of Shaun, the insensible body that dies in book III. While Shaun sinks down into a Yawn, Shem acts like a Gracehoper, making frenetic movements like those of an epileptic: "He took a round stroll, and he took a stroll round and he took a round stroll again till the grillies in his head, and the leivnits in his hair made him thought he had the Tossmania" (*Finnegans Wake*, p. 416).

Shem is naturally sinister, for the left is the direction of Th'Other, of one who like Thoth is illegitimate. The right is for Shaun the Same, who is seen as "Undivided reawlity," the single cruelty of the "Same Patholic". Shem's inferiority becomes a secret superiority and strength insofar as it is "the inside true inwardness of reality" that is true. The white light of Shaun and the shining prism of Shem becomes mingled together, as man is "nother man, wheile he is asame" (*Finnegans Wake*, p. 356). The bitterness of the discussions in which Shem and Shaun confront each other is explained by their need to differentiate themselves and to attribute guilt to each other; yet because they only have one non-identity made up of the coincidence of contraries, they are no sooner distinguised from each other than they try to replace each other. Shaun claims for himself the gift of language, which is Shem's, and Shem attempts to seduce the world of women who idolise Shaun.

IV. Writing as Poison or Cure

Is writing a good or a bad thing? Plato asks this question in the *Phaedrus*, and Joyce answers it throughout his work, particularly in *Ulysses* and *Finnegans Wake*, in terms analogous to those Socrates uses in his arguments; but he reaches a completely different conclusion. Socrates, like the Egyptian god-king whose words he reports, condemns writing as a poison, while Joyce for the same reasons defends it as a good thing, a cure. Both make use of the myth of Thoth and of his invention of the art of writing; he comes to offer it to King Thamous in his palace at Thebes, advising him to confer this gift on his people and claiming that it will make them more learned and more capable of remembering things. "It is a specific both for the memory and for the wit," King Thamous is the representative of the king of the gods, Amon Ra; he does not know the art of writing, but this is not a mere ignorant omission. Writing is a specific for inferior beings, for mortal men, and the king of the gods has no need of it; Thamous, like Amon Ra, needs only to speak and the world is created. Thus Thoth stands before Amon, through the intermediary of Thamous, like Stephen in the world of Dublin where the Divinity dwells.

This is not expressed clearly in *Ulysses*, but becomes evident in *Finnegan* when the word-play on Ani or Anu, the Egyptian name for Heliopolis, reveals the identification of Dublin with the city of the sun and (by a bitter oblique allusion) with the city of treachery, Healyopolis. One must move away from such a city, along the celestial and lunar paths of art; Stephen, obeying his vocation as a writer, moves away at the end of *Ulysses* vertically (like Shem), towards the "heaventree" of the night sky (like Thoth). Stephen, Thoth, and Shem are rejected or banished from the city, because the gift they bring is not appreciated; they have offered an art *(techné)* and a remedy *(pharmakon)*. But Thamous demonstrates that writing as presented by Thoth, although it seems to be good for the memory, is in fact a bad thing because it is exterior to the memory and because it is productive of opinion rather than of learning. Here the author of *Ulysses* dissociates himself from all forms of paternity, theology, or truth connected with the word; the episode 'Eolus' may be opposed to the *Phaedrus*, with its mockery of the spoken word which is ineffectual because it falls into the "porches" of thousands of ears without reaching the memory. The artist, as Stephen says, is a Moses bearing the law engraved upon tablets of stone. Joyce's pessimism and his mistrust of the man who forgets as soon as the voice is silent, of Ireland where the voice of Parnell has died away so completely, justify his deep respect for the inscribed word that cannot pass away. The words of Thamous, "This discovery of yours will create forgetfulness in the learners' souls, because they will not use their memories; they will trust to the external written character and not remember of themselves . . . they will appear to be omniscient and will generally know nothing; they will be tiresome company, having acquired not wisdom, but the show of wisdom," are perhaps valid in a Socratic world; and Socrates approves of them.

In *Finnegans Wake* it is Shaun, the idiot Christ, who makes the Socratic speech which Joyce has disfigured and devalued, accusing Shem of dissimulation, craft, and false teaching; to the question, "Since you rose to the use of money have you not . . . millions of moods used up slanguage tun times as words as the penmarks used out in sinscript with such hesitancy by your cerebrated brother?" (*Finnegans Wake*, p. 421), Sham replies furiously that he has nothing but scorn for Shem, relating the latter's life-story from his painful birth in "litterery bed" to cheating adolescence. "One temp when he foiled to be killed, the freak wanted to put his bilingual head intentionally through the Ikish Tames and go and join the clericy as a demonican skyterrier" (*Finnegans Wake*, p. 424). Shem is excommunicated for the "root language" he has planted in his "lettruce invrention".

The relationship between Shaun and Shem reproduces on a grotesque plane that between Thamous and Thoth. The majesty of the Egyptian king is replaced by the farcical indignation of a man who thinks he has been robbed: "every dimmed letter in it is a copy and not a few of the sibils and wholly words I can show you in my Kingdom of Heaven. The lowquacity of him! With his threestar monothong! . . . The last words is stolentelling! And what's more rightdown schisthematic robblemint! Yes".

To which the insidiously naïf chorus replies that Shaum is doubtless as "well letterread in yourshelves as ever were the Shamous Shamonous, Limited!" (*Finnegans Wake*, p. 425), and that thus he could not lose any contest with Shem. Shaum's reply is an involuntary admission of his own impotence, and this is shown by the shift from one meaning to another that destroys him: "Undoubtedly but that is show, Shaun replied . . . the authordux Book of Lief would, if given to daylight . . . far exceed what that bogus bolshy of a shame . . . is conversant with . . . Acomedy of letters! I have them all, tame and deep and harried, in my mine's I". *(Ibid.)* Shaun boasts of being the possessor of all words as he is the master of all men, and thus establishes his allegiance to capitalism and patriarchy. Joyce takes pleasure in making jokes about the opposition between capital and distribution; a whole pattern of jokes centres round the theme of "soviet" as opposed to the theme of money,[5] and this proceeds in parallel with the conflict between the Ondt who is not "a sommerfool" and the wasteful Gracehoper, "hoppy on akkant of his joyicity". If Shem is suspected of hoarding, his greed is for words, and this brings us back to the Socratic argument, for if he has such a "verbigracious" appetite, it can only be because "he was in his bardic memory low".

The ambiguous nature of this "remedy," then, as condemned by

---

[5]The chorus cries "so vi et!" at the beginning of Shem's trial (*Finnegans Wake*, p. 415).

Plato, is reproduced in the dichotomy of Shem and Shaun. The written word is thought out, beginning from a series of opposing values in both cases. Yet the accomplishment of *Finnegans Wake* is a sign that certain values have been chosen in preference to others. Joyce was well aware that his book would meet with a hostile reception from those who considered writing as a secondary thing, a mere instrument for the reproduction of reality, to be used by the Shauncritics to whom it is ironically dedicated as a challenge on every page. Shem is not an imitator but truly the inventor of a writing that does not seek to help or displace memory, but to live on its own perpetual contradiction, holding the reader always in attentive suspense.

NOTES

For this study we have made use of the following:

(1) *Finnegans Wake.*

(2) Frazer, *The Golden Bough*, in particular the chapters dealing with Attis, Adonis, Osiris.

(3) The appearance of Thoth in *Portrait of the Artist*.

(4) Atherton, *The Books at the Wake* (Viking Press, New York, 1960), chapter II, 'The Book of the Dead'.

(5) Festugière, *Les Révélations d'Hermès Trismégiste*, vol. I.

(6) S. Morenz, *La Religion égyptienne* (Payot, 1962).

(7) J. Vandier, *La Religion égyptienne* (P.U.F., 1949).

(8) Especially, Jacques Derrida's remarkable study of the origins of writing and of the opposition between the living *logos*, son of one who sustains him by speaking him as word, and the *techné* of inscription, the art which needs no father and which claims to be a specific *(pharmakon)* for the memory. This study is a critical analysis of Plato's *Phaedrus*, which appeared with the title *"La Pharmacie de Platon"* in *Tel Quel*, no. 32, winter 1967, pp. 3–48, "the whole of this essay being nothing more than a reading of *Finnegans Wake*, as the reader will quickly have realised" (Note 17, p. 22).

(9) The studies of Shem and Shaun in Clive Hart, *Structure and Motif in 'Finnegans Wake'* (London, 1962), especially pp. 114–142, and in Bernard Benstock, *Joyce Again's Wake* (Washington U.P., 1965).

Joyce's real knowledge of Egyptology was probably derived, as Atherton suggests, from study of the *Book of the Dead* and from numerous books by Sir E. A. Wallis Budge, who published in 1890 a facsimile of the Papyrus of Ani, and in 1895 *The Book of the Dead, The Papyrus of Ani, the Egyptian text with interlinear translation* (both published by the British Museum). Budge's *Osiris and the Egyptian Resurrection* (London, The Medici Society, 1891) seems to have been the source of the most useful information. Jackson I. Cope thinks that Joyce had read attentively a small popularising volume, *From Egyptian Rubbish-Heap,* by James Hope Moulton, (London, 1916), in which the author explains that papyri were not burned but thrown away in heaps which the winds scattered throughout the desert; thus, the motif of Kate the hen who finds the Letter in an "old dumplan," "that fatal midden," and begins the genealogy of writing with the substitution of letter for egg, seems to originate in the Egyptian rubbish-heap. Joyce's pun on "letter" and "litter" will be recalled in this context. See *James Joyce Quarterly* vol. III, no. 3, Spring 1966, pp. 166–70.

Bibliography

There are already several comprehensive books of bibliography on Joyce studies. The abundance of articles or studies about Joyce's life and work, dealing with details in one book or the whole of a book or of his entire work, is such that it would properly require a book of critical bibliography to itself, including a bibliography of bibliographies.

We have consulted more than two thousand studies in the course of our researches, as well as the rich collections of notes, rough-books, exercise books, first, second and third versions of *Ulysses* or of *Finnegans Wake* that are kept in the University Libraries of Yale, Buffalo, Cornell, New York, and at the British Museum.

We shall give here a selected list of works which seem essential to an understanding of Joyce's work, a list which for all its exiguity will suffice —through the quality of the works quoted or their authors—to support or to enlighten the propositions put forward in this book.

I. Bibliographies

Parker, A., *James Joyce: A bibliography of his writings, critical material and miscellanies* (Boston, 1948).

Slocum, J., and Cahoon, H., *A Bibliography of James Joyce* (New Haven, 1953).

Spoerri, James F., *James Joyce: Books and Pamphlets relating to the author and his works*, University of Virginia, Secretary's News Sheet, October 1955, September 1957, June 1962, February 1964.

Deming, Robert H., *A Bibliography of James Joyce Studies* (University of Kansas Libraries, 1964).

These works have been successively enlarged and completed by four specialists in Joyce bibliography: William White, Richard M. Kain, Alan M. Cohn, and Dr. Croessmann, firstly in the *James Joyce Review* until 1959, and then in the *James Joyce Quarterly* from 1964 onwards. These accumulative lists are to be used with the annual list in *PMLA*, which claims to be complementary to them, and that in the *Annual Bibliography of English Language and Literature*, published in Cambridge.

Maurice Beebe and Walton Litz also summed up the state of Joyce criticism clearly and methodically in no. IV (Spring 1958) of *Modern Fiction Studies*, with 'Criticism of James Joyce: A selected checklist with an Index to studies of Separate Works,' pp. 71–99.

II. Reviews

The James Joyce Review, ed. Edmund L. Epstein, 1957–9.

A James Joyce Miscellany, ed. Marvin Magalaner. Series I (1957) - Series 3 (1962). Published by Southern Illinois U.P.

A Wake Newslitter, ed. Clive Hart and Fritz Senn. No. 1 (March 1962) onwards. From Clive Hart, Newcastle University, N.S.W., Australia.

James Joyce Quarterly, ed. Thomas F. Staley. Vol. I, no. 1 (Autumn 1963) onwards. Still being regularly published by the University of Tulsa.

Since 1947 the James Joyce Society has been holding meetings four or five times a year in the bookshop of Frances Steloff, Gotham Book Mart, New York.

III. Works by Joyce

Chamber Music (Elkin Mathews, London, 1907).

Dubliners (Grant Richards, London, 1914).

A Portrait of the Artist as a Young Man (Huebsch, New York, 1916).

Exiles (Richards, London, and Huebsch, New York, 1918).

Ulysses (Shakespeare and Co., Paris, 1922). The best edition is that from the Odyssey Press, Hamburg, 1939.

Pomes Penyeach (Shakespeare and Co., Paris, 1927).

Finnegans Wake (Faber, London, and Viking, New York, 1939).

Fragments appeared in *Transition* between 1927 and 1938.

IV. Posthumous Works

Stephen Hero, ed. T. Spencer (New York, 1944).

Epiphanies, ed. O. Silvermann (Lockwood Memorial Library, University of Buffalo, 1956).

Letters, vol I, ed. S. Gilbert (New York, 1957).

Critical Writings, ed. Mason and Ellmann (New York, 1959).

Anna Livia Plurabelle, variorum edition, ed. F. H. Higginson (Minneapolis, 1960).

Letters, vol. II & III, ed. R. Ellmann (New York, 1966).

Giacomo Joyce, ed. R. Ellmann (Viking Press, 1968).

V. Biographies

Ellmann, R., *James Joyce* (New York and Oxford, 1959).

Byrne, J. F., *Silent Years: An Autobiography with Memoirs of James Joyce and Our Ireland* (New York, 1953).

Curran, C. P., *James Joyce Remembered* (Oxford University Press, 1968).

Hutchins, Patricia, *James Joyce's Dublin* (London, 1950).

_____. *James Joyce's World* (London, 1957).

VI. Critical Studies

Adams, R. M., *Surface and Symbol* (Oxford University Press, New York, 1962).

Atherton, J. S., *The Books at the Wake* (Viking Press, New York, 1960).

Beckett, Samuel, and others, *Our Exagmination Round his Factification for Incamination of Work in Progress* (Shakespeare and Co., Paris, 1929).

Benstock, B., *Joyce Again's Wake* (Washington U.P., 1965).

Budgen, F., *James Joyce and the Making of Ulysses* (London, 1934).

Campbell, Joseph, and Robinson, Henry M., *A Skeleton Key to Finnegans Wake* (Faber, London, and Harcourt Brace, New York, 1944).

Colum, Mary and Padraic, *Our Friend James Joyce* (New York, 1958).

Dujardin, Edouard, *Les Lauriers sont Coupés*, with preface by Valéry Larbaud, pp. 5–16 (Paris, 1925).

Ellmann, R., *Eminent Domain* (Oxford University Press, New York, 1967).

Gilbert, S., *James Joyce's Ulysses, A Study* (New York, 1930).

Gillet, Louis, *Stèle pour James Joyce* (Ed. du Sagittaire, Marseille, 1941).

Givens, S., *James Joyce: Two Decades of Criticism* (New York, 1948).

Goldberg, S. L., *The Classical Temper* (Barnes and Noble, New York, and Chatto and Windus, London, 1961).

Guidi, Augusto, 'Il Primo Joyce', in *Settimanale di Cultura* VI (1954) (Editions *Storia e Letteratura*, Roma, 1954).

Hart, C., *Structure and Motif in Finnegans Wake* (London, 1962).

Hayman, D., *Joyce et Mallarmé* (Les Lettres Modernes, Paris, 1956).

Jacquot, Jean, 'Joyce ou l'exil de l'artiste' in *Visages et perspectives de l'art moderne* (Ed. du C.N.R.S., Paris, 1956), pp. 79–112.

Mélanges Georges Jamati (Ed. du C.N.R.S., Paris, 1956), pp. 135–59.

Jolas, Maria, *A James Joyce Yearbook* (Transition Press, Paris, 1949).

Joyce, Stanislaus, *My Brother's Keeper* (New York, 1958).

———. *The Dublin Diary of Stanislaus Joyce* (London, 1962).

Kain, R. M., *Fabulous Voyager: James Joyce's Ulysses* (Chicago U.P. 1947; Viking, New York, and Macmillan, London, 1959).

———. *Dublin in the Age of William Butler Yeats and James Joyce* (Oklahoma U.P., 1962).

Kenner, H., *Dublin's Joyce* (Indiana U.P., 1956).

———. *The Stoic Comedians* (London, 1964).

Levin, H., *James Joyce, A Critical Introduction* (New Directions Books, Norfolk, 1941; later enlarged edition, 1960).

———. Editor's Introduction to *The Portable James Joyce* (Viking Press, 1947). The English edition of this work appeared as *The Essential James Joyce* (Cape, London, 1948).

Litz, W., *The Art of James Joyce* (Oxford University Press, 1961).

Magalaner, M., *James Joyce Miscellany* (James Joyce Society, New York, 1957).

———. *A James Joyce Miscellany*, series 2 (Southern Illinois U.P., Carbondale, Illinois, 1959).

———. *A James Joyce Miscellany*, series 3 (Southern Illinois U.P., 1962).

———. *Time of Apprenticeship* (New York, 1959).

———. (with Richard M. Kain) *Joyce: The Man, The Work, The Reputation* (New York U.P., 1956).

Mayoux, J.-J., *Joyce* (Gallimard, Paris, 1965).

Mercier, V., 'James Joyce and Irish Tradition' in *Society and Self in the Novel: English Institute Essays*, ed. Mark Schorer (Columbia U.P., New York, 1956).

Noon, William T., S. J., *Joyce and Aquinas* (Yale University Press, New Haven, 1957).

Paris, Jean, *James Joyce par lui-même* (Ecrivains de Toujours, no. 39, Ed. du Seuil, Paris, 1957).

Prescott, J., *Exploring James Joyce* (Southern Illinois U.P., 1964).

Schutte, W. M., *Joyce and Shakespeare, A Study in the Meaning of Ulysses* (Yale U.P., 1957).

Smidt, Kristian, *James Joyce and the Cultic Use of Fiction* (Oslo Studies in English, IV, Akademisk Forlag, Oslo, 1955).

Scholes, R., and Kain, R. M., *The Workshop of Daedalus* (Northwestern University Press, 1965).

Soupault, Phillippe, *Souvenirs de James Joyce* (Paris, 1945).

Sultan, S., *The Argument of Ulysses* (Ohio U.P., 1965).

Strong, L. A. G., *The Sacred River: An Approach to James Joyce* (Pelle-grini and Cudahy, New York, 1951).

Sullivan, K., *Joyce among the Jesuits* (Columbia U.P., 1958).

Tindall, W. Y., *James Joyce: His Way of Interpreting the Modern World* (New York, 1950).

_____. *James Joyce, Chamber Music*, edited with an introduction and notes (Columbia U.P., 1954).

_____. *The Literary Symbol* (Indiana U.P., 1955).

_____. *Reader's Guide to James Joyce* (New York, 1959).

Wilson, Edmund, *Axel's Castle*, (New York, 1931), pp. 191–236.

Index

The publisher wishes to thank the following for their cooperation in making this book possible: Cody Barnard, Wendy Weiss, Sally A.J. Purcell, Malcolm Wright, Ronald Gordon, Stephanie Gordon, Patric Farrell, Robert Kastor, John Wain, Constance Lowson, Jean Naggar, Marilyn Eiges, Jonathan Brent, and last but not least, Andrea Lewis.